SHELLEY'S POETRY AND PROSE

AUTHORITATIVE TEXTS
CRITICISM

W. W. NORTON & COMPANY, INC.
also publishes

THE NORTON ANTHOLOGY OF ENGLISH LITERATURE
edited by M. H. Abrams et al.

THE NORTON ANTHOLOGY OF MODERN POETRY
edited by Richard Ellmann and Robert O'Clair

THE NORTON ANTHOLOGY OF POETRY
edited by Arthur M. Eastman et al.

THE NORTON INTRODUCTION TO LITERATURE
edited by Carl E. Bain, Jerome Beaty, and J. Paul Hunter

THE NORTON READER
edited by Arthur M. Eastman et al.

WORLD MASTERPIECES
edited by Maynard Mack et al.

THE NORTON FACSIMILE OF
THE FIRST FOLIO OF SHAKESPEARE
prepared by Charlton Hinman

and the

NORTON CRITICAL EDITIONS

➤➤ A NORTON CRITICAL EDITION ◀◀

SHELLEY'S POETRY

AND PROSE

AUTHORITATIVE TEXTS
CRITICISM

➤➤◀◀

Selected and Edited by

DONALD H. REIMAN

THE CARL H. PFORZHEIMER LIBRARY

and

SHARON B. POWERS

W · W · NORTON & COMPANY · INC · *New York*

Published simultaneously in Canada
by George J. McLeod Limited, Toronto.

Printed in the United States of America.

FIRST EDITION

Library of Congress Cataloging in Publication Data
Shelley, Percy Bysshe, 1792–1822.
    Shelley's poetry and prose.
    (A Norton critical edition)
    Bibliography: p.
    I. Reiman, Donald H.   II. Powers, Sharon B.
PR5403.R4   821'.7   76–26929
ISBN 0–393–04436–X
ISBN 0–393–09164–3 pbk.

1 2 3 4 5 6 7 8 9 0

Contents

The Prose

Criticism

Preface

This edition includes all of Shelley's greatest poetry and other poems frequently taught or discussed (including *Queen Mab*, *Alastor*, and all the book-length poems Shelley wrote in Italy except *Swellfoot the Tyrant*), as well as three of his most important prose works. The critical selections include what we believe to be among the best and most helpful scholarly and critical studies that elucidate Shelley's art and thought and his most difficult poems. These selections are all recent because it is in the nature of scholarship that the best new work absorbs and builds upon the true elements of earlier scholarship and in the nature of criticism that the most sensitive current voices raise and attempt to answer the literary and philosophical questions that concern present readers.

We have reedited the texts of Shelley's writings from the primary authorities according to the principles stated in the Textual Introduction, and we have annotated the works with the aim of making the meaning of the words and allusions in the text immediately comprehensible without sending the reader to a reference library. Beyond glossing individual words and allusions, we provide brief accounts of the circumstances under which each poem was written and published. We also comment succinctly on the structural divisions of those poems which teaching experience and the history of Shelley criticism have shown us to require such elucidation. Finally, for some poems that lend themselves to interpretation at more than one level, we have mentioned the directions taken by allegorical or symbolic interpretations that seem to us consonant with Shelley's thought and artistic methods. Detailed interpretation of the poems remains the task and the privilege of students and teachers.

The texts of Shelley's poetry and prose presented here are closer to the primary authorities (and, we believe, to Shelley's intention) than those found in any previous edition. Our annotation—though not embodying all that has been known and thought about Shelley—is far more detailed and precise than that in earlier editions and contains considerable information not available otherwise in Shelley studies. Like all works of scholarship, however, the Norton Critical Edition of Shelley exists to be used, tested, and corrected.

New York, New York DONALD H. REIMAN
Montclair, New Jersey SHARON B. POWERS

Acknowledgments

We wish to thank M. H. Abrams of Cornell University and John Benedict of W. W. Norton & Company, who have generously provided thoughtful advice and guidance since the inception of this book. And we are grateful to the following libraries for permission to consult and utilize manuscripts in their collections to establish the texts of Shelley's poems (as specified in the textual notes to individual poems):

Bodleian Library, Oxford
The British Library, London
Cambridge University Library
Edinburgh University Library
The Houghton Library, Harvard University
The Huntington Library, San Marino, California
John Rylands University Library of Manchester
The Library of Congress
The Pierpont Morgan Library, New York
Yale University Library

Transcriptions of manuscripts in The Carl H. Pforzheimer Library from the texts published in *Shelley and his Circle* and *The Esdaile Notebook* have been utilized by permission of The Carl and Lily Pforzheimer Foundation, Inc., New York.

Textual Introduction

The texts of Shelley's poems in this edition have been reedited after a comparison of the primary authorities—extant holograph manuscripts, transcripts, the first editions, and later editions (especially those of Mary Shelley) that may have incorporated authorial emendations.[1] The resulting texts were then compared with one another and with the better critical editions: the collected editions of H. Buxton Forman, C. D. Locock, Thomas Hutchinson (corrected by G. M. Matthews), and Roger Ingpen and Walter E. Peck, as well as specialized editions and textual studies by Irving Massey, G. M. Matthews, Judith Chernaik, Neville Rogers, Lawrence John Zillman, and John E. Jordan. During these steps we observed certain peculiarities of punctuation and orthography that seemed persistent (though not universal) in Shelley's holographs and in texts printed under his direct supervision; all the texts have been regularized to these preferred forms.

Spelling: Where it can be established that Shelley employed two distinct forms of a word with a probable or demonstrable difference in pronunciation like "sat" (rhymed with "hat") and "sate" (rhymed with "hate") or a possible difference in meaning or function, like "desert" (which seems usually reserved for the adjectival meaning) as opposed to "desart" (noun), these distinctions have been maintained. In all cases Shelley's original preferred spellings—as nearly as they could be determined—have been incorporated, except in the case of certain repeatedly misspelled words ("thier" for "their," "recieve" for "receive") and certain abbreviations like the ampersand ("&") or "w^{ch}" (for "which"), often found in Shelley's manuscripts but not appearing in his printed texts. The shortened forms "tho'," "altho'," and "thro'" ("though," "although," and "through") were not abbreviations in this sense, but were standard alternative forms found in the printed books of many writers well into the nineteenth century; but though these abbreviations appear frequently in both Shelley's manuscripts and his printed books of certain periods, they are not in evidence in his late manuscripts or editions (like *Adonais*), and we have, therefore, normalized these words to their unabbreviated forms.

---

1. On criteria for determining the relative authority of various kinds of textual evidence, see Donald H. Reiman, review of vol. I of *The Complete Works of Percy Bysshe Shelley*, ed. Neville Rogers, *JEGP*, 73:250–260 (April 1974).

The student should find himself less confused by Shelley's few archaic spellings (e.g., "antient" for "ancient," "controul" for "control," "gulph" for "gulf") than by the changed pronunciation in modern American English of words like "again" (which Shelley rhymed with "pain"), words ending in "-ing" (which were shortened so that "pursuing" rhymed with "ruin"), and the noun "wind" (which Shelley often rhymed with "kind" and "find").

Punctuation: The punctuation found in Shelley's surviving holograph manuscripts has been supplemented but has not ordinarily been altered, unless the change originated in a printed text of similar authority. The function of Shelley's commas, semicolons, and dashes differs from that of standard modern usage. But just as twentieth-century poets like e. e. cummings and T. S. Eliot often break their poetry into short lines that identify the patterned grouping of phrases and clauses, so Shelley and the poets of his day often punctuated their poetry to show the reader how the words are to be grouped when recited aloud. These usages were recognized by the rhetoric and elocution manuals of the day. William Scott wrote, for example, in his *Elements of Elocution* (2nd ed., Edinburgh, 1808):

> The comma generally admits of a very short pause; in some situations, none: the semicolon requires a pause somewhat longer than the comma; the colon a still longer pause; and the period a longer still. The pause at the end of a paragraph, or where a dash is added to the period, should be greater than at the end of an ordinary sentence.—It has been said, that the pauses at the comma, semicolon, colon, and period, should be in the proportion of the numbers 1, 2, 3, 4; which may, in general, be pretty near the truth." [p. 57]

In *Mont Blanc*, Shelley inserts commas between the subject and the verb in lines 115 and 118 (as William Scott does in the last sentence quoted above) to show where he wants the break in phrasing. This practice was recognized by the leading grammarian Lindley Murray, who wrote:

> The Comma usually separates those parts of a sentence, which, though very closely connected in sense and construction, require a pause between them. . . . A simple sentence, . . . when it is a long one, and the nominative case is accompanied with inseparable adjuncts, may admit of a pause immediately before the verb: as, "The good taste of the present age, has not allowed us to neglect the cultivation of the English language." "To be totally indifferent to praise or censure, is a real defect in character." [*English Grammar*, 2nd ed., improved, York, London, & Edinburgh, 1809, I, 376]

In his draft manuscripts Shelley often omitted commas at the ends of poetic lines (and sometimes full stops at the ends of stanzas) simply because the natural pause at the end of the line (or stanza) obviated the need for any punctuation at that early stage of composition, when the manuscript was meant merely as a guide to the poet. In his fair copies destined for the press (or for friends to whom the poems were addressed) Shelley is much more careful in punctuating, but even in these he often depended on the natural pause at the end of the line to serve instead of an optional comma; and in the same position he sometimes employed a comma to indicate a pause where modern usage would require a colon or semicolon. While this practice is, again, analogous to that of T. S. Eliot and other subsequent poets and could easily be accepted by readers, the printers of Shelley's day generally supplemented his punctuation and, by not deleting their additions from the volumes for which he read proofs, Shelley seems to have endorsed, in a general way, the somewhat more heavily punctuated style of his day. We must remember, however, that the pointing was primarily rhetorical rather than grammatical and that it was usually not as heavy as subsequent editors have tried to impose on Shelley's poems. In treating those texts for which the primary authority is either a rough draft manuscript or a safekeeping copy (like *The Harvard Shelley Notebook*), we have attempted to approximate the spirit of the punctuation in Shelley's press copy manuscripts and in *The Cenci* and *Adonais*, which were printed under his direct supervision by Italian printers who would have been less likely than their English colleagues to "correct" Shelley's style. By the same rationale, we have slightly reduced the punctuation of some poems (particularly those for which the primary authority is the *Prometheus Unbound* volume) that seem to have been overpunctuated without Shelley's acquiescence.

Capitalization: Though the significance of Shelley's practice of capitalization is not yet fully understood in all details, he probably followed the practice of his time in capitalizing common nouns to indicate rhetorical emphasis. In "A Plain and Compendious Grammar of the English Tongue" prefixed to *The Complete Letter-Writer* (London: J. Brambles, A. Meggitt, and J. Waters, 1804), the anonymous author writes, under the heading "Of Capitals, or great Letters" (rule 2): "It is become customary to begin any substantive in a sentence with a capital, if it bears some considerable stress of the author's sense upon it, to make it the more remarkable." This rule is reinforced by rule 6, which states: "Sometimes capitals are used in whole words and sentences, when something extraordinary great is expressed" (p. 27). This latter mode of emphasis is clearly used by Shelley in "Hymn to Intellectual Beauty," lines

13, 71, and 83. In any case, it seems best to follow Shelley's own usage (as nearly as that can be determined from the surviving evidence) rather than to impose the usage of either a typesetter or a later editor. In every instance where a later editor has attempted to revise capitalization, he has merely replaced Shelley's usage with his own equally erratic and personal one.

Outline of Shelley's Life

1792   Percy Bysshe Shelley born August 4 at Field Place, near Horsham, Sussex, the son of Timothy Shelley, member of Parliament, and grandson of Bysshe Shelley, a wealthy landowner (baronet, 1806).

1798   Studies with his clergyman, the Reverend Evan Edwards.

1802–1804   Attends Syon House Academy at Isleworth, near London.

1804–1810   Studies at Eton.

1808   Begins corresponding with his cousin Harriet Grove (their "engagement" ends in 1810).

1810   *Zastrozzi*, a Gothic novel, published (spring). *Original Poetry by Victor and Cazire* published and withdrawn (autumn). Enters University College, Oxford, and meets Thomas Jefferson Hogg, a college classmate (Oct.). *Posthumous Fragments of Margaret Nicholson* published (Nov.). *St. Irvyne*, a second Gothic novel, published (Dec.).

1811   Meets Harriet Westbrook (Jan.). *The Necessity of Atheism* published (Feb.). Expelled with Hogg from Oxford (March 25). Elopes with Harriet Westbrook; married in Edinburgh on Aug. 29. At York, Hogg tries to seduce Harriet; the Shelleys move to Keswick.

1812   Political activities in Dublin. Two pamphlets, *Address to the Irish People* and *Proposals for an Association . . .* published (Feb.). *Declaration of Rights* printed. Returns to Wales (April 6); moves to Lynmouth, Devon; writes *Letter to Lord Ellenborough*. Joined by Elizabeth Hitchener, a spinster schoolteacher, in July (she leaves in Nov.). Goes to North Wales (Sept.). Meets William Godwin in London (Oct.).

1813   Flees Tremadoc, Wales (Feb. 27); goes to Ireland. Returns to London (April 5). *Queen Mab* issued

(May). Ianthe Shelley born (June 23). Settles at Bracknell (July).

1814　A *Refutation of Deism* printed. Elopes with Mary Wollstonecraft Godwin (July 27). They (with Jane "Claire" Clairmont, Mary's stepsister) tour the Continent, returning Sept. 13. First son, Charles, born to Harriet (Nov. 30).

1815　Sir Bysshe Shelley dies (Jan. 5). Mary's first child born (Feb. 22; dies two weeks later). In June, Shelley begins to receive annual income £1,000 (£200 paid directly to Harriet). Moves to cottage near Windsor Great Park (Aug.).

1816　William Shelley born (Jan. 24). *Alastor* published (Feb.). Visits Switzerland; lives near Lord Byron; writes "Hymn to Intellectual Beauty" and "Mont Blanc" (May-Aug.). Returns to England (Sept. 8). Suicide of Fanny Imlay, Mary's half sister (Oct. 9). Harriet Shelley drowns herself (Nov. 9; discovered Dec. 10). Marries Mary (Dec. 30).

1817　Develops friendship with Leigh Hunt, poet and editor of the *Examiner*. Allegra, Claire's daughter by Byron, born (Jan. 12). Denied custody of Ianthe and Charles (March 27). Settles at Marlow near his friend Thomas Love Peacock, poet and comic novelist (March). *Proposal for Putting Reform to the Vote* published (March). Finishes *Laon and Cythna* and begins *Rosalind and Helen* (Sept.). Clara Shelley born (Sept. 2). *History of a Six Weeks' Tour* published. Writes *Address . . . on the Death of the Princess Charlotte* (Nov.). *Laon and Cythna* published and withdrawn (Dec.); reissued as *The Revolt of Islam* (Jan. 1818).

1818　Sails to Continent (March 11). Sends Allegra to Byron (April 28). At Leghorn meets John and Maria Gisborne and Maria's son Henry Reveley (May-June). At Baths of Lucca completes *Rosalind and Helen* (July; published spring 1819). Goes to Venice with Claire; Mary follows with children (Aug.-Sept.). Clara Shelley dies (Sept. 24). At Este, begins *Julian and Maddalo*, "Euganean Hills," *Prometheus Unbound*, Act I. Visits Rome; settles at Naples (Dec.).

1819   Leaves Naples (Feb. 28). Writes Acts II-III of *Prometheus* in Rome (March-April). William Shelley dies (June 7). Moves to Leghorn; writes *The Cenci* (summer; published spring 1820) and "Mask of Anarchy" (Sept.). Moves to Florence (Oct. 2); son Percy Florence born (Nov. 12). Writes *Peter Bell the Third*, "West Wind," and *Philosophical View of Reform*; finishes *Julian and Maddalo* (published 1824) and *Prometheus Unbound* (published Aug. 1820).

1820   Moves to Pisa (Jan. 26) and becomes friendly with Lady Mount Cashell and George Tighe ("Mr. and Mrs. Mason"); writes "Sensitive-Plant" (March). At Leghorn (June-Aug.) writes "Ode to Liberty," "Sky-lark," "Letter to Maria Gisborne." At Baths of San Giuliano (Aug.-Oct.) writes "Witch of Atlas," "Ode to Naples," *Swellfoot the Tyrant* (published and suppressed, Dec.). Returns to Pisa (Oct. 31).

1821   Visits Teresa Viviani; writes *Epipsychidion* (Jan.-Feb.; published anonymously, May). Meets Edward and Jane Williams (Jan. 13). Writes *A Defence of Poetry* (Feb.-March). News of Keats's death (Rome, Feb. 23) arrives on April 11 from Horace Smith, London stockbroker and writer. Writes *Adonais* (May-June; printed July). Visits Byron at Ravenna (Aug.) and persuades him to live at Pisa (arrives Nov. 1). Writes *Hellas* (Oct.; published Feb. 1822).

1822   Works on "Charles the First." Edward John Trelawny arrives (Jan. 14). Writes poems to Jane (Jan. ff.). Allegra Byron dies (April 20). Shelleys and Williamses move to San Terenzo (April 30). Receives the *Don Juan*, his boat (May 12). Writes "Triumph of Life" (May-June). He and Williams sail to Leghorn to meet Leigh Hunt (July 1) and drown on return voyage (July 8).

The Poems

From THE ESDAILE NOTEBOOK[1]

Zeinab and Kathema[2]

Upon the lonely beach Kathema lay;
   Against his folded arm his heart beat fast.
Through gathering tears the Sun's departing ray
   In coldness o'er his shuddering spirit past
And all unfelt the breeze of evening came   5
That fanned with quivering wing his wan cheek's feeble flame.

"Oh!" cried the mourner, "could this widowed soul
   But fly where yonder Sun now speeds to dawn."
He paused—a thousand thoughts began to roll;
   Like waves they swept in restless tumult on,   10
Like those fast waves that quick-succeeding beat
Without one lasting shape the beach beneath his feet.

And now the beamless, broad and yellow sphere
   Half sinking lingered on the crimson sea;
A shape of darksome distance does appear   15
   Within its semicircled radiancy.

1. In 1813 Shelley planned to have two volumes of poetry published—*Queen Mab* and the volume of miscellaneous short poems that has become known as *The Esdaile Notebook*. Thomas Hookham declined to publish either volume. Shelley, even in proposing the volume to Hookham, showed his mixed feelings about it: "My poems, will, I fear, little stand the criticism even of friendship. Some of the later ones have the merit of conveying a meaning in every word, and these are all faithful pictures of my feelings at the time of writing them. But they are, in a great measure, abrupt and obscure—all breathing hatred to government and religion, but I think not too openly for publication" (*Letters*, I, 348).

  Shelley gave the notebook in which the fifty-seven poems had been transcribed to his current wife, Harriet Westbrook Shelley. When Shelley left Harriet to elope with Mary Godwin, the notebook remained with Harriet, and after Harriet's suicide in November or December 1816 (see *Shelley and his Circle*, IV, 769–802), it was preserved for her children, becoming the possession of Shelley's daughter Eliza Ianthe, who in 1837 married Edward Jeffries Esdaile. In the nineteenth century Edward Dowden was granted access to the notebook and, with the owner's permission, published excerpts from the poems in his two-volume *Life of Percy Bysshe Shelley* (1886). These poems were collected by T. J.

Wise and H. Buxton Forman, who issued thirty copies of a thin volume entitled *Poems and Sonnets* with a false Philadelphia imprint in 1887, probably in an attempt to provoke the Esdaile family into permitting publication of the whole. Though Neville Rogers included imperfect texts of a few more in *Shelley at Work* (1956), most of the poems continued unpublished until Mrs. Lettice A. Worrall (nee Esdaile), Shelley's great-granddaughter, sold the notebook at public auction. It was purchased by The Carl H. Pforzheimer Library, and two years later Alfred A. Knopf published Kenneth Neill Cameron's edition, *The Esdaile Notebook: A Volume of Early Poems by Percy Bysshe Shelley*. In 1966 Oxford University Press published Rogers' version of *The Esdaile Poems* (based largely on a photocopy of the notebook obtained some years before), which corrected some errors in Cameron's edition, while introducing others. Cameron then presented an exact transcription of the notebook in an Appendix to vol. IV of *Shelley and his Circle* (1970).

2. "Zeinab and Kathema" was probably composed in 1810 or 1811. It fuses wild incidents of Gothic and oriental romances with a violent attack on British imperialism abroad and social injustice at home. The name "Zeinab" comes from Southey's *Thalaba the Destroyer*, where Zeinab is Thalaba's widowed mother.

All sense[3] was gone to his betrothed one—
His eye fell on the form that dimmed the setting sun,—

He thought on his betrothed . . . for his youth
    With her that was its charm to ripeness grew.   20
All that was dear in love, or fair in truth,
    With her was shared as childhood's moments flew,
And mingled with sweet memories of her
Was life's unveiling morn with all its bliss and care.

A wild and lovely Superstition's[4] spell,   25
    Love for the friend that life and freedom gave,
Youth's growing hopes that watch themselves so well,
    Passion, so prompt to blight, so strong to save,
And childhood's host of memories combine
Her life and love around his being to entwine.   30

And to their wishes with its joy-mixed pain
    Just as the veil of hope began to fall,
The Christian murderers over-ran the plain,
    Ravaging, burning and polluting all.
Zeinab was reft[5] to grace the robbers' land;   35
Each drop of kindred blood stained the invaders' brand.

Yes! they had come their holy book to bring
    Which God's own son's apostles had compiled
That charity and peace, and love might spring
    Within a world by God's blind ire defiled,   40
But rapine,[6] war and treachery rushed before
Their hosts, and murder dyed Kathema's bower in gore.

Therefore his soul was widowed, and alone
    He stood in the world's wide and drear expanse.
No human ear could shudder at his groan,   45
    No heart could thrill with his unspeaking glance;
One only hope yet lingering dared to burn,
Urging to high emprize[7] and deeds that danger spurn.

The glow has failed on Ocean's western line,
    Faded from every moveless cloud above.   50
The moon is up—she that was wont to shine
    And bless thy childish nights of guileless love,
Unhappy one, ere Christian rapine tore
All ties, and stain'd thy hopes in a dear mother's gore.

The form that in the setting Sun was seen   55
    Now in the moonlight slowly nears the shore,
The white sails gleaming o'er the billows green
    That sparkle into foam its prow before;

---

3. Emotional consciousness.
4. False or pagan religion.
5. Stolen.

6. Pillage, robbery.
7. An undertaking, especially one of adventure or chivalry.

A wanderer of the deep it seems to be,
On high adventures bent, and feats of chivalry.   60

Then hope and wonder filled the mourner's mind.
   He gazed till vision even began to fail,
When to the pulses of the evening wind
   A little boat approaching gave its sail,
Rode o'er the slow raised surges near the strand,   65
Ran up the beach and gave some stranger men to land.

"If thou wilt bear me to far England's shore
   Thine is this heap—the Christian's God!"
The chief with gloating rapture viewed the ore
   And his pleased avarice gave the willing nod.   70
They reach the ship, the fresh'ning breezes rise
And smooth and fast they speed beneath the moonlight skies.

What heart e'er felt more ardent longings now?
   What eye than his e'er beamed with riper hope
As curbed impatience on his open brow   75
   There painted fancy's unsuspected scope,
As all that's fair the foreign land appeared
By ever present love, wonder and hope endeared?

Meanwhile through calm and storm, through night and day,
   Unvarying in her aim the vessel went   80
As if some inward spirit ruled her way
   And her tense sails were conscious of intent
Till Albion's[8] cliffs gleamed o'er her plunging bow
And Albion's river floods bright sparkled round her prow.

Then on the land in joy Kathema leaped   85
   And kissed the soil in which his hopes were sown;
These even now in thought his heart has reaped.
   Elate of body and soul he journeyed on
And the strange things of a strange land past by
Like motes[9] and shadows prest upon his charmed eye.   90

Yet Albion's changeful skies and chilling wind
   The change from Cashmire's vale might well denote.
There Heaven and Earth are ever bright and kind;
   Here, blights and storms and damp forever float
Whilst hearts are more ungenial than the zone—   95
Gross, spiritless, alive to no pangs but their own.

There flowers and fruits are ever fair and ripe;
   Autumn there mingles with the bloom of spring
And forms unpinched by frost or hunger's gripe
   A natural veil o'er natural spirits fling;   100
Here, woe on all but wealth has set its foot.
Famine, disease and crime even wealth's proud gates pollute.

---

8. England's.
9. Particles of dust; especially the in-
numerable minute specks seen in a sun-
beam.

Unquiet death and premature decay,
  Youth tottering on the crutches of old age,
And, ere the noon of manhood's riper day,   105
  Pangs that no art of medicine can assuage,
Madness and passion ever mingling flames,
And souls that well become such miserable frames—

These are the bribes which Art to man has given
  To yield his taintless nature to her sway.   110
So might dank night with meteors[1] tempt fair Heav'n
  To blot the sunbeam and forswear the day
Till gleams of baleful light alone might shew
The pestilential mists, the darkness and the woe.

Kathema little felt the sleet and wind,   115
  He little heeded the wide altered scene;
The flame that lived within his eager mind
  There kindled all the thoughts that once had been.
He stood alone in England's varied woe,
Safe, mid the flood of crime that round his steps did flow.   120

It was an evening when the bitterest breath
  Of dark December swept the mists along
That the lone wanderer came to a wild heath.
  Courage and hope had staid[2] his nature long;
Now cold, and unappeased hunger spent   125
His strength; sensation failed in total languishment.

When he awaked to life cold horror crept
  Even to his heart, for a damp deathy smell
Had slowly come around him while he slept.
  He started . . . lo! the fitful moonbeams fell   130
Upon a dead and naked female form
That from a gibbet[3] high swung to the sullen storm.

And wildly in the wind its dark hair swung,
  Low mingling with the clangor of the chain
Whilst ravenous birds of prey that on it clung   135
  In the dull ear of night poured their sad strain,
And ghastlily her shapeless visage shone
In the unsteady light, half mouldered through the bone.

Then madness seized Kathema, and his mind
  A prophecy of horror filled. He scaled   140
The gibbet which swung slowly in the wind
  High o'er the heath.—Scarcely his strength avail'd
To grasp the chain, when by the moonlight's gleam
His palsied gaze was fixed on Zeinab's altered frame.

---

1. Any luminous optical phenomenon in the earth's atmosphere.
2. Sustained.

3. An upright post with projecting arm from which the bodies of criminals were hung in chains or irons after execution.

Yes! in those orbs once bright with life and love   145
   Now full-fed worms bask in unnatural light;
That neck on which his eyes were wont to rove
   In rapture, changed by putrefaction's blight,
Now rusts the ponderous links that creak beneath
Its weight, and turns to life the frightful sport of death.   150

Then in the moonlight played Kathema's smile
   Calmly.—In peace his spirit seemed to be.
He paused, even like a man at ease awhile,
   Then spoke—"My love! I will be like to thee,
A mouldering carcase or a spirit blest,   155
With thee corruption's prey, or Heaven's happy guest."

He twined the chain around his neck, then leaped
   Forward, in haste to meet the life to come.
An iron-souled son of Europe might have wept
   To witness such a noble being's doom   160
As on the death scene Heaven indignant frowned
And Night in horror drew her veil the dead around.

For they had torn his Zeinab from her home—
   Her innocent habits were all rudely shriven[4]—
And dragged to live in love's untimely tomb   165
   To prostitution, crime and woe was driven.
The human race seemed leagued against her weal
And indignation cased her naked heart in steel.

Therefore against them she waged ruthless war
   With their own arms of bold and bloody crime,—   170
Even like a mild and sweetly-beaming star
   Whose rays were wont to grace the matin prime[5]
Changed to a comet, horrible and bright,
Which wild careers[6] awhile then sinks in dark-red night.

Thus, like its God, unjust and pityless,   175
   Crimes first are made and then avenged by man,
For where's the tender heart, whose hope can bless
   Or man's, or God's, unprofitable plan—
A universe of horror and decay,
Gibbets, disease, and wars and hearts as hard as they.   180

---

4. Confessed, absolved; here used ironically. The penance for Zeinab's "innocent habits" was "prostitution, crime and woe."

5. The order for public morning prayer in the Church of England includes matins, lauds, and prime: *matin prime* would be morning prayers generally.

6. Moves at full speed.

The Retrospect.[1]

Cwm Elan

1812

To trace Duration's lone career,
To check the chariot of the year,[2]
Whose burning wheels forever sweep
The boundaries of oblivion's deep. . . .
To snatch from Time, the monster's, jaw   5
The children which she just had borne
And, ere entombed within her maw,[3]
To drag them to the light of morn
And mark each feature with an eye
Of cold and fearless scrutiny. . . .   10
It asks a soul not formed to feel,
An eye of glass, a hand of steel,
Thoughts that have passed and thoughts that are
With truth and feeling to compare;
A scene which wildered[4] fancy viewed   15
In the soul's coldest solitude,
With that same scene when peaceful love
Flings rapture's colour o'er the grove
When mountain, meadow, wood and stream
With unalloying glory gleam   20
And to the spirit's ear and eye
Are unison and harmony.

The moonlight was my dearer day:—
Then would I wander far away
And lingering on the wild brook's shore   25
To hear its unremitting roar,
Would lose in the ideal flow
All sense of overwhelming woe;
Or at the noiseless noon of night
Would climb some heathy[5] mountain's height   30
And listen to the mystic sound
That stole in fitful gasps around.
I joyed to see the streaks of day
Above the purple peaks decay

---

1. In July and August 1811, Shelley visited Cwm Elan, the Welsh estate of his cousin Thomas Grove, just before he returned to London and eloped with Harriet Westbrook. In June 1812 he returned to Cwm Elan—this time with Harriet. The poem may owe its name and the theme of its opening lines to Southey's "The Retrospect" (1794), but Wordsworth's "Tintern Abbey" (1798) is the chief analogue and exerted the strongest influence on Shelley's poem.

2. The image of the chariot of being appears repeatedly in Shelley's poetry; see footnotes to *Queen Mab,* I.134 and IX.154.

3. Cf. the story of Kronos (Saturn), who devoured his children; through confusion of his name with Chronos, he was identified with Time.

4. Lost, straying.

5. Covered with heather or other low herbage.

And watch the latest line of light   35
Just mingling with the shades of night;
For day with me, was time of woe
When even tears refused to flow;
Then would I stretch my languid frame
Beneath the wild-woods' gloomiest shade   40
And try to quench the ceaseless flame
That on my withered vitals preyed;
Would close mine eyes and dream I were
On some remote and friendless plain
And long to leave existence there   45
If with it I might leave the pain
That with a finger cold and lean
Wrote madness on my withering mien.

It was not unrequited love
That bade my wildered spirit rove;   50
'Twas not the pride, disdaining life,
That with this mortal world at strife
Would yield to the soul's inward sense,
Then groan in human impotence,
And weep, because it is not given   55
To taste on Earth the peace of Heaven.
'Twas not, that in the narrow sphere
Where Nature fixed my wayward fate
There was no friend or kindred dear
Formed to become that spirit's mate,   60
Which, searching on tired pinion,[6] found
Barren and cold repulse around. . . .
Ah no! yet each one sorrow gave
New graces to the narrow grave:

For broken vows had early quelled   65
The stainless spirit's vestal[7] flame.
Yes! whilst the faithful bosom swelled,
Then the envenomed arrow came
And apathy's unaltering eye
Beamed coldness on the misery;   70
And early I had learned to scorn
The chains of clay that bound a soul
Panting to seize the wings of morn,[8]
And where its vital fires were born
To soar, and spurn the cold control   75
Which the vile slaves of earthly night
Would twine around its struggling flight.
O, many were the friends whom fame
Had linked with the unmeaning name[9]

6. Wing.
7. Chaste or virgin.
8. Cf. Psalms 139:9: "If I take the wings of the morning . . ."
9. Shelley refers to the gossip or public notice (*fame*) that had suggested marriage between various *friends* and himself, heir of a baronet, a title that he considered *unmeaning*.

Whose magic marked among mankind 80
The casket of my unknown mind,
Which hidden from the vulgar glare
Imbibed[1] no fleeting radiance there.
My darksome spirit sought. It found
A friendless solitude around.— 85
For who, that might undaunted stand
The saviour of a sinking land,
Would crawl, its ruthless tyrant's slave,
And fatten upon freedom's grave,[2]
Though doomed with her to perish where 90
The captive clasps abhorred despair.[3]

They could not share the bosom's feeling,
Which, passion's every throb revealing,
Dared force on the world's notice cold
Thoughts of unprofitable mould, 95
Who bask in Custom's fickle ray,—
Fit sunshine of such wintry day!
They could not in a twilight walk
Weave an impassioned web of talk
Till mysteries the spirit press 100
In wild yet tender awfulness,[4]
Then feel within our narrow sphere
How little yet how great we are!
But they might shine in courtly glare,
Attract the rabble's cheapest stare, 105
And might command where'er they move
A thing that bears the name of love;
They might be learned, witty, gay,
Foremost in fashion's gilt array,
On Fame's emblazoned pages shine, 110
Be princes' friends, but never mine!

Ye jagged peaks that frown sublime,
Mocking the blunted scythe of Time,
Whence I would watch its lustre pale
Steal from the moon o'er yonder vale! 115

Thou rock, whose bosom black and vast
Bared to the stream's unceasing flow,
Ever its giant shade doth cast
On the tumultuous surge below!

Woods, to whose depth retires to die 120
The wounded echo's melody,
And whither this lone spirit bent
The footstep of a wild intent—

1. Absorbed or received.
2. I.e., continue to enjoy the material benefits and prerogatives that the aristocracy enjoyed.
3. I.e., even if he were doomed to die in prison, filled with ("embracing") despair.
4. Impressive solemnity; dreadfulness.

Meadows! Whose green and spangled breast
These fevered limbs have often pressed   125
Until the watchful fiend despair
Slept in the soothing coolness there!
Have not your varied beauties seen
The sunken eye, the withering mien,
Sad traces of the unuttered pain   130
That froze my heart and burned my brain?

How changed since nature's summer form
Had last the power my grief to charm
Since last ye soothed my spirit's sadness—
Strange chaos of a mingled madness!   135
Changed!—not the loathsome worm that fed
In the dark mansions of the dead,
Now soaring through the fields of air
And gathering purest nectar there,
A butterfly whose million hues   140
The dazzled eye of wonder views,
Long lingering on a work so strange,
Has undergone so bright a change!

How do I feel my happiness?
I cannot tell, but they may guess   145
Whose every gloomy feeling gone,
Friendship and passion feel alone;
Who see mortality's dull clouds
Before affection's murmur fly,
Whilst the mild glances of her eye   150
Pierce the thin veil of flesh that shrouds
The spirit's radiant sanctuary.

O thou![5] whose virtues latest known,
First in this heart yet claim'st a throne;
Whose downy sceptre still shall share   155
The gentle sway with virtue there;
Thou fair in form and pure in mind,
Whose ardent friendship rivets fast
The flowery band our fates that bind,
Which incorruptible shall last   160
When duty's hard and cold control
Had thawed around the burning soul;
The gloomiest retrospects that bind
With crowns of thorn the bleeding mind,
The prospects of most doubtful hue   165
That rise on Fancy's shuddering view,
Are gilt by the reviving ray
Which thou hast flung upon my day.

5. Harriet Westbrook Shelley.

Sonnet[1]

To a balloon, laden with Knowledge

Bright ball of flame that through the gloom of even
Silently takest thine etherial way
And with surpassing glory dimm'st each ray
Twinkling amid the dark blue Depths of Heaven:
Unlike the Fire thou bearest,[2] soon shalt thou   5
Fade like a meteor in surrounding gloom
Whilst that,[3] unquencheable, is doomed to glow—
A watch light by the patriot's lonely tomb,
A ray of courage to the opprest and poor,
A spark, though gleaming on the hovel's hearth,   10
Which through the tyrant's gilded domes shall roar,
A beacon in the darkness of the Earth,
A Sun which o'er the renovated scene
Shall dart like Truth where Falshood yet has been.

To the Emperors of Russia and Austria who eyed the battle of Austerlitz from the heights whilst Buonaparte was active in the thickest of the fight[1]

Coward Chiefs! who while the fight
   Rages in the plain below
Hide the shame of your affright
   On yon distant mountain's brow,
Does one human feeling creep   5
Through your hearts' remorseless sleep
On that silence cold and deep?
   Does one impulse flow
Such as fires the Patriot's breast,
Such as breaks the Hero's rest?[2]   10

1. In August 1812, Shelley was in Devonshire distributing his broadsides (single-sheet publications) entitled *The Devil's Walk* (a poem) and *Declaration of Rights* (prose). One method he used to disseminate these works was to seal them in empty wine bottles and set these afloat in the sea. Shelley commemorated this gesture in a sonnet entitled, "On launching some bottles filled with knowledge into the Bristol Channel." If he also launched one or more of his broadsides in "a balloon," there is no outside evidence.
2. Shelley regularly uses fire as the symbol of spiritual energy—here as knowledge that can overcome evil error; he held the Socratic view that evil resulted from ignorance.
3. Fire (line 5).

1. Napoleon Bonaparte defeated the combined armies of Russia and Austria at Austerlitz in Moravia on December 2, 1805. Shelley completed another poem in the same relatively sophisticated stanza form in February 1812; this attack on the emperors of Austria and Russia probably dates from after August 1813, when they were once again allies in England's anti-French coalition. For the classic fictional description of the battle of Austerlitz, see Tolstoy's *War and Peace*, Part III, chaps. XIIff.
2. In lines 5–10 Shelley supplied no end punctuation except for a period at the end of the stanza. One editor has inserted a question mark at the end of line 6, after *sleep*, instead of after *deep* in line 7.

No, cowards! ye are calm[3] and still,
   Keen frosts that blight the human bud,
Each opening petal blight and kill
   And bathe its tenderness in blood.
Ye hear the groans of those who die,   15
Ye hear the whistling death shots fly
And when the yells of Victory
   Float o'er the murdered good
Ye smile secure.—On yonder plain
The game if lost begins again.   20

Think ye the restless fiend[4] who haunts
   The tumult of yon gory field,
Whom neither shame nor danger daunts,
   Who dares not fear, who cannot yield,
Will not with Equalizing blow   25
Exalt the high, abase the low
And in one mighty shock o'erthrow
   The slaves that sceptres wield
Till from the ruin of the storm
Ariseth Freedom's awful form?   30

Hushed below the battle's jar
   Night rests silent on the Heath,
Silent save when vultures soar
   Above the wounded warrior's death.
How sleep ye now, unfeeling Kings!   35
Peace seldom folds her snowy wings
On poisoned memory's conscience-stings
   Which lurk bad hearts beneath:
Nor downy beds procure repose
Where crime and terror mingle throes.   40

Yet may your terrors rest secure.
   Thou, Northern chief,[5] why startest thou?
Pale Austria,[6] calm those fears. Be sure
   The tyrant needs such slaves as you.
Think ye the world would bear his sway   45
Were dastards such as you away?
No! they would pluck his plumage gay
   Torn from a nation's woe
And lay him in the oblivious gloom
Where Freedom now prepares your tomb.   50

---

3. When speaking of human emotions, Shelley occasionally uses *calm* in a negative sense to mean "unmoved," or "insensitive" (e.g., *Prometheus Unbound*, I.238, 259).
4. Napoleon, portrayed as a "restless fiend," resembles Satan in *Paradise Lost*; Cf. Shelley's remarks on *Paradise Lost* in the Preface to *Prometheus Unbound*.
5. Czar Alexander I (reigned 1801–1825).
6. Francis Hapsburg reigned as Holy Roman Emperor Francis II from 1792 to 1806, when Napoleon dissolved the Holy Roman Empire, and as Francis I, Emperor of Austria, 1804–1835.

Queen Mab;[1]

A Philosophical Poem

ECRASEZ L'INFAME![2]
Correspondance de Voltaire.

Avia Pieridum peragro loca, nullius ante
Trita solo; juvat integros accedere fonteis;
Atque haurire: juvatque novos decerpere flores.

   . . . .

Unde prius nulli velarint tempora musæ.
Primum quod magnis doceo de rebus; et arctis
Religionum animos nodis exsolvere pergo.[3]
Lucret. lib. iv.

Δὸς ποῦ στῶ, καὶ κόσμον κινήσω.[4]
Archimedes.

To Harriet * * * * *[5]

Whose is the love that, gleaming through the world,
Wards off the poisonous arrow of its scorn?
 Whose is the warm and partial praise,
 Virtue's most sweet reward?

1. Shelley conceived *Queen Mab*, his first major poem, in December 1811, and composed it between June 1812 and February 19, 1813. On February 19, 1813, Shelley wrote to his publisher friend Thomas Hookham that it was "finished & transcribed," though the notes were then still in progress. By May 21, 1813, it was in press, but Shelley was by that date convinced that the poem was too radical to be published. Instead he distributed about 70 of the 250 copies printed to individuals he believed would be sympathetic, cutting out his name and address, which appeared as those of the printer.

The poem got some notice in 1817, when its moral quality figured in the decision of the Chancery Court to deprive Shelley of custody of his children by Harriet. In 1821, *Queen Mab* was pirated by William Clark of 201 Strand. Clark was prosecuted by the Society for the Suppression of Vice; his edition was turned over for sale to Richard Carlile, the most courageous of all the radical booksellers, who also discovered, advertised, and (probably) sold the 180 remaining copies of Shelley's original 1813 edition of the poem.

Thereafter *Queen Mab* was reprinted frequently in various editions. It became the Bible of the Chartist movement and later had great influence on British Marxists, including George Bernard Shaw. Shelley himself, however, when he heard of the 1821 reprinting, wrote from Italy in a public letter: "I regret this publication, not so much from literary vanity, as because I fear it is better fitted to injure than to serve the cause of freedom."

Queen Mab, "the fairies' midwife," appears in a famous speech by Mercutio in Shakespeare's *Romeo and Juliet* (I.iv. 53–94), in which her mischievous dreammaking is described in terms that Shelley was later to echo in "The Witch of Atlas," lines 617ff. During the eighteenth century Queen Mab was the title character (like Mother Goose) in numerous collections of children's stories. Shelley's choice of this innocent-sounding name for the intermediary between the divine and the human who teaches the soul of Ianthe the revolutionary lessons of the past, situation of the present, and hopes of the future is in keeping with his directions to his publisher to have the poem printed "on fine paper & so as to catch the aristocrats: They will not read it, but their sons & daughters may" (Shelley to Hookham, March 1813; *Letters*, I, 361).
2. "Crush the demon!" In his later years

Beneath whose looks did my reviving soul 5
Riper in truth and virtuous daring grow?
   Whose eyes have I gazed fondly on,
   And loved mankind the more?

Harriet! on thine:—thou wert my purer mind;
Thou wert the inspiration of my song; 10
   Thine are these early wilding flowers,
   Though garlanded by me.

Then press into thy breast this pledge of love,
And know, though time may change and years may roll,
   Each flowret gathered in my heart 15
   It consecrates to thine.

I.[6]

   How wonderful is Death,
   Death and his brother Sleep!
One, pale as yonder waning moon
   With lips of lurid blue;
The other, rosy as the morn 5
   When throned on ocean's wave
   It blushes o'er the world:
Yet both so passing wonderful!

Hath then the gloomy Power
Whose reign is in the tainted sepulchres 10
   Seized on her sinless soul?
   Must then that peerless form
Which love and admiration cannot view
Without a beating heart, those azure veins

---

at Ferney, near Geneva, Voltaire included the phrase in most of his letters. Shelley himself used the phrase at least twice in his letters, once in French (Dec. 20, 1810; *Letters*, I, 29) and again in English (Jan. 3, 1811; *Letters*, I, 35). According to Peter Gay, Voltaire, like Shelley, meant Christianity rather than "religion" by the term *l'infame*.
3. The Latin epigraph comes from the opening of Book IV of Lucretius' Epicurean poem *De rerum natura* (*Of the Nature of Things*). The lines may be translated "I blaze a trail through pathless tracks of the Pierian realm, where no foot has ever trod before. What joy it is to discover virgin springs and drink their waters, and what joy to gather new flowers . . . never before wreathed by the Muses around anyone's head! First, I teach of great matters, and [secondly] I free men's minds from the crippling bonds of superstition." The main subject of Book IV is the nature of sensation and erotic love. Shelley later wrote of Lucretius' poem: "The 4th book is per-

haps the finest. The whole of that passage about love is full of irresistible energy of language as well as the profoundest truth" (*Letters*, I, 545).
4. "Give me somewhere to stand, and I will move the earth," attributed to the Syracusan Greek scientist Archimedes (287–212 B.C.), refers to his enthusiasm for the power of the lever.
5. Shelley first intended this tribute to his first wife, Harriet Westbrook Shelley, to stand as the dedicatory poem in the collection of shorter works now known as *The Esdaile Notebook*; when he failed to find a publisher for that volume, he transferred it (slightly revised) to *Queen Mab*.
6. Shelley described his choice of verse form in a letter to Hogg: "The didactic is in blank heroic verse, & the descriptive in blank lyrical measure. If authority is of any weight in support of this singularity, Miltons Samson Agonistes, the Greek Choruses, & (you will laugh) Southeys Thalaba may be adduced" (Feb. 7, 1813; *Letters*, I, 352).

Which steal like streams along a field of snow,   15
    That lovely outline, which is fair
        As breathing marble, perish?
        Must putrefaction's breath
    Leave nothing of this heavenly sight
        But loathsomeness and ruin?   20
    Spare nothing but a gloomy theme,
On which the lightest heart might moralize?
    Or is it only a sweet slumber
        Stealing o'er sensation,
    Which the breath of roseate morning   25
        Chaseth into darkness?
Will Ianthe[7] wake again,
And give that faithful bosom joy
Whose sleepless spirit waits to catch
Light, life and rapture from her smile?   30

    Yes! she will wake again,
Although her glowing limbs are motionless,
    And silent those sweet lips,
    Once breathing eloquence,
That might have soothed a tyger's rage,   35
Or thawed the cold heart of a conqueror.
    Her dewy eyes are closed,
And on their lids, whose texture fine
Scarce hides the dark blue orbs beneath,
    The baby Sleep is pillowed: 40
    Her golden tresses shade
    The bosom's stainless pride,
Curling like tendrils of the parasite[8]
    Around a marble column.

    Hark! whence that rushing sound?   45
    'Tis like the wondrous strain
That round a lonely ruin swells,
Which, wandering on the echoing shore,
    The enthusiast hears at evening:
'Tis softer than the west wind's sigh;   50
'Tis wilder than the unmeasured notes
Of that strange lyre[9] whose strings
    The genii of the breezes sweep:
    Those lines of rainbow light
Are like the moonbeams when they fall   55

7. The character is modeled on Harriet Shelley (Ianthe's name was given to Shelley's and Harriet's first child, a daughter born June 23, 1813).
8. I.e., ivy.
9. The Aeolian harp or wind lyre was an instrument popular in Shelley's time; designed to be placed in an open window or on a porch, its strings would vibrate in the wind, producing musical sounds (like wind chimes). The image of the poet as an Aeolian harp moved by the winds of a spiritual force or being is prominent in Romantic poetry.

Through some cathedral window, but the teints[1]
    Are such as may not find
    Comparison on earth.

Behold the chariot of the Fairy Queen!
Celestial coursers paw the unyielding air;[2]   60
Their filmy pennons[3] at her word they furl,
And stop obedient to the reins of light:
    These the Queen of spells drew in,
    She spread a charm around the spot,
And leaning graceful from the etherial car,   65
    Long did she gaze, and silently,
        Upon the slumbering maid.

Oh! not the visioned poet in his dreams,
When silvery clouds float through the 'wildered brain,
When every sight of lovely, wild and grand   70
    Astonishes, enraptures, elevates,
        When fancy at a glance combines
        The wondrous and the beautiful,—
So bright, so fair, so wild a shape
    Hath ever yet beheld,   75
As that which reined the coursers of the air,
    And poured the magic of her gaze
        Upon the maiden's sleep.

    The broad and yellow moon
    Shone dimly through her form—   80
That form of faultless symmetry;
The pearly and pellucid[4] car
    Moved not the moonlight's line:
    'Twas not an earthly pageant:
Those who had looked upon the sight,   85
    Passing all human glory,
    Saw not the yellow moon,
    Saw not the mortal scene,
    Heard not the night-wind's rush,
    Heard not an earthly sound,   90
    Saw but the fairy pageant,
    Heard but the heavenly strains
    That filled the lonely dwelling.

The Fairy's frame was slight, yon fibrous cloud,
That catches but the palest tinge of even,   95
And which the straining eye can hardly seize
When melting into eastern twilight's shadow,
Were scarce so thin, so slight; but the fair star
That gems the glittering coronet of morn,[5]

1. Hues or tints.
2. The air gives solid footing to the hooves of "celestial coursers," whose density is no greater than that of air.
3. I.e., wings ("pinions").
4. Translucent or transparent.
5. The planet Venus as morning star.

Sheds not a light so mild, so powerful, 100
As that which, bursting from the Fairy's form,
Spread a purpureal[6] halo round the scene,
  Yet with an undulating motion,
  Swayed to her outline gracefully.

    From her celestial car 105
    The Fairy Queen descended,
    And thrice she waved her wand
Circled with wreaths of amaranth:[7]
    Her thin and misty form
    Moved with the moving air, 110
    And the clear silver tones,
    As thus she spoke, were such
As are unheard by all but gifted ear.

FAIRY.

Stars! your balmiest influence shed!
Elements! your wrath suspend! 115
Sleep, Ocean, in the rocky bounds
    That circle thy domain!
Let not a breath be seen to stir
Around yon grass-grown ruin's height,
    Let even the restless gossamer 120
    Sleep on the moveless air!
    Soul of Ianthe! thou,
Judged alone worthy of the envied boon,
That waits the good and the sincere; that waits
Those who have struggled, and with resolute will 125
Vanquished earth's pride and meanness, burst the chains,
The icy chains of custom, and have shone
The day-stars[8] of their age;—Soul of Ianthe!
    Awake! arise!

    Sudden arose[9] 130
    Ianthe's Soul; it stood
All beautiful in naked purity,
The perfect semblance of its bodily frame,
Instinct[1] with inexpressible beauty and grace;
    Each stain of earthliness 135
    Had passed away, it reassumed
    Its native dignity, and stood
    Immortal amid ruin.

6. Purple; a poetic usage also found in Wordsworth and Byron.
7. From the Greek meaning "unfading" or "incorruptible," the name given to a mythical flower whose blossoms never die.
8. Stars so bright that they are visible during the day; Milton uses the phrase (*Lycidas*, 168) to refer to the sun.
9. The sharp distinction found in lines 130–156 between a perishable body and an immortal, everlasting (*sempiternal*, 149) soul is strongly present in Shelley's early poetry through *Queen Mab*, but appears to be more figurative in later poems like *Adonais*.
1. Animated, impelled; the word appears in Milton's description of the Chariot of Paternal Deitie (*Paradise Lost*, VI. 749ff.), which underlies this and several other descriptions of chariots in Shelley's poetry.

Upon the couch the body lay
   Wrapt in the depth of slumber: 140
Its features were fixed and meaningless.
      Yet animal life was there,
   And every organ yet performed
   Its natural functions: 'twas a sight
Of wonder to behold the body and soul   145
   The self-same lineaments, the same
   Marks of identity were there:
Yet, oh, how different! One aspires to Heaven,
Pants for its sempiternal heritage,
And ever-changing, ever-rising still,   150
      Wantons in endless being.
The other, for a time the unwilling sport
Of circumstance and passion, struggles on;
Fleets through its sad duration rapidly;
Then, like an useless and worn-out machine,   155
      Rots, perishes, and passes.

FAIRY.

   Spirit! who hast dived so deep;
   Spirit! who hast soared so high;
   Thou the fearless, thou the mild,
Accept the boon thy worth hath earned,   160
      Ascend the car with me.

SPIRIT.

Do I dream? is this new feeling
But a visioned ghost of slumber?
   If indeed I am a soul,
A free, a disembodied soul,   165
      Speak again to me.

FAIRY.

I am the Fairy MAB: to me 'tis given
The wonders of the human world to keep:
The secrets of the immeasurable past,
In the unfailing consciences of men,   170
Those stern, unflattering chroniclers, I find:
The future, from the causes which arise
In each event, I gather: not the sting
Which retributive memory implants
In the hard bosom of the selfish man;   175
Nor that extatic and exulting throb
Which virtue's votary feels when he sums up
The thoughts and actions of a well-spent day,
Are unforeseen, unregistered by me:
And it is yet permitted me, to rend   180
The veil of mortal frailty, that the spirit
Clothed in its changeless purity, may know

How soonest to accomplish the great end
For which it hath its being, and may taste
That peace, which in the end all life will share.   185
This is the meed of virtue; happy Soul,
    Ascend the car with me!

    The chains of earth's immurement
      Fell from Ianthe's spirit;
They shrank and brake² like bandages of straw   190
    Beneath a wakened giant's strength.
      She knew her glorious change,
    And felt in apprehension uncontrolled
      New raptures opening round:
Each day-dream of her mortal life,   195
Each frenzied vision of the slumbers
    That closed each well-spent day,
    Seemed now to meet reality.

    The Fairy and the Soul proceeded;
      The silver clouds disparted;   200
And as the car of magic they ascended,
    Again the speechless music swelled,
    Again the coursers of the air
Unfurled their azure pennons, and the Queen
    Shaking the beamy reins   205
    Bade them pursue their way.

    The magic car moved on.
    The night was fair, and countless stars
Studded heaven's dark blue vault,—
    Just o'er the eastern wave   210
Peeped the first faint smile of morn:—
    The magic car moved on—
    From the celestial hoofs
The atmosphere in flaming sparkles flew,
    And where the burning wheels   215
Eddied above the mountain's loftiest peak,
    Was traced a line of lightning.
    Now it flew far above a rock,
      The utmost verge of earth,
The rival of the Andes,³ whose dark brow   220
    Lowered o'er the silver sea.

    Far, far below the chariot's path,
      Calm as a slumbering babe,
    Tremendous Ocean lay.
    The mirror of its stillness shewed   225
      The pale and waning stars,

2. Broke.
3. In Shelley's day natural historians believed that the Andes were the highest mountains in the world and that the mountains of Japan were among those that rivaled them in height (Buffon, *Natural History*).

The chariot's fiery track,
And the grey light of morn
Tinging those fleecy clouds
That canopied the dawn.   230
    Seemed it, that the chariot's way
Lay through the midst of an immense concave,
Radiant with million constellations, tinged
    With shades of infinite colour,
    And semicircled with a belt   235
    Flashing incessant meteors.

The magic car moved on.
    As they approached their goal
The coursers seemed to gather speed;
The sea no longer was distinguished; earth   240
    Appeared a vast and shadowy sphere;
    The sun's unclouded orb
    Rolled through the black concave;[4]
    Its rays of rapid light
Parted around the chariot's swifter course,   245
    And fell, like ocean's feathery spray
    Dashed from the boiling surge
    Before a vessel's prow.

The magic car moved on.
    Earth's distant orb appeared   250
The smallest light that twinkles in the heaven;
    Whilst round the chariot's way
    Innumerable systems rolled,[5]
    And countless spheres diffused
    An ever-varying glory.   255
It was a sight of wonder: some
Were horned like the crescent moon;
Some shed a mild and silver beam
Like Hesperus[6] o'er the western sea;
Some dash'd athwart with trains of flame,   260
Like worlds to death and ruin driven;
Some shone like suns, and as the chariot passed,
    Eclipsed all other light.

    Spirit of Nature! here!
In this interminable wilderness   265
Of worlds, at whose immensity

4. "Beyond our atmosphere the sun would appear a rayless orb of fire in the midst of a black concave. The equal diffusion of its light on earth is owing to the refraction of the rays by the atmosphere, and their reflection from other bodies" (the beginning of Shelley's note).
5. "The plurality of worlds,—the indefinite immensity of the universe is a most awful subject of contemplation. He who rightly feels its mystery and grandeur, is in no danger of seduction from the falsehoods of religious systems, or of deifying the principle of the universe. . . . Millions and millions of suns are ranged around us, all attended by innumerable worlds, all keeping the paths of immutable necessity" (from Shelley's note).
6. The planet Venus as the evening star; also called Vesper.

Even soaring fancy staggers,
Here is thy fitting temple.
    Yet not the lightest leaf
That quivers to the passing breeze   270
    Is less instinct with thee:
    Yet not the meanest worm
That lurks in graves and fattens on the dead
    Less shares thy eternal breath.
        Spirit of Nature! thou!   275
    Imperishable as this scene,
        Here is thy fitting temple.

II.

If solitude hath ever led thy steps
    To the wild ocean's echoing shore,
        And thou hast lingered there,
        Until the sun's broad orb
    Seemed resting on the burnished wave,   5
        Thou must have marked the lines
Of purple gold, that motionless
        Hung o'er the sinking sphere:
Thou must have marked the billowy clouds
Edged with intolerable radiancy   10
        Towering like rocks of jet
        Crowned with a diamond wreath.
        And yet there is a moment,
        When the sun's highest point
Peeps like a star o'er ocean's western edge,   15
When those far clouds of feathery gold,
    Shaded with deepest purple, gleam
    Like islands on a dark blue sea;
Then has thy fancy soared above the earth,
        And furled its wearied wing   20
        Within the Fairy's fane.[7]

    Yet not the golden islands
    Gleaming in yon flood of light,
        Nor the feathery curtains
    Stretching o'er the sun's bright couch,   25
    Nor the burnished ocean waves
        Paving that gorgeous dome,
    So fair, so wonderful a sight
As Mab's etherial palace could afford.
Yet likest evening's vault, that faery Hall!   30
As Heaven, low resting on the wave, it spread
        Its floors of flashing light,
        Its vast and azure dome,
        Its fertile golden islands
        Floating on a silver sea;   35

7. Temple.

Whilst suns their mingling beamings darted
Through clouds of circumambient[8] darkness,
   And pearly battlements around
   Looked o'er the immense of Heaven.

   The magic car no longer moved.   40
     The Fairy and the Spirit
     Entered the Hall of Spells:
       Those golden clouds
    That rolled in glittering billows
    Beneath the azure canopy   45
With the etherial footsteps trembled not:
    The light and crimson mists,
Floating to strains of thrilling melody
    Through that unearthly dwelling,
Yielded to every movement of the will.   50
Upon their passive swell the Spirit leaned,
And, for the varied bliss that pressed around,
    Used not the glorious privilege
    Of virtue and of wisdom.

    "Spirit!" the Fairy said,   55
  And pointed to the gorgeous dome,
    "This is a wondrous sight
   And mocks all human grandeur;
But, were it virtue's only meed,[9] to dwell
In a celestial palace, all resigned   60
To pleasurable impulses, immured
Within the prison of itself, the will
Of changeless nature would be unfulfilled.
Learn to make others happy. Spirit, come!
This is thine high reward:—the past shall rise;   65
Thou shalt behold the present; I will teach
    The secrets of the future."

    The Fairy and the Spirit
Approached the overhanging battlement.—
    Below lay stretched the universe!   70
    There, far as the remotest line
    That bounds imagination's flight,
     Countless and unending orbs
     In mazy motion intermingled,
    Yet still fulfilled immutably   75
      Eternal nature's law.
     Above, below, around,
     The circling systems formed
    A wilderness of harmony;
    Each with undeviating aim,   80
In eloquent silence, through the depths of space
    Pursued its wondrous way.

8. Surrounding.   9. Reward.

There was a little light
That twinkled in the misty distance:
   None but a spirit's eye   85
   Might ken[1] that rolling orb;
   None but a spirit's eye,
   And in no other place
But that celestial dwelling, might behold
Each action of this earth's inhabitants.   90
   But matter, space and time
In those aërial mansions cease to act;
And all-prevailing wisdom, when it reaps
The harvest of its excellence, o'erbounds
Those obstacles, of which an earthly soul   95
   Fears to attempt the conquest.

The Fairy pointed to the earth.
The Spirit's intellectual eye
Its kindred beings recognized.
The thronging thousands, to a passing view,   100
   Seemed like an anthill's citizens.
   How wonderful! that even
The passions, prejudices, interests,
That sway the meanest being, the weak touch
   That moves the finest nerve,   105
   And in one human brain
Causes the faintest thought, becomes a link
   In the great chain of nature.

   "Behold," the Fairy cried,
"Palmyra's ruined palaces![2]—   110
   Behold! where grandeur frowned;
   Behold! where pleasure smiled;
What now remains?—the memory
   Of senselessness and shame—
   What is immortal there?   115
   Nothing—it stands to tell
   A melancholy tale, to give
   An awful warning: soon
Oblivion will steal silently
   The remnant of its fame.   120
   Monarchs and conquerors there
Proud o'er prostrate millions trod—
The earthquakes of the human race;
Like them, forgotten when the ruin
   That marks their shock is past.   125

1. Recognize.
2. Palmyra, in what is now Syria, was once a flourishing city. Under its princess Zenobia Septima (who became first the wife and then the heir of Odenatus, co-ruler of the Roman Empire) Palmyra challenged Rome itself, but the city was totally destroyed in 273 A.D. after Aure-lian successfully besieged Zenobia there. Palmyra's ruins were invoked by authors, especially in Volney's *Ruins of Empire*, as an illustration of the ephemeral nature of human glory; Shelley's friend Thomas Love Peacock published a poem entitled *Palmyra* on this theme in 1806.

"Beside the eternal Nile,
The Pyramids have risen.
Nile shall pursue his changeless way:
Those pyramids shall fall;
Yea! not a stone shall stand to tell   130
The spot whereon they stood!
Their very site shall be forgotten,
As is their builder's name!

"Behold yon sterile spot;
Where now the wandering Arab's tent   135
Flaps in the desart-blast.
There once old Salem's haughty fane[3]
Reared high to heaven its thousand golden domes,
And in the blushing face of day
Exposed its shameful glory.   140
Oh! many a widow, many an orphan cursed
The building of that fane; and many a father,
Worn out with toil and slavery, implored
The poor man's God to sweep it from the earth,
And spare his children the detested task   145
Of piling stone on stone, and poisoning
The choicest days of life,
To soothe a dotard's[4] vanity.
There an inhuman and uncultured race
Howled hideous praises to their Demon-God;   150
They rushed to war, tore from the mother's womb
The unborn child,—old age and infancy
Promiscuous[5] perished; their victorious arms
Left not a soul to breathe.[6] Oh! they were fiends:
But what was he who taught them that the God   155
Of nature and benevolence hath given
A special sanction to the trade of blood?
His name and theirs are fading, and the tales
Of this barbarian nation, which imposture
Recites till terror credits,[7] are pursuing   160
Itself into forgetfulness.

"Where Athens, Rome, and Sparta stood,
There is a moral desart now:
The mean and miserable huts,
The yet more wretched palaces,   165
Contrasted with those antient fanes,
Now crumbling to oblivion;

3. The Temple at Jerusalem, sacked by the Emperor Vespasian and his son Titus in 70 A.D.
4. The dotard is King Solomon.
5. Indiscriminately.
6. Shelley's attack on the religion of the Jews grew out of similar attacks by moralistic skeptics throughout the eighteenth century, from Voltaire to Thomas Paine. Attacks on the Jews were more acceptable in England than attacks on Christianity, which was Shelley's ultimate target.
7. *tales . . . credits:* The Old Testament and perhaps the Apocrypha, sacred writings of the Jews.

The long and lonely colonnades,
Through which the ghost of Freedom stalks,[8]
    Seem like a well-known tune,   170
Which, in some dear scene we have loved to hear,
    Remembered now in sadness.
        But, oh! how much more changed,
        How gloomier is the contrast
        Of human nature there!   175
Where Socrates expired, a tyrant's slave,
A coward and a fool, spreads death around—
    Then, shuddering, meets his own.
Where Cicero and Antoninus lived,[9]
    A cowled and hypocritical monk   180
        Prays, curses and deceives.

        "Spirit! ten thousand years
        Have scarcely past away,
Since, in the waste where now the savage drinks
His enemy's blood, and aping Europe's sons,   185
    Wakes the unholy song of war,
    Arose a stately city,[1]
Metropolis of the western continent:
    There, now, the mossy column-stone,
Indented by time's unrelaxing grasp,   190
        Which once appeared to brave
        All, save its country's ruin;
        There the wide forest scene,
Rude in the uncultivated loveliness
        Of gardens long run wild,   195
Seems, to the unwilling sojourner, whose steps
    Chance in that desert has delayed,
Thus to have stood since earth was what it is.
    Yet once it was the busiest haunt,
Whither, as to a common centre, flocked   200
    Strangers, and ships, and merchandise:
        Once peace and freedom blest
        The cultivated plain:
        But wealth, that curse of man,
Blighted the bud of its prosperity: 205
Virtue and wisdom, truth and liberty,
Fled, to return not, until man shall know
        That they alone can give the bliss
            Worthy a soul that claims
            Its kindred with eternity.   210

---

8. The spirit of Freedom from the Greek and Roman republics haunts the monuments of their past glories.
9. Cicero, republican orator and Stoic philosopher, and the good emperor Marcus Aurelius Antoninus, also a Stoic philosopher, are named as the virtuous spirits of ancient Rome.
1. Lines 182–210 probably refer to the ruins of Mayan cities in Central America.

"There's not one atom of yon earth
  But once was living man;
Nor the minutest drop of rain,
That hangeth in its thinnest cloud,
  But flowed in human veins: 215
  And from the burning plains
  Where Libyan monsters yell,
  From the most gloomy glens
  Of Greenland's sunless clime,
  To where the golden fields   220
  Of fertile England spread
  Their harvest to the day,
  Thou canst not find one spot
  Whereon no city stood.

  "How strange is human pride!   225
I tell thee that those living things,
To whom the fragile blade of grass,
  That springeth in the morn
  And perisheth ere noon,
  Is an unbounded world;   230
I tell thee that those viewless[2] beings,
Whose mansion is the smallest particle
Of the impassive[3] atmosphere,
  Think, feel and live like man;
That their affections and antipathies,   235
  Like his, produce the laws
  Ruling their moral state;
  And the minutest throb
That through their frame diffuses
  The slightest, faintest motion,   240
  Is fixed and indispensable
  As the majestic laws
  That rule yon rolling orbs."[4]

The Fairy paused. The Spirit,
In extacy of admiration, felt   245
All knowledge of the past revived; the events
  Of old and wondrous times,
Which dim tradition interruptedly
Teaches the credulous vulgar, were unfolded
  In just perspective to the view;   250
  Yet dim from their infinitude.
    The Spirit seemed to stand
High on an isolated pinnacle;
The flood of ages combating below,

---

2. Invisible.
3. Insensate; unable to feel pain.
4. Shelley's conception that there are minute universes within atoms comparable to the universe men inhabit (lines 225–243) is given another form in his "Ode to Heaven."

The depth of the unbounded universe 255
    Above, and all around
  Nature's unchanging harmony.

III.

  "FAIRY!" the Spirit said,
  And on the Queen of spells
  Fixed her etherial eyes,
  "I thank thee. Thou hast given
A boon which I will not resign, and taught 5
A lesson not to be unlearned. I know
The past, and thence I will essay to glean
A warning for the future, so that man
May profit by his errors, and derive
  Experience from his folly: 10
For, when the power of imparting joy
Is equal to the will, the human soul
  Requires no other Heaven"[5]

MAB.

  Turn thee, surpassing Spirit!
  Much yet remains unscanned. 15
  Thou knowest how great is man,
  Thou knowest his imbecility:[6]
  Yet learn thou what he is:
  Yet learn the lofty destiny
  Which restless time prepares 20
  For every living soul.

Behold a gorgeous palace, that amid
Yon populous city, rears its thousand towers
And seems itself a city. Gloomy troops
Of sentinels, in stern and silent ranks, 25
Encompass it around: the dweller there
Cannot be free and happy; hearest thou not
The curses of the fatherless, the groans
Of those who have no friend? He passes on:
The King, the wearer of a gilded chain 30
That binds his soul to abjectness, the fool
Whom courtiers nickname monarch, whilst a slave
Even to the basest appetites—that man
Heeds not the shriek of penury; he smiles
At the deep curses which the destitute 35
Mutter in secret, and a sullen joy
Pervades his bloodless heart when thousands groan

---

5. The discrepancy between the will to do good and the power of doing so is a major theme throughout Shelley's poetry; in *Queen Mab* he advocates increasing the human power for doing good by in-creasing men's knowledge, and he finds no absolute need for Heaven or an after-life.
6. Weakness, feebleness.

But for those morsels which his wantonness
Wastes in unjoyous revelry, to save
All that they love from famine: when he hears   40
The tale of horror, to some ready-made face
Of hypocritical ascent he turns,
Smothering the glow of shame, that, spite of him,
Flushes his bloated cheek.
                 Now to the meal
Of silence, grandeur, and excess, he drags   45
His palled[7] unwilling appetite. If gold,
Gleaming around, and numerous viands[8] culled
From every clime, could force the loathing sense
To overcome satiety,—if wealth
The spring it draws from poisons not,—or vice,   50
Unfeeling, stubborn vice, converteth not
Its food to deadliest venom; then that king
Is happy; and the peasant who fulfils
His unforced task, when he returns at even,
And by the blazing faggot[9] meets again   55
Her welcome for whom all his toil is sped,
Tastes not a sweeter meal.
                Behold him now
Stretched on the gorgeous couch; his fevered brain
Reels dizzily awhile: but ah! too soon
The slumber of intemperance subsides,   60
And conscience, that undying serpent, calls
Her venomous brood to their nocturnal task.
Listen! he speaks! oh! mark that frenzied eye—
Oh! mark that deadly visage.

KING.

            No cessation!
Oh! must this last for ever? Awful death,   65
I wish, yet fear to clasp thee!—Not one moment
Of dreamless sleep! O dear and blessed peace!
Why dost thou shroud thy vestal purity
In penury and dungeons? wherefore lurkest
With danger, death, and solitude; yet shunn'st   70
The palace I have built thee? Sacred peace!
Oh visit me but once, but pitying shed
One drop of balm upon my withered soul.

THE FAIRY.

Vain man! that palace is the virtuous heart,
And peace defileth not her snowy robes   75
In such a shed as thine. Hark! yet he mutters;
His slumbers are but varied agonies,
They prey like scorpions on the springs of life.

---

7. Weakened, enfeebled.
8. Articles of food, victuals.

9. A bundle of twigs or small sticks tied
together for use as fuel.

There needeth not the hell that bigots frame
To punish those who err: earth in itself   80
Contains at once the evil and the cure;
And all-sufficing nature can chastise
Those who transgress her law,—she only knows
How justly to proportion to the fault.
The punishment it merits.
                 Is it strange   85
That this poor wretch should pride him in his woe?
Take pleasure in his abjectness, and hug
The scorpion that consumes him? Is it strange
That, placed on a conspicuous throne of thorns,
Grasping an iron sceptre, and immured   90
Within a splendid prison, whose stern bounds
Shut him from all that's good or dear on earth,
His soul asserts not its humanity?
That man's mild nature rises not in war
Against a king's employ? No—'tis not strange.   95
He, like the vulgar, thinks, feels, acts and lives
Just as his father did; the unconquered powers
Of precedent and custom interpose
Between a *king* and virtue. Stranger yet,
To those who know not nature, nor deduce   100
The future from the present, it may seem,
That not one slave, who suffers from the crimes
Of this unnatural being; not one wretch,
Whose children famish, and whose nuptial bed
Is earth's unpitying bosom, rears an arm   105
To dash him from his throne!
                 Those gilded flies[1]
That, basking in the sunshine of a court,
Fatten on its corruption!—what are they?
—The drones[2] of the community; they feed
On the mechanic's labour: the starved hind   110
For them compels the stubborn glebe[3] to yield
Its unshared harvests; and yon squalid form,
Leaner than fleshless misery, that wastes
A sunless life in the unwholesome mine,
Drags out in labour a protracted death,   115
To glut their grandeur; many faint with toil,
That few may know the cares and woe of sloth.

Whence, thinkest thou, kings and parasites arose?
Whence that unnatural line of drones, who heap
Toil and unvanquishable penury   120

1. The kings' courtiers; the literary allusion is to the description of Sporus in Pope's *Epistle to Dr. Arbuthnot*, 305–333, especially 309–311.
2. The natural analogy is to a beehive community and the literary allusion to
Bernard de Mandeville's *The Fable of the Bees* (1714).
3. *hind . . . glebe:* The hired agricultural laborer plows the stubborn soil or clod of earth.

On those who build their palaces, and bring
Their daily bread?—From vice, black loathsome vice;
From rapine, madness, treachery, and wrong;
From all that genders misery, and makes
Of earth this thorny wilderness; from lust,   125
Revenge, and murder. . . . And when reason's voice,
Loud as the voice of nature, shall have waked
The nations; and mankind perceive that vice
Is discord, war, and misery; that virtue
Is peace, and happiness and harmony;   130
When man's maturer nature shall disdain
The playthings of its childhood;—kingly glare
Will lose its power to dazzle; its authority
Will silently pass by; the gorgeous throne
Shall stand unnoticed in the regal hall,   135
Fast falling to decay; whilst falsehood's trade
Shall be as hateful and unprofitable
As that of truth is now.
     Where is the fame
Which the vainglorious mighty of the earth
Seek to eternize? Oh! the faintest sound   140
From time's light footfall, the minutest wave
That swells the flood of ages, whelms in nothing
The unsubstantial bubble. Aye! to-day
Stern is the tyrant's mandate, red the gaze
That flashes desolation, strong the arm   145
That scatters multitudes. To-morrow comes!
That mandate is a thunder-peal that died
In ages past; that gaze, a transient flash
On which the midnight closed, and on that arm
The worm has made his meal.
      The virtuous man,   150
Who, great in his humility, as kings
Are little in their grandeur; he who leads
Invincibly a life of resolute good,
And stands amid the silent dungeon-depths
More free and fearless than the trembling judge,   155
Who, clothed in venal power, vainly strove
To bind the impassive[4] spirit;—when he falls,
His mild eye beams benevolence no more:
Withered the hand outstretched but to relieve;
Sunk Reason's simple eloquence, that rolled   160
But to appal the guilty. Yes! the grave
Hath quenched that eye, and death's relentless frost
Withered that arm: but the unfading fame
Which virtue hangs upon its votary's tomb;
The deathless memory of that man, whom kings   165
Call to their mind and tremble; the remembrance

4. Unyielding (cf. II.233).

With which the happy spirit contemplates
Its well-spent pilgrimage on earth,
Shall never pass away.

Nature rejects the monarch, not the man;   170
The subject, not the citizen: for kings
And subjects, mutual foes, for ever play
A losing game into each other's hands,
Whose stakes are vice and misery. The man
Of virtuous soul commands not, nor obeys.   175
Power, like a desolating pestilence,
Pollutes whate'er it touches; and obedience,
Bane of all genius, virtue, freedom, truth,
Makes slaves of men, and, of the human frame,
A mechanized automaton.
                When Nero,   180
High over flaming Rome, with savage joy
Lowered[5] like a fiend, drank with enraptured ear
The shrieks of agonizing death, beheld
The frightful desolation spread, and felt
A new-created sense within his soul   185
Thrill to the sight, and vibrate to the sound;
Thinkest thou his grandeur had not overcome
The force of human kindness? and, when Rome,
With one stern blow, hurled not the tyrant down,
Crushed not the arm red with her dearest blood,   190
Had not submissive abjectness destroyed
Nature's suggestions?
                Look on yonder earth:
The golden harvests spring; the unfailing sun
Sheds light and life; the fruits, the flowers, the trees,
Arise in due succession; all things speak   195
Peace, harmony, and love. The universe,
In nature's silent eloquence, declares
That all fulfil the works of love and joy,—
All but the outcast man. He fabricates[6]
The sword which stabs his peace; he cherisheth   200
The snakes that gnaw his heart; he raiseth up
The tyrant, whose delight is in his woe,
Whose sport is in his agony. Yon sun,
Lights it the great alone? Yon silver beams,
Sleep they less sweetly on the cottage thatch,   205
Than on the dome of kings? Is mother earth
A step-dame to her numerous sons, who earn
Her unshared gifts with unremitting toil;
A mother only to those puling[7] babes
Who, nursed in ease and luxury, make men   210

5. Frowned.   7. Whining or complaining.
6. Makes.

The playthings of their babyhood, and mar,
In self-important childishness, that peace
Which men alone appreciate?

      Spirit of Nature! no.
The pure diffusion of thy essence throbs   215
  Alike in every human heart.
    Thou, aye, erectest there
  Thy throne of power unappealable:
Thou art the judge beneath whose nod
Man's brief and frail authority   220
    Is powerless as the wind
      That passeth idly by.
Thine the tribunal which surpasseth
    The shew of human justice,
      As God surpasses man.   225

      Spirit of Nature! thou
Life of interminable multitudes;
  Soul of those mighty spheres
Whose changeless paths through Heaven's deep silence lie;
  Soul of that smallest being,   230
    The dwelling of whose life
  Is one faint April sun-gleam;—
  Man, like these passive things,
Thy will unconsciously fulfilleth:
  Like theirs, his age of endless peace,   235
    Which time is fast maturing,
    Will swiftly, surely come;
And the unbounded frame, which thou pervadest,
    Will be without a flaw
Marring its perfect symmetry.   240

IV.

[THE FAIRY CONTINUES:]

How beautiful this night! the balmiest sigh,
Which vernal zephyrs breathe in evening's ear,
Were discord to the speaking quietude
That wraps this moveless scene. Heaven's ebon vault,[8]
Studded with stars unutterably bright,   5
Through which the moon's unclouded grandeur rolls,
Seems like a canopy which love had spread
To curtain her sleeping world. Yon gentle hills,
Robed in a garment of untrodden snow;
Yon darksome rocks, whence icicles depend,[9]   10
So stainless, that their white and glittering spires
Tinge not the moon's pure beam; yon castled steep,
Whose banner hangeth o'er the time-worn tower

8. Black (ebony) arch.   9. Hang down.

So idly, that rapt fancy deemeth it
A metaphor of peace;—all form a scene   15
Where musing solitude might love to lift
Her soul above this sphere of earthliness;
Where silence undisturbed might watch alone,
So cold, so bright, so still.
                        The orb of day,
In southern climes, o'er ocean's waveless field   20
Sinks sweetly smiling: not the faintest breath
Steals o'er the unruffled deep; the clouds of eve
Reflect unmoved the lingering beam of day;
And vesper's[1] image on the western main
Is beautifully still. To-morrow comes: 25
Cloud upon cloud, in dark and deepening mass,
Roll o'er the blackened waters; the deep roar
Of distant thunder mutters awfully;
Tempest unfolds its pinion o'er the gloom
That shrouds the boiling surge; the pityless fiend,   30
With all his winds and lightnings, tracks his prey;
The torn deep yawns,—the vessel finds a grave
Beneath its jugged gulph.
                  Ah! whence yon glare
That fires the arch of heaven?—that dark red smoke
Blotting the silver moon? The stars are quenched   35
In darkness, and the pure and spangling snow
Gleams faintly through the gloom that gathers round!
Hark to that roar, whose swift and deaf'ning peals
In countless echoes through the mountains ring,
Startling pale midnight on her starry throne!   40
Now swells the intermingling din; the jar
Frequent and frightful of the bursting bomb;
The falling beam, the shriek, the groan, the shout,
The ceaseless clangor, and the rush of men
Inebriate with rage:—loud, and more loud   45
The discord grows; till pale death shuts the scene,
And o'er the conqueror and the conquered draws
His cold and bloody shroud.—Of all the men
Whom day's departing beam saw blooming there,
In proud and vigorous health; of all the hearts   50
That beat with anxious life at sun-set there;
How few survive, how few are beating now!
All is deep silence, like the fearful calm
That slumbers in the storm's portentous pause;
Save when the frantic wail of widowed love   55
Comes shuddering on the blast, or the faint moan
With which some soul bursts from the frame of clay
Wrapt round its struggling powers.

---

1. The planet Venus as the evening star (see I.259).

The grey morn
Dawns on the mournful scene; the sulphurous smoke
Before the icy wind slow rolls away,   60
And the bright beams of frosty morning dance
Along the spangling snow. There tracks of blood
Even to the forest's depth, and scattered arms,
And lifeless warriors, whose hard lineaments
Death's self could change not, mark the dreadful path   65
Of the outsallying[2] victors: far behind,
Black ashes note where their proud city stood.
Within yon forest is a gloomy glen—
Each tree which guards its darkness from the day,
Waves o'er a warrior's tomb.

                  I see thee shrink,   70
Surpassing Spirit!—wert thou human else?
I see a shade of doubt and horror fleet
Across thy stainless features: yet fear not;
This is no unconnected misery,
Nor stands uncaused, and irretrievable.   75
Man's evil nature, that apology
Which kings who rule, and cowards who crouch, set up
For their unnumbered crimes, sheds not the blood
Which desolates the discord-wasted land.
From kings, and priests, and statesmen, war arose,   80
Whose safety is man's deep unbettered woe,
Whose grandeur his debasement. Let the axe
Strike at the root, the poison-tree will fall;
And where its venomed exhalations spread
Ruin, and death, and woe, where millions lay   85
Quenching the serpent's famine, and their bones
Bleaching unburied in the putrid blast,
A garden shall arise, in loveliness
Surpassing fabled Eden.

             Hath Nature's soul,
That formed this world so beautiful, that spread   90
Earth's lap with plenty, and life's smallest chord
Strung to unchanging unison, that gave
The happy birds their dwelling in the grove,
That yielded to the wanderers of the deep
The lovely silence of the unfathomed main,   95
And filled the meanest worm that crawls in dust
With spirit, thought, and love; on Man alone,
Partial in causeless malice, wantonly
Heaped ruin, vice, and slavery; his soul
Blasted with withering curses; placed afar   100
The meteor-happiness, that shuns his grasp,

---

2. A *sally* was a sudden charge out of a besieged place in an attack upon the besiegers.

But serving on the frightful gulph to glare,
Rent wide beneath his footsteps?
                    Nature!—no!
Kings, priests, and statesmen, blast the human flower
Even in its tender bud; their influence darts   105
Like subtle poison through the bloodless veins
Of desolate society. The child,
Ere he can lisp his mother's sacred name,
Swells with the unnatural pride of crime, and lifts
His baby-sword even in a hero's mood.   110
This infant-arm becomes the bloodiest scourge
Of devastated earth; whilst specious names,
Learnt in soft childhood's unsuspecting hour,
Serve as the sophisms[3] with which manhood dims
Bright reason's ray, and sanctifies the sword   115
Upraised to shed a brother's innocent blood.
Let priest-led slaves cease to proclaim that man
Inherits vice and misery, when force
And falshood hang even o'er the cradled babe,
Stifling with rudest grasp all natural good.   120

Ah! to the stranger-soul, when first it peeps
From its new tenement,[4] and looks abroad
For happiness and sympathy, how stern
And desolate a tract is this wide world!
How withered all the buds of natural good!   125
No shade, no shelter from the sweeping storms
Of pityless power! On its wretched frame,
Poisoned, perchance, by the disease and woe
Heaped on the wretched parent whence it sprung
By morals, law, and custom, the pure winds   130
Of heaven, that renovate the insect tribes,[5]
May breathe not. The untainting light of day
May visit not its lodgings.[6] It is bound
Ere it has life: yea, all the chains are forged
Long ere its being: all liberty and love   135
And peace is torn from its defencelessness;
Cursed from its birth, even from its cradle doomed
To abjectness and bondage!

Throughout this varied and eternal world
Soul is the only element; the block   140
That for uncounted ages has remained
The moveless pillar of a mountain's weight
Is active, living spirit. Every grain
Is sentient both in unity and part,

---

3. False yet plausible arguments, especially those urging expediency.
4. *stranger-soul . . . tenement:* The image is that of a complete soul coming from another realm to enter the "house" or "dwelling-place" of the human body.
5. *pure winds . . . insect tribes:* According to Pliny's *Natural History*, locusts.
6. Though the first edition reads *longings*, the context would suggest that this was a typographical error that slipped through unnoticed.

And the minutest atom comprehends   145
A world of loves and hatreds; these beget
Evil and good: hence truth and falshood spring;
Hence will and thought and action, all the germs
Of pain or pleasure, sympathy or hate,
That variegate the eternal universe.   150
Soul is not more polluted than the beams
Of heaven's pure orb, ere round their rapid lines
The taint of earth-born atmospheres arise.[7]

Man is of soul and body, formed for deeds
Of high resolve, on fancy's boldest wing   155
To soar unwearied, fearlessly to turn
The keenest pangs to peacefulness, and taste
The joys which mingled sense and spirit yield.
Or he is formed for abjectness and woe,
To grovel on the dunghill of his fears,   160
To shrink at every sound, to quench the flame
Of natural love in sensualism, to know
That hour as blest when on his worthless days
The frozen hand of death shall set its seal,
Yet fear the cure, though hating the disease.   165
The one is man that shall hereafter be;
The other, man as vice has made him now.

War is the statesman's game, the priest's delight,
The lawyer's jest, the hired assassin's trade,
And, to those royal murderers, whose mean thrones   170
Are bought by crimes of treachery and gore,
The bread they eat, the staff on which they lean.
Guards, garbed in blood-red livery, surround
Their palaces, participate[8] the crimes
That force defends, and from a nation's rage   175
Secure the crown, which all the curses reach
That famine, frenzy, woe and penury breathe.
These are the hired bravos who defend
The tyrant's throne—the bullies of his fear:[9]
These are the sinks and channels of worst vice,   180
The refuse of society, the dregs
Of all that is most vile: their cold hearts blend
Deceit with sternness, ignorance with pride,
All that is mean and villainous, with rage
Which hopelessness of good, and self-contempt,   185
Alone might kindle; they are decked in wealth,

7. Shelley's doctrine in lines 139–153 is that good and evil arise from the nature of soul, or active, living spirit, which is *sentient* and exhibits *loves* and *hatreds* (attractions and repulsions), whence spring all moral qualities.
8. Share, take part in.
9. Shelley, in a long note, quotes from Essay V of William Godwin's *Enquirer:*

"A soldier is a man whose business it is to kill those who never offended him, and who are the innocent martyrs of other men's iniquities. Whatever may become of the abstract question of the justifiableness of war, it seems impossible that the soldier should not be a depraved and unnatural being."

Honour and power, then are sent abroad
To do their work. The pestilence that stalks
In gloomy triumph through some eastern land
Is less destroying. They cajole with gold,   190
And promises of fame, the thoughtless youth
Already crushed with servitude: he knows
His wretchedness too late, and cherishes
Repentance for his ruin, when his doom
Is sealed in gold and blood!   195
Those too the tyrant serve, who, skilled to snare
The feet of justice in the toils of law,
Stand, ready to oppress the weaker still;
And, right or wrong, will vindicate for gold,
Sneering at public virtue, which beneath   200
Their pityless tread lies torn and trampled, where
Honour sits smiling at the sale of truth.

Then grave and hoary-headed hypocrites,
Without a hope, a passion, or a love,
Who, through a life of luxury and lies,   205
Have crept by flattery to the seats of power,
Support the system whence their honours flow. . . .
They have three words:—well tyrants know their use,
Well pay them for the loan, with usury
Torn from a bleeding world!—God, Hell, and Heaven.   210
A vengeful, pityless, and almighty fiend,
Whose mercy is a nickname for the rage
Of tameless tygers hungering for blood.
Hell, a red gulph of everlasting fire,
Where poisonous and undying worms prolong   215
Eternal misery to those hapless slaves
Whose life has been a penance for its crimes.
And Heaven, a meed for those who dare belie
Their human nature, quake, believe, and cringe
Before the mockeries of earthly power.   220

These tools the tyrant tempers to his work,
Wields in his wrath, and as he wills destroys,
Omnipotent in wickedness: the while
Youth springs, age moulders, manhood tamely does
His bidding, bribed by short-lived joys to lend   225
Force to the weakness of his trembling arm.

They rise, they fall; one generation comes
Yielding its harvest to destruction's scythe.
It fades, another blossoms: yet behold!
Red glows the tyrant's stamp-mark on its bloom,   230
Withering and cankering deep its passive prime.
He has invented lying words and modes,
Empty and vain as his own coreless heart;

Evasive meanings, nothings of much sound,
To lure the heedless victim to the toils   235
Spread round the valley of its paradise.

Look to thyself, priest, conqueror, or prince!
Whether thy trade is falshood, and thy lusts
Deep wallow in the earnings of the poor,
With whom thy master[1] was:—or thou delight'st   240
In numbering o'er the myriads of thy slain,
All misery weighing nothing in the scale
Against thy short-lived fame: or thou dost load
With cowardice and crime the groaning land,
A pomp-fed king. Look to thy wretched self!   245
Aye, art thou not the veriest slave that e'er
Crawled on the loathing earth? Are not thy days
Days of unsatisfying listlessness?
Dost thou not cry, ere night's long rack[2] is o'er,
"When will the morning come?" Is not thy youth   250
A vain and feverish dream of sensualism?
Thy manhood blighted with unripe disease?
Are not thy views of unregretted death
Drear, comfortless, and horrible? Thy mind,
Is it not morbid as thy nerveless frame,   255
Incapable of judgment, hope, or love?
And dost thou wish the errors to survive
That bar thee from all sympathies of good,
After the miserable interest
Thou hold'st in their protraction? When the grave   260
Has swallowed up thy memory and thyself,
Dost thou desire the bane that poisons earth
To twine its roots around thy coffined clay,
Spring from thy bones, and blossom on thy tomb,
That of its fruit thy babes may eat and die?   265

V.

[THE FAIRY CONTINUES:]

Thus do the generations of the earth
Go to the grave, and issue from the womb,
Surviving still the imperishable change
That renovates the world; even as the leaves
Which the keen frost-wind of the waning year   5
Has scattered on the forest soil, and heaped
For many seasons there, though long they choke,
Loading with loathsome rottenness the land,
All germs of promise. Yet when the tall trees
From which they fell, shorn of their lovely shapes,   10

1. Jesus Christ.
2. The would-be sleeper's bed is here compared to the instrument of torture on which victims were stretched.

Lie level with the earth to moulder there,
They fertilize the land they long deformed,
Till from the breathing lawn a forest springs
Of youth, integrity, and loveliness,
Like that which gave it life, to spring and die.   15
Thus suicidal selfishness, that blights
The fairest feelings of the opening heart,
Is destined to decay, whilst from the soil
Shall spring all virtue, all delight, all love,
And judgment cease to wage unnatural war   20
With passion's unsubduable array.

Twin-sister of religion, selfishness!
Rival in crime and falshood, aping all
The wanton horrors of her bloody play;
Yet frozen, unimpassioned, spiritless,   25
Shunning the light, and owning not its name;
Compelled, by its deformity, to screen
With flimsy veil of justice and of right,
Its unattractive lineaments, that scare
All, save the brood of ignorance: at once   30
The cause and the effect of tyranny;
Unblushing, hardened, sensual, and vile;
Dead to all love but of its abjectness,
With heart impassive[3] to more noble powers
Than unshared pleasure, sordid gain, or fame;   35
Despising its own miserable being,
Which still it longs, yet fears to disenthrall.

Hence commerce springs, the venal interchange
Of all that human art or nature yield;
Which wealth should purchase not, but want demand,   40
And natural kindness hasten to supply
From the full fountain of its boundless love,
For ever stifled, drained, and tainted now.
Commerce! beneath whose poison-breathing shade
No solitary virtue dares to spring,[4]   45
But poverty and wealth with equal hand
Scatter their withering curses, and unfold
The doors of premature and violent death,
To pining famine and full-fed disease,
To all that shares the lot of human life,   50
Which poisoned, body and soul, scarce drags the chain,
That lengthens as it goes and clanks behind.

Commerce has set the mark of selfishness,
The signet of its all-enslaving power
Upon a shining ore, and called it gold: 55

3. Impassible; Shelley uses the word with two different meanings at II.233 and III.157.
4. The mythical upas tree of Java, a poisonous tree that killed all life within miles of it, figures prominently in similes in Shelley's early poetry (see also IV.82–83). Its story was invented ca. 1783 and appears in Erasmus Darwin's *Loves of the Plants* (1789).

Before whose image bow the vulgar great,
The vainly rich, the miserable proud,
The mob of peasants, nobles, priests, and kings,
And with blind feelings reverence the power
That grinds them to the dust of misery.[5]   60
But in the temple of their hireling hearts
Gold is a living god, and rules in scorn
All earthly things but virtue.

Since tyrants, by the sale of human life,
Heap luxuries to their sensualism, and fame   65
To their wide-wasting and insatiate pride,
Success has sanctioned to a credulous world
The ruin, the disgrace, the woe of war.
His hosts of blind and unresisting dupes
The despot numbers; from his cabinet   70
These puppets of his schemes he moves at will,
Even as the slaves by force or famine driven,
Beneath a vulgar master, to perform
A task of cold and brutal drudgery;—
Hardened to hope, insensible to fear,   75
Scarce living pullies of a dead machine,
Mere wheels of work and articles of trade,
That grace the proud and noisy pomp of wealth!

The harmony and happiness of man
Yields to the wealth of nations;[6] that which lifts   80
His nature to the heaven of its pride,
Is bartered for the poison of his soul;
The weight that drags to earth his towering hopes,
Blighting all prospect but of selfish gain,
Withering all passion but of slavish fear,   85
Extinguishing all free and generous love
Of enterprize and daring, even the pulse
That fancy kindles in the beating heart
To mingle with sensation, it destroys,—
Leaves nothing but the sordid lust of self,   90
The groveling hope of interest and gold,
Unqualified, unmingled, unredeemed
Even by hypocrisy.
                           And statesmen boast
Of wealth![7] The wordy eloquence, that lives
After the ruin of their hearts, can gild   95
The bitter poison of a nation's woe,

5. In a note Shelley quotes the first fourteen lines of book II of Lucretius' *De rerum natura*, ending: "O wretched minds of men! O blinded hearts!"
6. Shelley alludes here to the title of Adam Smith's classic rationale for laissez-faire capitalism.
7. "There is no real wealth but the labour of man. Where the mountains of gold and the vallies of silver, the world would not be one grain of corn the richer; no one comfort would be added to the human race. . . .

"I will not insult common sense by insisting on the doctrine of the natural equality of man. The question is not concerning its desirableness, but its practicability: so far as it is practicable, it

Can turn the worship of the servile mob
To their corrupt and glaring idol, fame,
From virtue, trampled by its iron tread,
Although its dazzling pedestal be raised   100
Amid the horrors of a limb-strewn field,
With desolated dwellings smoking round.
The man of ease, who, by his warm fire-side,
To deeds of charitable intercourse
And bare fulfilment of the common laws   105
Of decency and prejudice, confines
The struggling nature of his human heart,
Is duped by their cold sophistry; he sheds
A passing tear perchance upon the wreck
Of earthly peace, when near his dwelling's door   110
The frightful waves are driven,—when his son
Is murdered by the tyrant, or religion
Drives his wife raving mad.[8] But the poor man,
Whose life is misery, and fear, and care;
Whom the morn wakens but to fruitless toil;   115
Who ever hears his famished offsprings' scream,
Whom their pale mother's uncomplaining gaze
For ever meets, and the proud rich man's eye
Flashing command, and the heart-breaking scene
Of thousands like himself;—he little heeds   120
The rhetoric of tyranny; his hate
Is quenchless as his wrongs; he laughs to scorn
The vain and bitter mockery of words,
Feeling the horror of the tyrant's deeds,
And unrestrained but by the arm of power,   125
That knows and dreads his enmity.

The iron rod of penury still compels
Her wretched slave to bow the knee to wealth,
And poison, with unprofitable toil,
A life too void of solace to confirm   130
The very chains that bind him to his doom.
Nature, impartial in munificence,
Has gifted man with all-subduing will.
Matter, with all its transitory shapes,
Lies subjected and plastic[9] at his feet,   135
That, weak from bondage, tremble as they tread.
How many a rustic Milton has past by,
Stifling the speechless longings of his heart,

---

is desirable. That state of human society
which approaches nearer to an equal
partition of its benefits and evils should
. . . be preferred . . ." (from Shelley's
note).
8. "I am acquainted with a lady of
considerable accomplishments, and the
mother of a numerous family, whom the
Christian religion has goaded to incurable
insanity. A parallel case is, I believe,
within the experience of every physician"
(Shelley's note).
9. Susceptible of being molded or shaped.

In unremitting drudgery and care!
How many a vulgar Cato has compelled   140
His energies, no longer tameless then,
To mould a pin, or fabricate a nail!
How many a Newton, to whose passive ken
Those mighty spheres that gem infinity
Were only specks of tinsel, fixed in heaven   145
To light the midnights of his native town![1]

Yet every heart contains perfection's germ:
The wisest of the sages of the earth,
That ever from the stores of reason drew
Science and truth, and virtue's dreadless tone,   150
Were but a weak and inexperienced boy,
Proud, sensual, unimpassioned, unimbued
With pure desire and universal love,
Compared to that high being, of cloudless brain,
Untainted passion, elevated will,   155
Which death (who even would linger long in awe
Within his noble presence, and beneath
His changeless eyebeam) might alone subdue.
Him, every slave now dragging through the filth
Of some corrupted city his sad life,   160
Pining with famine, swoln with luxury,
Blunting the keenness of his spiritual sense
With narrow schemings and unworthy cares,
Or madly rushing through all violent crime,
To move the deep stagnation of his soul,—   165
Might imitate and equal.
                         But mean lust[2]
Has bound its chains so tight around the earth,
That all within it but the virtuous man
Is venal: gold or fame will surely reach
The price prefixed by selfishness, to all   170
But him of resolute and unchanging will;
Whom, nor the plaudits of a servile crowd,
Nor the vile joys of tainting luxury,
Can bribe to yield his elevated soul
To tyranny or falshood, though they wield   175
With blood-red hand the sceptre of the world.

All things are sold: the very light of heaven
Is venal; earth's unsparing gifts of love,
The smallest and most despicable things
That lurk in the abysses of the deep,   180

1. John Milton, Marcus Porcius Cato Uticensis (140), a staunch defender of the Roman Republic against Catiline and Julius Caesar, and Sir Isaac Newton (143) are representatives of noble achievements in writing, political life, and scientific inquiry, respectively.
2. In the broad sense of strong desire for *mean* (small, low, unexalted) things.

All objects of our life, even life itself,
And the poor pittance which the laws allow
Of liberty, the fellowship of man,
Those duties which his heart of human love
Should urge him to perform instinctively,   185
Are bought and sold as in a public mart
Of undisguising selfishness, that sets
On each its price, the stamp-mark of her reign.
Even love is sold;[3] the solace of all woe
Is turned to deadliest agony, old age   190
Shivers in selfish beauty's loathing arms,
And youth's corrupted impulses prepare
A life of horror from the blighting bane
Of commerce; whilst the pestilence that springs
From unenjoying sensualism, has filled   195
All human life with hydra-headed[4] woes.

Falshood[5] demands but gold to pay the pangs
Of outraged conscience; for the slavish priest
Sets no great value on his hireling faith:
A little passing pomp, some servile souls,   200
Whom cowardice itself might safely chain,
Or the spare mite of avarice could bribe
To deck the triumph of their languid zeal,
Can make him minister to tyranny.
More daring crime requires a loftier meed: 205
Without a shudder, the slave-soldier lends
His arm to murderous deeds, and steels his heart,
When the dread eloquence of dying men,
Low mingling on the lonely field of fame,
Assails that nature, whose applause he sells   210
For the gross blessings of a patriot mob,
For the vile gratitude of heartless kings,
And for a cold world's good word,—viler still!

There is a nobler glory, which survives
Until our being fades, and, solacing   215
All human care, accompanies its change;
Deserts not virtue in the dungeon's gloom,
And, in the precincts of the palace, guides
Its footsteps through that labyrinth of crime;
Imbues his lineaments with dauntlessness,   220

3. "Not even the intercourse of the sexes is exempt from the despotism of positive institution. . . . Love withers under constraint: its very essence is liberty. . . . A husband and wife ought to continue so long united as they love each other: any law which should bind them to cohabitation for one moment after the decay of their affection, would be a most intolerable tyranny . . ." (from Shelley's note).

4. The Hydra was a monster in Greek mythology that had many heads (various authorities number them from nine to one hundred); whenever one head was cut off, two grew unless the neck was immediately cauterized by fire.

5. Shelley uses the word "falsehood" (usually spelled by him without the silent "e") to mean organized Christian religion.

Even when, from power's avenging hand, he takes
Its sweetest, last and noblest title—death;
—The consciousness of good, which neither gold,
Nor sordid fame, nor hope of heavenly bliss
Can purchase; but a life of resolute good,   225
Unalterable will, quenchless desire
Of universal happiness, the heart
That beats with it in unison, the brain,
Whose ever wakeful wisdom toils to change
Reason's rich stores for its eternal weal.   230

This commerce of sincerest virtue needs
No mediative signs of selfishness,
No jealous intercourse of wretched gain,
No balancings of prudence, cold and long;
In just and equal measure all is weighed,   235
One scale contains the sum of human weal,
And one, the good man's heart.
                          How vainly seek
The selfish for that happiness denied
To aught but virtue! Blind and hardened, they,
Who hope for peace amid the storms of care,   240
Who covet power they know not how to use,
And sigh for pleasure they refuse to give,—
Madly they frustrate still their own designs;
And, where they hope that quiet to enjoy
Which virtue pictures, bitterness of soul,   245
Pining regrets, and vain repentances,
Disease, disgust, and lassitude, pervade
Their valueless and miserable lives.

But hoary-headed selfishness has felt
Its death-blow, and is tottering to the grave: 250
A brighter morn awaits the human day,
When every transfer of earth's natural gifts
Shall be a commerce of good words and works;
When poverty and wealth, the thirst of fame,
The fear of infamy, disease and woe,   255
War with its million horrors, and fierce hell
Shall live but in the memory of time,
Who, like a penitent libertine, shall start,
Look back, and shudder at his younger years.

                          VI.
        All touch, all eye, all ear,
The Spirit felt the Fairy's burning speech.
    O'er the thin texture of its frame,
The varying periods painted changing glows,
        As on a summer even,   5

When soul-enfolding music floats around,
   The stainless mirror of the lake
   Re-images the eastern gloom,
Mingling convulsively its purple hues
     With sunset's burnished gold.   10

     Then thus the Spirit spoke:
"It is a wild and miserable world!
   Thorny, and full of care,
Which every fiend can make his prey at will.
   O Fairy! in the lapse of years,   15
     Is there no hope in store?
     Will yon vast suns roll on
Interminably, still illuming
   The night of so many wretched souls,
     And see no hope for them?   20
Will not the universal Spirit e'er
Revivify this withered limb of Heaven?"

     The Fairy calmly smiled
In comfort, and a kindling gleam of hope
   Suffused the Spirit's lineaments.   25
"Oh! rest thee tranquil; chase those fearful doubts,
Which ne'er could rack an everlasting soul,
That sees the chains which bind it to its doom.
Yes! crime and misery are in yonder earth,
     Falshood, mistake, and lust;   30
     But the eternal world
Contains at once the evil and the cure.
Some eminent in virtue shall start up,
     Even in perversest time:
The truths of their pure lips, that never die,   35
Shall bind the scorpion falshood with a wreath
     Of ever-living flame,
Until the monster sting itself to death.[6]

"How sweet a scene will earth become!
Of purest spirits, a pure dwelling-place,   40
Symphonious with the planetary spheres;[7]
When man, with changeless Nature coalescing,
Will undertake regeneration's work,
When its ungenial poles no longer point
     To the red and baleful sun   45
     That faintly twinkles there.[8]

6. *scorpion . . . death:* Pliny and other natural historians of antiquity wrote that scorpions commit suicide if surrounded by fire; Shelley used the metaphor more than once for the self-destructive nature of evil. (See *The Cenci,* II.ii.70–71.)
7. An allusion to the music of the spheres, the harmonious sound that, according to classical and Renaissance authorities, the planets make in their courses.
8. "The north polar star, to which the axis of the earth . . . points" (from Shelley's note). Shelley goes on to suggest that the angle of the earth's axis is gradually diminishing and that someday,

"Spirit! on yonder earth,
Falshood now triumphs; deadly power
Has fixed its seal upon the lip of truth!
Madness and misery are there!   50
The happiest is most wretched! Yet confide,
Until pure health-drops, from the cup of joy,
Fall like a dew of balm upon the world.
Now, to the scene I shew, in silence turn,
And read the blood-stained charter of all woe,   55
Which nature soon, with recreating hand,
Will blot in mercy from the book of earth.
How bold the flight of passion's wandering wing,
How swift the step of reason's firmer tread,
How calm and sweet the victories of life,   60
How terrorless the triumph of the grave!
How powerless were the mightiest monarch's arm,
Vain his loud threat, and impotent his frown!
How ludicrous the priest's dogmatic roar!
The weight of his exterminating curse,   65
How light! and his affected charity,
To suit the pressure of the changing times,
What palpable deceit!—but for thy aid,
Religion![9] but for thee, prolific fiend,
Who peoplest earth with demons, hell with men,   70
And heaven with slaves!

"Thou taintest all thou lookest upon!—the stars,
Which on thy cradle beamed so brightly sweet,
Were gods to the distempered playfulness
Of thy untutored infancy: the trees,   75
The grass, the clouds, the mountains, and the sea,
All living things that walk, swim, creep, or fly,
Were gods: the sun had homage, and the moon
Her worshipper. Then thou becamest, a boy,
More daring in thy frenzies: every shape,   80
Monstrous or vast, or beautifully wild,
Which, from sensation's relics, fancy culls;
The spirits of the air, the shuddering ghost,
The genii of the elements, the powers
That give a shape to nature's varied works,   85
Had life and place in the corrupt belief
Of thy blind heart: yet still thy youthful hands

---

when "the equator coincides with the
ecliptic" (the line marking the points
closest to the sun), "the nights and days
will then become equal on the earth
during the year, and probably the sea-
sons also." He quotes contemporary
scientists in support of his idea, but his
real motivation (like that of some of the
scientists) was the mythical notion, re-
flected by Milton in *Paradise Lost*, Book
X. 668–687, that the discrepancy be-
tween the equator and the ecliptic—the
variation in the seasons and in the length
of days and nights—was a physical
manifestation of the moral Fall of Man.
9. In lines 72–145, Shelley personifies
Religion and addresses "him" on his life
cycle.

Were pure of human blood. Then manhood gave
Its strength and ardour to thy frenzied brain;
Thine eager gaze scanned the stupendous scene, 90
Whose wonders mocked the knowledge of thy pride:
Their everlasting and unchanging laws
Reproached thine ignorance. Awhile thou stoodst
Baffled and gloomy; then thou didst sum up
The elements of all that thou didst know; 95
The changing seasons, winter's leafless reign,
The budding of the heaven-breathing trees,
The eternal orbs that beautify the night,
The sun-rise, and the setting of the moon,
Earthquakes and wars, and poisons and disease, 100
And all their causes, to an abstract point
Converging, thou didst bend, and called it GOD!
The self-sufficing, the omnipotent,
The merciful, and the avenging God!
Who, prototype of human misrule, sits 105
High in heaven's realm, upon a golden throne,
Even like an earthly king; and whose dread work,
Hell, gapes for ever for the unhappy slaves
Of fate, whom he created, in his sport,
To triumph in their torments when they fell! 110
Earth heard the name; earth trembled, as the smoke
Of his revenge ascended up to heaven,
Blotting the constellations; and the cries
Of millions, butchered in sweet confidence
And unsuspecting peace, even when the bonds 115
Of safety were confirmed by wordy oaths
Sworn in his dreadful name, rung through the land;
Whilst innocent babes writhed on thy stubborn spear,
And thou didst laugh to hear the mother's shriek
Of maniac gladness, as the sacred steel 120
Felt cold in her torn entrails!

"Religion! thou wert then in manhood's prime:
But age crept on: one God would not suffice
For senile puerility; thou framedst
A tale to suit thy dotage, and to glut 125
Thy misery-thirsting soul, that the mad fiend
Thy wickedness had pictured, might afford
A plea for sating the unnatural thirst
For murder, rapine, violence, and crime,
That still consumed thy being, even when 130
Thou heardst the step of fate;—that flames might light
Thy funeral scene, and the shrill horrent[1] shrieks
Of parents dying on the pile that burned
To light their children to thy paths, the roar
Of the encircling flames, the exulting cries 135

1. Shuddering, expressing horror.

Of thine apostles, loud commingling there,
  Might sate thine hungry ear
  Even on the bed of death!

"But now contempt is mocking thy gray hairs;
Thou art descending to the darksome grave,   140
Unhonoured and unpitied, but by those
Whose pride is passing by like thine, and sheds,
Like thine, a glare that fades before the sun
Of truth, and shines but in the dreadful night
That long has lowered above the ruined world.   145

"Throughout these infinite orbs of mingling light,
Of which yon earth is one, is wide diffused
A spirit of activity and life,
That knows no term, cessation, or decay;
That fades not when the lamp of earthly life,   150
Extinguished in the dampness of the grave,
Awhile there slumbers, more than when the babe
In the dim newness of its being feels
The impulses of sublunary[2] things,
And all is wonder to unpractised sense: 155
But, active, steadfast, and eternal, still
Guides the fierce whirlwind, in the tempest roars,
Cheers in the day, breathes in the balmy groves,
Strengthens in health, and poisons in disease;
And in the storm of change, that ceaselessly   160
Rolls round the eternal universe, and shakes
Its undecaying battlement, presides,
Apportioning with irresistible law
The place each spring of its machine shall fill;
So that when waves on waves tumultuous heap   165
Confusion to the clouds, and fiercely driven
Heaven's lightnings scorch the uprooted ocean-fords,
Whilst, to the eye of shipwrecked mariner,
Lone sitting on the bare and shuddering rock,
All seems unlinked contingency and chance: 170
No atom of this turbulence fulfils
A vague and unnecessitated task,
Or acts but as it must and ought to act.[3]
Even the minutest molecule of light,
That in an April sunbeam's fleeting glow   175
Fulfils its destined, though invisible work,
The universal Spirit guides; nor less,
When merciless ambition, or mad zeal,
Has led two hosts of dupes to battle-field,
That, blind, they there may dig each other's graves,   180

---

2. Because, in classical and Renaissance thought, all things beneath the moon were subject to change and decay, *sub-lunar(y)* came to mean "mortal," "mundane."

3. In a note to lines 171–173, Shelley quotes from Baron d'Holbach's *Système de la nature*, illustrating the operation of Necessity in the realms of physical nature and social interaction.

And call the sad work glory, does it rule
All passions: not a thought, a will, an act,
No working of the tyrant's moody mind,
Nor one misgiving of the slaves who boast
Their servitude, to hide the shame they feel,   185
Nor the events enchaining every will,
That from the depths of unrecorded time
Have drawn all-influencing virtue, pass
Unrecognized, or unforeseen by thee,
Soul of the Universe! eternal spring   190
Of life and death, of happiness and woe,
Of all that chequers the phantasmal scene
That floats before our eyes in wavering light,
Which gleams but on the darkness of our prison,
  Whose chains and massy[4] walls   195
  We feel, but cannot see.

"Spirit of Nature! all-sufficing Power,
Necessity![5] thou mother of the world!
Unlike the God of human error, thou
Requirest no prayers or praises; the caprice   200
Of man's weak will belongs no more to thee
Than do the changeful passions of his breast
To thy unvarying harmony: the slave,
Whose horrible lusts spread misery o'er the world,
And the good man, who lifts, with virtuous pride,   205
His being, in the sight of happiness,
That springs from his own works; the poison-tree,
Beneath whose shade all life is withered up,
And the fair oak, whose leafy dome affords
A temple where the vows of happy love   210
Are registered, are equal in thy sight:
No love, no hate thou cherishest; revenge
And favoritism, and worst desire of fame
Thou knowst not: all that the wide world contains
Are but thy passive instruments, and thou   215
Regardst them all with an impartial eye,
Whose joy or pain thy nature cannot feel,
  Because thou hast not human sense,
  Because thou art not human mind.

---

4. Solid, weighty.
5. "He who asserts the doctrine of Necessity means that, contemplating the events which compose the moral and material universe, he beholds only an immense and uninterrupted chain of causes and effects, no one of which could occupy any other place than it does occupy. . . . Motive is, to voluntary action in the human mind, what cause is to effect in the material universe. The word liberty, as applied to mind, is analogous to the word chance, as applied to matter: they spring from an ignorance of the certainty of the conjunction of antecedents and consequents. . . . The doctrine of Necessity tends to introduce a great change into the established notions of morality, and utterly destroy religion. . . . we are taught, by the doctrine of Necessity, that there is neither good nor evil in the universe, otherwise than as the events to which we apply these epithets have relation to our own peculiar mode of being" (from Shelley's note).

"Yes! when the sweeping storm of time   220
Has sung its death-dirge o'er the ruined fanes
And broken altars of the almighty fiend,[6]
Whose name usurps thy honors, and the blood
Through centuries clotted there, has floated down
The tainted flood of ages, shalt thou live   225
Unchangeable! A shrine is raised to thee,
   Which, nor the tempest-breath of time,
   Nor the interminable flood,
   Over earth's slight pageant rolling,
    Availeth to destroy,—   230
The sensitive extension of the world.
   That wondrous and eternal fane,
Where pain and pleasure, good and evil join,
To do the will of strong necessity,
   And life, in multitudinous shapes,   235
Still pressing forward where no term can be,
   Like hungry and unresting flame
Curls round the eternal columns of its strength."

VII.

SPIRIT.

I was an infant when my mother went
To see an atheist burned. She took me there:
The dark-robed priests were met around the pile;
The multitude was gazing silently;
And as the culprit passed with dauntless mien,   5
Tempered disdain in his unaltering eye,
Mixed with a quiet smile, shone calmly forth:
The thirsty fire crept round his manly limbs;
His resolute eyes were scorched to blindness soon;
His death-pang rent my heart! the insensate[7] mob   10
Uttered a cry of triumph, and I wept.
"Weep not, child!" cried my mother, "for that man
Has said, 'There is no God.'"

FAIRY.

               There is no God![8]
Nature confirms the faith his death-groan sealed:
Let heaven and earth, let man's revolving race,   15
His ceaseless generations tell their tale;
Let every part depending on the chain
That links it to the whole, point to the hand

---

6. The ordinary conception of God.
7. Unfeeling; devoid of moral feeling.
8. "This negation must be understood solely to affect a creative Deity. The hypothesis of a pervading Spirit co-eternal with the universe remains unshaken. . . . God is an hypothesis, and, as such, stands in need of proof. . . . From the phenomena, which are the objects of our senses, we attempt to infer a cause, which we call God. . . . From this hypothesis we invent this general name, to conceal our ignorance of causes and essences . . ." (from Shelley's note).

That grasps its term! let every seed that falls
In silent eloquence unfold its store   20
Of argument; infinity within,
Infinity without, belie creation;
The exterminable spirit it contains
Is nature's only God; but human pride
Is skilful to invent most serious names   25
To hide its ignorance.
                            The name of God
Has fenced about all crime with holiness,
Himself the creature of his worshippers,
Whose names and attributes and passions change,
Seeva, Buddh, Foh, Jehovah, God, or Lord,[9]   30
Even with the human dupes who build his shrines,
Still serving o'er the war-polluted world
For desolation's watch-word; whether hosts
Stain his death-blushing chariot wheels, as on
Triumphantly they roll, whilst Brahmins raise   35
A sacred hymn to mingle with the groans;[1]
Or countless partners of his power divide
His tyranny to weakness; or the smoke
Of burning towns, the cries of female helplessness,
Unarmed old age, and youth, and infancy,   40
Horribly massacred, ascend to heaven
In honor of his name; or, last and worst,
Earth groans beneath religion's iron age,[2]
And priests dare babble of a God of peace,
Even whilst their hands are red with guiltless blood,   45
Murdering the while, uprooting every germ
Of truth, exterminating, spoiling all,
Making the earth a slaughter-house!

            O Spirit! through the sense
By which thy inner nature was apprised   50
    Of outward shows, vague dreams have rolled,
    And varied reminiscences have waked
        Tablets that never fade;
    All things have been imprinted there,
    The stars, the sea, the earth, the sky,   55

9. *Seeva*, or Shiva, is the Hindu name for God in his role as destroyer; *Buddh* is the Buddha; *Foh*, or *Fohi*, was the name used in England in Shelley's day for Fu Hsi, the legendary or quasi-historical "first king of China, who is said to have founded this empire soon after the deluge" (George Crabb, *Universal Historical Dictionary*, London, 1833); *Jehovah* (or "Yahweh"), the Hebrew god; *Lord* (the Hebrew "Adonai"), the name used instead of "Yahweh" when the name was pronounced.

1. *hosts . . . groans:* The reference is to the massive car of Vishnu, a title of whom is Jagannāth (hence "Juggernaut"), under whose wheels devotees were said sometimes to have immolated themselves; in general, an overwhelming force. *Brahmins* are highest caste Hindus.
2. There were four traditional ages in classical thought: the Golden Age, the Silver Age, the Bronze Age, and the Iron Age; Shelley implies that religion has descended to its last, least noble phase.

Even the unshapeliest lineaments
Of wild and fleeting visions
 Have left a record there
 To testify of earth.

These are my empire, for to me is given   60
The wonders of the human world to keep,
And fancy's thin creations to endow
With manner, being, and reality;
Therefore a wondrous phantom, from the dreams
Of human error's dense and purblind[3] faith,   65
I will evoke, to meet thy questioning.
 Ahasuerus,[4] rise!

 A strange and woe-worn wight[5]
Arose beside the battlement,
 And stood unmoving there.   70
His inessential figure cast no shade
 Upon the golden floor;
His port and mien bore mark of many years,
And chronicles of untold antientness
Were legible within his beamless eye: 75
 Yet his cheek bore the mark of youth;
Freshness and vigor knit his manly frame;
The wisdom of old age was mingled there
 With youth's primæval dauntlessness;
 And inexpressible woe,   80
Chastened by fearless resignation, gave
An awful grace to his all-speaking brow.

SPIRIT.

Is there a God?

AHASUERUS.

Is there a God!—aye, an almighty God,
And vengeful as almighty! Once his voice   85
Was heard on earth: earth shuddered at the sound
The fiery-visaged firmament expressed
Abhorrence, and the grave of nature yawned
To swallow all the dauntless and the good
That dared to hurl defiance at his throne,   90

---

3. Of impaired or defective vision.
4. The Wandering Jew of ancient legend. Shelley's note, quoting from a German source, reads in part: "When our Lord was wearied with the burthen of his ponderous cross, and wanted to rest before the door of Ahasuerus, the unfeeling wretch drove him away with brutality. The Savior of mankind staggered, sinking under the heavy load, but uttered no complaint. An angel of death appeared before Ahasuerus, and exclaimed indignantly, 'Barbarian! thou has denied rest to the Son of Man: be it denied thee also, until he comes to judge the world.' . . .
"A black demon . . . goads him now from country to country: he is denied the consolation which death affords, and precluded from the rest of the peaceful grave."
5. A human being; usually used to express either contempt or sympathy.

Girt as it was with power. None but slaves
Survived,—cold-blooded slaves, who did the work
Of tyrannous omnipotence; whose souls
No honest indignation ever urged
To elevated daring, to one deed   95
Which gross and sensual self did not pollute.
These slaves built temples for the omnipotent fiend,
Gorgeous and vast: the costly altars smoked
With human blood, and hideous pæans[6] rung
Through all the long-drawn aisles. A murderer[7] heard   100
His voice in Egypt, one whose gifts and arts
Had raised him to his eminence in power,
Accomplice of omnipotence in crime,
And confidant of the all-knowing one.
       These were Jehovah's words.   105

"From an eternity of idleness
I, God, awoke; in seven days' toil made earth
From nothing; rested, and created man:
I placed him in a paradise, and there
Planted the tree of evil, so that he   110
Might eat and perish, and my soul procure
Wherewith to sate its malice, and to turn,
Even like a heartless conqueror of the earth,
All misery to my fame. The race of men
Chosen to My honor, with impunity   115
May sate the lusts I planted in their heart.
Here I command thee hence to lead them on,
Until, with hardened feet, their conquering troops
Wade on the promised soil through woman's blood,
And make my name be dreaded through the land.   120
Yet ever-burning flame and ceaseless woe
Shall be the doom of their eternal souls,
With every soul on this ungrateful earth,
Virtuous or vicious, weak or strong,—even all
Shall perish, to fulfil the blind revenge   125
(Which you, to men, call justice) of their God."

         The murderer's brow
Quivered with horror.
           "God omnipotent,
Is there no mercy? must our punishment
Be endless? will long ages roll away,   130
And see no term? Oh! wherefore hast thou made
In mockery and wrath this evil earth?
Mercy becomes the powerful—be but just:
O God! repent and save."

---

6. Songs of praise or thanksgiving; shouts   7. Moses.
of joy.

"One way remains:
I will beget a son, and he shall bear   135
The sins of all the world;[8] he shall arise
In an unnoticed corner of the earth,
And there shall die upon a cross, and purge
The universal crime; so that the few
On whom my grace descends, those who are marked   140
As vessels to the honor of their God,
May credit this strange sacrifice, and save
Their souls alive: millions shall live and die,
Who ne'er shall call upon their Saviour's name,
But, unredeemed, go to the gaping grave.   145
Thousands shall deem it an old woman's tale,
Such as the nurses frighten babes withal:
These in a gulph of anguish and of flame
Shall curse their reprobation endlessly,
Yet tenfold pangs shall force them to avow,   150
Even on their beds of torment, where they howl,
My honor, and the justice of their doom.
What then avail their virtuous deeds, their thoughts
Of purity, with radiant genius bright,
Or lit with human reason's earthly ray?   155
Many are called, but few will I elect.
Do thou my bidding, Moses!"

                              Even the murderer's cheek
Was blanched with horror, and his quivering lips
Scarce faintly uttered—"O almighty One,
I tremble and obey!"   160

O Spirit! centuries have set their seal
On this heart of many wounds, and loaded brain,
Since the Incarnate came: humbly he came,
Veiling his horrible Godhead in the shape
Of man, scorned by the world, his name unheard,   165
Save by the rabble of his native town,
Even as a parish demagogue. He led
The crowd; he taught them justice, truth, and peace,
In semblance; but he lit within their souls
The quenchless flames of zeal, and blest the sword   170
He brought on earth to satiate with the blood

8. Shelley attacks Christianity and the Bible in a long note that reads, in part: "A Roman governor of Judea, at the instances of a priest-led mob, crucified a man called Jesus eighteen centuries ago. He was a man of pure life, who desired to rescue his countrymen from the tyranny of their barbarous and degrading superstitions. The common fate of all who desire to benefit mankind awaited him. . . . Jesus was sacrificed to the honour of that God with whom he was afterwards confounded. It is of importance, therefore, to distinguish between the pretended character of this being as the Son of God and the Saviour of the world, and his real character as a man, who, for a vain attempt to reform the world, paid the forfeit of his life to that overbearing tyranny which has since so long desolated the universe in his name."

Of truth and freedom his malignant soul.
At length his mortal frame was led to death.
I stood beside him: on the torturing cross
No pain assailed his unterrestrial sense;   175
And yet he groaned. Indignantly I summed
The massacres and miseries which his name
Had sanctioned in my country, and I cried,
"Go! go!" in mockery.
A smile of godlike malice reillumed   180
His fading lineaments.—"I go," he cried,
"But thou shalt wander o'er the unquiet earth
Eternally."——The dampness of the grave
Bathed my imperishable front. I fell,
And long lay tranced upon the charmed soil.   185
When I awoke hell burned within my brain,
Which staggered on its seat; for all around
The mouldering relics of my kindred lay,
Even as the Almighty's ire arrested them,
And in their various attitudes of death   190
My murdered children's mute and eyeless sculls
Glared ghastily upon me.
                              But my soul,
From sight and sense of the polluting woe
Of tyranny, had long learned to prefer
Hell's freedom to the servitude of heaven.   195
Therefore I rose, and dauntlessly began
My lonely and unending pilgrimage,
Resolved to wage unweariable war
With my almighty tyrant, and to hurl
Defiance at his impotence to harm   200
Beyond the curse I bore. The very hand
That barred my passage to the peaceful grave
Has crushed the earth to misery, and given
Its empire to the chosen of his slaves.
These have I seen, even from the earliest dawn   205
Of weak, unstable and precarious power,
Then preaching peace, as now they practise war;
So, when they turned but from the massacre
Of unoffending infidels, to quench
Their thirst for ruin in the very blood   210
That flowed in their own veins, and pityless zeal
Froze every human feeling, as the wife
Sheathed in her husband's heart the sacred steel,
Even whilst its hopes were dreaming of her love;
And friends to friends, brothers to brothers stood   215
Opposed in bloodiest battle-field, and war,
Scarce satiable by fate's last death-draught, waged,
Drunk from the winepress of the Almighty's wrath;
Whilst the red cross, in mockery of peace,

Pointed to victory! When the fray was done,   220
No remnant of the exterminated faith
Survived to tell its ruin, but the flesh,
With putrid smoke poisoning the atmosphere,
That rotted on the half-extinguished pile.

Yes! I have seen God's worshippers unsheathe   225
The sword of his revenge, when grace descended,
Confirming all unnatural impulses,
To sanctify their desolating deeds;
And frantic priests waved the ill-omened cross
O'er the unhappy earth: then shone the sun   230
On showers of gore from the upflashing steel
Of safe assassination, and all crime
Made stingless by the spirits of the Lord,
And blood-red rainbows canopied the land.

Spirit! no year of my eventful being   235
Has passed unstained by crime and misery,
Which flows from God's own faith. I've marked his slaves
With tongues whose lies are venomous, beguile
The insensate mob, and, whilst one hand was red
With murder, feign to stretch the other out   240
For brotherhood and peace; and that they now
Babble of love and mercy, whilst their deeds
Are marked with all the narrowness and crime
That freedom's young arm dare not yet chastise,
Reason may claim our gratitude, who now   245
Establishing the imperishable throne
Of truth, and stubborn virtue, maketh vain
The unprevailing malice of my foe,
Whose bootless rage heaps torments for the brave,
Adds impotent eternities to pain,   250
Whilst keenest disappointment racks his breast
To see the smiles of peace around them play,
To frustrate or to sanctify their doom.

Thus have I stood,—through a wild waste of years
Struggling with whirlwinds of mad agony,   255
Yet peaceful, and serene, and self-enshrined,
Mocking my powerless tyrant's horrible curse
With stubborn and unalterable will,
Even as a giant oak, which heaven's fierce flame
Had scathed in the wilderness, to stand   260
A monument of fadeless ruin there;
Yet peacefully and movelessly it braves
The midnight conflict of the wintry storm,
    As in the sun-light's calm it spreads
    Its worn and withered arms on high   265
To meet the quiet of a summer's noon.

The Fairy waved her wand:
Ahasuerus fled
Fast as the shapes of mingled shade and mist,
That lurk in the glens of a twilight grove,   270
Flee from the morning beam:
The matter of which dreams are made
Not more endowed with actual life
Than this phantasmal portraiture
Of wandering human thought.[9]   275

VIII.

THE FAIRY.

The present and the past thou hast beheld:
It was a desolate sight. Now, Spirit, learn
The secrets of the future.—Time!
Unfold the brooding pinion of thy gloom,
Render thou up thy half-devoured babes,   5
And from the cradles of eternity,
Where millions lie lulled to their portioned sleep
By the deep murmuring stream of passing things,
Tear thou that gloomy shroud.—Spirit, behold
Thy glorious destiny!   10

Joy to the Spirit came.
Through the wide rent in Time's eternal veil,
Hope was seen beaming through the mists of fear:
Earth was no longer hell;
Love, freedom, health, had given   15
Their ripeness to the manhood of its prime,
And all its pulses beat
Symphonious to the planetary spheres:
Then dulcet music swelled
Concordant[1] with the life-strings of the soul;   20
It throbbed in sweet and languid beatings there,
Catching new life from transitory death,—
Like the vague sighings of a wind at even,
That wakes the wavelets of the slumbering sea
And dies on the creation of its breath,   25
And sinks and rises, fails and swells by fits:
Was the pure stream of feeling
That sprung from these sweet notes,
And o'er the Spirit's human sympathies
With mild and gentle motion calmly flowed.   30

Joy to the Spirit came,—
Such joy as when a lover sees
The chosen of his soul in happiness,
And witnesses her peace

9. That is, Ahasuerus has reality only as   1. Harmonious; *dulcet* means sweet.
an aberrant human idea.

Whose woe to him were bitterer than death,   35
    Sees her unfaded cheek
Glow mantling[2] in first luxury of health,
    Thrills with her lovely eyes,
Which like two stars amid the heaving main
    Sparkle through liquid bliss.   40

Then in her triumph spoke the Fairy Queen:
"I will not call the ghost of ages gone
To unfold the frightful secrets of its lore;
    The present now is past,
And those events that desolate the earth   45
Have faded from the memory of Time,
Who dares not give reality to that
Whose being I annul. To me is given
The wonders of the human world to keep,
Space, matter, time, and mind. Futurity   50
Exposes now its treasure; let the sight
Renew and strengthen all thy failing hope.
O human Spirit! spur thee to the goal
Where virtue fixes universal peace,
And midst the ebb and flow of human things,   55
Show somewhat stable, somewhat certain still,
A lighthouse o'er the wild of dreary waves.

"The habitable earth is full of bliss;
Those wastes of frozen billows that were hurled
By everlasting snow-storms round the poles,   60
Where matter dared not vegetate or live,
But ceaseless frost round the vast solitude
Bound its broad zone of stillness, are unloosed;
And fragrant zephyrs there from spicy isles
Ruffle the placid ocean-deep, that rolls   65
Its broad, bright surges to the sloping sand,
Whose roar is wakened into echoings sweet
To murmur through the heaven-breathing groves
And melodize with man's blest nature there.

"Those desarts of immeasurable sand,   70
Whose age-collected fervors scarce allowed
A bird to live, a blade of grass to spring,
Where the shrill chirp of the green lizard's love
Broke on the sultry silentness alone,
Now teem with countless rills and shady woods,   75
Corn-fields and pastures and white cottages;
And where the startled wildnerness beheld
A savage conqueror stained in kindred blood,
A tygress sating with the flesh of lambs
The unnatural famine of her toothless cubs,   80

2. Suffused with color, blushes.

Whilst shouts and howlings through the desart rang,
Sloping and smooth the daisy-spangled lawn,
Offering sweet incense to the sun-rise, smiles
To see a babe before his mother's door,
    Sharing his morning's meal   85
  With the green and golden basilisk[3]
    That comes to lick his feet.

"Those trackless deeps, where many a weary sail
Has seen above the illimitable plain,
Morning on night, and night on morning rise,   90
Whilst still no land to greet the wanderer spread
Its shadowy mountains on the sun-bright sea,
Where the loud roarings of the tempest-waves
So long have mingled with the gusty wind
In melancholy loneliness, and swept   95
The desart of those ocean solitudes,
But vocal to the sea-bird's harrowing shriek,
The bellowing monster, and the rushing storm,
Now to the sweet and many mingling sounds
Of kindliest human impulses respond.   100
Those lonely realms bright garden-isles begem,
With lightsome clouds and shining seas between,
And fertile vallies, resonant with bliss,
Whilst green woods overcanopy the wave,
Which like a toil-worn labourer leaps to shore,   105
To meet the kisses of the flowrets there.

"All things are recreated, and the flame
Of consentaneous[4] love inspires all life:
The fertile bosom of the earth gives suck
To myriads, who still grow beneath her care,   110
Rewarding her with their pure perfectness:
The balmy breathings of the wind inhale
Her virtues, and diffuse them all abroad:
Health floats amid the gentle atmosphere,
Glows in the fruits, and mantles[5] on the stream: 115
No storms deform the beaming brow of heaven,
Nor scatter in the freshness of its pride
The foliage of the ever verdant trees;
But fruits are ever ripe, flowers ever fair,
And autumn proudly bears her matron grace,   120
Kindling a flush on the fair cheek of spring,
Whose virgin bloom beneath the ruddy fruit
Reflects its tint, and blushes into love.

"The lion now forgets to thirst for blood:
There might you see him sporting in the sun   125
Beside the dreadless kid; his claws are sheathed,

---

3. A mythical reptile, also called a "cockatrice," whose breath and even its look were supposed to be fatal.

4. Simultaneous, mutual.
5. Foams or bubbles (see also VIII.132).

His teeth are harmless, custom's force has made
His nature as the nature of a lamb.[6]
Like passion's fruit, the nightshade's[7] tempting bane
Poisons no more the pleasure it bestows: 130
All bitterness is past; the cup of joy
Unmingled mantles to the goblet's brim,
And courts the thirsty lips it fled before.

"But chief, ambiguous man, he that can know
More misery, and dream more joy than all;   135
Whose keen sensations thrill within his breast
To mingle with a loftier instinct there,
Lending their power to pleasure and to pain,
Yet raising, sharpening, and refining each;
Who stands amid the ever-varying world,   140
The burthen or the glory of the earth;
He chief perceives the change, his being notes
The gradual renovation, and defines
Each movement of its progress on his mind.

"Man, where the gloom of the long polar night   145
Lowers o'er the snow-clad rocks and frozen soil,
Where scarce the hardiest herb that braves the frost
Basks in the moonlight's ineffectual glow,
Shrank with the plants, and darkened with the night;
His chilled and narrow energies, his heart,   150
Insensible to courage, truth, or love,
His stunted stature and imbecile frame,
Marked him for some abortion of the earth,
Fit compeer of the bears that roamed around,
Whose habits and enjoyments were his own: 155
His life a feverish dream of stagnant woe,
Whose meagre wants, but scantily fulfilled,
Apprised him ever of the joyless length
Which his short being's wretchedness had reached;
His death a pang which famine, cold and toil,   160
Long on the mind, whilst yet the vital spark
Clung to the body stubbornly, had brought:
All was inflicted here that earth's revenge
Could wreak on the infringers of her law;
One curse alone was spared—the name of God.   165

"Nor where the tropics bound the realms of day
With a broad belt of mingling cloud and flame,
Where blue mists through the unmoving atmosphere
Scattered the seeds of pestilence, and fed

---

6. Shelley's two chief precedents for this peaceable vision of the future are Isaiah 11 and Virgil's Fourth Eclogue.
7. A poisonous plant, either of the genus *Solanum*, including black nightshade (which has white flowers and black berries) or woody nightshade (purple flowers and red berries), or else of the genus *Atropa*, deadly nightshade (belladonna).

Unnatural vegetation, where the land   170
Teemed with all earthquake, tempest and disease,
Was man a nobler being; slavery
Had crushed him to his country's bloodstained dust;
Or he was bartered for the fame of power,
Which all internal impulses destroying,   175
Makes human will an article of trade;
Or he was changed with Christians for their gold,
And dragged to distant isles, where to the sound
Of the flesh-mangling scourge, he does the work
Of all-polluting luxury and wealth,   180
Which doubly visits on the tyrants' heads
The long-protracted fulness of their woe;
Or he was led to legal butchery,
To turn to worms beneath that burning sun,
Where kings first leagued against the rights of men,   185
And priests first traded with the name of God.

"Even where the milder zone afforded man
A seeming shelter, yet contagion there,
Blighting his being with unnumbered ills,
Spread like a quenchless fire; nor truth till late   190
Availed to arrest its progress, or create
That peace which first in bloodless victory waved
Her snowy standard o'er this favoured clime:
There man was long the train-bearer of slaves,
The mimic of surrounding misery,   195
The jackal of ambition's lion-rage,
The bloodhound of religion's hungry zeal.

"Here now the human being stands adorning
This loveliest earth with taintless body and mind;
Blest from his birth with all bland impulses,   200
Which gently in his noble bosom wake
All kindly passions and all pure desires.
Him, still from hope to hope the bliss pursuing
Which from the exhaustless lore of human weal
Dawns on the virtuous mind, the thoughts that rise   205
In time-destroying infiniteness, gift
With self-enshrined eternity, that mocks
The unprevailing hoariness of age,
And man, once fleeting o'er the transient scene
Swift as an unremembered vision, stands   210
Immortal upon earth:[8] no longer now

8. "Time is our consciousness of the succession of ideas in our mind. Vivid sensation, of either pain or pleasure, makes the time seem long. . . . If, therefore, the human mind . . . should become conscious of an infinite number of ideas in a minute, that minute would be eternity. I do not hence infer that the actual space between the birth and death of a man will ever be prolonged; but that his sensibility is perfectible. . . . the life of a man of virtue and talent, who should die in his thirtieth year, is, with regard to his own feelings, longer than that of a miserable priest-ridden slave, who dreams out a century of dulness" (from Shelley's note; Shelley actually died in his thirtieth year).

He slays the lamb that looks him in the face,
And horribly devours his mangled flesh,
Which still avenging nature's broken law,
Kindled all putrid humours in his frame,   215
All evil passions, and all vain belief,
Hatred, despair, and loathing in his mind,
The germs of misery, death, disease, and crime.[9]
No longer now the winged habitants,
That in the woods their sweet lives sing away,   220
Flee from the form of man; but gather round,
And prune their sunny feathers on the hands
Which little children stretch in friendly sport
Towards these dreadless partners of their play.
All things are void of terror: man has lost   225
His terrible prerogative, and stands
An equal amidst equals: happiness
And science dawn though late upon the earth;
Peace cheers the mind, health renovates the frame;
Disease and pleasure cease to mingle here,   230
Reason and passion cease to combat there;
Whilst each unfettered o'er the earth extend
Their all-subduing energies, and wield
The sceptre of a vast dominion there;
Whilst every shape and mode of matter lends   235
Its force to the omnipotence of mind,
Which from its dark mine drags the gem of truth
To decorate its paradise of peace."

IX.

"O happy Earth! reality of Heaven!
To which those restless souls that ceaselessly
Throng through the human universe, aspire;
Thou consummation of all mortal hope!
Thou glorious prize of blindly-working will!   5
Whose rays, diffused throughout all space and time,
Verge to one point and blend for ever there:
Of purest spirits thou pure dwelling-place!

9. In Shelley's day comparative anat-
omists studying man and apes, none of
which has meat as a staple of its diet,
concluded that man was naturally an
eater of fruits and nuts—a vegetarian.
Shelley was a vegetarian on both medical
and moral grounds and remained one
most of his life. Shelley's note states:
"I hold that the depravity of the physical
and moral nature of man originated in
his unnatural habits of life. . . . All
vice arose from the ruin of healthful
innocence. Tyranny, superstition, com-
merce, and inequality, were then first
known, when reason vainly attempted to
guide the wanderings of exacerbated
passion. . . .
"Comparative anatomy teaches us that
man resembles frugivorous animals in
everything, and carnivorous in nothing;
he has neither claws wherewith to seize
his prey, nor distinct and pointed teeth
to tear the living fibre. . . .
"The intestines are also identical with
those of herbivorous animals. . . . On a
natural system of diet, we should require
no spices from India; no wines from
Portugal, Spain, France, or Madeira;
none of those multitudinous articles of
luxury, for which every corner of the
globe is rifled, and which are the causes
of so much individual rivalship, such
calamitous and sanguinary national dis-
putes. . . .
"The advantage of a reform in diet is
obviously greater than that of any other.
It strikes at the root of the evil."

Where care and sorrow, impotence and crime,
Languor, disease, and ignorance dare not come: 10
O happy Earth, reality of Heaven!

"Genius has seen thee in her passionate dreams,
And dim forebodings of thy loveliness
Haunting the human heart, have there entwined
Those rooted hopes of some sweet place of bliss   15
Where friends and lovers meet to part no more.
Thou art the end of all desire and will,
The product of all action; and the souls
That by the paths of an aspiring change
Have reached thy haven of perpetual peace,   20
There rest from the eternity of toil
That framed the fabric of thy perfectness.

"Even Time, the conqueror, fled thee in his fear;
That hoary giant, who, in lonely pride,
So long had ruled the world, that nations fell   25
Beneath his silent footstep. Pyramids,
That for millenniums had withstood the tide
Of human things, his storm-breath drove in sand
Across that desert where their stones survived
The name of him whose pride had heaped them there.   30
Yon monarch, in his solitary pomp,
Was but the mushroom of a summer day,
That his light-winged footstep pressed to dust:
Time was the king of earth: all things gave way
Before him, but the fixed and virtuous will,   35
The sacred sympathies of soul and sense,
That mocked his fury and prepared his fall.

"Yet slow and gradual dawned the morn of love;
Long lay the clouds of darkness o'er the scene,
Till from its native heaven they rolled away: 40
First, crime triumphant o'er all hope careered
Unblushing, undisguising, bold and strong;
Whilst falshood, tricked in virtue's attributes,
Long sanctified all deeds of vice and woe,
Till done by her own venomous sting to death,   45
She left the moral world without a law,
No longer fettering passion's fearless wing,
Nor searing reason with the brand of God.
Then steadily the happy ferment worked;
Reason was free; and wild though passion went   50
Through tangled glens and wood-embosomed meads,[1]
Gathering a garland of the strangest flowers,
Yet like the bee returning to her queen,
She bound the sweetest on her sister's brow,
Who meek and sober kissed the sportive child,   55
No longer trembling at the broken rod.

1. Meadows enclosed by woods.

"Mild was the slow necessity of death:
The tranquil Spirit failed beneath its grasp,
Without a groan, almost without a fear,
Calm as a voyager to some distant land,   60
And full of wonder, full of hope as he.
The deadly germs of languor and disease
Died in the human frame, and purity
Blest with all gifts her earthly worshippers.
How vigorous then the athletic form of age!   65
How clear its open and unwrinkled brow!
Where neither avarice, cunning, pride, or care,
Had stamped the seal of grey deformity
On all the mingling lineaments of time.
How lovely the intrepid front of youth!   70
Which meek-eyed courage decked with freshest grace;
Courage of soul, that dreaded not a name,
And elevated will, that journeyed on
Through life's phantasmal scene in fearlessness,
With virtue, love, and pleasure, hand in hand.   75

"Then, that sweet bondage which is freedom's self,
And rivets with sensation's softest tie
The kindred sympathies of human souls,
Needed no fetters of tyrannic law:
Those delicate and timid impulses   80
In nature's primal modesty arose,
And with undoubted confidence disclosed
The growing longings of its dawning love,
Unchecked by dull and selfish chastity,
That virtue of the cheaply virtuous,   85
Who pride themselves in senselessness[2] and frost.
No longer prostitution's venomed bane
Poisoned the springs of happiness and life;
Woman and man, in confidence and love,
Equal and free and pure together trod   90
The mountain-paths of virtue, which no more
Were stained with blood from many a pilgrim's feet.

"Then, where, through distant ages, long in pride
The palace of the monarch-slave had mocked
Famine's faint groan, and penury's silent tear,   95
A heap of crumbling ruins stood, and threw
Year after year their stones upon the field,
Wakening a lonely echo; and the leaves
Of the old thorn, that on the topmost tower
Usurped the royal ensign's grandeur, shook   100
In the stern storm that swayed the topmost tower
And whispered strange tales in the whirlwind's ear.

2. An absence of sensuous feelings.

"Low through the lone cathedral's roofless aisles
The melancholy winds a death-dirge sung:
It were a sight of awfulness to see   105
The works of faith and slavery, so vast,
So sumptuous, yet so perishing withal![3]
Even as the corpse that rests beneath its wall.
A thousand mourners deck the pomp of death
To-day, the breathing marble glows above   110
To decorate its memory, and tongues
Are busy of its life: to-morrow, worms
In silence and in darkness seize their prey.

"Within the massy prison's mouldering courts,
Fearless and free the ruddy children played,   115
Weaving gay chaplets[4] for their innocent brows
With the green ivy and the red wall-flower,
That mock the dungeon's unavailing gloom;
The ponderous chains, and gratings of strong iron,
There rusted amid heaps of broken stone   120
That mingled slowly with their native earth:
There the broad beam of day, which feebly once
Lighted the cheek of lean captivity
With a pale and sickly glare, then freely shone
On the pure smiles of infant playfulness: 125
No more the shuddering voice of hoarse despair
Pealed through the echoing vaults, but soothing notes
Of ivy-fingered winds and gladsome birds
And merriment were resonant around.

"These ruins soon left not a wreck[5] behind: 130
Their elements, wide scattered o'er the globe,
To happier shapes were moulded, and became
Ministrant to all blissful impulses:
Thus human things were perfected, and earth,
Even as a child beneath its mother's love,   135
Was strengthened in all excellence, and grew
Fairer and nobler with each passing year.

"Now Time his dusky pennons o'er the scene
Closes in stedfast darkness, and the past
Fades from our charmed sight. My task is done: 140
Thy lore is learned. Earth's wonders are thine own,
With all the fear and all the hope they bring.
My spells are past: the present now recurs.
Ah me! a pathless wilderness remains
Yet unsubdued by man's reclaiming hand.   145

---

3. Nonetheless, in spite of everything.
Lines 107–108 form an accidentally
rhymed couplet; in revising the poem as
Queen of the Universe, Shelley eliminated
this imperfection by inserting *withal* be-
tween *yet* and *so*.
4. Garlands or wreaths worn on the head.

5. The *Oxford English Dictionary* gives
this use (with one from Wordsworth's
Evening Walk) as an example of the
mistaken use of "wreck" for "wrack"
(sb.[15].B), meaning vestige or trace left
after a destructive process.

"Yet, human Spirit, bravely hold thy course,
Let virtue teach thee firmly to pursue
The gradual paths of an aspiring change:
For birth and life and death, and that strange state
Before the naked soul has found its home,   150
All tend to perfect happiness, and urge
The restless wheels of being on their way,
Whose flashing spokes, instinct with infinite life,
Bicker[6] and burn to gain their destined goal:
For birth but wakes the spirit to the sense   155
Of outward shows, whose unexperienced shape
New modes of passion to its frame may lend;
Life is its state of action, and the store
Of all events is aggregated there
That variegate the eternal universe;   160
Death is a gate of dreariness and gloom,
That leads to azure isles and beaming skies
And happy regions of eternal hope.
Therefore, O Spirit! fearlessly bear on:
Though storms may break the primrose on its stalk,   165
Though frosts may blight the freshness of its bloom,
Yet spring's awakening breath will woo the earth
To feed with kindliest dews its favorite flower,
That blooms in mossy banks and darksome glens,
Lighting the green wood with its sunny smile.   170

"Fear not then, Spirit, death's disrobing hand,
So welcome when the tyrant is awake,
So welcome when the bigot's hell-torch burns;
'Tis but the voyage of a darksome hour,
The transient gulph-dream of a startling sleep.   175
Death is no foe to virtue: earth has seen
Love's brightest roses on the scaffold bloom,
Mingling with freedom's fadeless laurels there,
And presaging the truth of visioned bliss.
Are there not hopes within thee, which this scene   180
Of linked and gradual being has confirmed?
Whose stingings bade thy heart look further still,
When to the moonlight walk by Henry[7] led,
Sweetly and sadly thou didst talk of death?
And wilt thou rudely tear them from thy breast,   185
Listening supinely to a bigot's creed,
Or tamely crouching to the tyrant's rod,
Whose iron thongs are red with human gore?
Never: but bravely bearing on, thy will
Is destined an eternal war to wage   190
With tyranny and falshood, and uproot
The germs of misery from the human heart.

6. Flash, gleam, quiver (see *Paradise Lost*, VI.766, in the description of the Chariot of Paternal Deitie alluded to in the note to I.134).
7. Ianthe's lover, i.e., Shelley himself.

Thine is the hand whose piety would soothe
The thorny pillow of unhappy crime,
Whose impotence an easy pardon gains,   195
Watching its wanderings as a friend's disease:
Thine is the brow whose mildness would defy
Its fiercest rage, and brave its sternest will,
When fenced by power and master of the world.
Thou art sincere and good; of resolute mind,   200
Free from heart-withering custom's cold control,
Of passion lofty, pure and unsubdued.
Earth's pride and meanness could not vanquish thee,
And therefore art thou worthy of the boon
Which thou hast now received: virtue shall keep   205
Thy footsteps in the path that thou hast trod,
And many days of beaming hope shall bless
Thy spotless life of sweet and sacred love.
Go, happy one, and give that bosom joy
   Whose sleepless spirit waits to catch   210
   Light, life and rapture from thy smile."

   The Fairy waves her wand of charm.
Speechless with bliss the Spirit mounts the car,
   That rolled beside the battlement,
Bending her beamy eyes in thankfulness.   215
   Again the enchanted steeds were yoked,
   Again the burning wheels inflame
The steep descent of heaven's untrodden way.
   Fast and far the chariot flew:
   The vast and fiery globes that rolled   220
   Around the Fairy's palace-gate
Lessened by slow degrees, and soon appeared
Such tiny twinklers as the planet orbs
That there attendant on the solar power
With borrowed light pursued their narrower way.   225

   Earth floated then below:
   The chariot paused a moment there;
   The Spirit then descended:
The restless coursers pawed the ungenial soil,
Snuffed the gross air, and then, their errand done,   230
Unfurled their pinions to the winds of heaven.

   The Body and the Soul united then,
A gentle start convulsed Ianthe's frame:
Her veiny eyelids quietly unclosed;
Moveless awhile the dark blue orbs remained: 235
She looked around in wonder and beheld
Henry, who kneeled in silence by her couch,
Watching her sleep with looks of speechless love,
   And the bright beaming stars
   That through the casement shone.   240

Alastor; or, The Spirit of Solitude

Preface

The poem entitled "ALASTOR," may be considered as allegorical of one of the most interesting situations of the human mind. It represents a youth of uncorrupted feelings and adventurous genius led forth by an imagination inflamed and purified through familiarity with all that is excellent and majestic, to the contemplation of the universe. He drinks deep of the fountains of knowledge, and is still insatiate. The magnificence and beauty of the external world sinks profoundly into the frame of his conceptions, and affords to their modifications a variety not to be exhausted. So long as it is possible for his desires to point towards objects thus infinite and unmeasured, he is joyous, and tranquil, and self-possessed. But the period arrives when these objects cease to suffice. His mind is at length suddenly awakened and thirsts for intercourse with an intelligence similar to itself. He images to himself the Being whom he loves. Conversant with speculations of the sublimest and most perfect natures, the vision in which he embodies his own imaginations unites all of wonderful, or wise, or beautiful, which the poet, the philosopher, or the lover could depicture. The intellectual faculties, the imagination, the functions of sense, have their respective requisitions on the sympathy of corresponding powers in other human beings. The Poet is represented as uniting these requisitions, and attaching them to a single image. He seeks in vain for a prototype of his conception. Blasted by his disappointment, he descends to an untimely grave.

The picture is not barren of instruction to actual men. The Poet's self-centred seclusion was avenged by the furies of an irresistible passion pursuing him to speedy ruin. But that Power which strikes the luminaries of the world with sudden darkness and extinction, by awakening them to too exquisite a perception of its influences, dooms to a slow and poisonous decay those meaner spirits that dare to abjure its dominion. Their destiny is more abject and inglorious as their delinquency is more contemptible and pernicious. They who, deluded by no generous error, instigated by no sacred thirst of doubtful knowledge, duped by no illustrious superstition, loving nothing on this earth, and cherishing no hopes beyond, yet keep aloof from sympathies with their kind, rejoicing neither in human joy nor mourning with human grief; these, and such as they, have their apportioned curse. They languish, because none feel with them their common nature. They are morally dead. They are neither friends, nor lovers, nor fathers, nor citizens of the world, nor benefactors of their country. Among those who attempt to exist without human sympathy, the pure and tender-hearted perish through the intensity and passion of their search after its communities, when the vacancy of their spirit suddenly makes itself felt. All else, selfish, blind, and torpid, are those unforeseeing multitudes who constitute, together with their own, the lasting misery and loneliness of the world. Those who love not their fellow-beings live unfruitful lives, and prepare for their old age a miserable grave.

> "The good die first,
> And those whose hearts are dry as summer dust,
> Burn to the socket!"

December 14, 1815.

Alastor; or, The Spirit of Solitude[1]

Nondum amabam, et amare amabam, quærebam quid amarem, amans amare.—*Confess. St. August.*

Earth, ocean, air, beloved brotherhood!
If our great Mother has imbued my soul
With aught of natural piety[2] to feel
Your love, and recompense the boon with mine;[3]
If dewy morn, and odorous noon, and even,   5
With sunset and its gorgeous ministers,[4]

1. For a detailed explication of *Alastor* and its Preface see Evan K. Gibson's essay (pp. 545–569, below). At the end of the Preface, Shelley slightly misquotes Wordsworth's *The Excursion*, I.500–502; the epigraph from St. Augustine's *Confessions*, III.i, has been translated: "Not yet did I love, yet I was in love with loving; . . . I sought what I might love, loving to love." *Alastor* explores the interrelations between the universal human need for love and social ties and the idealist's solitary search for ultimate truths and ideal love. Earl R. Wasserman has recently suggested that the poem contains two chief characters, neither of whom is named: (1) the Narrator, who invokes the elements of nature and tells of his own early search for knowledge of the Ultimate (lines 1–49), and (2) the idealistic "Poet," whose story the Narrator tells in the main body of the poem and whose fate he regrets in the closing 49 lines. The numerous echoes of Wordsworth's poems are concentrated in the opening and closing addresses by the Narrator, leading Wasserman to consider the Narrator not Shelley's personal voice, but a Wordsworthian poet who compromises with mortal limitations and who, therefore, contrasts with the absolutism

of the visionary young Poet.
   Shelley wrote *Alastor* in the fall and early winter of 1815 while he and Mary Godwin were living quietly in a cottage at Bishopsgate, one of the eastern entrances to the Great Park of Windsor, in the Thames Valley west of London. It was published, together with ten shorter poems, in March 1816 by Baldwin, Cradock and Joy, an important London bookselling-publishing firm of the period. Though the volume was no best seller, by the time of Shelley's death in 1822 all copies had been sold, and Mary Shelley, who had difficulty obtaining a copy for her own use, reprinted *Alastor* with Shelley's *Posthumous Poems* (1824). No manuscript of the poem survives, though there is a copy of the *Alastor* volume containing Shelley's corrections for one of the poems published with it (see *Shelley and his Circle*, IV, 592–594). The only significant textual authorities are, therefore, the first edition and Mary's reprint in *Posthumous Poems*.
2. From Wordsworth's "My Heart Leaps Up": "And I could wish my days to be/ Bound each to each by natural piety."
3. I.e., "repay your gift [of love] with my love."
4. Colors accompanying the sunset.

And solemn midnight's tingling silentness;
If autumn's hollow sighs in the sere wood,
And winter robing with pure snow and crowns
Of starry ice the grey grass and bare boughs;   10
If spring's voluptuous pantings when she breathes
Her first sweet kisses, have been dear to me;
If no bright bird, insect, or gentle beast
I consciously have injured, but still loved
And cherished these my kindred; then forgive   15
This boast, beloved brethren, and withdraw
No portion of your wonted favour now!

   Mother of this unfathomable world!
Favour my solemn song, for I have loved
Thee ever, and thee only; I have watched   20
Thy shadow, and the darkness of thy steps,
And my heart ever gazes on the depth
Of thy deep mysteries. I have made my bed
In charnels and on coffins, where black death
Keeps record of the trophies won from thee.   25
Hoping to still these obstinate questionings[5]
Of[6] thee and thine, by forcing some lone ghost,
Thy messenger, to render up the tale
Of what we are. In lone and silent hours,
When night makes a weird sound of its own stillness,   30
Like an inspired and desperate alchymist
Staking his very life on some dark hope,
Have I mixed awful talk and asking looks
With my most innocent love, until strange tears
Uniting with those breathless kisses, made   35
Such magic as compels the charmed night
To render up thy charge: . . . and, though ne'er yet
Thou hast unveil'd thy inmost sanctuary,[7]
Enough from incommunicable dream,
And twilight phantasms, and deep noonday thought,   40
Has shone within me, that serenely now
And moveless, as a long-forgotten lyre
Suspended in the solitary dome
Of some mysterious and deserted fane,[8]
I wait thy breath, Great Parent, that my strain   45
May modulate with murmurs of the air,
And motions of the forests and the sea,
And voice of living beings, and woven hymns
Of night and day, and the deep heart of man.

---

5. From Wordsworth, *Ode: Intimations of Immortality*, 142: "those obstinate questionings/Of sense and outward things."
6. I.e., about, concerning.

7. Shelley in his youth actually hunted ghosts and tried to raise the Devil and spirits of the dead in churchyards and burial vaults.
8. A sanctuary or temple.

There was a Poet whose untimely tomb   50
No human hands with pious reverence reared,
But the charmed eddies of autumnal winds
Built o'er his mouldering bones a pyramid
Of mouldering leaves in the waste wilderness:—
A lovely youth,—no mourning maiden decked   55
With weeping flowers, or votive cypress wreath,[9]
The lone couch of his everlasting sleep:—
Gentle, and brave, and generous,—no lorn[1] bard
Breathed o'er his dark fate one melodious sigh:
He lived, he died, he sung, in solitude.   60
Strangers have wept to hear his passionate notes,
And virgins, as unknown he past, have pined
And wasted for fond love of his wild eyes.
The fire of those soft orbs has ceased to burn,
And Silence, too enamoured of that voice,   65
Locks its mute music in her rugged cell.

By solemn vision, and bright silver dream,
His infancy was nutured. Every sight
And sound from the vast earth and ambient[2] air,
Sent to his heart its choicest impulses.   70
The fountains of divine philosophy[3]
Fled not his thirsting lips, and all of great
Or good, or lovely, which the sacred past
In truth or fable consecrates, he felt
And knew. When early youth had past, he left   75
His cold fireside and alienated home
To seek strange truths in undiscovered lands.
Many a wide waste and tangled wilderness
Has lured his fearless steps; and he has bought
With his sweet voice and eyes, from savage men,   80
His rest and food. Nature's most secret steps
He like her shadow has pursued, where'er
The red volcano overcanopies
Its fields of snow and pinnacles of ice
With burning smoke, or where bitumen lakes[4]   85
On black bare pointed islets ever beat
With sluggish surge, or where the secret caves
Rugged and dark, winding among the springs
Of fire and poison, inaccessible
To avarice or pride, their starry domes   90
Of diamond and of gold expand above
Numberless and immeasurable halls,

9. The cypress tree was sacred to mourn-
ers (Ovid, *Metamorphoses*, Book X),
who offered wreaths of cypress boughs
to the gods on behalf of the dead.
1. Forsaken, abandoned.
2. Surrounding.
3. An echo of Milton's *Comus*, 476:

"How charming is divine Philosophy!"
4. Molten lava flows; the exact phrase
appears in Southey's *Thalaba*, VI.15, but
the significance possibly derives from
Milton's *Paradise Lost*, X.562 and XII.
41, where bituminous lakes are associated
with Hell.

Frequent with[5] crystal column, and clear shrines
Of pearl, and thrones radiant with chrysolite.[6]
Nor had that scene of ampler majesty   95
Than gems or gold, the varying roof of heaven
And the green earth lost in his heart its claims
To love and wonder; he would linger long
In lonesome vales, making the wild his home,
Until the doves and squirrels would partake   100
From his innocuous hand his bloodless food,[7]
Lured by the gentle meaning of his looks,
And the wild antelope, that starts whene'er
The dry leaf rustles in the brake,[8] suspend
Her timid steps to gaze upon a form   105
More graceful than her own.

               His wandering step
Obedient to high thoughts, has visited
The awful ruins of the days of old:
Athens, and Tyre, and Balbec, and the waste
Where stood Jerusalem, the fallen towers   110
Of Babylon, the eternal pyramids,
Memphis and Thebes, and whatsoe'er of strange[9]
Sculptured on alabaster obelisk,
Or jasper tomb, or mutilated sphynx,
Dark Æthiopia in her desert hills   115
Conceals. Among the ruined temples there,
Stupendous columns, and wild images
Of more than man, where marble dæmons[1] watch
The Zodiac's brazen mystery, and dead men
Hang their mute thoughts on the mute walls around,   120
He lingered, poring on memorials
Of the world's youth, through the long burning day
Gazed on those speechless shapes, nor, when the moon
Filled the mysterious halls with floating shades
Suspended he that task, but ever gazed   125
And gazed, till meaning on his vacant mind
Flashed like strong inspiration, and he saw
The thrilling secrets of the birth of time.[2]

    Meanwhile an Arab maiden brought his food,
Her daily portion, from her father's tent,   130
And spread her matting for his couch, and stole

5. Crowded with (see *Paradise Lost*, I.797).
6. Olivine, a greenish semi-precious stone.
7. Shelley was a vegetarian.
8. A thicket of bushes, brushwood, or briers.
9. The unusual or the mysterious; a noun.
1. Intermediate spirits with ability to communicate between the gods and men (from Plato and Greek mythology).
2. The Poet's journey in lines 106–128 carries him to the sites of great civilizations of the past in search of knowledge; he moves backward in time from the Greeks to the Phoenicians (Tyre and Balbec or Heliopolis), the Jews, the Babylonians, the Egyptians (Memphis and Thebes), and finally to Ethiopia, which the French writer Volney in his *Ruins of Empire* (1791) described as the "cradle of the sciences." In the temple of Dendera in Upper Egypt, the gods were arranged within the pattern of the Zodiac.

From duties and repose to tend his steps:—
Enamoured, yet not daring for deep awe
To speak her love:—and watched his nightly sleep,
Sleepless herself, to gaze upon his lips   135
Parted in slumber, whence the regular breath
Of innocent dreams arose: then, when red morn
Made paler the pale moon, to her cold home
Wildered,[3] and wan, and panting, she returned.

    The Poet wandering on, through Arabie   140
And Persia, and the wild Carmanian waste,
And o'er the aërial mountains which pour down
Indus and Oxus from their icy caves,
In joy and exultation held his way;[4]
Till in the vale of Cashmire, far within   145
Its loneliest dell, where odorous plants entwine
Beneath the hollow rocks a natural bower,
Beside a sparkling rivulet he stretched
His languid limbs. A vision[5] on his sleep
There came, a dream of hopes that never yet   150
Had flushed his cheek. He dreamed a veiled maid
Sate near him, talking in low solemn tones.
Her voice was like the voice of his own soul
Heard in the calm of thought; its music long,
Like woven sounds of streams and breezes, held   155
His inmost sense suspended in its web
Of many-coloured woof and shifting hues.
Knowledge and truth and virtue were her theme,
And lofty hopes of divine liberty,
Thoughts the most dear to him, and poesy,   160
Herself a poet. Soon the solemn mood
Of her pure mind kindled through all her frame
A permeating fire: wild numbers then
She raised, with voice stifled in tremulous sobs
Subdued by its own pathos: her fair hands   165
Were bare alone, sweeping from some strange harp
Strange symphony, and in their branching veins
The eloquent blood told an ineffable tale.
The beating of her heart was heard to fill
The pauses of her music, and her breath   170
Tumultuously accorded with those fits
Of intermitted song. Sudden she rose,
As if her heart impatiently endured
Its bursting burthen: at the sound he turned,
And saw by the warm light of their own life   175

3. Lost or perplexed.
4. The Poet journeys eastward through Arabia, Persia, the Desert of Karmin (southeast Iran), across the Hindu Kush Mountains (the Indian Caucasus of *Prometheus Unbound*) and the source of the Rivers Indus and Oxus, to the fabled Vale of Kashmir in northwest India (see *Prometheus Unbound*, II.i).
5. On the nature and significance of the dream-vision in lines 148–191, see Gibson, pp. 551–554, below.

Her glowing limbs beneath the sinuous veil
Of woven wind, her outspread arms now bare,
Her dark locks floating in the breath of night,
Her beamy bending eyes, her parted lips
Outstretched, and pale, and quivering eagerly.   180
His strong heart sunk and sickened with excess
Of love. He reared his shuddering limbs and quelled
His gasping breath, and spread his arms to meet
Her panting bosom: . . . she drew back a while,
Then, yielding to the irresistible joy,   185
With frantic gesture and short breathless cry
Folded his frame in her dissolving arms.
Now blackness veiled his dizzy eyes, and night
Involved[6] and swallowed up the vision; sleep,
Like a dark flood suspended in its course,   190
Rolled back its impulse on his vacant brain.

　　Roused by the shock he started from his trance—
The cold white light of morning, the blue moon
Low in the west, the clear and garish hills,
The distinct valley and the vacant woods,   195
Spread round him where he stood. Whither have fled
The hues of heaven that canopied his bower
Of yesternight? The sounds that soothed his sleep,
The mystery and the majesty of Earth,
The joy, the exultation? His wan eyes   200
Gaze on the empty scene as vacantly
As ocean's moon looks on the moon in heaven.
The spirit of sweet human love has sent
A vision to the sleep of him who spurned
Her choicest gifts. He eagerly pursues   205
Beyond the realms of dream that fleeting shade;
He overleaps the bounds. Alas! alas!
Were limbs, and breath, and being intertwined
Thus treacherously? Lost, lost, for ever lost,
In the wide pathless desart of dim sleep,   210
That beautiful shape! Does the dark gate of death
Conduct to thy mysterious paradise,
O Sleep? Does the bright arch of rainbow clouds,
And pendent mountains seen in the calm lake,
Lead only to a black and watery depth,   215
While death's blue vault, with loathliest vapours hung,
Where every shade which the foul grave exhales
Hides its dead eye from the detested day,
Conduct, O Sleep, to thy delightful realms?
This doubt with sudden tide flowed on his heart,   220
The insatiate hope which it awakened, stung
His brain even like despair.

6. Wrapped up, obscured.

While day-light held
The sky, the Poet kept mute conference
With his still soul. At night the passion came,
Like the fierce fiend of a distempered dream,   225
And shook him from his rest, and led him forth
Into the darkness.—As an eagle grasped
In folds of the green serpent, feels her breast
Burn with the poison, and precipitates[7]
Through night and day, tempest, and calm, and cloud,   230
Frantic with dizzying anguish, her blind flight
O'er the wide aëry wilderness: thus driven
By the bright shadow of that lovely dream,
Beneath the cold glare of the desolate night,
Through tangled swamps and deep precipitous dells,   235
Startling with careless step the moon-light snake,
He fled. Red morning dawned upon his flight,
Shedding the mockery of its vital hues
Upon his cheek of death. He wandered on
Till vast Aornos seen from Petra's steep   240
Hung o'er the low horizon like a cloud;
Through Balk, and where the desolated tombs
Of Parthian kings scatter to every wind
Their wasting dust, wildly he wandered on,[8]
Day after day, a weary waste of hours,   245
Bearing within his life the brooding care
That ever fed on its decaying flame.
And now his limbs were lean; his scattered hair
Sered by the autumn of strange suffering
Sung dirges in the wind; his listless hand   250
Hung like dead bone within its withered skin;
Life, and the lustre that consumed it, shone

7. Hastens.
8. The Poet flees from Kashmir to the northwest into what is now Afghanistan and then into the central Asian areas that in classical times (whose geographical terms Shelley employs) were Persian provinces; some of these areas are now parts of the USSR. *Aornos* (240) was a mountain fortress on the upper Indus River captured by Alexander the Great; its name means "without birds." *Petra* (240), the Sogdian Rock, is part of the Pamir Range in the Tadzhik SSR. *Balk* (242), the ancient Persian province of Bactria, was south of the River Oxus (now Amu Darya). Though at some periods Bactria and Parthia (which was to the southwest, in the heartland of modern Iran) were distinct provinces, after the decline of the post-Alexandrian Seleucid empire, a strong independent Parthian kingdom spread over the region; its kings were buried at the city of Nysa (modern Nisa) in Bactria proper. The Chorasmia was the swampy region between the Caspian and the Aral Sea, but here the latter body of water seems intended; in classical times the Oxus River flowed into the Aral Sea.

If we understand the Poet to embark on the Aral Sea, his shallop, a small open boat, would be carried by a supernatural impulse up the Oxus to its headwaters in the Hindu Kush Mountains (see note to 144). In Shelley's day the scientist Buffon and others believed that the Hindu Kush (Indian Caucasus) region was the cradle of the human race. Because of the ambiguity of several geographical terms (especially *Chorasmian*, 272, and *Caucasus*, 353, 377), it is possible that Shelley may have intended the Poet to embark on the Caspian Sea and end up in the western Caucasus Mountains, between the Caspian and the Black Sea. In the latter case, his journey would end somewhere near the traditional site of the Garden of Eden. (See note to Luther L. Scales, Jr., *KSJ*, 21–22: 137–139 [1972–73]).

As in a furnace burning secretly
From his dark eyes alone. The cottagers,
Who ministered with human charity   255
His human wants, beheld with wondering awe
Their fleeting visitant. The mountaineer,
Encountering on some dizzy precipice
That spectral form, deemed that the Spirit of wind
With lightning eyes, and eager breath, and feet   260
Disturbing not the drifted snow, had paused
In its career: the infant would conceal
His troubled visage in his mother's robe
In terror at the glare of those wild eyes,
To remember their strange light in many a dream   265
Of after-times; but youthful maidens, taught
By nature, would interpret half the woe
That wasted him, would call him with false names
Brother, and friend, would press his pallid hand
At parting, and watch, dim through tears, the path   270
Of his departure from their father's door.

    At length upon the lone Chorasmian shore
He paused, a wide and melancholy waste
Of putrid marshes. A strong impulse urged
His steps to the sea-shore. A swan was there,   275
Beside a sluggish stream among the reeds.
It rose as he approached, and with strong wings
Scaling the upward sky, bent its bright course
High over the immeasurable main.
His eyes pursued its flight.—"Thou hast a home,   280
Beautiful bird; thou voyagest to thine home,
Where thy sweet mate will twine her downy neck
With thine, and welcome thy return with eyes
Bright in the lustre of their own fond joy.
And what am I that I should linger here,   285
With voice far sweeter than thy dying notes,
Spirit more vast than thine, frame more attuned
To beauty, wasting these surpassing powers
In the deaf air, to the blind earth, and heaven
That echoes not my thoughts?" A gloomy smile   290
Of desperate hope wrinkled his quivering lips.
For sleep, he knew, kept most relentlessly
Its precious charge, and silent death exposed,
Faithless perhaps as sleep, a shadowy lure,
With doubtful smile mocking its own strange charms.   295

    Startled by his own thoughts he looked around.
There was no fair fiend[9] near him, not a sight
Or sound of awe but in his own deep mind.

---

9. The Poet fears he has been tempted to suicide (285–295) by a seductive "fiend" external to his mind.

A little shallop floating near the shore
Caught the impatient wandering of his gaze.   300
It had been long abandoned, for its sides
Gaped wide with many a rift, and its frail joints
Swayed with the undulations of the tide.
A restless impulse urged him to embark
And meet lone Death on the drear ocean's waste;   305
For well he knew that mighty Shadow loves
The slimy caverns of the populous deep.

The day was fair and sunny; sea and sky
Drank its inspiring radiance, and the wind
Swept strongly from the shore, blackening the waves.   310
Following his eager soul, the wanderer
Leaped in the boat, he spread his cloak aloft
On the bare mast, and took his lonely seat,
And felt the boat speed o'er the tranquil sea
Like a torn cloud before the hurricane.   315

As one that in a silver vision floats
Obedient to the sweep of odorous winds
Upon resplendent clouds, so rapdily
Along the dark and ruffled waters fled
The straining boat.—A whirlwind swept it on,   320
With fierce gusts and precipitating force,
Through the white ridges of the chafed sea.
The waves arose. Higher and higher still
Their fierce necks writhed beneath the tempest's scourge
Like serpents struggling in a vulture's grasp.   325
Calm and rejoicing in the fearful war
Of wave running on wave, and blast on blast
Descending, and black flood on whirlpool driven
With dark obliterating course, he sate:
As if their genii were the ministers   330
Appointed to conduct him to the light
Of those beloved eyes, the Poet sate
Holding the steady helm. Evening came on,
The beams of sunset hung their rainbow hues
High 'mid the shifting domes of sheeted spray   335
That canopied his path o'er the waste deep;
Twilight, ascending slowly from the east,
Entwin'd in duskier wreaths her braided locks
O'er the fair front and radiant eyes of day;
Night followed, clad with stars. On every side   340
More horribly the multitudinous streams
Of ocean's mountainous waste to mutual war
Rushed in dark tumult thundering, as to mock
The calm and spangled sky. The little boat
Still fled before the storm; still fled, like foam   345
Down the steep cataract of a wintry river;

Now pausing on the edge of the riven wave;
Now leaving far behind the bursting mass
That fell, convulsing ocean. Safely fled—
As if that frail and wasted human form,   350
Had been an elemental god.
              At midnight
The moon arose: and lo! the etherial[1] cliffs
Of Caucasus, whose icy summits shone
Among the stars like sunlight, and around
Whose cavern'd base the whirlpools and the waves   355
Bursting and eddying irresistibly
Rage and resound for ever.—Who shall save?—
The boat fled on,—the boiling torrent drove,—
The crags closed round with black and jagged arms,
The shattered mountain overhung the sea,   360
And faster still, beyond all human speed,
Suspended on the sweep of the smooth wave,
The little boat was driven. A cavern there
Yawned, and amid its slant and winding depths
Ingulphed the rushing sea. The boat fled on   365
With unrelaxing speed.—"Vision and Love!"
The Poet cried aloud, "I have beheld
The path of thy departure. Sleep and death
Shall not divide us long!"

              The boat pursued
The winding of the cavern. Day-light shone   370
At length upon that gloomy river's flow;
Now, where the fiercest war among the waves
Is calm, on the unfathomable stream
The boat moved slowly. Where the mountain, riven,
Exposed those black depths to the azure sky,   375
Ere yet the flood's enormous volume fell
Even to the base of Caucasus, with sound
That shook the everlasting rocks, the mass
Filled with one whirlpool all that ample chasm;
Stair above stair the eddying waters rose,   380
Circling immeasurably fast, and laved
With alternating dash the knarled roots
Of mighty trees, that stretched their giant arms
In darkness over it. I' the midst was left,
Reflecting, yet distorting every cloud,   385
A pool of treacherous and tremendous calm.
Seized by the sway of the ascending stream,
With dizzy swiftness, round, and round, and round,
Ridge after ridge the straining boat arose,
Till on the verge of the extremest curve,   390
Where, through an opening of the rocky bank,

1. Rising high in the air.

The waters overflow, and a smooth spot
Of glassy quiet mid those battling tides
Is left, the boat paused shuddering.—Shall it sink
Down the abyss? Shall the reverting stress   395
Of that resistless gulph embosom it?
Now shall it fall?—A wandering stream of wind,
Breathed from the west, has caught the expanded sail,
And lo! with gentle motion, between banks
Of mossy slope, and on a placid stream,   400
Beneath a woven grove it sails, and, hark!
The ghastly torrent mingles its far roar,
With the breeze murmuring in the musical woods.
Where the embowering trees recede, and leave
A little space of green expanse, the cove   405
Is closed by meeting banks, whose yellow flowers[2]
For ever gaze on their own drooping eyes,
Reflected in the crystal calm. The wave
Of the boat's motion marred their pensive task,
Which nought but vagrant bird, or wanton wind,   410
Or falling spear-grass, or their own decay
Had e'er disturbed before. The Poet longed
To deck with their bright hues his withered hair,
But on his heart its solitude returned,
And he forbore. Not the strong impulse hid   415
In those flushed cheeks, bent eyes, and shadowy frame,
Had yet performed its ministry: it hung
Upon his life, as lightning in a cloud
Gleams, hovering ere it vanish, ere the floods
Of night close over it.   420
                 The noonday sun
Now shone upon the forest, one vast mass
Of mingling shade, whose brown magnificence
A narrow vale embosoms. There, huge caves,
Scooped in the dark base of their aëry rocks
Mocking[3] its[4] moans, respond and roar for ever.   425
The meeting boughs and implicated[5] leaves
Wove twilight o'er the Poet's path, as led
By love, or dream, or god, or mightier Death,
He sought in Nature's dearest haunt, some bank,
Her cradle, and his sepulchre. More dark   430
And dark the shades accumulate. The oak,
Expanding its immense and knotty arms,
Embraces the light beech. The pyramids
Of the tall cedar overarching, frame
Most solemn domes within, and far below.   435
Like clouds suspended in an emerald sky,

---

2. The narcissi recall the legend of the Greek youth who pined away for self-love.

3. Imitating or mimicking.
4. The *forest* of 421.
5. Intertwined.

The ash and the acacia floating hang
Tremulous and pale. Like restless serpents, clothed
In rainbow and in fire, the parasites,
Starred with ten thousand blossoms, flow around   440
The grey trunks, and, as gamesome infants' eyes,
With gentle meanings, and most innocent wiles,
Fold their beams round the hearts of those that love,
These twine their tendrils with the wedded boughs
Uniting their close union; the woven leaves   445
Make net-work of the dark blue light of day,
And the night's noontide clearness, mutable
As shapes in the weird clouds. Soft mossy lawns
Beneath these canopies extend their swells,
Fragrant with perfumed herbs, and eyed with blooms   450
Minute yet beautiful. One darkest glen
Sends from its woods of musk-rose, twined with jasmine,
A soul-dissolving odour, to invite
To some more lovely mystery. Through the dell,
Silence and Twilight here, twin-sisters, keep   455
Their noonday watch, and sail among the shades,
Like vaporous shapes half seen; beyond, a well,
Dark, gleaming, and of most translucent wave,
Images all the woven boughs above,
And each depending leaf, and every speck   460
Of azure sky, darting between their chasms;
Nor aught else in the liquid mirror laves
Its portraiture, but some inconstant star
Between one foliaged lattice twinkling fair,
Or, painted bird, sleeping beneath the moon,   465
Or gorgeous insect floating motionless,
Unconscious of the day, ere yet his wings
Have spread their glories to the gaze of noon.

    Hither the Poet came. His eyes beheld
Their own wan light through the reflected lines   470
Of his thin hair, distinct in the dark depth
Of that still fountain; as the human heart,
Gazing in dreams over the gloomy grave,
Sees its own treacherous likeness there. He heard
The motion of the leaves, the grass that sprung   475
Startled and glanced and trembled even to feel
An unaccustomed presence, and the sound
Of the sweet brook that from the secret springs
Of that dark fountain rose. A Spirit seemed
To stand beside him—clothed in no bright robes   480
Of shadowy silver or enshrining light,
Borrowed from aught the visible world affords
Of grace, or majesty, or mystery;—
But, undulating woods, and silent well,
And leaping rivulet, and evening gloom   485

Now deepening the dark shades, for speech assuming
Held commune with him, as if he and it
Were all that was,—only . . . when his regard
Was raised by intense pensiveness, . . . two eyes,
Two starry eyes, hung in the gloom of thought,   490
And seemed with their serene and azure smiles
To beckon him.

        Obedient to the light
That shone within his soul, he went, pursuing
The windings of the dell.—The rivulet
Wanton and wild, through many a green ravine   495
Beneath the forest flowed. Sometimes it fell
Among the moss with hollow harmony
Dark and profound. Now on the polished stones
It danced; like childhood laughing as it went:
Then, through the plain in tranquil wanderings crept,   500
Reflecting every herb and drooping bud
That overhung its quietness.—"O stream!
Whose source is inaccessibly profound,
Whither do thy mysterious waters tend?
Thou imagest my life. Thy darksome stillness,   505
Thy dazzling waves, thy loud and hollow gulphs,
Thy searchless[6] fountain, and invisible course
Have each their type in me: and the wide sky,
And measureless ocean may declare as soon
What oozy cavern or what wandering cloud   510
Contains thy waters, as the universe
Tell where these living thoughts reside, when stretched
Upon thy flowers my bloodless limbs shall waste
I' the passing wind!"

        Beside the grassy shore
Of the small stream he went; he did impress   515
On the green moss his tremulous step, that caught
Strong shuddering from his burning limbs. As one
Roused by some joyous madness from the couch
Of fever, he did move; yet, not like him,
Forgetful of the grave, where, when the flame   520
Of his frail exultation shall be spent,
He must descend. With rapid steps he went
Beneath the shade of trees, beside the flow
Of the wild babbling rivulet; and now
The forest's solemn canopies were changed   525
For the uniform and lightsome[7] evening sky.
Grey rocks did peep from the spare moss, and stemmed
The struggling brook: tall spires of windlestrae[8]
Threw their thin shadows down the rugged slope,

6. Undiscoverable.
7. Luminous, evidently from light re-
fracted by the atmosphere after sunset.

8. Dry stalks left from flowering plants
after blossoms have died.

And nought but knarled roots[9] of antient pines 530
Branchless and blasted, clenched with grasping roots
The unwilling soil. A gradual change was here,
Yet ghastly. For, as fast years flow away,
The smooth brow gathers, and the hair grows thin
And white, and where irradiate dewy eyes 535
Had shone, gleam stony orbs:—so from his steps
Bright flowers departed, and the beautiful shade
Of the green groves, with all their odorous winds
And musical motions. Calm, he still pursued
The stream, that with a larger volume now 540
Rolled through the labyrinthine dell; and there
Fretted a path through its descending curves
With its wintry speed. On every side now rose
Rocks, which, in unimaginable forms,
Lifted their black and barren pinnacles 545
In the light of evening, and its precipice[1]
Obscuring the ravine, disclosed above,
Mid toppling stones, black gulphs and yawning caves,
Whose windings gave ten thousand various tongues
To the loud stream. Lo! where the pass expands 550
Its stony jaws, the abrupt mountain breaks,
And seems, with its accumulated crags,
To overhang the world: for wide expand
Beneath the wan stars and descending moon
Islanded seas, blue mountains, mighty streams, 555
Dim tracts and vast, robed in the lustrous gloom
Of leaden-coloured even, and fiery hills
Mingling their flames with twilight, on the verge
Of the remote horizon. The near scene,
In naked and severe simplicity, 560
Made contrast with the universe. A pine,[2]
Rock-rooted, stretched athwart the vacancy
Its swinging boughs, to each inconstant blast
Yielding one only response, at each pause
In most familiar cadence, with the howl 565
The thunder and the hiss of homeless streams
Mingling its solemn song, whilst the broad river,
Foaming and hurrying o'er its rugged path,
Fell into that immeasurable void
Scattering its waters to the passing winds. 570

    Yet the grey precipice and solemn pine
And torrent, were not all;—one silent nook
Was there. Even on the edge of that vast mountain,
Upheld by knotty roots and fallen rocks,

---

9. Shelley must have meant *knarled* (gnarled) *trunks*, since these are said to clench the soil *with grasping roots* (531–532).
1. Headlong descent—*its* referring to *stream*, 540.
2. In Shelley's poetry pine trees recur as emblems of human hopes and symbolize the persistence of life in the face of adversity.

It overlooked in its serenity   575
The dark earth, and the bending vault of stars.
It was a tranquil spot, that seemed to smile
Even in the lap of horror. Ivy clasped
The fissured stones with its entwining arms,
And did embower with leaves for ever green,   580
And berries dark, the smooth and even space
Of its inviolated floor, and here
The children of the autumnal whirlwind bore,
In wanton sport, those bright leaves, whose decay,
Red, yellow, or etherially pale,   585
Rivals the pride of summer. 'Tis the haunt
Of every gentle wind, whose breath can teach
The wilds to love tranquillity. One step,
One human step alone, has ever broken
The stillness of its solitude:—one voice   590
Alone inspired its echoes,—even that voice
Which hither came, floating among the winds,
And led the loveliest among human forms
To make their wild haunts the depository
Of all the grace and beauty that endued   595
Its motions, render up its majesty,
Scatter its music on the unfeeling storm,
And to the damp leaves and blue cavern mould,
Nurses of rainbow flowers and branching moss,
Commit the colours of that varying cheek,   600
That snowy breast, those dark and drooping eyes.

      The dim and horned moon[3] hung low, and poured
A sea of lustre on the horizon's verge
That overflowed its mountains. Yellow mist
Filled the unbounded atmosphere, and drank   605
Wan moonlight even to fulness: not a star
Shone, not a sound was heard; the very winds,
Danger's grim playmates, on that precipice
Slept, clasped in his embrace.—O, storm of death!
Whose sightless[4] speed divides this sullen night: 610
And thou, colossal Skeleton, that, still
Guiding its irresistible career
In thy devastating omnipotence,
Art king of this frail world, from the red field
Of slaughter, from the reeking hospital,   615
The patriot's sacred couch, the snowy bed
Of innocence, the scaffold and the throne,
A mighty voice invokes thee. Ruin calls

---

3. The moon is crescent-shaped with the points rising; the image is that in Coleridge's *Dejection: An Ode* of "the new Moon/With the old Moon in her arms" (see also "The Triumph of Life," 79–85).
4. Some critics have glossed this word as "invisible," but "blind" or "unseeing" seems to be the more likely meaning; like the charioteers in *Hellas* (711ff.) and "The Triumph of Life" (86–105), Death is blind in not apprehending moral distinctions.

His brother Death. A rare and regal prey
He hath prepared, prowling around the world;   620
Glutted with which thou mayst repose, and men
Go to their graves like flowers or creeping worms,
Nor ever more offer at thy dark shrine
The unheeded tribute of a broken heart.

    When on the threshold of the green recess   625
The wanderer's footsteps fell, he knew that death
Was on him. Yet a little, ere it fled,
Did he resign his high and holy soul
To images of the majestic past,
That paused within his passive being now,   630
Like winds that bear sweet music, when they breathe
Through some dim latticed chamber. He did place
His pale lean hand upon the rugged trunk
Of the old pine. Upon an ivied stone
Reclined his languid head, his limbs did rest,   635
Diffused and motionless, on the smooth brink
Of that obscurest chasm;—and thus he lay,
Surrendering to their final impulses
The hovering powers of life. Hope and despair,
The torturers, slept; no mortal pain or fear   640
Marred his repose, the influxes of sense,
And his own being unalloyed by pain,
Yet feebler and more feeble, calmly fed
The stream of thought, till he lay breathing there
At peace, and faintly smiling:—his last sight   645
Was the great moon, which o'er the western line
Of the wide world her mighty horn suspended,
With whose dun[5] beams inwoven darkness seemed
To mingle. Now upon the jagged hills
It rests, and still as the divided frame   650
Of the vast meteor[6] sunk, the Poet's blood,
That ever beat in mystic sympathy
With nature's ebb and flow, grew feebler still:
And when two lessening points of light alone
Gleamed through the darkness,[7] the alternate gasp   655
Of his faint respiration scarce did stir
The stagnate night:—till the minutest ray
Was quenched, the pulse yet lingered in his heart.
It paused—it fluttered. But when heaven remained
Utterly black, the murky shades involved   660
An image, silent, cold, and motionless,
As their own voiceless earth and vacant air.
Even as a vapour[8] fed with golden beams

5. Brownish; as the moon sinks lower, its light is more refracted and turns from a whitish to a dark yellow or orange color.
6. The term originally meant any phenomenon (including weather) within the earth's atmosphere, whose outer limits were thought to be marked by the moon.
7. As the moon sets, its center sinks first below the horizon, leaving eventually *two lessening points of light* (654).
8. Cloud.

That ministered[9] on sunlight, ere the west
Eclipses it, was now that wonderous frame—   665
No sense, no motion, no divinity—
A fragile lute, on whose harmonious strings
The breath of heaven did wander—a bright stream
Once fed with many-voiced waves—a dream
Of youth, which night and time have quenched for ever,   670
Still, dark, and dry, and unremembered now.

   O, for Medea's[1] wondrous alchemy,
Which wheresoe'er it fell made the earth gleam
With bright flowers, and the wintry boughs exhale
From vernal blooms fresh fragrance! O, that God,   675
Profuse of poisons, would concede the chalice
Which but one living man[2] has drained, who now,
Vessel of deathless wrath, a slave that feels
No proud exemption in the blighting curse
He bears, over the world wanders for ever,   680
Lone as incarnate death! O, that the dream
Of dark magician[3] in his visioned cave,
Raking the cinders of a crucible
For life and power, even when his feeble hand
Shakes in its last decay, were the true law   685
Of this so lovely world! But thou art fled
Like some frail exhalation; which the dawn
Robes in its golden beams,—ah! thou hast fled!
The brave, the gentle, and the beautiful,
The child of grace and genius. Heartless things   690
Are done and said i' the world, and many worms
And beasts and men live on, and mighty Earth
From sea and mountain, city and wilderness,
In vesper low or joyous orison,
Lifts still its solemn voice:—but thou art fled—   695
Thou canst no longer know or love the shapes
Of this phantasmal scene, who have to thee
Been purest ministers, who are, alas!
Now thou art not. Upon those pallid lips
So sweet even in their silence, on those eyes   700
That image sleep in death, upon that form
Yet safe from the worm's outrage, let no tear
Be shed—not even in thought. Nor, when those hues
Are gone, and those divinest lineaments,
Worn by the senseless[4] wind, shall live alone   705

---

9. Attended, as a servant.
1. While Medea, the sorceress of Greek legend and tragedy, brewed a magic potion to revive Aeson, she spilled some on the ground, whereupon flowers and grass sprang up (Ovid, *Metamorphoses*, VII.275ff.).
2. Ahasuerus, the Wandering Jew, doomed to eternal life, who appears also in *Queen Mab* (VII.66ff.) and *Hellas* (137–185, 638–640, 738ff.), among other works by Shelley.
3. An alchemist searching for the elixir of life and the power to change base metals into gold within a cave in which he sees visions.
4. Lacking sensation, insensate.

In the frail pauses of this simple strain,
Let not high verse, mourning the memory
Of that which is no more, or painting's woe
Or sculpture, speak in feeble imagery
Their own cold powers. Art and eloquence,   710
And all the shews o' the world are frail and vain
To weep a loss that turns their lights to shade.
It is a woe too "deep for tears,"[5] when all
Is reft at once, when some surpassing Spirit,
Whose light adorned the world around it, leaves   715
Those who remain behind, not sobs or groans,
The passionate tumult of a clinging hope;
But pale despair and cold tranquillity,
Nature's vast frame, the web of human things,
Birth and the grave, that are not as they were.   720

Stanzas.—April, 1814.[1]

Away! the moor is dark beneath the moon,
   Rapid clouds have drank the last pale beam of even:
Away! the gathering winds will call the darkness soon,
   And profoundest midnight shroud the serene lights of heaven.

Pause not! The time is past! Every voice cries, Away!   5
   Tempt not with one last tear thy friend's ungentle mood:
Thy lover's eye, so glazed and cold, dares not entreat thy stay:
   Duty and dereliction[2] guide thee back to solitude.

Away, away! to thy sad and silent home;
   Pour bitter tears on its desolated hearth;   10
Watch the dim shades as like ghosts they go and come,
   And complicate strange webs of melancholy mirth.[3]

The leaves of wasted autumn woods shall float around thine head:
   The blooms of dewy spring shall gleam beneath thy feet:
But thy soul or this world must fade[4] in the frost that binds the
   dead,   15
   Ere midnight's frown and morning's smile, ere thou and peace
   may meet.

The cloud shadows of midnight possess their own repose,
   For the weary winds are silent, or the moon is in the deep:
Some respite to its turbulence unresting ocean knows;
   Whatever moves, or toils, or grieves, hath its appointed sleep. 20

5. Wordsworth, *Ode: Intimations of Immortality*, 203.
1. Composed at Bracknell, a village west of London, in April 1814, this poem refers to Shelley's infatuation with Cornelia Boinville Turner, daughter of Shelley's friend Harriet Collins de Boinville and wife of Thomas Turner, a lawyer and protégé of Godwin. The poem was published with *Alastor* in 1816.
2. The condition of being forsaken or abandoned.
3. Lines 9–12 signal the deterioration of Shelley's first marriage to Harriet Westbrook Shelley. *Complicate:* form in an intricate way.
4. If the soul is immortal, then the world will fade first.

Thou in the grave shalt rest—yet till the phantoms flee
  Which that house and heath and garden made dear to thee
    erewhile,[5]
Thy remembrance, and repentance, and deep musings are not free
  From the music of two voices and the light of one sweet smile.

Mutability.[6]

  We are as clouds that veil the midnight moon;
    How restlessly they speed, and gleam, and quiver,
  Streaking the darkness radiantly!—yet soon
    Night closes round, and they are lost for ever:

  Or like forgotten lyres,[7] whose dissonant strings   5
    Give various response to each varying blast,
  To whose frail frame no second motion brings
    One mood or modulation like the last.

  We rest.—A dream has power to poison sleep;
    We rise.—One wandering thought pollutes the day;   10
  We feel, conceive or reason, laugh or weep;
    Embrace fond woe, or cast our cares away:

  It is the same!—For, be it joy or sorrow,
    The path of its departure still is free:
  Man's yesterday may ne'er be like his morrow;   15
    Nought may endure but Mutability.

                 1816

To Wordsworth.[8]

  Poet of Nature, thou hast wept to know
  That things depart which never may return:
  Childhood and youth, friendship and love's first glow,
  Have fled like sweet dreams, leaving thee to mourn.
  These common woes I feel. One loss is mine   5
  Which thou too feel'st, yet I alone deplore.
  Thou wert as a lone star, whose light did shine
  On some frail bark in winter's midnight roar:
  Thou hast like to a rock-built refuge stood
  Above the blind and battling multitude: 10
  In honoured poverty thy voice did weave
  Songs consecrate to truth and liberty,—
  Deserting these, thou leavest me to grieve,
  Thus having been, that thou shouldst cease to be.

                 1816

5. A while before, formerly.
6. "Mutability," like "To Wordsworth," was published with *Alastor* (1816).
7. Aeolian harps or wind lyres (cf. *Alastor*, 41–49, 663–668).
8. Shelley's comment on the growing political and religious conservatism of both William Wordsworth (whom he knew only through his writings) and Wordsworth's friend Robert Southey (whom Shelley had known well during his stay at Keswick, Cumberland, from November 1812 through January 1813). On September 14, 1814, Mary Shelley recorded in her journal: "Shelley . . . brings home Wordsworth's Excursion, of which we read a part, much disappointed. He is a slave."

Mont Blanc[1]

LINES WRITTEN IN THE VALE OF CHAMOUNI

I

The everlasting universe of things
Flows through the mind, and rolls its rapid waves,
Now dark—now glittering—now reflecting gloom—
Now lending splendour, where from secret springs
The source of human thought its tribute brings   5
Of waters,—with a sound but half its own.
Such as a feeble brook will oft assume   *— individual human mind*
In the wild woods, among the mountains lone,
Where waterfalls around it leap for ever,
Where woods and winds contend, and a vast river   10
Over its rocks ceaselessly bursts and raves.

II

Thus thou, Ravine of Arve—dark, deep Ravine—   *Universal mind*
Thou many-coloured, many-voiced vale,
Over whose pines, and crags, and caverns sail
Fast cloud shadows and sunbeams: awful[2] scene,   15
Where Power in likeness of the Arve comes down
From the ice gulphs that gird his secret throne,
Bursting through these dark mountains like the flame
Of lightning through the tempest;—thou dost lie,

1. According to the interpretation advanced by Earl R. Wasserman in *The Subtler Language* (1959), Shelley distinguishes between the Universal Mind (represented in Part II by the Ravine) and the individual human mind (compared in line 7 with the channel of a "feeble brook"). (See also *Alastor*, 668–669.) The streams passing through these respective channels (the River Arve and the brook itself) would represent the stream of sensations or impressions that pass through the mind, universal or individual. Under this reading (which gains support from lines 34ff.) the poet explores (1) the relationship of his own seeming individual identity ("my own separate phantasy") to the Universal or One Mind, of which all minds are parts, and (2) the relationship of Mind to the unknown first cause or motive force that sends the impressions of "things" (line 1) to the Mind. This unknown actuating force—referred to as "Power" in the poem (lines 16, 96)—is represented by the top of Mont Blanc, the highest mountain in Europe, hidden high above the clouds. The actual scene of the poem—the place where Shelley stood when he was inspired to write it—is on a bridge over the Arve River in the Valley of Chamonix in Savoy, now southeastern France, not far from Geneva, Switzerland. Shelley sees only the rushing river and the Arve Valley; he hears the falling of the streams melting off the glacier, Mer de Glace, above; but he images to himself and in the poem snows and the lightning storms, unseen and unheard, at the upper reaches of the mountain which feed the glacier and start the chain of Necessity that first destroys life as the glacier moves down the mountain and then supports life as the River Arve and, later, the River Rhone carry water and life to peoples far away (lines 100–126).

Power and the cycle of Necessity generated by Power are unconcerned with human values; what the scene teaches the attentive ("adverting") mind, that mind which can learn from observing the cycle of destruction and rebirth found in natural Necessity, is that "Power" (the First Cause) is not a personal God, but an Unmoved Mover quite alien in nature to mutable mortal creatures. This knowledge can "repeal/Large codes of fraud and woe" (80–81), because it destroys old dogmatic ideas (the Divine Right of kings, for example) and the hierarchies and tyrannies that spring from them. For a reading of "Mont Blanc" that laid the foundation for modern understanding of the poem, see Charles H. Vivian's "The One 'Mont Blanc,' " reprinted pp. 569–579, below.

2. Filled with awe, reverence.

Thy giant brood of pines[3] around thee clinging,   20
Children of elder time, in whose devotion
The chainless winds still come and ever came
To drink their odours, and their mighty swinging
To hear—an old and solemn harmony;
Thine earthly rainbows stretched across the sweep   25
Of the etherial waterfall, whose veil
Robes some unsculptured image;[4] the strange sleep
Which when the voices of the desart fail
Wraps all in its own deep eternity;—
Thy caverns echoing to the Arve's commotion,   30
A loud, lone sound no other sound can tame;
Thou art pervaded with that ceaseless motion,
Thou art the path of that unresting sound—
Dizzy Ravine! and when I gaze on thee[5]
I seem as in a trance sublime and strange   35
To muse on my own separate phantasy,[6]
My own, my human mind, which passively
Now renders and receives fast influencings,
Holding an unremitting interchange
With the clear universe of things around;   40
One legion of wild thoughts, whose wandering wings
Now float above thy darkness, and now rest
Where that or thou art no unbidden guest,
In the still cave of the witch Poesy,[7]
Seeking among the shadows[8] that pass by   45
Ghosts of all things that are, some shade of thee,
Some phantom, some faint image; till the breast
From which they fled[9] recalls them,[1] thou art there!

III

Some say that gleams of a remoter world
Visit the soul in sleep,—that death is slumber,   50
And that its shapes the busy thoughts outnumber
Of those who wake and live.—I look on high;
Has some unknown omnipotence unfurled

---

3. Shelley uses the pine tree in several poems to symbolize the persistence of human values in the face of obstacles. (But see lines 109–111.)
4. The image that appears in the rocks behind the veil of the waterfall has not been sculptured by man.
5. The poet addresses the Ravine of Arve in personal terms (thee, thy, thou) because, as the analogies of the opening twenty lines have established, the Ravine has become the emblem of the Universal Mind.
6. The phrase *my own separate phantasy* is in apposition to *My own, my human mind* (37) and *One legion of wild thoughts* (41). These identifications distinguish the individual human mind from the Universal Mind.

7. The witch Poesy personifies the imagination; only in the stillness of her cave —within the mind—can the individual communicate with "that" (43), "the clear universe of *things*" (40), *or* "thou" (43), the Universal Mind; note that the syntax is ambiguous, leaving the possibility that these may be either two separate entities or only one.
8. In apposition to *Ghosts* (46).
9. *breast . . . fled:* The *Ghosts of all things that are* found in the imaginative mind must come from a source, here anthropomorphized as a *breast;* the poet explores the nature of this source in lines 49–57.
1. *they . . . them* refers to *shadows . . . Ghosts* (45–46).

The veil of life and death?[2] or do I lie
In dream, and does the mightier world of sleep   55
Spread far around and inaccessibly
Its circles? For the very spirit fails,
Driven like a homeless cloud from steep to steep
That vanishes among the viewless gales!
Far, far above, piercing the infinite sky,   60
Mont Blanc appears,—still, snowy, and serene—
Its subject mountains their unearthly forms
Pile around it, ice and rock; broad vales between
Of frozen floods, unfathomable deeps,
Blue as the overhanging heaven, that spread   65
And wind among the accumulated steeps;
A desert peopled by the storms alone,
Save when the eagle brings some hunter's bone,
And the wolf tracts[3] her there—how hideously
Its shapes are heaped around! rude, bare, and high,   70
Ghastly, and scarred, and riven.—Is this the scene
Where the old Earthquake-dæmon[4] taught her young
Ruin? Were these their toys? or did a sea
Of fire, envelope once this silent snow?
None can reply—all seems eternal now.   75
The wilderness has a mysterious tongue
Which teaches awful doubt,[5] or faith so mild,
So solemn, so serene, that man may be
But for such faith[6] with nature reconciled,
Thou hast a voice, great Mountain, to repeal   80
Large codes of fraud and woe; not understood
By all, but which the wise, and great, and good
Interpret, or make felt, or deeply feel.

IV

The fields, the lakes, the forests, and the streams,
Ocean, and all the living things that dwell   85
Within the dædal[7] earth; lightning, and rain,
Earthquake, and fiery flood, and hurricane,
The torpor of the year when feeble dreams

2. As E. B. Murray has argued (*KSJ*, 18:39–48 [1969]), Shelley here records the anticlimactic moment at the end of the poet's vision in the cave of Poesy, when the veil is lowered again between the realms of life and death.
3. Pursues, traces.
4. A daemon, in Greek mythology, is a spirit intermediate between the gods and men, usually personifying natural forces.
5. Reverent open-mindedness.
6. *But for such faith* probably means "only through such faith"; in the manuscript draft this passage reads (canceled words in italics):
Which teaches awful,—or a *belief* faith
  so mild
So solemn, so serene, that man *again*
may be
To such high thoughts of **With such**
  a faith
In such wise faith with Nature reconciled!—
On the basis of this evidence both Wasserman and Judith Chernaik have concluded that *But* is used here not as a preposition meaning "except," but rather as an adverb meaning "only" or "merely."
7. Intricately, cleverly fashioned; this favorite adjective of Shelley comes ultimately from Daedalus, the craftsman of Greek mythology who built the Cretan labyrinth and, later, wings to escape from it.

Visit the hidden buds, or dreamless sleep
Holds every future leaf and flower;—the bound   90
With which from that detested trance they leap;
The works and ways of man, their death and birth,
And that of him and all that his may be;
All things that move and breathe with toil and sound
Are born and die; revolve, subside and swell.   95
Power dwells apart in its tranquillity
Remote, serene, and inaccessible:[8]
And *this*,[9] the naked countenance of earth,
On which I gaze, even these primæval mountains
Teach the adverting mind. The glaciers creep   100
Like snakes that watch their prey, from their far fountains,
Slow rolling on; there, many a precipice,
Frost and the Sun in scorn of mortal power
Have piled: dome, pyramid, and pinnacle,
A city of death, distinct with many a tower   105
And wall impregnable of beaming ice.
Yet not a city, but a flood of ruin
Is there, that from the boundaries of the sky
Rolls its perpetual stream; vast pines are strewing
Its destined path, or in the mangled soil   110
Branchless and shattered stand: the rocks, drawn down
From yon remotest waste, have overthrown
The limits of the dead and living world,
Never to be reclaimed. The dwelling-place
Of insects, beasts, and birds, becomes its spoil;   115
Their food and their retreat for ever gone,
So much of life and joy is lost. The race
Of man, flies far in dread; his work and dwelling
Vanish, like smoke before the tempest's stream,
And their place is not known.[10] Below, vast caves   120
Shine in the rushing torrents' restless gleam,
Which from those secret chasms in tumult welling
Meet in the vale, and one majestic River,
The breath and blood of distant lands,[1] for ever
Rolls its loud waters to the ocean waves,   125
Breathes its swift vapours to the circling air.

v

Mont Blanc yet gleams on high:—the power is there,
The still and solemn power of many sights,
And many sounds, and much of life and death.
In the calm darkness of the moonless nights,   130

---

8. The bald statement of the aloof nature
of *Power* contrasts with the endless cycli-
cal activities of mortal creatures de-
scribed in lines 84–95.
9. I.e., the contrast drawn in lines 84–97,
but especially the nature of *Power* stated
in 96–97.
10. "As for man, his days are as grass.
. . . For the wind passeth over it, and

it is gone; and the place thereof shall
know it no more" (Psalms 103:15–16).
1. The River Arve, which originates in
the Valley of Chamonix at the foot of
Mont Blanc, flows into Lake Geneva
near the city of Geneva; nearby, the
River Rhone flows out of Lake Geneva
to begin its course through France to
the Mediterranean Sea.

In the lone glare of day, the snows descend
Upon that Mountain; none beholds them there,
Nor when the flakes burn in the sinking sun,
Or the star-beams dart through them:—Winds contend
Silently there, and heap the snow with breath   135
Rapid and strong, but silently! Its home
The voiceless lightning in these solitudes
Keeps innocently, and like vapour broods
Over the snow. The secret strength of things
Which governs thought, and to the infinite dome   140
Of heaven is as a law,[2] inhabits thee![3]
And what were thou, and earth, and stars, and sea,
If to the human mind's imaginings
Silence and solitude were vacancy?

Hymn to Intellectual Beauty[1]

1

The awful shadow of some unseen Power
   Floats though unseen amongst us,—visiting
   This various world with as inconstant wing
As summer winds that creep from flower to flower.—
Like moonbeams that behind some piny mountain shower,   5
   It visits with inconstant glance
   Each human heart and countenance;
Like hues and harmonies of evening,—
   Like clouds in starlight widely spread,—
   Like memory of music fled,—   10
   Like aught that for its grace may be
Dear, and yet dearer for its mystery.

2

Spirit of BEAUTY, that dost[2] consecrate
   With thine own hues all thou dost shine upon
   Of human thought or form,—where art thou gone?   15
Why dost thou pass away and leave our state,

2. The clause, *The secret strength . . . law*, states that the *Power* that generates *things* and is the law of nature also *governs thought*—that mind is ultimately subordinate to the *remote, serene, and inaccessible* (97) force that originates the amoral cycles of Necessity.

3. Mont Blanc; this personification of the symbol of the nonanthropomorphic, amoral Power prepares for the final rhetorical question (142–144). The very power of imagination to realize the nature of Power, so remote and foreign to all mortal experience, illustrates the supremacy of that imagination over the *silence and solitude* that threaten it. The poet is equal to Mont Blanc, for though the amoral Power can destroy him, only he can comprehend its meaning.

1. Composed in the summer of 1816 during his stay with Byron on the shores of Lake Geneva, Shelley's "Hymn" was first published in Leigh Hunt's weekly newspaper the *Examiner* on January 19, 1817; a revised version was printed, along with "Lines written among the Euganean Hills" and "Ozymandias," in *Rosalind and Helen* (1819). "Intellectual," as used in the title, means nonmaterial.

2. Though some editors follow the *Examiner* text, which reads *that doth*, the second person familiar form is correct in this situation; see parallel usages in the Collects of the *Book of Common Prayer* (e.g., "Almighty God, who *hast* given thine only Son . . .") and in Milton's sonnets, many of which are modeled on the Collects of the prayer book.

This dim vast vale of tears, vacant and desolate?
　　Ask why the sunlight not forever
　　Weaves rainbows o'er yon mountain river,
Why aught should fail and fade that once is shewn,　　　20
　　Why fear and dream and death and birth
　　Cast on the daylight of this earth
　　Such gloom,—why man has such a scope
For love and hate, despondency and hope?

3

No voice from some sublimer world hath ever　　　25
　　To sage or poet these responses given—
　　Therefore the name of God and ghosts and Heaven,
Remain the records of their[3] vain endeavour,
Frail spells—whose utttered charm might not avail to sever,
　　From all we hear and all we see,　　　30
　　Doubt, chance, and mutability.
Thy light alone—like mist o'er mountains driven,
　　Or music by the night wind sent
　　Through strings of some still instrument,[4]
　　Or moonlight on a midnight stream,　　　35
Gives grace and truth to life's unquiet dream.

4

Love, Hope, and Self-esteem, like clouds depart
　　And come, for some uncertain moments lent.
　　Man were immortal, and omnipotent,
Didst thou, unknown and awful as thou art,[5]　　　40
Keep with thy glorious train firm state within his heart.[6]
　　Thou messenger of sympathies,
　　That wax and wane in lovers' eyes—
Thou—that to human thought art nourishment,
　　Like darkness to a dying flame![7]　　　45
　　Depart not as thy shadow came,
　　Depart not—lest the grave should be,
Like life and fear, a dark reality.

5

While yet a boy I sought for ghosts, and sped
　　Through many a listening chamber, cave and ruin,　　　50
　　And starlight wood, with fearful steps pursuing
Hopes of high talk with the departed dead.

---

3. Sage and poet (line 26).
4. The Aeolian harp or wind lyre.
5. I.e., "Man would be . . . If thou didst. . . ."
6. Shelley's hyperbole in lines 39–41 derives from his belief in the primary importance of psychological, rather than chronological, time. In his note to *Queen Mab*, VIII.203–207, he asserts the perfectibility of the human sensibility and, therefore, the possibility of virtual (not literal) immortality.
7. The Spirit Shelley invokes is said to nourish human thought as darkness nourishes a dying flame; i.e., the Spirit does not really feed human thought at all, but sets off and calls attention to it because of its opposite, antithetical nature. This contrast is also found in "Mont Blanc."

I called on poisonous names[8] with which our youth is fed;
   I was not heard—I saw them not—
   When musing deeply on the lot   55
Of life, at that sweet time when winds are wooing
   All vital things that wake to bring
   News of buds and blossoming,—
   Sudden, thy shadow fell on me;
I shrieked, and clasped my hands in extacy!   60

6

I vowed that I would dedicate my powers
   To thee and thine—have I not kept the vow? *his poetry?*
   With beating heart and streaming eyes, even now
I call the phantoms of a thousand hours
Each from his voiceless grave: they have in visioned bowers   65
   Of studious zeal or love's delight
   Outwatched with me the envious night—
They know that never joy illumed my brow
   Unlinked with hope that thou wouldst free
   This world from its dark slavery,   70
   That thou—O awful LOVELINESS,
Wouldst give whate'er these words cannot express.

7

The day becomes more solemn and serene
   When noon is past—there is a harmony
   In autumn, and a lustre in its sky,   75
Which through the summer is not heard or seen,
As if it could not be, as if it had not been!
   Thus let thy power, which like the truth
   Of nature on my passive youth
Descended, to my onward life supply   80
   Its calm—to one who worships thee,
   And every form containing thee,
   Whom, SPIRIT fair, thy spells did bind
To fear[9] himself, and love all human kind.

8. Religious terms such as "God,"   9. Revere, have respect.
"ghosts," and "Heaven" (line 27).

From Laon and Cythna; or
The Revolution of the Golden City[1]
DEDICATION
TO
MARY —— ——

1.

So now my summer task is ended, Mary,
    And I return to thee, mine own heart's home;
As to his Queen some victor Knight of Faëry,[2]
    Earning bright spoils for her inchanted dome;
    Nor thou disdain, that ere my fame become   5
A star among the stars of mortal night,
    If it indeed may cleave its natal gloom,
Its doubtful promise thus I would unite
With thy beloved name, thou Child of love and light.

2.

The toil which stole from thee so many an hour   10
    Is ended,—and the fruit is at thy feet!
No longer where the woods to frame a bower
    With interlaced branches mix and meet,
    Or where with sound like many voices sweet
Water-falls leap among wild islands green,   15
    Which framed for my lone boat a lone retreat
Of moss-grown trees and weeds, shall I be seen:
But beside thee, where still my heart has ever been.

3.

Thoughts of great deeds were mine, dear Friend, when first
    The clouds which wrap this world from youth did pass.   20
I do remember well the hour which burst
    My spirit's sleep: a fresh May-dawn it was,
    When I walked forth upon the glittering grass,
And wept, I knew not why; until there rose
    From the near school-room, voices, that, alas!   25
Were but one echo from a world of woes—
The harsh and grating strife of tyrants and of foes.

4.

And then I clasped my hands and looked around—
    —But none was near to mock my streaming eyes,
Which poured their warm drops on the sunny ground—   30

1. *Laon and Cythna* (later retitled *The Revolt of Islam*), Shelley's longest poem, is a symbolic epic of twelve cantos in Spenserian stanzas. Uniting Shelley's philosophical, social, and personal concerns, it tells the story of two lovers (also brother and sister in the original version) who inspire and lead a bloodless revolution against the sultan of Turkey— an idealized portrayal of the French Revolution. Shelley composed the poem between March or April and September 1817; the Dedication "To Mary" (i.e., Mary Wollstonecraft Shelley) was written after this "summer's task" had been completed.

2. The poem owes much to Spenser's *The Faerie Queen.*

So without shame, I spake:—"I will be wise,
  And just, and free, and mild, if in me lies
Such power, for I grow weary to behold
  The selfish and the strong still tyrannise
  Without reproach or check." I then controuled   35
My tears, my heart grew calm, and I was meek and bold.

5.

And from that hour did I with earnest thought
  Heap knowledge from forbidden mines of lore,
Yet nothing that my tyrants knew or taught
  I cared to learn, but from that secret store   40
  Wrought linked armour for my soul, before
It might walk forth to war among mankind;
  Thus power and hope were strengthened more and more
  Within me, till there came upon my mind
A sense of loneliness, a thirst with which I pined.[3]   45

6.

Alas, that love should be a blight and snare
  To those who seek all sympathies in one!—
Such once I sought in vain; then black despair,
  The shadow of a starless night, was thrown
  Over the world in which I moved alone:—   50
Yet never found I one not false to me,
  Hard hearts, and cold, like weights of icy stone
  Which crushed and withered mine, that could not be
Aught but a lifeless clog, until revived by thee.

7.

Thou Friend, whose presence on my wintry heart   55
  Fell, like bright Spring upon some herbless plain;
How beautiful and calm and free thou wert
  In thy young wisdom, when the mortal chain
  Of Custom thou didst burst and rend in twain,[4]
And walked as free as light the clouds among,   60
  Which many an envious slave then breathed in vain
From his dim dungeon, and my spirit sprung
To meet thee from the woes which had begirt it long.

8.

No more alone through the world's wilderness,
  Although I trod the paths of high intent,   65
I journeyed now: no more companionless,
  Where solitude is like despair, I went.—

3. Lines 21–45 give Shelley's most specific and detailed account of his conversion to revolutionary principles; the circumstances of the scene seem to fit aristocratic Eton College (a leading "public school" or endowed private preparatory school), where Shelley studied from 1804 to 1810.
4. Mary Godwin was sixteen years old when she declared her love to Shelley, who was then twenty-one and married to Harriet Westbrook Shelley.

There is the wisdom of a stern content
When Poverty can blight the just and good,
    When Infamy dares mock the innocent,   70
And cherished friends turn with the multitude
To trample: this was ours, and we unshaken stood!

9.

Now has descended a serener hour,
    And with inconstant fortune, friends return;
Though suffering leaves the knowledge and the power   75
    Which says:—Let scorn be not repaid with scorn.
And from thy side two gentle babes are born
    To fill our home with smiles,[5] and thus are we
    Most fortunate beneath life's beaming morn;
And these delights, and thou, have been to me   80
The parents of the Song I consecrate to thee.

10.

Is it, that now my inexperienced fingers
    But strike the prelude of a loftier strain?
Or, must the lyre on which my spirit lingers
    Soon pause in silence, ne'er to sound again,[6]   85
    Though it might shake the Anarch Custom's reign,
And charm the minds of men to Truth's own sway
    Holier than was Amphion's?[7] I would fain
Reply in hope—but I am worn away,
And Death and Love are yet contending for their prey.   90

11.

And what art thou? I know, but dare not speak:
    Time may interpret to his silent years.
Yet in the paleness of thy thoughtful cheek,
    And in the light thine ample forehead wears,
    And in thy sweetest smiles, and in thy tears,   95
And in thy gentle speech, a prophecy
    Is whispered, to subdue my fondest fears:
And through thine eyes, even in thy soul I see
A lamp of vestal fire[8] burning internally.

12.

They say that thou wert lovely from thy birth,   100
    Of glorious parents, thou aspiring Child.
I wonder not—for One then left this Earth[9]
    Whose life was like a setting planet mild

---

5. William (born Jan. 24, 1816) and Clara Everina (born Sept. 2, 1817).
6. Shelley, who thought he might be dying at this time.
7. In Greek myth Amphion, a son of Zeus, was so creative with his lyre that stones formed themselves into the walls of Thebes in response to his music. (His unholy acts were to avenge his human mother by conquering Thebes and putting to death her husband and that man's second wife.)
8. Sacred fire tended by vestal virgins in the temple of Vesta, Roman goddess of the hearth and household.
9. Mary Wollstonecraft Godwin, mother of Mary Wollstonecraft Godwin Shelley, had died in 1797 from complications connected with the birth of her namesake.

Which clothed thee in the radiance undefiled
Of its departing glory; still her fame   105
    Shines on thee, through the tempests dark and wild
Which shake these latter days; and thou canst claim
The shelter, from thy Sire,[1] of an immortal name.

13.

One voice[2] came forth from many a mighty spirit,
    Which was the echo of three thousand years;   110
And the tumultuous world stood mute to hear it,
    As some lone man who in a desert hears
    The music of his home:—unwonted fears
Fell on the pale oppressors of our race,
    And Faith, and Custom, and low-thoughted cares,   115
Like thunder-stricken dragons, for a space
Left the torn human heart, their food and dwelling-place.

14.

Truth's deathless voice pauses among mankind!
    If there must be no response to my cry—
If men must rise and stamp with fury blind   120
    On his pure name who loves them,—thou and I,
    Sweet Friend! can look from our tranquillity
Like lamps into the world's tempestuous night,—
    Two tranquil stars, while clouds are passing by
Which wrap them from the foundering[3] seaman's sight,   125
That burn from year to year with unextinguished light.

From CANTO IX[4]

*   *   *

20.

"We know not what will come—yet Laon, dearest,   3640
    Cythna shall be the prophetess of love,
Her lips shall rob thee of the grace thou wearest,
    To hide thy heart, and clothe the shapes which rove
    Within the homeless future's wintry grove;—
For I now, sitting thus beside thee, seem   3645
    Even with thy breath and blood to live and move,
And violence and wrong are as a dream
Which rolls from stedfast truth, an unreturning stream.

1. William Godwin was regarded by young liberals as England's greatest political theorist and novelist of the decade following 1792.
2. Godwin's *An Enquiry concerning Political Justice* (1793).
3. Stumbling; sinking because the ship is filled with water.
4. Laon and his sister Cythna, after escaping the counter-revolutionary armies sent by reactionary powers, have told each other how, after their separation years before, each had come to participate in the bloodless Revolution of the Golden City. In this speech Cythna assures Laon that they have not struggled in vain. Shelley later reused the imagery in "Ode to the West Wind."

21.

"The blasts of autumn drive the winged seeds
    Over the Earth,—next come the snows, and rain,   3650
And frosts, and storms, which dreary winter leads
    Out of his Scythian[5] cave, a savage train;
    Behold! Spring sweeps over the world again,
Shedding soft dews from her æthereal wings;
    Flowers on the mountains, fruits over the plain,   3655
And music on the waves and woods she flings,
And love on all that lives, and calm on lifeless things.

22.

"O Spring, of hope, and love, and youth, and gladness
    Wind-winged emblem! brightest, best and fairest!
Whence comest thou, when, with dark Winter's sadness   3660
    The tears that fade in sunny smiles thou sharest?
    Sister of joy, thou art the child who wearest
Thy mother's dying smile, tender and sweet;
    Thy mother Autumn, for whose grave thou bearest
Fresh flowers, and beams like flowers, with gentle feet,   3665
Disturbing not the leaves which are her winding-sheet.

23.

"Virtue, and Hope, and Love, like light and Heaven,
    Surround the world.—We are their chosen slaves.
Has not the whirlwind of our spirit driven
    Truth's deathless germs to thought's remotest caves?   3670
    Lo, Winter comes!—the grief of many graves,
The frost of death, the tempest of the sword,
    The flood of tyranny, whose sanguine waves
Stagnate like ice at Faith, the inchanter's word,
And bind all human hearts in its repose abhorred.   3675

24.

"The seeds are sleeping in the soil: meanwhile
    Thy tyrant peoples dungeons with his prey,
Pale victims on the guarded scaffold smile
    Because they cannot speak; and, day by day,
    The moon of wasting Science[6] wanes away   3680
Among her stars, and in that darkness vast
    The sons of Earth to their foul idols pray,
And grey priests triumph, and like blight or blast
A shade of selfish care o'er human looks is cast.

25.

"This is the winter of the world;—and here   3685
    We die, even as the winds of Autumn fade,
Expiring in the frore[7] and foggy air.—
    Behold! Spring comes, though we must pass, who made

5. Classical Scythia included regions of central Asia east of the Aral Sea (Scythia intra Imaum) and what are now Tibet and Sinkiang province of western China (Scythia extra Imaum).
6. Knowledge and reasoned discourse.
7. Intensely cold, frosty.

The promise of its birth,—even as the shade
  Which from our death, as from a mountain, flings   3690
    The future, a broad sunrise; thus arrayed
  As with the plumes of overshadowing wings,
From its dark gulphs of chains, Earth like an eagle springs.

26.

"O dearest love! we shall be dead and cold
  Before this morn may on the world arise;   3695
Wouldst thou the glory of its dawn behold?
  Alas! gaze not on me, but turn thine eyes
  On thine own heart—it is a Paradise
Which everlasting Spring has made its own,
  And while drear Winter fills the naked skies,   3700
Sweet streams of sunny thought, and flowers fresh-blown,
Are there, and weave their sounds and odours into one.

27.

"In their own hearts the earnest of the hope
  Which made them great, the good will ever find;
And though some envious shades may interlope   3705
  Between the effect and it, One comes behind,
  Who aye the future to the past will bind—
Necessity,[8] whose sightless strength forever
  Evil with evil, good with good must wind
In bands of union, which no power may sever: 3710
They must bring forth their kind, and be divided never!

28.

"The good and mighty of departed ages
  Are in their graves, the innocent and free
Heroes, and Poets, and prevailing Sages,
  Who leave the vesture[9] of their majesty   3715
  To adorn and clothe this naked world;—and we
Are like to them—such perish, but they leave
  All hope, or love, or truth, or liberty,
Whose forms their mighty spirits could conceive,
To be a rule and law to ages that survive."[10]   3720

*   *   *

To Constantia[1]

Thy voice, slow rising like a Spirit, lingers
O'ershadowing me with soft and lulling wings;
The blood and life within thy snowy fingers
Teach witchcraft to the instrumental strings.

8. See note to *Queen Mab*, VI.198.
9. Clothing, raiment.
10. Cf. the end of *A Defence of Poetry:*
"Poets are the unacknowledged legislators of the world."
1. Written at Marlow between mid-1817 and January 19, 1818, "To Constantia" celebrates Claire Clairmont, one of whose nicknames was "Constantia" (a character in *Ormond*, by the American novelist Charles Brockden Brown). It was first published in the *Oxford University and City Herald* on January 31, 1818, over the name "Pleyel," the name not only of a famous piano maker of the day but also of a character in *Wieland*, Brown's best-known novel.

My brain is wild, my breath comes quick,   5
The blood is listening in my frame,
And thronging shadows fast and thick
Fall on my overflowing eyes,
My heart is quivering like a flame;
As morning dew, that in the sunbeam dies,   10
I am dissolved in these consuming extacies.

I have no life, Constantia, but in thee;
Whilst, like the world-surrounding air, thy song
Flows on, and fills all things with melody:
Now is thy voice a tempest, swift and strong,   15
 On which, as one in trance upborne,
 Secure o'er woods and waves I sweep
 Rejoicing, like a cloud of morn:
 Now 'tis the breath of summer's night[2]
 Which, where the starry waters sleep   20
Round western isles with incense blossoms bright,
Lingering, suspends my soul in its voluptuous flight.

A deep and breathless awe, like the swift change
Of dreams unseen, but felt in youthful slumbers;
Wild, sweet, yet incommunicably strange,   25
Thou breathest now, in fast ascending numbers:
 The cope of Heaven seems rent and cloven[3]
 By the inchantment of thy strain,
 And o'er my shoulders wings are woven
 To follow its sublime career,   30
 Beyond the mighty moons that wane
Upon the verge of Nature's utmost sphere,
Till the world's shadowy walls are past, and disappear.

Cease, cease—for such wild lessons madmen learn:
Long thus to sink,—thus to be lost and die   35
Perhaps is death indeed—Constantia turn!
Yes! in thine eyes a power like light doth lie,
 Even though the sounds, its voice, that were
 Between thy lips are laid to sleep—
 Within thy breath and on thy hair   40
 Like odour it is lingering yet—
 And from thy touch like fire doth leap:
Even while I write my burning cheeks are wet—
Such things the heart can feel and learn, but not forget![4]

2. A metaphor for the quality of her
voice (not a reference to the season of
the poem's composition, as has some-
times been assumed).
3. I.e., "The vault of Heaven seems torn
and split." In traditional artistic repre-
sentations of St. Cecilia, patron saint of

music, the heavens are opened by the
power of her singing while accompanied
by the organ.
4. In the Bodleian manuscript of Shelley's
first draft this line reads: "Alas, that the
torn heart can bleed but not forget."

Ozymandias[5]

I met a traveller from an antique land,
Who said—"Two vast and trunkless legs of stone
Stand in the desert. . . . Near them, on the sand,
Half sunk a shattered visage lies, whose frown,
And wrinkled lip, and sneer of cold command,
Tell that its sculptor well those passions read
Which yet survive,[6] stamped on these lifeless things,[7]
The hand that mocked them, and the heart that fed:[8]
And on the pedestal, these words appear:
My name is Ozymandias, King of Kings,
Look on my Works, ye Mighty, and despair!
Nothing beside remains. Round the decay
Of that colossal Wreck, boundless and bare
The lone and level sands stretch far away."

Lines written among the Euganean Hills[1]

October, 1818.

Many a green isle needs must be
In the deep wide sea of Misery,
Or the mariner, worn and wan,
Never thus could voyage on—
Day and night, and night and day,   5
Drifting on his dreary way,
With the solid darkness black
Closing round his vessel's track;

5. Ozymandias (the Greek name for Ramses II, 1304–1237 B.C.) was the pharaoh of Egypt with whom Moses contended during the Exodus. Shelley's sonnet was written—probably late in 1817—in a contest with his friend Horace (Horatio) Smith. Shelley's sonnet was published in Leigh Hunt's *Examiner* for January 11, 1818, and Smith's sonnet, also titled "Ozymandias" at first, but later reprinted as "On a Stupendous Leg of Granite, Discovered Standing by Itself in the Deserts of Egypt, with the Inscription Inserted Below," appeared in the *Examiner* for February 1, 1818. Discrepancies between Shelley's and Smith's poems make it clear that they were responding independently to a conversation about the scene and not relying on a single written description. H. M. Richmond argues cogently (*KSJ*, 11:65–71 [1962]) that Shelley's poem may reflect recollection of a description and an illustration in Richard Pocoke's *A Description of the East and Some Other Countries* (London, 1743). Our substantive text derives from the two printings during Shelley's lifetime, punctuation and orthography from Shelley's holograph.
6. Outlive.
7. The phrase, *stamped . . . things*, is almost parenthetical, identifying the medium through which the *passions* survive.
8. The sculptor's *hand mocked* (imitated and derided) the *passions* that Ozymandias' *heart fed*.
1. Shelley began writing this poem while living at Este, amid the Euganean Hills near Padua, in October 1818. In December 1818 or January 1819 he mailed it to his publisher Charles Ollier, who published it with *Rosalind and Helen* (May 1819). Fragments of the press copy manuscript survive at the Huntington Library and in the Tinker Collection at Yale University Library. For a detailed reading of the poem, see Donald H. Reiman, "Structure, Symbol, and Theme in 'Lines written among the Euganean Hills,' " pages 579–596.

Whilst above the sunless sky,
Big with clouds, hangs heavily,   10
And behind the tempest fleet
Hurries on with lightning feet,
Riving² sail, and cord, and plank,
Till the ship has almost drank
Death from the o'er-brimming deep;   15
And sinks down, down, like that sleep
When the dreamer seems to be
Weltering³ through eternity;
And the dim low line before
Of a dark and distant shore   20
Still recedes, as ever still
Longing with divided will,
But no power to seek or shun,
He is ever drifted on
O'er the unreposing wave   25
To the haven of the grave.

What, if there no friends will greet;
What, if there no heart will meet
His with love's impatient beat;
Wander wheresoe'er he may,   30
Can he dream before that day
To find refuge from distress
In friendship's smile, in love's caress?
Then 'twill wreak⁴ him little woe
Whether such there be or no: 35
Senseless⁵ is the breast, and cold,
Which relenting love would fold;
Bloodless are the veins and chill
Which the pulse of pain did fill;
Every little living nerve   40
That from bitter words did swerve
Round the tortured lips and brow,
Are like sapless leaflets now
Frozen upon December's bough.

On the beach of a northern sea   45
Which tempests shake eternally,
As once the wretch⁶ there lay to sleep,
Lies a solitary heap,
One white skull and seven dry bones,⁷
On the margin of the stones   50
Where a few grey rushes⁸ stand,
Boundaries of the sea and land:

---

2. Tearing or pulling apart, rending.
3. Tossing and tumbling; floundering.
4. Cause harm or damage.
5. Incapable of perception or emotion.
6. A poor and hapless being.
7. See Reiman, page 583.
8. Plants having naked stalks growing in marshy ground; used as a type of something with no value.

Nor is heard one voice of wail
But the sea-mews,[9] as they sail
O'er the billows of the gale;   55
Or the whirlwind up and down
Howling, like a slaughtered town,
When a King in glory rides
Through the pomp of fratricides:
Those unburied bones around   60
There is many a mournful sound;
There is no lament for him
Like a sunless vapour dim
Who once clothed with life and thought
What now moves nor murmurs not.   65

Aye, many flowering islands lie
In the waters of wide Agony.
To such a one this morn was led
My bark by soft winds piloted—
'Mid the mountains Euganean[1]   70
I stood listening to the pæan
With which the legioned rooks did hail
The sun's uprise majestical;
Gathering round with wings all hoar,
Through the dewy mist they soar   75
Like grey shades, till th'eastern heaven
Bursts, and then, as clouds of even
Flecked with fire and azure lie
In the unfathomable sky,
So their plumes of purple grain,   80
Starred with drops of golden rain,
Gleam above the sunlight woods,
As in silent multitudes
On the morning's fitful gale
Through the broken mist they sail,   85
And the vapours cloven and gleaming
Follow down the dark steep streaming,
Till all is bright, and clear, and still,
Round the solitary hill.

Beneath is spread like a green sea   90
The waveless plain of Lombardy,
Bounded by the vaporous air,
Islanded by cities fair;
Underneath day's azure eyes
Ocean's nursling Venice lies,   95
A peopled labyrinth of walls,
Amphitrite's[2] destined halls

---

9. See Reiman, page 586.
1. This line shows how Shelley pro-
nounced Euganean (yoo-gä-ne′-un);
paean: song of thanksgiving.

2. In Greek mythology Amphitrite was
the daughter of Oceanus (*sire*, 98) and
the wife of Poseidon (Neptune), the
god of the sea.

Which her hoary sire now paves
With his blue and beaming waves.—
Lo! the sun upsprings behind,   100
Broad, red, radiant, half-reclined
On the level quivering line
Of the waters chrystalline;
And before that chasm of light,
As within a furnace bright,   105
Column, tower, and dome, and spire,
Shine like obelisks of fire,
Pointing with inconstant motion
From the altar of dark ocean
To the sapphire-tinted skies;   110
As the flames of sacrifice
From the marble shrines did rise,
As to pierce the dome of gold
Where Apollo spoke of old.[3]

Sun-girt City, thou hast been   115
Ocean's child, and then his queen;
Now is come a darker day,
And thou soon must be his prey,
If the power that raised thee here
Hallow so thy watery bier.   120
A less drear ruin then than now,
With thy conquest-branded brow[4]
Stooping to the slave of slaves
From thy throne, among the waves
Wilt thou be, when the sea-mew   125
Flies, as once before it flew,
O'er thine isles depopulate,
And all is in its antient state,
Save where many a palace gate
With green sea-flowers overgrown   130
Like a rock of ocean's own,
Topples o'er the abandoned sea
As the tides change sullenly.
The fisher on his watery way,
Wandering at the close of day,   135
Will spread his sail and seize his oar
Till he pass the gloomy shore,
Lest thy dead should, from their sleep
Bursting o'er the starlight deep,
Lead a rapid masque[5] of death   140
O'er the waters of his path.

---

3. *dome . . . old:* the oracle of Apollo at Delphi.
4. Venice is disfigured both by having in the past been a conqueror and recently by having been conquered by Napoleonic France and Austria.
5. An elaborately staged dramatic performance.

Those who alone thy towers behold
Quivering through aerial gold,
As I now behold them here,
Would imagine not they were   145
Sepulchres, where human forms,
Like pollution-nourished worms,
To the corpse of greatness cling,
Murdered, and now mouldering:
But if Freedom should awake   150
In her omnipotence, and shake
From the Celtic Anarch's⁶ hold
All the keys of dungeons cold,
Where a hundred cities lie
Chained like thee, ingloriously,   155
Thou and all thy sister band
Might adorn this sunny land,
Twining memories of old time
With new virtues more sublime;
If not, perish thou and they!—   160
Clouds which stain truth's rising day
By her sun consumed away—
Earth can spare ye: while like flowers,
In the waste of years and hours,
From your dust new nations spring   165
With more kindly blossoming.

Perish—let there only be
Floating o'er thy heartless sea,
As the garment of thy sky
Clothes the world immortally,   170
One remembrance, more sublime
Than the tattered pall⁷ of time,
Which scarce hides thy visage wan;—
That a tempest-cleaving Swan⁸
Of the songs of Albion,⁹   175
Driven from his ancestral streams
By the might of evil dreams,
Found a nest in thee; and Ocean
Welcomed him with such emotion
That its joy grew his, and sprung   180
From his lips like music flung
O'er a mighty thunder-fit,
Chastening terror:—what though yet
Poesy's unfailing River,
Which through Albion winds forever   185

6. Austrian tyrant; in Shelley's day *Celtic* (pronounced in the Greek manner "Keltic") referred to all northern, non-Mediterranean barbarian tribes, and *Anarch* had gained associations from Milton's and Pope's use of it to char- acterize chaos (*Paradise Lost*, II.988, and *Dunciad*, IV.655).
7. Robe or cloak.
8. Lord Byron.
9. England.

Lashing with melodious wave
Many a sacred Poet's grave,
Mourn its latest nursling fled?
What though thou with all thy dead
Scarce can for this fame repay   190
Aught thine own? oh, rather say
Though thy sins and slaveries foul
Overcloud a sunlike soul?
As the ghost of Homer clings
Round Scamander's[1] wasting springs;   195
As divinest Shakespeare's might
Fills Avon[2] and the world with light
Like Omniscient power which he
Imaged 'mid mortality;
As the love from Petrarch's urn[3]   200
Yet amid yon hills doth burn,
A quenchless lamp by which the heart
Sees things unearthly;—so thou art,
Mighty Spirit—so shall be
The City that did refuge thee.   205

Lo, the sun floats up the sky
Like thought-winged Liberty,
Till the universal light
Seems to level plain and height;
From the sea a mist has spread,   210
And the beams of morn lie dead
On the towers of Venice now,
Like its glory long ago.
By the skirts of that grey cloud
Many-domed Padua proud   215
Stands, a peopled solitude,
'Mid the harvest-shining plain,
Where the peasant heaps his grain
In the garner[4] of his foe,
And the milk-white oxen slow   220
With the purple vintage strain,
Heaped upon the creaking wain,[5]
That the brutal Celt[6] may swill
Drunken sleep with savage will;
And the sickle to the sword   225
Lies unchanged, though many a lord,
Like a weed whose shade is poison,
Overgrows this region's foizon,[7]

1. Scamander was a river near Troy in Homer's *Iliad*.
2. The river near Shakespeare's birthplace, Stratford-on-Avon.
3. The last home and the burial place of the great Italian poet and humanist Francis Petrarch (1304–1374) were at the village of Arqua in the Euganean Hills.
4. Storehouse, granary.
5. A large open wagon for carrying heavy loads, especially of agricultural produce.
6. See note to line 152.
7. A plentiful crop or harvest.

Sheaves of whom are ripe to come
To destruction's harvest home: 230
Men must reap the things they sow,
Force from force must ever flow—
Or worse; but 'tis a bitter woe
That love or reason cannot change
The despot's rage, the slave's revenge. 235

Padua, thou within whose walls
Those mute guests at festivals,
Son and Mother, Death and Sin,[8]
Played at dice for Ezzelin,
Till Death cried, "I win, I win!"[9] 240
And Sin cursed to lose the wager,
But Death promised, to assuage her,
That he would petition for
Her to be made Vice-Emperor,
When the destined years were o'er, 245
Over all between the Po
And the eastern Alpine snow,
Under the mighty Austrian.
Sin smiled so as Sin only can,
And since that time, aye, long before, 250
Both have ruled from shore to shore,—
That incestuous pair, who follow
Tyrants as the sun the swallow,
As Repentance follows Crime,
And as changes follow Time. 255

In thine halls the lamp of learning,
Padua, now no more is burning;[1]
Like a meteor, whose wild way
Is lost over the grave of day,
It gleams betrayed and to betray: 260
Once remotest nations came
To adore that sacred flame,
When it lit not many a hearth
On this cold and gloomy earth:
Now new fires from antique light 265
Spring beneath the wide world's might;
But their spark lies dead in thee,
Trampled out by tyranny.
As the Norway woodman quells,
In the depth of piny dells, 270

8. Cf. Milton's allegory of Sin and Death in *Paradise Lost*, Book II.
9. Cf. Coleridge's "Rime of the Ancient Mariner," lines 196–197, where Death and Life-in-Death cast dice for the soul of the Ancient Mariner. *Ezzelin:* Ezzelino da Romano, tyrannical ruler of Padua in the thirteenth century.
1. Padua's university was one of the oldest and most famous in medieval Europe.

One light flame among the brakes,[2]
While the boundless forest shakes,
And its mighty trunks are torn
By the fire thus lowly born:
The spark beneath his feet is dead,   275
He starts to see the flames it fed
Howling through the darkened sky
With a myriad tongues victoriously,
And sinks down in fear: so thou,
O tyranny, beholdest now   280
Light around thee, and thou hearest
The loud flames ascend, and fearest:
Grovel on the earth; aye, hide
In the dust thy purple pride!

Noon descends around me now: 285
'Tis the noon of autumn's glow,
When a soft and purple mist
Like a vaporous amethyst,
Or an air-dissolved star
Mingling light and fragrance, far   290
From the curved horizon's bound
To the point of heaven's profound,[3]
Fills the overflowing sky;
And the plains that silent lie
Underneath, the leaves unsodden   295
Where the infant frost has trodden
With his morning-winged feet,
Whose bright print is gleaming yet;
And the red and golden vines,
Piercing with their trellised lines   300
The rough, dark-skirted wilderness;
The dun and bladed grass no less,
Pointing from this hoary tower
In the windless air; the flower
Glimmering at my feet; the line   305
Of the olive-sandalled Apennine
In the south dimly islanded;
And the Alps, whose snows are spread
High between the clouds and sun;
And of living things each one;   310
And my spirit which so long
Darkened this swift stream of song,—
Interpenetrated lie
By the glory of the sky:
Be it love, light, harmony,   315
Odour, or the soul of all
Which from heaven like dew doth fall,

---

2. Thickets, clumps of bushes.   3. A vast depth or abyss.

Or the mind which feeds this verse
Peopling the lone universe.

Noon descends, and after noon   320
Autumn's evening meets me soon,
Leading the infantine moon,
And that one star,[4] which to her
Almost seems to minister
Half the crimson light she brings   325
From the sunset's radiant springs:
And the soft dreams of the morn
(Which like winged winds had borne
To that silent isle, which lies
'Mid remembered agonies,   330
The frail bark[5] of this lone being)
Pass, to other sufferers fleeing,
And its antient pilot, Pain,
Sits beside the helm again.

Other flowering isles must be   335
In the sea of Life and Agony:
Other spirits float and flee
O'er that gulph: even now, perhaps,
On some rock the wild wave wraps,
With folded wings they waiting sit   340
For my bark, to pilot it
To some calm and blooming cove,
Where for me, and those I love,
May a windless bower be built,
Far from passion, pain, and guilt,   345
In a dell 'mid lawny hills,
Which the wild sea-murmur fills,
And soft sunshine, and the sound
Of old forests echoing round,
And the light and smell divine   350
Of all flowers that breathe and shine:
We may live so happy there,
That the Spirits of the Air,
Envying us, may even entice
To our healing Paradise   355
The polluting multitude;
But their rage would be subdued
By that clime divine and calm,
And the winds whose wings rain balm
On the uplifted soul, and leaves   360
Under which the bright sea heaves;
While each breathless interval
In their whisperings musical

4. Venus as the evening star (Vesper,   5. A small ship or rowing boat.
Hesperus).

The inspired soul supplies
With its own deep melodies,   365
And the love which heals all strife
Circling, like the breath of life,
All things in that sweet abode
With its own mild brotherhood:
They, not it, would change;[6] and soon   370
Every sprite[7] beneath the moon
Would repent its envy vain,
And the earth grow young again.

Julian and Maddalo;

A Conversation[1]

The meadows with fresh streams, the bees with thyme,
The goats with the green leaves of budding spring,
Are saturated not—nor Love with tears.
                        VIRGIL'S *Gallus*.

Count Maddalo is a Venetian nobleman of antient family and of
great fortune, who, without mixing much in the society of his
countrymen, resides chiefly at his magnificent palace in that city.
He is a person of the most consummate genius, and capable, if he
would direct his energies to such an end, of becoming the redeemer
of his degraded country. But it is his weakness to be proud: he
derives, from a comparison of his own extraordinary mind with the

6. The literary analogues underlying Shel-
ley's thought in lines 352–370 are Shake-
speare's *The Tempest* and Dante's sonnet
to Guido Cavalcanti beginning, "Guido,
I would that Lappo, thou, and I,/ Led by
some strong enchantment, might ascend/
A magic ship . . ." of which Shelley
published a translation with *Alastor*.
7. Spirit.
1. Late in 1818, Shelley commenced a
drama on the love and madness of the
Italian epic poet Torquato Tasso. Then
abandoning that drama, he began to
write, early in 1819, a dialogue between
himself (Julian) and Byron (Maddalo),
reflecting their conversations in Venice of
August 1818 (possibly stimulated by his
reading of *Childe Harold*, Canto IV).
Finally, while writing *The Cenci* near
Leghorn during the summer of 1819, he
took the materials thus far composed,
incorporated within the Maniac's speeches
some emotional lines that probably re-
flect his own estrangement from Mary
Shelley following the death of their son
William Shelley at Rome, June 7, 1819,
and shaped them into a philosophical
dialogue in the conversational or
"familiar" style. Shelley sent the poem
to Leigh Hunt to have it published
anonymously and—while affirming the im-
personal nature of his portrait of the
Maniac—told Hunt that the poem had
been "composed last year at Este," a
remark probably designed to screen the
personal origin of parts of the madman's
speech. The poem remained unpublished,
however, during Shelley's lifetime, and
first appeared in his *Posthumous Poems*
(1824). This version is from the author's
manuscript in the Pierpont Morgan Li-
brary.
   In his letter to Hunt of August 15,
1819, Shelley included some sentences on
the poetic style of the poem that he had
originally drafted in a notebook, perhaps
intending to include them in the preface:
"I have employed a certain familiar style
of language to express the actual way in
which people talk with each other whom
education and a certain refinement of
sentiment have placed above the use of
vulgar idioms. I use the word *vulgar* in
its most extensive sense; the vulgarity of
rank and fashion is as gross in its way
as that of Poverty, and its cant terms
equally expressive of base conceptions,
and therefore equally unfit for Poetry.
Not that the familiar style is to be
admitted in the treatment of a subject
wholly ideal, or in that part of any
subject which relates to common life,
where the passion exceeding a certain
limit touches the boundaries of that
which is ideal. Strong passion expresses
itself in metaphor borrowed from ob-
jects alike remote or near, and casts over
all the shadow of its own greatness"
(Shelley, *Letters*, II, 108).

dwarfish intellects that surround him, an intense apprehension of the nothingness of human life. His passions and his powers are incomparably greater than those of other men; and, instead of the latter having been employed in curbing the former, they have mutually lent each other strength. His ambition preys upon itself, for want of objects which it can consider worthy of exertion. I say that Maddalo is proud, because I can find no other word to express the concentered and impatient feelings which consume him; but it is on his own hopes and affections only that he seems to trample, for in social life no human being can be more gentle, patient, and unassuming than Maddalo. He is cheerful, frank, and witty. His more serious conversation is a sort of intoxication; men are held by it as by a spell. He has travelled much; and there is an inexpressible charm in his relation of his adventures in different countries.

Julian is an Englishman of good family, passionately attached to those philosophical notions which assert the power of man over his own mind, and the immense improvements of which, by the extinction of certain moral superstitions, human society may be yet susceptible. Without concealing the evil in the world, he is for ever speculating how good may be made superior. He is a complete infidel, and a scoffer at all things reputed holy; and Maddalo takes a wicked pleasure in drawing out his taunts against religion. What Maddalo thinks on these matters is not exactly known. Julian, in spite of his heterodox opinions, is conjectured by his friends to possess some good qualities. How far this is possible the pious reader will determine. Julian is rather serious.

Of the Maniac I can give no information. He seems by his own account to have been disappointed in love. He was evidently a very cultivated and amiable person when in his right senses. His story, told at length, might be like many other stories of the same kind: the unconnected exclamations of his agony will perhaps be found a sufficient comment for the text of every heart.

> I rode one evening with Count Maddalo[2]
> Upon the bank of land which breaks the flow
> Of Adria towards Venice:[3]—a bare strand
> Of hillocks, heaped from ever-shifting sand,
> Matted with thistles and amphibious weeds,　　　　　5
> Such as from earth's embrace the salt ooze breeds,
> Is this;—an uninhabitable sea-side
> Which the lone fisher, when his nets are dried,
> Abandons; and no other object breaks
> The waste, but one dwarf tree and some few stakes　　10
> Broken and unrepaired, and the tide makes

---

2. At least some details of the scene in lines 1–140 are based on Shelley's conversation with Byron of August 23, 1818 (described by Shelley, *Letters*, II, 36).
3. The *bank of land* is the Lido of Venice; *Adria*: the Adriatic Sea.

A narrow space of level sand thereon,—
Where 'twas our wont[4] to ride while day went down.
This ride was my delight.—I love all waste
And solitary places; where we taste   15
The pleasure of believing what we see
Is boundless, as we wish our souls to be:
And such was this wide ocean, and this shore
More barren than its billows;—and yet more
Than all, with a remembered friend I love   20
To ride as then I rode;—for the winds drove
The living spray along the sunny air
Into our faces; the blue heavens were bare,
Stripped to their depths by the awakening North;
And, from the waves, sound like delight broke forth   25
Harmonizing with solitude, and sent
Into our hearts aërial merriment . . .
So, as we rode, we talked; and the swift thought,
Winging itself with laughter, lingered not,
But flew from brain to brain,—such glee was ours—   30
Charged with light memories of remembered hours,
None slow enough for sadness: till we came
Homeward, which always makes the spirit tame.
This day had been cheerful but cold, and now
The sun was sinking, and the wind also.   35
Our talk grew somewhat serious, as may be
Talk interrupted with such raillery
As mocks itself, because it cannot scorn
The thoughts it would extinguish:—'twas forlorn
Yet pleasing, such as once, so poets tell,   40
The devils held within the dales of Hell
Concerning God, freewill and destiny:[5]
Of all that earth has been or yet may be,
All that vain men imagine or believe,
Or hope can paint or suffering may atchieve,   45
We descanted,[6] and I (for ever still
Is it not wise to make the best of ill?)
Argued against despondency, but pride
Made my companion take the darker side.
The sense that he was greater than his kind   50
Had struck, methinks, his eagle spirit blind
By gazing on its own exceeding light.[7]
—Meanwhile the sun paused ere it should alight,[8]

4. Custom, habit.
5. The allusion in lines 40–42 is to *Paradise Lost*, II.555–561, where the fallen angels in Hell "reason'd high/ Of Providence, Foreknowledge, Will, and Fate, . . . And found no end, in wandring mazes lost."
6. Discussed at length, discoursed about.
7. *eagle spirit . . . light:* According to tradition, the eagle not only possessed the keenest vision of all creatures, but it could renew its vision by flying directly into the sun, which burned the scales from its eyes.
8. *light . . . alight:* The exact repetition of the phonetic syllable in two rhyme words, called *rime riche,* though considered a virtue in French and Italian poetry, is avoided by most English poets; Shelley, however, employs it with some frequency.

Over the horizon of the mountains;—Oh,
How beautiful is sunset, when the glow   55
Of Heaven descends upon a land like thee,
Thou Paradise of exiles, Italy!
Thy mountains, seas and vineyards and the towers
Of cities they encircle!—it was ours
To stand on thee, beholding it; and then   60
Just where we had dismounted, the Count's men
Were waiting for us with the gondola.⁹—
As those who pause on some delightful way
Though bent on pleasant pilgrimage, we stood
Looking upon the evening and the flood   65
Which lay between the city and the shore
Paved with the image of the sky . . . the hoar
And aery Alps towards the North appeared
Through mist, an heaven-sustaining bulwark reared
Between the East and West; and half the sky   70
Was roofed with clouds of rich emblazonry
Dark purple at the zenith, which still grew
Down the steep West into a wondrous hue
Brighter than burning gold, even to the rent
Where the swift sun yet paused in his descent   75
Among the many folded hills: they were
Those famous Euganean hills, which bear
As seen from Lido through the harbour piles
The likeness of a clump of peaked isles—
And then—as if the Earth and Sea had been   80
Dissolved into one lake of fire, were seen
Those mountains towering as from waves of flame
Around the vaporous sun, from which there came
The inmost purple spirit of light, and made
Their very peaks transparent. "Ere it fade,"   85
Said my Companion, "I will shew you soon
A better station"—so, o'er the lagune
We glided, and from that funereal bark¹
I leaned, and saw the City, and could mark
How from their many isles, in evening's gleam,   90
Its temples and its palaces did seem
Like fabrics of enchantment piled to Heaven.
I was about to speak, when—"We are even
Now at the point I meant," said Maddalo,
And bade the gondolieri cease to row.   95
"Look, Julian, on the West, and listen well
If you hear not a deep and heavy bell."
I looked, and saw between us and the sun
A building on an island; such a one

9. That Shelley, here and at lines 139–
140, rhymes "gondola" with "way" sug-
gests the contemporary British pronuncia-
tion of the word.
1. "These gondolas are . . . finely car-

peted & furnished with black & painted
black" (Shelley to Mary Shelley, Aug.
23, 1818). "It glides along the water
looking blackly,/ Just like a coffin clapt
in a canoe" (Byron, *Beppo*, 150–151).

As age to age might add, for uses vile,   100
A windowless, deformed and dreary pile;
And on the top an open tower, where hung
A bell, which in the radiance swayed and swung;
We could just hear its hoarse and iron tongue:
The broad sun sunk behind it, and it tolled   105
In strong and black relief.—"What we behold
Shall be the madhouse and its belfry tower,"
Said Maddalo, "and ever at this hour
Those who may cross the water, hear that bell
Which calls the maniacs each one from his cell   110
To vespers."—"As much skill as need to pray
In thanks or hope for their dark lot have they
To their stern maker,"[2] I replied. "O ho!
You talk as in years past," said Maddalo.
" 'Tis strange men change not. You were ever still   115
Among Christ's flock a perilous infidel,
A wolf for the meek lambs—if you can't swim
Beware of Providence." I looked on him,
But the gay smile had faded in his eye.
"And such,"—he cried, "is our mortality   120
And this must be the emblem and the sign
Of what should be eternal and divine!—
And like that black and dreary bell, the soul,
Hung in a heaven-illumined tower, must toll
Our thoughts and our desires to meet below   125
Round the rent heart and pray—as madmen do
For what? they know not,—till the night of death
As sunset that strange vision, severeth
Our memory from itself, and us from all
We sought and yet were baffled!" I recall   130
The sense of what he said, although I mar
The force of his expressions. The broad star
Of day meanwhile had sunk behind the hill
And the black bell became invisible
And the red tower looked grey, and all between   135
The churches, ships and palaces were seen
Huddled in gloom;—into the purple sea
The orange hues of heaven sunk silently.
We hardly spoke, and soon the gondola
Conveyed me to my lodging by the way.   140

    The following morn was rainy, cold and dim:
Ere Maddalo arose, I called on him,
And whilst I waited with his child[3] I played;
A lovelier toy sweet Nature never made,

---

2. The tone in lines 111–113 is ironic.
3. Allegra Byron (or Biron), natural child of Byron and Mary Jane Clara "Claire" Clairmont, Mary Shelley's stepsister. Allegra had been raised by Claire under Shelley's care from her birth on January 12, 1817, until she was sent to Byron in Venice on April 28, 1818. (Thus, line 155 refers to the *six months or so* of separation from the child.)

A serious, subtle, wild, yet gentle being,   145
Graceful without design and unforeseeing,
With eyes—oh speak not of her eyes!—which seem
Twin mirrors of Italian Heaven, yet gleam
With such deep meaning, as we never see
But in the human countenance: with me   150
She was a special favourite: I had nursed
Her fine and feeble limbs when she came first
To this bleak world; and she yet seemed to know
On second sight her antient playfellow,
Less changed than she was by six months or so;   155
For after her first shyness was worn out
We sate there, rolling billiard balls about.
When the Count entered—salutations past[4]—
"The word you spoke last night might well have cast
A darkness on my spirit—if man be   160
The passive thing you say, I should not see
Much harm in the religions and old saws
(Though I may never own[5] such leaden laws)
Which break a teachless[6] nature to the yoke:
Mine is another faith"—thus much I spoke   165
And noting he replied not, added: "See
This lovely child, blithe, innocent and free;
She spends a happy time with little care
While we to such sick thoughts subjected are
As came on you last night—it is our will   170
That thus enchains us to permitted ill—
We might be otherwise—we might be all
We dream of happy, high, majestical.
Where is the love, beauty and truth we seek
But in our mind? and if we were not weak   175
Should we be less in deed than in desire?"
"Ay, if we were not weak—and we aspire
How vainly to be strong!" said Maddalo;
"You talk Utopia." "It remains to know,"[7]
I then rejoined, "and those who try may find   180
How strong the chains are which our spirit bind;
Brittle perchance as straw . . . We are assured
Much may be conquered, much may be endured
Of what degrades and crushes us. We know
That we have power over ourselves to do   185
And suffer—what, we know not till we try;
But something nobler than to live and die—
So taught those kings of old philosophy
Who reigned, before Religion made men blind;
And those who suffer with their suffering kind   190

4. In Shelley's draft this word replaced "o'er" to rhyme with *cast*.
5. Acknowledge.
6. Unteachable.

7. In Shelley's fair copy manuscript the word is "see"; but *know* completes the rhyme, and all printed texts include it.

Yet feel their faith, religion." "My dear friend,"
Said Maddalo, "my judgement will not bend
To your opinion, though I think you might
Make such a system refutation-tight
As far as words go. I knew one like you   195
Who to this city came some months ago
With whom I argued in this sort, and he
Is now gone mad,—and so he answered me,—
Poor fellow! but if you would like to go
We'll visit him, and his wild talk will show   200
How vain are such aspiring theories."
"I hope to prove the induction otherwise,
And that a want of that true theory, still,
Which seeks a 'soul of goodness'[8] in things ill
Or in himself or others has thus bowed   205
His being—there are some by nature proud,
Who patient in all else demand but this:
To love and be beloved with gentleness;
And being scorned, what wonder if they die
Some living death? this is not destiny   210
But man's own wilful ill." As thus I spoke[9]
Servants announced the gondola, and we
Through the fast-falling rain and high-wrought sea
Sailed to the island where the madhouse stands.
We disembarked. The clap of tortured hands,   215
Fierce yells and howlings and lamentings keen,
And laughter where complaint had merrier been,
Moans, shrieks and curses and blaspheming prayers
Accosted us. We climbed the oozy stairs
Into an old courtyard. I heard on high,   220
Then, fragments of most touching melody,
But looking up saw not the singer there—
Through the black bars in the tempestuous air
I saw, like weeds on a wrecked palace growing,
Long tangled locks flung wildly forth, and flowing, 225
Of those who on a sudden were beguiled
Into strange silence, and looked forth and smiled
Hearing sweet sounds.—Then I: "Methinks there were
A cure of these with patience and kind care,
If music can thus move . . . but what is he   230
Whom we seek here?" "Of his sad history
I know but this," said Maddalo: "he came
To Venice a dejected man, and fame
Said he was wealthy, or he had been so;
Some thought the loss of fortune wrought him woe; 235
But he was ever talking in such sort

---

8. Shakespeare, *King Henry V*, IV.i.4.
9. G. M. Matthews has explained how this came to be the only unrhymed line in the poem when Shelley elected to drop three and a half lines from the draft.

As you do—far more sadly—he seemed hurt,
Even as a man with his peculiar wrong,
To hear but of the oppression of the strong,
Or those absurd deceits (I think with you   240
In some respects, you know) which carry through
The excellent impostors of this Earth
When they outface detection—he had worth,
Poor fellow! but a humourist[1] in his way"—
"Alas, what drove him mad?" "I cannot say;   245
A Lady came with him from France, and when
She left him and returned, he wandered then
About yon lonely isles of desart sand
Till he grew wild—he had no cash or land
Remaining,—the police had brought him here—   250
Some fancy took him and he would not bear
Removal; so I fitted up for him
Those rooms beside the sea, to please his whim,
And sent him busts and books and urns for flowers,
Which had adorned his life in happier hours,   255
And instruments of music—you may guess
A stranger could do little more or less
For one so gentle and unfortunate;
And those are his sweet strains which charm the weight
From madmen's chains, and make this Hell appear   260
A heaven of sacred silence, hushed to hear."—
"Nay, this was kind of you—he had no claim,
As the world says"—"None—but the very same
Which I on all mankind were I as he
Fallen to such deep reverse;—his melody   265
Is interrupted now—we hear the din
Of madmen, shriek on shriek again begin;
Let us now visit him; after this strain
He ever communes with himself again,
And sees nor hears not any." Having said   270
These words we called the keeper, and he led
To an apartment opening on the sea—
There the poor wretch was sitting mournfully
Near a piano, his pale fingers twined
One with the other, and the ooze and wind   275
Rushed through an open casement, and did sway
His hair, and starred it with the brackish[2] spray;
His head was leaning on a music book,
And he was muttering, and his lean limbs shook;
His lips were pressed against a folded leaf   280
In hue too beautiful for health, and grief

---

1. One who exhibits strong peculiarities in a particular direction, supposedly caused by the predominance of one of the four "humours" or vital fluids of classical medieval physiology—blood, phlegm, choler (yellow bile), and melancholy (black bile).
2. Somewhat salty.

Smiled in their motions as they lay apart—
As one who wrought from his own fervid heart
The eloquence of passion, soon he raised
His sad meek face and eyes lustrous and glazed   285
And spoke—sometimes as one who wrote and thought
His words might move some heart that heeded not
If sent to distant lands; and then as one
Reproaching deeds never to be undone
With wondering self-compassion; then his speech   290
Was lost in grief, and then his words came each
Unmodulated, cold, expressionless;
But that from one jarred accent you might guess
It was despair made them so uniform:
And all the while the loud and gusty storm   295
Hissed through the window, and we stood behind
Stealing his accents from the envious wind
Unseen. I yet remember what he said
Distinctly: such impression his words made.

"Month after month," he cried, "to bear this load   300
And as a jade[3] urged by the whip and goad
To drag life on, which like a heavy chain
Lengthens behind with many a link of pain!—
And not to speak my grief—o not to dare
To give a human voice to my despair,   305
But live and move, and wretched thing! smile on
As if I never went aside to groan
And wear this mask of falshood even to those
Who are most dear—not for my own repose—
Alas, no scorn or pain or hate could be   310
So heavy as that falshood is to me—
But that I cannot bear more altered faces
Than needs must be, more changed and cold embraces,
More misery, disappointment and mistrust
To own me for their father . . . Would the dust   315
Were covered in upon my body now!
That the life ceased to toil within my brow!
And then these thoughts would at the least be fled;
Let us not fear such pain can vex the dead.

"What Power delights to torture us? I know   320
That to myself I do not wholly owe
What now I suffer, though in part I may.
Alas, none strewed sweet flowers upon the way
Where wandering heedlessly, I met pale Pain
My shadow, which will leave me not again—   325
If I have erred, there was no joy in error,
But pain and insult and unrest and terror;

---

3. A cart horse or a worn-out, inferior horse.

I have not as some do, bought penitence
With pleasure, and a dark yet sweet offence,
For then,—if love and tenderness and truth   330
Had overlived hope's momentary youth,
My creed should have redeemed me from repenting;
But loathed scorn and outrage unrelenting
Met love excited by far other seeming
Until the end was gained . . . as one from dreaming   335
Of sweetest peace, I woke, and found my state
Such as it is.——
            "O Thou, my spirit's mate
Who, for thou art compassionate and wise,
Wouldst pity me from thy most gentle eyes
If this sad writing thou shouldst ever see—   340
My secret groans must be unheard by thee,
Thou wouldst weep tears bitter as blood to know
Thy lost friend's incommunicable woe.

    "Ye few by whom my nature has been weighed
In friendship, let me not that name degrade   345
By placing on your hearts the secret load
Which crushes mine to dust. There is one road
To peace and that is truth, which follow ye!
Love sometimes leads astray to misery.
Yet think not though subdued—and I may well   350
Say that I am subdued—that the full Hell
Within me would infect the untainted breast
Of sacred nature with its own unrest;
As some perverted beings think to find
In scorn or hate a medicine for the mind   355
Which scorn or hate have wounded—o how vain!
The dagger heals not but may rend again . . . .
Believe that I am ever still the same
In creed as in resolve, and what may tame
My heart, must leave the understanding free   360
Or all would sink in this keen agony—
Nor dream that I will join the vulgar cry,
Or with my silence sanction tyranny,
Or seek a moment's shelter from my pain
In any madness which the world calls gain,   365
Ambition or revenge or thoughts as stern
As those which make me what I am, or turn
To avarice or misanthropy or lust . . . .
Heap on me soon, o grave, thy welcome dust!
Till then the dungeon may demand its prey,   370
And poverty and shame may meet and say—
Halting beside me on the public way—
'That love-devoted[4] youth is ours—let's sit

4. Sacrificed to love.

Beside him—he may live some six months yet.'
Or the red scaffold, as our country bends,   375
May ask some willing victim, or ye friends
May fall under some sorrow which this heart
Or hand may share or vanquish or avert;
I am prepared: in truth with no proud joy
To do or suffer aught, as when a boy   380
I did devote to justice and to love
My nature, worthless now!⁵ . . .
                                "I must remove
A veil from my pent⁶ mind. 'Tis torn aside!
O, pallid as death's dedicated bride,
Thou mockery which art sitting by my side,   385
Am I not wan like thee? at the grave's call
I haste, invited to thy wedding ball
To greet the ghastly paramour, for whom
Thou hast deserted me . . . and made the tomb
Thy bridal bed . . . But I beside your feet   390
Will lie and watch ye from my winding sheet—
Thus . . . wide awake, though dead . . . yet stay, o stay!
Go not so soon—I know not what I say—
Hear but my reasons . . . I am mad, I fear,
My fancy is o'erwrought . . . thou art not here . . .   395
Pale art thou, 'tis most true . . . but thou art gone,
Thy work is finished . . . I am left alone!—

*   *   *   *   *   *   *7

    "Nay, was it I who wooed thee to this breast
Which, like a serpent, thou envenomest
As in repayment of the warmth it lent?   400
Didst thou not seek me for thine own content?
Did not thy love awaken mine? I thought
That thou wert she who said, 'You kiss me not
Ever, I fear you do not love me now'—
In truth I loved even to my overthrow   405
Her, who would fain forget these words: but they
Cling to her mind, and cannot pass away.

*   *   *   *   *   *   *

    "You say that I am proud—that when I speak
My lip is tortured with the wrongs which break
The spirit it expresses . . . Never one   410
Humbled himself before, as I have done!
Even the instinctive worm on which we tread
Turns, though it wound not—then with prostrate head
Sinks in the dust and writhes like me—and dies?
No: wears a living death of agonies!   415

5. Cf. lines 380–382 with "Hymn to In-
tellectual Beauty" and the Dedication to
Laon and Cythna.
6. Locked up, imprisoned.

7. The lines of asterisks indicate breaks
in the intermittent outcries of the Maniac;
none of Shelley's poem is here omitted.

As the slow shadows of the pointed grass
Mark the eternal periods, his pangs pass
Slow, ever-moving,—making moments be
As mine seem—each an immortality!

*   *   *   *   *   *   *

"That you had never seen me—never heard   420
My voice, and more than all had ne'er endured
The deep pollution of my loathed embrace—
That your eyes ne'er had lied love in my face—
That, like some maniac monk, I had torn out
The nerves of manhood by their bleeding root   425
With mine own quivering fingers, so that ne'er
Our hearts had for a moment mingled there
To disunite in horror—these were not
With thee, like some suppressed and hideous thought
Which flits athwart our musings, but can find   430
No rest within a pure and gentle mind . . .
Thou sealedst them with many a bare broad word,
And cearedst[8] my memory o'er them,—for I heard
And can forget not . . . they were ministered
One after one, those curses. Mix them up   435
Like self-destroying poisons in one cup,
And they will make one blessing which thou ne'er
Didst imprecate for, on me,—death.

*   *   *   *   *   *   *

                                        "It were
A cruel punishment for one most cruel,
If such can love, to make that love the fuel   440
Of the mind's hell; hate, scorn, remorse, despair:
But *me*—whose heart a stranger's tear might wear
As water-drops the sandy fountain-stone,
Who loved and pitied all things, and could moan
For woes which others hear not, and could see   445
The absent with the glance of phantasy,
And with the poor and trampled sit and weep,
Following the captive to his dungeon deep;
Me—who am as a nerve o'er which do creep
The else unfelt oppressions of this earth   450
And was to thee the flame upon thy hearth
When all beside was cold—that thou on me
Shouldst rain these plagues of blistering agony—
Such curses are from lips once eloquent
With love's too partial praise—let none relent   455
Who intend deeds too dreadful for a name
Henceforth, if an example for the same

---

8. Wrapped in waxed cloth, embalmed; previous editors have changed the word to "searedst."

They seek . . . for thou on me lookedst so, and so—
And didst speak thus . . . and thus . . . I live to shew
How much men bear and die not!

     *   *   *   *   *   *   *

                         "Thou wilt tell   460
With the grimace of hate how horrible
It was to meet my love when thine grew less;
Thou wilt admire how I could e'er address
Such features to love's work . . . this taunt, though true,
(For indeed nature nor in form nor hue   465
Bestowed on me her choicest workmanship)
Shall not be thy defence . . . for since thy lip
Met mine first, years long past, since thine eye kindled
With soft fire under mine, I have not dwindled
Nor changed in mind or body, or in aught   470
But as love changes what it loveth not
After long years and many trials.
                         "How vain
Are words! I thought never to speak again,
Not even in secret,—not to my own heart—
But from my lips the unwilling accents start   475
And from my pen the words flow as I write,
Dazzling my eyes with scalding tears . . . my sight
Is dim to see that charactered in vain
On this unfeeling leaf which burns the brain
And eats into it . . . blotting all things fair   480
And wise and good which time had written there.

"Those who inflict must suffer, for they see
The work of their own hearts and this must be
Our chastisement or recompense—O child!
I would that thine were like to be more mild   485
For both our wretched sakes . . . for thine the most
Who feelest already all that thou hast lost
Without the power to wish it thine again;
And as slow years pass, a funereal train
Each with the ghost of some lost hope or friend   490
Following it like its shadow, wilt thou bend
No thought on my dead memory?

     *   *   *   *   *   *   *

                        "Alas, love,
Fear me not . . . against thee I would not move
A finger in despite. Do I not live
That thou mayst have less bitter cause to grieve?   495
I give thee tears for scorn and love for hate,
And that thy lot may be less desolate
Than his on whom thou tramplest, I refrain
From that sweet sleep[9] which medicines all pain.

9. I.e., death.

Then, when thou speakest of me, never say,   500
'He could forgive not.' Here I cast away
All human passions, all revenge, all pride;
I think, speak, act no ill; I do but hide
Under these words like embers, every spark
Of that which has consumed me—quick and dark   505
The grave is yawning . . . as its roof shall cover
My limbs with dust and worms under and over
So let Oblivion hide this grief . . . the air
Closes upon my accents, as despair
Upon my heart—let death upon despair!"   510

He ceased, and overcome leant back awhile,
Then rising, with a melancholy smile
Went to a sofa, and lay down, and slept
A heavy sleep, and in his dreams he wept
And muttered some familiar name, and we   515
Wept without shame in his society.
I think I never was impressed so much;
The man who were not, must have lacked a touch
Of human nature . . . then we lingered not,
Although our argument was quite forgot,   520
But calling the attendants, went to dine
At Maddalo's; yet neither cheer nor wine
Could give us spirits, for we talked of him
And nothing else, till daylight made stars dim;
And we agreed his was some dreadful ill   525
Wrought on him boldly, yet unspeakable
By a dear friend; some deadly change in love
Of one vowed deeply which he dreamed not of;
For whose sake he, it seemed, had fixed a blot
Of falshood on his mind which flourished not   530
But in the light of all-beholding truth;
And having stamped this canker[1] on his youth
She had abandoned him—and how much more
Might be his woe, we guessed not—he had store
Of friends and fortune once, as we could guess   535
From his nice[2] habits and his gentleness;
These were now lost . . . it were a grief indeed
If he had changed one unsustaining reed
For all that such a man might else adorn.
The colours of his mind seemed yet unworn;   540
For the wild language of his grief was high,
Such as in measure were called poetry;
And I remember one remark which then
Maddalo made. He said: "Most wretched men
Are cradled into poetry by wrong,   545
They learn in suffering what they teach in song."

1. A consuming, spreading sore or ulcer   2. Refined, cultured.
(cf. cancer).

    If I had been an unconnected man[3]
I, from this moment, should have formed some plan
Never to leave sweet Venice,—for to me
It was delight to ride by the lone sea;   550
And then, the town is silent—one may write
Or read in gondolas by day or night,
Having the little brazen[4] lamp alight,
Unseen, uninterrupted; books are there,
Pictures, and casts from all those statues fair   555
Which were twin-born with poetry, and all
We seek in towns, with little to recall
Regrets for the green country. I might sit
In Maddalo's great palace, and his wit
And subtle talk would cheer the winter night   560
And make me know myself, and the firelight
Would flash upon our faces, till the day
Might dawn and make me wonder at my stay:
But I had friends in London too: the chief
Attraction here, was that I sought relief   565
From the deep tenderness that maniac wrought
Within me—'twas perhaps an idle thought,
But I imagined that if day by day
I watched him, and but seldom went away,
And studied all the beatings of his heart   570
With zeal, as men study some stubborn art
For their own good, and could by patience find
An entrance to the caverns of his mind,
I might reclaim him from his dark estate:
In friendships I had been most fortunate—   575
Yet never saw I one whom I would call
More willingly my friend; and this was all
Accomplished not; such dreams of baseless[5] good
Oft come and go in crowds or solitude
And leave no trace—but what I now designed 580
Made for long years impression on my mind.
The following morning, urged by my affairs,
I left bright Venice.

             After many years
And many changes I returned; the name
Of Venice, and its aspect, was the same;   585
But Maddalo was travelling far away
Among the mountains of Armenia.[6]
His dog was dead. His child had now become
A woman; such as it has been my doom[7]
To meet with few, a wonder of this earth,   590
Where there is little of transcendent worth,

---

3. A man without family or other responsibilities.
4. Made of brass.
5. Having no foundation; see Shakespeare, *The Tempest*, IV.151.
6. Byron was in 1817–1818 studying the Armenian language in Venice.
7. Fate.

Like one of Shakespeare's women: kindly she
And with a manner beyond courtesy
Received her father's friend; and when I asked
Of the lorn[8] maniac, she her memory tasked   595
And told as she had heard the mournful tale:
"That the poor sufferer's health began to fail
Two years from my departure, but that then
The Lady who had left him, came again.
Her mien had been imperious, but she now   600
Looked meek—perhaps remorse had brought her low.
Her coming made him better, and they stayed
Together at my father's—for I played
As I remember with the lady's shawl—
I might be six years old—but after all   605
She left him" . . . "Why, her heart must have been tough:
How did it end?" "And was not this enough?
They met—they parted"—"Child, is there no more?"
"Something within that interval which bore
The stamp of *why* they parted, *how* they met: 610
Yet if thine aged eyes disdain to wet
Those wrinkled cheeks with youth's remembered tears,
Ask me no more, but let the silent years
Be closed and ceared[9] over their memory
As yon mute marble where their corpses lie."   615
I urged and questioned still, she told me how
All happened—but the cold world shall not know.

Stanzas written in Dejection— December 1818, Near Naples[1]

The Sun is warm, the sky is clear,
The waves are dancing fast and bright,
Blue isles and snowy mountains wear
The purple noon's transparent might,
The breath of the moist earth is light   5
Around its unexpanded buds;
Like many a voice of one delight
The winds, the birds, the Ocean-floods;
   The City's voice itself is soft, like Solitude's.

I see the Deep's untrampled floor   10
With green and purple seaweeds strown;
I see the waves upon the shore
Like light dissolved in star-showers, thrown;

8. Abandoned, desolate.
9. Sealed up, embalmed (cf. line 433).
1. In the title Shelley gives us a place and date of one of his most despairing lyrics, the personal nature of which might give him reason to disguise the circumstances of its composition from Mary or other intimates. It is fairly certain that Shelley enclosed this and other poems in his letter to Charles Ollier of November 10, 1820, urging him to publish most of them ("my saddest verses raked up into one heap") with *Julian and Maddalo*, but all remained unpublished until *Posthumous Poems* (1824). This version is from the author's manuscript in the Pierpont Morgan Library.

I sit upon the sands alone;
The lightning of the noontide Ocean 15
Is flashing round me, and a tone
Arises from its measured motion,
How sweet! did any heart now share in my emotion.

Alas, I have nor hope nor health
Nor peace within nor calm around, 20
Nor that content surpassing wealth
The sage in meditation found,
And walked with inward glory crowned;[2]
Nor fame nor power nor love nor leisure—
Others I see whom these surround, 25
Smiling they live and call life pleasure:[3]
To me that cup has been dealt in another measure.

Yet now despair itself is mild,
Even as the winds and waters are;
I could lie down like a tired child 30
And weep away the life of care
Which I have borne and yet must bear
Till Death like Sleep might steal on me,
And I might feel in the warm air
My cheek grow cold, and hear the Sea 35
Breathe o'er my dying brain its last monotony.

Some might lament that I were cold,
As I, when this sweet day is gone,[4]
Which my lost heart, too soon grown old,
Insults with this untimely moan— 40
They might lament,—for I am one
Whom men love not, and yet regret;
Unlike this day, which, when the Sun
Shall on its stainless glory set,
Will linger though enjoyed, like joy in Memory yet.[5] 45

The Two Spirits—An Allegory[6]

FIRST SPIRIT

O Thou who plumed with strong desire
Would float above the Earth—beware!
A shadow tracks thy flight of fire—
Night is coming!

2. *content . . . crowned:* M. H. Abrams has plausibly suggested that the allusion in lines 21–23 is to the Roman emperor and Stoic philosopher Marcus Aurelius (A.D. 121–180), whose *Meditations* Shelley admired.
3. If lines 25–26 were indeed written on the date and at the place Shelley gives, the chief reference is surely to Lord Byron and his circle at Venice.
4. I.e., Some might lament my death as

I will lament the passing of this sweet day.
5. Lines 43–45: the stainless day, unlike the poet, will leave a joyful memory that will reproduce its original enjoyment.
6. At the time of Shelley's death this poetic dialogue between optimistic and pessimistic views of human destiny existed only in Shelley's original draft (Bodleian MS. Shelley adds. e.12, pp. 13–17). Mary Shelley then transcribed

Bright are the regions of the air   5
And when winds and beams [   ]
It were delight to wander there—
    Night is coming!

SECOND SPIRIT

The deathless stars are bright above;
If I should cross the shade of night   10
Within my heart is the torch of love
    And that is day—
And the moon will smile with gentle light
On my golden plumes where'er they move;
The meteors[7] will linger around my flight   15
    And make night day.

FIRST SPIRIT

But if the whirlwinds of darkness waken
Hail and Lightning and stormy rain—
See, the bounds of the air are shaken,
    Night is coming.   20
The red swift clouds of the hurricane
Yon declining sun have overtaken,
The clash of the hail sweeps o'er the plain—
    Night is coming.

SECOND SPIRIT

I see the glare and I hear the sound—   25
I'll sail on the flood of the tempest dark
With the calm within and light around
    Which make night day;
And thou when the gloom is deep and stark,
Look from thy dull earth slumberbound—   30
My moonlike flight thou then mayst mark
    On high, far away.

———

Some say there is a precipice
Where one vast pine hangs frozen to ruin
O'er piles of snow and chasms of ice   35
    Mid Alpine mountains;
And that the languid storm pursuing
That winged shape forever flies
Round those hoar branches, aye renewing
    Its aery[8] fountains.   40

---

it (with some errors) and published it in Shelley's *Posthumous Poems* (1824), later placing it among his poems of 1820. Judith Chernaik reedited it, along with most of Shelley's other major lyrical poems, in *The Lyrics of Shelley* (1972); she and Earl R. Wasserman (*Shelley: A Critical Reading*, pp. 42–44) are both convinced the poem is earlier—possibly as early as 1818. We agree that the position in the Bodleian notebook suggests a date earlier than 1820 and date it tentatively between October 1818 and February 1819. Our text, based on the Bodleian draft, differs verbally from Chernaik's redaction in lines 11 and 21.

7. Probably shooting stars.
8. Ethereal.

Some say when the nights are dry [and] clear
And the death dews sleep on the morass,
Sweet whispers are heard by the traveller
  Which make night day—
And a shape like his early love doth pass   45
Upborne by her wild and glittering hair,
And when he awakes on the fragrant grass
  He finds night day.

Prometheus Unbound Shelley began drafting *Prometheus Un-*
bound at Este in September 1818 and, after an apparent hiatus at Naples, resumed work on it at Rome in March and April of 1819, completing most of the first three acts before he undertook work on *The Cenci* in mid-May. Late in 1819 Shelley again took up work on his drama, writing Act IV and a few "lyrical insertions" for Acts I–III, among them the song at II.iii.54–98.

Though he had first sent *Prometheus Unbound* to be published in England in its three-act original version, Shelley's late additions broadened the scope of his most ambitious work from a myth of the renovation of the human psyche to a renewing of the whole cosmos. Given Shelley's ethics and his theory of knowledge (epistemology), it seems likely that he believed that when human beings saw the universe correctly, it would appear to be beneficent rather than hostile. *Queen Mab*, VIII–IX, provides a clearer, more literal representation of such universal amelioration and can be used to gloss and gauge the significance of the vision embodied in Act IV.

In its final form *Prometheus Unbound* exhibits Shelley's preferred symmetrical structure. Act I and Act IV each consists of a single scene that has three clear-cut divisions (Act I, 1–305, 306–634, and 635–833; Act IV, 1–184, 185–502, 503–578); these acts flank two acts divided into nine scenes, of which the central one—Act II, scene v—depicts the journey and transformation of Asia as she moves backwards through time, reversing the gyres of history to make "the world grow young again." Another obvious structural parallel comprises the dialogues of mythological characters in II.ii and III.ii. And whereas Acts I and III deal primarily with conditions in the human world—with the psychology of tyranny (Act I) and of freedom (Act III)—the other two acts explore the metaphysical implications of human bondage—how a slave psychology distorts the human view of the universe.

Woven into these abstract structures is the action of the drama itself, which Shelley drew—with modifications, as he explains in his Preface—from Aeschylus' drama *Prometheus Bound* and what is known of his lost sequel entitled *Prometheus Unbound*. In Shelley's version Act I sees Prometheus' curse of Jupiter repeated to him, Prometheus repents it, he resists the psychological torments sent by the tyrant, and he is comforted by human hopes and ideals.

In Act II Panthea communicates to Asia two dreams she has had which presage the release of Prometheus and the renewal of the world; Asia and

Panthea are called away and drawn down to the realm of Demogorgon, the ultimate motive source of the chain of events known as Necessity. Asia questions him on the nature of things. Demogorgon ascends the chariot of the Hour in which Jupiter is destined to be overthrown and directs the Oceanides to the car of the following Hour that will redeem Prometheus.

In Act III Jupiter, having married and raped Thetis, awaits the offspring of their union; this proves to be Demogorgon, who drags Jupiter down into the abyss of chaos. Hercules releases Prometheus, and—after directing the Spirit of the Hour of redemption to spread the good news around the world and after hearing that Spirit's report of the effects of the proclamation—Prometheus and Asia retire to an oracular cave to cultivate the arts. The action itself having come to an end, Act IV is a hymn of rejoicing—first by a chorus of Spirits of the Hours and another chorus of Spirits of the Human Mind; then by the Spirit of the Earth (male) and the Spirit of the Moon (female). Finally, as in his opening speech Prometheus had described his situation in relation to past events, so Demogorgon, addressing the spirits of all creatures in the Universe, summarizes the present joy and tells how to recapture freedom, should it be lost again.

There have been several books and dozens of scholarly articles devoted solely or chiefly to explaining *Prometheus Unbound* or parts of it. For a summary and liberal sampling of interpretations up through the mid-1950s, students can consult Lawrence John Zillman's *Shelley's "Prometheus Unbound": A Variorum Edition* (University of Washington Press, 1959), and for supplementary references, page 367 of Donald H. Reiman's chapter "Shelley" in *The English Romantic Poets: A Review of Research and Criticism*, ed. Frank Jordan, Jr. (3rd ed., Modern Language Association, 1972). In this volume, see the critical selections from Earl R. Wasserman, M. H. Abrams, and D. J. Hughes (pp. 524–530, 596–603, 603–620).

The textual difficulty of *Prometheus Unbound* is an anvil that has already broken many hammers. We must admit that considerable bafflement and frustration accompanied our attempts to edit a text that would mediate between the three imperfect authorities—Shelley's intermediate fair copy manuscript in the Bodleian Library (MSS. Shelley e.1, e.2, and e.3), the first edition of 1820, and Mary Shelley's edition of 1839, which incorporates some (though *how many* remains the problem) authoritative corrections of the imperfect first edition. The present text, which we cannot claim approaches definitiveness, has been edited on the following principles: (1) Because the (now lost) manuscript copied by Shelley and/or Mary that served as press copy for the first edition certainly contained his final choices of words, which neither the compositors nor Shelley's friend Thomas Love Peacock (who corrected the proofs) would have felt free to alter, we have retained the verbal text of 1820, unless either 1839 returns to the reading of *MS*, or the *MS* reading makes much better sense than 1820. (2) Because the punctuation—especially in the lyric passages—is much heavier than that in either Shelley's surviving press copy manuscripts or those poems that he personally saw through the press (but resembles the punctuation of Peacock's own poetry), we have made Shelley's *MS* the chief authority for punctuation, capitalization, and spelling; in numerous cases, where the *MS* was manifestly underpunctuated, we have added pointing either from 1820 or on analogy with punctuation in parallel lines and passages in MS itself. (3) We have regularized spellings and, to a lesser extent, capitalization in those instances where the *Prometheus Unbound MS* and his other MSS and authorized printed texts show that Shelley maintained a reasonably consistent practice.

The punctuation, especially in the lyrics, is primarily rhetorical, not grammatical (see Textual Introduction, p. xiv). For example, Shelley's manuscript invariably contains a comma after internal rhyme words in lyric passages (e.g., "To stay steps proud, o'er the slow cloud [I.236]); and in other passages Shelley inserted commas, semicolons, and full stops, to indicate pauses at the beginnings and ends of phrases to be read as units, as well as suspension points (. . .) to mark sentences interrupted by another speaker or longer pauses. Thus, if the meaning is not immediately clear to the silent reader, he should read the passage aloud, with pauses whose length is governed by the heaviness of the punctuation.

The capitalization in the Bodleian holograph manuscript does not seem as erratic to us now as it first appeared. Since Peacock or the compositors at Marchant, the printer, obviously lower-cased many capitals in Shelley's manuscript (of the type that appear in print in those volumes that he saw through the press), we have preferred Shelley's manuscript *except* that we have included capitals found in the first edition (and not in the MS) where they are congruent with the pattern of capitalization found in the Bodleian MS—and hence may have been added to the lost press copy.

Prometheus Unbound

A *Lyrical Drama in Four Acts*

AUDISNE HÆC AMPHIARAE, SUB TERRAM ABDITE?

PREFACE.

The Greek tragic writers, in selecting as their subject any portion of their national history or mythology, employed in their treatment of it a certain arbitrary discretion. They by no means conceived themselves bound to adhere to the common interpretation or to imitate in story as in title their rivals and predecessors. Such a system would have amounted to a resignation of those claims to preference over their competitors which incited the composition. The Agamemnonian story was exhibited on the Athenian theatre with as many variations as dramas.

I have presumed to employ a similar licence.—The *Prometheus Unbound* of Æschylus, supposed the reconciliation of Jupiter with his victim as the price of the disclosure of the danger threatened to his empire by the consummation of his marriage with Thetis. Thetis, according to this view of the subject, was given in marriage to Peleus, and Prometheus by the permission of Jupiter delivered from his captivity by Hercules.—Had I framed my story on this model I should have done no more than have attempted to restore the lost drama of Æschylus; an ambition, which, if my preference to this mode of treating the subject had incited me to cherish, the recollection of the high comparison such an attempt would challenge, might well abate. But in truth I was averse from a catastrophe so feeble as that of reconciling the Champion with the Oppressor of mankind. The moral interest of the fable which is so powerfully sustained by the sufferings and endurance of Prometheus, would be annihilated if we could conceive of him as unsaying his high language, and quailing before his successful and perfidious adversary. The only imaginary being resembling in any degree Prometheus, is Satan; and Prometheus is, in my judgement, a more poetical character than Satan because, in addition to courage and majesty and firm and patient opposition to omnipotent force, he is susceptible of being described as exempt from the taints of ambition, envy, revenge, and a desire for personal aggrandisement, which in the Hero of *Paradise Lost*, interfere with the interest. The character of Satan engenders in the mind a pernicious casuistry which leads us to weigh his faults with his wrongs and to excuse the former because the latter exceed all measure. In the minds of those who consider that magnificent fiction with a religious feeling, it engenders something worse. But Prometheus is, as it were, the type of the highest perfection of moral and intellectual nature, impelled by the purest` and the truest motives to the best and noblest ends.

This Poem was chiefly written upon the mountainous ruins of the Baths of Caracalla, among the flowery glades, and thickets of odoriferous blossoming trees which are extended in ever winding labyrinths upon its immense platforms and dizzy arches suspended in the air. The bright blue sky of Rome, and the effect of the vigorous awakening of spring in that divinest climate, and the new life with which it drenches the spirits even to intoxication, were the inspiration of this drama.

The imagery which I have employed will be found in many instances to have been drawn from the operations of the human mind, or from those external actions by which they are expressed. This is unusual in modern Poetry; although Dante and Shakespeare are full of instances of the same kind: Dante indeed more than any other poet and with greater success. But the Greek poets, as writers to whom no resource of awakening the sympathy of their contemporaries was unknown, were in the habitual use of this power, and it is the study of their works (since a higher merit would probably be denied me) to which I am willing that my readers should impute this singularity.

One word is due in candour to the degree in which the study of contemporary writings may have tinged my composition, for such has been a topic of censure with regard to poems far more popular, and indeed more deservedly popular than mine. It is impossible that any one who inhabits the same age with such writers as those who stand in the foremost ranks of our own, can conscientiously assure himself, that his language and tone of thought may not have been modified by the study of the productions of those extraordinary intellects. It is true, that, not the spirit of their genius, but the forms in which it has manifested itself, are due, less to the peculiarities of their own minds, than to the peculiarity of the moral and intellectual condition of the minds among which they have been produced. Thus a number of writers possess the form, whilst they want the spirit of those whom, it is alleged, they imitate; because the former is the endowment of the age in which they live, and the latter must be the uncommunicated lightning of their own mind.

The peculiar style of intense and comprehensive imagery which distinguishes the modern literature of England, has not been, as a general power, the product of the imitation of any particular writer. The mass of capabilities remains at every period materially the same; the circumstances which awaken it to action perpetually change. If England were divided into forty republics, each equal in population and extent to Athens, there is no reason to suppose but that, under institutions not more perfect than those of Athens, each would produce philosophers and poets equal to those who (if we except Shakespeare) have never been surpassed. We owe the great writers of the golden age of our literature to that fervid awakening of the public mind which shook to dust the oldest and most oppressive form of the Christian Religion. We owe Milton to the progress and developement of the same spirit; the sacred Milton was, let it ever be remembered, a Republican, and a bold enquirer into morals and religion. The great writers of our own age are, we have reason to suppose, the companions and forerunners of some unimagined change in our social condition or the opinions which cement it. The cloud of mind is discharging its collected lightning, and the equilibrium between institutions and opinions is now restoring, or is about to be restored.

As to imitation; Poetry is a mimetic art. It creates, but it creates by combination and representation. Poetical abstractions are beautiful and new, not because the portions of which they are composed had no previous existence in the mind of man or in nature, but because the whole produced by their combination has some intelligible and beautiful analogy with those sources of emotion and thought, and with the contemporary condition of them: one great poet is a masterpiece of nature, which another not only ought to study but must study. He might as wisely and as easily determine that his mind should no longer be the mirror of all that is lovely in the visible universe, as exclude from his contemplation the beautiful which exists in the writings of a great contemporary. The pretence of doing it would be a presumption in any but the greatest; the effect, even in him, would be strained, unnatural and ineffectual. A Poet, is the combined product of such internal powers as modify the nature of others, and of such external influences as excite and sustain these powers; he is not one, but both. Every man's mind is in this respect modified by all the objects of nature and art, by every word and every suggestion which he ever admitted to act upon his consciousness; it is the mirror upon which all forms are reflected, and in which they compose one form. Poets, not otherwise than philosophers, painters, sculptors and musicians, are in one sense the creators and in another the creations of their age. From this subjection the loftiest do not escape. There is a similarity between Homer and Hesiod, between Æschylus and Euripides, between Virgil and Horace, between Dante and Petrarch, between Shakespeare and Fletcher, between Dryden and Pope; each has a generic resemblance under which their specific distinctions are arranged. If this similarity be the result of imitation, I am willing to confess that I have imitated.

Let this opportunity be conceded to me of acknowledging that I have, what a Scotch philosopher characteristically terms, 'a passion for reforming the world:' what passion incited him to write and publish his book, he omits to explain. For my part I had rather be damned with Plato and Lord Bacon, than go to Heaven with Paley and Malthus. But it is a mistake to suppose that I dedicate my poetical compositions solely to the direct enforcement of reform, or that I consider them in any degree as containing a reasoned system on the theory of human life. Didactic poetry is my abhorrence; nothing can be equally well expressed in prose that is not tedious and supererogatory in verse. My purpose has hitherto been simply to familiarise the highly refined imagination of the more select classes of poetical readers with beautiful idealisms of moral excellence; aware that until the mind can love, and admire, and trust, and hope, and endure, reasoned principles of moral conduct are seeds cast upon the highway of life which the unconscious passenger tramples into dust, although they would bear the harvest of his happiness. Should I live to accomplish what I purpose, that is, produce a systematical history of what appear to me to be the genuine elements of human society, let not the advocates of injustice and superstition flatter themselves that I should take Æschylus rather than Plato as my model.

The having spoken of myself with unaffected freedom will need little apology with the candid; and let the uncandid consider that they injure me less than their own hearts and minds by misrepresentation. Whatever talents a person may possess to amuse and instruct others, be they ever so inconsiderable, he is yet bound to exert them: if his attempt be ineffectual, let the punishment of an unaccomplished purpose have been sufficient; let none trouble themselves to heap the dust of oblivion upon his efforts; the pile they raise will betray his grave which might otherwise have been unknown.

Prometheus Unbound

ACT I

Scene: A Ravine of Icy Rocks in the Indian Caucasus. Prometheus *is discovered bound to the Precipice.* Panthea *and* Ione *are seated at his feet. Time, Night. During the Scene, Morning slowly breaks.*

PROMETHEUS

Monarch of Gods and Dæmons,[1] and all Spirits
But One, who throng those bright and rolling Worlds
Which Thou and I alone of living things
Behold with sleepless eyes! regard this Earth
Made multitudinous with thy slaves, whom thou   5
Requitest for knee-worship, prayer and praise,
And toil, and hecatombs[2] of broken hearts,
With fear and self contempt and barren hope;
Whilst me, who am thy foe, eyeless[3] in hate,
Hast thou made reign and triumph, to thy scorn,   10
O'er mine own misery and thy vain revenge.—
Three thousand years[4] of sleep-unsheltered hours
And moments—aye[5] divided by keen pangs
Till they seemed years, torture and solitude,
Scorn and despair,—these are mine empire:—   15
More glorious far than that which thou surveyest
From thine unenvied throne, O Mighty God!
Almighty, had I deigned to share the shame
Of thine ill tyranny, and hung not here
Nailed to this wall of eagle-baffling mountain,   20
Black, wintry, dead, unmeasured; without herb,
Insect, or beast, or shape or sound of life.
Ah me, alas, pain, pain ever, forever!

No change, no pause, no hope!—Yet I endure.
I ask the Earth, have not the mountains felt?   25
I ask yon Heaven—the all-beholding Sun,

1. Supernatural beings of secondary rank who could communicate with both gods and men.
2. Sacrifices of many victims presented as offerings.
3. Blind.

4. The time span nineteenth-century scientists believed separated the development of early civilizations (Egypt, etc.) from their own time.
5. Continually.

Has it not seen? The Sea, in storm or calm,
Heaven's ever-changing Shadow, spread below—
Have its deaf waves not heard my agony?
Ah me, alas, pain, pain ever, forever!   30

The crawling glaciers pierce me with the spears
Of their moon-freezing chrystals; the bright chains
Eat with their burning cold into my bones.
Heaven's winged hound,[6] polluting from thy lips
His beak in poison not his own, tears up   35
My heart; and shapeless sights come wandering by,
The ghastly people of the realm of dream,
Mocking me: and the Earthquake-fiends are charged
To wrench the rivets from my quivering wounds
When the rocks split and close again behind;   40
While from their loud abysses howling throng
The genii of the storm, urging the rage
Of whirlwind, and afflict me with keen hail.
And yet to me welcome is Day and Night,
Whether one breaks the hoar frost of the morn,   45
Or starry, dim, and slow, the other climbs
The leaden-coloured East; for then they lead
Their wingless, crawling Hours,[7] one among whom
—As some dark Priest hales[8] the reluctant victim—
Shall drag thee, cruel King, to kiss the blood   50
From these pale feet, which then might trample thee
If they disdained not such a prostrate slave.
Disdain? Ah no! I pity thee.—What Ruin
Will hunt thee undefended through wide Heaven!
How will thy soul, cloven to its depth with terror,   55
Gape like a Hell within! I speak in grief,
Not exultation, for I hate no more,
As then, ere misery made me wise.—The Curse
Once breathed on thee I would recall.[9] Ye Mountains,
Whose many-voiced Echoes, through the mist   60
Of cataracts,[1] flung the thunder of that spell!
Ye icy Springs, stagnant with wrinkling frost,
Which vibrated to hear me, and then crept
Shuddering through India![2] Thou serenest Air,
Through which the Sun walks burning without beams!   65
And ye swift Whirlwinds, who on poised wings

---

6. The eagle or vulture of Jupiter that daily tortured Prometheus.
7. In classical art and myth the Horae, representations of the hours and seasons, are winged human figures.
8. Hauls or drags by force.
9. Remember; the word also foreshadows his *revoking* the curse.
1. Large waterfalls.
2. As the stage direction indicates, Shelley has relocated the scene of the play from the European Caucasus (between the Black and Caspian seas) to the Hindu Kush, or Indian Caucasus, which some writers identified with the Himalayas. Shelley's reasons for the shift have been much speculated on, but he was certainly reflecting current ideas that human life originated in central Asia; he was attempting to universalize the Greek myth to a generally human myth.

Hung mute and moveless o'er yon hushed abyss,
As thunder louder than your own made rock[3]
The orbed world! If then my words had power
—Though I am changed so that aught evil wish   70
Is dead within, although no memory be
Of what is hate—let them not lose it now!
What was that curse? for ye all heard me speak.

FIRST VOICE: *from the Mountains*
Thrice three hundred thousand years
   O'er the Earthquake's couch we stood: 75
Oft as men convulsed with fears
   We trembled in our multitude.

SECOND VOICE: *from the Springs*
Thunderbolts had parched our water,
   We had been stained with bitter blood,
And had run mute 'mid shrieks of slaughter   80
   Through a city and a solitude!

THIRD VOICE: *from the Air*
I had clothed since Earth uprose
   Its wastes in colours not their own,
And oft had my serene repose
   Been cloven by many a rending groan.   85

FOURTH VOICE: *from the Whirlwinds*
We had soared beneath these mountains
   Unresting ages; nor had thunder
Nor yon volcano's flaming fountains
   Nor any power above or under
   Ever made us mute with wonder!   90

FIRST VOICE
   But never bowed our snowy crest
   As at the voice of thine unrest.

SECOND VOICE
Never such a sound before
To the Indian waves we bore.—
A pilot asleep on the howling sea   95
Leaped up from the deck in agony
And heard, and cried, "Ah, woe is me!"
And died as mad as the wild waves be.

THIRD VOICE
By such dread words from Earth to Heaven
My still realm was never riven: 100
When its wound was closed, there stood
Darkness o'er the Day like blood.

3. Though *rock* functions as a verb, it can also be a pun on the meaning of the word
as a noun.

FOURTH VOICE

And we shrank back—for dreams of ruin
To frozen caves our flight pursuing[4]
Made us keep silence—thus—and thus—   105
Though silence is as hell to us.

THE EARTH

The tongueless Caverns of the craggy hills
Cried "Misery!" then; the hollow Heaven replied,
"Misery!" And the Ocean's purple waves,
Climbing the land, howled to the lashing winds.   110
And the pale nations heard it,—"Misery!"

PROMETHEUS

I hear a sound of voices—not the voice
Which I gave forth.—Mother,[5] thy sons and thou
Scorn him, without whose all-enduring will
Beneath the fierce omnipotence of Jove   115
Both they and thou had vanished like thin mist
Unrolled on the morning wind!—Know ye not me,
The Titan, he who made his agony
The barrier to your else all-conquering foe?
O rock-embosomed lawns and snow-fed streams   120
Now seen athwart frore[6] vapours deep below,
Through whose o'er-shadowing woods I wandered once
With Asia, drinking life from her loved eyes;
Why scorns the spirit which informs ye, now
To commune with me? me alone, who checked,   125
As one who checks a fiend-drawn charioteer,
The falshood and the force of Him who reigns
Supreme, and with the groans of pining slaves
Fills your dim glens and liquid wildernesses?
Why answer ye not, still? brethren!

THE EARTH

                                   They dare not.   130

PROMETHEUS

Who dares? for I would hear that curse again. . . .
Ha, what an awful whisper rises up!
'Tis scarce like sound, it tingles through the frame
As lightning tingles, hovering ere it strike.—
Speak, Spirit! from thine inorganic voice   135
I only know that thou art moving near
And love. How cursed I him?

---

4. In Shelley's day, *ruin* and *pursuing* were an exact rhyme ("pursuin"). According to William Scott's *Elements of Elocution* (1808), apart from a few exceptions (which he lists), "G is silent before and after *n* in the same syllable, as gnat, gnarl, resign, . . . thinking, learning" (p. 11).

5. The Earth; in Hesiod's *Theogony*, Earth (Gaea or Tithea) was the mother and Sky (Uranus) the father of the Titans.

6. Frosty.

THE EARTH
                    How canst thou hear
Who knowest not the language of the dead?

PROMETHEUS
Thou art a living spirit—speak as they.

THE EARTH
I dare not speak like life, lest Heaven's fell King   140
Should hear, and link me to some wheel of pain
More torturing than the one whereon I roll.—
Subtle thou art and good, and though the Gods
Hear not this voice—yet thou art more than God,
Being wise and kind—earnestly hearken now.—   145

PROMETHEUS
Obscurely through my brain like shadows dim
Sweep awful[7] thoughts, rapid and thick.—I feel
Faint, like one mingled in entwining love,
Yet 'tis not pleasure.

THE EARTH
                    No, thou canst not hear:
Thou art immortal, and this tongue is known   150
Only to those who die . . .

PROMETHEUS
                    And what art thou,
O melancholy Voice?

THE EARTH
                    I am the Earth,
Thy mother, she within whose stony veins
To the last fibre of the loftiest tree
Whose thin leaves trembled in the frozen air   155
Joy ran, as blood within a living frame,
When thou didst from her bosom, like a cloud
Of glory, arise, a spirit of keen joy!
And at thy voice her pining sons uplifted
Their prostrate brows from the polluting dust   160
And our almighty Tyrant with fierce dread
Grew pale, until his thunder chained thee here.
Then—see those million worlds which burn and roll
Around us: their inhabitants beheld
My sphered light wane in wide Heaven; the sea   165
Was lifted by strange tempest, and new fire
From earthquake-rifted mountains of bright snow
Shook its portentous hair beneath Heaven's frown;
Lightning and Inundation vexed the plains;
Blue thistles bloomed in cities; foodless toads   170
Within voluptuous chambers panting crawled;

7. Awe-inspiring.

When plague had fallen on man and beast and worm,
And Famine, and black blight on herb and tree,
And in the corn and vines and meadow grass
Teemed ineradicable poisonous weeds   175
Draining their growth, for my wan breast was dry
With grief; and the thin air, my breath, was stained
With the contagion of a mother's hate
Breathed on her child's destroyer—aye, I heard
Thy curse, the which if thou rememberest not   180
Yet my innumerable seas and streams,
Mountains and caves and winds, and yon wide Air
And the inarticulate people of the dead
Preserve, a treasured spell. We meditate
In secret joy and hope those dreadful words   185
But dare not speak them.

    PROMETHEUS
            Venerable mother!
All else who live and suffer take from thee
Some comfort; flowers and fruits and happy sounds
And love, though fleeting; these may not be mine.
But mine own words, I pray, deny me not.   190

    THE EARTH
They shall be told.—Ere Babylon was dust,
The Magus Zoroaster,[8] my dead child,
Met his own image walking in the garden.
That apparition, sole of men, he saw.
For know, there are two worlds of life and death: 195
One that which thou beholdest, but the other
Is underneath the grave, where do inhabit
The shadows of all forms that think and live
Till death unite them, and they part no more;
Dreams and the light imaginings of men   200
And all that faith creates, or love desires,
Terrible, strange, sublime and beauteous shapes.
There thou art, and dost hang, a writhing shade
'Mid whirlwind-peopled mountains; all the Gods
Are there, and all the Powers of nameless worlds,   205
Vast, sceptred phantoms; heroes, men, and beasts;
And Demogorgon,[9] a tremendous Gloom;

---

8. Zoroaster (sixth or seventh century B.C.), a king of Bactria in what became part of Persia, founded a dualistic religion that worshiped fire and light in opposition to the evil principle of darkness. Priests of the religion were called Magi (singular: Magus). The exact source of Shelley's reference has not yet been discovered, but there had been a revival of interest in Zoroaster in France in the eighteenth century, and Peacock was much interested in the subject.
9. The name originated from a medieval error in transcribing the word "Demiourgos" (Demiurge) from Plato's myth of the creation in *Timaeus* (28–40). In a note to the name in a poem written and published in 1817 while he and Shelley both lived at Marlow and conversed daily, Thomas Love Peacock alludes to Milton's mention of Demogorgon (*Paradise Lost*, II.965), and outlines the available information, from which we abstract: "Pronapides . . . makes Pan and the three sister Fates the offspring of Dæmogorgon. Boccaccio . . . gives

And he, the Supreme Tyrant,[1] on his throne
Of burning Gold. Son, one of these shall utter
The curse which all remember. Call at will   210
Thine own ghost, or the ghost of Jupiter,
Hades or Typhon,[2] or what mightier Gods
From all-prolific Evil, since thy ruin
Have sprung, and trampled on my prostrate sons.—
Ask and they must reply—so the revenge   215
Of the Supreme may sweep through vacant shades
As rainy wind through the abandoned gate
Of a fallen palace.

PROMETHEUS
    Mother, let not aught
Of that which may be evil, pass again
My lips, or those of aught resembling me.—   220
Phantasm of Jupiter, arise, appear![3]

IONE
My wings are folded o'er mine ears,
My wings are crossed over mine eyes,
Yet through their silver shade appears
And through their lulling plumes arise   225
 A Shape, a throng of sounds:
  May it be, no ill to thee[4]
 O thou of many wounds!
Near whom for our sweet sister's sake
Ever thus we watch and wake.   230

PANTHEA
The sound is of whirlwind underground,
Earthquake and fire, and mountains cloven;
The Shape is awful like the sound,
Clothed in dark purple, star-inwoven.
 A sceptre of pale gold   235
  To stay steps proud, o'er the slow cloud
 His veined hand doth hold.
Cruel he looks but calm and strong
Like one who does, not suffers wrong.

---

some account of him. . . . He was the Genius of the Earth, and the Sovereign Power of the Terrestrial Dæmons. He dwelt originally with Eternity and Chaos, till, becoming weary of inaction, he organised the chaotic elements, and surrounded the earth with the heavens. In addition to Pan and the Fates, his children were Uranus, Titæa, Pytho, Eris, and Erebus" (*Rhododaphne* [London, 1818], pp. 179–180). Thus, in Peacock's account, Demogorgon is the father of the Sky, the Earth, and the Underworld, as well as the Fates.
1. The shadow of Jupiter.

2. *Hades* (Pluto), brother of Zeus (Jupiter) and king of the underworld; *Typhon*, a hundred-headed giant, warred with *Jupiter* and was finally imprisoned beneath volcanic Mt. Aetna.
3. Critics have suggested that Prometheus, when he cursed Jupiter, resembled the tyrant—that, in fact, Jupiter may be merely a distortion of Prometheus himself—and that it is therefore appropriate to have the Phantasm of Jupiter repeat the curse.
4. Shelley uses the comma in the middle of lines like these to emphasize the internal rhyme.

PHANTASM OF JUPITER

Why have the secret powers of this strange world   240
Driven me, a frail and empty phantom, hither
On direst storms? What unaccustomed sounds
Are hovering on my lips, unlike the voice
With which our pallid race hold ghastly talk
In darkness? And, proud Sufferer, who art thou?   245

PROMETHEUS

Tremendous Image! as thou art must be
He whom thou shadowest forth. I am his foe
The Titan. Speak the words which I would hear,
Although no thought inform thine empty voice.

THE EARTH

Listen! and though your echoes must be mute,   250
Grey mountains and old woods and haunted springs,
Prophetic caves and isle-surrounding streams
Rejoice to hear what yet ye cannot speak.

PHANTASM

A spirit seizes me, and speaks within:
It tears me as fire tears a thunder-cloud!   225

PANTHEA

See how he lifts his mighty looks, the Heaven
Darkens above.

IONE

            He speaks! O shelter me—

PROMETHEUS

I see the curse on gestures proud and cold,
And looks of firm defiance, and calm hate,
And such despair as mocks itself with smiles,   260
Written as on a scroll . . . yet speak—O speak!

PHANTASM

Fiend, I defy thee! with a calm, fixed mind,
    All that thou canst inflict I bid thee do;
Foul Tyrant both of Gods and Humankind,
    One only being shalt thou not subdue.   265
        Rain then thy plagues upon me here,
        Ghastly disease and frenzying fear;
        And let alternate frost and fire
        Eat into me, and be thine ire
Lightning and cutting hail and legioned[5] forms   270
Of furies, driving by upon the wounding storms.

Aye, do thy worst. Thou art Omnipotent.
    O'er all things but thyself I gave thee power,
And my own will. Be thy swift mischiefs sent
    To blast mankind, from yon etherial tower.   275

5. Arrayed in legions, as armies.

Let thy malignant spirit move
Its darkness over those I love:
On me and mine I imprecate[6]
The utmost torture of thy hate
And thus devote to sleepless agony   280
This undeclining head while thou must reign on high.

But thou who art the God and Lord—O thou
    Who fillest with thy soul this world of woe,
To whom all things of Earth and Heaven do bow
    In fear and worship—all-prevailing foe!   285
        I curse thee! let a sufferer's curse
        Clasp thee, his torturer, like remorse,
        Till thine Infinity shall be
        A robe of envenomed agony;
And thine Omnipotence a crown of pain   290
To cling like burning gold round thy dissolving brain.[7]

Heap on thy soul by virtue of this Curse
    Ill deeds, then be thou damned, beholding good,
Both infinite as is the Universe,
    And thou, and thy self-torturing solitude.   295
        An awful Image of calm power
        Though now thou sittest, let the hour
        Come, when thou must appear to be
        That which thou art internally.
And after many a false and fruitless crime   300
Scorn track thy lagging fall through boundless space and time.
                                          [*The Phantasm vanishes.*]

              PROMETHEUS
Were these my words, O Parent?

          THE EARTH
                                    They were thine.

              PROMETHEUS
    It doth repent me: words are quick and vain;
Grief for awhile is blind, and so was mine.
    I wish no living thing to suffer pain.   305

              THE EARTH
    Misery, O misery to me,
    That Jove at length should vanquish thee.
    Wail, howl aloud, Land and Sea,
    The Earth's rent heart shall answer ye.
Howl, Spirits of the living and the dead,   310
Your refuge, your defence lies fallen and vanquished.

6. Invoke or call down evil or calamity.
7. In lines 286–291 Shelley combines
tortures from Greek myths (a poisoned
shirt or tunic from the centaur Nessus
caused the death of Hercules) and the
mocking of Jesus with a "gorgeous robe"
and a crown of thorns (Matthew 27:28–
29; Mark 15:17; Luke 23:11).

FIRST ECHO
Lies fallen and vanquished?

SECOND ECHO
Fallen and vanquished!

IONE
Fear not—'tis but some passing spasm,
    The Titan is unvanquished still.   315
But see, where through the azure chasm
    Of yon forked and snowy hill,
Trampling the slant winds on high
    With golden-sandalled feet, that glow
Under plumes of purple dye   320
Like rose-ensanguined[8] ivory,
    A Shape comes now,
Stretching on high from his right hand
    A serpent-cinctured[9] wand.

PANTHEA
'Tis Jove's world-wandering Herald, Mercury.   325

IONE
And who are those with hydra tresses[1]
    And iron wings that climb the wind,
Whom the frowning God represses,
    Like vapours streaming up behind,
Clanging loud, an endless crowd—   330

PANTHEA
These are Jove's tempest-walking hounds,[2]
    Whom he gluts with groans and blood
When, charioted on sulphurous cloud,
    He bursts Heaven's bounds.

IONE
Are they now led from the thin dead,   335
    On new pangs to be fed?

PANTHEA
The Titan looks as ever, firm, not proud.

FIRST FURY
Ha! I scent life!

SECOND FURY
    Let me but look into his eyes!

THIRD FURY
The hope of torturing him smells like a heap
Of corpses, to a death-bird after battle.   340

8. Stained blood color.   note to 346).
9. Encircled or girdled.   2. I.e., the Furies.
1. Hair of snakes like a Gorgon's (see

FIRST FURY

Darest thou delay, O Herald? take cheer, Hounds
Of Hell—what if the Son of Maia[3] soon
Should make us food and sport? Who can please long
The Omnipotent?

MERCURY

Back to your towers of iron
And gnash, beside the streams of fire, and wail[3a]   345
Your foodless teeth! . . . Geryon, arise! and Gorgon,
Chimæra,[4] and thou Sphinx, subtlest of fiends,
Who ministered to Thebes Heaven's poisoned wine,
Unnatural love and more unnatural hate:[5]
These shall perform your task.

FIRST FURY

O mercy! mercy!   350
We die with our desire—drive us not back!

MERCURY

Crouch then in silence.—

Awful[6] Sufferer!
To thee unwilling, most unwillingly
I come, by the great Father's will driven down
To execute a doom of new revenge.   355
Alas! I pity thee, and hate myself
That I can do no more.—Aye from thy sight
Returning, for a season, Heaven seems Hell,
So thy worn form pursues me night and day,
Smiling reproach. Wise art thou, firm and good,   360
But vainly wouldst stand forth alone in strife
Against the Omnipotent, as yon clear lamps
That measure and divide the weary years
From which there is no refuge, long have taught
And long must teach. Even now thy Torturer arms   365
With the strange might of unimagined pains
The powers who scheme slow agonies in Hell,

3. Mercury, whose father was Jupiter. Maia, the most luminous of the seven sisters in the constellation Pleiades, was the daughter of Atlas and Pleione.
3a. We have repunctuated this line according to the argument of E. B. Murray, *KSJ*, 24:17–20 (1975).
4. *Geryon*, a monster with three heads and three bodies, lived with his man-eating flocks and his three-headed dog on an island beyond the Straits of Gibraltar, where he was destroyed by Hercules. The three *Gorgons* were mythical personages, with snakes for hair, who turned beholders into stone. The only mortal one, Medusa, was slain by Perseus and her head fixed on Athena's (Minerva's) shield. The *Chimera*, a fabled fire-breathing monster of Greek mythology with three heads (lion, goat, and dragon), the body of a lion and a goat, and a dragon's tail, was killed by Bellerophon.
5. The Sphinx, a monster with the body of a lion, wings, and the face and breasts of a woman, besieged Thebes by devouring those who could not answer her riddle. Oedipus solved the riddle (causing the Sphinx to kill herself), only to marry his mother (*unnatural love*), leading to the tragic events depicted in the Greek Theban plays, in which first the royal family and then all Thebes are destroyed by mutual hatreds.
6. Inspiring reverence.

And my commission is, to lead them here,
Or what more subtle, foul or savage fiends
People the abyss, and leave them to their task.   370
Be it not so! . . . There is a secret known
To thee and to none else of living things
Which may transfer the sceptre of wide Heaven,
The fear of which perplexes the Supreme . . .
Clothe it in words, and bid it clasp his throne   375
In intercession; bend thy soul in prayer
And like a suppliant in some gorgeous fane[7]
Let the will kneel within thy haughty heart;
For benefits and meek submission tame
The fiercest and the mightiest.

                      PROMETHEUS
                              Evil minds   380
Change good to their own nature. I gave all
He has, and in return he chains me here
Years, ages, night and day: whether the Sun
Split my parched skin, or in the moony night
The chrystal-winged snow cling round my hair—   385
Whilst my beloved race is trampled down
By his thought-executing ministers.
Such is the tyrant's recompense: 'tis just:
He who is evil can receive no good;
And for a world bestowed, or a friend lost,   390
He can feel hate, fear, shame—not gratitude:
He but requites me for his own misdeed.
Kindness to such is keen reproach, which breaks
With bitter stings the light sleep of Revenge.
Submission, thou dost know, I cannot try: 395
For what submission but that fatal word,
The death-seal of mankind's captivity—
Like the Sicilian's hair-suspended sword[8]
Which trembles o'er his crown—would he accept
Or could I yield?—which yet I will not yield.   400
Let others flatter Crime where it sits thron'd
In brief Omnipotence; secure are they:
For Justice when triumphant will weep down
Pity not punishment on her own wrongs,
Too much avenged by those who err. I wait,   405
Enduring thus the retributive hour
Which since we spake is even nearer now.—
But hark, the hell-hounds clamour. Fear delay!
Behold! Heaven lowers[9] under thy Father's frown.

7. Temple.
8. Dionysius the Elder, pronounced by Damocles to be the happiest man on earth because of his wealth, persuaded the flatterer to take his place as sovereign. Amidst the splendor, Damocles perceived a sword hanging by one horsehair above his head and begged Dionysius to remove him from the terrifying situation.
9. Cowers.

MERCURY

O that we might be spared—I to inflict   410
And thou to suffer! Once more answer me:
Thou knowest not the period[1] of Jove's power?

PROMETHEUS

I know but this, that it must come.

MERCURY

Alas!
Thou canst not count thy years to come of pain?

PROMETHEUS

They last while Jove must reign: nor more nor less   415
Do I desire or fear.

MERCURY

Yet pause, and plunge
Into Eternity, where recorded time,
Even all that we imagine, age on age,
Seems but a point, and the reluctant mind
Flags wearily in its unending flight   420
Till it sink, dizzy, blind, lost, shelterless;
Perchance it has not numbered the slow years
Which thou must spend in torture, unreprieved.

PROMETHEUS

Perchance no thought can count them—yet they pass.

MERCURY

If thou might'st dwell among the Gods the while,   425
Lapped in voluptuous joy?—

PROMETHEUS

I would not quit
This bleak ravine, these unrepentant pains.

MERCURY

Alas! I wonder at, yet pity thee.

PROMETHEUS

Pity the self-despising slaves of Heaven,
Not me, within whose mind sits peace serene   430
As light in the sun, throned. . . . How vain is talk!
Call up the fiends.

IONE

O sister, look! White fire
Has cloven to the roots yon huge snow-loaded Cedar;
How fearfully God's thunder howls behind!

1. The end or conclusion.

MERCURY

I must obey his words and thine—alas!   435
Most heavily remorse hangs at my heart!

PANTHEA

See where the child of Heaven, with winged feet,
Runs down the slanted sunlight of the dawn.

IONE

Dear sister, close thy plumes over thine eyes
Lest thou behold and die—they come—they come   440
Blackening the birth of day with countless wings,
And hollow underneath, like death.

FIRST FURY

                          Prometheus!

SECOND FURY

Immortal Titan!

THIRD FURY

                Champion of Heaven's slaves!

PROMETHEUS

He whom some dreadful voice invokes is here.
Prometheus, the chained Titan.—Horrible forms,   445
What and who are ye? Never yet there came
Phantasms[2] so foul through monster-teeming Hell
From the all-miscreative brain of Jove;
Whilst I behold such execrable shapes,
Methinks I grow like what I contemplate   450
And laugh and stare in loathsome sympathy.

FIRST FURY

We are the ministers of pain and fear
And disappointment and mistrust and hate
And clinging[3] crime; and as lean dogs pursue
Through wood and lake some struck and sobbing fawn,   455
We track all things that weep and bleed and live
When the great King betrays them to our will.[4]

PROMETHEUS

O many fearful natures in one name!
I know ye, and these lakes and echoes know
The darkness and the clangour of your wings.   460
But why more hideous than your loathed selves
Gather ye up in legions from the deep?

2. Spirits or incorporeal beings; apparitions.
3. Clasping.
4. The comparison of human fears, hatreds, and evil thoughts with hunting dogs that pursue a deer embodies both the myth of Actaeon (a hunter who was turned into a deer and devoured by his own hounds for seeing Diana naked) and an image deriving from it in Shakespeare's *Twelfth Night:* "That instant was I turn'd into a hart;/ And my desires, like fell and cruel hounds,/ E'er since pursue me." (I.i.21–23).

SECOND FURY
We knew not that—Sisters, rejoice, rejoice!

PROMETHEUS
Can aught exult in its deformity?

SECOND FURY
The beauty of delight makes lovers glad,   465
Gazing on one another—so are we.
As from the rose which the pale priestess kneels
To gather for her festal crown of flowers
The aerial crimson falls, flushing her cheek—
So from our victim's destined agony   470
The shade which is our form invests us round,
Else are we shapeless as our Mother Night.[5]

PROMETHEUS
I laugh your power and his who sent you here
To lowest scorn.—Pour forth the cup of pain.

FIRST FURY
Thou thinkest we will rend thee bone from bone?   475
And nerve from nerve, working like fire within?

PROMETHEUS
Pain is my element as hate is thine;
Ye rend me now: I care not.

SECOND FURY
                              Dost imagine
We will but laugh into thy lidless eyes?

PROMETHEUS
I weigh not what ye do, but what ye suffer   480
Being evil. Cruel was the Power which called
You, or aught else so wretched, into light.

THIRD FURY
Thou think'st we will live through thee, one by one,
Like animal life; and though we can obscure not
The soul which burns within, that we will dwell   485
Beside it, like a vain loud multitude
Vexing the self-content of wisest men—
That we will be dread thought beneath thy brain
And foul desire round thine astonished heart
And blood within thy labyrinthine veins   490
Crawling like agony.

5. The children of Night (according to   Vengeance, Retribution, Deceit, Old Age,
Hesiod's *Theogony*) included Destruction, and Strife.
Death, Blame, Grief, the Specters of

PROMETHEUS
                    Why, ye are thus now;
Yet am I king over myself, and rule
The torturing and conflicting throngs within
As Jove rules you when Hell grows mutinous.

CHORUS OF FURIES
From the ends of the Earth, from the ends of the Earth,   495
Where the night has its grave and the morning its birth,
          Come, come, come!
O ye who shake hills with the scream of your mirth
When cities sink howling in ruin, and ye
Who with wingless footsteps[6] trample the Sea,   500
And close upon Shipwreck and Famine's track
Sit chattering with joy on the foodless wreck;
          Come, come, come!
     Leave the bed, low, cold and red,
     Strewed beneath a nation dead;   505
     Leave the hatred—as in ashes
          Fire is left for future burning,—
     It will burst in bloodier flashes
          When ye stir it, soon returning;
     Leave the self-contempt implanted   510
     In young spirits sense-enchanted,
          Misery's yet unkindled fuel;
     Leave Hell's secrets half-unchanted
          To the maniac dreamer: cruel
     More than ye can be with hate,   515
          Is he with fear.
          Come, come, come!
We are steaming up from Hell's wide gate
And we burthen the blasts of the atmosphere,
But vainly we toil till ye come here.   520

IONE
Sister, I hear the thunder of new wings.

PANTHEA
These solid mountains quiver with the sound
Even as the tremulous air: their shadows make
The space within my plumes more black than night.

FIRST FURY
     Your call was as a winged car   525
     Driven on whirlwinds fast and far;
     It rapt[7] us from red gulphs of war—

SECOND FURY
From wide cities, famine-wasted—

6. Heavy, evil.   7. Carried from one place to another.

THIRD FURY
Groans half heard, and blood untasted—

FOURTH FURY
Kingly conclaves, stern and cold,   530
Where blood with gold is bought and sold—

FIFTH FURY
From the furnace, white and hot,
In which—

A FURY
  Speak not—whisper not!
I know all that ye would tell,
But to speak might break the spell   535
Which must bend the Invincible,
  The stern of thought;
He yet defies the deepest power of Hell.

A FURY
Tear the veil!

ANOTHER FURY
  It is torn!

CHORUS
          The pale stars of the morn
Shine on a misery dire to be borne.   540
Dost thou faint, mighty Titan? We laugh thee to scorn.
Dost thou boast the clear knowledge thou waken'dst for man?
Then was kindled within him a thirst which outran
Those perishing waters; a thirst of fierce fever,
Hope, love, doubt, desire—which consume him forever. 545
  One[8] came forth, of gentle worth,
    Smiling on the sanguine earth;
  His words outlived him, like swift poison
    Withering up truth, peace and pity.
  Look! where round the wide horizon   550
    Many a million-peopled city
  Vomits smoke in the bright air.
  Hark that outcry of despair!
  'Tis his mild and gentle ghost
    Wailing for the faith he kindled.   555
  Look again, the flames almost
    To a glow-worm's lamp have dwindled:
  The survivors round the embers
    Gather in dread.
      Joy, joy, joy!   560
Past ages crowd on thee, but each one remembers,
And the future is dark, and the present is spread
Like a pillow of thorns for thy slumberless head.

8. Jesus Christ.

SEMICHORUS I
Drops of bloody agony flow
From his white and quivering brow.   565
Grant a little respite now—
See! a disenchanted nation[9]
Springs like day from desolation;
To truth its state, is dedicate,
And Freedom leads it forth, her mate;   570
A legioned band of linked brothers
Whom Love calls children—

SEMICHORUS II
                                    'Tis another's—
See how kindred murder kin!
'Tis the vintage-time for Death and Sin:
Blood, like new wine, bubbles within   575
        Till Despair smothers
The struggling World, which slaves and tyrants win.
                    [*All the* Furies *vanish, except one.*]

IONE
Hark, sister! what a low yet dreadful groan
Quite unsuppressed is tearing up the heart
Of the good Titan, as storms tear the deep,   580
And beasts hear the sea moan in inland caves.
Darest thou observe how the fiends torture him?

PANTHEA
Alas, I looked forth twice, but will no more.

IONE
What didst thou see?

PANTHEA
                A woeful sight—a youth[1]
With patient looks nailed to a crucifix.   585

IONE
What next?

PANTHEA
            The Heaven around, the Earth below
Was peopled with thick shapes of human death,
All horrible, and wrought by human hands,
And some appeared the work of human hearts,
For men were slowly killed by frowns and smiles: 590
And other sights too foul to speak and live
Were wandering by. Let us not tempt worse fear
By looking forth—those groans are grief enough.

9. France, when it was freed of its enchantment by monarchy during the French Revolution; subsequent lines recount the perversion of the Revolution into bloody civil strife and then wars of conquest.
1. Jesus Christ.

FURY

Behold, an emblem[2]—those who do endure
Deep wrongs for man, and scorn and chains, but heap   595
Thousand-fold torment on themselves and him.

PROMETHEUS

Remit the anguish of that lighted stare—
Close those wan lips—let that thorn-wounded brow
Stream not with blood—it mingles with thy tears!
Fix, fix those tortured orbs in peace and death   600
So thy sick throes shake not that crucifix,
So those pale fingers play not with thy gore.—
O horrible! Thy name I will not speak,
It hath become a curse. I see, I see
The wise, the mild, the lofty and the just,   605
Whom thy slaves hate for being like to thee,
Some hunted by foul lies from their heart's home,
An early-chosen, late-lamented home,
As hooded ounces[3] cling to the driven hind,
Some linked to corpses in unwholesome cells: 610
Some—hear I not the multitude laugh loud?—
Impaled in lingering fire: and mighty realms
Float by my feet like sea-uprooted isles
Whose sons are kneaded down in common blood
By the red light of their own burning homes.   615

FURY

Blood thou canst see, and fire; and canst hear groans;
Worse things, unheard, unseen, remain behind.

PROMETHEUS

Worse?

FURY

            In each human heart terror survives
The ravin it has gorged: the loftiest fear
All that they would disdain to think were true: 620
Hypocrisy and custom make their minds
The fanes of many a worship, now outworn.
They dare not devise good for man's estate
And yet they know not that they do not dare.
The good want power, but to weep barren tears.   625
The powerful goodness want: worse need for them.
The wise want love, and those who love want wisdom;
And all best things are thus confused to ill.
Many are strong and rich,—and would be just,—
But live among their suffering fellow men   630
As if none felt: they know not what they do.[4]

<hr>

2. A symbol; a fable or allegory such as might be expressed pictorially.
3. Cheetahs or hunting leopards; *hind:* a female deer in and after its third year.

4. Lines 625–631 show the moment of Prometheus' ultimate temptation to despair, ending with the words of Christ on the cross (Luke 23:34).

PROMETHEUS

Thy words are like a cloud of winged snakes
And yet, I pity those they torture not.

FURY

Thou pitiest them? I speak no more!

[*Vanishes.*]

PROMETHEUS

Ah woe!

Ah woe! Alas! pain, pain ever, forever!   635
I close my tearless eyes, but see more clear
Thy works within my woe-illumed mind,
Thou subtle Tyrant! . . . Peace is in the grave—
The grave hides all things beautiful and good—
I am a God and cannot find it there,   640
Nor would I seek it: for, though dread revenge,
This is defeat, fierce King, not victory.
The sights with which thou torturest gird my soul
With new endurance, till the hour arrives
When they shall be no types of things which are.   645

PANTHEA

Alas! what sawest thou?

PROMETHEUS

There are two woes:
To speak and to behold; thou spare me one.
Names are there, Nature's sacred watchwords—they
Were borne aloft in bright emblazonry.
The nations thronged around, and cried aloud   650
As with one voice, "Truth, liberty and love!"
Suddenly fierce confusion fell from Heaven
Among them—there was strife, deceit and fear;
Tyrants rushed in, and did divide the spoil.
This was the shadow of the truth I saw.   655

THE EARTH

I felt thy torture, Son, with such mixed joy
As pain and Virtue give.—To cheer thy state
I bid ascend those subtle and fair spirits
Whose homes are the dim caves of human thought
And who inhabit, as birds wing the wind,   660
Its world-surrounding ether; they behold
Beyond that twilight realm, as in a glass,
The future—may they speak comfort to thee!

PANTHEA

Look, Sister, where a troop of spirits gather
Like flocks of clouds in spring's delightful weather,   665
Thronging in the blue air!

IONE
                    And see! more come
Like fountain-vapours when the winds are dumb,
That climb up the ravine in scattered lines.
And hark! is it the music of the pines?
Is it the lake? is it the waterfall?   670

PANTHEA
'Tis something sadder, sweeter far than all.

CHORUS OF SPIRITS[5]
From unremembered ages we
Gentle guides and guardians be
Of Heaven-oppressed mortality—
And we breathe, and sicken not,   675
The atmosphere of human thought:
Be it dim and dank and grey
Like a storm-extinguished day
Travelled o'er by dying gleams;
    Be it bright as all between   680
Cloudless skies and windless streams,
    Silent, liquid and serene—
As the birds within the wind,
    As the fish within the wave,
As the thoughts of man's own mind   685
    Float through all above the grave,
We make there, our liquid lair,
Voyaging cloudlike and unpent[6]
Through the boundless element—
Thence we bear the prophecy   690
Which begins and ends in thee!

IONE
More yet come, one by one: the air around them
Looks radiant as the air around a star.

FIRST SPIRIT
On a battle-trumpet's blast
I fled hither, fast, fast, fast,   695
Mid the darkness upward cast—
From the dust of creeds outworn,
From the tyrant's banner torn,
Gathering round me, onward borne,
There was mingled many a cry—   700
Freedom! Hope! Death! Victory!
Till they faded through the sky
And one sound above, around,
One sound beneath, around, above,
Was moving; 'twas the soul of love;   705
'Twas the hope, the prophecy,
Which begins and ends in thee.

5. Identified by Earth at 658–663.   6. Unconfined.

SECOND SPIRIT

A rainbow's arch stood on the sea,
Which rocked beneath, immoveably;
And the triumphant storm did flee,   710
Like a conqueror swift and proud
Between, with many a captive cloud
A shapeless, dark and rapid crowd,
Each by lightning riven in half.—
I heard the thunder hoarsely laugh.—   715
Mighty fleets were strewn like chaff
And spread beneath, a hell of death
O'er the white waters, I alit
On a great ship lightning-split
And speeded hither on the sigh   720
Of one who gave an enemy
His plank—then plunged aside to die.

THIRD SPIRIT

I sate beside a sage's bed
And the lamp was burning red
Near the book where he had fed,   725
When a Dream with plumes of flame
To his pillow hovering came,
And I knew it was the same
Which had kindled long ago
Pity, eloquence and woe;   730
And the world awhile below
Wore the shade its lustre made.
It has borne me here as fleet
As Desire's lightning feet:
I must ride it back ere morrow,   735
Or the sage will wake in sorrow.

FOURTH SPIRIT

On a Poet's lips I slept
Dreaming like a love-adept
In the sound his breathing kept;
Nor seeks nor finds he mortal blisses   740
But feeds on the aerial kisses
Of shapes that haunt thought's wildernesses.
He will watch from dawn to gloom
The lake-reflected sun illume
The yellow bees i' the ivy-bloom   745
Nor heed nor see, what things they be;
But from these create he can
Forms more real than living man,
Nurslings of immortality!—
One of these awakened me   750
And I sped to succour thee.

IONE

Behold'st thou not two shapes from the East and West
Come, as two doves to one beloved nest,
Twin nurslings of the all-sustaining air,
On swift still wings glide down the atmosphere?   755
And hark! their sweet, sad voices! 'tis despair
Mingled with love, and then dissolved in sound.—

PANTHEA

Canst thou speak, sister? all my words are drowned.

IONE

Their beauty gives me voice. See how they float
On their sustaining wings of skiey grain,   760
Orange and azure, deepening into gold:
Their soft smiles light the air like a star's fire.

CHORUS OF SPIRITS

Hast thou beheld the form of Love?

FIFTH SPIRIT

As over wide dominions
I sped, like some swift cloud that wings the wide air's wildernesses,
That planet-crested Shape swept by on lightning-braided
      pinions,[7]   765
Scattering the liquid joy of life from his ambrosial[8] tresses:
His footsteps paved the world with light—but as I past 'twas fading
      And hollow Ruin yawned behind. Great Sages bound in madness
And headless patriots and pale youths who perished unupbraiding,
      Gleamed in the Night I wandered o'er—till thou, O King of
      sadness,   770
Turned by thy smile the worst I saw to recollected gladness.

SIXTH SPIRIT

Ah, sister! Desolation is a delicate thing:
It walks not on the Earth, it floats not on the air,
But treads with silent footstep, and fans with silent wing
The tender hopes which in their hearts the best and gentlest
      bear,   775
Who soothed to false repose by the fanning plumes above
And the music-stirring motion of its soft and busy feet,
Dream visions of aerial joy, and call the monster, Love,
And wake, and find the shadow Pain, as he whom now we greet.

CHORUS

Though Ruin now Love's[9] shadow be,   780
      Following him destroyingly
            On Death's white and winged steed,
      Which the fleetest cannot flee—
            Trampling down both flower and weed,

---

7. Wings.
8. Divine or worthy of the gods.
9. It may be relevant to the thought
here (and in 763 and 778) that in
Hesiod's *Theogony*, Love is among the
children of Night (along with those
mentioned in the note to line 472 above).
The Spirits here describe the effects of
Love in the imperfect, unredeemed world.

Man and beast and foul and fair,   785
Like a tempest through the air;
Thou shalt quell this Horseman grim,
Woundless though in heart or limb.—

PROMETHEUS
Spirits! how know ye this shall be?

CHORUS
In the atmosphere we breathe—   790
As buds grow red when snow-storms flee
From spring gathering up beneath,
Whose mild winds shake, the elder brake[1]
And the wandering herdsmen know
That the white-thorn soon will blow—   795
Wisdom, Justice, Love and Peace,
When they struggle to increase,
Are to us as soft winds be
To shepherd-boys—the prophecy
Which begins and ends in thee.   800

IONE
Where are the Spirits fled?

PANTHEA
                     Only a sense
Remains of them, like the Omnipotence
Of music when the inspired voice and lute
Languish, ere yet the responses are mute
Which through the deep and labyrinthine soul,   805
Like echoes through long caverns, wind and roll.

PROMETHEUS
How fair these air-born shapes! and yet I feel
Most vain all hope but love, and thou art far,
Asia! who when my being overflowed
Wert like a golden chalice to bright wine   810
Which else had sunk into the thirsty dust.[2]
All things are still—alas! how heavily
This quiet morning weighs upon my heart;
Though I should dream, I could even sleep with grief
If slumber were denied not . . . I would fain   815
Be what it is my destiny to be,
The saviour and the strength of suffering man,
Or sink into the original gulph of things. . . .
There is no agony and no solace left;
Earth can console, Heaven can torment no more.   820

1. Thicket.
2. The simile suggests that Asia is in some sense the creation of Prometheus— that the human conception of the Ideal or Intellectual Beauty comes from the overflow of man's spiritual imagination.

PANTHEA

Hast thou forgotten one who watches thee
The cold dark night, and never sleeps but when
The shadow of thy spirit falls on her?

PROMETHEUS

I said all hope was vain but love—thou lovest . . .

PANTHEA

Deeply in truth—but the Eastern star looks white,   825
And Asia waits in that far Indian vale,
The scene of her sad exile—rugged once
And desolate and frozen like this ravine,
But now invested with fair flowers and herbs
And haunted by sweet airs and sounds, which flow   830
Among the woods and waters, from the ether[3]
Of her transforming presence—which would fade
If it were mingled not with thine.—Farewell!

END OF THE FIRST ACT.

ACT II

SCENE I

Morning. A lovely Vale in the Indian Caucasus. Asia *alone.*

ASIA

From all the blasts of Heaven thou hast descended—
Yes, like a spirit, like a thought which makes
Unwonted[4] tears throng to the horny[5] eyes
And beatings haunt the desolated heart
Which should have learnt repose,—thou hast descended   5
Cradled in tempests; thou dost wake, O Spring!
O child of many winds! As suddenly
Thou comest as the memory of a dream
Which now is sad because it hath been sweet;
Like genius, or like joy which riseth up   10
As from the earth, clothing with golden clouds
The desart of our life. . . .
This is the season, this the day, the hour;
At sunrise thou shouldst come, sweet sister mine,
Too long desired, too long delaying, come!   15
How like death-worms the wingless moments crawl!
The point of one white star[6] is quivering still
Deep in the orange light of widening morn
Beyond the purple mountains; through a chasm
Of wind-divided mist the darker lake   20
Reflects it—now it wanes—it gleams again

---

3. The air breathed by the gods.
4. Not usual.
5. Semi-opaque like horn.
6. I.e., Venus, the morning star.

As the waves fade, and as the burning threads
Of woven cloud unravel in pale air. . . .
'Tis lost! and through yon peaks of cloudlike snow
The roseate sunlight quivers—hear I not   25
The Æolian music of her[7] sea-green plumes
Winnowing[8] the crimson dawn?

                        [Panthea *enters*.]
              I feel, I see
Those eyes which burn through smiles that fade in tears
Like stars half quenched in mists of silver dew.
Beloved and most beautiful, who wearest   30
The shadow of that soul by which I live,
How late thou art! the sphered sun had climbed
The sea, my heart was sick with hope, before
The printless air felt thy belated plumes.

          PANTHEA
Pardon, great Sister! but my wings were faint   35
With the delight of a remembered dream
As are the noontide plumes of summer winds
Satiate with sweet flowers. I was wont to sleep
Peacefully, and awake refreshed and calm
Before the sacred Titan's fall and thy   40
Unhappy love, had made through use and pity
Both love and woe familiar to my heart
As they had grown to thine . . . erewhile[9] I slept
Under the glaucous[1] caverns of old Ocean,
Within dim bowers of green and purple moss;   45
Our young Ione's soft and milky arms
Locked then as now behind my dark moist hair
While my shut eyes and cheek were pressed within
The folded depth of her life-breathing bosom . . .
But not as now since I am made the wind   50
Which fails beneath the music that I bear
Of thy most wordless converse; since dissolved
Into the sense with which love talks, my rest
Was troubled and yet sweet—my waking hours
Too full of care and pain.

         ASIA
                  Lift up thine eyes   55
And let me read thy dream.—

         PANTHEA
                As I have said,
With our sea-sister at his feet I slept.
The mountain mists, condensing at our voice
Under the moon, had spread their snowy flakes

---

7. I.e., Panthea (*sister*, line 14).
8. Beating or flapping.
9. Formerly or some time ago.

1. Of a dull or pale green color passing into grayish blue.

From the keen ice shielding our linked sleep . . .   60
Then two dreams came.[2] One I remember not.
But in the other, his pale, wound-worn limbs
Fell from Prometheus, and the azure night
Grew radiant with the glory of that form
Which lives unchanged within, and his voice fell   65
Like music which makes giddy the dim brain
Faint with intoxication of keen joy:
"Sister of her whose footsteps pave the world
With loveliness—more fair than aught but her
Whose shadow thou art—lift thine eyes on me!"   70
I lifted them—the overpowering light
Of that immortal shape was shadowed o'er
By love; which, from his soft and flowing limbs
And passion-parted lips, and keen faint eyes
Steam'd forth like vaporous fire; an atmosphere   75
Which wrapt me in its all-dissolving power
As the warm ether of the morning sun
Wraps ere it drinks some cloud of wandering dew.
I saw not—heard not—moved not—only felt
His presence flow and mingle through my blood   80
Till it became his life and his grew mine
And I was thus absorbed—until it past
And like the vapours when the sun sinks down,
Gathering again in drops upon the pines
And tremulous as they, in the deep night   85
My being was condensed, and as the rays
Of thought were slowly gathered, I could hear
His voice, whose accents lingered ere they died
Like footsteps of far melody. Thy name,
Among the many sounds alone I heard   90
Of what might be articulate; though still
I listened through the night when sound was none.
Ione wakened then, and said to me:
"Canst thou divine what troubles me tonight?
I always knew what I desired before   95
Nor ever found delight to wish in vain.
But now I cannot tell thee what I seek;
I know not—something sweet since it is sweet
Even to desire—it is thy sport, false sister!
Thou hast discovered some inchantment old   100
Whose spells have stolen my spirit as I slept
And mingled it with thine;—for when just now
We kissed, I felt within thy parted lips
The sweet air that sustained me; and the warmth
Of the life-blood for loss of which I faint   105
Quivered between our intertwining arms."

2. The communication of these two action in this scene.
dreams of Panthea to Asia is the main

I answered not, for the Eastern star grew pale,
But fled to thee.

ASIA
    Thou speakest, but thy words
Are as the air. I feel them not. . . . oh, lift
Thine eyes that I may read his written soul!   110

PANTHEA
I lift them, though they droop beneath the load
Of that they would express—what canst thou see
But thine own fairest shadow imaged there?

ASIA
Thine eyes are like the deep blue, boundless Heaven
Contracted to two circles underneath   115
Their long, fine lashes—dark, far, measureless,—
Orb within orb, and line through line inwoven.—

PANTHEA
Why lookest thou as if a spirit past?

ASIA
There is a change: beyond their inmost depth
I see a shade—a shape—'tis He, arrayed   120
In the soft light of his own smiles which spread
Like radiance from the cloud-surrounded moon.
Prometheus, it is thou—depart not yet!
Say not those smiles that we shall meet again
Within that bright pavilion which their beams   125
Shall build o'er the waste world? The dream is told.
What shape[3] is that between us? Its rude hair
Roughens the wind that lifts it; its regard
Is wild and quick, yet 'tis a thing of air
For through its grey robe gleams the golden dew   130
Whose stars the noon has quench'd not.

DREAM
        Follow, follow!

PANTHEA
It is mine other dream.—

ASIA
      It disappears.

PANTHEA
It passes now into my mind. Methought
As we sate here the flower-infolding buds

---

3. This is the second dream, which re-
lates to the Spirits of the Hours that
are to usher in the fall of Jupiter and
the release of Prometheus, and to the
course of necessity.

Burst on yon lightning-blasted almond tree,[4]   135
When swift from the white Scythian wilderness
A wind swept forth wrinkling the Earth with frost . . .
I looked, and all the blossoms were blown down;
But on each leaf was stamped—as the blue bells
Of Hyacinth tell Apollo's written grief[5]—   140
O *follow, follow!*

ASIA
                    As you speak, your words
Fill, pause by pause my own forgotten sleep
With shapes. Methought among these lawns together
We wandered, underneath the young grey dawn,
And multitudes of dense white fleecy clouds   145
Were wandering in thick flocks along the mountains
Shepherded by the slow, unwilling wind;
And the white dew on the new-bladed grass,
Just piercing the dark earth, hung silently—
And there was more which I remember not;   150
But, on the shadows of the morning clouds
Athwart the purple mountain slope was written
Follow, O follow! as they vanished by,
And on each herb from which Heaven's dew had fallen
The like was stamped as with a withering fire;   155
A wind arose among the pines—it shook
The clinging music from their boughs, and then
Low, sweet, faint sounds, like the farewell of ghosts,
Were heard—O *follow, follow, follow me!*
And then I said: "Panthea, look on me."   160
But in the depth of those beloved eyes
Still I saw, *follow, follow!*

ECHO
                    Follow, follow!

PANTHEA
The crags, this clear spring morning, mock our voices,
As they were spirit-tongued.

ASIA
                    It is some being
Around the crags.—What fine clear sounds! O list!   165

4. Earl R. Wasserman has pointed out that in Pliny's *Natural History* (a book Shelley knew well) the almond tree is mentioned as the first tree to bud in winter (January) and to bear fruit (March), and that the prophet Jeremiah puns on the Hebrew word for "almond," which also means "hasten" (Jeremiah 1:11–12).

5. After Hyacinthus, beloved of Apollo, was killed by the jealous Zephyrus, Apollo changed his blood into a flower and wrote his lament, "Ai" ("alas" or "woe!" in Greek) on the petals.

ECHOES *unseen*
Echoes we—listen!
　　We cannot stay
　As dew-stars glisten
　　Then fade away—
　　　Child of Ocean!⁶ 　　　　170

ASIA
Hark! Spirits speak! The liquid responses
Of their aerial tongues yet sound.

PANTHEA
　　　　　　　　　I hear.

ECHOES
　O follow, follow,
　　As our voice recedeth
　Through the caverns hollow 　　　　175
　　Where the forest spreadeth;
　　　[*More distant.*]
　O follow, follow,
　Through the caverns hollow,
As the song floats, thou pursue
Where the wild bee never flew, 　　　　180
Through the noontide darkness deep,
By the odour breathing sleep
Of faint night flowers, and the waves
At the fountain-lighted caves,
While our music, wild and sweet, 　　　　185
Mocks thy gently-falling feet,
　　　Child of Ocean!

ASIA
Shall we pursue the sound?—It grows more faint
And distant.

PANTHEA
　List! the strain floats nearer now.

ECHOES
In the world unknown 　　　　190
　Sleeps a voice unspoken;⁷
By thy step alone
　Can its rest be broken,
　　Child of Ocean!

ASIA
How the notes sink upon the ebbing wind! 　　　　195

6. Asia, Panthea, and Ione are Oceanides, daughters of Oceanus, one of the first gods in all classical theogonies.
7. Such descriptions in negatives (see *world unknown*, line 190) suggest that the echoes are leading Asia and Panthea from the realm of actuality into a world of potentiality (see D. J. Hughes' essay, pp. 603–620).

ECHOES

O follow, follow!
Through the caverns hollow,
As the song floats thou pursue,
By the woodland noontide dew,
By the forests, lakes and fountains,   200
Through the many-folded mountains,
To the rents and gulphs and chasms
Where the Earth reposed from spasms
On the day when He and thou
Parted—to commingle now,   205
     Child of Ocean!

ASIA

Come, sweet Panthea, link thy hand in mine,
And follow, ere the voices fade away.

SCENE II

A *Forest, intermingled with Rocks and Caverns. Asia and* Panthea
pass into it. Two young Fauns are sitting on a Rock, listening.

SEMICHORUS I OF SPIRITS

The path through which that lovely twain[8]
     Have past, by cedar, pine and yew,[9]
     And each dark tree that ever grew
     Is curtained out from Heaven's wide blue;
Nor sun nor moon nor wind nor rain   5
          Can pierce its interwoven bowers;
     Nor aught save when some cloud of dew,
Drifted along the earth-creeping breeze
Between the trunks of the hoar[1] trees,
     Hangs each a pearl in the pale flowers   10
     Of the green laurel,[2] blown anew;
And bends and then fades silently
One frail and fair anemone;[3]
Or when some star of many a one
That climbs and wanders through steep night,   15
Has found the cleft through which alone
Beams fall from high those depths upon,
Ere it is borne away, away,
By the swift Heavens that cannot stay—
It scatters drops of golden light   20
Like lines of rain that ne'er unite;
And the gloom divine is all around
And underneath is the mossy ground.

8. I.e., Asia and Panthea.
9. Though the yew tree is commonly
associated with death, the *cedar* and
pine—evergreens with more hopeful
symbolism—suggest that Shelley's de-
scription aims at a neutral portrayal of
the gloom divine (line 22) of the path
leading down to Demogorgon's under-
world.
1. Old and venerable.
2. Also called "bay," a symbol of suc-
cess in poetry; *blown:* blooming.
3. Windflower; it belongs to the butter-
cup family.

SEMICHORUS II
There the voluptuous nightingales
  Are awake through all the broad noonday.   25
When one with bliss or sadness fails—
    And through the windless ivy-boughs,
   Sick with sweet love, droops dying away
On its mate's music-panting bosom—
Another from the swinging blossom,   30
    Watching to catch the languid close
  Of the last strain, then lifts on high
  The wings of the weak melody,
Till some new strain of feeling bear
  The song, and all the woods are mute;   35
When there is heard through the dim air
The rush of wings, and rising there
  Like many a lake-surrounded flute,
Sounds overflow the listener's brain
So sweet that joy is almost pain.   40

    SEMICHORUS I
There those inchanted eddies play
  Of echoes, music-tongued, which draw,
  By Demogorgon's mighty law
  With melting rapture or sweet awe,
All spirits on that secret way,   45
  As inland boats are driven to Ocean
Down streams made strong with mountain-thaw;
    And first there comes a gentle sound
   To those in talk or slumber bound,
  And wakes the destined—soft emotion   50
Attracts, impels them: those who saw
  Say from the breathing Earth behind
  There steams a plume-uplifting wind
Which drives them on their path, while they
  Believe their own swift wings and feet   55
The sweet desires within obey:
And so they float upon their way,
Until still sweet but loud and strong
The storm of sound is driven along,
    Sucked up and hurrying—as they fleet   60
   Behind its gathering billows meet
And to the fatal mountain bear
Like clouds amid the yielding air.[4]

    FIRST FAUN
Canst thou imagine where those spirits live
Which make such delicate music in the woods?   65
We haunt within the least frequented caves
And closest coverts,[5] and we know these wilds,

4. Lines 24–63 deal with sounds—following the closing out of light and the sense of sight in the scene's opening lines.
5. Most secret shelters or thickets.

Yet never meet them, though we hear them oft:
Where may they hide themselves?

SECOND FAUN

'Tis hard to tell—
I have heard those more skilled in spirits say,   70
The bubbles which the enchantment of the sun
Sucks from the pale faint water-flowers that pave
The oozy bottom of clear lakes and pools
Are the pavilions where such dwell and float
Under the green and golden atmosphere   75
Which noontide kindles through the woven leaves,
And when these burst, and the thin fiery air,
The which they breathed within those lucent[6] domes,
Ascends to flow like meteors through the night,
They ride on it, and rein their headlong speed,   80
And bow their burning crests, and glide in fire
Under the waters of the Earth again.[7]

FIRST FAUN

If such live thus, have others other lives
Under pink blossoms or within the bells
Of meadow flowers, or folded violets deep,   85
Or on their dying odours, when they die,
Or in the sunlight of the sphered dew?

SECOND FAUN

Aye, many more, which we may well divine.
But should we stay to speak, noontide would come,
And thwart Silenus[8] find his goats undrawn   90
And grudge to sing those wise and lovely songs
Of fate and chance and God, and Chaos old,
And love and the chained Titan's woful doom
And how he shall be loosed, and make the Earth
One brotherhood—delightful strains which cheer   95
Our solitary twilights, and which charm
To silence the unenvying nightingales.

SCENE III

A *Pinnacle of Rock among Mountains.* Asia *and* Panthea.

PANTHEA

Hither the sound has borne us—to the realm
Of Demogorgon, and the mighty portal,
Like a volcano's meteor-breathing chasm,
Whence the oracular vapour is hurled up

6. Shining or luminous.
7. Lines 70–82 portray the hydrogen cycle, as it was understood in Shelley's day, explaining the origin of the swamp gas that, when ignited, becomes the *ignis fatuus* or will-o'-the-wisp.

8. A demigod who became the nurse, preceptor, and attendant of Bacchus, Silenus is generally represented as a fat and jolly old man riding an ass, crowned with flowers, and always intoxicated; *undrawn:* unmilked.

Which lonely men drink wandering in their youth   5
And call truth, virtue, love, genius or joy—
That maddening wine of life, whose dregs they drain
To deep intoxication, and uplift
Like Mænads who cry loud, Evoe! Evoe![9]
The voice which is contagion to the world.   10

ASIA

Fit throne for such a Power! Magnificent!
How glorious art thou, Earth! and if thou be
The shadow of some Spirit lovelier still,
Though evil stain its work and it should be
Like its creation, weak yet beautiful,   15
I could fall down and worship that and thee.[1]—
Even now my heart adoreth.—Wonderful!
Look Sister, ere the vapour dim thy brain;
Beneath is a wide plain of billowy mist,
As a lake, paving in the morning sky,   20
With azure waves which burst in silver light,
Some Indian vale . . . Behold it, rolling on
Under the curdling winds, and islanding
The peak whereon we stand—midway, around
Encinctured[2] by the dark and blooming forests,   25
Dim twilight lawns and stream-illumed caves
And wind-inchanted shapes of wandering mist;
And far on high the keen sky-cleaving mountains
From icy spires of sunlike radiance fling
The dawn, as lifted Ocean's dazzling spray,   30
From some Atlantic islet scattered up,
Spangles the wind with lamp-like water drops.
The vale is girdled with their walls—a howl
Of cataracts from their thaw-cloven ravines
Satiates the listening wind, continuous, vast,   35
Awful as silence.—Hark! the rushing snow!
The sun-awakened avalanche! whose mass,
Thrice sifted by the storm, had gathered there
Flake after flake, in Heaven-defying minds
As thought by thought is piled, till some great truth   40
Is loosened, and the nations echo round
Shaken to their roots: as do the mountains now.[3]

---

9. Maenads were fanatic female wor-
shipers of Dionysus, Greek god of wine
(Roman Bacchus); when in an intoxicated
frenzy, they would surge through the
wilderness, crying *"Evoe!"* and killing
every living thing in their path. (See
Euripides' late drama *The Bacchae*.)
1. The central imagery in lines 12–16
echoes *Paradise Lost*, where Raphael
implies to Adam that Earth may be "but
the shadow of Heav'n, and things therein/
Each to other like, more than on earth

is thought" (V.574–576).
2. Belted.
3. This simile is one of the best ex-
amples of the reversal of imagery that
Shelley mentions in the fourth paragraph
of the Preface, for here an external nat-
ural event (the avalanche, 36–38) is
compared to a figure "drawn from the
operations of the human mind"—in this
case, the slow growth of new concepts in
Heaven-defying minds until there is an
intellectual revolution.

PANTHEA

Look, how the gusty sea of mist is breaking
In crimson foam, even at our feet! it rises
As Ocean at the inchantment of the moon   45
Round foodless men wrecked on some oozy isle.

ASIA

The fragments of the cloud are scattered up—
The wind that lifts them disentwines my hair—
Its billows now sweep o'er mine eyes—my brain
Grows dizzy—I see thin shapes within the mist.   50

PANTHEA

A countenance with beckoning smiles—there burns
An azure fire within its golden locks—
Another and another—hark! they speak!

SONG OF SPIRITS

To the Deep, to the Deep,
        Down, down!   55
Through the shade of Sleep,
Through the cloudy strife
Of Death and of Life;
Through the veil and the bar
Of things which seem and are,   60
Even to the steps of the remotest Throne,
        Down, down!

While the sound,[4] whirls around,
        Down, down!
As the fawn draws the hound,   65
As the lightning the vapour,
As a weak moth the taper;
Death, Despair; Love, Sorrow;
Time both; to-day, to-morrow;
As steel obeys the Spirit of the stone,[5]   70
        Down, down!

Through the grey, void Abysm,
        Down, down!
Where the air is no prism[6]
And the moon and stars are not   75
And the cavern-crags wear not
The radiance of Heaven,
Nor the gloom to Earth given;
Where there is One pervading, One alone,
        Down, down!   80

---

4. Again, the comma is metrical (mark-
ing a pause after the internal rhyme)
rather than grammatical.
5. The magnet draws the steel; the fawn
attracts the hound (65); there is mutual
attraction between lightning and vapour,
moth and taper (candle), Death and
Despair, etc.
6. I.e., out of the earth's atmosphere,
which, acting as a prism, breaks the pure
white sunlight of eternity into the varie-
gated colors of mortal perception.

In the depth of the Deep,
            Down, down!
Like veil'd Lightning asleep,
Like the spark nursed in embers,
The last look Love remembers,   85
Like a diamond which shines
On the dark wealth of mines,[7]
A spell is treasured but for thee alone.
            Down, down!

We have bound thee, we guide thee   90
            Down, down!
With the bright form beside thee—
Resist not the weakness—
Such strength is in meekness—
That the Eternal, the Immortal,   95
Must unloose through life's portal
The snake-like Doom coiled underneath his throne
            By that alone!

SCENE IV

The Cave of Demogorgon. Asia *and* Panthea.

PANTHEA
What veiled form sits on that ebon throne?

ASIA
The veil has fallen! . . .

PANTHEA
                    I see a mighty Darkness
Filling the seat of power; and rays of gloom
Dart round, as light from the meridian Sun,
Ungazed upon and shapeless—neither limb   5
Nor form—nor outline;[8] yet we feel it is
A living Spirit.

DEMOGORGON
Ask what thou wouldst know.

ASIA
What canst thou tell?

DEMOGORGON
                    All things thou dar'st demand.

7. According to eighteenth-century scientists, the diamond was phosphorescent, first absorbing light and then glowing in the dark (see Robert A. Hartley, *Notes and Queries*, n.s. 20:293–294 [August 1973]).

8. Shelley's description of Demogorgon echoes Milton's description of Death in *Paradise Lost* (II.666–673), beginning, "The other shape,/ If shape it might be call'd that shape had none/ Distinguishable in member, joynt, or limb. . . ."

ASIA

Who made the living world?

DEMOGORGON
                    God.

ASIA
                                    Who made all
That it contains—thought, passion, reason, will,   10
Imagination?[9]

DEMOGORGON
God, Almighty God.

ASIA
Who made that sense which, when the winds of Spring
In rarest visitation, or the voice
Of one beloved heard in youth alone,
Fills the faint eyes with falling tears, which dim   15
The radiant looks of unbewailing flowers,
And leaves this peopled earth a solitude
When it returns no more?

DEMOGORGON
                    Merciful God.

ASIA
And who made terror, madness, crime, remorse,
Which from the links of the great chain of things   20
To every thought within the mind of man
Sway and drag heavily—and each one reels
Under the load towards the pit of death;
Abandoned hope, and love that turns to hate;
And self-contempt, bitterer to drink than blood;   25
Pain whose unheeded and familiar speech
Is howling and keen shrieks, day after day;
And Hell, or the sharp fear of Hell?

DEMOGORGON
                    He reigns.

ASIA
Utter his name—a world pining in pain
Asks but his name; curses shall drag him down.   30

DEMOGORGON
He reigns.

ASIA
I feel, I know it—who?

9. The metaphysical implication of Asia's statement is that all the universe is made up of mental activities, yet this—like Asia's other assertions—is neither con- firmed nor denied by Demogorgon and should be seen as a useful myth rather than a declaration of Shelley's beliefs about reality.

DEMOGORGON
He reigns.

ASIA

Who reigns? There was the Heaven and Earth at first
And Light and Love;—then Saturn, from whose throne
Time fell, an envious shadow;[1] such the state
Of the earth's primal spirits beneath his sway   35
As the calm joy of flowers and living leaves
Before the wind or sun has withered them
And semivital worms; but he refused
The birthright of their being, knowledge, power,
The skill which wields the elements, the thought   40
Which pierces this dim Universe like light,
Self-empire and the majesty of love,
For thirst of which they fainted. Then Prometheus
Gave wisdom, which is strength, to Jupiter
And with this law alone: "Let man be free,"   45
Clothed him with the dominion of wide Heaven.
To know nor faith nor love nor law, to be
Omnipotent but friendless, is to reign;
And Jove now reigned; for on the race of man
First famine and then toil and then disease,   50
Strife, wounds, and ghastly death unseen before,
Fell; and the unseasonable seasons drove,
With alternating shafts of frost and fire,
Their shelterless, pale tribes to mountain caves;
And in their desart[2] hearts fierce wants he sent   55
And mad disquietudes, and shadows idle
Of unreal good, which levied mutual war,
So ruining the lair wherein they raged.
Prometheus saw, and waked the legioned[3] hopes
Which sleep within folded Elysian flowers,   60
Nepenthe, Moly, Amaranth, fadeless blooms;[4]
That they might hide with thin and rainbow wings
The shape of Death; and Love he sent to bind
The disunited tendrils of that vine
Which bears the wine of life, the human heart;   65
And he tamed fire, which like some beast of prey
Most terrible, but lovely, played beneath
The frown of man, and tortured to his will
Iron and gold, the slaves and signs of power,

1. Shelley plays on the Greek names for Saturn (Kronos), in whose reign was the mythical Golden Age, and Time (Chronos).
2. Forsaken or lonely.
3. Arrayed in legions, as armies.
4. *Elysian:* conducive to complete happiness (from "Elysium," the abode of the virtuous Greeks after death); *Nepenthe:* a drug mentioned in the *Odyssey* (IV.220ff.) capable of banishing grief or trouble; *Moly:* a magical herb with a white flower and a black root, given to Odysseus by Hermes as a charm against the sorceries of Circe (*Odyssey*, X.302ff.); *Amaranth:* from the Greek adjective meaning "everlasting," "not fading," or "incorruptible" (Cf. *Paradise Lost*, III. 352–360).

And gems and poisons, and all subtlest forms 70
Hidden beneath the mountains and the waves.
He gave man speech, and speech created thought,
Which is the measure of the Universe;
And Science struck the thrones of Earth and Heaven
Which shook but fell not; and the harmonious mind 75
Poured itself forth in all-prophetic song,
And music lifted up the listening spirit
Until it walked, exempt from mortal care,
Godlike, o'er the clear billows of sweet sound;
And human hands first mimicked[5] and then mocked 80
With moulded limbs more lovely than its own
The human form, till marble grew divine,
And mothers, gazing, drank the love men see
Reflected in their race, behold, and perish.[6]
He told the hidden power of herbs and springs, 85
And Disease drank and slept—Death grew like sleep.—
He taught the implicated[7] orbits woven
Of the wide-wandering stars, and how the Sun
Changes his lair, and by what secret spell
The pale moon is transformed, when her broad eye 90
Gazes not on the interlunar[8] sea;
He taught to rule, as life directs the limbs,
The tempest-winged chariots of the Ocean,[9]
And the Celt[1] knew the Indian. Cities then
Were built, and through their snow-like columns flowed 95
The warm winds, and the azure æther shone,
And the blue sea and shadowy hills were seen . . .
Such the alleviations of his state
Prometheus gave to man—for which he hangs
Withering in destined pain—but who rains down 100
Evil, the immedicable plague, which while
Man looks on his creation like a God
And sees that it is glorious, drives him on,
The wreck of his own will, the scorn of Earth,
The outcast, the abandoned, the alone?— 105
Not Jove: while yet his frown shook Heaven, aye when
His adversary from adamantine[2] chains
Cursed him, he trembled like a slave. Declare
Who is his master? Is he too a slave?

---

5. Copied or faithfully reproduced.
6. Swinburne suggested that lines 83–84 describe the positive prenatal influence on children whose mothers had viewed sculptures that achieved such idealized beauty that men fell desperately in love with them. He compares Virgil's phrase on the sorcery of love: "Ut vidi, ut perii (*Eclogues*, VIII.41; "As I saw, how I was lost!").
7. Intertwined or entangled.

8. Dark; the time between the old and the new moon.
9. *tempest . . . Ocean:* a periphrasis for "boats."
1. From classical Greek times to Shelley's day the term "Celts" meant any of the barbarians to the north of the Graeco-Roman Mediterranean civilization.
2. Incapable of being broken.

DEMOGORGON

All spirits are enslaved who serve things evil: 110
Thou knowest if Jupiter be such or no.

ASIA

Whom calledst thou God?

DEMOGORGON

               I spoke but as ye speak—
For Jove is the supreme of living things.

ASIA

Who is the master of the slave?

DEMORORGON

               —If the Abysm
Could vomit forth its secrets:—but a voice   115
Is wanting, the deep truth is imageless;
For what would it avail to bid thee gaze
On the revolving world? what to bid speak
Fate, Time, Occasion, Chance and Change? To these
All things are subject but eternal Love.[3]   120

ASIA

So much I asked before, and my heart gave
The response thou hast given; and of such truths
Each to itself must be the oracle.—
One more demand . . . and do thou answer me
As my own soul would answer, did it know   125
That which I ask.—Prometheus shall arise
Henceforth the Sun of this rejoicing world:
When shall the destined hour arrive?

DEMORORGON

               Behold!

ASIA

The rocks are cloven, and through the purple night
I see Cars drawn by rainbow-winged steeds   130
Which trample the dim winds—in each there stands
A wild-eyed charioteer, urging their flight.
Some look behind, as fiends pursued them there
And yet I see no shapes but the keen stars:
Others with burning eyes lean forth, and drink   135
With eager lips the wind of their own speed
As if the thing they loved fled on before,

---

3. Demogorgon makes sense only if we read Shelley's use of "Love" here as Eros or Desire; the *desire* for good eternally outlasts all the evils of mortality.

And now—even now they clasped it; their bright locks
Stream like a comet's flashing hair: they all
Sweep onward.—

DEMOGORGON
                  These are the immortal Hours   140
Of whom thou didst demand.—One waits for thee.

ASIA
A Spirit with a dreadful countenance
Checks its dark chariot by the craggy gulph.
Unlike thy brethren, ghastly charioteer,
What art thou? whither wouldst thou bear me? Speak!   145

SPIRIT
I am the shadow of a destiny
More dread than is mine aspect—ere yon planet
Has set, the Darkness which ascends with me
Shall wrap in lasting night Heaven's kingless throne.

ASIA
What meanest thou?

PANTHEA
                  That terrible shadow⁴ floats   150
Up from its throne, as may the lurid⁵ smoke
Of earthquake-ruined cities o'er the sea.—
Lo! it ascends the Car . . . the coursers fly
Terrified; watch its path among the stars
Blackening the night!

ASIA
                  Thus I am answered—strange!   155

PANTHEA
See, near the verge⁶ another chariot stays;
An ivory shell inlaid with crimson fire
Which comes and goes within its sculptured rim
Of delicate strange tracery—the young Spirit
That guides it, has the dovelike eyes of hope.   160
How its soft smiles attract the soul!—as light
Lures winged insects through the lampless air.

SPIRIT
    My coursers are fed with the lightning,
        They drink of the whirlwind's stream
    And when the red morning is brightning   165
        They bathe in the fresh sunbeam;
        They have strength for their swiftness, I deem:
        Then ascend with me, daughter of Ocean.

---

4. I.e., Demogorgon.   darkness.
5. Shining with a red glow or glare amid   6. Outermost limits, horizon.

I desire—and their speed makes night kindle;
 I fear—they outstrip the Typhoon;   170
Ere the cloud piled on Atlas[7] can dwindle
  We encircle the earth and the moon:
  We shall rest from long labours at noon:
   Then ascend with me, daughter of Ocean.

SCENE V

The Car pauses within a Cloud on the Top of a snowy Mountain.
Asia, Panthea *and the* Spirit of the Hour.

SPIRIT

On the brink of the night and the morning
 My coursers are wont to respire,[8]
But the Earth has just whispered a warning
 That their flight must be swifter than fire:
 They shall drink the hot speed of desire!   5

ASIA

Thou breathest on their nostrils—but my breath
Would give them swifter speed.

SPIRIT

      Alas, it could not.

PANTHEA

O Spirit! pause and tell whence is the light
Which fills the cloud? the sun is yet unrisen.

SPIRIT

The sun will rise not until noon.—Apollo   10
Is held in Heaven by wonder—and the light
Which fills this vapour, as the aerial hue
Of fountain-gazing roses fills the water,
Flows from thy mighty sister.

PANTHEA

      Yes, I feel . . .

ASIA

What is it with thee, sister? Thou art pale.   15

PANTHEA

How thou art changed! I dare not look on thee;
I feel, but see thee not. I scarce endure
The radiance of thy beauty. Some good change
Is working in the elements which suffer

---

7. Atlas, a Titan and brother of Prometheus, refused hospitality to Perseus, who (by means of Medusa's head) changed Atlas into a mountain. (The real mountain was so high that the ancients believed the heavens rested on its top and Atlas supported the world on his shoulders.)

8. I.e., usually rest or slow down.

Thy presence thus unveiled.—The Nereids[9] tell   20
That on the day when the clear hyaline[1]
Was cloven at thy uprise, and thou didst stand
Within a veined shell, which floated on
Over the calm floor of the chrystal sea,
Among the Ægean isles, and by the shores   25
Which bear thy name,[2] love, like the atmosphere
Of the sun's fire filling the living world,
Burst from thee, and illumined Earth and Heaven
And the deep ocean and the sunless caves,
And all that dwells within them; till grief cast   30
Eclipse upon the soul from which it came:
Such art thou now, nor is it I alone,
Thy sister, thy companion, thine own chosen one,
But the whole world which seeks thy sympathy.
Hearest thou not sounds i' the air which speak the love 35
Of all articulate beings? Feelest thou not
The inanimate winds enamoured of thee?—List!

[*Music.*]

ASIA

Thy words are sweeter than aught else but his
Whose echoes they are—yet all love is sweet,
Given or returned; common as light is love   40
And its familiar voice wearies not ever.
Like the wide Heaven, the all-sustaining air,
It makes the reptile equal to the God . . .
They who inspire it most are fortunate
As I am now; but those who feel it most   45
Are happier still, after long sufferings
As I shall soon become.

PANTHEA
List! Spirits speak.

VOICE (*in the air, singing*)
Life of Life! thy lips enkindle
    With their love the breath between them
And thy smiles before they dwindle   50
    Make the cold air fire; then screen them
In those looks where whoso gazes
Faints, entangled in their mazes.

---

9. Water nymphs who were daughters of
Nereus (the Old Man of the Sea) and
Doris (Hesiod's *Theogony*).
1. The glassy, transparent surface of the
sea.
2. *shores . . . name:* In his syncretic way
of treating myths, Shelley draws upon
various traditions of Aphrodite/Venus
mentioned by Cicero. One saw her as the
daughter of Celus (Sky) and Light, an-
other saw her rising from the froth of
the sea and standing "within a veined
shell," and still another located her birth
near Tyre and identified her with Astarte
of the Phoenicians and Syrians. But by
naming her Asia, Shelley frees his crea-
tion from the specific limitations associ-
ated with the myths of Aphrodite/Venus.

Child of Light! thy limbs are burning
   Through the vest which seems to hide them   55
As the radiant lines of morning
   Through the clouds ere they divide them,
And this atmosphere divinest
Shrouds thee wheresoe'er thou shinest.

Fair are others;—none beholds thee   60
   But thy voice sounds low and tender
Like the fairest—for it folds thee
   From the sight, that liquid splendour,
And all feel, yet see thee never
As I feel now, lost forever!   65

Lamp of Earth! where'er thou movest
   Its dim shapes are clad with brightness
And the souls of whom thou lovest
   Walk upon the winds with lightness
Till they fail, as I am failing,   70
Dizzy, lost . . . yet unbewailing!

     ASIA
   My soul is an enchanted Boat
   Which, like a sleeping swan, doth float
Upon the silver waves of thy sweet singing,
   And thine doth like an Angel sit   75
   Beside the helm conducting it
Whilst all the winds with melody are ringing.
   It seems to float ever—forever—
   Upon that many winding River
   Between mountains, woods, abysses,   80
   A Paradise of wildernesses,
Till like one in slumber bound
Borne to the Ocean, I float down, around,
Into a Sea profound, of ever-spreading sound.

   Meanwhile thy Spirit lifts its pinions[3]   85
   In Music's most serene dominions,
Catching the winds that fan that happy Heaven.
   And we sail on, away, afar,
   Without a course—without a star—
But by the instinct of sweet Music driven   90
   Till, through Elysian garden islets
   By thee, most beautiful of pilots,
   Where never mortal pinnace[4] glided,
   The boat of my desire is guided—
Realms where the air we breathe is Love   95
Which in the winds and on the waves doth move,
Harmonizing this Earth with what we feel above.

---

3. Wings.   4. A small, light boat.

We have past Age's icy caves,
And Manhood's dark and tossing waves
And Youth's smooth ocean, smiling to betray;   100
Beyond the glassy gulphs we flee
Of shadow-peopled Infancy,
Through Death and Birth to a diviner day,[5]
A Paradise of vaulted bowers
Lit by downward-gazing flowers   105
And watery paths that wind between
Wildernesses calm and green,
Peopled by shapes too bright to see,
And rest, having beheld—somewhat like thee,
Which walk upon the sea, and chaunt melodiously!   110

END OF THE SECOND ACT.

ACT III

SCENE I

Heaven. Jupiter *on his Throne;* Thetis *and the other Deities assembled.*

JUPITER

Ye congregated Powers of Heaven who share
The glory and the strength of him ye serve,
Rejoice! henceforth I am omnipotent.
All else has been subdued to me—alone
The soul of man, like unextinguished fire,   5
Yet burns towards Heaven with fierce reproach and doubt
And lamentation and reluctant prayer,
Hurling up insurrection, which might make
Our antique empire insecure, though built
On eldest faith, and Hell's coeval,[6] fear.   10
And though my curses through the pendulous air
Like snow on herbless peaks, fall flake by flake[7]
And cling to it—though under my wrath's night
It climb the crags of life, step after step,
Which wound it, as ice wounds unsandalled feet,   15
It yet remains supreme o'er misery,
Aspiring . . . unrepressed; yet soon to fall:
Even now have I begotten a strange wonder,
That fatal Child,[8] the terror of the Earth,

---

5. The reversal of time and mortal aging described here parallels a myth in Plato's *Statesman* (270e and 271b).
6. Equal in antiquity or contemporary in origin.
7. Jupiter's picture of his curses, falling "flake by flake," echoes Asia's simile of the avalanche of change loosed after building up "flake after flake, in Heaven-defying minds" (II.iii.39), and thus prepares for Jupiter's overthrow; *pendulous:* floating in space or undulatory.
8. Jupiter describes at lines 37–48 more fully how he begot this child by raping Thetis. The present speech is an example of irony in the classical sense in which everything the speaker says is true in a way he does not comprehend.

Who waits but till the destined Hour arrive, 20
Bearing from Demogorgon's vacant throne
The dreadful might of ever living limbs
Which clothed that awful spirit unbeheld—
To redescend and trample out the spark . . .

Pour forth Heaven's wine, Idæan Ganymede,[9] 25
And let it fill the dædal[1] cups like fire
And from the flower-inwoven soil divine
Ye all triumphant harmonies arise
As dew from Earth under the twilight stars;
Drink! be the nectar circling through your veins 30
The soul of joy, ye everliving Gods,
Till exultation burst in one wide voice
Like music from Elysian winds.—
                              And thou
Ascend beside me, veiled in the light
Of the desire which makes thee one with me, 35
Thetis,[2] bright Image of Eternity!—
When thou didst cry, "Insufferable might!
God! spare me! I sustain not the quick flames,
The penetrating presence;[3] all my being,
Like him whom the Numidian seps did thaw 40
Into a dew with poison,[4] is dissolved,
Sinking through its foundations"—even then
Two mighty spirits, mingling, made a third
Mightier than either—which unbodied now
Between us, floats, felt although unbeheld, 45
Waiting the incarnation, which ascends—
Hear ye the thunder of the fiery wheels
Griding[5] the winds?—from Demogorgon's throne.—
Victory! victory! Feel'st thou not, O World,
The Earthquake of his chariot thundering up 50
Olympus?
[*The Car of the* Hour *arrives.* Demogorgon *descends
    and moves towards the Throne of* Jupiter.]
          Awful Shape, what art thou? Speak!

                  DEMOGORGON
Eternity—demand no direr name.
Descend, and follow me down the abyss;
I am thy child, as thou wert Saturn's child,

---

9. While tending his father's flocks on Mt. Ida, *Ganymede* was carried away by an eagle to satisfy Jupiter's lust; he replaced Hebe as cupbearer to the gods.
1. Displaying artistic cunning or fertile invention; variously adorned (from Daedalus, the mythical craftsman).
2. A sea nymph (nereid) who was also the mother of Achilles by Peleus.
3. *sustain . . . presence:* Semele, daughter of Cadmus, was consumed by fire

when—through a trick of Hera (Juno)—Zeus (Jupiter) was bound by an oath to lie with her in his own undisguised form. (The child of the union was Dionysus [Bacchus]).
4. *him . . . poison:* In Lucan's *Pharsalia* (IX.762–788) Sabellus dissolves when bitten by a seps, a legendary poisonous snake, while crossing the Numidian desert.
5. Clashing or grating against.

Mightier than thee;[6] and we must dwell together　　　　55
Henceforth in darkness.—Lift thy lightnings not.
The tyranny of Heaven none may retain,
Or reassume, or hold succeeding thee . . .
Yet if thou wilt—as 'tis the destiny
Of trodden worms to writhe till they are dead—　　　　60
Put forth thy might.

JUPITER

　　　　　　　Detested prodigy!
Even thus beneath the deep Titanian prisons[7]
I trample thee! . . . Thou lingerest?

　　　　　　　　　　　　Mercy! mercy!
No pity—no release, no respite! . . . Oh,
That thou wouldst make mine enemy my judge.　　　　65
Even where he hangs, seared by my long revenge
On Caucasus—he would not doom me thus.—
Gentle and just and dreadless, is he not
The monarch of the world?—what then art thou? . . .
No refuge! no appeal— . . .

　　　　　　　　　　Sink with me then—　　　　70
We two will sink in the wide waves of ruin
Even as a vulture and a snake outspent
Drop, twisted in inextricable fight,
Into a shoreless sea.—Let Hell unlock
Its mounded Oceans of tempestuous fire,　　　　75
And whelm on them into the bottomless void
The desolated world and thee and me,
The conqueror and the conquered, and the wreck
Of that for which they combated.

　　　　　　　　　　Ai! Ai!
The elements obey me not . . . I sink . . .　　　　80
Dizzily down—ever, forever, down—
And, like a cloud, mine enemy above
Darkens my fall with victory!—Ai! Ai!

SCENE II

The Mouth of a great River in the Island Atlantis. Ocean *is discovered reclining near the Shore;* Apollo *stands beside him.*

OCEAN

He fell, thou sayest, beneath his conqueror's frown?

6. *I am thy child . . . than thee:* In Hesiod's *Theogony* (lines 886–900)—and, hence, at the very beginning of the literary transmission of the Greek myths—there is the stated possibility that Zeus (Jupiter) will be overthrown by his second child by Metis (Wisdom), an "unruly son, the future king of gods and men."

7. The Titans, after their overthrow by Jupiter and the Olympian gods, were imprisoned in Tartarus, so far below the earth that it would take an anvil ten days to fall there from the earth (the same distance as from heaven to earth).

APOLLO

Aye, when the strife was ended which made dim
The orb I rule, and shook the solid stars.[8]
The terrors of his eye illumined Heaven
With sanguine[9] light, through the thick ragged skirts   5
Of the victorious Darkness, as he fell;
Like the last glare of day's red agony
Which from a rent among the fiery clouds
Burns far along the tempest-wrinkled Deep.

OCEAN

He sunk to the abyss? to the dark void?   10

APOLLO

An eagle so, caught in some bursting cloud
On Caucasus, his thunder-baffled wings
Entangled in the whirlwind, and his eyes
Which gazed on the undazzling sun, now blinded
By the white lightning, while the ponderous hail   15
Beats on his struggling form which sinks at length
Prone, and the aerial ice clings over it.

OCEAN

Henceforth the fields of Heaven-reflecting sea
Which are my realm, will heave, unstain'd with blood
Beneath the uplifting winds—like plains of corn   20
Swayed by the summer air; my streams will flow
Round many-peopled continents and round
Fortunate isles; and from their glassy thrones
Blue Proteus and his humid Nymphs shall mark
The shadow of fair ships, as mortals see   25
The floating bark of the light-laden moon
With that white star,[10] its sightless pilot's crest,
Borne down the rapid sunset's ebbing sea;
Tracking their path no more by blood and groans;
And desolation, and the mingled voice   30
Of slavery and command—but by the light
Of wave-reflected flowers, and floating odours,
And music soft, and mild, free, gentle voices,
That sweetest music, such as spirits love.

APOLLO

And I shall gaze not on the deeds which make   35
My mind obscure with sorrow, as Eclipse
Darkens the sphere I guide—but list, I hear
The small, clear, silver lute of the young spirit
That sits i' the Morning star.

---

8. The *orb* is the sun, and the *solid stars*
are the fixed stars (those which were
thought not to move).

9. Blood-red.
10. Venus, the *morning star* of line 39.

OCEAN

Thou must away?

Thy steeds will pause at even—till when, farewell.   40
The loud Deep calls me home even now, to feed it
With azure calm out of the emerald urns
Which stand forever full beside my throne.
Behold the Nereids under the green sea,
Their wavering limbs borne on the windlike stream,   45
Their white arms lifted o'er their streaming hair
With garlands pied[1] and starry sea-flower crowns,
Hastening to grace their mighty Sister's joy.

[A sound of waves is heard.]

It is the unpastured Sea hung'ring for Calm.
Peace, Monster—I come now! Farewell.

APOLLO

Farewell!—   50

SCENE III

Caucasus. Prometheus, Hercules,[2] Ione, *the* Earth, Spirits. Asia *and* Panthea *borne in the Car with the* Spirit of the Hour. Hercules *unbinds* Prometheus, *who descends*.

HERCULES

Most glorious among Spirits, thus doth strength
To wisdom, courage, and long suffering love,
And thee, who art the form they animate,
Minister, like a slave.

PROMETHEUS

Thy gentle words

Are sweeter even than freedom long desired   5
And long delayed.

Asia, thou light of life,

Shadow of beauty unbeheld; and ye
Fair sister nymphs, who made long years of pain
Sweet to remember through your love and care:
Henceforth we will not part. There is a Cave   10
All overgrown with trailing odorous plants
Which curtain out the day with leaves and flowers
And paved with veined emerald, and a fountain
Leaps in the midst with an awakening sound;
From its curved roof the mountain's frozen tears   15
Like snow or silver or long diamond spires
Hang downward, raining forth a doubtful light;

1. With variegated colors.
2. In the Greek legend Herakles (Roman Hercules), the human hero who has been made immortal, kills the eagle (or vulture) that tortures Prometheus and frees him after Prometheus had made his peace with Zeus (Jupiter). Shelley omits the killing of the bird because, as III.ii had made clear, bloodshed was banished after Jupiter's fall.

And there is heard the ever-moving air
Whispering without from tree to tree, and birds,
And bees; and all around are mossy seats   20
And the rough walls are clothed with long soft grass;
A simple dwelling, which shall be our own,
Where we will sit and talk of time and change
As the world ebbs and flows, ourselves unchanged—
What can hide man from Mutability?—   25
And if ye sigh, then I will smile, and thou
Ione, shall chant fragments of sea-music,
Until I weep, when ye shall smile away
The tears she brought, which yet were sweet to shed;
We will entangle buds and flowers, and beams   30
Which twinkle on the fountain's brim, and make
Strange combinations out of common things
Like human babes in their brief innocence;
And we will search, with looks and words of love
For hidden thoughts each lovelier than the last,   35
Our unexhausted spirits, and like lutes
Touched by the skill of the enamoured wind,
Weave harmonies divine, yet ever new,
From difference sweet where discord cannot be.
And hither come, sped on the charmed winds   40
Which meet from all the points of Heaven, as bees
From every flower aerial Enna[3] feeds
At their known island-homes in Himera,
The echoes of the human world, which tell
Of the low voice of love, almost unheard,   45
And dove-eyed pity's murmured pain and music,
Itself the echo of the heart, and all
That tempers or improves man's life, now free.
And lovely apparitions dim at first
Then radiant—as the mind, arising bright   50
From the embrace of beauty (whence the forms
Of which these are the phantoms) casts on them
The gathered rays which are reality—
Shall visit us, the progeny immortal
Of Painting, Sculpture and rapt Poesy   55
And arts, though unimagined, yet to be.
The wandering voices and the shadows these
Of all that man becomes, the mediators
Of that best worship, love, by him and us
Given and returned, swift shapes and sounds which grow   60
More fair and soft as man grows wise and kind,
And veil by veil evil and error fall . . .
Such virtue has the cave and place around.

---

3. The famous meadow in Sicily from which Hades abducted Persephone was *aerial* because it was in the air of earth (rather than in the underworld); not far from it in Sicily are two rivers and a town named *Himera*.

[*Turning to the* Spirit of the Hour.]
For thee, fair Spirit, one toil remains. Ione,
Give her that curved shell which Proteus oid[4]   65
Made Asia's nuptial boon, breathing within it
A voice to be accomplished, and which thou
Didst hide in grass under the hollow rock.

IONE

Thou most desired Hour, more loved and lovely
Than all thy sisters, this is the mystic shell;   70
See the pale azure fading into silver,
Lining it with a soft yet glowing light.
Looks it not like lulled music sleeping there?

SPIRIT

It seems in truth the fairest shell of Ocean:
Its sound must be at once both sweet and strange.   75

PROMETHEUS

Go, borne over the cities of mankind
On whirlwind-footed coursers! once again
Outspeed the sun around the orbed world
And as thy chariot cleaves the kindling air,
Thou breathe into the many-folded Shell,   80
Loosening its mighty music; it shall be
As thunder mingled with clear echoes.—Then
Return and thou shalt dwell beside our cave.

[*Kissing the ground.*]

And thou, O Mother Earth!—

THE EARTH

             I hear—I feel—
Thy lips are on me, and their touch runs down   85
Even to the adamantine central gloom
Along these marble nerves—'tis life, 'tis joy,
And through my withered, old and icy frame
The warmth of an immortal youth shoots down
Circling.—Henceforth the many children fair   90
Folded in my sustaining arms—all plants,

4. Proteus was a sea deity who could not only change himself into various forms, but could also predict future events. In Francis Bacon's explanation of classical myths, Proteus represents physical nature and natural law. That Proteus gives Asia the wedding gift of a conch shell to proclaim the fall of Jupiter and the beginning of a new Golden Age may be explained by a legend surrounding three conch shells in the Shelleys' coat of arms (probably deriving from the magic bugle of Arthur's squire in Spenser's *Fairie Queene*, Book I, VIII). Shelley's college friend and biographer, Thomas Jefferson Hogg, writes: "Sir Guyon de Shelley, one of the most famous of the Paladins . . . carried about with him at all times three conchs fastened to the inside of his shield. . . . When he blew the first shell, all giants, however huge, fled before him. When he put the second to his lips, all spells were broken, all enchantments dissolved; and when he made the third conch, the golden one, vocal, the law of God was immediately exalted, and the law of the Devil annulled and abrogated, wherever the potent sound reached." (Hogg, *Life of . . . Shelley*, ed. Edward Dowden [1906], p. 18.)

And creeping forms, and insects rainbow-winged
And birds and beasts and fish and human shapes
Which drew disease and pain from my wan bosom,
Draining the poison of despair—shall take   95
And interchange sweet nutriment; to me
Shall they become like sister-antelopes
By one fair dam, snowwhite and swift as wind
Nursed among lilies near a brimming stream;
The dewmists of my sunless sleep shall float   100
Under the stars like balm; night-folded flowers
Shall suck unwithering hues in their repose;
And men and beasts in happy dreams shall gather
Strength for the coming day and all its joy:
And death shall be the last embrace of her   105
Who takes the life she gave, even as a mother
Folding her child, says, "Leave me not again!"

ASIA

O mother! wherefore speak the name of death?
Cease they to love and move and breathe and speak
Who die?

THE EARTH

          It would avail not to reply: 110
Thou art immortal and this tongue is known
But to the uncommunicating dead.—
Death is the veil which those who live call life:
They sleep—and it is lifted[5] . . . and meanwhile
In mild variety the seasons mild   115
With rainbow-skirted showers, and odorous winds
And long blue meteors cleansing the dull night,
And the life-kindling shafts of the keen Sun's
All-piercing bow, and the dew-mingled rain
Of the calm moonbeams, a soft influence mild;   120
Shall clothe the forests and the fields—aye, even
The crag-built desarts of the barren deep—
With ever-living leaves and fruits and flowers.
And Thou! There is a Cavern[6] where my spirit
Was panted forth in anguish whilst thy pain   125
Made my heart mad, and those who did inhale it
Became mad too, and built a Temple there
And spoke and were oracular, and lured
The erring nations round to mutual war
And faithless faith, such as Jove kept with thee;   130
Which breath now rises as among tall weeds
A violet's exhalation, and it fills

5. *Death is the veil . . . lifted:* Cf. Shel-
ley's sonnet: "Lift not the painted
veil . . ." (p. 312).
6. This cavern is, apparently, the "mighty
portal" described by Panthea at II.iii.2–

10, now redeemed from its former un-
happy role. At lines 127–130, Shelley
identifies this location with oracles, like
that at Delphi.

With a serener light and crimson air
Intense yet soft the rocks and woods around;
It feeds the quick growth of the serpent vine   135
And the dark linked ivy tangling wild
And budding, blown, or odour-faded blooms
Which star the winds with points of coloured light
As they rain through them, and bright, golden globes
Of fruit, suspended in their own green heaven;   140
And, through their veined leaves and amber stems,
The flowers whose purple and translucid bowls
Stand ever mantling with aerial dew,
The drink of spirits; and it circles round
Like the soft waving wings of noonday dreams,   145
Inspiring calm and happy thoughts, like mine
Now thou art thus restored . . . This Cave is thine.
Arise! Appear!

[A *Spirit rises in the likeness of a winged child.*]
                    This is my torch-bearer,
Who let his lamp out in old time, with gazing
On eyes from which he kindled it anew   150
With love which is as fire, sweet Daughter mine,
For such is that within thine own.—Run, Wayward!
And guide this company beyond the peak
Of Bacchic Nysa,[7] Mænad-haunted mountain,
And beyond Indus and its tribute rivers,   155
Trampling the torrent streams and glassy lakes
With feet unwet, unwearied, undelaying;
And up the green ravine, across the vale,
Beside the windless and chrystalline pool
Where ever lies, on unerasing waves,   160
The image of a temple built above,
Distinct with column, arch and architrave[8]
And palm-like capital, and overwrought,
And populous most with living imagery—
Praxitelean shapes,[9] whose marble smiles   165
Fill the hushed air with everlasting love.
It is deserted now, but once it bore
Thy name, Prometheus; there the emulous youths
Bore to thine honour through the divine gloom
The lamp, which was thine emblem[1] . . . even as those   170
Who bear the untransmitted torch of hope

7. In classical geography and legend there were no less than ten places named Nysa, all associated with Dionysus (Bacchus). One, a city in India, was the reputed birthplace of Dionysus and his capital during his legendary conquest of the East.
8. The main beam that rests on the tops of the capitals (column tops) in post and lintel architecture.
9. Statues by or exhibiting the perfection of the fourth-century B.C. Greek sculptor Praxiteles.
1. At Athens there was a cult that annually celebrated Prometheus' exploits as fire bringer in the Lampadephoria, a race by torch-bearing youths (who thus *emulated* the feat of Prometheus). The lost third play of Aeschylus' Promethean trilogy was called *Prometheus the Fire Bringer.*

Into the grave across the night of life . . .
As thou hast borne it most triumphantly
To this far goal of Time . . . Depart, farewell.
Beside that Temple is the destined Cave . . .   175

SCENE IV

A *Forest. In the Background a Cave.* Prometheus, Asia, Panthea,
Ione, *and the* Spirit of the Earth.

IONE

Sister, it is not Earthly . . . how it glides
Under the leaves! how on its head there burns
A light like a green star, whose emerald beams
Are twined with its fair hair! how, as it moves
The splendour drops in flakes upon the grass!   5
Knowest thou it?

PANTHEA

      It is the delicate spirit
That guides the earth through Heaven. From afar
The populous constellations call that light
The loveliest of the planets, and sometimes
It floats along the spray of the salt sea   10
Or makes its chariot of a foggy cloud
Or walks through fields or cities while men sleep
Or o'er the mountain tops, or down the rivers,
Or through the green waste wilderness, as now,
Wondering at all it sees. Before Jove reigned   15
It loved our sister Asia, and it came
Each leisure hour to drink the liquid light
Out of her eyes, for which it said it thirsted
As one bit by a dipsas;[2] and with her
It made its childish confidence, and told her   20
All it had known or seen, for it saw much,
Yet idly reasoned what it saw; and called her—
For whence it sprung it knew not nor do I—
"Mother, dear Mother."

SPIRIT OF THE EARTH [*running to* Asia]
      Mother, dearest Mother;
May I then talk with thee as I was wont?   25
May I then hide mine eyes in thy soft arms
After thy looks have made them tired of joy?
May I then play beside thee the long noons
When work is none in the bright silent air?

2. A poisonous snake of classical legend (mentioned in Lucan's *Pharsalia*, IX.737–760, and Milton's *Paradise Lost*, X.526), the bite of which caused an unquenchable thirst (cf. dipsomaniac).

ASIA

I love thee, gentlest being, and henceforth   30
Can cherish thee unenvied.—Speak, I pray:
Thy simple talk once solaced, now delights.

SPIRIT OF THE EARTH

Mother, I am grown wiser, though a child
Cannot be wise like thee, within this day
And happier too, happier and wiser both.   35
Thou knowest that toads and snakes and loathly worms
And venomous and malicious beasts, and boughs
That bore ill berries in the woods, were ever
An hindrance to my walks o'er the green world,
And that, among the haunts of humankind   40
Hard-featured men, or with proud, angry looks
Or cold, staid gait, or false and hollow smiles
Or the dull sneer of self-loved ignorance
Or other such foul masks with which ill thoughts
Hide that fair being whom we spirits call man;   45
And women too, ugliest of all things evil,
Though fair, even in a world where thou art fair
When good and kind, free and sincere like thee,
When false or frowning made me sick at heart
To pass them, though they slept, and I unseen.   50
Well—my path lately lay through a great City
Into the woody hills surrounding it.
A sentinel was sleeping at the gate:
When there was heard a sound, so loud, it shook
The towers amid the moonlight, yet more sweet   55
Than any voice but thine, sweetest of all,
A long long sound, as it would never end:
And all the inhabitants leapt suddenly
Out of their rest, and gathered in the streets,
Looking in wonder up to Heaven, while yet   60
The music pealed along. I hid myself
Within a fountain in the public square
Where I lay like the reflex[3] of the moon
Seen in a wave under green leaves—and soon
Those ugly human shapes and visages   65
Of which I spoke as having wrought me pain,
Past floating through the air, and fading still
Into the winds that scattered them;[4] and those
From whom they past seemed mild and lovely forms
After some foul disguise had fallen—and all   70
Were somewhat changed, and after brief surprise

3. Reflection.
4. *Those ugly human shapes . . . scattered them:* This image of the masks of ugly human nature floating away from the creatures that produced and wore them derives (with a reversal of emphasis) from the passage on the *simulacra,* or "images," in Lucretius' *De rerum natura,* IV.46ff. See also "The Triumph of Life," 480–516.

And greetings of delighted wonder, all
Went to their sleep again: and when the dawn
Came—wouldst thou think that toads and snakes and efts[5]
Could e'er be beautiful?—yet so they were   75
And that with little change of shape or hue:
All things had put their evil nature off.
I cannot tell my joy, when o'er a lake,
Upon a drooping bough with nightshade twined,
I saw two azure halcyons clinging downward   80
And thinning one bright bunch of amber berries
With quick, long beaks, and in the deep there lay
Those lovely forms imaged as in a sky.[6]—
So with my thoughts full of these happy changes
We meet again, the happiest change of all.   85

ASIA

And never will we part, till thy chaste Sister[7]
Who guides the frozen and inconstant moon
Will look on thy more warm and equal light
Till her heart thaw like flakes of April snow
And love thee.

SPIRIT OF THE EARTH
What, as Asia loves Prometheus?   90

ASIA

Peace, Wanton[8]—thou art yet not old enough.
Think ye, by gazing on each other's eyes
To multiply your lovely selves, and fill
With sphered fires the interlunar[9] air?

SPIRIT OF THE EARTH
Nay, Mother, while my sister trims[1] her lamp   95
'Tis hard I should go darkling—

ASIA

—Listen! look!
[*The* Spirit of the Hour *enters.*]

PROMETHEUS
We feel what thou hast heard and seen—yet speak.

SPIRIT OF THE HOUR
Soon as the sound had ceased whose thunder filled
The abysses of the sky, and the wide earth,
There was a change . . . the impalpable thin air   100

---

5. Small lizards or lizardlike animals;
newts.
6. *I cannot tell my joy . . . as in a sky:*
The double point of lines 78–83 is that
the berries of the deadly nightshade are
no longer poisonous (cf. *Queen Mab*,
VIII.129–130) and that the halcyons, or
kingfishers, have turned vegetarian.
7. Selene, the moon goddess of Greek

mythology.
8. A spoiled child (with overtones of
lasciviousness).
9. Dark; the time between the old and
the new moon.
1. Puts into proper order for lighting by
cleaning, cutting the wick, or adding
fresh fuel.

And the all-circling sunlight were transformed
As if the sense of love dissolved in them
Had folded itself round the sphered world.
My vision then grew clear and I could see
Into the mysteries of the Universe.[2]   105
Dizzy as with delight I floated down,
Winnowing[3] the lightsome air with languid plumes,
My coursers sought their birthplace in the sun
Where they henceforth will live exempt from toil,
Pasturing flowers of vegetable fire—   110
And where my moonlike car will stand within
A temple, gazed upon by Phidian forms,[4]
Of thee, and Asia and the Earth, and me
And you fair nymphs, looking the love we feel,
In memory of the tidings it has borne,   115
Beneath a dome fretted with graven flowers,
Poised on twelve columns of resplendent stone
And open to the bright and liquid sky.
Yoked to it by an amphisbænic snake
The likeness of those winged steeds will mock   120
The flight from which they find repose.[5]—Alas,
Whither has wandered now my partial[6] tongue
When all remains untold which ye would hear!—
As I have said, I floated to the Earth:
It was, as it is still, the pain of bliss   125
To move, to breathe, to be; I wandering went
Among the haunts and dwellings of mankind
And first was disappointed not to see
Such mighty change as I had felt within
Expressed in outward things; but soon I looked,   130
And behold! thrones were kingless, and men walked
One with the other even as spirits do,
None fawned, none trampled; hate, disdain or fear,
Self-love or self-contempt on human brows
No more inscribed, as o'er the gate of hell,   135
"All hope abandon, ye who enter here";[7]
None frowned, none trembled, none with eager fear
Gazed on another's eye of cold command
Until the subject of a tyrant's will
Became, worse fate, the abject[8] of his own   140

2. In the general regeneration the earth's atmosphere ceases to act as a prism, thus no longer distorting sunlight into varied colors and a glare that hides realities.
3. Flapping or beating.
4. Statues by or approaching the quality of the great Athenian sculptor Phidias (fifth century B.C.).
5. The scene described in lines 111–121 is based on the Pantheon and the Sala della Biga in the Vatican Museum—both places Shelley visited in Rome. The *biga*, two-horse chariot, was the emblem of the moon (*my moonlike car*), as opposed to the four-horse chariot of the sun-god; in the museum the yoke of the two-horse chariot is a snake with a head on each end—the legendary *amphisbaena*.
6. Biased in favor of.
7. This line translates literally the last words of the inscription written above the gate leading into Dante's Inferno (III.9).
8. Outcast or degraded person.

Which spurred him, like an outspent horse, to death.
None wrought his lips in truth-entangling lines
Which smiled the lie his tongue disdained to speak;
None with firm sneer trod out in his own heart
The sparks of love and hope, till there remained   145
Those bitter ashes, a soul self-consumed,
And the wretch crept, a vampire among men,
Infecting all with his own hideous ill.
None talked that common, false, cold, hollow talk
Which makes the heart deny the *yes* it breathes   150
Yet question that unmeant hypocrisy
With such a self-mistrust as has no name.
And women too, frank, beautiful and kind
As the free Heaven which rains fresh light and dew
On the wide earth, past: gentle, radiant forms,   155
From custom's evil taint exempt and pure;
Speaking the wisdom once they could not think,
Looking emotions once they feared to feel
And changed to all which once they dared not be,
Yet being now, made Earth like Heaven—nor pride   160
Nor jealousy nor envy nor ill shame,
The bitterest of those drops of treasured gall,
Spoilt the sweet taste of the nepenthe,[9] love.

Thrones, altars, judgement-seats and prisons; wherein
And beside which, by wretched men were borne   165
Sceptres, tiaras, swords and chains, and tomes
Of reasoned wrong glozed[1] on by ignorance,
Were like those monstrous and barbaric shapes,
The ghosts of a no more remembered fame,
Which from their unworn obelisks look forth   170
In triumph o'er the palaces and tombs
Of those who were their conquerors, mouldering round.[2]
Those imaged to the pride of Kings and Priests
A dark yet mighty faith, a power as wide
As is the world it wasted, and are now   175
But an astonishment; even so the tools
And emblems of its last captivity
Amid the dwellings of the peopled Earth,
Stand, not o'erthrown, but unregarded now.
And those foul shapes,[3] abhorred by God and man—   180
Which under many a name and many a form
Strange, savage, ghastly, dark and execrable

9. A magic drink that banished grief and pain.
1. Glossed; commented on or explained.
2. The Egyptian *obelisks*, brought to Rome by the conquering armies of the empire, had in the Renaissance been erected in the principal piazzas of the city, while the palaces of their conquerors (the ancient Romans) had fallen into decay. The *shapes* on the obelisks seemed *monstrous and barbaric* (168) because, when Shelley wrote, hieroglyphics could not be deciphered.
3. A generalized term for all gods of vengeance who inspired fear.

Were Jupiter, the tyrant of the world;
And which the nations panic-stricken served
With blood, and hearts broken by long hope, and love   185
Dragged to his altars soiled and garlandless
And slain amid men's unreclaiming tears,
Flattering the thing they feared, which fear was hate—
Frown, mouldering fast, o'er their abandoned shrines.
The painted veil, by those who were, called life,   190
Which mimicked,[4] as with colours idly spread,
All men believed and hoped, is torn aside—
The loathsome mask has fallen, the man remains
Sceptreless, free, uncircumscribed—but man:
Equal, unclassed, tribeless and nationless,   195
Exempt from awe, worship, degree,—the King
Over himself; just, gentle, wise—but man:
Passionless? no—yet free from guilt or pain
Which were, for his will made, or suffered them,
Nor yet exempt, though ruling them like slaves,   200
From chance and death and mutability,
The clogs[5] of that which else might oversoar
The loftiest star of unascended Heaven
Pinnacled dim in the intense inane.[6]

END OF THE THIRD ACT.

ACT IV

Scene: A Part of the Forest near the Cave of Prometheus. Panthea
and Ione *are sleeping: they awaken gradually during the first Song.*

VOICE OF UNSEEN SPIRITS
    The pale Stars are gone,—
    For the Sun, their swift Shepherd,
    To their folds them compelling
    In the depths of the Dawn
Hastes, in meteor-eclipsing array, and they flee   5
    Beyond his blue dwelling,
    As fawns flee the leopard . . .
      But where are ye?

[A *Train of dark Forms and Shadows passes by confusedly, singing.*]
      Here, oh here!
      We bear the bier   10
Of the Father of many a cancelled year!
      Spectres we
      Of the dead Hours be,
We bear Time to his tomb in eternity.

4. Mocked (because the appearance is copied ineffectively).

5. Impediments or encumbrances.
6. The formless void of infinite space.

Strew, oh strew 15
Hair, not yew!
Wet the dusty pall with tears, not dew!
Be the faded flowers
Of Death's bare bowers
Spread on the corpse of the King of Hours! 20

Haste, oh haste!
As shades are chased
Trembling, by Day, from Heaven's blue waste,
We melt away
Like dissolving spray 25
From the children of a diviner day,
With the lullaby
Of winds that die
On the bosom of their own harmony!

IONE
What dark forms were they? 30

PANTHEA
The past Hours weak and grey
With the spoil, which their toil
Raked together
From the conquest but One could foil.

IONE
Have they past?

PANTHEA
They have past; 35
They outspeeded the blast;
While 'tis said, they are fled—

IONE
Whither, oh whither?

PANTHEA
To the dark, to the past, to the dead.

VOICE OF UNSEEN SPIRITS
Bright clouds float in Heaven, 40
Dew-stars gleam on Earth,
Waves assemble on Ocean,
They are gathered and driven
By the Storm of delight, by the panic of glee!
They shake with emotion— 45
They dance in their mirth—
But where are ye?

The pine boughs are singing
Old songs with new gladness,
The billows and fountains 50
Fresh music are flinging

Like the notes of a spirit from land and from sea;
   The storms mock the mountains
    With the thunder of gladness.
     But where are ye?   55

IONE

What charioteers are these?

PANTHEA

                 Where are their chariots?

SEMICHORUS OF HOURS I

The voice of the Spirits of Air and of Earth
Has drawn back the figured curtain of sleep
Which covered our being and darkened our birth
In the deep—

A VOICE

       In the deep?

SEMICHORUS II

           Oh, below the deep.   60

SEMICHORUS I

An hundred ages we had been kept
Cradled in visions of hate and care
And each one who waked as his brother slept
Found the truth—

SEMICHORUS II

        Worse than his visions were!

SEMICHORUS I

We have heard the lute of Hope in sleep,   65
We have known the voice of Love in dreams,
We have felt the wand of Power, and leap—

SEMICHORUS II

As the billows leap in the morning beams!

CHORUS

Weave the dance on the floor of the breeze,
   Pierce with song Heaven's silent light,   70
Enchant the Day that too swiftly flees,
   To check its flight, ere the cave of Night.

Once the hungry Hours were hounds
   Which chased the Day, like a bleeding deer
And it limped and stumbled with many wounds   75
   Through the nightly dells of the desart year.

But now—oh weave the mystic measure
   Of music and dance and shapes of light,
Let the Hours, and the Spirits of might and pleasure
   Like the clouds and sunbeams unite.

A VOICE

Unite! 80

PANTHEA

See where the Spirits of the human mind
Wrapt in sweet sounds as in bright veils, approach.

CHORUS OF SPIRITS

We join the throng
Of the dance and the song
By the whirlwind of gladness borne along; 85
As the flying-fish leap
From the Indian deep,
And mix with the sea birds half asleep.

CHORUS OF HOURS

Whence come ye so wild and so fleet,
For sandals of lightning are on your feet 90
And your wings are soft and swift as thought,
And your eyes are as Love which is veiled not?

CHORUS OF SPIRITS

We come from the mind
Of human kind
Which was late so dusk and obscene and blind; 95
Now 'tis an Ocean
Of clear emotion,
A Heaven of serene and mighty motion.

From that deep Abyss
Of wonder and bliss 100
Whose caverns are chrystal palaces;
From those skiey towers
Where Thought's crowned Powers
Sit watching your dance, ye happy Hours!

From the dim recesses 105
Of woven caresses
Where lovers catch ye by your loose tresses—
From the azure isles
Where sweet Wisdom smiles,
Delaying your ships with her siren wiles; 110

From the temples high
Of man's ear and eye,
Roofed over Sculpture and Poesy;
From the murmurings
Of the unsealed springs, 115
Where Science bedews his Dædal wings.

Years after years
Through blood and tears,
And a thick hell of hatreds and hopes and fears,
We waded and flew   120
And the islets were few
Where the bud-blighted flowers of happiness grew.

Our feet now, every palm,
Are sandalled with calm,
And the dew of our wings is a rain of balm;   125
And beyond our eyes
The human love lies
Which makes all it gazes on, Paradise.

CHORUS OF SPIRITS AND HOURS

Then weave the web of the mystic measure;
From the depths of the sky and the ends of the Earth   130
Come, swift Spirits of might and of pleasure,
Fill the dance and the music of mirth,
As the waves of a thousand streams rush by
To an Ocean of splendour and harmony!

CHORUS OF SPIRITS

Our spoil is won,   135
Our task is done,
We are free to dive or soar or run . . .
Beyond and around
Or within the bound
Which clips the world with darkness round.   140

We'll pass the Eyes
Of the starry skies
Into the hoar Deep to colonize;
Death, Chaos and Night,
From the sound of our flight   145
Shall flee, like mist from a Tempest's might.

And Earth, Air and Light
And the Spirit of Might
Which drives round the stars in their fiery flight;
And Love, Thought, and Breath,   150
The powers that quell Death,
Wherever we soar shall assemble beneath!

And our singing shall build,
In the Void's loose field,
A world for the Spirit of Wisdom to wield;   155
We will take our plan
From the new world of man
And our work shall be called the Promethean.

CHORUS OF HOURS

Break the dance, and scatter the song;
Let some depart and some remain.   160

SEMICHORUS I

We, beyond Heaven, are driven along—

SEMICHORUS II

Us, the inchantments of Earth retain—

SEMICHORUS I

Ceaseless and rapid and fierce and free
With the spirits which build a new earth and sea
And a Heaven where yet Heaven could never be—   165

SEMICHORUS II

Solemn and slow and serene and bright
Leading the Day and outspeeding the Night
With the Powers of a world of perfect light—

SEMICHORUS I

We whirl, singing loud, round the gathering sphere
Till the trees and the beasts, and the clouds appear   170
From its chaos made calm by love, not fear—

SEMICHORUS II

We encircle the Oceans and Mountains of Earth
And the happy forms of its death and birth
Change to the music of our sweet mirth.

CHORUS OF HOURS AND SPIRITS

Break the dance and scatter the song—   175
    Let some depart and some remain;
Wherever we fly we lead along
In leashes, like starbeams, soft yet strong,
    The clouds that are heavy with Love's sweet rain.

PANTHEA

Ha, they are gone!

IONE

                Yet feel you no delight   180
From the past sweetness?

PANTHEA

                As the bare green hill
When some soft cloud vanishes into rain
Laughs with a thousand drops of sunny water
To the unpavilioned sky!

IONE

                Even whilst we speak
New notes arise . . . What is that awful sound?   185

PANTHEA

'Tis the deep music of the rolling world,
Kindling within the strings of the waved air
Æolian modulations.

IONE

Listen too,
How every pause is filled with under-notes,
Clear, silver, icy, keen, awakening tones   190
Which pierce the sense and live within the soul
As the sharp stars pierce Winter's chrystal air
And gaze upon themselves within the sea.

PANTHEA

But see, where through two openings in the forest
Which hanging branches overcanopy,   195
And where two runnels[7] of a rivulet
Between the close moss violet-inwoven
Have made their path of melody, like sisters
Who part with sighs that they may meet in smiles,
Turning their dear disunion to an isle   200
Of lovely grief, a wood of sweet sad thoughts;
Two visions of strange radiance float upon
The Ocean-like inchantment of strong sound
Which flows intenser, keener, deeper yet
Under the ground and through the windless air.   205

IONE

I see a chariot like that thinnest boat
In which the Mother of the Months[8] is borne
By ebbing light into her western cave
When she upsprings from interlunar dreams,
O'er which is curved an orblike canopy   210
Of gentle darkness, and the hills and woods
Distinctly seen through that dusk aery veil
Regard[9] like shapes in an enchanter's glass;
Its wheels are solid clouds, azure and gold,
Such as the genii of the thunderstorm   215
Pile on the floor of the illumined sea
When the Sun rushes under it; they roll
And move and grow as with an inward wind.
Within it sits a winged Infant, white
Its countenance, like the whiteness of bright snow,   220
Its plumes are as feathers of sunny frost,
Its limbs gleam white, through the wind-flowing folds
Of its white robe, woof of ætherial pearl.
Its hair is white,—the brightness of white light[1]

---

7. Small streams.
8. The moon, seen as the thin crescent of the new moon bearing the shadowy old moon.
9. Appear or look.

1. The multiple references to the *whiteness* of the moon emphasize both its cold sterility and the beauty of its light undistorted by an atmosphere. It is potentiality to the earth's actuality.

Scattered in strings, yet its two eyes are Heavens   225
Of liquid darkness, which the Deity
Within, seems pouring, as a storm is poured
From jagged clouds, out of their arrowy lashes,
Tempering the cold and radiant air around
With fire that is not brightness;[2] in its hand   230
It sways a quivering moonbeam, from whose point
A guiding power directs the chariot's prow
Over its wheeled clouds, which as they roll
Over the grass and flowers and waves, wake sounds
Sweet as a singing rain of silver dew.   235

PANTHEA

And from the other opening in the wood
Rushes with loud and whirlwind harmony
A sphere, which is as many thousand spheres,
Solid as chrystal, yet through all its mass
Flow, as through empty space, music and light: 240
Ten thousand orbs involving and involved,[3]
Purple and azure, white and green and golden,
Sphere within sphere, and every space between
Peopled with unimaginable shapes
Such as ghosts dream dwell in the lampless deep   245
Yet each intertranspicuous,[4] and they whirl
Over each other with a thousand motions
Upon a thousand sightless[5] axles spinning
And with the force of self-destroying swiftness,
Intensely, slowly, solemnly roll on—   250
Kindling with mingled sounds, and many tones,
Intelligible words and music wild.—
With mighty whirl the multidinous Orb
Grinds the bright brook into an azure mist
Of elemental subtlety, like light,   255
And the wild odour of the forest flowers,
The music of the living grass and air,
The emerald light of leaf-entangled beams
Round its intense, yet self-conflicting[6] speed,
Seem kneaded into one aerial mass   260
Which drowns the sense. Within the Orb itself,
Pillowed upon its alabaster arms
Like to a child o'erwearied with sweet toil,
On its own folded wings and wavy hair

2. As Shelley knew from Sir Humphry Davy's account of the findings of Herschel (1800), there are "dark rays"—infrared emanations that produce heat without light—which, Davy suggested, might be given off by the moon.
3. This description of the earth and the spirit asleep within it draws heavily on Milton's descriptions of angels (*Paradise Lost*, V.620–624) and of the Chariot of Paternal Deitie (*Paradise Lost*, VI.

749ff.), which in turn echo visions in Ezekiel (chaps. 1 and 10) and Dante (*Purgatorio*, Canto XXIX); *involving and involved*: entwining and enfolded or enwrapped.
4. That can be seen through or between each other.
5. Blind morally.
6. Because its various component spheres are spinning in different directions.

The Spirit of the Earth is laid asleep, 265
And you can see its little lips are moving
Amid the changing light of their own smiles
Like one who talks of what he loves in dream—

IONE
'Tis only mocking the Orb's harmony . . .

PANTHEA
And from a star upon its forehead, shoot, 270
Like swords of azure fire, or golden spears
With tyrant-quelling myrtle[7] overtwined,
Embleming Heaven and Earth united now,
Vast beams like spokes of some invisible wheel
Which whirl as the Orb whirls, swifter than thought, 275
Filling the abyss with sunlike lightenings,
And perpendicular now, and now transverse,
Pierce the dark soil, and as they pierce and pass
Make bare the secrets of the Earth's deep heart,
Infinite mine of adamant[8] and gold, 280
Valueless[9] stones and unimagined gems,
And caverns on chrystalline columns poised
With vegetable silver[1] overspread,
Wells of unfathomed fire, and watersprings
Whence the great Sea, even as a child, is fed 285
Whose vapours clothe Earth's monarch mountain-tops
With kingly, ermine snow; the beams flash on
And make appear the melancholy ruins
Of cancelled cycles;[2] anchors, beaks of ships,
Planks turned to marble, quivers, helms and spears 290
And gorgon-headed targes,[3] and the wheels
Of scythed chariots,[4] and the emblazonry
Of trophies, standards and armorial beasts
Round which Death laughed, sepulchred emblems
Of dead Destruction, ruin within ruin! 295
The wrecks beside of many a city vast,
Whose population which the Earth grew over
Was mortal but not human; see, they lie,
Their monstrous works and uncouth skeletons,
Their statues, homes, and fanes;[5] prodigious shapes 300
Huddled in grey annihilation, split,
Jammed in the hard black deep; and over these

---

7. The myrtle was associated with Venus and love.
8. Extremely hard rock.
9. Valuable beyond calculation.
1. In Milton's Eden the Tree of Life bore "Ambrosial Fruit/ Of vegetable Gold" (IV.218–220).
2. On this passage and what follows, see D. J. Hughes, "Potentiality in *Prometheus Unbound*," pp. 605–612. Many de-
tails come from a book Shelley read in 1812: James Parkinson's *Organic Remains of a Former World* (3 vols., 1804–1811).
3. Light shields or bucklers carried by archers, embossed with gorgon's head; *helms:* helmets.
4. War chariots with scythes fastened to the axles.
5. Temples.

The anatomies[6] of unknown winged things,
And fishes which were isles of living scale,
And serpents, bony chains, twisted around   305
The iron crags, or within heaps of dust
To which the tortuous strength of their last pangs
Had crushed the iron crags;—and over these
The jagged alligator and the might
Of earth-convulsing behemoth,[7] which once   310
Were monarch beasts, and on the slimy shores
And weed-overgrown continents of Earth
Increased and multiplied like summer worms
On an abandoned corpse, till the blue globe
Wrapt Deluge round it like a cloak, and they   315
Yelled, gaspt and were abolished; or some God
Whose throne was in a Comet, past, and cried—
"Be not!"—and like my words they were no more.

THE EARTH

The joy, the triumph, the delight, the madness,
The boundless, overflowing bursting gladness,   320
The vaporous exultation, not to be confined!
  Ha! ha! the animation of delight
  Which wraps me, like an atmosphere of light,
And bears me as a cloud is borne by its own wind!

THE MOON

        Brother mine, calm wanderer,   325
        Happy globe of land and air,
Some Spirit is darted like a beam from thee,
        Which penetrates my frozen frame
        And passes with the warmth of flame—
With love and odour and deep melody   330
        Through me, through me!—

THE EARTH

Ha! ha! the caverns of my hollow mountains,
My cloven fire-crags,[8] sound-exulting fountains
Laugh with a vast and inextinguishable laughter.
  The Oceans and the Desarts and the Abysses   335
  And the deep air's unmeasured wildernesses
Answer from all their clouds and billows, echoing after.

  They cry aloud as I do—"Sceptred Curse,[9]
  Who all our green and azure Universe
Threatenedst to muffle round with black destruction, sending   340
  A solid cloud to rain hot thunderstones,
  And splinter and knead down my children's bones,
All I bring forth, to one void mass battering and blending,

6. Skeletons.
7. A general expression for one of the largest and strongest animals.
8. Volcanoes.
9. Jupiter—or, rather, the more general principle of tyrannical rule.

"Until each craglike tower and storied column,
Palace and Obelisk and Temple solemn,   345
My imperial mountains crowned with cloud and snow and fire,
My sea-like forests, every blade and blossom
Which finds a grave or cradle in my bosom,
Were stamped by thy strong hate into a lifeless mire,

"How art thou sunk, withdrawn, cover'd—drunk up   350
By thirsty nothing, as the brackish[1] cup
Drained by a Desart-troop—a little drop for all;
And from beneath, around, within, above,
Filling thy void annihilation, Love
Bursts in like light on caves cloven by the thunderball."   355

THE MOON

The snow upon my lifeless mountains
Is loosened into living fountains,
My solid Oceans flow and sing and shine
A spirit from my heart bursts forth,
It clothes with unexpected birth   360
My cold bare bosom: Oh! it must be thine
        On mine, on mine!

Gazing on thee I feel, I know,
Green stalks burst forth, and bright flowers grow
And living shapes upon my bosom move: 365
Music is in the sea and air,
Winged clouds soar here and there,
Dark with the rain new buds are dreaming of:
        'Tis Love, all Love!

THE EARTH

It interpenetrates my granite mass,   370
Through tangled roots and trodden clay doth pass
Into the utmost leaves and delicatest flowers;
Upon the winds, among the clouds 'tis spread,
It wakes a life in the forgotten dead,
They breathe a spirit up from their obscurest bowers   375

And like a storm, bursting its cloudy prison
With thunder and with whirlwind, has arisen
Out of the lampless caves of unimagined being,
With earthquake shock and swiftness making shiver
Thought's stagnant chaos, unremoved forever,   380
Till Hate and Fear and Pain, light-vanquished shadows, fleeing,

Leave Man, who was a many-sided mirror
Which could distort to many a shape of error
This true fair world of things—a Sea reflecting Love;
Which over all his kind, as the Sun's Heaven   385
Gliding o'er Ocean, smooth, serene and even,
Darting from starry depths radiance and light, doth move,

1. Salty.

Leave Man, even as a leprous child is left
Who follows a sick beast to some warm cleft
Of rocks, through which the might of healing springs is poured; 390
   Then when it wanders home with rosy smile
   Unconscious, and its mother fears awhile
It is a Spirit—then weeps on her child restored.[2]

   Man, oh, not men! a chain of linked thought,
   Of love and might to be divided not, 395
Compelling the elements with adamantine stress—
   As the Sun rules, even with a tyrant's gaze,
   The unquiet Republic of the maze
Of Planets, struggling fierce towards Heaven's free wilderness.

   Man, one harmonious Soul of many a soul 400
   Whose nature is its own divine controul
Where all things flow to all, as rivers to the sea;
   Familiar acts are beautiful through love;
   Labour and Pain and Grief in life's green grove
Sport like tame beasts—none knew how gentle they could be! 405

   His Will, with all mean passions, bad delights,
   And selfish cares, its trembling satellites,
A spirit ill to guide, but mighty to obey,
   Is as a tempest-winged ship, whose helm
   Love rules, through waves which dare not overwhelm, 410
Forcing life's wildest shores to own its sovereign sway.

   All things confess his strength.—Through the cold mass
   Of marble and of colour his dreams pass;
Bright threads, whence mothers weave the robes their children wear;[3]
   Language is a perpetual Orphic song,[4] 415
   Which rules with Dædal harmony a throng
Of thoughts and forms, which else senseless and shapeless were.

   The Lightning is his slave; Heaven's utmost deep
   Gives up her stars, and like a flock of sheep
They pass before his eye, are numbered, and roll on! 420
   The Tempest is his steed,—he strides the air;
   And the abyss shouts from her depth laid bare,
"Heaven, hast thou secrets? Man unveils me, I have none."

THE MOON

The shadow of white Death has past
From my path in Heaven at last, 425

2. The stanza alludes to the legend of King Bladud, mythical king of Britain, a banished leper who, while following a lost swine, stumbled upon the healing hot springs of the English town of Bath and returned home cured (Richard Warner's *History of Bath* [Bath, 1801]).
3. That is, the ideals that parents give their children are influenced by their artistic heritage.
4. *Orphic song . . . Dædal harmony:* Orpheus, the mythical Greek bard, sang so beautifully that he tamed wild beasts and even stopped the tortures of Hades; Daedalus was the mythical Athenian artist; both represent the creative human spirit.

A clinging shroud of solid frost and sleep—
  And through my newly-woven bowers
  Wander happy paramours
Less mighty, but as mild as those who keep
    Thy vales more deep.   430

THE EARTH

  As the dissolving warmth of Dawn may fold
  A half-unfrozen dewglobe, green and gold
And chrystalline, till it becomes a winged mist
  And wanders up the vault of the blue Day,
  Outlives the noon, and on the Sun's last ray   435
Hangs o'er the Sea—a fleece of fire and amethyst—

THE MOON

  Thou art folded, thou art lying
  In the light which is undying
Of thine own joy and Heaven's smile divine;
  All suns and constellations shower   440
  On thee a light, a life, a power
Which doth array thy sphere—thou pourest thine
    On mine, on mine!

THE EARTH

I spin beneath my pyramid of night[5]
Which points into the Heavens, dreaming delight,   445
Murmuring victorious joy in my enchanted sleep;
  As a youth lulled in love-dreams, faintly sighing,
  Under the shadow of his beauty lying
Which round his rest a watch of light and warmth doth keep.

THE MOON

  As in the soft and sweet eclipse   450
  When soul meets soul on lovers' lips,
High hearts are calm and brightest eyes are dull;
  So when thy shadow falls on me
  Then am I mute and still,—by thee
Covered; of thy love, Orb most beautiful,   455
    Full, oh, too full!—

  Thou art speeding round the Sun,
  Brightest World of many a one,
  Green and azure sphere, which shinest
  With a light which is divinest   460
  Among all the lamps of Heaven
  To whom life and light is given;
  I, thy chrystal paramour,
  Borne beside thee by a power
  Like the polar Paradise,   465

5. The cone-shaped shadow a planet casts out into space on the side away from the sun.

Magnet-like, of lovers' eyes;
I, a most enamoured maiden
Whose weak brain is overladen
With the pleasure of her love—
Maniac-like around thee move,   470
Gazing, an insatiate bride,
On thy form from every side[6]
Like a Mænad round the cup
Which Agave lifted up
In the weird Cadmæan forest.[7]—   475
Brother, wheresoe'er thou soarest
I must hurry, whirl and follow
Through the Heavens wide and hollow,
Sheltered by the warm embrace
Of thy soul, from hungry space,   480
Drinking, from thy sense and sight
Beauty, majesty, and might,
As a lover or chameleon
Grows like what it looks upon,
As a violet's gentle eye   485
Gazes on the azure sky
Until its hue grows like what it beholds,
As a grey and watery mist
Glows like solid amethyst
Athwart the western mountains it enfolds,   490
When the sunset sleeps
Upon its snow—

THE EARTH

And the weak day weeps
That it should be so.
O gentle Moon, the voice of thy delight   495
Falls on me like thy clear and tender light
Soothing the seaman, borne the summer night
Through isles forever calm;
O gentle Moon, thy chrystal accents pierce
The caverns of my Pride's deep Universe,   500
Charming the tyger Joy, whose tramplings fierce
Made wounds, which need thy balm.

PANTHEA

I rise as from a bath of sparkling water,
A bath of azure light, among dark rocks,
Out of the stream of sound—

6. The moon, in circling the earth, always keeps the same side toward the earth because the period of its rotation exactly equals that of its revolution.
7. Agave, daughter of Cadmus, became a maenad (one of the female devotees of Dionysus); in a fit of blind intoxication, she killed her own son Pentheus. See Euripides, *The Bacchae*.

IONE

Ah me, sweet sister,   505

The stream of sound has ebbed away from us
And you pretend to rise out of its wave
Because your words fall like the clear soft dew
Shaken from a bathing wood-nymph's limbs and hair.

PANTHEA

Peace! peace! a mighty Power, which is as Darkness, 510
Is rising out o' Earth, and from the sky
Is showered like Night, and from within the air
Bursts, like eclipse which had been gathered up
Into the pores[8] of sunlight—the bright Visions
Wherein the singing spirits rode and shone 515
Gleam like pale meteors through a watery night.

IONE

There is a sense of words upon mine ear—

PANTHEA

A universal sound like words . . . O list!

DEMOGORGON

Thou Earth, calm empire of a happy Soul,
 Sphere of divinest shapes and harmonies,
Beautiful orb! gathering as thou dost roll 520
 The Love which paves thy path along the skies:

THE EARTH

I hear,—I am as a drop of dew that dies!

DEMOGORGON

Thou Moon, which gazest on the nightly Earth
 With wonder, as it gazes upon thee,
Whilst each to men and beasts and the swift birth 525
 Of birds, is beauty, love, calm, harmony:

THE MOON

I hear—I am a leaf shaken by thee!

DEMOGORGON

Ye Kings of suns and stars, Dæmons and Gods,
 Ætherial Dominations, who possess 530
Elysian, windless, fortunate abodes
 Beyond Heaven's constellated wilderness:[9]

---

8. Minute spaces between the particles of light.
9. Shelley, in creating a hierarchy of Heaven like those described in Dante's *Paradiso* (XXVIII.121–126, for example) and *Paradise Lost* (II.310–311, V.772), uses just three classes—*Daemons* and *Gods*, ruling heavenly bodies within human ken; and *Dominations*, who exist at rest beyond the active universe. As Carl Grabo notes, even Newton had allowed for the possibility of "some body absolutely at rest," though this region would be beyond human power to identify.

A VOICE: *from above*
Our great Republic hears . . . we are blest, and bless.

DEMOGORGON
Ye happy dead, whom beams of brightest verse
   Are clouds to hide, not colours to portray,   535
Whether your nature is that Universe
   Which once ye saw and suffered—

A VOICE: *from beneath*
                      Or as they
Whom we have left, we change and pass away.—

DEMOGORGON
Ye elemental Genii,[1] who have homes
   From man's high mind even to the central stone   540
Of sullen lead, from Heaven's star-fretted domes
   To the dull weed some sea-worm battens[2] on—

A *confused* VOICE
We hear: thy words waken Oblivion.

DEMOGORGON
Spirits whose homes are flesh—ye beasts and birds—
   Ye worms and fish—ye living leaves and buds—   545
Lightning and Wind—and ye untameable herds,
   Meteors and mists, which throng Air's solitudes:

A VOICE
Thy voice to us is wind among still woods.

DEMOGORGON
Man, who wert once a despot and a slave,—
   A dupe and a deceiver,—a Decay,   550
A Traveller from the cradle to the grave
   Through the dim night of this immortal Day:

ALL
Speak—thy strong words may never pass away.

DEMOGORGON
This is the Day which down the void Abysm
At the Earth-born's spell yawns for Heaven's Despotism,   555
   And Conquest is dragged Captive through the Deep;
Love from its awful throne of patient power
In the wise heart, from the last giddy hour
   Of dread endurance, from the slippery, steep,
And narrow verge of crag-like Agony, springs   560
And folds over the world its healing wings.

1. The animating spirits of the elements.   2. Feeds gluttonously.

Gentleness, Virtue, Wisdom and Endurance,—
These are the seals of that most firm assurance
   Which bars the pit over Destruction's strength;
And if, with infirm hand, Eternity,   565
Mother of many acts and hours, should free
   The serpent that would clasp her with his length—
These are the spells by which to reassume
An empire o'er the disentangled Doom.

To suffer woes which Hope thinks infinite;   570
To forgive wrongs darker than Death or Night;
   To defy Power which seems Omnipotent;
To love, and bear;[3] to hope, till Hope creates
From its own wreck the thing it contemplates;
   Neither to change nor falter nor repent:[4]   575
This, like thy glory, Titan! is to be
Good, great and joyous, beautiful and free;
This is alone Life, Joy, Empire and Victory.

The Sensitive-Plant[1]

PART FIRST

A Sensitive-plant in a garden grew,
And the young winds fed it with silver dew,
And it opened its fan-like leaves to the light
And closed them beneath the kisses of night.

And the Spring arose on the garden fair   5
Like the Spirit of love felt every where;
And each flower and herb on Earth's dark breast
Rose from the dreams of its wintry rest.

But none ever trembled and panted with bliss
In the garden, the field or the wilderness,   10

3. Appropriately, Demogorgon expresses these timeless admonitions in timeless infinitives.
4. Here Shelley has adapted Satan's sentiment from Milton's *Paradise Lost* and reversed its moral implications: "yet not for those/ Nor what the Potent Victor in his rage/ Can else inflict, do I repent or change" (I.94–96).
1. Shelley composed "The Sensitive-Plant" in the spring of 1820. It was the first of the "other poems" included in the *Prometheus Unbound* volume, perhaps because it is both the longest of these poems and a mythopoeic fable that harmonizes with *Prometheus* itself. There is a fair copy in the hand of Mary Shelley in *The Harvard Shelley Notebook*, which we have consulted in revising the orthography and punctuation to approximate Shelley's customary practice. The first edition remains authoritative for the words of the text.

The sensitive-plant itself is a small variety of mimosa (*Mimosa pudica*), native to Brazil, that closes up and recoils when touched; it is hermaphroditic—needing only a single plant to reproduce (hence, "companionless," line 12). Earl Wasserman has noted that late-eighteenth-century biologists were debating the sensitive-plant's place as a bridge between the animal and vegetable kingdoms.

Though interpretations of the poem's fable have varied, it seems likely that the sensitive-plant represents, not Shelley or any individual, but either mankind amid natural creation or else the type of the poet with creative sensibility amid general mankind.

Like a doe in the noontide with love's sweet want
As the companionless Sensitive-plant.[2]

The snow-drop and then the violet
Arose from the ground with warm rain wet
And their breath was mixed with fresh odour, sent   15
From the turf, like the voice and the instrument.

Then the pied[3] wind-flowers and the tulip tall,
And narcissi, the fairest among them all
Who gaze on their eyes in the stream's recess
Till they die of their own dear loveliness;[4]   20

And the Naiad-like[5] lily of the vale
Whom youth makes so fair and passion so pale,
That the light of its tremulous bells is seen
Through their pavilions of tender green;

And the hyacinth[6] purple, and white, and blue,   25
Which flung from its bells a sweet peal anew
Of music so delicate, soft and intense,
It was felt like an odour within the sense;

And the rose like a nymph to the bath addresst,
Which unveiled the depth of her glowing breast,   30
Till, fold after fold, to the fainting air
The soul of her beauty and love lay bare:

And the wand-like lily, which lifted up,
As a Mænad,[7] its moonlight-coloured cup
Till the fiery star, which is its eye,   35
Gazed through clear dew on the tender sky;

And the jessamine faint, and the sweet tuberose,
The sweetest flower for scent that blows;[8]
And all rare blossoms from every clime
Grew in that garden in perfect prime.   40

And on the stream whose inconstant bosom
Was prankt[9] under boughs of embowering blossom
With golden and green light, slanting through
Their heaven of many a tangled hue,

---

2. Whereas the sensitive-plant is an annual, all of the other flowers mentioned in Part First, 13–57, are perennials.
3. Of varied colors.
4. *narcissi . . . loveliness:* An allusion to the myth of Narcissus, who fell in love with his own beautiful image in a pool and killed himself in despair because he could not communicate with the image he believed to be a nymph. He was transformed into a flower.
5. A *Naiad* was a nymph of a stream or fountain; naiads, according to Hesiod, initiated youths into sexual experience.
6. According to Greek legend, Hyacin-

thus was a youth beloved by both Apollo and Zephyrus, one of the winds; the latter, in a fit of jealousy, blew a quoit that Apollo had thrown out of its course, killing the young man. Apollo changed his blood into a flower.
7. A fanatical female devotee of Bacchus. Note that all the mythical creatures compared with the flowers are highly passionate and sexual, whereas the sensitive-plant, being unisexual, has no such relations with the other flowers.
8. Blooms.
9. Spangled or brightened with colors.

Broad water-lilies lay tremulously,   45
And starry river-buds glimmered by,
And around them the soft stream did glide and dance
With a motion of sweet sound and radiance.

And the sinuous paths of lawn and of moss,
Which led through the garden along and across—   50
Some open at once to the sun and the breeze,
Some lost among bowers of blossoming trees—

Were all paved with daisies and delicate bells
As fair as the fabulous asphodels[1]
And flowrets which drooping as day drooped too   55
Fell into pavilions, white, purple and blue,
To roof the glow-worm from the evening dew.

And from this undefiled Paradise
The flowers, as an infant's awakening eyes
Smile on its mother, whose singing sweet   60
Can first lull, and at last must awaken it,

When Heaven's blithe winds had unfolded them,
As mine-lamps enkindle a hidden gem,
Shone smiling to Heaven; and every one
Shared joy in the light of the gentle sun,   65

For each one was interpenetrated
With the light and the odour its neighbour shed
Like young lovers, whom youth and love makes dear
Wrapt and filled by their mutual atmosphere.

But the Sensitive-plant which could give small fruit   70
Of the love which it felt from the leaf to the root,
Received more than all—it loved more than ever,
Where none wanted but it, could belong to the giver.

For the Sensitive-Plant has no bright flower;
Radiance and odour are not its dower—   75
It loves—even like Love—its deep heart is full—
It desires what it has not—the beautiful![2]

The light winds which from unsustaining wings
Shed the music of many murmurings;
The beams which dart from many a star   80
Of the flowers whose hues they bear afar;

1. A common flower in Italy; in poetic usage from Homer through Milton and Pope it has been the name given to the immortal flowers that bloom in the Elysian fields.
2. This stanza closely parallels a passage in Plato's *Symposium* that Shelley cited with approval in his review of Peacock's *Rhododaphne* (1817). Shelley translated *The Symposium* in July 1818, rendering the relevant passage (in which Socrates records his earlier conversation with Diotima) thus: " 'It is conceded, then, that Love loves that which he wants but possesses not?'—'Yes, certainly.'—'But Love wants and does not possess beauty?' —'Indeed it must necessarily follow" (Notopoulos, *Platonism of Shelley*, p. 440).

The plumed[3] insects swift and free
Like golden boats on a sunny sea,
Laden with light and odour which pass
Over the gleam of the living grass;   85

The unseen clouds of the dew which lie
Like fire in the flowers till the Sun rides high,
Then wander like spirits among the spheres,
Each cloud faint with the fragrance it bears;

The quivering vapours of dim noontide,   90
Which like a sea o'er the warm earth glide
In which every sound, and odour, and beam
Move, as reeds in a single stream;

Each, and all, like ministering angels were
For the Sensitive-plant sweet joy to bear   95
Whilst the lagging hours of the day went by
Like windless clouds o'er a tender sky.

And when evening descended from Heaven above,
And the Earth was all rest, and the Air was all love;
And delight, though less bright, was far more deep,   100
And the day's veil fell from the world of sleep,

And the beasts, and the birds, and the insects were drowned
In an ocean of dreams without a sound
Whose waves never mark, though they ever impress
The light sand which paves it-Consciousness.   105

(Only over head the sweet nightingale
Ever sang more sweet as the day might fail
And snatches of its Elysian[4] chant
Were mixed with the dreams of the Sensitive-plant).

The Sensitive-plant was the earliest   110
Upgathered into the bosom of rest;
A sweet child weary of its delight,
The feeblest and yet the favourite,
Cradled within the embrace of night.

PART SECOND

There was a Power in this sweet place,
An Eve in this Eden; a ruling grace
Which to the flowers did they waken or dream
Was as God[5] is to the starry scheme:

3. Delicately winged.
4. Glorious or perfect, like Elysium, Greek mythological abode of the blessed dead.
5. In Shelley's conception God did not create matter but merely organized it into a universe. In letters and conversa- tions Shelley compared two women with the *Lady* in this poem—Margaret, Countess of Mount Cashell ("Mrs. Mason") and Jane Williams. His references seem to imply that they gave emotional support and harmony to those about them.

A Lady—the wonder of her kind,   5
Whose form was upborne by a lovely mind
Which, dilating, had moulded her mien and motion,
Like a sea-flower unfolded beneath the Ocean—

Tended the garden from morn to even:
And the meteors[6] of that sublunar Heaven   10
Like the lamps of the air when night walks forth,
Laughed round her footsteps up from the Earth.

She had no companion of mortal race,
But her tremulous breath and her flushing face
Told, whilst the morn kissed the sleep from her eyes   15
That her dreams were less slumber than Paradise:

As if some bright Spirit for her sweet sake
Had deserted heaven while the stars were awake
As if yet around her he lingering were,
Though the veil of daylight concealed him from her.   20

Her step seemed to pity the grass it prest;
You might hear by the heaving of her breast,
That the coming and going of the wind
Brought pleasure there and left passion behind,

And wherever her aery footstep trod,   25
Her trailing hair from the grassy sod
Erased its light vestige, with shadowy sweep
Like a sunny storm o'er the dark green deep.

I doubt not the flowers of that garden sweet
Rejoiced in the sound of her gentle feet;   30
I doubt not they felt the spirit that came
From her glowing fingers through all their frame.

She sprinkled bright water from the stream
On those that were faint with the sunny beam;
And out of the cups of the heavy flowers   35
She emptied the rain of the thunder showers.

She lifted their heads with her tender hands
And sustained them with rods and ozier bands;[7]
If the flowers had been her own infants she
Could never have nursed them more tenderly.   40

And all killing insects and gnawing worms
And things of obscene and unlovely forms
She bore, in a basket of Indian woof,[8]
Into the rough woods far aloof,

6. Any atmospheric phenomenon; in this context, healthful winds (cf. Part Third, line 78); *sublunar:* earthly; in the realm of mutability.
7. Slender willow branches.
8. A woven pattern.

In a basket of grasses and wild flowers full,   45
The freshest her gentle hands could pull
For the poor banished insects, whose intent,
Although they did ill, was innocent.

But the bee and the beam-like ephemeris[9]
Whose path is the lightning's, and soft moths that kiss   50
The sweet lips of the flowers, and harm not, did she
Make her attendant angels be.

And many an antenatal tomb
Where butterflies dream of the life to come
She left clinging round the smooth and dark   55
Edge of the odorous cedar bark.

This fairest creature from earliest spring
Thus moved through the garden ministering
All the sweet season of summertide,
And ere the first leaf looked brown—she died!   60

PART THIRD

Three days the flowers of the garden fair,
Like stars when the moon is awakened, were;
Or the waves of Baiæ,[1] ere luminous
She floats up through the smoke of Vesuvius.

And on the fourth, the Sensitive-plant   5
Felt the sound of the funeral chaunt
And the steps of the bearers heavy and slow,
And the sobs of the mourners deep and low,

The weary sound and the heavy breath
And the silent motions of passing death   10
And the smell, cold, oppressive and dank,
Sent through the pores of the coffin plank.

The dark grass and the flowers among the grass
Were bright with tears as the crowd did pass;
From their sighs the wind caught a mournful tone,   15
And sate in the pines and gave groan for groan.

The garden once fair became cold and foul
Like the corpse of her who had been its soul
Which at first was lovely as if in sleep,
Then slowly changed, till it grew a heap   20
To make men tremble who never weep.

9. The ephemerid, dayfly or mayfly, has a slender body and small, transparent wings. In its imago or winged stage, it lives only for a single day. Shelley mentions the insect in his note to *Queen Mab*, VIII.203–207, and alludes to it in *Adonais*, 254.

1. Baiae is a small bay of the Gulf of Naples, west of the city itself; volcanic Mt. Vesuvius is within sight of the bay, though on the other side of Naples.

Swift summer into the autumn flowed,
And frost in the mist of the morning rode,
Though the noonday sun looked clear and bright,
Mocking the spoil of the secret night.   25

The rose leaves like flakes of crimson snow
Paved the turf and the moss below:
The lilies were drooping, and white, and wan,
Like the head and the skin of a dying man.

And Indian plants, of scent and hue   30
The sweetest that ever were fed on dew;
Leaf by leaf, day after day,
Were massed into the common clay.

And the leaves, brown, yellow, and grey, and red,
And white, with the whiteness of what is dead,   35
Like troops of ghosts on the dry wind past—
Their whistling noise made the birds aghast.

And the gusty winds waked the winged seeds
Out of their birthplace of ugly weeds,
Till they clung round many a sweet flower's stem   40
Which rotted into the earth with them.

The water blooms under the rivulet
Fell from the stalks on which they were set;
And the eddies drove them here and there
As the winds did those of the upper air.   45

Then the rain came down, and the broken stalks
Were bent and tangled across the walks;
And the leafless network of parasite bowers
Massed into ruin; and all sweet flowers.

Between the time of the wind and the snow   50
All loathliest weeds began to grow,
Whose coarse leaves were splashed with many a speck
Like the water-snake's belly and the toad's back.

And thistles, and nettles, and darnels[2] rank,
And the dock, and henbane, and hemlock dank,[3]   55
Stretched out its long and hollow shank
And stifled the air, till the dead wind stank.

And plants, at whose names the verse feels loath,
Filled the place with a monstrous undergrowth,
Prickly, and pulpous,[4] and blistering, and blue,   60
Livid, and starred with a lurid[5] dew.

---

2. Harmful grasses.
3. *Dock* is the common name for several thick-rooted, coarse plants; both *henbane* and *hemlock* are poisonous.
4. Soft or fleshy; flabby.
5. *Livid:* bruised; *lurid:* pale and sickly in color.

And agarics[6] and fungi with mildew and mould
Started like mist from the wet ground cold;
Pale, fleshy,—as if the decaying dead
With a spirit of growth had been animated!   65

Their moss rotted off them, flake by flake,
Till the thick stalk stuck like a murderer's stake,
Where rags of loose flesh yet tremble on high,
Infecting the winds that wander by.[7]

Spawn,[8] weeds and filth, a leprous scum,   70
Made the running rivulet thick and dumb
And at its outlet flags[9] huge as stakes
Dammed it up with roots knotted like water snakes.

And hour by hour when the air was still
The vapours arose which have strength to kill: 75
At morn they were seen, at noon they were felt,
At night they were darkness no star could melt.

And unctuous[1] meteors from spray to spray
Crept and flitted in broad noonday
Unseen; every branch on which they alit   80
By a venomous blight was burned and bit.

The Sensitive-plant like one forbid
Wept, and the tears, within each lid
Of its folded leaves which together grew,
Were changed to a blight of frozen glue.   85

For the leaves soon fell, and the branches soon
By the heavy axe of the blast were hewn;
The sap shrank to the root through every pore
As blood to a heart that will beat no more.

For Winter came—the wind was his whip—   90
One choppy finger was on his lip:
He had torn the cataracts[2] from the hills
And they clanked at his girdle like manacles;

6. Gill mushrooms. Lines 64–69 describe in detail (Hélène Dworzan informs us) the maturing of the *Amanita phalloides* ("Death Cap") and the *Amanita virosa* ("Destroying Angel"), two of the deadliest agarics.
7. Some editors have omitted this stanza (which describes a body rotting on a gibbet) on the grounds that it is canceled in Mary's transcript in *The Harvard Shelley Notebook* and that Mary omits it from her collected editions. But the first fact probably explains the second, and since all editors follow the other substantive features of the first edition rather than Mary's quite different safe-keeping transcript, it seems logical to retain this stanza also. The gibbet was a sort of gallows on which the body of a criminal executed for a particularly heinous crime was, by order of the sentencing judge, chained to an iron frame near the scene of the crime as a warning to others. Its use was legal in England from 1752 to 1834. See another use of the gibbet at the end of "Zeinab and Kathema."
8. The vegetative part (white filamentous tubes) of mushrooms or other fungi.
9. Reeds or rushes.
1. *unctuous:* oily; *meteors:* bad air or winds; *spray:* a slender twig or shoot.
2. Large waterfalls.

His breath was a chain which without a sound
The earth and the air and the water bound;   95
He came, fiercely driven, in his Chariot-throne
By the tenfold blasts of the arctic zone.

Then the weeds which were forms of living death
Fled from the frost to the Earth beneath.
Their decay and sudden flight from frost   100
Was but like the vanishing of a ghost!

And under the roots of the Sensitive-plant
The moles and the dormice died for want.
The birds dropped stiff from the frozen air
And were caught in the branches naked and bare.   105

First there came down a thawing rain
And its dull drops froze on the boughs again;
Then there steamed up a freezing dew
Which to the drops of the thaw-rain grew;

And a northern whirlwind, wandering about   110
Like a wolf that had smelt a dead child out,
Shook the boughs thus laden and heavy and stiff
And snapped them off with his rigid griff.[3]

When winter had gone and spring came back
The Sensitive-plant was a leafless wreck;   115
But the mandrakes and toadstools and docks and darnels
Rose like the dead from their ruined charnels.

CONCLUSION

Whether the Sensitive-plant, or that
Which within its boughs like a spirit sat
Ere its outward form had known decay,
Now felt this change,—I cannot say.

Whether that Lady's gentle mind,   5
No longer with the form combined
Which scattered love—as stars do light,
Found sadness, where it left delight,

I dare not guess; but in this life
Of error, ignorance and strife—   10
Where nothing is—but all things seem,
And we the shadows of the dream,

It is a modest creed, and yet
Pleasant if one considers it,
To own that death itself must be,   15
Like all the rest,—a mockery.

3. A claw.

That garden sweet, that lady fair
And all sweet shapes and odours there
In truth have never past away—
'Tis we, 'tis ours, are changed—not they.   20

For love, and beauty, and delight
There is no death nor change: their might
Exceeds our organs—which endure
No light—being themselves obscure.[4]

Ode to Heaven[1]

CHORUS OF SPIRITS

Palace-roof of cloudless nights,
Paradise of golden lights,
　　Deep, Immeasurable, Vast,
　　　　Which art now, and which wert then;
　　Of the present and the past,   5
　　　　Of the eternal Where and When,
　　　　　　Presence chamber, Temple, Home,
　　　　　　Ever-canopying Dome
　　　　　　Of acts and ages yet to come!

Glorious shapes have life in thee—   10
Earth and all Earth's company,
　　Living globes which ever throng
　　　　Thy deep chasms and wildernesses,
　　And green worlds that glide along,
　　　　And swift stars with flashing tresses,   15
　　　　　　And icy moons most cold and bright,
　　　　　　And mighty suns, beyond the Night,
　　　　　　Atoms[2] of intensest light!

4. *their might . . . obscure:* The statement of the conclusion is simply that, since we know *our organs* (of sensation, reasoning, etc.) to be *obscure* (dark, dim), the sequence of events related in Parts First, Second, and Third may not be the true picture. Because he knows human perceptions to be fallible, the poet can still hold his *modest creed* (13), even after relating the apparent death of the Lady and the destruction of the beautiful garden.
1. In *The Harvard Shelley Notebook*, Mary Shelley concluded her transcript of "Ode to Heaven," "Florence—December. 1819." The poem, an obvious outgrowth of the same mythopoeic impulse that inspired Act IV of *Prometheus Unbound*, was published in 1820 in the *Prometheus* volume. Our text, which differs considerably in form from those

in the collected editions, is based on a detailed comparison of the first edition with the holograph manuscripts at the Huntington and Bodleian libraries and with the transcript in *The Harvard Shelley Notebook*. The three parts of the poem represent three perspectives on man's place in the universe. The first is the viewpoint of eighteenth-century deists, represented by Joseph Addison's famous hymn, "The Spacious Firmament on High." The second enunciates the Platonic doctrine that the present world is an imperfect and darkened delusion compared to the spiritual reality. The third deplores the presumption of thinking that human existence is so important in the scheme of things. Cf. the opening canto of *Queen Mab*.
2. The smallest conceivable portions or fragments of anything.

Even thy name is as a God,
Heaven! for thou art the abode   20
   Of that Power which is the glass
     Wherein man his nature sees;—
Generations as they pass
     Worship thee with bended knees—
       Their unremaining Gods and they   25
      Like a river roll away—
      Thou remainest such—alway!—

A REMOTER VOICE

Thou art but the Mind's first chamber,
Round which its young fancies[3] clamber
   Like weak insects in a cave   30
     Lighted up by stalactites;
But the portal of the grave,
     Where a world of new delights
      Will make thy best glories seem
      But a dim and noonday gleam   35
      From the shadow of a dream.

A LOUDER AND STILL REMOTER VOICE

Peace! the abyss is wreathed with scorn
At your presumption, Atom-born![4]
   What is Heaven? and what are ye
     Who its brief expanse inherit?   40
   What are suns and spheres which flee
     With the instinct of that spirit
      Of which ye are but a part?
      Drops which Nature's mighty heart
      Drives through thinnest veins. Depart!   45

What is Heaven? a globe of dew
Filling in the morning new
   Some eyed flower[5] whose young leaves waken
     On an unimagined world.
   Constellated suns unshaken,   50
     Orbits measureless, are furled
      In that frail and fading sphere
      With ten million gathered there
      To tremble, gleam, and disappear![6]—

3. Fantasies.
4. I.e., born of one of the dust particles rendered visible by light, a mote in a sunbeam.
5. Probably the flower called cosmos.
6. In lines 44–54 the entire visible universe is seen as a microcosm existing as a tiny part of a dewdrop in an infinitely bigger universe.

Ode to the West Wind[1]

I

O wild West Wind, thou breath of Autumn's being,
Thou, from whose unseen presence the leaves dead
Are driven, like ghosts from an enchanter fleeing,

Yellow, and black, and pale, and hectic[2] red,
Pestilence-stricken multitudes:[3] O Thou,   5
Who chariotest to their dark wintry bed

The winged seeds, where they lie cold and low,
Each like a corpse within its grave, until
Thine azure sister of the Spring[4] shall blow

Her clarion[5] o'er the dreaming earth, and fill   10
(Driving sweet buds like flocks to feed in air)
With living hues and odours plain and hill:

Wild Spirit, which art moving everywhere;
Destroyer and Preserver;[6] hear, O hear!

II

Thou on whose stream, 'mid the steep sky's commotion,   15
Loose clouds[7] like Earth's decaying leaves are shed,
Shook from the tangled boughs of Heaven and Ocean,[8]

1. Though the basic imagery of this poem dates from at least 1817, when Shelley developed it in Canto IX of *Laon and Cythna* (see pp. 99–101), this best known of all Shelley's shorter poems was begun October 20–25, 1819, under circumstances described in the poet's own note: "This poem was conceived and chiefly written in a wood that skirts the Arno, near Florence, and on a day when that tempestuous wind, whose temperature is at once mild and animating, was collecting the vapours which pour down the autumnal rains. They began, as I foresaw, at sunset with a violent tempest of hail and rain, attended by that magnificent thunder and lightning peculiar to the Cisalpine regions." "Ode to the West Wind" was first published in the *Prometheus Unbound* volume of 1820.

Structurally the poem consists of five *terza-rima* sonnets, the first three of which describe the effect of autumn on the foliage of the land, the sea, and (figuratively) the sky. The fourth stanza contrasts the poet's situation with these natural elements, and the final stanza is a prayer or request to the West Wind, as mover of the seasonal cycle, to assist the poet's aims by spreading his message and, thereby, helping him to contribute to a moral or political revolution paralleling the seasonal change.

2. Wasting or consuming (referring to the "hectic flush" of tuberculosis).

3. *the leaves dead . . . multitudes:* Shelley embodies in lines 2–5 the traditional epic simile found in Homer, Virgil, Dante, and Milton, in which souls of the dead are compared to fallen leaves driven by the wind (see also "The Triumph of Life," 49–51). G. M. Matthews notes that the four colors are not only actually found in dead leaves, but are those traditionally representing the four races of man—Mongoloid, Negroid, Caucasian, and American Indian.

4. The traditional name of the autumnal west wind was Ausonius. (Italy was poetically known as Ausonia.) Though the spring west wind was masculine in both Greek (Zephyrus) and Latin (Favonius) mythology, Shelley revises the tradition by making the restorative force of the spring mildly feminine.

5. A narrow shrill-sounding war trumpet.

6. These titles come directly from the titles of the Hindu gods Siva the Destroyer and Vishnu the Preserver, known to Shelley from both the translations and writings of Sir William Jones and Edward Moor's *Hindu Pantheon* (1810).

7. High, wispy cirrus clouds (the word means "curl" or "lock of hair" in Latin).

8. Along the coasts of the Mediterranean from Genoa to Leghorn the autumn brought storms accompanied by waterspouts that rose like tree trunks on the horizon. (Shelley and other travelers of his time describe them.)

Angels[9] of rain and lightning: there are spread
On the blue surface of thine aery surge,
Like the bright hair uplifted from the head   20

Of some fierce Mænad,[1] even from the dim verge
Of the horizon to the zenith's height,
The locks of the approaching storm. Thou Dirge[2]

Of the dying year, to which this closing night
Will be the dome of a vast sepulchre,   25
Vaulted with all thy congregated might

Of vapours,[3] from whose solid atmosphere
Black rain and fire and hail will burst: O hear!

                              III
Thou who didst waken from his summer dreams
The blue Mediterranean, where he lay,   30
Lulled by the coil of his chrystalline streams,

Beside a pumice isle in Baiæ's bay,[4]
And saw in sleep old palaces and towers
Quivering within the wave's intenser day,

All overgrown with azure moss and flowers   35
So sweet, the sense faints picturing them! Thou
For whose path the Atlantic's level powers

Cleave themselves into chasms, while far below
The sea-blooms and the oozy woods which wear
The sapless foliage of the ocean,[5] know   40

Thy voice, and suddenly grow grey with fear,
And tremble and despoil themselves: O hear!

                              IV
If I were a dead leaf thou mightest bear;
If I were a swift cloud to fly with thee;
A wave to pant beneath thy power, and share   45

---

9. Literally, "messengers."
1. *hair . . . Mænad:* The cirrus clouds seem scattered ahead of the storm like locks thrown forward by the wild orgiastic dance of a maenad. Shelley had seen four depicted in a relief sculpture at Florence, which he described thus: "The tremendous spirit of superstition aided by drunkenness . . . seems to have caught them in its whirlwinds, and to bear them over the earth as the rapid volutions of a tempest bear the ever-changing trunk of a water-spout. . . . Their hair loose and floating seems caught in the tempest of their own tumultuous motion, their heads are thrown back leaning with a strange inanity upon their necks, and looking up to Heaven, while they totter and stumble even in the energy of their

tempestuous dance" (Julian Edition, VI, 323). See "The Triumph of Life," 137–147.
2. A song of mourning.
3. Clouds.
4. From a boat beside an island of *pumice* (porous lava) Shelley had the previous December seen the overgrown ruins of villas from the days of imperial Rome reflected in the waters of the Bay of Baiae (Shelley, *Letters*, II, 61).
5. "The phenomenon alluded to at the conclusion of the third stanza is well known to naturalists. The vegetation at the bottom of the sea, of rivers, and of lakes, sympathizes with that of the land in the change of seasons, and is consequently influenced by the winds which announce it" (Shelley's note).

The impulse of thy strength, only less free
Than thou, O Uncontrollable! If even
I were as in my boyhood, and could be

The comrade of thy wanderings over Heaven,
As then, when to outstrip thy skiey speed   50
Scarce seemed a vision; I would ne'er have striven

As thus with thee in prayer in my sore need.
Oh! lift me as a wave, a leaf, a cloud!
I fall upon the thorns of life!6 I bleed!

A heavy weight of hours has chained and bowed   55
One too like thee: tameless, and swift, and proud.

v

Make me thy lyre, even as the forest is:
What if my leaves are falling like its own!
The tumult of thy mighty harmonies

Will take from both a deep, autumnal tone,   60
Sweet though in sadness. Be thou, Spirit fierce,
My spirit! Be thou me, impetuous one!

Drive my dead thoughts over the universe
Like withered leaves to quicken a new birth!
And, by the incantation of this verse,   65

Scatter, as from an unextinguished hearth
Ashes and sparks, my words among mankind!
Be through my lips to unawakened Earth

The trumpet of a prophecy!7 O Wind,
If Winter comes, can Spring be far behind?   70

The Cloud1

I bring fresh showers for the thirsting flowers,
    From the seas and the streams;
I bear light shade for the leaves when laid
    In their noon-day dreams.

6. Behind Shelley's image—besides other literary references—lie Jesus' crown of thorns and Dante's metaphor of life as "a dark wood . . . rough and stubborn" (*Inferno*, I.1–5).

7. *Be . . . prophecy!:* "It is impossible to read the productions of our most celebrated writers . . . without being startled with the electric life which there is in their words. . . . They are the priests of an unapprehended inspiration, the mirrors of gigantic forms which futurity casts upon the present, the words which express what they conceive not, the trumpet which sings to battle and feels not what it inspires; the influence which is moved not but moves" (*A Philosophical View of Reform*; see also *A Defence of Poetry*, p. 508).

1. "The Cloud," written in 1820 and published with *Prometheus Unbound*, was inspired, not so much by an event or scene in Italy, as by the first-person plural song of the Nepheliads (cloud nymphs) in Part II of Leigh Hunt's poem "The Nymphs," which was admired by Shelley at least from its publication in *Foliage* (1818), and probably before. That song begins:

Ho! We are the Nepheliads, we,
Who bring the clouds from the great sea,
And have within our happy care
All the love 'twixt earth and air.
We it is with soft new showers
Wash the eyes of the young flowers. . . .
                    (*Foliage*, p. xxxi)

From my wings are shaken the dews that waken   5
    The sweet buds every one,
When rocked to rest on their mother's[2] breast,
    As she dances about the Sun.
I wield the flail[3] of the lashing hail,
    And whiten the green plains under,   10
And then again I dissolve it in rain,
    And laugh as I pass in thunder.

I sift the snow on the mountains below,
    And their great pines groan aghast;
And all the night 'tis my pillow white,   15
    While I sleep in the arms of the blast.
Sublime on the towers of my skiey bowers,
    Lightning my pilot sits;[4]
In a cavern under is fettered the thunder,
    It struggles and howls at fits;[5]   20
Over Earth and Ocean, with gentle motion,
    This pilot is guiding me,
Lured by the love of the genii that move
    In the depths of the purple sea;
Over the rills, and the crags, and the hills,   25
    Over the lakes and the plains,
Wherever he dream, under mountain or stream,
    The Spirit he loves remains;
And I all the while bask in Heaven's blue smile,
    Whilst he is dissolving in rains.   30

The sanguine Sunrise, with his meteor eyes,[6]
    And his burning plumes[7] outspread,
Leaps on the back of my sailing rack,[8]
    When the morning star shines dead;
As on the jag of a mountain crag,   35
    Which an earthquake rocks and swings,

Throughout the song are lines like these that suggest ideas that Shelley develops in "The Cloud." As Desmond King-Hele points out (*Shelley: His Thought and Work*, pp. 219–227), Luke Howard's *Essay on Clouds*, published in a journal in 1803, established the modern system of classification and generated interest in describing clouds. Reiman has argued (*Percy Bysshe Shelley*, pp. 116–117) that, besides creating the mythopoeic auto-biography of a cloud, Shelley uses the cloud here, as in other poems, as "an analogue of the human mind" and that the poem portrays "the life-cycle of the human soul."

2. I.e., the earth's.

3. A military weapon consisting of an iron handle, at the end of which a stouter striking part armed with spikes swings freely; also a similarly constructed implement for threshing grain.

4. In his published lectures entitled *A System of Familiar Philosophy* (2 vols., 1799), Adam Walker (who lectured at both Syon House Academy and Eton during Shelley's school days there) argued that "water rises through the air, flying on the wings of electricity" and that rains are caused when positively charged clouds react with the negatively charged earth, either in a violent electrical storm (lines 19–20) or in more gentle precipitation (line 30). The attraction of the two kinds of electrical charge Shelley personifies as love (23–28).

5. Spasmodically or at varying intervals.

6. I.e., like a fireball or shooting star; *sanguine:* blood-red.

7. A poetic description of the sun's corona.

8. A mass of clouds driven before the wind in the upper air.

An eagle alit one moment may sit
  In the light of its golden wings.
And when Sunset may breathe, from the lit Sea beneath,
  Its ardours of rest and of love,   40
And the crimson pall⁹ of eve may fall
  From the depth of Heaven above,
With wings folded I rest, on mine aëry nest,
  As still as a brooding dove.¹

That orbed maiden with white fire laden   *internal* 45
  Whom mortals call the Moon,   *rhyme*
Glides glimmering o'er my fleece-like floor,
  By the midnight breezes strewn;
And wherever the beat of her unseen feet,
  Which only the angels hear,   50
May have broken the woof,² of my tent's thin roof,
  The stars peep behind her, and peer;
And I laugh to see them whirl and flee,
  Like a swarm of golden bees,
When I widen the rent in my wind-built tent,   55
  Till the calm rivers, lakes, and seas,
Like strips of the sky fallen through me on high,
  Are each paved with the moon and these.³

I bind the Sun's throne with a burning zone
  And the Moon's with a girdle of pearl;⁴   60
The volcanos are dim and the stars reel and swim
  When the whirlwinds my banner unfurl.
From cape to cape, with a bridge-like shape,
  Over a torrent sea,
Sunbeam-proof, I hang like a roof—   65
  The mountains its columns be!
The triumphal arch, through which I march
  With hurricane, fire, and snow,
When the Powers of the Air, are chained to my chair,
  Is the million-coloured Bow;   70
The sphere-fire above its soft colours wove
  While the moist Earth was laughing below.

---

9. A canopy or coverlet of rich cloth.
1. *With wings . . . brooding dove:* A significant echo of the invocation in Book I of *Paradise Lost*, in which the "Heav'nly Muse," whom Milton identifies with the Holy Spirit, is described at the creation as sitting "Dove-like . . . brooding on the vast Abyss" (I.21).
2. Fabric.
3. That is, the earthly waters reflect the images of the moon and stars (*these*).
4. *I bind . . . girdle of pearl:* Cirrostratus nebulosus clouds—high, transparent, whitish cloud-veils covering the sky— produce the halo phenomenon when the sun or moon shines behind them. Shel-

ley's universalized Cloud changes constantly throughout the poem, assuming roles played by different types of clouds; for example, the cloud described in lines 45–58 is probably the middle-altitude altocumulus radiatus, a sheet of cloud that seems to be torn in *strips*, that *Sunbeam-proof . . . roof* in 65 is the low gray sheet stratocumulus opacus, and that which marches through *the triumphal arch* of the rainbow (67–70) is probably a cumulonimbus capillatus, a low rain-cloud, often featuring an anvilshaped "thunderhead." *zone* (59): *girdle*, belt.

I am the daughter of Earth and Water,
    And the nursling of the Sky;[5]
I pass through the pores, of the ocean and shores;   75
    I change, but I cannot die—
For after the rain, when with never a stain
    The pavilion of Heaven is bare,
And the winds and sunbeams, with their convex gleams,[6]
    Build up the blue dome of Air—   80
I silently laugh at my own cenotaph,[7]
    And out of the caverns of rain,
Like a child from the womb, like a ghost from the tomb,
    I arise, and unbuild it again.—

To a Sky-Lark[1]

Hail to thee, blithe Spirit!
    Bird thou never wert—
That from Heaven, or near it,
    Pourest thy full heart
In profuse strains of unpremeditated art.   5

Higher still and higher
    From the earth thou springest
Like a cloud of fire;
    The blue deep thou wingest,
And singing still dost soar, and soaring ever singest.   10

In the golden lightning
    Of the sunken Sun—
O'er which clouds are brightning,
    Thou dost float and run;
Like an unbodied joy whose race is just begun.   15

The pale purple even
    Melts around thy flight,
Like a star of Heaven[2]
    In the broad day-light,
Thou art unseen,—but yet I hear thy shrill delight,   20

5. As in the parentage of "The Witch of Atlas," the emphasis is on the Cloud's middle station on the metaphysical scale of being, between earth and heaven.
6. The course of sunlight is refracted by the earth's atmosphere, bending around the earth in a convex arc, when viewed from above. Violet and blue, at the end of the visible color spectrum with the shortest wave length, dominate in the sky when the sunbeams are least distorted by clouds of dust or moisture.
7. A sepulchral monument erected in honor of a deceased person whose body is elsewhere.

1. This poem was composed near Leghorn (Livorno) in late June 1820 and published with *Prometheus Unbound*. Thematically, it can be divided into three parts: lines 1–30; 31–60; and 61–105. The first describes the flight of an actual skylark (*Alauda arvensis*), a small European bird that sings only in flight, usually when it is too high to be clearly visible. The second part attempts but fails to find a fitting analogue for the bird and its song; the third asks the bird to teach men its secret joy.
2. Venus as the evening star.

Keen as are the arrows
    Of that silver sphere,[3] *Venus in morning*
Whose intense lamp narrows
    In the white dawn clear
Until we hardly see—we feel that it is there.   25

All the earth and air
    With thy voice is loud, *flight of the skylark described*
As when Night is bare
    From one lonely cloud
The moon rains out her beams—and Heaven is overflowed.   30

What thou art we know not;
    What is most like thee?
From rainbow clouds there flow not
    Drops so bright to see
As from thy presence showers a rain of melody.   35

Like a Poet[4] hidden
    In the light of thought,
Singing hymns unbidden,
    Till the world is wrought
To sympathy with hopes and fears it heeded not: 40

Like a high-born maiden
    In a palace-tower,
Soothing her love-laden
    Soul in secret hour,
With music sweet as love—which overflows her bower: 45

Like a glow-worm golden
    In a dell of dew,
Scattering unbeholden
    Its aerial hue
Among the flowers and grass which screen it from the view: 50

Like a rose embowered
    In its own green leaves—
By warm winds deflowered—
    Till the scent it gives
Makes faint with too much sweet heavy-winged thieves: 55

Sound of vernal showers
    On the twinkling grass, *attempt to compare skylark to something earthy*
Rain-awakened flowers,
    All that ever was
Joyous, and clear and fresh, thy music doth surpass.   60

3. Venus as the morning star.
4. The similes in stanzas 8–12 both descend from human poet and lover through the animal, vegetable, and mineral realms and involve all five senses.

Teach us, Sprite or Bird,
    What sweet thoughts are thine;
I have never heard
    Praise of love or wine[5]   *poems*
That panted forth a flood of rapture so divine: 65

Chorus Hymeneal[6]   *these poems don't come*
    Or triumphal chaunt   *near your song*
Matched with thine would be all
    But an empty vaunt,
A thing wherein we feel there is some hidden want.   70

What objects are the fountains
    Of thy happy strain?
What fields or waves or mountains?
    What shapes of sky or plain?
What love of thine own kind? what ignorance of pain?   75

With thy clear keen joyance
    Languor cannot be—
Shadow of annoyance
    Never came near thee;
XX Thou lovest—but ne'er knew love's sad satiety.   80

Waking or asleep,
    Thou of death must deem
Things more true and deep
    Than we mortals dream,
Or how could thy notes flow in such a chrystal stream?   85

We look before and after,
    And pine for what is not[7]—
Our sincerest laughter
    With some pain is fraught—
his Our sweetest songs are those that tell of saddest thought.   90

Yet if we could scorn   *must have one to*
    Hate and pride and fear;   *Nach the other*
If we were things born
    Not to shed a tear,
I know not how thy joy we ever should come near.   95

Better than all measures
    Of delightful sound—
Better than all treasures
    That in books are found—
X X X Thy skill to poet were, thou Scorner of the ground!   100

5. Short poems in *praise of love or wine*, called Anacreontics, were an established tradition descending from the Greek poet Anacreon (ca. 563–478 B.C.).
6. Wedding song; Hymen was the Greek god of marriage.
7. Shelley echoes *Hamlet*, IV.iv.33–39, where Hamlet distinguishes between human beings' "god-like reason" and mere animal life.

Teach me half the gladness
    That thy brain must know,
Such harmonious madness
    From my lips would flow
The world should listen then—as I am listening now.[8]   105

[handwritten: if the world would listen to my poems like I am listening to your song, then would be better understanding of ideal]

[handwritten: p.125]

Ode to Liberty[1]

Yet, Freedom, yet thy banner torn but flying,
Streams like a thunder-storm against the wind.[2]
                                        BYRON

I.

A glorious people vibrated again
    The lightning of the nations:[3] Liberty
From heart to heart, from tower to tower, o'er Spain,
    Scattering contagious fire into the sky,
Gleamed. My soul spurned the chains of its dismay,   5
        And in the rapid plumes of song
        Clothed itself, sublime and strong;
As a young eagle soars the morning clouds among,
    Hovering in verse o'er its accustomed prey;
        Till from its station in the heaven of fame   10
    The Spirit's whirlwind rapt it, and the ray
        Of the remotest sphere of living flame
Which paves the void was from behind it flung,
    As foam from a ship's swiftness, when there came
A voice out of the deep: I will record the same.   15

II.

The Sun and the serenest Moon sprang forth:
    The burning stars of the abyss were hurled
Into the depths of heaven. The dædal[4] earth,
    That island in the ocean of the world,
Hung in its cloud of all-sustaining air: 20
        But this divinest universe
        Was yet a chaos and a curse,
For thou wert not: but power from worst producing worse,
    The spirit of the beasts was kindled there,
        And of the birds, and of the watery forms,   25
    And there was war among them, and despair
        Within them, raging without truce or terms:

8. Shelley's estimate of the effects of poetic joy in lines 101–105 contrasts with the isolation that Coleridge sees as its result in "Kubla Khan," 42–54. See also *Julian and Maddalo,* 544–546.
1. This ode was written between March and July 1820 in celebration of the Spanish liberal revolution of that spring. Published later that year with *Prometheus Unbound,* it traces the progress of liberty as Thomas Gray had earlier traced the "Progress of Poesy." Except for the first and last stanzas, which frame the poem, the poet addresses the personified goddess of Liberty directly as "thou" in the form of a prayer.
2. Byron's *Childe Harold's Pilgrimage,* IV.XCVIII.1–2; the lines begin the last of twenty-one stanzas in which Byron traces the struggle between tyranny and liberty.
3. The spontaneous resistance to the French by the Spanish people in 1807–1808 had inspired the British to engage in the Peninsular Campaign in Portugal and Spain, the prelude to the downfall of Napoleon's empire.
4. Intricately wrought (from Daedalus, the Greek craftsman).

The bosom of their violated nurse
  Groan'd, for beasts warr'd on beasts, and worms on worms,
  And men on men; each heart was a hell of storms.   30

III.

Man, the imperial shape, then multiplied
  His generations under the pavilion
Of the Sun's throne: palace and pyramid,
  Temple and prison, to many a swarming million
Were, as to mountain-wolves their ragged caves.   35
      This human living multitude
      Was savage, cunning, blind, and rude,
For thou wert not; but o'er the populous solitude,
  Like one fierce cloud over a waste of waves
    Hung tyranny; beneath, sate deified   40
  The sister-pest,[5] congregator of slaves;
    Into the shadow of her pinions[6] wide
Anarchs[7] and priests, who feed on gold and blood
  Till with the stain their inmost souls are dyed,
  Drove the astonished herds of men from every side.   45

IV.

The nodding promontories, and blue isles,
  And cloud-like mountains, and dividuous[8] waves
Of Greece, basked glorious in the open smiles
  Of favouring heaven: from their enchanted caves
Prophetic echoes flung dim melody   50
      On the unapprehensive wild.
      The vine, the corn, the olive mild,
Grew savage yet, to human use unreconciled;
  And, like unfolded flowers beneath the sea,
    Like the man's thought dark in the infant's brain,   55
  Like aught that is which wraps what is to be,
Art's deathless dreams lay veiled by many a vein
  Of Parian stone;[9] and, yet a speechless child,
    Verse murmured, and Philosophy did strain
    Her lidless eyes for thee; when o'er the Ægean main   60

V.

Athens arose: a city such as vision
  Builds from the purple crags and silver towers
Of battlemented cloud, as in derision
  Of kingliest masonry: the ocean-floors
Pave it; the evening sky pavilions it;   65
      Its portals are inhabited
      By thunder-zoned winds, each head
Within its cloudy wings with sunfire garlanded,—

---

5. Fideistic religion exaggerating the importance of blind faith.
6. Wings.
7. Tyrants.

8. Separate, individual.
9. Fine white marble from the island of Paros, one of the Cyclades.

A divine work! Athens diviner yet
　　Gleamed with its crest of columns, on the will　　　70
Of man, as on a mount of diamond, set;
　　For thou[1] wert, and thine all-creative skill
Peopled with forms that mock the eternal dead
　　In marble immortality that hill[2]
Which was thine earliest throne and latest oracle.　　　75

VI.

Within the surface of Time's fleeting river
　　Its[3] wrinkled image lies, as then it lay
Immovably unquiet, and for ever
　　It trembles, but it cannot pass away!
The voices of its bards and sages thunder　　　80
　　　　With an earth-awakening blast
　　　　Through the caverns of the past;
Religion veils her eyes; Oppression shrinks aghast:
　　A winged sound of joy, and love, and wonder,
　　　Which soars where Expectation never flew,　　　85
　　Rending the veil of space and time asunder!
　　　One ocean feeds the clouds, and streams, and dew;
One sun illumines heaven; one spirit vast
　　With life and love makes chaos ever new,
　　As Athens doth the world with thy delight renew.　　　90

VII.

Then Rome was, and from thy deep bosom fairest,
　　Like a wolf-cub from a Cadmæan Mænad,[4]
She drew the milk of greatness, though thy dearest
　　From that Elysian food was yet unweaned;[5]
And many a deed of terrible uprightness　　　95
　　　　By thy sweet love was sanctified;
　　　　And in thy smile, and by thy side,
Saintly Camillus lived, and firm Atilius died.[6]
　　But when tears stained thy robe of vestal whiteness,
　　　And gold prophaned thy Capitolian throne,[7]　　　100
　　Thou didst desert, with spirit-winged lightness,
　　　The senate of the tyrants: they sunk prone
Slaves of one tyrant: Palatinus sighed
　　　Faint echoes of Ionian song; that tone
　　Thou didst delay to hear, lamenting to disown.　　　105

1. Athens, treated as a permanent idea of human civilization made possible by the spirit of Liberty.
2. The Acropolis.
3. Athens'.
4. In Euripides' play *The Bacchae*, the maenads, who are worshipers of Dionysus, are led by Cadmus' daughter Agave. (See *Prometheus Unbound*, IV.473–475.)
5. *thy dearest . . . yet unweaned:* Athens was still nourished by Liberty from which Rome now also drew inspiration.
6. Camillus, the Roman general, rejected the proposal by a traitorous teacher that Camillus secure the surrender of Falerii by using the teacher's pupils—the sons of that city's leading men—as hostages (Livy, 5.27). According to Roman legend Atilius Regulus (third century B.C.) urged Rome to continue the war with Carthage even though failure of the peace mission meant his own cruel death. Cf. "A Defence of Poetry," p. 494.
7. The Capitoline and Palatine (103), two of Rome's seven hills, represent republican Rome and imperial Rome, respectively.

VIII.

From what Hyrcanian[8] glen or frozen hill,
   Or piny promontory of the Arctic main,
Or utmost islet inaccessible,
   Didst thou lament the ruin of thy reign,
Teaching the woods and waves, and desert rocks,   110
      And every Naiad's[9] ice-cold urn,
      To talk in echoes sad and stern
Of that sublimest lore which man had dared unlearn?
   For neither didst thou watch the wizard flocks
      Of the Scald's dreams, nor haunt the Druid's sleep.[1]   115
What if the tears rained through thy scattered locks
   Were quickly dried? for thou didst groan, not weep,
When from its sea of death, to kill and burn,
   The Galilean serpent[2] forth did creep,
   And made thy world an undistinguishable heap.   120

IX.

A thousand years the Earth cried, Where art thou?
   And then the shadow of thy coming fell
On Saxon Alfred's olive-cinctured brow:[3]
   And many a warrior-peopled citadel,
Like rocks which fire lifts out of the flat deep,   125
      Arose in sacred Italy,
      Frowning o'er the tempestuous sea
Of kings, and priests, and slaves, in tower-crowned majesty;
   That multitudinous anarchy did sweep
      And burst around their walls, like idle foam,   130
   Whilst from the human spirit's deepest deep
      Strange melody with love and awe struck dumb
Dissonant arms; and Art, which cannot die,
   With divine wand traced on our earthly home
   Fit imagery to pave heaven's everlasting dome.[4]   135

X.

Thou huntress swifter than the Moon![5] thou terror
   Of the world's wolves! thou bearer of the quiver,
Whose sunlike shafts pierce tempest-winged Error,
   As light may pierce the clouds when they dissever
In the calm regions of the orient day!   140
      Luther[6] caught thy wakening glance,
      Like lightning, from his leaden lance

8. Hyrcania was a province of Persia near the Caspian (Hyrcanian) Sea.
9. Nymphs of fountains and streams.
1. Scalds (skalds) were Norwegian and Icelandic poets of the Viking period and down to about 1250 A.D.; *Druids:* Celtic priests.
2. The Christian religion.
3. Alfred the Great (870–901), the West Saxon king and scholar who made peace with the raiding Danes, united the English people, and encouraged the intellectual growth of his nation. He is circled or crowned with olive leaves, traditionally the highest tribute that could be paid to the honorable and brave.
4. The rise of the communes, independent city-state republics in medieval Italy, led to a revival of the arts.
5. The moon as the goddess Diana, virgin huntress.
6. Cf. *A Defence of Poetry*, p. 499.

Reflected, it dissolved the visions of the trance
   In which, as in a tomb, the nations lay;
      And England's prophets hailed thee as their queen,   145
   In songs whose music cannot pass away,
      Though it must flow for ever: not unseen
Before the spirit-sighted countenance
   Of Milton didst thou pass, from the sad scene
   Beyond whose night he saw, with a dejected mien.   150

XI.

The eager hours and unreluctant years
   As on a dawn-illumined mountain stood,
Trampling to silence their loud hopes and fears,
   Darkening each other with their multitude,
And cried aloud, Liberty! Indignation   155
      Answered Pity from her cave;
      Death grew pale within the grave,
And Desolation howled to the destroyer,[7] Save!
   When like heaven's sun girt by the exhalation
      Of its own glorious light, thou didst arise,   160
   Chasing thy foes from nation unto nation
      Like shadows: as if day had cloven the skies
At dreaming midnight o'er the western wave,
   Men started, staggering with a glad surprise,
   Under the lightnings of thine unfamiliar eyes.[8]   165

XII.

Thou heaven of earth! what spells could pall thee then
   In ominous eclipse? a thousand years
Bred from the slime of deep oppression's den,
   Dyed all thy liquid light with blood and tears,
Till thy sweet stars could weep the stain away;   170
      How like Bacchanals of blood
      Round France, the ghastly vintage, stood
Destruction's sceptred slaves, and Folly's mitred brood![9]
   When one, like them, but mightier far than they,
      The Anarch[1] of thine own bewildered powers,   175
   Rose: armies mingled in obscure array,
      Like clouds with clouds, darkening the sacred bowers
Of serene heaven. He, by the past pursued,
   Rests with those dead, but unforgotten hours,
   Whose ghosts scare victor kings in their ancestral towers.   180

XIII.

England yet sleeps: was she not called of old?
   Spain calls her now, as with its thrilling thunder
Vesuvius wakens Ætna,[2] and the cold
   Snow-crags by its reply are cloven in sunder:[3]

---

7. Death (157).
8. Lines 159–165 depict the Enlightenment and subsequent reform and revolutionary movements of the eighteenth century.
9. The French Revolution.
1. Napoleon.
2. Volcanoes near Naples and in eastern Sicily, respectively.
3. Split apart.

O'er the lit waves every Æolian isle   185
     From Pithecusa to Pelorus[4]
      Howls, and leaps, and glares in chorus:
They cry, Be dim; ye lamps of heaven suspended o'er us.
    Her[5] chains are threads of gold, she need but smile
      And they dissolve; but Spain's were links of steel,   190
Till bit to dust by virtue's keenest file.
     Twins of a single destiny! appeal
To the eternal years enthroned before us
    In the dim West; impress as from a seal
    All ye have thought and done! Time cannot dare conceal.   195

XIV.

Tomb of Arminius![6] render up thy dead.
    Till, like a standard from a watch-tower's staff,
His soul may stream over the tyrant's head;
    Thy victory shall be his epitaph,
Wild Bacchanal[7] of truth's mysterious wine,   200
     King-deluded Germany,
      His dead spirit lives in thee.
    Why do we fear or hope? thou art already free!
    And thou,[8] lost Paradise of this divine
     And glorious world! thou flowery wilderness!   205
Thou island of eternity! thou shrine
    Where desolation, clothed with loveliness,
Worships the thing thou wert! O Italy,
    Gather thy blood into thy heart; repress
    The beasts who make their dens thy sacred palaces.   210

XV.

O, that the free would stamp the impious name
    Of KING into the dust! or write it there,
So that this blot upon the page of fame
    Were as a serpent's path, which the light air
Erases, and the flat sands close behind!   215
     Ye[9] the oracle have heard:
      Lift the victory-flashing sword,
And cut the snaky knots of this foul gordian word,[1]
    Which weak itself as stubble, yet can bind
     Into a mass, irrefragably[2] firm,   220
The axes and the rods which awe mankind;
    The sound has poison in it, 'tis the sperm
Of what makes life foul, cankerous, and abhorred;
    Disdain not thou,[3] at thine appointed term,
    To set thine armed heel on this reluctant worm.   225

4. *Aeolian isles:* islands north of eastern Sicily, including Stromboli; *Pithecusa:* island of Ischia, west of Naples and Cumae; *Pelorus:* Cape Faro, the northeast point in Sicily.
5. England's.
6. Germanic tribal leader (18 B.C.–19 A.D.), who annihilated a Roman army (9 A.D.) and freed Germany from foreign domination.
7. An occasion of drunken revelry.
8. Italy.
9. The free (211).
1. "King" (212).
2. Indisputably.
3. Liberty.

XVI.

O, that the wise from their bright minds would kindle
  Such lamps within the dome of this dim world,
That the pale name of PRIEST might shrink and dwindle
  Into the hell from which it first was hurled,
A scoff of impious pride from fiends impure;   230
      Till human thoughts might kneel alone,
      Each before the judgement-throne
Of its own aweless soul, or of the power[4] unknown!
  O, that the words which make the thoughts obscure
    From which they spring, as clouds of glimmering dew   235
  From a white lake blot heaven's blue portraiture,
    Were stript of their thin masks and various hue
And frowns and smiles and splendours not their own,
    Till in the nakedness of false and true
    They stand before their Lord,[5] each to receive its due!   240

XVII.

He[6] who taught man to vanquish whatsoever
  Can be between the cradle and the grave
Crowned him the King of Life. Oh, vain endeavour!
  If on his own high will, a willing slave,
He has enthroned the oppression and the oppressor.   245
      What if earth can clothe and feed
      Amplest millions at their need,
And power in thought be as the tree within the seed?
  Or what if Art, an ardent intercessor,
    Diving on fiery wings to Nature's throne,   250
  Checks the great mother stooping to caress her,
    And cries: Give me, thy child, dominion
Over all height and depth?[7] if Life can breed
    New wants, and wealth from those who toil and groan
    Rend of thy gifts and hers[8] a thousandfold for one!   255

XVIII.

Come Thou, but lead out of the inmost cave
  Of man's deep spirit, as the morning-star
Beckons the Sun from the Eoan[9] wave,
  Wisdom. I hear the pennons of her car
Self-moving, like cloud charioted by flame;   260
      Comes she not, and come ye not,
      Rulers of eternal thought,
To judge, with solemn truth, life's ill-apportioned lot?
    Blind Love, and equal Justice, and the Fame
    Of what has been, the Hope of what will be?   265

---

4. See general note to "Mont Blanc," p. 89.
5. Either *aweless soul* or *power unknown* (233); Shelley may be purposely (skeptically) ambiguous here.
6. Lord (240).
7. In lines 249–253, Art intercedes between Nature (*the great mother*) and men.
8. *thy:* Liberty's; *hers:* Art's.
9. Eastern; Eos was the Greek name of Aurora, goddess of the dawn.

O, Liberty! if such could be thy name
   Wert thou disjoined from these, or they from thee:
If thine or theirs were treasures to be bought
By blood or tears, have not the wise and free
Wept tears, and blood like tears?—The solemn harmony   270

XIX.

Paused, and the spirit of that mighty singing
   To its abyss was suddenly withdrawn;
Then, as a wild swan, when sublimely winging
   Its path athwart the thunder-smoke of dawn,
Sinks headlong through the aerial golden light   275
      On the heavy-sounding plain,
      When the bolt has pierced its brain;
As summer clouds dissolve, unburthened of their rain;
   As a far taper fades with fading night,[1]
     As a brief insect dies with dying day,—   280
   My song, its pinions disarrayed of might,
     Drooped; o'er it closed the echoes far away
Of the great voice which did its flight sustain,
   As waves which lately paved his watery way
Hiss round a drowner's head in their tempestuous play.   285

The Cenci   Shelley began to compose this tragedy in May 1819, probably inspired by viewing the supposed Guido Reni portrait of Beatrice Cenci at the Palazzo Colonna in Rome. (The painting, which cannot be by Guido, is now exhibited at the Corsini Palace.) This portrait and a visit to the Palazzo Cenci stimulated Shelley to reread a manuscript version of the Cenci family history that Mary had copied in May 1818 from a copy owned by John Gisborne. Composition was interrupted by the death of William Shelley (June 7, 1819), but continued through late June and July after the Shelleys' move to the Villa Valsovano, near Leghorn. By July 25, Shelley could write to Peacock, "I have written a tragedy" (Shelley, *Letters*, II, 102; for the date of the letter, see *Shelley and his Circle*, VI, 897n.). On August 11, Shelley was copying his drama for the press, and on August 20, Mary notes, she was copying it; by September 21, 1819, the Leghorn printer Glauco Masi had produced 250 copies ready to ship to England.

In the meantime, on September 10, Shelley had mailed to Thomas Love Peacock a single printed copy (without the Dedication and Preface) with which he was to submit the play anonymously to the Theatre Royal, Covent Garden—where Beatrice would be played, Shelley hoped, by Eliza O'Neill (1791–1872), the leading female tragedian of the day. Miss O'Neill, unknown to Shelley, had just married and retired from the stage, and Thomas Harris—who had managed Covent Garden since 1774 and was not noted for his theatrical innovations—refused even to consider producing the play because of its emphasis on incest. His opinion was

---

1. Compare this simile with "Hymn to Intellectual Beauty," lines 44–45: "Thou   —that to human thought art nourishment,/Like darkness to a dying flame!"

echoed by theatrical censors in Britain throughout the nineteenth century; in 1886 *The Cenci* received its first staging in a private performance sponsored by the Shelley Society and was not produced on the London public stage until 1922, the centenary of Shelley's death. Prior to that date the play had been produced professionally in Paris (1891), Coburg, Germany (1919), Moscow (1919–1920), and Prague (1922); subsequent professional productions in Europe and America have confirmed Shelley's confidence that *The Cenci* is "fitted for the stage." (See Stuart Curran, *Shelley's "Cenci": Scorpions Ringed with Fire* [Princeton, 1970].)

When it became clear to Shelley that the play would not be staged, he secured its publication in 1820. It alone of Shelley's books went into an authorized second edition during his lifetime—one for which he corrected verbal errors in the first edition.

Our text is based on the first edition, as corrected from the errata leaf in the hand of Mary Shelley. Because Shelley himself saw the play through the press and inasmuch as the Italian compositors are unlikely to have taken as many liberties with the forms of Shelley's words and punctuation as British printers, *The Cenci* and *Adonais* (similarly produced) provide the best evidence of how Shelley wished his poetry to appear in print. We have, therefore, made only the most sparing changes in the first edition where obvious errors appeared (Æ instead of Œ at the beginning of "Œdipus") or where the printed punctuation is not only inadequate but also fails to conform with Shelley's own practice in his polished fair copy manuscripts.

The Cenci
A Tragedy, in Five Acts

DEDICATION[1]
TO LEIGH HUNT, Esq.

MY DEAR FRIEND—I inscribe with your name, from a distant country, and after an absence whose months have seemed years, this the latest of my literary efforts.

Those writings which I have hitherto published,[2] have been little else than visions which impersonate my own apprehensions of the beautiful and the just. I can also perceive in them the literary defects incidental to youth and impatience; they are dreams of what ought to be, or may be. The drama which I now present to you is a sad reality. I lay aside the presumptuous attitude of an instructor, and am content to paint, with such colours as my own heart furnishes, that which has been.

1. The rough draft of this Dedication to Shelley's closest friend was written at Villa Valsovano sometime in the period August 16–19, 1819; for the rough draft version and Shelley's possible reasons for dating it May 29, 1819, see Donald H. Reiman, *Shelley and his Circle*, VI, 865–874.
2. Shelley alludes especially to *Queen Mab, Alastor*, and *Laon and Cythna*, the last composed while Hunt was visiting him at Marlow.

Had I known a person more highly endowed than yourself with all that it becomes a man to possess, I had solicited for this work the ornament of his name. One more gentle, honourable, innocent and brave; one of more exalted toleration for all who do and think evil, and yet himself more free from evil; one who knows better how to receive, and how to confer a benefit though he must ever confer far more than he can receive; one of simpler, and, in the highest sense of the word, of purer life and manners I never knew: and I had already been fortunate in friendships when your name was added to the list.

In that patient and irreconcileable enmity with domestic and political tyranny and imposture which the tenor of your life has illustrated, and which, had I health and talents should illustrate mine, let us, comforting each other in our task, live and die.

All happiness attend you! Your affectionate friend,

PERCY B. SHELLEY.

ROME, *May* 29, 1819.

PREFACE

A Manuscript was communicated to me during my travels in Italy which was copied from the archives of the Cenci Palace at Rome, and contains a detailed account of the horrors which ended in the extinction of one of the noblest and richest families of that city during the Pontificate of Clement VIII,[3] in the year 1599. The story is, that an old man having spent his life in debauchery and wickedness, conceived at length an implacable hatred towards his children; which shewed itself towards one daughter under the form of an incestuous passion, aggravated by every circumstance of cruelty and violence. This daughter, after long and vain attempts to escape from what she considered a perpetual contamination both of body and mind, at length plotted with her mother-in-law[4] and brother to murder their common tyrant. The young maiden who was urged to this tremendous deed by an impulse which overpowered its horror, was evidently a most gentle and amiable being, a creature formed to adorn and be admired, and thus violently thwarted from her nature by the necessity of circumstance and opinion. The deed was quickly discovered and in spite of the most earnest prayers made to the Pope by the highest persons in Rome the criminals were put to death. The old man had during his life repeatedly bought his pardon from the Pope for capital crimes of the most enormous and unspeakable kind, at the price of a hundred thousand crowns; the

---

3. Clement VIII (Ippolito Aldobrandino) was pope from 1592 to 1605.
4. Stepmother; in Shelley's day the word could mean either "stepmother" or "spouse's mother."

death therefore of his victims can scarcely be accounted for by the love of justice. The Pope, among other motives for severity, probably felt that whoever killed the Count Cenci deprived his treasury of a certain and copious source of revenue.[5] Such a story, if told so as to present to the reader all the feelings of those who once acted it, their hopes and fears, their confidences and misgivings, their various interests, passions and opinions acting upon and with each other, yet all conspiring to one tremendous end, would be as a light to make apparent some of the most dark and secret caverns of the human heart.

On my arrival at Rome I found that the story of the Cenci was a subject not to be mentioned in Italian society without awakening a deep and breathless interest; and that the feelings of the company never failed to incline to a romantic pity for the wrongs, and a passionate exculpation of the horrible deed to which they urged her, who has been mingled two centuries with the common dust. All ranks of people knew the outlines of this history, and participated in the overwhelming interest which it seems to have the magic of exciting in the human heart. I had a copy of Guido's picture of Beatrice which is preserved in the Colonna Palace, and my servant instantly recognized it as the portrait of *La Cenci*.

This national and universal interest which the story produces and has produced for two centuries and among all ranks of people in a great City, where the imagination is kept for ever active and awake, first suggested to me the conception of its fitness for a dramatic purpose. In fact it is a tragedy which has already received, from its capacity of awakening and sustaining the sympathy of men, approbation and success. Nothing remained as I imagined, but to clothe it to the apprehensions of my countrymen in such language and action as would bring it home to their hearts. The deepest and the sublimest tragic compositions, *King Lear* and the two plays in which the tale of Œdipus is told, were stories which already existed in tradition, as matters of popular belief and interest, before Shakspeare and Sophocles made them familiar to the sympathy of all succeeding generations of mankind.

This story of the Cenci is indeed eminently fearful and monstrous: any thing like a dry exhibition of it on the stage would be insupportable. The person who would treat such a subject must increase the ideal, and diminish the actual horror of the events, so that the pleasure which arises from the poetry which exists in these tempestuous sufferings and crimes may mitigate the pain of the contemplation

5. "The Papal government formerly took the most extraordinary precautions against the publicity of facts which offer so tragical a demonstration of its own wickedness and weakness; so that the communication of the MS. had become, until very lately, a matter of some difficulty" (Shelley's note).

of the moral deformity from which they spring. There must also be nothing attempted to make the exhibition subservient to what is vulgarly termed a moral purpose. The highest moral purpose aimed at in the highest species of the drama, is the teaching the human heart, through its sympathies and antipathies, the knowledge of itself; in proportion to the possession of which knowledge, every human being is wise, just, sincere, tolerant and kind. If dogmas can do more, it is well: but a drama is no fit place for the enforcement of them. Undoubtedly, no person can be truly dishonoured by the act of another; and the fit return to make to the most enormous injuries is kindness and forbearance, and a resolution to convert the injurer from his dark passions by peace and love. Revenge, retaliation, atonement, are pernicious mistakes. If Beatrice had thought in this manner she would have been wiser and better; but she would never have been a tragic character: the few whom such an exhibition would have interested, could never have been sufficiently interested for a dramatic purpose, from the want of finding sympathy in their interest among the mass who surround them. It is in the restless and anatomizing casuistry[6] with which men seek the justification of Beatrice, yet feel that she has done what needs justification; it is in the superstitious horror with which they contemplate alike her wrongs and their revenge; that the dramatic character of what she did and suffered, consists.

I have endeavoured as nearly as possible to represent the characters as they probably were, and have sought to avoid the error of making them actuated by my own conceptions of right or wrong, false or true, thus under a thin veil converting names and actions of the sixteenth century into cold impersonations of my own mind. They are represented as Catholics, and as Catholics deeply tinged with religion. To a Protestant apprehension there will appear something unnatural in the earnest and perpetual sentiment of the relations between God and man which pervade the tragedy of the Cenci. It will especially be startled at the combination of an undoubting persuasion of the truth of the popular religion with a cool and determined perseverance in enormous guilt. But religion in Italy is not, as in Protestant countries, a cloak to be worn on particular days; or a passport which those who do not wish to be railed at carry with them to exhibit; or a gloomy passion for penetrating the impenetrable mysteries of our being, which terrifies its possessor at the darkness of the abyss to the brink of which it has conducted him. Religion coexists, as it were, in the mind of an Italian Catholic with

---

6. The analytic reasoning of the casuist; casuistry is that part of ethics which resolves cases of conscience, applying the general rules of religion and morality to particular instances in which circumstances alter cases, or in which there appears to be a conflict of duties.

a faith in that of which all men have the most certain knowledge. It is interwoven with the whole fabric of life. It is adoration, faith, submission, penitence, blind admiration; not a rule for moral conduct. It has no necessary connexion with any one virtue. The most atrocious villain may be rigidly devout, and without any shock to established faith, confess himself to be so. Religion pervades intensely the whole frame of society, and is according to the temper of the mind which it inhabits, a passion, a persuasion, an excuse, a refuge; never a check. Cenci himself built a chapel in the court of his Palace, and dedicated it to St. Thomas the Apostle, and established masses for the peace of his soul. Thus in the first scene of the fourth act Lucretia's design in exposing herself to the consequences of an expostulation with Cenci after having administered the opiate, was to induce him by a feigned tale to confess himself before death; this being esteemed by Catholics as essential to salvation; and she only relinquishes her purpose when she perceives that her perseverance would expose Beatrice to new outrages.

I have avoided with great care in writing this play the introduction of what is commonly called mere poetry, and I imagine there will scarcely be found a detached simile or a single isolated description, unless Beatrice's description of the chasm appointed for her father's murder should be judged to be of that nature.[7]

In a dramatic composition the imagery and the passion should interpenetrate one another, the former being reserved simply for the full development and illustration of the latter. Imagination is as the immortal God which should assume flesh for the redemption of mortal passion. It is thus that the most remote and the most familiar imagery may alike be fit for dramatic purposes when employed in the illustration of strong feeling, which raises what is low, and levels to the apprehension that which is lofty, casting over all the shadow of its own greatness. In other respects I have written more carelessly; that is, without an over-fastidious and learned choice of words. In this respect I entirely agree with those modern critics who assert that in order to move men to true sympathy we must use the familiar language of men. And that our great ancestors the antient English poets are the writers, a study of whom might incite us to do that for our own age which they have done for theirs. But it must be the real language of men in general and not that of any

7. "An idea in this speech was suggested by a most sublime passage in *El Purgatorio de San Patricio* of Calderon: the only plagiarism which I have intentionally committed in the whole piece" (Shelley's note). As Stuart Curran points out, most of Shelley's supposed verbal and situational "plagiarisms" from Shakespeare, Webster, and other Elizabethan dramatists derive from the Italian manuscript *Relation of the Death of the Family of the Cenci* that was Shelley's chief source. (Curran also notes that Shakespeare himself, by the time he wrote *Macbeth* and *Measure for Measure*, could have known the story of the Cenci murder and trial of 1599 through accounts transmitted from Rome.)

particular class to whose society the writer happens to belong. So much for what I have attempted; I need not be assured that success is a very different matter; particularly for one whose attention has but newly been awakened to the study of dramatic literature.

I endeavoured whilst at Rome to observe such monuments of this story as might be accessible to a stranger. The portrait of Beatrice at the Colonna Palace is admirable as a work of art: it was taken by Guido during her confinement in prison. But it is most interesting as a just representation of one of the loveliest specimens of the workmanship of Nature. There is a fixed and pale composure upon the features: she seems sad and stricken down in spirit, yet the despair thus expressed is lightened by the patience of gentleness. Her head is bound with folds of white drapery from which the yellow strings of her golden hair escape, and fall about her neck. The moulding of her face is exquisitely delicate; the eye brows are distinct and arched: the lips have that permanent meaning of imagination and sensibility which suffering has not repressed and which it seems as if death scarcely could extinguish. Her forehead is large and clear; her eyes, which we are told were remarkable for their vivacity, are swollen with weeping and lustreless, but beautifully tender and serene. In the whole mien there is a simplicity and dignity which united with her exquisite loveliness and deep sorrow are inexpressibly pathetic. Beatrice Cenci appears to have been one of those rare persons in whom energy and gentleness dwell together without destroying one another: her nature was simple and profound. The crimes and miseries in which she was an actor and a sufferer are as the mask and the mantle in which circumstances clothed her for her impersonation on the scene of the world.

The Cenci Palace is of great extent; and though in part modernized, there yet remains a vast and gloomy pile of feudal architecture in the same state as during the dreadful scenes which are the subject of this tragedy. The Palace is situated in an obscure corner of Rome, near the quarter of the Jews, and from the upper windows you see the immense ruins of Mount Palatine half hidden under their profuse overgrowth of trees. There is a court in one part of the palace (perhaps that in which Cenci built the Chapel to St. Thomas), supported by granite columns and adorned with antique friezes of fine workmanship and built up, according to the antient Italian fashion, with balcony over balcony of open work. One of the gates of the palace formed of immense stones and leading through a passage, dark and lofty and opening into gloomy subterranean chambers, struck me particularly.

Of the Castle of Petrella, I could obtain no further information than that which is to be found in the manuscript.

DRAMATIS PERSONÆ

COUNT FRANCESCO CENCI.
GIACOMO. }
BERNARDO. } *his sons.*
CARDINAL CAMILLO.
ORSINO, *a Prelate.*

SAVELLA, *the Pope's Legate.*
OLIMPIO. }
MARZIO. } *Assassins.*
ANDREA, *servant to Cenci.*
Nobles—Judges—Guards—Servants.

LUCRETIA, W*ife of* CENCI, *and step-mother of his children.*
BEATRICE, *his daughter.*

The Scene lies principally in Rome, but changes during the Fourth
Act to Petrella, a castle among the Apulia Apennines.

Time. During the Pontificate of Clement VIII.

ACT I

SCENE I.—*An apartment in the Cenci Palace.*
Enter COUNT CENCI, *and* CARDINAL CAMILLO.
Camillo. That matter of the murder is hushed up
If you consent to yield his Holiness
Your fief that lies beyond the Pincian gate.[8]—
It needed all my interest in the conclave
To bend him to this point: he said that you   5
Bought perilous impunity with your gold;
That crimes like yours if once or twice compounded
Enriched the Church, and respited from hell
An erring soul which might repent and live:—
But that the glory and the interest   10
Of the high throne he fills, little consist
With making it a daily mart of guilt
As manifold and hideous as the deeds
Which you scarce hide from men's revolted eyes.
  Cenci. The third of my possessions—let it go!   15
Aye, I once heard the nephew of the Pope[9]
Had sent his architect to view the ground,
Meaning to build a villa on my vines
The next time I compounded[1] with his uncle:
I little thought he should outwit me so!   20
Henceforth no witness—not the lamp—shall see
That which the vassal threatened to divulge
Whose throat is choked with dust for his reward.
The deed he saw could not have rated higher
Than his most worthless life:—it angers me!   25
Respited me from Hell!—So may the Devil

---

8. The gate at the north end of the Via
Veneto and now leading to the Borghese
Gardens; *fief*: an estate.
9. The illegitimate children of Roman

Catholic clergy were euphemistically
called "nephews" and "nieces."
1. Accepted terms of settlement in lieu
of prosecution.

Respite their souls from Heaven. No doubt Pope Clement,
And his most charitable nephews, pray
That the apostle Peter and the saints
Will grant for their sake that I long enjoy   30
Strength, wealth, and pride, and lust, and length of days
Wherein to act the deeds which are the stewards
Of their revenue.—But much yet remains
To which they shew no title.
    Camillo.   Oh, Count Cenci!
So much that thou migh'st honourably live   35
And reconcile thyself with thine own heart
And with thy God, and with the offended world.
How hideously look deeds of lust and blood
Through those snow white and venerable hairs!—
Your children should be sitting round you now,   40
But that you fear to read upon their looks
The shame and misery you have written there.
Where is your wife? Where is your gentle daughter?
Methinks her sweet looks, which make all things else
Beauteous and glad, might kill the fiend within you.   45
Why is she barred from all society
But her own strange and uncomplaining wrongs?[2]
Talk with me, Count,—you know I mean you well.
I stood beside your dark and fiery youth
Watching its bold and bad career, as men   50
Watch meteors, but it vanished not—I marked
Your desperate and remorseless manhood; now
Do I behold you in dishonoured age
Charged with a thousand unrepented crimes.
Yet I have ever hoped you would amend,   55
And in that hope have saved your life three times.
    Cenci. For which Aldobrandino[3] owes you now
My fief beyond the Pincian.—Cardinal,
One thing, I pray you, recollect henceforth,
And so we shall converse with less restraint.   60
A man you knew spoke of my wife and daughter—
He was accustomed to frequent my house;
So the next day *his* wife and daughter came
And asked if I had seen him; and I smiled:
I think they never saw him any more.   65
    Camillo. Thou execrable man, beware!—
    Cenci.   Of thee?
Nay this is idle:—We should know each other.
As to my character for what men call crime
Seeing I please my senses as I list,[4]
And vindicate that right with force or guile,   70
It is a public matter, and I care not

2. The evils done to Beatrice.   4. Wish or choose.
3. I.e., the Pope (his family name).

If I discuss it with you. I may speak
Alike to you and my own conscious heart—
For you give out that you have half reformed me,
Therefore strong vanity will keep you silent   75
If fear should not; both will, I do not doubt.
All men delight in sensual luxury,
All men enjoy revenge; and most exult
Over the tortures they can never feel—
Flattering their secret peace with others' pain.   80
But I delight in nothing else. I love
The sight of agony, and the sense of joy,
When this shall be another's, and that mine.
And I have no remorse and little fear,
Which are, I think, the checks of other men.   85
This mood has grown upon me, until now
Any design my captious[5] fancy makes
The picture of its wish, and it forms none
But such as men like you would start to know.
Is as my natural food and rest debarred   90
Until it be accomplished.
    Camillo.   Art thou not
Most miserable?
    Cenci.   Why, miserable?—
No.—I am what your theologians call
Hardened;—which they must be in impudence,
So to revile a man's peculiar taste.   95
True, I was happier than I am, while yet
Manhood remained to act the thing I thought;
While lust was sweeter than revenge; and now
Invention palls:—Aye, we must all grow old—
And but that there remains a deed to act   100
Whose horror might make sharp an appetite
Duller than mine—I'd do,—I know not what.
When I was young I thought of nothing else
But pleasure; and I fed on honey sweets:
Men, by St. Thomas! cannot live like bees   105
And I grew tired:—yet, till I killed a foe,
And heard his groans, and heard his children's groans,
Knew I not what delight was else on earth,
Which now delights me little. I the rather
Look on such pangs as terror ill conceals,   110
The dry fixed eye ball; the pale quivering lip,
Which tell me that the spirit weeps within
Tears bitterer than the bloody sweat of Christ.
I rarely kill the body which preserves,
Like a strong prison, the soul within my power,   115
Wherein I feed it with the breath of fear
For hourly pain.

---

5. Designed to entrap or entangle by subtlety.

Camillo.   Hell's most abandoned fiend
Did never, in the drunkenness of guilt,
Speak to his heart as now you speak to me;
I thank my God that I believe you not.   120

Enter ANDREA.

   Andrea. My Lord, a gentleman from Salamanca[6]
Would speak with you.
   Cenci.   Bid him attend me in
The grand saloon.[7]   [*Exit* ANDREA
   Camillo.   Farewell; and I will pray
Almighty God that thy false, impious words
Tempt not his spirit to abandon thee.   [*Exit* CAMILLO.
   Cenci. The third of my possessions! I must use   126
Close husbandry,[8] or gold, the old man's sword,
Falls from my withered hand. But yesterday
There came an order from the Pope to make
Fourfold provision for my cursed sons;   130
Whom I had sent from Rome to Salamanca,
Hoping some accident might cut them off;
And meaning if I could to starve them there.
I pray thee, God, send some quick death upon them!
Bernardo and my wife could not be worse   135
If dead and damned:—then, as to Beatrice—
              [*Looking around him suspiciously.*
I think they cannot hear me at that door;
What if they should? And yet I need not speak
Though the heart triumphs with itself in words.
O, thou most silent air, that shalt not hear   140
What now I think! Thou, pavement, which I tread
Towards her chamber,—let your echoes talk
Of my imperious step scorning surprise,
But not of my intent!—Andrea!

Enter ANDREA.

   Andrea.   My lord?
   Cenci. Bid Beatrice attend me in her chamber   145
This evening:—no, at midnight and alone.   [*Exeunt.*

SCENE II.—*A garden of the Cenci Palace. Enter* BEATRICE *and*
ORSINO, *as in conversation.*

   Beatrice. Pervert not truth,
Orsino. You remember where we held
That conversation;—nay, we see the spot
Even from this cypress;—two long years are past
Since, on an April midnight, underneath   5
The moon-light ruins of mount Palatine,
I did confess to you my secret mind.

6. A city in Old Castile, Spain—not far
from northern Portugal.
7. A principal reception room in a palace
or great house; salon.
8. Secret or careful thrift, economy.

Orsino. You said you loved me then.
Beatrice. You are a Priest,
Speak to me not of love.
Orsino. I may obtain
The dispensation of the Pope to marry.   10
Because I am a Priest do you believe
Your image, as the hunter some struck deer,
Follows me not whether I wake or sleep?
Beatrice. As I have said, speak to me not of love;
Had you a dispensation I have not;   15
Nor will I leave this home of misery
Whilst my poor Bernard, and that gentle lady
To whom I owe life, and these virtuous thoughts,
Must suffer what I still have strength to share.
Alas, Orsino! All the love that once   20
I felt for you, is turned to bitter pain.
Ours was a youthful contract, which you first
Broke, by assuming vows no Pope will loose.
And thus I love you still, but holily,
Even as a sister or a spirit might;   25
And so I swear a cold fidelity.
And it is well perhaps we shall not marry.
You have a sly, equivocating vein
That suits me not.—Ah, wretched that I am!
Where shall I turn? Even now you look on me   30
As you[9] were not my friend, and as if you
Discovered that I thought so, with false smiles
Making my true suspicion seem your wrong.
Ah! No, forgive me; sorrow makes me seem
Sterner than else my nature might have been;   35
I have a weight of melancholy thoughts,
And they forbode,—but what can they forbode
Worse than I now endure?
Orsino. All will be well.
Is the petition yet prepared? You know
My zeal for all you wish, sweet Beatrice;   40
Doubt not but I will use my utmost skill
So that the Pope attend to your complaint.
Beatrice. Your zeal for all I wish;—Ah me, you are cold!
Your utmost skill . . . speak but one word . . . (*aside*) Alas!
Weak and deserted creature that I am,   45
Here I stand bickering with my only friend!   [*To* ORSINO.
This night my father gives a sumptuous feast,
Orsino; he has heard some happy news
From Salamanca, from my brothers there,
And with this outward shew of love he mocks   50
His inward hate. 'Tis bold hypocrisy
For he would gladlier celebrate their deaths,

9. I.e., As if you.

Which I have heard him pray for on his knees:
Great God! that such a father should be mine!
But there is mighty preparation made, 55
And all our kin, the Cenci, will be there,
And all the chief nobility of Rome.
And he has bidden me and my pale Mother
Attire ourselves in festival array.
Poor lady! She expects some happy change 60
In his dark spirit from this act; I none.
At supper I will give you the petition:
Till when—farewell.
    Orsino.   Farewell. (*Exit* BEATRICE.) I know the Pope
Will ne'er absolve me from my priestly vow
But by absolving me from the revenue 65
Of many a wealthy see;[1] and, Beatrice,
I think to win thee at an easier rate.
Nor shall he read her eloquent petition:
He might bestow her on some poor relation
Of his sixth cousin, as he did her sister, 70
And I should be debarred from all access.
Then as to what she suffers from her father,
In all this there is much exaggeration:—
Old men are testy and will have their way;
A man may stab his enemy, or his vassal, 75
And live a free life as to wine or women,
And with a peevish temper may return
To a dull home, and rate[2] his wife and children;
Daughters and wives call this, foul tyranny.
I shall be well content if on my conscience 80
There rest no heavier sin than what they suffer
From the devices of my love—a net
From which she shall escape not. Yet I fear
Her subtle mind, her awe-inspiring gaze,
Whose beams anatomize[3] me nerve by nerve 85
And lay me bare, and make me blush to see
My hidden thoughts.—Ah, no! A friendless girl
Who clings to me, as to her only hope:—
I were a fool, not less than if a panther
Were panic-stricken by the Antelope's eye, 90
If she escape me.   [*Exit.*

SCENE III.—*A magnificent Hall in the Cenci Palace. A Banquet.*
  Enter CENCI, LUCRETIA, BEATRICE, ORSINO, CAMILLO, NOBLES.

    Cenci. Welcome my friends and Kinsmen; welcome ye,
Princes and Cardinals, pillars of the church,
Whose presence honours our festivity.

---

1. *revenue/ Of many a wealthy see:* Orsino, a clergyman from an influential Roman family, has been given nominal charge of several churches; he receives their revenues and hires common priests to perform all duties.
2. Scold, reprove angrily or vehemently.
3. Analyze minutely.

I have too long lived like an Anchorite,[4]
And in my absence from your merry meetings   5
An evil word is gone abroad of me;
But I do hope that you, my noble friends,
When you have shared the entertainment here,
And heard the pious cause for which 'tis given,
And we have pledged a health or two together,   10
Will think me flesh and blood as well as you;
Sinful indeed, for Adam made all so,
But tender-hearted, meek and pitiful.
    First Guest. In truth, my Lord, you seem too light of heart,
Too sprightly and companionable a man,   15
To act the deeds that rumour pins on you.
(*To his Companion.*) I never saw such blithe and open cheer
In any eye!
    Second Guest. Some most desired event,
In which we all demand a common joy,
Has brought us hither; let us hear it, Count.   20
    Cenci. It is indeed a most desired event.
If, when a parent from a parent's heart
Lifts from this earth to the great father of all
A prayer, both when he lays him down to sleep,
And when he rises up from dreaming it;   25
One supplication, one desire, one hope,
That he would grant a wish for his two sons
Even all that he demands in their regard—
And suddenly beyond his dearest hope,
It is accomplished, he should then rejoice,   30
And call his friends and kinsmen to a feast,
And task their love to grace his merriment,
Then honour me thus far—for I am he.
    Beatrice (*to* LUCRETIA). Great God! How horrible! Some
      dreadful ill
Must have befallen my brothers.
    Lucretia.   Fear not, Child,   35
He speaks too frankly.
    Beatrice.   Ah! My blood runs cold.
I fear that wicked laughter round his eye
Which wrinkles up the skin even to the hair.
    Cenci. Here are the letters brought from Salamanca;
Beatrice, read them to your mother. God!   40
I thank thee! In one night didst thou perform,
By ways inscrutable, the thing I sought.
My disobedient and rebellious sons
Are dead!—Why, dead!—What means this change of cheer?
You hear me not, I tell you they are dead;   45
And they will need no food or raiment more:
The tapers that did light them the dark way

4. One who has secluded himself from the world, usually for religious reasons.

Are their last cost. The Pope, I think, will not
Expect I should maintain them in their coffins.
Rejoice with me—my heart is wondrous glad.   50
        [LUCRETIA *sinks, half fainting;* BEATRICE *supports her.*
  Beatrice. It is not true!—Dear lady, pray look up.
Had it been true, there is[5] a God in Heaven,
He would not live to boast of such a boon.
Unnatural man, thou knowest that it is false.
  Cenci. Aye, as the word of God; whom here I call   55
To witness that I speak the sober truth;—
And whose most favouring Providence was shewn
Even in the manner of their deaths. For Rocco[6]
Was kneeling at the mass, with sixteen others,
When the Church fell and crushed him to a mummy,[7]   60
The rest escaped unhurt. Cristofano[8]
Was stabbed in error by a jealous man,
Whilst she he loved was sleeping with his rival,
All in the self-same hour of the same night;
Which shews that Heaven has special care of me.   65
I beg those friends who love me, that they mark
The day a feast upon their calendars.
It was the twenty-seventh of December:[9]
Aye, read the letters if you doubt my oath.
       [*The assembly appears confused; several of the guests rise.*
  First Guest. Oh, horrible! I will depart—
  Second Guest.   And I.—
  Third Guest.   No, stay! 70
I do believe it is some jest; though faith!
'Tis mocking us somewhat too solemnly.
I think his son has married the Infanta,
Or found a mine of gold in El Dorado;[1]
'Tis but to season some such news; stay, stay!   75
I see 'tis only raillery by his smile.
  Cenci (*filling a bowl of wine, and lifting it up*).
Oh, thou bright wine whose purple splendor leaps
And bubbles gaily in this golden bowl
Under the lamp light, as my spirits do,
To hear the death of my accursed sons!   80
Could I believe thou wert their mingled blood,
Then would I taste thee like a sacrament,
And pledge with thee the mighty Devil in Hell,
Who, if a father's curses, as men say,
Climb with swift wings after their children's souls,   85
And drag them from the very throne of Heaven,
Now triumphs in my triumph!—But thou art

---

5. I.e., because there is.
6. One of Cenci's sons.
7. A pulpy substance or mass.
8. Another of Cenci's sons.
9. The feast day of John the Evangelist, who wrote "God is love" (1 John 4:8).

1. A fictitious country or city abounding in gold, believed by the Spaniards and Sir Walter Ralegh to exist upon the Amazon; *Infanta:* the title given a daughter of the king of Spain.

Superfluous; I have drunken deep of joy
And I will taste no other wine to-night.
Here, Andrea! Bear the bowl around.

 A Guest (*rising*).   Thou wretch! 90
Will none among this noble company
Check the abandoned villain?

 Camillo.   For God's sake
Let me dismiss the guests! You are insane,
Some ill will come of this.

 Second Guest.   Seize, silence him!

 First Guest. I will!

 Third Guest. And I!

 Cenci (*addressing those who rise with a threatening gesture*).
       Who moves? Who speaks?
       (*turning to the Company*)
          'tis nothing, 95
Enjoy yourselves.—Beware! For my revenge
Is as the sealed commission of a king
That kills, and none dare name the murderer.

 [*The Banquet is broken up; several of the Guests are departing.*

 Beatrice. I do entreat you, go not, noble guests;
What although tyranny, and impious hate 100
Stand sheltered by a father's hoary hair?
What, if 'tis he who clothed us in these limbs
Who tortures them, and triumphs? What, if we,
The desolate and the dead, were his own flesh,
His children and his wife, whom he is bound 105
To love and shelter? Shall we therefore find
No refuge in this merciless wide world?
Oh, think what deep wrongs must have blotted out
First love, then reverence in a child's prone mind
Till it thus vanquish shame and fear! O, think! 110
I have borne much, and kissed the sacred hand
Which crushed us to the earth, and thought its stroke
Was perhaps some paternal chastisement!
Have excused much, doubted; and when no doubt
Remained, have sought by patience, love and tears 115
To soften him, and when this could not be
I have knelt down through the long sleepless nights
And lifted up to God, the father of all,
Passionate prayers: and when these were not heard
I have still borne,—until I meet you here, 120
Princes and kinsmen, at this hideous feast
Given at my brothers' deaths. Two yet remain,
His wife remains and I, whom if ye save not,
Ye may soon share such merriment again
As fathers make over their children's graves. 125
Oh! Prince Colonna,[2] thou art our near kinsman,

2. The Colonna family, great rivals of the Orsinis for centuries, were at this period at the height of their power.

Cardinal, thou art the Pope's chamberlain,
Camillo, thou art chief justiciary,
Take us away!

    Cenci. (*He has been conversing with* CAMILLO *during the first
    part of* BEATRICE'S *speech; he hears the conclusion, and now
                     advances.*)

            I hope my good friends here
Will think of their own daughters—or perhaps   130
Of their own throats—before they lend an ear
To this wild girl.

    Beatrice (*not noticing the words of Cenci*). Dare no one look
    on me
None answer? Can one tyrant overbear
The sense of many best and wisest men?
Or is it that I sue not in some form   135
Of scrupulous law, that ye deny my suit?
Oh, God! That I were buried with my brothers!
And that the flowers of this departed spring
Were fading on my grave! And that my father
Were celebrating now one feast for all!   140

    Camillo. A bitter wish for one so young and gentle;
Can we do nothing—

    Colonna.   Nothing that I see.
Count Cenci were a dangerous enemy:
Yet I would second any one.

    A Cardinal.   And I.

    Cenci. Retire to your chamber, insolent girl!   145

    Beatrice. Retire thou, impious man! Aye hide thyself
Where never eye can look upon thee more!
Wouldst thou have honour and obedience
Who art a torturer? Father, never dream
Though thou mayst overbear this company,   150
But ill must come of ill.—Frown not on me!
Haste, hide thyself, lest with avenging looks
My brothers' ghosts should hunt thee from thy seat!
Cover thy face from every living eye,
And start if thou but hear a human step: 155
Seek out some dark and silent corner, there,
Bow thy white head before offended God,
And we will kneel around, and fervently
Pray that he pity both ourselves and thee.

    Cenci. My friends, I do lament this insane girl   160
Has spoilt the mirth of our festivity.
Good night, farewell; I will not make you longer
Spectators of our dull domestic quarrels.
Another time.—   [*Exeunt all but* CENCI *and* BEATRICE.
            My brain is swimming round;
Give me a bowl of wine!   [*To* BEATRICE.

Thou painted viper!   165
Beast that thou art! Fair and yet terrible!
I know a charm shall make thee meek and tame,
Now get thee from my sight!   [*Exit* BEATRICE.
                          Here, Andrea,
Fill up this goblet with Greek wine. I said
I would not drink this evening; but I must;   170
For, strange to say, I feel my spirits fail
With thinking what I have decreed to do.—
                              [*Drinking the wine.*
Be thou the resolution of quick youth
Within my veins, and manhood's purpose stern,
And age's firm, cold, subtle villainy;   175
As if thou wert indeed my children's blood
Which I did thirst to drink! The charm works well;
It must be done; it shall be done, I swear!   [*Exit.*

END OF THE FIRST ACT.

ACT II

SCENE I.—*An apartment in the Cenci Palace. Enter* LUCRETIA *and*
BERNARDO.

Lucretia. Weep not, my gentle boy; he struck but me
Who have borne deeper wrongs. In truth, if he
Had killed me, he had done a kinder deed.
O, God Almighty, do thou look upon us,
We have no other friend but only thee!   5
Yet weep not; though I love you as my own
I am not your true mother.
    Bernardo.   O more, more,
Than ever mother was to any child,
That have you been to me! Had he not been
My father, do you think that I should weep?   10
    Lucretia. Alas! Poor boy, what else could'st thou have done?

Enter BEATRICE.

Beatrice (in a hurried voice). Did he pass this way? Have you
    seen him, brother?
Ah! No, that is his step upon the stairs;
'Tis nearer now; his hand is on the door;
Mother, if I to thee have ever been   15
A duteous child, now save me! Thou, great God,
Whose image upon earth a father is,
Dost thou indeed abandon me! He comes;
The door is opening now; I see his face;
He frowns on others, but he smiles on me,   20
Even as he did after the feast last night.

Enter a Servant.

Almighty God, how merciful thou art!
'Tis but Orsino's servant.—Well, what news?
   Servant. My master bids me say, the Holy Father
Has sent back your petition thus unopened.   [*Giving a paper.*
And he demands at what hour 'twere secure   26
To visit you again?
   Lucretia.   At the Ave Mary.[3]   [*Exit Servant.*
So, daughter, our last hope has failed; Ah me!
How pale you look; you tremble, and you stand
Wrapped in some fixed and fearful meditation,   30
As if one thought were over strong for you:
Your eyes have a chill glare; O, dearest child!
Are you gone mad? If not, pray speak to me.
   Beatrice. You see I am not mad. I speak to you.
   Lucretia. You talked of something that your father did   35
After that dreadful feast? Could it be worse
Than when he smiled, and cried, "My sons are dead!"
And every one looked in his neighbour's face
To see if others were as white as he?
At the first word he spoke I felt the blood   40
Rush to my heart, and fell into a trance;
And when it past I sat all weak and wild;
Whilst you alone stood up, and with strong words
Checked his unnatural pride; and I could see
The devil was rebuked that lives in him.   45
Until this hour thus you have ever stood
Between us and your father's moody wrath
Like a protecting presence: your firm mind
Has been our only refuge and defence:
What can have thus subdued it? What can now   50
Have given you that cold melancholy look,
Succeeding to your unaccustomed fear?
   Beatrice. What is it that you say? I was just thinking
'Twere better not to struggle any more.
Men, like my father, have been dark and bloody,   55
Yet never—O! Before worse comes of it
'Twere wise to die: it ends in that at last.
   Lucretia. Oh, talk not so, dear child! Tell me at once
What did your father do or say to you?
He stayed not after that accursed feast   60
One moment in your chamber.—Speak to me.
   Bernardo. Oh, sister, sister, prithee, speak to us!
   Beatrice (*speaking very slowly with a forced calmness*).
It was one word, Mother, one little word;
One look, one smile. (*Wildly.*) Oh! He has trampled me
Under his feet, and made the blood stream down   65

---

3. I.e., at the hour when the bell is rung for the recitation of the salutation (*Ave*) to the Virgin.

My pallid cheeks. And he has given us all
Ditch water, and the fever-stricken flesh
Of buffaloes, and bade us eat or starve,
And we have eaten.—He has made me look
On my beloved Bernado, when the rust   70
Of heavy chains has gangrened his sweet limbs,
And I have never yet despaired—but now!
What would I say?   *[Recovering herself.*
      Ah! No, 'tis nothing new.
The sufferings we all share have made me wild:
He only struck and cursed me as he passed;   75
He said, he looked, he did;—nothing at all
Beyond his wont, yet it disordered me.
Alas! I am forgetful of my duty,
I should preserve my senses for your sake.
    Lucretia. Nay, Beatrice; have courage, my sweet girl,   80
If any one despairs it should be I
Who loved him once, and now must live with him
Till God in pity call for him or me.
For you may, like your sister, find some husband,
And smile, years hence, with children round your knees;   85
Whilst I, then dead, and all this hideous coil[4]
Shall be remembered only as a dream.
    Beatrice. Talk not to me, dear lady, of a husband.
Did you not nurse me when my mother died?
Did you not shield me and that dearest boy?   90
And had we any other friend but you
In infancy, with gentle words and looks,
To win our father not to murder us?
And shall I now desert you? May the ghost
Of my dead Mother plead against my soul   95
If I abandon her who filled the place
She left, with more, even, than a mother's love!
    Bernardo. And I am of my sister's mind. Indeed
I would not leave you in this wretchedness,
Even though the Pope should make me free to live   100
In some blithe place, like others of my age,
With sports, and delicate food, and the fresh air.
Oh, never think that I will leave you, Mother!
    Lucretia. My dear, dear children!

      Enter CENCI, *suddenly.*
   Cenci.   What, Beatrice here!
Come hither!   *[She shrinks back, and covers her face.*
      Nay, hide not your face, 'tis fair;   105
Look up! Why, yesternight you dared to look
With disobedient insolence upon me,
Bending a stern and an inquiring brow

4. Turmoil, confusion; cf. "mortal coil" (*Hamlet*, III.i.67).

On what I meant; whilst I then sought to hide
That which I came to tell you—but in vain.   110
   Beatrice (*wildly, staggering towards the door*).
Oh, that the earth would gape! Hide me, O God!
   Cenci. Then it was I whose inarticulate words
Fell from my lips, and who with tottering steps
Fled from your presence, as you now from mine.
Stay, I command you—from this day and hour   115
Never again, I think, with fearless eye,
And brow superior, and unaltered cheek,
And that lip made for tenderness or scorn,
Shalt thou strike dumb the meanest of mankind;
Me least of all. Now get thee to thy chamber!   120
Thou too, loathed image of thy cursed mother,   [*To* BERNARDO.
Thy milky, meek face makes me sick with hate!
                    [*Exeunt* BEATRICE *and* BERNARDO.
   (*Aside.*) So much has passed between us as must make
Me bold, her fearful.—'Tis an awful[5] thing
To touch such mischief as I now conceive: 125
So men sit shivering on the dewy bank,
And try the chill stream with their feet; once in . . .
How the delighted spirit pants for joy!
   Lucretia (*advancing timidly towards him*).
Oh, husband! Pray forgive poor Beatrice.
She meant not any ill.
   Cenci.   Nor you perhaps?   130
Nor that young imp, whom you have taught by rote
Parricide with his alphabet? Nor Giacomo?
Nor those two most unnatural sons, who stirred
Enmity up against me with the Pope?
Whom in one night merciful God cut off: 135
Innocent lambs! They thought not any ill.
You were not here conspiring? You said nothing
Of how I might be dungeoned as a madman;
Or be condemned to death for some offence,
And you would be the witnesses?—This failing,   140
How just it were to hire assassins, or
Put sudden poison in my evening drink?
Or smother me when overcome by wine?
Seeing we had no other judge but God,
And he had sentenced me, and there were none   145
But you to be the executioners
Of his decree enregistered in heaven?
Oh, no! You said not this?
   Lucretia.   So help me God,
I never thought the things you charge me with!
   Cenci. If you dare speak that wicked lie again   150
I'll kill you. What! It was not by your counsel
That Beatrice disturbed the feast last night?

---

5. Awe-inspiring.

You did not hope to stir some enemies
Against me, and escape, and laugh to scorn
What every nerve of you now trembles at? 155
You judged that men were bolder than they are;
Few dare to stand between their grave and me.
    Lucretia. Look not so dreadfully! By my salvation
I knew not aught that Beatrice designed;
Nor do I think she designed any thing 160
Until she heard you talk of her dead brothers.
    Cenci. Blaspheming liar! You are damned for this!
But I will take you where you may persuade
The stones you tread on to deliver you:
For men shall there be none but those who dare 165
All things—not question that which I command.
On Wednesday next I shall set out: you know
That savage rock, the Castle of Petrella,
'Tis safely walled, and moated round about:
Its dungeons underground, and its thick towers 170
Never told tales; though they have heard and seen
What might make dumb things speak.—Why do you linger?
Make speediest preparation for the journey!   [*Exit* LUCRETIA.
The all-beholding sun yet shines; I hear
A busy stir of men about the streets; 175
I see the bright sky through the window panes:
It is a garish, broad, and peering day;
Loud, light, suspicious, full of eyes and ears,
And every little corner, nook, and hole
Is penetrated with the insolent light. 180
Come darkness! Yet, what is the day to me?
And wherefore should I wish for night, who do
A deed which shall confound both night and day?
'Tis she shall grope through a bewildering mist
Of horror: if there be a sun in heaven 185
She shall not dare to look upon its beams;
Nor feel its warmth. Let her then wish for night;
The act I think shall soon extinguish all
For me: I bear a darker deadlier gloom
Than the earth's shade,[6] or interlunar air, 190
Or constellations quenched in murkiest cloud,
In which I walk secure and unbeheld
Towards my purpose.—Would that it were done!   [*Exit.*

SCENE II.—*A chamber in the Vatican. Enter* CAMILLO *and* GIACOMO,
in conversation.

    Camillo. There is an obsolete and doubtful law
By which you might obtain a bare provision
Of food and clothing—
    Giacomo.   Nothing more? Alas!

6. The shadow that the earth casts away
from the sun; *interlunar:* pertaining to
the dark period between the old and new
moon.

Bare must be the provision which strict law
Awards, and aged, sullen avarice pays.   5
Why did my father not apprentice me
To some mechanic trade? I should have then
Been trained in no highborn necessities
Which I could meet not by my daily toil.
The eldest son of a rich nobleman   10
Is heir to all his incapacities;
He has wide wants, and narrow powers. If you,
Cardinal Camillo, were reduced at once
From thrice-driven beds of down,[7] and delicate food,
An hundred servants, and six palaces,   15
To that which nature doth indeed require?—
   Camillo. Nay, there is reason in your plea; 'twere hard.
   Giacomo. 'Tis hard for a firm man to bear: but I
Have a dear wife, a lady of high birth,
Whose dowry in ill hour I lent my father   20
Without a bond or witness to the deed:
And children, who inherit her fine senses,
The fairest creatures in this breathing world;
And she and they reproach me not. Cardinal,
Do you not think the Pope would interpose   25
And stretch authority beyond the law?
   Camillo. Though your peculiar case is hard, I know
The Pope will not divert the course of law.
After that impious feast the other night
I spoke with him, and urged him then to check   30
Your father's cruel hand; he frowned and said,
"Children are disobedient, and they sting
Their fathers' hearts to madness and despair
Requiting years of care with contumely.[8]
I pity the Count Cenci from my heart;   35
His outraged love perhaps awakened hate,
And thus he is exasperated to ill.
In the great war between the old and young
I, who have white hairs and a tottering body,
Will keep at least blameless neutrality."   40

            Enter ORSINO.
You, my good Lord Orsino, heard those words.
   Orsino. What words?
   Giacomo.   Alas, repeat them not again!
There then is no redress for me, at least
None but that which I may atchieve myself,
Since I am driven to the brink.—But, say,   45
My innocent sister and my only brother

---

7. Apparently down (the soft under-feathers of birds) that has been separated from larger, coarser feathers by beating the feathers until the lightest are blown away from the others (see V.ii. 169–170).

8. Insulting or offensively contemptuous language or treatment.

Are dying underneath my father's eye.
The memorable torturers of this land,
Galeaz Visconti, Borgia, Ezzelin,[9]
Never inflicted on their meanest slave   50
What these endure; shall they have no protection?
  Camillo. Why, if they would petition to the Pope
I see not how he could refuse it—yet
He holds it of most dangerous example
In aught to weaken the paternal power,   55
Being, as 'twere, the shadow of his own.
I pray you now excuse me. I have business
That will not bear delay.   [*Exit* CAMILLO.
  Giacomo.   But you, Orsino,
Have the petition: wherefore not present it?
  Orsino. I have presented it, and backed it with   60
My earnest prayers, and urgent interest;
It was returned unanswered. I doubt not
But that the strange and execrable deeds
Alledged in it—in truth they might well baffle
Any belief—have turned the Pope's displeasure   65
Upon the accusers from the criminal:
So I should guess from what Camillo said.
  Giacomo. My friend, that palace-walking devil Gold
Has whispered silence to his Holiness:
And we are left, as scorpions ringed with fire,   70
What should we do but strike ourselves to death?[1]
For he who is our murderous persecutor
Is shielded by a father's holy name,
Or I would—   [*Stops abruptly.*
  Orsino.   What? Fear not to speak your thought.
Words are but holy as the deeds they cover: 75
A priest who has forsworn the God he serves;
A judge who makes truth weep at his decree;
A friend who should weave counsel, as I now,
But as the mantle of some selfish guile;
A father who is all a tyrant seems,   80
Were the prophaner for his sacred name.
  Giacomo. Ask me not what I think; the unwilling brain
Feigns often what it would not; and we trust
Imagination with such phantasies
As the tongue dares not fashion into words,   85

---

9. Three noted Italian tyrants featured as villains in Sismondi's *History of the Italian Republics in the Middle Ages.* Gian Galeazzo Visconti (1351–1402), first Duke of Milan, imprisoned or killed his relatives and then conquered much of northern Italy; Cesare Borgia (1475–1507), the son of Pope Alexander VI, a Spaniard, tried to carve out a personal state in Romagna, the marches of Ancona, and Tuscany by cruelly suppressing the warring petty rulers of the region; Ezzelino (Eccelino) da Romano (1194–1259), vicar and son-in-law of Holy Roman Emperor Frederick II, led the Ghibelline faction in Lombardy as ruler of Verona, Vicenza, and Padua.
1. According to bestiary tradition, when scorpions are surrounded by fire, they commit suicide by stinging themselves. (See *Queen Mab*, VI.36–38 and note.)

Which have no words, their horror makes them dim
To the mind's eye.—My heart denies itself
To think what you demand.
    Orsino.   But a friend's bosom
Is as the inmost cave of our own mind
Where we sit shut from the wide gaze of day,   90
And from the all-communicating air.
You look what I suspected—
    Giacomo.   Spare me now!
I am as one lost in a midnight wood,
Who dares not ask some harmless passenger
The path across the wilderness, lest he,   95
As my thoughts are, should be—a murderer.
I know you are my friend, and all I dare
Speak to my soul that will I trust with thee.
But now my heart is heavy and would take
Lone counsel from a night of sleepless care.   100
Pardon me, that I say farewell—farewell!
I would that to my own suspected self
I could address a word so full of peace.
    Orsino. Farewell!—Be your thoughts better or more bold.
                          [*Exit* GIACOMO.
I had disposed the Cardinal Camillo   105
To feed his hope with cold encouragement:
It fortunately serves my close designs
That 'tis a trick of this same family
To analyse their own and other minds.
Such self-anatomy[2] shall teach the will   110
Dangerous secrets: for it tempts our powers,
Knowing what must be thought, and may be done,
Into the depth of darkest purposes:
So Cenci fell into the pit; even I,
Since Beatrice unveiled me to myself,   115
And made me shrink from what I cannot shun,
Shew a poor figure to my own esteem,
To which I grow half reconciled. I'll do
As little mischief as I can; that thought
Shall fee[3] the accuser conscience.
    (*After a pause.*)   Now what harm   120
If Cenci should be murdered?—Yet, if murdered,
Wherefore by me? And what if I could take
The profit, yet omit the sin and peril
In such an action? Of all earthly things
I fear a man whose blows outspeed his words;   125
And such is Cenci: and while Cenci lives
His daughter's dowry were a secret grave
If a priest wins her.—Oh, fair Beatrice!
Would that I loved thee not, or loving thee

2. Self-dissection or analysis.   3. Pay, bribe.

Could but despise danger and gold and all   130
That frowns between my wish and its effect,
Or smiles beyond it! There is no escape . . .
Her bright form kneels beside me at the altar,
And follows me to the resort of men,
And fills my slumber with tumultuous dreams,   135
So when I wake my blood seems liquid fire;
And if I strike my damp and dizzy head
My hot palm scorches it: her very name,
But spoken by a stranger, makes my heart
Sicken and pant; and thus unprofitably   140
I clasp the phantom of unfelt delights
Till weak imagination half possesses
The self-created shadow. Yet much longer
Will I not nurse this life of feverous hours:
From the unravelled hopes of Giacomo   145
I must work out my own dear purposes.
I see, as from a tower, the end of all:
Her father dead; her brother bound to me
By a dark secret, surer than the grave;
Her mother scared and unexpostulating   150
From the dread manner of her wish atchieved:
And she!—Once more take courage, my faint heart;
What dares a friendless maiden matched with thee?
I have such foresight as assures success:
Some unbeheld divinity doth ever,   155
When dread events are near, stir up men's minds
To black suggestions; and he prospers best,
Not who becomes the instrument of ill,
But who can flatter the dark spirit, that makes
Its empire and its prey of other hearts   160
Till it become his slave . . . as I will do.   [*Exit.*

END OF THE SECOND ACT.

ACT III

SCENE I.—*An apartment in the Cenci Palace.* LUCRETIA, *to her
enter* BEATRICE.

Beatrice. (She enters staggering, and speaks wildly.)
Reach me that handkerchief!—My brain is hurt;
My eyes are full of blood; just wipe them for me . . .
I see but indistinctly . . .
   Lucretia.   My sweet child,
You have no wound; 'tis only a cold dew
That starts from your dear brow . . . Alas! Alas!   5
What has befallen?
   Beatrice.   How comes this hair undone?
Its wandering strings must be what blind me so,

And yet I tied it fast.—O, horrible!
The pavement sinks under my feet! The walls
Spin round! I see a woman weeping there,   10
And standing calm and motionless, whilst I
Slide giddily as the world reels. . . . My God!
The beautiful blue heaven is flecked with blood!
The sunshine on the floor is black! The air
Is changed to vapours such as the dead breathe   15
In charnel pits! Pah! I am choked! There creeps
A clinging, black, contaminating mist
About me . . . 'tis substantial, heavy, thick,
I cannot pluck it from me, for it glues
My fingers and my limbs to one another,   20
And eats into my sinews, and dissolves
My flesh to a pollution, poisoning
The subtle, pure, and inmost spirit of life!
My God! I never knew what the mad felt
Before; for I am mad beyond all doubt!   25
(*More wildly.*) No, I am dead! These putrefying limbs
Shut round and sepulchre the panting soul
Which would burst forth into the wandering air! (*A pause.*)
What hideous thought was that I had even now?
'Tis gone; and yet its burthen remains here   30
O'er these dull eyes . . . upon this weary heart!
O, world! O, life! O, day! O, misery!
   Lucretia. What ails thee, my poor child? She answers not:
Her spirit apprehends the sense of pain,.
But not its cause; suffering has dried away   35
The source from which it sprung . . .
   Beatrice (franticly).   Like Parricide . . .
Misery has killed its father: yet its father
Never like mine . . .O, God! What thing am I?
   Lucretia. My dearest child, what has your father done?
   Beatrice (doubtfully). Who art thou, questioner? I have no
    father.   40
(*Aside.*) She is the madhouse nurse who tends on me,
It is a piteous office.   [*To* LUCRETIA, *in a slow, subdued voice.*
               Do you know
I thought I was that wretched Beatrice
Men speak of, whom her father sometimes hales[4]
From hall to hall by the entangled hair;   45
At others, pens up naked in damp cells
Where scaly reptiles crawl, and starves her there,
Till she will eat strange flesh. This woful story
So did I overact in my sick dreams,
That I imagined . . . no, it cannot be!   50
Horrible things have been in this wide world,
Prodigious mixtures, and confusions strange

---

4. Drags, especially by force or violence.

Of good and ill; and worse have been conceived
Than ever there was found a heart to do.
But never fancy imaged such a deed   55
As . . .   [*Pauses, suddenly recollecting herself.*
      Who art thou? Swear to me, ere I die
With fearful expectation, that indeed
Thou art not what thou seemest . . . Mother!
  Lucretia.   Oh!
My sweet child, know you . . .
  Beatrice.   Yet speak it not:
For then if this be truth, that other too   60
Must be a truth, a firm enduring truth,
Linked with each lasting circumstance of life,
Never to change, never to pass away.
Why so it is. This is the Cenci palace;
Thou art Lucretia; I am Beatrice.   65
I have talked some wild words, but will no more.
Mother, come near me: from this point of time,
I am . . .   [*Her voice dies away faintly.*
  Lucretia. Alas! What has befallen thee, child?
What has thy father done?
  Beatrice.   What have I done?
Am I not innocent? Is it my crime   70
That one with white hair, and imperious brow,
Who tortured me from my forgotten years,
As parents only dare, should call himself
My father, yet should be!—Oh, what am I?
What name, what place, what memory shall be mine?   75
What retrospects, outliving even despair?
  Lucretia. He is a violent tyrant, surely, child:
We know that death alone can make us free;
His death or ours. But what can he have done
Of deadlier outrage or worse injury?   80
Thou art unlike thyself; thine eyes shoot forth
A wandering and strange spirit. Speak to me,
Unlock those pallid hands whose fingers twine
With one another.
  Beatrice.   'Tis the restless life
Tortured within them. If I try to speak   85
I shall go mad. Aye, something must be done;
What, yet I know not . . . something which shall make
The thing that I have suffered but a shadow
In the dread lightning which avenges it;
Brief, rapid, irreversible, destroying   90
The consequence of what it cannot cure.
Some such thing is to be endured or done:
When I know what, I shall be still and calm,
And never any thing will move me more.
But now!—O blood, which art my father's blood,   95

Circling through these contaminated veins,
If thou, poured forth on the polluted earth,
Could wash away the crime, and punishment
By which I suffer . . . no, that cannot be!
Many might doubt there were a God above   100
Who sees and permits evil, and so die:
That faith no agony shall obscure in me.
    Lucretia. It must indeed have been some bitter wrong;
Yet what, I dare not guess. Oh, my lost child,
Hide not in proud impenetrable grief   105
Thy sufferings from my fear.
    Beatrice.   I hide them not.
What are the words which you would have me speak?
I, who can feign no image in my mind
Of that which has transformed me. I, whose thought
Is like a ghost shrouded and folded up   110
In its own formless horror. Of all words,
That minister to mortal intercourse,[5]
Which wouldst thou hear? For there is none to tell
My misery: if another ever knew
Aught like to it, she died as I will die,   115
And left it, as I must, without a name.
Death! Death! Our law and our religion call thee
A punishment and a reward . . . Oh, which
Have I deserved?
    Lucretia.   The peace of innocence;
Till in your season you be called to heaven.   120
Whate'er you may have suffered, you have done
No evil. Death must be the punishment
Of crime, or the reward of trampling down
The thorns which God has strewed upon the path
Which leads to immortality.
    Beatrice.   Aye, death . . .   125
The punishment of crime. I pray thee, God,
Let me not be bewildered while I judge.
If I must live day after day, and keep
These limbs, the unworthy temple of thy spirit,
As a foul den from which what thou abhorrest   130
May mock thee, unavenged . . . it shall not be!
Self-murder . . . no, that might be no escape,
For thy decree yawns like a Hell between
Our will and it:—O! In this mortal world
There is no vindication and no law   135
Which can adjudge and execute the doom
Of that through which I suffer.

              Enter ORSINO.
(*She approaches him solemnly.*)   Welcome, Friend!
I have to tell you that, since last we met,

---

5. Conversation; social communication.

I have endured a wrong so great and strange,
That neither life or death can give me rest.   140
Ask me not what it is, for there are deeds
Which have no form, sufferings which have no tongue.
   Orsino. And what is he who has thus injured you?
   Beatrice. The man they call my father: a dread name.
   Orsino. It cannot be . . .
   Beatrice.   What it can be, or not,   145
Forbear to think. It is, and it has been;
Advise me how it shall not be again.
I thought to die; but a religious awe
Restrains me, and the dread lest death itself
Might be no refuge from the consciousness   150
Of what is yet unexpiated. Oh, speak!
   Orsino. Accuse him of the deed, and let the law
Avenge thee.
   Beatrice.   Oh, ice-hearted counsellor!
If I could find a word that might make known
The crime of my destroyer; and that done   155
My tongue should like a knife tear out the secret
Which cankers[6] my heart's core; aye, lay all bare
So that my unpolluted fame should be
With vilest gossips a stale mouthed story;
A mock, a bye-word, an astonishment:—   160
If this were done, which never shall be done,
Think of the offender's gold, his dreaded hate,
And the strange horror of the accuser's tale,
Baffling belief, and overpowering speech;
Scarce whispered, unimaginable, wrapt   165
In hideous hints . . . Oh, most assured redress!
   Orsino. You will endure it then?
   Beatrice.   Endure?—Orsino,
It seems your counsel is small profit.
                      [*Turns from him, and speaks half to herself.*
                     Aye,
All must be suddenly resolved and done.
What is this undistinguishable mist   170
Of thoughts, which rise, like shadow after shadow,
Darkening each other?
   Orsino.   Should the offender live?
Triumph in his misdeed? and make, by use,
His crime, whate'er it is, dreadful no doubt,
Thine element; until thou mayst become   175
Utterly lost; subdued even to the hue
Of that which thou permittest?
   Beatrice (*to herself*).   Mighty death!
Thou double visaged shadow![7] Only judge!

---

6. Corrupts; consumes slowly and se-
cretly.
7. Shelley here associates the image of
death with the myth of Janus, the Roman
god of beginnings and endings, who is
usually depicted with two faces, one to
view the past and one the future.

Rightfullest arbiter!   [*She retires absorbed in thought.*
    Lucretia.   If the lightning
Of God has e'er descended to avenge . . .   180
    Orsino. Blaspheme not! His high Providence commits
Its glory on this earth, and their own wrongs
Into the hands of men; if they neglect
To punish crime . . .
    Lucretia.   But if one, like this wretch,
Should mock, with gold, opinion, law and power?   185
If there be no appeal to that which makes
The guiltiest tremble? If because our wrongs,
For that they are, unnatural, strange and monstrous,
Exceed all measure of belief? O God!
If, for the very reasons which should make   190
Redress most swift and sure, our injurer triumphs?
And we the victims, bear worse punishment
Than that appointed for their torturer?
    Orsino.   Think not
But that there is redress where there is wrong,
So we be bold enough to seize it.
    Lucretia.   How?   195
If there were any way to make all sure,
I know not . . . but I think it might be good
To . . .
    Orsino. Why, his late outrage to Beatrice;
For it is such, as I but faintly guess,
As makes remorse dishonour, and leaves her   200
Only one duty, how she may avenge:
You, but one refuge from ills ill endured;
Me, but one counsel . . .
    Lucretia.   For we cannot hope
That aid, or retribution, or resource
Will arise thence, where every other one   205
Might find them with less need.   [BEATRICE *advances.*
    Orsino.   Then . . .
    Beatrice.   Peace, Orsino!
And, honoured Lady, while I speak, I pray,
That you put off, as garments overworn,
Forbearance and respect, remorse and fear,
And all the fit restraints of daily life,   210
Which have been borne from childhood, but which now
Would be a mockery to my holier plea.
As I have said, I have endured a wrong,
Which, though it be expressionless, is such
As asks atonement; both for what is past,   215
And lest I be reserved, day after day,
To load with crimes an overburthened soul,
And be . . . what ye can dream not. I have prayed
To God, and I have talked with my own heart,

And have unravelled my entangled will,   220
And have at length determined what is right.
Art thou my friend, Orsino? False or true?
Pledge thy salvation ere I speak.
    Orsino.   I swear
To dedicate my cunning, and my strength,
My silence, and whatever else is mine,   225
To thy commands.
    Lucretia.   You think we should devise
His death?
    Beatrice. And execute what is devised,
And suddenly. We must be brief and bold.
    Orsino. And yet most cautious.
    Lucretia.   For the jealous laws
Would punish us with death and infamy   230
For that which it became themselves to do.
    Beatrice. Be cautious as ye may, but prompt. Orsino,
What are the means?
    Orsino.   I know two dull, fierce outlaws,
Who think man's spirit as a worm's, and they
Would trample out, for any slight caprice,   235
The meanest or the noblest life. This mood
Is marketable here in Rome. They sell
What we now want. .
    Lucretia.   To-morrow before dawn,
Cenci will take us to that lonely rock,
Petrella, in the Apulian Apennines.[8]   240
If he arrive there . . .
    Beatrice.   He must not arrive.
    Orsino. Will it be dark before you reach the tower?
    Lucretia. The sun will scarce be set.
    Beatrice.   But I remember
Two miles on this side of the fort, the road
Crosses a deep ravine; 'tis rough and narrow,   245
And winds with short turns down the precipice;
And in its depth there is a mighty rock,
Which has, from unimaginable years,
Sustained itself with terror and with toil
Over a gulph, and with the agony   250
With which it clings seems slowly coming down;
Even as a wretched soul hour after hour,
Clings to the mass of life; yet clinging, leans;
And leaning, makes more dark the dread abyss
In which it fears to fall: beneath this crag   255
Huge as despair, as if in weariness,
The melancholy mountain yawns . . . below,
You hear but see not an impetuous torrent
Raging among the caverns, and a bridge

8. Mountains in Apulia, a region of southeast Italy.

Crosses the chasm; and high above there grow,   260
With intersecting trunks, from crag to crag,
Cedars, and yews, and pines; whose tangled hair
Is matted in one solid roof of shade
By the dark ivy's twine. At noon day here
'Tis twilight, and at sunset blackest night.[9]   265
    Orsino. Before you reach that bridge make some excuse
For spurring on your mules, or loitering
Until . . .
    Beatrice. What sound is that?
    Lucretia. Hark! No, it cannot be a servant's step;
It must be Cenci, unexpectedly   270
Returned . . . Make some excuse for being here.
    Beatrice. (*To* ORSINO, *as she goes out*.)
That step we hear approach must never pass
The bridge of which we spoke.   [*Exeunt* LUCRETIA *and* BEATRICE.
    Orsino.   What shall I do?
Cenci must find me here, and I must bear
The imperious inquisition of his looks   275
As to what brought me hither: let me mask
Mine own in some inane and vacant smile.

          Enter GIACOMO, *in a hurried manner*.
How! Have you ventured hither? Know you then
That Cenci is from home?
    Giacomo.   I sought him here;
And now must wait till he returns.
    Orsino.   Great God!   280
Weigh you the danger of this rashness?
    Giacomo.   Aye!
Does my destroyer know his danger? We
Are now no more, as once, parent and child,
But man to man; the oppressor to the oppressed;
The slanderer to the slandered; foe to foe: 285
He has cast Nature off, which was his shield,
And Nature casts him off, who is her shame;
And I spurn both. Is it a father's throat
Which I will shake, and say, I ask not gold;
I ask not happy years; nor memories   290
Of tranquil childhood; nor home-sheltered love;
Though all these hast thou torn from me, and more;
But only my fair fame; only one hoard
Of peace, which I thought hidden from thy hate,
Under the penury heaped on me by thee,   295
Or I will . . . God can understand and pardon,
Why should I speak with man?

---

9. Lines 243–265 contain the description which, Shelley says in his Preface, he modeled on a passage near the end of the second act of *El Purgatorio de San Patricio* by the Spanish dramatist Pedro Calderón de la Barca (1600–1681); in Calderón's play the description is that of the entrance to Hell.

Orsino.   Be calm, dear friend.
   Giacomo. Well, I will calmly tell you what he did.
This old Francesco Cenci, as you know,
Borrowed the dowry of my wife from me,   300
And then denied the loan; and left me so
In poverty, the which I sought to mend
By holding a poor office in the state.
It had been promised to me, and already
I bought new clothing for my ragged babes,   305
And my wife smiled; and my heart knew repose.
When Cenci's intercession, as I found,
Conferred this office on a wretch, whom thus
He paid for vilest service. I returned
With this ill news, and we sate sad together   310
Solacing our despondency with tears
Of such affection and unbroken faith
As temper life's worst bitterness; when he,
As he is wont, came to upbraid and curse,
Mocking our poverty, and telling us   315
Such was God's scourge for disobedient sons.
And then, that I might strike him dumb with shame,
I spoke of my wife's dowry; but he coined
A brief yet specious tale, how I had wasted
The sum in secret riot; and he saw   320
My wife was touched, and he went smiling forth.
And when I knew the impression he had made,
And felt my wife insult with silent scorn
My ardent truth, and look averse and cold,
I went forth too: but soon returned again;   325
Yet not so soon but that my wife had taught
My children her harsh thoughts, and they all cried,
"Give us clothes, father! Give us better food!
What you in one night squander were enough
For months!" I looked, and saw that home was hell.   330
And to that hell will I return no more
Until mine enemy has rendered up
Atonement, or, as he gave life to me
I will, reversing nature's law . . .
   Orsino.   Trust me,
The compensation which thou seekest here   335
Will be denied.
   Giacomo.   Then . . . Are you not my friend?
Did you not hint at the alternative,
Upon the brink of which you see I stand,
The other day when we conversed together?
My wrongs were then less. That word parricide,   340
Although I am resolved, haunts me like fear.
   Orsino. It must be fear itself, for the bare word
Is hollow mockery. Mark, how wisest God

Draws to one point the threads of a just doom,
So sanctifying it: what you devise   345
Is, as it were, accomplished.
    Giacomo.   Is he dead?
    Orsino. His grave is ready. Know that since we met
Cenci has done an outrage to his daughter.
    Giacomo. What outrage?
    Orsino.   That she speaks not, but you may
Conceive such half conjectures as I do,   350
From her fixed paleness, and the lofty grief
Of her stern brow bent on the idle air,
And her severe unmodulated voice,
Drowning both tenderness and dread; and last
From this; that whilst her step-mother and I,   355
Bewildered in our horror, talked together
With obscure hints; both self-misunderstood
And darkly guessing, stumbling, in our talk,
Over the truth, and yet to its revenge,
She interrupted us, and with a look   360
Which told before she spoke it, he must die . . .
    Giacomo. It is enough. My doubts are well appeased;
There is a higher reason for the act
Than mine; there is a holier judge than me,
A more unblamed avenger. Beatrice,   365
Who in the gentleness of thy sweet youth
Hast never trodden on a worm, or bruised
A living flower, but thou hast pitied it
With needless tears! Fair sister, thou in whom
Men wondered how such loveliness and wisdom   370
Did not destroy each other! Is there made
Ravage of thee? O, heart, I ask no more
Justification! Shall I wait, Orsino,
Till he return, and stab him at the door?
    Orsino. Not so; some accident might interpose   375
To rescue him from what is now most sure;
And you are unprovided where to fly,
How to excuse or to conceal. Nay, listen:
All is contrived; success is so assured
That . . .

Enter BEATRICE.

    Beatrice. 'Tis my brother's voice! You know me not?   380
    Giacomo. My sister, my lost sister!
    Beatrice.   Lost indeed!
I see Orsino has talked with you, and
That you conjecture things too horrible
To speak, yet far less than the truth. Now, stay not,
He might return: yet kiss me; I shall know   385
That then thou hast consented to his death.
Farewell, Farewell! Let piety to God,

Brotherly love, justice and clemency,
And all things that make tender hardest hearts
Make thine hard, brother. Answer not . . . farewell.   390
                                   [*Exeunt severally.*

SCENE II.—*A mean apartment in* GIACOMO'S *house.* GIACOMO, *alone.*

Giacomo. 'Tis midnight, and Orsino comes not yet.
                     [*Thunder, and the sound of a storm.*
What! can the everlasting elements
Feel with a worm like man? If so the shaft
Of mercy-winged lightning would not fall
On stones and trees. My wife and children sleep: 5
They are now living in unmeaning dreams:
But I must wake, still doubting if that deed
Be just which is most necessary. O,
Thou unreplenished lamp! whose narrow fire
Is shaken by the wind, and on whose edge   10
Devouring darkness hovers! Thou small flame,
Which, as a dying pulse rises and falls,
Still flickerest up and down, how very soon,
Did I not feed thee, wouldst thou fail and be
As thou hadst never been! So wastes and sinks   15
Even now, perhaps, the life that kindled mine:
But that no power can fill with vital oil
That broken lamp of flesh. Ha! 'tis the blood
Which fed these veins that ebbs till all is cold:
It is the form that moulded mine that sinks   20
Into the white and yellow spasms of death:
It is the soul by which mine was arrayed
In God's immortal likeness which now stands
Naked before Heaven's judgement seat!   [*A bell strikes.*
                     One! Two!
The hours crawl on; and when my hairs are white,   25
My son will then perhaps be waiting thus,
Tortured between just hate and vain remorse;
Chiding the tardy messenger of news
Like those which I expect. I almost wish
He be not dead, although my wrongs are great;   30
Yet . . . 'tis Orsino's step . . .

                     Enter ORSINO.
                     Speak!
Orsino.   I am come
To say he has escaped.
    Giacomo.   Escaped!
    Orsino.   And safe
Within Petrella. He past by the spot
Appointed for the deed an hour too soon.

Giacomo. Are we the fools of such contingencies?   35
And do we waste in blind misgivings thus
The hours when we should act? Then wind and thunder,
Which seemed to howl his knell, is the loud laughter
With which Heaven mocks our weakness! I henceforth
Will ne'er repent of aught designed or done   40
But my repentance.
    Orsino.   See, the lamp is out.
    Giacomo. If no remorse is ours when the dim air
Has drank this innocent flame, why should we quail
When Cenci's life, that light by which ill spirits
See the worst deeds they prompt, shall sink for ever?   45
No, I am hardened.
    Orsino.   Why, what need of this?
Who feared the pale intrusion of remorse
In a just deed? Although our first plan failed
Doubt not but he will soon be laid to rest.
But light the lamp; let us not talk i' the dark.   50
    Giacomo (*lighting the lamp*). And yet once quenched I cannot
        thus relume[1]
My father's life: do you not think his ghost
Might plead that argument with God?
    Orsino.   Once gone
You cannot now recall your sister's peace;
Your own extinguished years of youth and hope;   55
Nor your wife's bitter words; nor all the taunts
Which, from the prosperous, weak misfortune takes;
Nor your dead mother; nor . . .
    Giacomo.   O, speak no more!
I am resolved, although this very hand
Must quench the life that animated it.   60
    Orsino. There is no need of that. Listen: you know
Olimpio, the castellan[2] of Petrella
In old Colonna's time; him whom your father
Degraded from his post? And Marzio,
That desperate wretch, whom he deprived last year   65
Of a reward of blood, well earned and due?
    Giacomo. I know Olimpio; and they say he hated
Old Cenci so, that in his silent rage
His lips grew white only to see him pass.
Of Marzio I know nothing.
    Orsino.   Marzio's hate   70
Matches Olimpio's. I have sent these men,
But in your name, and as at your request,
To talk with Beatrice and Lucretia.
    Giacomo. Only to talk?
    Orsino.   The moments which even now
Pass onward to to-morrow's midnight hour   75

---

1. Relight, rekindle.   2. The governor or constable of a castle.

May memorize[3] their flight with death: ere then
They must have talked, and may perhaps have done,
And made an end . . .
    Giacomo.   Listen! What sound is that?
    Orsino. The house-dog moans, and the beams crack: nought
    else.
    Giacomo. It is my wife complaining in her sleep: 80
I doubt not she is saying bitter things
Of me; and all my children round her dreaming
That I deny them sustenance.
    Orsino.   Whilst he
Who truly took it from them, and who fills
Their hungry rest with bitterness, now sleeps   85
Lapped in bad pleasures, and triumphantly
Mocks thee in visions of successful hate
Too like the truth of day.
    Giacomo.   If e'er he wakes
Again, I will not trust to hireling hands . . .
    Orsino. Why, that were well. I must be gone; good-night!   90
When next we meet may all be done—
    Giacomo.   And all
Forgotten—Oh, that I had never been!   [*Exeunt.*

END OF THE THIRD ACT.

ACT IV

SCENE I.—*An apartment in the Castle of Petrella.*
Enter CENCI.

    Cenci. She comes not; yet I left her even now
Vanquished and faint. She knows the penalty
Of her delay: yet what if threats are vain?
Am I now not within Petrella's moat?
Or fear I still the eyes and ears of Rome?   5
Might I not drag her by the golden hair?
Stamp on her? Keep her sleepless till her brain
Be overworn? Tame her with chains and famine?
Less would suffice. Yet so to leave undone
What I most seek! No, 'tis her stubborn will   10
Which by its own consent shall stoop as low
As that which drags it down.

               Enter LUCRETIA.
               Thou loathed wretch!
Hide thee from my abhorrence, Fly, begone!
Yet stay! Bid Beatrice come hither.
    Lucretia.   Oh,
Husband! I pray for thine own wretched sake   15

3. Memorialize.

Heed what thou dost. A man who walks like thee
Through crimes, and through the danger of his crimes,
Each hour may stumble o'er a sudden grave.
And thou art old; thy hairs are hoary grey;
As thou wouldst save thyself from death and hell, 20
Pity thy daughter; give her to some friend
In marriage: so that she may tempt thee not
To hatred, or worse thoughts, if worse there be.
Cenci. What! like her sister who has found a home
To mock my hate from with prosperity? 25
Strange ruin shall destroy both her and thee
And all that yet remain. My death may be
Rapid—her destiny outspeeds it. Go,
Bid her come hither, and before my mood
Be changed, lest I should drag her by the hair. 30
Lucretia. She sent me to thee, husband. At thy presence
She fell, as thou dost know, into a trance;
And in that trance she heard a voice which said,
"Cenci must die! Let him confess himself!
Even now the accusing Angel waits to hear 35
If God, to punish his enormous crimes,
Harden his dying heart!"
Cenci. Why—such things are . . .
No doubt divine revelings may be made.
'Tis plain I have been favoured from above,
For when I cursed my sons they died.—Aye . . . so . . . 40
As to the right or wrong that's talk . . . repentance . . .
Repentance is an easy moment's work
And more depends on God than me. Well . . . well . . .
I must give up the greater point, which was
To poison and corrupt her soul.
 [A *pause;* LUCRETIA *approaches anxiously, and*
 then shrinks back as he speaks.
 One, two; 45
Aye . . . Rocco and Cristofano my curse
Strangled: and Giacomo, I think, will find
Life a worse Hell than that beyond the grave:
Beatrice shall, if there be skill in hate
Die in despair, blaspheming: to Bernardo, 50
He is so innocent, I will bequeath
The memory of these deeds, and make his youth
The sepulchre of hope, where evil thoughts
Shall grow like weeds on a neglected tomb.
When all is done, out in the wide Campagna,[4] 55
I will pile up my silver and my gold;
My costly robes, paintings and tapestries;
My parchments and all records of my wealth,

4. The Roman Campagna is the level valley of the Tiber River surrounding Rome; in Count Cenci's (and in Shelley's) day it was almost deserted because of its unhealthy climate—malaria was rife there—and because Italian warlords, like the Orsini and Colonna families, had ravaged it.

And make a bonfire in my joy, and leave
Of my possessions nothing but my name;   60
Which shall be an inheritance to strip
Its wearer bare as infamy. That done,
My soul, which is a scourge,[5] will I resign
Into the hands of him who wielded it;
Be it for its own punishment or theirs,   65
He will not ask it of me till the lash[6]
Be broken in its last and deepest wound;
Until its hate be all inflicted. Yet,
Lest death outspeed my purpose, let me make
Short work and sure . . .   [*Going.*
    Lucretia (*Stops him.*) Oh, stay! It was a feint: 70
She had no vision, and she heard no voice.
I said it but to awe thee.
    Cenci.   That is well.
Vile palterer[7] with the sacred truth of God,
Be thy soul choked with that blaspheming lie!
For Beatrice worse terrors are in store   75
To bend her to my will.
    Lucretia.   Oh! to what will?
What cruel sufferings more than she has known
Canst thou inflict?
    Cenci.   Andrea! Go call my daughter,
And if she comes not tell her that I come.
What sufferings? I will drag her, step by step,   80
Through infamies unheard of among men:
She shall stand shelterless in the broad noon
Of public scorn, for acts blazoned[8] abroad,
One among which shall be . . . What? Canst thou guess?
She shall become (for what she most abhors   85
Shall have a fascination to entrap
Her loathing will), to her own conscious self
All she appears to others; and when dead,
As she shall die unshrived[9] and unforgiven,
A rebel to her father and her God,   90
Her corpse shall be abandoned to the hounds;[1]
Her name shall be the terror of the earth;
Her spirit shall approach the throne of God
Plague-spotted with my curses. I will make
Body and soul a monstrous lump of ruin.   95

          Enter ANDREA.
    Andrea. The lady Beatrice . . .
    Cenci.   Speak, pale slave! What
Said she?
    Andrea. My Lord, 'twas what she looked; she said:

---

5. A person seen as an instrument of divine chastisement.
6. I.e., the *soul* of line 63.
7. An equivocator or trifler with serious matters.

8. Conspicuously displayed, proclaimed.
9. Unconfessed.
1. "And the dogs shall eat Jezebel . . . and there shall be none to bury her" (2 Kings 9:10).

"Go tell my father that I see the gulph
Of Hell between us two, which he may pass,
I will not."   [*Exit* ANDREA.
   Cenci.   Go thou quick, Lucretia,   100
Tell her to come; yet let her understand
Her coming is consent: and say, moreover,
That if she come not I will curse her.   [*Exit* LUCRETIA.
               Ha!
With what but with a father's curse doth God
Panic-strike armed victory, and make pale   105
Cities in their prosperity? The world's Father
Must grant a parent's prayer against his child
Be he who asks even what men call me.
Will not the deaths of her rebellious brothers
Awe her before I speak? For I on them   110
Did imprecate quick ruin, and it came.

          Enter LUCRETIA.
Well; what? Speak, wretch!
   Lucretia.   She said, "I cannot come;
Go tell my father that I see a torrent
Of his own blood raging between us."
   Cenci (kneeling).   God!
Hear me! If this most specious mass of flesh,   115
Which thou hast made my daughter; this my blood,
This particle of my divided being;
Or rather, this my bane and my disease,
Whose sight infects and poisons me; this devil
Which sprung from me as from a hell, was meant   120
To aught good use; if her bright loveliness
Was kindled to illumine this dark world;
If nursed by thy selectest dew of love   ·
Such virtues blossom in her as should make
The peace of life, I pray thee for my sake,   125
As thou the common God and Father art
Of her, and me, and all; reverse that doom!
Earth, in the name of God, let her food be
Poison, until she be encrusted round
With leprous stains! Heaven, rain upon her head 130
The blistering drops of the Maremma's dew,[2]
Till she be speckled like a toad; parch up
Those love-enkindled lips, warp those fine limbs
To loathed lameness! All-beholding sun,
Strike in thine envy those life-darting eyes   135
With thine own blinding beams!
   Lucretia.   Peace! Peace!
For thine own sake unsay those dreadful words.
When high God grants He punishes such prayers.

---

2. The Maremma, a coastal plain and tidewater swamp near Pisa, was noted for its
unhealthy climate.

Cenci (leaping up, and throwing his right hand towards Heaven).
    He does his will, I mine! This in addition,
That if she have a child . . .
    Lucretia.   Horrible thought!   140
    Cenci. That if she ever have a child; and thou,
Quick Nature! I adjure thee by thy God,
That thou be fruitful in her, and encrease
And multiply, fulfilling his command,
And my deep imprecation! May it be   145
A hideous likeness of herself, that as
From a distorting mirror, she may see
Her image mixed with what she most abhors,
Smiling upon her from her nursing breast.
And that the child may from its infancy   150
Grow, day by day, more wicked and deformed,
Turning her mother's love to misery:
And that both she and it may live until
It shall repay her care and pain with hate,
Or what may else be more unnatural.   155
So he may hunt her through the clamorous scoffs
Of the loud world to a dishonoured grave.
Shall I revoke this curse? Go, bid her come,
Before my words are chronicled in heaven.   [*Exit* LUCRETIA.
I do not feel as if I were a man,   160
But like a fiend appointed to chastise
The offences of some unremembered world.
My blood is running up and down my veins;
A fearful pleasure makes it prick and tingle:
I feel a giddy sickness of strange awe;   165
My heart is beating with an expectation
Of horrid joy.

               Enter LUCRETIA.
           What? Speak!
    Lucretia.   She bids thee curse;
And if thy curses, as they cannot do,
Could kill her soul . . .
    Cenci.   She would not come. 'Tis well,
I can do both: first take what I demand,   170
And then extort concession. To thy chamber!
Fly ere I spurn[3] thee: and beware this night
That thou cross not my footsteps. It were safer
To come between the tyger and his prey.   [*Exit* LUCRETIA.
It must be late; mine eyes grow weary dim   175
With unaccustomed heaviness of sleep.
Conscience! Oh, thou most insolent of lies!
They say that sleep, that healing dew of heaven,
Steeps not in balm the foldings of the brain

3. Kick.

Which thinks thee an impostor. I will go   180
First to belie thee with an hour of rest,
Which will be deep and calm, I feel: and then . . .
O, multitudinous Hell, the fiends will shake
Thine arches with the laughter of their joy!
There shall be lamentation heard in Heaven   185
As o'er an angel fallen; and upon Earth
All good shall droop and sicken, and ill things
Shall with a spirit of unnatural life
Stir and be quickened[4] . . . even as I am now.   [*Exit.*

SCENE II.—*Before the Castle of Petrella. Enter* BEATRICE *and*
LUCRETIA *above on the ramparts.*

Beatrice. They come not yet.
Lucretia.   'Tis scarce midnight.
Beatrice.   How slow
Behind the course of thought, even sick with speed,
Lags leaden-footed time!
Lucretia.   The minutes pass . . .
If he should wake before the deed is done?
Beatrice. O, Mother! He must never wake again.   5
What thou hast said persuades me that our act
Will but dislodge a spirit of deep hell
Out of a human form.
Lucretia.   'Tis true he spoke
Of death and judgement with strange confidence
For one so wicked; as a man believing   10
In God, yet recking[5] not of good or ill.
And yet to die without confession! . . .
Beatrice.   Oh!
Believe that heaven is merciful and just,
And will not add our dread necessity[6]
To the amount of his offences.

Enter OLIMPIO *and* MARZIO, *below.*
Lucretia.   See,   15
They come.
Beatrice. All mortal things must hasten thus
To their dark end. Let us go down.
             [*Exeunt* LUCRETIA *and* BEATRICE *from above.*
Olimpio. How feel you to this work?
Marzio   As one who thinks
A thousand crowns excellent market price
For an old murderer's life. Your cheeks are pale.   20
Olimpio. It is the white reflexion of your own,
Which you call pale.

4. Brought to life.
5. Heeding the consequences, caring.
6. Though Beatrice's use of the word "necessity" is ordinary, to comprehend

the ironic deeper meaning the word must be read in the context of Shelley's belief in Necessity as proclaimed in *Queen Mab*, VI.198ff. and note.

Marzio.   Is that their natural hue?
Olimpio. Or 'tis my hate and the deferred desire
To wreak[7] it, which extinguishes their blood.
    Marzio. You are inclined then to this business?
    Olimpio.   Aye.   25
If one should bribe me with a thousand crowns
To kill a serpent which had stung my child,
I could not be more willing.

            Enter BEATRICE *and* LUCRETIA, *below.*
                            Noble ladies!
    Beatrice. Are ye resolved?
    Olimpio.   Is he asleep?
    Marzio.   Is all
Quiet?
    Lucretia. I mixed an opiate with his drink: 30
He sleeps so soundly . . .
    Beatrice.   That his death will be
But as a change of sin-chastising dreams,
A dark continuance of the Hell within him,
Which God extinguish! But ye are resolved?
Ye know it is a high and holy deed?   35
    Olimpio. We are resolved.
    Marzio.   As to the how this act
Be warranted, it rests with you.
    Beatrice.   Well, follow!
    Olimpio. Hush! Hark! What noise is that?
    Marzio.   Ha! some one comes!
    Beatrice. Ye conscience-stricken cravens,[8] rock to rest
Your baby hearts. It is the iron gate,   40
Which ye left open, swinging to the wind,
That enters whistling as in scorn. Come, follow!
And be your steps like mine, light, quick and bold.   [*Exeunt.*

SCENE III.—*An apartment in the Castle. Enter* BEATRICE *and*
                        LUCRETIA.
    Lucretia. They are about it now.
    Beatrice.   Nay, it is done.
    Lucretia. I have not heard him groan.
    Beatrice.   He will not groan.
    Lucretia. What sound is that?
    Beatrice.   List! 'tis the tread of feet
About his bed.
    Lucretia.   My God!
If he be now a cold stiff corpse . . .
    Beatrice.   O, fear not   5
What may be done, but what is left undone:
The act seals all.

---

7. Give vent or expression to.   8. Confessed or acknowledged cowards.

Enter OLIMPIO *and* MARZIO.
                     Is it accomplished?
Marzio.   What?
Olimpio. Did you not call?
Beatrice.   When?
Olimpio.   Now.
Beatrice.   I ask if all is over?
  Olimpio. We dare not kill an old and sleeping man;
His thin grey hair, his stern and reverent brow,   10
His veined hands crossed on his heaving breast,
And the calm innocent sleep in which he lay,
Quelled me. Indeed, indeed, I cannot do it.
  Marzio. But I was bolder; for I chid Olimpio,
And bade him bear his wrongs to his own grave   15
And leave me the reward. And now my knife
Touched the loose wrinkled throat, when the old man
Stirred in his sleep, and said, "God! hear, O, hear,
A father's curse! What, art thou not our father?"
And then he laughed. I knew it was the ghost   20
Of my dead father speaking through his lips,
And could not kill him.
  Beatrice.   Miserable slaves!
Where, if ye dare not kill a sleeping man,
Found ye the boldness to return to me
With such a deed undone? Base palterers!   25
Cowards and traitors! Why, the very conscience
Which ye would sell for gold and for revenge
Is an equivocation:[9] it sleeps over
A thousand daily acts disgracing men;
And when a deed where mercy insults heaven . . .   30
Why do I talk?
              [*Snatching a dagger from one of them and raising it.*
              Hadst thou a tongue to say,
"She murdered her own father," I must do it!
But never dream ye shall outlive him long!
  Olimpio. Stop, for God's sake!
  Marzio.   I will go back and kill him.
  Olimpio. Give me the weapon, we must do thy will.   35
  Beatrice. Take it! Depart! Return!
                          [*Exeunt* OLIMPIO *and* MARZIO.
                          How pale thou art!
We do but that which 'twere a deadly crime
To leave undone.
  Lucretia.   Would it were done!
  Beatrice.   Even whilst
That doubt is passing through your mind, the world
Is conscious of a change. Darkness and Hell   40
Have swallowed up the vapour they sent forth

---

9. The expression of a falsehood in a form that is verbally true.

To blacken the sweet light of life. My breath
Comes, methinks, lighter, and the jellied blood
Runs freely through my veins. Hark!

Enter OLIMPIO *and* MARZIO.
                He is . . .
  Olimpio.   Dead!
  Marzio. We strangled him that there might be no blood;   45
And then we threw his heavy corpse i' the garden
Under the balcony; 'twill seem it fell.
  Beatrice (*giving them a bag of coin*). Here take this gold, and
    hasten to your homes.
And, Marzio, because thou wast only awed
By that which made me tremble, wear thou this!   50
                    [*Clothes him in a rich mantle.*
It was the mantle which my grandfather
Wore in his high prosperity, and men
Envied his state: so may they envy thine.
Thou wert a weapon in the hand of God
To a just use. Live long and thrive! And, mark,   55
If thou hast crimes, repent: this deed is none. [*A horn is sounded.*
  Lucretia. Hark, 'tis the castle horn; my God! it sounds
Like the last trump.[1]
  Beatrice.   Some tedious guest is coming.
  Lucretia. The drawbridge is let down; there is a tramp
Of horses in the court; fly, hide yourselves!   60
                  [*Exeunt* OLIMPIO *and* MARZIO.
  Beatrice. Let us retire to counterfeit deep rest;
I scarcely need to counterfeit it now:
The spirit which doth reign within these limbs
Seems strangely undisturbed. I could even sleep   64
Fearless and calm: all ill is surely past.   [*Exeunt.*

SCENE IV.—*Another apartment in the Castle. Enter on one side the*
LEGATE SAVELLA *introduced by a servant, and on the other*
LUCRETIA *and* BERNARDO.

  Savella. Lady, my duty to his Holiness
Be my excuse that thus unseasonably
I break upon your rest. I must speak with
Count Cenci; doth he sleep?
  Lucretia (*in a hurried and confused manner*). I think he sleeps;
Yet wake him not, I pray, spare me awhile,   5
He is a wicked and a wrathful man;
Should he be roused out of his sleep to-night,
Which is, I know, a hell of angry dreams,
It were not well; indeed it were not well.
Wait till day break. . . . (*aside*) O, I am deadly sick!   10

1. The end of the world when Gabriel's trumpet will announce the Last Judgment.

Savella. I grieve thus to distress you, but the Count
Must answer charges of the gravest import,
And suddenly;[2] such my commission is.
 Lucretia (*with increased agitation*). I dare not rouse him: I know
  none who dare . . .
'Twere perilous; . . . you might as safely waken   15
A serpent; or a corpse in which some fiend
Were laid to sleep.
 Savella.   Lady, my moments here
Are counted. I must rouse him from his sleep,
Since none else dare.
 Lucretia (*aside*). O, terror! O, despair!
(*To* BERNARDO.) Bernardo, conduct you the Lord Legate to 20
Your father's chamber.   [*Exeunt* SAVELLA *and* BERNARDO.

     Enter BEATRICE.
 Beatrice.   'Tis a messenger
Come to arrest the culprit who now stands
Before the throne of unappealable God.
Both Earth and Heaven, consenting arbiters,
Acquit our deed.
 Lucretia. Oh, agony of fear!   25
Would that he yet might live! Even now I heard
The Legate's followers whisper as they passed
They had a warrant for his instant death.
All was prepared by unforbidden means
Which we must pay so dearly, having done.   30
Even now they search the tower, and find the body;
Now they suspect the truth; now they consult
Before they come to tax us with the fact;
O, horrible, 'tis all discovered!
 Beatrice.   Mother,
What is done wisely, is done well. Be bold   35
As thou art just. 'Tis like a truant child
To fear that others know what thou hast done,
Even from thine own strong consciousness, and thus
Write on unsteady eyes and altered cheeks
All thou wouldst hide. Be faithful to thyself,   40
And fear no other witness but thy fear.
For if, as cannot be, some circumstance
Should rise in accusation, we can blind
Suspicion with such cheap[3] astonishment,
Or overbear[4] it with such guiltless pride,   45
As murderers cannot feign. The deed is done,
And what may follow now regards not me.
I am as universal as the light;
Free as the earth-surrounding air; as firm

2. Immediately.   4. Overcome.
3. Easily accomplished.

As the world's centre. Consequence, to me,   50
Is as the wind which strikes the solid rock
But shakes it not.   [*A cry within and tumult.*
  Voices.   Murder! Murder! Murder!

  Enter BERNARDO *and* SAVELLA.
 Savella (*to his followers*). Go search the castle round; sound the alarm;
Look to the gates that none escape!
 Beatrice.   What now?
 Bernardo. I know not what to say . . . my father's dead. 55
 Beatrice. How; dead! he only sleeps; you mistake, brother.
His sleep is very calm, very like death;
'Tis wonderful how well a tyrant sleeps.
He is not dead?
 Bernardo. Dead; murdered.
 Lucretia (*with extreme agitation*). Oh no, no,
He is not murdered though he may be dead; 60
I have alone the keys of those apartments.
 Savella. Ha! Is it so?
 Beatrice.   My Lord, I pray excuse us;
We will retire; my mother is not well:
She seems quite overcome with this strange horror.
     [*Exeunt* LUCRETIA *and* BEATRICE.
 Savella. Can you suspect who may have murdered him? 65
 Bernardo. I know not what to think.
 Savella.   Can you name any
Who had an interest in his death?
 Bernardo.   Alas!
I can name none who had not, and those most
Who most lament that such a deed is done;
My mother, and my sister, and myself. 70
 Savella. 'Tis strange! There were clear marks of violence.
I found the old man's body in the moonlight
Hanging beneath the window of his chamber
Among the branches of a pine: he could not
Have fallen there, for all his limbs lay heaped 75
And effortless; 'tis true there was no blood . . .
Favour me, Sir; it much imports your house
That all should be made clear; to tell the ladies
That I request their presence. [*Exit* BERNARDO.

  Enter GUARDS *bringing in* MARZIO.
 Guard.   We have one.
 Officer. My Lord, we found this ruffian and another 80
Lurking among the rocks; there is no doubt
But that they are the murderers of Count Cenci:
Each had a bag of coin; this fellow wore
A gold-inwoven robe, which shining bright
Under the dark rocks to the glimmering moon 85

Betrayed them to our notice: the other fell
Desperately fighting.
  Savella.   What does he confess?
Officer. He keeps firm silence; but these lines found on him
May speak.
  Savella. Their language is at least sincere.   [*Reads.*
"To the Lady Beatrice.   90
That the atonement of what my nature
Sickens to conjecture may soon arrive,
I send thee, at thy brother's desire, those
Who will speak and do more than I dare
Write. . . .
     Thy devoted servant, Orsino."

    Enter LUCRETIA, BEATRICE, *and* BERNARDO.
Knowest thou this writing, Lady?
  Beatrice.   No.
  Savella.   Nor thou?   95
  Lucretia. (*Her conduct throughout the scene is marked by extreme agitation.*) Where was it found? What is it? It should be
Orsino's hand! It speaks of that strange horror
Which never yet found utterance, but which made
Between that hapless child and her dead father
A gulph of obscure hatred.
  Savella.   Is it so?   100
Is it true, Lady, that thy father did
Such outrages as to awaken in thee
Unfilial hate?
  Beatrice. Not hate, 'twas more than hate:
This is most true, yet wherefore question me?
  Savella. There is a deed demanding question done; 105
Thou hast a secret which will answer not.
Beatrice. What sayest? My Lord, your words are bold and rash.
  Savella. I do arrest all present in the name
Of the Pope's Holiness. You must to Rome.
  Lucretia. O, not to Rome! Indeed we are not guilty. 110
  Beatrice. Guilty! Who dares talk of guilt? My Lord,
I am more innocent of parricide
Than is a child born fatherless . . . Dear Mother,
Your gentleness and patience are no shield
For this keen judging world, this two-edged lie, 115
Which seems, but is not. What! will human laws,
Rather will ye who are their ministers,
Bar all access to retribution first,
And then, when heaven doth interpose to do
What ye neglect, arming familiar things 120
To the redress of an unwonted[5] crime,

---

5. Unusual.

Make ye the victims who demanded it
Culprits? 'Tis ye are culprits! That poor wretch
Who stands so pale, and trembling, and amazed,
If it be true he murdered Cenci, was   125
A sword in the right hand of justest God,
Wherefore should I have wielded it? Unless
The crimes which mortal tongue dare never name
God therefore scruples to avenge.
    Savella.   You own
That you desired his death?
    Beatrice.   It would have been   130
A crime no less than his, if for one moment
That fierce desire had faded in my heart.
'Tis true I did believe, and hope, and pray,
Aye, I even knew . . . for God is wise and just,
That some strange sudden death hung over him.   135
'Tis true that this did happen, and most true
There was no other rest for me on earth,
No other hope in Heaven . . . now what of this?
    Savella. Strange thoughts beget strange deeds; and here are
        both:
I judge thee not.
    Beatrice.   And yet, if you arrest me,   140
You are the judge and executioner
Of that which is the life of life: the breath
Of accusation kills an innocent name,
And leaves for lame acquittal the poor life
Which is a mask without it.[6] 'Tis most false   145
That I am guilty of foul parricide;
Although I must rejoice, for justest cause,
That other hands have sent my father's soul
To ask the mercy he denied to me.
Now leave us free; stain not a noble house   150
With vague surmises of rejected crime;
Add to our sufferings and your own neglect
No heavier sum: let them have been enough:
Leave us the wreck we have.
    Savella.   I dare not, Lady.
I pray that you prepare yourselves for Rome: 155
There the Pope's further pleasure will be known.
    Lucretia. O, not to Rome! O, take us not to Rome!
    Beatrice. Why not to Rome, dear mother? There as here
Our innocence is as an armed heel
To trample accusation. God is there   160
As here, and with his shadow ever clothes
The innocent, the injured and the weak;

6. The sense of lines 140–145 is that good reputation (*an innocent name*) is the *life of life*, which will be killed by the accusation of so serious a crime, leaving only *acquittal* to give insufficient substance to the life that would, without acquittal, be merely a *mask*.

And such are we. Cheer up, dear Lady, lean
On me; collect your wandering thoughts. My Lord,
As soon as you have taken some refreshment,   165
And had all such examinations made
Upon the spot, as may be necessary
To the full understanding of this matter,
We shall be ready. Mother; will you come?
    Lucretia. Ha! they will bind us to the rack, and wrest   170
Self-accusation from our agony!
Will Giacomo be there? Orsino? Marzio?
All present; all confronted; all demanding
Each from the other's countenance the thing
Which is in every heart! O, misery!   175
                              [*She faints, and is borne out.*
    Savella. She faints: an ill appearance this.
    Beatrice.   My Lord,
She knows not yet the uses of the world.
She fears that power is as a beast which grasps
And loosens not: a snake whose look transmutes
All things to guilt which is its nutriment.   180
She cannot know how well the supine slaves
Of blind authority read the truth of things
When written on a brow of guilelessness:
She sees not yet triumphant Innocence
Stand at the judgement-seat of mortal man,   185
A judge and an accuser of the wrong
Which drags it there. Prepare yourself, my Lord;
Our suite[7] will join yours in the court below.   [*Exeunt.*

END OF THE FOURTH ACT.

ACT V

SCENE I.—*An apartment in* ORSINO's *Palace. Enter* ORSINO *and*
GIACOMO.

    Giacomo. Do evil deeds thus quickly come to end?
O, that the vain remorse which must chastise
Crimes done, had but as loud a voice to warn
As its keen sting is mortal to avenge!
O, that the hour when present had cast off   5
The mantle of its mystery, and shewn
The ghastly form with which it now returns
When its scared game is roused, cheering the hounds
Of conscience to their prey! Alas! Alas!
It was a wicked thought, a piteous deed,   10
To kill an old and hoary-headed father.
    Orsino. It has turned out unluckily, in truth.
    Giacomo. To violate the sacred doors of sleep;

---
7. Retinue; train of followers or servants.

To cheat kind nature of the placid death
Which she prepares for overwearied age;   15
To drag from Heaven an unrepentant soul
Which might have quenched in reconciling prayers
A life of burning crimes . . .
    Orsino.   You cannot say
I urged you to the deed.
    Giacomo.   O, had I never
Found in thy smooth and ready countenance   20
The mirror of my darkest thoughts; hadst thou
Never with hints and questions made me look
Upon the monster of my thought, until
It grew familiar to desire . . .
    Orsino.   'Tis thus
Men cast the blame of their unprosperous acts   25
Upon the abettors of their own resolve;
Or anything but their weak, guilty selves.
And yet, confess the truth, it is the peril
In which you stand that gives you this pale sickness
Of penitence; confess 'tis fear disguised   30
From its own shame that takes the mantle now
Of thin remorse. What if we yet were safe?
    Giacomo. How can that be? Already Beatrice,
Lucretia and the murderer are in prison.
I doubt not officers are, whilst we speak,   35
Sent to arrest us.
    Orsino.   I have all prepared
For instant flight. We can escape even now,
So we take fleet occasion by the hair.[8]
    Giacomo. Rather expire in tortures, as I may.
What! will you cast by self-accusing flight   40
Assured conviction upon Beatrice?
She, who alone in this unnatural work,
Stands like God's angel ministered upon
By fiends; avenging such a nameless wrong
As turns black parricide to piety;   45
Whilst we for basest ends . . . I fear, Orsino,
While I consider all your words and looks,
Comparing them with your proposal now,
That you must be a villain. For what end
Could you engage in such a perilous crime,   50
Training me on with hints, and signs, and smiles,
Even to this gulph? Thou art no liar? No,
Thou art a lie! Traitor and murderer!
Coward and slave! But, no, defend thyself;   [*Drawing.*
Let the sword speak what the indignant tongue   55
Disdains to brand thee with.
    Orsino.   Put up your weapon.

8. Gain power or leverage over, while the time is right.

Is it the desperation of your fear
Makes you thus rash and sudden with a friend,
Now ruined for your sake? If honest anger
Have moved you, know, that what I just proposed   60
Was but to try you. As for me, I think,
Thankless affection led me to this point,
From which, if my firm temper could repent,
I cannot now recede. Even whilst we speak
The ministers of justice wait below: 65
They grant me these brief moments. Now if you
Have any word of melancholy comfort
To speak to your pale wife, 'twere best to pass
Out at the postern,⁹ and avoid them so.
    Giacomo. O, generous friend! How canst thou pardon me?   70
Would that my life could purchase thine!
    Orsino.   That wish
Now comes a day too late. Haste; fare thee well!
Hear'st thou not steps along the corridor?   [*Exit* GIACOMO.
I'm sorry for it; but the guards are waiting
At his own gate, and such was my contrivance   75
That I might rid me both of him and them.
I thought to act a solemn comedy
Upon the painted scene of this new world,
And to attain my own peculiar ends
By some such plot of mingled good and ill   80
As others weave; but there arose a Power
Which graspt and snapped the threads of my device
And turned it to a net of ruin . . . Ha!   [*A shout is heard.*
Is that my name I hear proclaimed abroad?
But I will pass, wrapt in a vile disguise;   85
Rags on my back, and a false innocence
Upon my face, through the misdeeming crowd
Which judges by what seems. 'Tis easy then
For a new name and for a country new,
And a new life, fashioned on old desires,   90
To change the honours of abandoned Rome.
And these must be the masks of that within,
Which must remain unaltered . . . Oh, I fear
That what is past will never let me rest!
Why, when none else is conscious, but myself,   95
Of my misdeeds, should my own heart's contempt
Trouble me? Have I not the power to fly
My own reproaches? Shall I be the slave
Of . . . what? A word? which those of this false world
Employ against each other, not themselves;   100
As men wear daggers not for self-offence.
But if I am mistaken, where shall I
Find the disguise to hide me from myself,
As now I skulk from every other eye?   [*Exit.*

9. Back or side door.

SCENE II.—A *Hall of Justice.* CAMILLO, JUDGES, *etc., are discovered seated;* MARZIO *is led in.*

 First Judge. Accused, do you persist in your denial?
I ask you, are you innocent, or guilty?
I demand who were the participators
In your offence? Speak truth and the whole truth.
 Marzio. My God! I did not kill him; I know nothing; 5
Olimpio sold the robe to me from which
You would infer my guilt.
 Second Judge.   Away with him!
 First Judge. Dare you, with lips yet white from the rack's kiss
Speak false? Is it so soft a questioner,
That you would bandy lover's talk with it 10
Till it wind out your life and soul? Away!
 Marzio. Spare me! O, spare! I will confess.
 First Judge.   Then speak.
 Marzio. I strangled him in his sleep.
 First Judge.   Who urged you to it?
 Marzio. His own son Giacomo, and the young prelate
Orsino sent me to Petrella; there 15
The ladies Beatrice and Lucretia
Tempted me with a thousand crowns, and I
And my companion forthwith murdered him.
Now let me die.
 First Judge. This sounds as bad as truth. Guards, there,
Lead forth the prisoners!

   Enter LUCRETIA, BEATRICE, *and* GIACOMO, *guarded.*
       Look upon this man; 20
When did you see him last?
 Beatrice.   We never saw him.
 Marzio. You know me too well, Lady Beatrice.
 Beatrice. I know thee! How? where? when?
 Marzio.   You know 'twas I
Whom you did urge with menaces and bribes
To kill your father. When the thing was done 25
You clothed me in a robe of woven gold
And bade me thrive: how I have thriven, you see.
You, my Lord Giacomo, Lady Lucretia,
You know that what I speak is true.
 [BEATRICE *advances towards him; he covers his face, and shrinks*
               back.
       Oh, dart
The terrible resentment of those eyes 30
On the dead earth! Turn them away from me!
They wound: 'twas torture forced the truth. My Lords,
Having said this let me be led to death.
 Beatrice. Poor wretch, I pity thee: yet stay awhile.
 Camillo. Guards, lead him not away.
 Beatrice.   Cardinal Camillo, 35

You have a good repute for gentleness
And wisdom: can it be that you sit here
To countenance a wicked farce like this?
When some obscure and trembling slave is dragged
From sufferings which might shake the sternest heart   40
And bade to answer, not as he believes,
But as those may suspect or do desire
Whose questions thence suggest their own reply:
And that in peril of such hideous torments
As merciful God spares even the damned. Speak now   45
The thing you surely know, which is that you,
If your fine frame were stretched upon that wheel,
And you were told: "Confess that you did poison
Your little nephew; that fair blue-eyed child
Who was the lodestar[1] of your life:"—and though   50
All see, since his most swift and piteous death,
That day and night, and heaven and earth, and time,
And all the things hoped for or done therein
Are changed to you, through your exceeding grief,
Yet you would say, "I confess any thing:"   55
And beg from your tormentors, like that slave,
The refuge of dishonourable death.
I pray thee, Cardinal, that thou assert
My innocence.
  Camillo (much moved). What shall we think, my lords?
Shame on these tears! I thought the heart was frozen   60
Which is their fountain. I would pledge my soul
That she is guiltless.
  Judge.   Yet she must be tortured.
  Camillo. I would as soon have tortured mine own nephew:
(If he now lived he would be just her age;
His hair, too, was her colour, and his eyes   65
Like hers in shape, but blue and not so deep)
As that most perfect image of God's love
That ever came sorrowing upon the earth.
She is as pure as speechless infancy!
  Judge. Well, be her purity on your head, my Lord,   70
If you forbid the rack. His Holiness
Enjoined us to pursue this monstrous crime
By the severest forms of law; nay even
To stretch a point against the criminals.
The prisoners stand accused of parricide   75
Upon such evidence as justifies
Torture.
  Beatrice. What evidence? This man's?
  Judge.   Even so.
  Beatrice (to MARZIO). Come near. And who art thou thus chosen
   forth

---

1. A "guiding star"; that on which one's attentions or hopes are fixed.

Out of the multitude of living men
To kill the innocent?
    Marzio.   I am Marzio,   80
Thy father's vassal.
    Beatrice.   Fix thine eyes on mine;
Answer to what I ask.   [*Turning to the* JUDGES.
                I prithee mark
His countenance: unlike bold calumny
Which sometimes dares not speak the thing it looks,
He dares not look the thing he speaks, but bends   85
His gaze on the blind earth.
(*To* MARZIO.)   What! wilt thou say
That I did murder my own father?
    Marzio.   Oh!
Spare me! My brain swims round . . . I cannot speak . . .
It was that horrid torture forced the truth.
Take me away! Let her not look on me!   90
I am a guilty miserable wretch;
I have said all I know; now, let me die!
    Beatrice. My Lords, if by my nature I had been
So stern, as to have planned the crime alledged,
Which your suspicions dictate to this slave,   95
And the rack makes him utter, do you think
I should have left this two edged instrument
Of my misdeed; this man, this bloody knife
With my own name engraven on the heft,
Lying unsheathed amid' a world of foes,   100
For my own death? That with such horrible need
For deepest silence, I should have neglected
So trivial a precaution, as the making
His tomb the keeper of a secret written
On a thief's memory? What is his poor life?   105
What are a thousand lives? A parricide
Had trampled them like dust; and, see, he lives!
(*Turning to* MARZIO.) And thou . . .
    Marzio.   Oh, spare me! Speak to me no more!
That stern yet piteous look, those solemn tones,
Wound worse than torture.
    (*To the* JUDGES.)   I have told it all;   110
For pity's sake lead me away to death.
    Camillo. Guards, lead him nearer the Lady Beatrice,
He shrinks from her regard like autumn's leaf
From the keen breath of the serenest north.
    Beatrice. Oh, thou who tremblest on the giddy[2] verge   115
Of life and death, pause ere thou answerest me;
So mayest thou answer God with less dismay:
What evil have we done thee? I, alas!
Have lived but on this earth a few sad years,

2. Apt to cause dizziness.

And so my lot was ordered, that a father   120
First turned the moments of awakening life
To drops, each poisoning youth's sweet hope; and then
Stabbed with one blow my everlasting soul;
And my untainted fame; and even that peace
Which sleeps within the core of the heart's heart;   125
But the wound was not mortal; so my hate
Became the only worship I could lift
To our great father, who in pity and love,
Armed thee, as thou dost say, to cut him off;
And thus his wrong becomes my accusation;   130
And art thou the accuser? If thou hopest
Mercy in heaven, shew justice upon earth:
Worse than a bloody hand is a hard heart.
If thou hast done murders, made thy life's path
Over the trampled laws of God and man,   135
Rush not before thy Judge, and say: "My maker,
I have done this and more; for there was one
Who was most pure and innocent on earth;
And because she endured what never any
Guilty or innocent endured before: 140
Because her wrongs could not be told, not thought;
Because thy hand at length did rescue her;
I with my words killed her and all her kin."
Think, I adjure you, what it is to slay
The reverence living in the minds of men   145
Towards our antient house, and stainless fame!
Think what it is to strangle infant pity,
Cradled in the belief of guileless looks,
Till it become a crime to suffer. Think
What 'tis to blot with infamy and blood   150
All that which shows like innocence, and is,
Hear me, great God! I swear, most innocent,
So that the world lose all discrimination
Between the sly, fierce, wild regard of guilt,
And that which now compels thee to reply   155
To what I ask: Am I, or am I not
A parricide?
    Marzio.   Thou art not!
    Judge.   What is this?
    Marzio. I here declare those whom I did accuse
Are innocent. 'Tis I alone am guilty.
    Judge. Drag him away to torments; let them be   160
Subtle and long drawn out, to tear the folds
Of the heart's inmost cell. Unbind him not
Till he confess.
    Marzio.   Torture me as ye will:
A keener pain has wrung a higher truth
From my last breath. She is most innocent!   165

Bloodhounds, not men, glut yourselves well with me;
I will not give you that fine piece of nature
To rend and ruin.   [*Exit* MARZIO, *guarded.*
   Camillo.   What say ye now, my Lords?
   Judge. Let tortures strain the truth till it be white
As snow thrice sifted by the frozen wind.   170
   Camillo. Yet stained with blood.
   Judge (*to* BEATRICE).   Know you this paper, Lady?
   Beatrice. Entrap me not with questions. Who stands here
As my accuser? Ha! wilt thou be he,
Who art my judge? Accuser, witness, judge,
What, all in one? Here is Orsino's name;   175
Where is Orsino? Let his eye meet mine.
What means this scrawl? Alas! ye know not what,
And therefore on the chance that it may be
Some evil, will ye kill us?
                Enter an Officer.
   Officer.   Marzio's dead.
   Judge. What did he say?
   Officer.   Nothing. As soon as we   180
Had bound him on the wheel, he smiled on us,
As one who baffles a deep[3] adversary;
And holding his breath, died.
   Judge.   There remains nothing
But to apply the question to those prisoners,
Who yet remain stubborn.
   Camillo.   I overrule   185
Further proceedings, and in the behalf
Of these most innocent and noble persons
Will use my interest with the Holy Father.
   Judge. Let the Pope's pleasure then be done. Meanwhile
Conduct these culprits each to separate cells;   190
And be the engines[4] ready: for this night
If the Pope's resolution be as grave,
Pious,[5] and just as once, I'll wring the truth
Out of those nerves and sinews, groan by groan.   [*Exeunt.*

SCENE III.—*The cell of a prison.* BEATRICE *is discovered asleep
on a couch. Enter* BERNARDO.

   Bernardo. How gently slumber rests upon her face,
Like the last thoughts of some day sweetly spent
Closing in night and dreams, and so prolonged.
After such torments as she bore last night,
How light and soft her breathing comes. Ay, me!   5

3. Profoundly cunning.
4. Machines of torture, especially the rack.
5. *Pope's resolution . . . Pious:* While Shelley was in Italy, Pope Pius VII (1740–1823) ruled Rome and the Papal States with a reactionary government employing spies, secret police and assassins, torture, execution, slavery in the galleys, and exile.

Methinks that I shall never sleep again.
But I must shake the heavenly dew of rest
From this sweet folded flower, thus . . . wake! awake!
What, sister, canst thou sleep?
    Beatrice (awaking).   I was just dreaming
That we were all in Paradise. Thou knowest   10
This cell seems like a kind of Paradise
After our father's presence.
    Bernardo.   Dear, dear sister,
Would that thy dream were not a dream! O, God!
How shall I tell?
    Beatrice.   What would'st thou tell, sweet brother?
    Bernardo. Look not so calm and happy, or even whilst   15
I stand considering what I have to say
My heart will break.
    Beatrice.   See now, thou mak'st me weep:
How very friendless thou wouldst be, dear child,
If I were dead. Say what thou hast to say.
    Bernardo. They have confessed; they could endure no more 20
The tortures . . .
    Beatrice.   Ha! What was there to confess?
They must have told some weak and wicked lie
To flatter their tormentors. Have they said
That they were guilty? O white innocence,
That thou shouldst wear the mask of guilt to hide   25
Thine awful and serenest countenance
From those who know thee not!

      Enter JUDGE *with* LUCRETIA *and* GIACOMO, *guarded.*
                        Ignoble hearts!
For some brief spasms of pain, which are at least
As mortal as the limbs through which they pass,
Are centuries of high splendour laid in dust?   30
And that eternal honour which should live
Sunlike, above the reek of mortal fame,
Changed to a mockery and a bye-word? What!
Will you give up these bodies to be dragged
At horse's heels, so that our hair should sweep   35
The footsteps of the vain and senseless crowd,
Who, that they may make our calamity
Their worship and their spectacle, will leave
The churches and the theatres as void
As their own hearts? Shall the light multitude   40
Fling, at their choice, curses or faded pity,
Sad funeral flowers to deck a living corpse,
Upon us as we pass to pass away,
And leave . . . what memory of our having been?
Infamy, blood, terror, despair? O thou,   45
Who wert a mother to the parentless,
Kill not thy child! Let not her wrongs kill thee!

Brother, lie down with me upon the rack,
And let us each be silent as a corpse;
It soon will be as soft as any grave.   50
'Tis but the falsehood it can wring from fear
Makes the rack cruel.
    Giacomo.   They will tear the truth
Even from thee at last, those cruel pains:
For pity's sake say thou art guilty now.
    Lucretia. O, speak the truth! Let us all quickly die;   55
And after death, God is our judge, not they;
He will have mercy on us.
    Bernardo.   If indeed
It can be true, say so, dear sister mine;
And then the Pope will surely pardon you,
And all be well.
    Judge.   Confess, or I will warp   60
Your limbs with such keen tortures . . .
    Beatrice.   Tortures! Turn
The rack henceforth into a spinning-wheel!
Torture your dog, that he may tell when last
He lapped the blood his master shed . . . not me!
My pangs are of the mind, and of the heart,   65
And of the soul; aye, of the inmost soul,
Which weeps within tears as of burning gall
To see, in this ill world where none are true,
My kindred false to their deserted selves.
And with considering all the wretched life   70
Which I have lived, and its now wretched end,
And the small justice shown by Heaven and Earth
To me or mine; and what a tyrant thou art,
And what slaves these; and what a world we make,
The oppressor and the oppressed . . . such pangs compel   75
My answer. What is it thou wouldst with me?
    Judge. Art thou not guilty of thy father's death?
    Beatrice. Or wilt thou rather tax high judging God
That he permitted such an act as that
Which I have suffered, and which he beheld;   80
Made it unutterable, and took from it
All refuge, all revenge, all consequence,
But that which thou hast called my father's death?
Which is or is not what men call a crime,
Which either I have done, or have not done;   85
Say what ye will. I shall deny no more.
If ye desire it thus, thus let it be,
And so an end of all. Now do your will;
No other pains shall force another word.
    Judge. She is convicted, but has not confessed.   90
Be it enough. Until their final sentence
Let none have converse with them. You, young Lord,

Linger not here!
 Beatrice. Oh, tear him not away!
 Judge. Guards, do your duty.
 Bernardo (embracing BEATRICE). Oh! would ye divide
Body from soul?
 Officer. That is the headsman's business. 95
    [*Exeunt all but* LUCRETIA, BEATRICE, *and* GIACOMO.
 Giacomo. Have I confessed? Is it all over now?
No hope! No refuge! O weak, wicked tongue
Which hast destroyed me, would that thou hadst been
Cut out and thrown to dogs first! To have killed
My father first, and then betrayed my sister; 100
Aye, thee! the one thing innocent and pure
In this black guilty world, to that which I
So well deserve! My wife! my little ones!
Destitute, helpless, and I . . . Father! God!
Canst Thou forgive even the unforgiving, 105
When their full hearts break thus, thus! . . .
     [*Covers his face and weeps.*
 Lucretia.   O my child!
To what a dreadful end are we all come!
Why did I yield? Why did I not sustain
Those torments? Oh, that I were all dissolved
Into these fast and unavailing tears, 110
Which flow and feel not!
 Beatrice.   What 'twas weak to do,
'Tis weaker to lament, once being done;
Take cheer! The God who knew my wrong, and made
Our speedy act the angel of his wrath,
Seems, and but seems to have abandoned us. 115
Let us not think that we shall die for this.
Brother, sit near me; give me your firm hand,
You had a manly heart. Bear up! Bear up!
O, dearest Lady, put your gentle head
Upon my lap, and try to sleep a while: 120
Your eyes look pale, hollow and overworn,
With heaviness of watching and slow grief.
Come, I will sing you some low, sleepy tune,
Not cheerful, nor yet sad; some dull old thing,
Some outworn and unused monotony, 125
Such as our country gossips sing and spin,
Till they almost forget they live: lie down!
So, that will do. Have I forgot the words?
Faith! They are sadder than I thought they were.

      SONG
   False friend, wilt thou smile or weep 130
   When my life is laid asleep?
   Little cares for a smile or a tear,
   The clay-cold corpse upon the bier!

Farewell! Heigho!
    What is this whispers low?   135
There is a snake in thy smile, my dear;
And bitter poison within thy tear.

Sweet sleep, were death like to thee,
Or if thou couldst mortal be,
I would close these eyes of pain;   140
When to wake? Never again.
    O, World! Farewell!
    Listen to the passing bell!
It says, thou and I must part,   144
With a light and a heavy heart.   *[The scene closes.*

SCENE IV.—*A Hall of the Prison. Enter* CAMILLO *and* BERNARDO.

   Camillo. The Pope is stern; not to be moved or bent.
He looked as calm and keen as is the engine
Which tortures and which kills, exempt itself
From aught that it inflicts; a marble form,
A rite, a law, a custom: not a man.   5
He frowned, as if to frown had been the trick
Of his machinery,[6] on the advocates
Presenting the defences, which he tore
And threw behind, muttering with hoarse, harsh voice:
"Which among ye defended their old father   10
Killed in his sleep?" Then to another: "Thou
Dost this in virtue of thy place; 'tis well."
He turned to me then, looking deprecation,
And said these three words, coldly: "They must die."
   Bernardo. And yet you left him not?
   Camillo.   I urged him still;   15
Pleading, as I could guess, the devilish wrong
Which prompted your unnatural parent's death.
And he replied: "Paolo Santa Croce
Murdered his mother yester evening,
And he is fled. Parricide grows so rife   20
That soon, for some just cause no doubt, the young
Will strangle us all, dozing in our chairs.
Authority, and power, and hoary hair
Are grown crimes capital. You are my nephew,
You come to ask their pardon; stay a moment;   25
Here is their sentence; never see me more
Till, to the letter, it be all fulfilled."
   Bernardo. O God, not so! I did believe indeed
That all you said was but sad preparation
For happy news. O, there are words and looks   30
To bend the sternest purpose! Once I knew them,

---

6. Those who plead a case in court.

Now I forget them at my dearest need.
What think you if I seek him out, and bathe
His feet and robe with hot and bitter tears?
Importune him with prayers, vexing his brain   35
With my perpetual cries, until in rage
He strike me with his pastoral cross, and trample
Upon my prostrate head, so that my blood
May stain the senseless dust on which he treads,
And remorse waken mercy? I will do it!   40
O, wait till I return!   [*Rushes out.*
   Camillo.   Alas! poor boy!
A wreck-devoted seaman thus might pray
To the deaf sea.

     Enter LUCRETIA, BEATRICE, *and* GIACOMO, *guarded.*
   Beatrice.   I hardly dare to fear
That thou bring'st other news than a just pardon.
   Camillo. May God in heaven be less inexorable   45
To the Pope's prayers, than he has been to mine.
Here is the sentence and the warrant.
   Beatrice (*wildly*).   Oh,
My God! Can it be possible I have
To die so suddenly? So young to go
Under the obscure, cold, rotting, wormy ground!   50
To be nailed down into a narrow place;
To see no more sweet sunshine; hear no more
Blithe voice of living thing; muse not again
Upon familiar thoughts, sad, yet thus lost—
How fearful! to be nothing! Or to be . . .   55
What? O, where am I? Let me not go mad!
Sweet Heaven, forgive weak thoughts! If there should be
No God, no Heaven, no Earth in the void world;
The wide, grey, lampless, deep, unpeopled world!
If all things then should be . . . my father's spirit   60
His eye, his voice, his touch surrounding me;
The atmosphere and breath of my dead life!
If sometimes, as a shape more like himself,
Even the form which tortured me on earth,
Masked in grey hairs and wrinkles, he should come   65
And wind me in his hellish arms, and fix
His eyes on mine, and drag me down, down, down!
For was he not alone omnipotent
On Earth, and ever present? Even though dead,
Does not his spirit live in all that breathe,   70
And work for me and mine still the same ruin,
Scorn, pain, despair? Who ever yet returned
To teach the laws of death's untrodden realm?
Unjust perhaps as those which drive us now,
O, whither, whither?
Lucretia.   Trust in God's sweet love,   75

The tender promises of Christ: ere night
Think we shall be in Paradise.
    Beatrice.   'Tis past!
Whatever comes my heart shall sink no more.
And yet, I know not why, your words strike chill:
How tedious, false and cold seem all things. I   80
Have met with much injustice in this world;
No difference has been made by God or man,
Or any power moulding my wretched lot,
'Twixt good or evil, as regarded me.
I am cut off from the only world I know,   85
From light, and life, and love, in youth's sweet prime.
You do well telling me to trust in God,
I hope I do trust in him. In whom else
Can any trust? And yet my heart is cold.
          [*During the latter speeches* GIACOMO *has retired conversing
           with* CAMILLO, *who now goes out;* GIACOMO *advances.*
    Giacomo. Know you not, Mother . . . Sister, know you not? 90
Bernardo even now is gone to implore
The Pope to grant our pardon.
    Lucretia.   Child, perhaps
It will be granted. We may all then live
To make these woes a tale for distant years:
O, what a thought! It gushes to my heart   95
Like the warm blood.
    Beatrice.   Yet both will soon be cold.
O, trample out that thought! Worse than despair,
Worse than the bitterness of death, is hope:
It is the only ill which can find place
Upon the giddy, sharp and narrow hour   100
Tottering beneath us. Plead with the swift frost
That it should spare the eldest flower of spring:
Plead with awakening Earthquake, o'er whose couch
Even now a city stands, strong, fair and free;
Now stench and blackness yawns, like death. O, plead   105
With famine, or wind-walking Pestilence,
Blind lightning, or the deaf sea, not with man!
Cruel, cold, formal man; righteous in words,
In deeds a Cain.[7] No, Mother, we must die:
Since such is the reward of innocent lives;   110
Such the alleviation of worst wrongs.
And whilst our murderers live, and hard, cold men,
Smiling and slow, walk through a world of tears
To death as to life's sleep; 'twere just the grave
Were some strange joy for us. Come, obscure Death,   115
And wind me in thine all-embracing arms!
Like a fond mother hide me in thy bosom,

---

7. The first fratricide and murderer gave
his name to the area of Hell (Caina) in
Dante's *Inferno* where those who mur-
dered relatives were punished.

And rock me to the sleep from which none wake.
Live ye, who live, subject to one another
As we were once, who now . . .

BERNARDO *rushes in.*
Bernardo.   Oh, horrible!   120
That tears, that looks, that hope poured forth in prayer,
Even till the heart is vacant and despairs,
Should all be vain! The ministers of death
Are waiting round the doors. I thought I saw
Blood on the face of one . . . what if 'twere fancy?   125
Soon the heart's blood of all I love on earth
Will sprinkle him, and he will wipe it off
As if 'twere only rain. O, life! O, world!
Cover me! let me be no more! To see
That perfect mirror of pure innocence   130
Wherein I gazed, and grew happy and good,
Shivered[8] to dust! To see thee, Beatrice,
Who made all lovely thou didst look upon . . .
Thee, light of life . . . dead, dark! while I say, sister,
To hear I have no sister; and thou, Mother,   135
Whose love was a bond to all our loves . . .
Dead! The sweet bond broken!

Enter CAMILLO *and* GUARDS.
                  They come! Let me
Kiss those warm lips before their crimson leaves
Are blighted . . . white . . . cold. Say farewell, before
Death chokes that gentle voice! O, let me hear   140
You speak!
   Beatrice. Farewell, my tender brother. Think
Of our sad fate with gentleness, as now:
And let mild, pitying thoughts lighten for thee
Thy sorrow's load. Err not in harsh despair,
But tears and patience. One thing more, my child,   145
For thine own sake be constant to the love
Thou bearest us; and to the faith that I,
Though wrapped in a strange cloud of crime and shame,
Lived ever holy and unstained. And though
Ill tongues shall wound me, and our common name   150
Be as a mark stamped on thine innocent brow
For men to point at as they pass, do thou
Forbear, and never think a thought unkind
Of those, who perhaps love thee in their graves.
So mayest thou die as I do; fear and pain   155
Being subdued. Farewell! Farewell! Farewell!
   Bernardo. I cannot say, farewell!
   Camillo.   O, Lady Beatrice!
   Beatrice. Give yourself no unnecessary pain,

8. Shattered.

My dear Lord Cardinal. Here, Mother, tie
My girdle for me, and bind up this hair   160
In any simple knot; aye, that does well.
And yours I see is coming down. How often
Have we done this for one another; now
We shall not do it any more. My Lord,
We are quite ready. Well, 'tis very well.   165

THE END.

The Mask of Anarchy[1]

Written on the Occasion of the Massacre at Manchester

As I lay asleep in Italy
There came a voice from over the Sea,
And with great power it forth led me
To walk in the visions of Poesy.

I met Murder on the way—   5
He had a mask like Castlereagh[2]—
Very smooth he looked, yet grim;
Seven bloodhounds[3] followed him:

All were fat; and well they might
Be in admirable plight,   10
For one by one, and two by two,
He tossed them human hearts to chew
Which from his wide cloak he drew.

1. On August 16, 1819, in St. Peter's Field, near Manchester, a group of drunken mounted militiamen and cavalrymen misinterpreted their orders and charged into a peaceful crowd of men, women, and children who were attending a rally in support of Parliamentary reform. At least six persons were killed and more than eighty wounded. (Some authorities give figures as high as eleven killed and five-hundred injured.) Shelley, isolated in Italy, first learned of the so-called Peterloo Massacre (a name alluding to the Tories' great pride in the victory at Waterloo) in a letter from Thomas Love Peacock that reached him on September 5. Writing to Charles Ollier, his publisher, Shelley said that the "torrent of my indignation has not yet done boiling in my veins." He drafted "The Mask of Anarchy" and reworked it into an intermediate fair copy, and Mary Shelley recopied it for the press and mailed it to Leigh Hunt to publish in the *Examiner* on September 23, 1819. Hunt—fearful of prosecution because of the volatile temper of the country and the new repressive legislation passed late in 1819 and 1820—refrained from publishing the poem until 1832, after the battle had been won for which Shelley had intended his poem as a rallying cry.

The poem, utilizing irregular ballad stanzas of four and five lines, embodies Shelley's characteristic symbols and imagery, but aims for more immediate effects from a less educated audience. It is a kind of rallying hymn to nonviolent resistance.

The two authoritative manuscripts, Shelley's intermediate holograph and Mary's fair copy with Shelley's corrections, are in the Ashley Collection of the British Library and in the Manuscript Division of the Library of Congress.

2. Robert Stewart, Viscount Castlereagh, at this time Foreign Secretary and leader of the Tories in the House of Commons, had earlier been infamous for his bloody suppression of unrest in Ireland; now Shelley (and Byron) blamed him for his support of Austria and the reactionary Holy Alliance in Europe.

3. In 1815, Britain joined seven other nations (Austria, France, Russia, Prussia, Portugal, Spain, and Sweden) in agreeing to postpone final abolition of the slave trade; the pro-war advocates in Pitt's administration had been popularly known as the "bloodhounds" (cf. "hawks").

Next came Fraud, and he had on,
Like Eldon,[4] an ermined gown;   15
His big tears, for he wept well,
Turned to mill-stones as they fell.

And the little children, who
Round his feet played to and fro,
Thinking every tear a gem,   20
Had their brains knocked out by them.

Clothed with the Bible, as with light,[5]
And the shadows of the night,
Like Sidmouth,[6] next, Hypocrisy
On a crocodile[7] rode by.   25

And many more Destructions played
In this ghastly masquerade,
All disguised, even to the eyes,
Like Bishops, lawyers, peers, or spies.

Last came Anarchy:[8] he rode   30
On a white horse, splashed with blood;
He was pale even to the lips,
Like Death in the Apocalypse.

And he wore a kingly crown,
And in his grasp a sceptre shone;   35
On his brow this mark I saw—
"I AM GOD, AND KING, AND LAW!"

With a pace stately and fast,
Over English land he past,
Trampling to a mire of blood   40
The adoring multitude.

And a mighty troop around,
With their trampling shook the ground,
Waving each a bloody sword,
For the service of their Lord.   45

4. John Scott, Baron Eldon, was the Lord Chancellor (hence the *ermined gown*); his decision in court had deprived Shelley of his children by Harriet. He was notorious for weeping in public.
5. Shelley had marked an "x" in his manuscript, as if to indicate the reference to a footnote (which remained unwritten).
6. Henry Addington, Viscount Sidmouth, was as Home Secretary responsible for internal security. He hired spies and agents who first provoked discontented workingmen to illegal acts and then betrayed them to be hanged or deported. In 1818 he persuaded Parliament to vote a million pounds for new churches to help pacify the half-starved workers in the new industrial towns.
7. The crocodile, which according to legend wept in order to attract or while devouring its prey, was a symbol of hypocrisy.
8. Shelley's personification of Anarchy, besides drawing on Revelation 6:8, alludes to Benjamin West's celebrated painting of *Death on the Pale Horse*, in which Death is portrayed as wearing a crown and, with sword-bearing followers, is trampling a crowd. In using the name Anarchy for the supreme personification of evil, Shelley was following Milton and Pope, who termed Chaos (*Paradise Lost*, II.988; *Dunciad*, IV.655) Anarch.

And with glorious triumph, they
Rode through England proud and gay
Drunk as with intoxication
Of the wine of desolation.

O'er fields and towns, from sea to sea.   50
Passed the Pageant swift and free,
Tearing up, and trampling down;
Till they came to London town.

And each dweller, panic-stricken,
Felt his heart with terror sicken   55
Hearing the tempestuous cry
Of the triumph of Anarchy.

For with pomp to meet him came
Clothed in arms like blood and flame,
The hired Murderers, who did sing   60
"Thou art God, and Law, and King.

"We have waited, weak and lone
For thy coming, Mighty One!
Our purses are empty, our swords are cold,
Give us glory, and blood, and gold."   65

Lawyers and priests, a motley crowd,
To the earth their pale brows bowed;
Like a bad prayer not over loud,
Whispering—"Thou art Law and God."—

Then all cried with one accord;   70
"Thou art King, and God, and Lord;
Anarchy, to Thee we bow,
Be thy name made holy now!"

And Anarchy, the Skeleton,
Bowed and grinned to every one,   75
As well as if his education
Had cost ten millions to the Nation.

For he knew the Palaces
Of our Kings were rightly his;
His the sceptre, crown, and globe,[9]   80
And the gold-inwoven robe.

So he sent his slaves before
To seize upon the Bank and Tower,[1]
And was proceeding with intent
To meet his pensioned[2] Parliament   85

9. The golden ball or orb borne along with the scepter as a sign of sovereignty. 1. *Bank:* The Bank of England, which manages the government's money; *Tower:* the Tower of London, where the crown jewels are kept. 2. Retired on a pension; the word implies that Parliament was open to corruption, especially bribery.

When one fled past, a maniac maid,
And her name was Hope, she said:
But she looked more like Despair,
And she cried out in the air:

"My father Time is weak and grey   90
With waiting for a better day;
See how idiot-like he stands,
Fumbling with his palsied hands!

"He has had child after child
And the dust of death is piled   95
Over every one but me—
Misery, oh, Misery!"

Then she lay down in the street,
Right before the horses' feet,
Expecting, with a patient eye,   100
Murder, Fraud and Anarchy.

When between her and her foes
A mist, a light, an image rose,
Small at first, and weak, and frail
Like the vapour of a vale: 105

Till as clouds grow on the blast,
Like tower-crowned giants striding fast
And glare with lightnings as they fly,
And speak in thunder to the sky,

It grew—a Shape arrayed in mail   110
Brighter than the Viper's scale,
And upborne on wings whose grain
Was as the light of sunny rain.

On its helm, seen far away,
A planet, like the Morning's,[3] lay;   115
And those plumes its light rained through
Like a shower of crimson dew.

With step as soft as wind it past
O'er the heads of men—so fast
That they knew the presence there,   120
And looked,—but all was empty air.

As flowers beneath May's footstep waken
As stars from Night's loose hair are shaken
As waves arise when loud winds call
Thoughts sprung where'er that step did fall.   125

And the prostrate multitude
Looked—and ankle-deep in blood,
Hope that maiden most serene
Was walking with a quiet mien:

3. Venus as the morning star.

And Anarchy, the ghastly birth,   130
Lay dead earth upon the earth
The Horse of Death tameless as wind
Fled, and with his hoofs did grind
To dust, the murderers thronged behind.

A rushing light of clouds and splendour,   135
A sense awakening and yet tender
Was heard and felt—and at its close
These words of joy and fear arose

As if their Own indignant Earth
Which gave the sons of England birth   140
Had felt their blood upon her brow,
And shuddering with a mother's throe

Had turned every drop of blood
By which her face had been bedewed
To an accent unwithstood,—   145
As if her heart had cried aloud:

"Men of England, heirs of Glory,
Heroes of unwritten story,
Nurslings of one mighty Mother,
Hopes of her, and one another;   150

"Rise like Lions after slumber
In unvanquishable number
Shake your chains to Earth like dew
Which in sleep had fallen on you—
Ye are many—they are few.   155

"What is Freedom?—ye can tell
That which slavery is, too well—
For its very name has grown
To an echo of your own.

"'Tis to work and have such pay   160
As just keeps life from day to day
In your limbs, as in a cell
For the tyrants' use to dwell

"So that ye for them are made
Loom, and plough, and sword, and spade,   165
With or without your own will bent
To their defence and nourishment.

"'Tis to see your children weak
With their mothers pine and peak,[4]
When the winter winds are bleak,—
They are dying whilst I speak.   171

4. Wasting away in health and spirits.

"'Tis to hunger for such diet
As the rich man in his riot
Casts to the fat dogs that lie
Surfeiting beneath his eye;   175

"'Tis to let the Ghost of Gold[5]
Take from Toil a thousand fold
More than e'er its substance could
In the tyrannies of old.

"Paper coin—that forgery   180
Of the title deeds, which ye
Hold to something of the worth
Of the inheritance of Earth.

"'Tis to be a slave in soul
And to hold no strong controul   185
Over your own wills, but be
All that others make of ye.

"And at length when ye complain
With a murmur weak and vain
'Tis to see the Tyrant's crew   190
Ride over your wives and you—
Blood is on the grass like dew.

"Then it is to feel revenge
Fiercely thirsting to exchange
Blood for blood—and wrong for wrong—   195
Do not thus when ye are strong.

"Birds find rest, in narrow nest
When weary of their winged quest;
Beasts find fare, in woody lair
When storm and snow are in the air.   200

"Asses, swine, have litter spread
And with fitting food are fed;
All things have a home but one—
Thou, Oh, Englishman, hast none![6]

"This is Slavery—savage men,   205
Or wild beasts within a den
Would endure not as ye do—
But such ills they never knew.

"What art thou Freedom? O! could slaves
Answer from their living graves   210
This demand—tyrants would flee
Like a dream's dim imagery:

5. Paper money, which Shelley con-
sidered a trick to inflate currency, there-
by depressing the relative cost of labor.
6. Shelley alludes ironically to a saying
of Jesus: "The foxes have holes, and
the birds of the air have nests; but the
Son of man hath not where to lay his
head" (Matthew 8:20; Luke 9:58).

"Thou art not, as impostors say,
A shadow soon to pass away,
A superstition, and a name   215
Echoing from the cave of Fame.[7]

"For the labourer thou art bread,
And a comely table spread
From his daily labour come
In a neat and happy[8] home.   220

"Thou art clothes, and fire, and food
For the trampled multitude—
No—in countries that are free
Such starvation cannot be
As in England now we see.   225

"To the rich thou art a check,
When his foot is on the neck
Of his victim, thou dost make
That he treads upon a snake.[9]

"Thou art Justice—ne'er for gold   230
May thy righteous laws be sold
As laws are in England—thou
Shield'st alike the high and low.

"Thou art Wisdom—Freemen never
Dream that God will damn for ever   235
All who think those things untrue
Of which Priests make such ado.

"Thou art Peace—never by thee
Would blood and treasure wasted be
As tyrants wasted them, when all   240
Leagued to quench thy flame in Gaul.[1]

"What if English toil and blood
Was poured forth, even as a flood?
It availed, Oh, Liberty!
To dim, but not extinguish thee.   245

"Thou art Love—the rich[2] have kist
Thy feet, and like him following Christ,
Give their substance to the free
And through the rough world follow thee

"Or turn their wealth to arms, and make   250
War for thy beloved sake
On wealth, and war, and fraud—whence they
Drew the power which is their prey.

---

7. Common talk or rumor.
8. Free from want.
9. This image had been used by the American Revolutionists in their "Don't Tread on Me" flag picturing a coiled rattlesnake. Shelley—and/or the English radicals who used the image earlier— may have adopted it from the Americans.
1. France, during the Revolution.
2. Shelley obviously includes himself in this group dedicated to Liberty through Love.

"Science, Poetry, and Thought
Are thy lamps; they make the lot   255
Of the dwellers in a cot[3]
So serene, they curse it not.

Spirit, Patience, Gentleness,
All that can adorn and bless
Art thou—let deeds, not words, express   260
Thine exceeding loveliness.

"Let a great Assembly be
Of the fearless and the free
On some spot of English ground
Where the plains stretch wide around.   265

"Let the blue sky overhead,
The green earth on which ye tread,
All that must eternal be
Witness the solemnity.

"From the corners uttermost   270
Of the bounds of English coast,
From every hut, village and town
Where those who live and suffer moan
For others' misery or their own,

"From the workhouse and the prison   275
Where pale as corpses newly risen,
Women, children, young and old
Groan for pain, and weep for cold—

"From the haunts of daily life
Where is waged the daily strife   280
With common wants and common cares
Which sows the human heart with tares[4]—

"Lastly from the palaces
Where the murmur of distress
Echoes, like the distant sound   285
Of a wind alive around

"Those prison halls of wealth and fashion,
Where some few feel such compassion
For those who groan, and toil, and wail
As must make their brethren pale—   290

"Ye who suffer woes untold,
Or to feel, or to behold
Your lost country bought and sold
With a price of blood and gold—

3. Cottage.
4. Deleterious weeds; see Matthew 13: 24ff. for the parable of the wheat and the tares.

"Let a vast assembly be,   295
And with great solemnity
Declare with measured words that ye
Are, as God has made ye, free—

"Be your strong and simple words
Keen to wound as sharpened swords,   300
And wide as targes⁵ let them be
With their shade to cover ye.

"Let the tyrants pour around
With a quick and startling sound,
Like the loosening of a sea   305
Troops of armed emblazonry.

"Let the charged artillery drive
Till the dead air seems alive
With the clash of clanging wheels,
And the tramp of horses' heels.   310

"Let the fixed bayonet
Gleam with sharp desire to wet
Its bright point in English blood
Looking keen as one for food.

"Let the horsemen's scimitars   315
Wheel and flash, like sphereless stars
Thirsting to eclipse their burning
In a sea of death and mourning.

"Stand ye calm and resolute,
Like a forest close and mute,   320
With folded arms and looks which are
Weapons of unvanquished war,

"And let Panic, who outspeeds
The career of armed steeds
Pass, a disregarded shade   325
Through your phalanx undismayed.

"Let the Laws of your own land,
Good or ill, between ye stand
Hand to hand, and foot to foot,
Arbiters of the dispute,   330

"The old laws of England—they
Whose reverend heads with age are grey,
Children of a wiser day;
And whose solemn voice must be
Thine own echo—Liberty!   335

5. **Large lightweight shields or bucklers.**

"On those who first should violate
Such sacred heralds in their state
Rest the blood that must ensue,
And it will not rest on you.

"And if then the tyrants dare   340
Let them ride among you there,
Slash, and stab, and maim, and hew,—
What they like, that let them do.

"With folded arms and steady eyes,
And little fear, and less surprise   345
Look upon them as they slay
Till their rage has died away.

"Then they will return with shame
To the place from which they came
And the blood thus shed will speak   350
In hot blushes on their cheek.

"Every woman in the land
Will point at them as they stand—
They will hardly dare to greet
Their acquaintance in the street.   355

"And the bold, true warriors
Who have hugged Danger in wars
Will turn to those who would be free,
Ashamed of such base company.

"And that slaughter to the Nation   360
Shall steam up like inspiration,
Eloquent, oracular;
A volcano heard afar.

"And these words shall then become
Like oppression's thundered doom   365
Ringing through each heart and brain,
Heard again—again—again—

"Rise like lions after slumber
In unvanquishable number—
Shake your chains to earth like dew   370
Which in sleep had fallen on you—
Ye are many—they are few."

THE END.

England in 1819[1]

An old, mad, blind, despised, and dying King;[2]
Princes, the dregs of their dull race, who flow
Through public scorn,—mud from a muddy spring;[3]
Rulers who neither see nor feel nor know,
But leechlike to their fainting country cling   5
Till they drop, blind in blood, without a blow.
A people starved and stabbed in th'untilled field;[4]
An army, whom liberticide[5] and prey
Makes as a two-edged sword to all who wield;
Golden and sanguine[6] laws which tempt and slay;   10
Religion Christless, Godless—a book sealed;
A senate, Time's worst statute, unrepealed[7]—
Are graves from which a glorious Phantom may
Burst, to illumine our tempestuous day.

Sonnet: To the Republic of Benevento[8]

Nor[9] happiness nor majesty nor fame
Nor peace nor strength nor skill in arms or arts
Shepherd[1] those herds whom Tyranny makes tame;
Verse echoes not one beating of their hearts,
History is but the shadow of their shame—   5
Art veils her glass, or from the pageant starts
As to Oblivion their blind millions fleet,[2]
Staining that Heaven with obscene imagery

1. Shelley sent this sonnet to Leigh Hunt from Florence on December 23, 1819 (*Letters*, II, 167). Mary Shelley first published it in her edition of Shelley's *Poetical Works*, 1839.
2. King George III, who had reigned since 1760, had been acknowledged violently insane in 1811; he died on January 29, 1820.
3. The sons of George III had among them sired numerous illegitimate children and only two legitimate ones. In addition, they had engaged in such diverse activities as gluttony, gambling, incest with a sister, and selling army commands to those who bribed a favorite mistress.
4. An allusion to the Peterloo Massacre (see "The Mask of Anarchy").
5. The killing of liberty.
6. Gold and blood are recurring emblems of the twin roots and forms of tyranny. (See *Queen Mab*, IV.195; *Cenci*, I.i.127; "Written on . . . the Death of Napoleon," 35; *Hellas*, 1094; "The Mask of Anarchy," 65, 294; "The Triumph of Life," 287.)
7. Shelley details his objections to Parliament for being unrepresentative of the

British people in his *Philosophical View of Reform* (see *Shelley and his Circle*, VI, 997ff.).
8. Better known as "Political Greatness," the title that Mary Shelley gave it when she published it in *Posthumous Poems* (1824), this sonnet records Shelley's interest in the revival of one of the medieval Italian communes that Sismondi celebrates in his *History of the Italian Republics in the Middle Ages*. (See "Ode to Liberty.") After a popular revolt in July 1820 drove the reactionary Bourbon Ferdinand, King of the Two Sicilies, from absolute rule in Naples, the town of Benevento northeast of Naples established a short-lived "republic," until the entire revolutionary movement was crushed by an Austrian army in the spring of 1821.
9. The first *nor* in a series of this kind means "neither."
1. Though each subject of this verb is technically discrete and singular, grammarians of Shelley's day accepted the practice of using plural verbs in such situations.
2. Speed or hasten.

Of their own likeness.[3]—What are numbers knit
By force or custom? Man who man would be,   10
Must rule the empire of himself; in it
Must be supreme, establishing his throne
On vanquished will,—quelling the anarchy
Of hopes and fears,—being himself alone.—

Sonnet[4]

Lift not the painted veil[5] which those who live
Call Life; though unreal shapes be pictured there
And it but mimic all we would believe
With colours idly spread,—behind, lurk Fear
And Hope, twin Destinies, who ever weave   5
Their shadows o'er the chasm, sightless[6] and drear.
I knew one who had lifted it . . . . he sought,
For his lost heart was tender, things to love
But found them not, alas; nor was there aught
The world contains, the which he could approve.   10
Through the unheeding many he did move,
A splendour among shadows—a bright blot
Upon this gloomy scene—a Spirit that strove
For truth, and like the Preacher,[7] found it not.—

Sonnet[8]

Ye hasten to the grave! What seek ye there,
Ye restless thoughts, and busy purposes
Of the idle brain, which the world's livery wear?
O thou quick Heart, which pantest to possess
All that pale Expectation feigneth fair!   5
Thou vainly curious mind which wouldest guess
Whence thou didst come, and whither thou must go,
And all that never yet was known, would[9] know,

3. *Staining . . . likeness:* See *Queen Mab*, VI.88–107 and "The Triumph of Life," 288–292.
4. The date Shelley composed this sonnet is uncertain, but probably before the end of 1819. The Morgan manuscript on which our text is based is written on the back of a leaf containing the concluding lines of "Stanzas Written in Dejection"; both poems, torn from *The Harvard Shelley Notebook*, were probably among what Shelley called "all my saddest verses raked up into one heap" that he sent to Ollier on November 10, 1820, to publish with *Julian and Maddalo*. Because Ollier failed to issue *Julian and Maddalo*, this sonnet was first published, in a different text, in Shelley's *Posthumous Poems* of 1824.
5. Compare and contrast the veil figure in *Prometheus Unbound*, III.iv.190–192.

6. Lacking anything to see.
7. I.e., the skeptical speaker in Ecclesiastes, who begins by saying "Vanity of vanities . . . all is vanity" (emptiness). In Shelley's rough draft lines 13 and 14 read: "I should be happier had I ne'er known/This mornful man—he was himself alone."
8. Leigh Hunt first published this sonnet in *The Literary Pocket-Book for 1823* (1822). Mary Shelley reprinted it in *Posthumous Poems* (1824). In her collected edition of Shelley's *Poetical Works* (1839) Mary placed this sonnet among Shelley's poems of 1820. Our text follows the holograph press copy manuscript in the Pierpont Morgan Library.
9. The verb is subjunctive (*thou . . . wouldst* being the correct indicative form).

O whither hasten ye, that thus ye press,
With such swift feet life's green and pleasant path,   10
Seeking alike from happiness and woe
A refuge in the cavern of grey death?
O Heart and Mind and Thoughts what thing do you
Hope to inherit in the grave below?

Letter to Maria Gisborne[1]

Leghorn, July 1, 1820

The spider spreads her webs, whether she be
In poet's tower, cellar, or barn, or tree;
The silkworm in the dark green mulberry leaves
His winding sheet and cradle ever weaves;
So I, a thing whom moralists call worm,[2]   5
Sit spinning still round this decaying form,
From the fine threads of rare and subtle thought—
No net of words in garish colours wrought
To catch the idle buzzers of the day—
But a soft cell, where when that fades away,   10
Memory may clothe in wings my living name
And feed it with the asphodels[3] of fame,
Which in those hearts which must remember me
Grow, making love an immortality.

Whoever should behold me now, I wist,[4]   15
Would think I were a mighty mechanist,
Bent with sublime Archimedean[5] art
To breathe a soul into the iron heart

1. Shelley's verse letter to Maria James Reveley Gisborne—obviously meant to be read also by her husband John and by Henry Reveley, her son by an earlier marriage—was written at the Leghorn home of the Gisbornes, which the Shelleys were occupying while the Gisbornes were in London attempting to find a suitable professional position for Henry, an aspiring engineer. The poem was written late in June 1820 and probably mailed on July 1, 1820. The original verse letter that Shelley mailed does not, apparently, survive, but both Shelley's draft and a transcript by Mary Shelley do. The poem was first published in *Posthumous Poems* (1824), with some of the personal references omitted and others disguised. It first reached its present general shape in Harry Buxton Forman's edition of 1876. Our text is based on Forman's, with punctuation generally lightened on the basis of Shelley's draft and with a few verbal emendations from the draft and from Mary's transcription of it, which—though it contains errors—seems to embody a few revisions prob-

ably attributable to Shelley.
   The poem has an air of easy, conversational informality, as Shelley describes the objects in Henry Reveley's study and then imagines the Gisbornes and Henry in London and those they would be seeing there. But running through it is a strong unifying theme in which Shelley contrasts mechanical and scientific knowledge with the magical powers of the imagination.
2. Shelley alludes to personal attacks on his morals in reviews of his and Hunt's poems in the *Quarterly Review* and to personal criticisms of him with which, as Shelley suspected, William Godwin was at the time filling the Gisbornes' ears. (Godwin was bitter because Shelley refused to lend—really give—him more money.)
3. The immortal flowers of the Elysian fields.
4. "I know" or "certainly."
5. Here, mechanical or scientific, from Archimedes (ca. 287–212 B.C.), the Greek mathematician and inventor who lived at Syracuse in Sicily.

Of some machine portentous, or strange gin,[6]
Which by the force of figured spells might win   20
Its way over the sea,[7] and sport therein;
For round the walls are hung dread engines, such
As Vulcan never wrought for Jove to clutch
Ixion or the Titan:[8]—or the quick
Wit of that man of God, St. Dominic,[9]   25
To convince Atheist, Turk or Heretic
Or those in philanthropic council[1] met,
Who thought to pay some interest for the debt
They owed to Jesus Christ for their salvation,
By giving a faint foretaste of damnation   30
To Shakespeare, Sidney, Spenser and the rest
Who made our land an island of the blest,
When lamp-like Spain, who now relumes her fire
On Freedom's hearth, grew dim with Empire:—
With thumbscrews, wheels, with tooth and spike and jag,   35
Which fishers found under the utmost crag
Of Cornwall and the storm-encompassed isles,[2]
Where to the sky the rude sea rarely smiles
Unless in treacherous wrath, as on the morn
When the exulting elements in scorn   40
Satiated with destroyed destruction, lay
Sleeping in beauty on their mangled prey,
As Panthers sleep;—and other strange and dread
Magical forms the brick floor overspread,—
Proteus[3] transformed to metal did not make   45
More figures, or more strange; nor did he take
Such shapes of unintelligible brass,
Or heap himself in such a horrid mass
Of tin and iron not to be understood,
And forms of unimaginable wood,   50
To puzzle Tubal Cain[4] and all his brood:
Great screws, and cones, and wheels, and grooved blocks,
The elements of what will stand the shocks

6. Engine; the word *gin* is frequently used in Shakespeare and other Renaissance writers to refer to traps or snares.
7. Henry Reveley had been building, with Shelley's financial help, a steamboat to travel between Leghorn and Marseilles.
8. Vulcan (Greek Hephaestus) made both an ever-turning wheel on which Ixion was tied in Hades and the bands that chained Prometheus to his mountain of torture.
9. The Spanish founder of the Dominican order (lived 1170–1221) took a leading role in the bloody suppression of the Albigensian heresy in southern France, an activity which eventually brought the Dominicans into a leading role in the Inquisition.
1. Syntactically parallel to *Vulcan* and *St. Dominic*, this allusion is to the ecumenical councils of the Roman Catholic Church—especially the Council of Trent (1545–1563), which initiated the Counter-Reformation.
2. The Hebrides, north of Scotland, where many ships from the Spanish Armada, which sailed against England in 1588, were wrecked. Some of these ships contained instruments of torture (line 35) that the Spanish Inquisition intended to use against English Protestants.
3. A Greek mythological sea-god who could assume numerous different forms.
4. Tubal Cain, the first metalsmith of biblical myth (Genesis 4:22), was the third son of Lamech, who was the great-great-great-grandson of Cain, the son of Adam.

Of wave and wind and time.—Upon the table
More knacks and quips there be than I am able   55
To catalogize in this verse of mine:—
A pretty bowl of wood—not full of wine,
But quicksilver; that dew which the gnomes drink
When at their subterranean toil they swink,[5]
Pledging the demons of the earthquake, who   60
Reply to them in lava—cry halloo!
And call out to the cities o'er their head,—
Roofs, towers, and shrines, the dying and the dead,
Crash through the chinks of earth—and then all quaff
Another rouse,[6] and hold their sides and laugh.   65
This quicksilver no gnome has drunk—within
The walnut bowl it lies, veined and thin,
In colour like the wake of light that stains
The Tuscan deep, when from the moist moon rains
The inmost shower of its white fire—the breeze   70
Is still—blue Heaven smiles over the pale seas.
And in this bowl of quicksilver—for I
Yield to the impulse of an infancy
Outlasting manhood—I have made to float
A rude idealism of a paper boat[7]—   75
A hollow screw with cogs—Henry will know
The thing I mean and laugh at me,—if so
He fears not I should do more mischief.—Next
Lie bills and calculations much perplext,
With steam-boats, frigates and machinery quaint   80
Traced over them in blue and yellow paint.
Then comes a range of mathematical
Instruments, for plans nautical and statical;[8]
A heap of rosin, a queer broken glass
With ink in it;—a china cup that was   85
What it will never be again, I think,
A thing from which sweet lips were wont to drink
The liquor doctors rail at—and which I
Will quaff in spite of them—and when we die
We'll toss up[9] who died first of drinking tea,   90
And cry out, heads or tails? where'er we be.
Near that a dusty paint box, some odd hooks,
A half-burnt match, an ivory block, three books,
Where conic sections, spherics, logarithms,
To great Laplace, from Sanderson and Sims,[1]   95

5. Gnomes are diminutive spirits fabled to inhabit the interior of the earth and to be the guardians of its treasures; *swink:* labor.
6. A full draught of liquor.
7. Shelley was famous among his friends for sailing paper boats on any body of water he happened to encounter.
8. Referring to matters of state.
9. I.e., toss a coin to settle the question.

1. Marquis Pierre Simon de Laplace (1749–1827), French mathematician and astronomer, most famous in Shelley's day for his theory of the universe (1796) that introduced the nebular hypothesis; Nicholas Saunderson or Sanderson (1682–1739), an early teacher of Newtonian science at Cambridge and eventually professor of mathematics who wrote important books on algebra and elementary

Lie heaped in their harmonious disarray
Of figures,—disentangle them who may.
Baron de Tott's Memoirs[2] beside them lie,
And some odd volumes of old chemistry.
Near those a most inexplicable thing,   100
With lead in the middle—I'm conjecturing
How to make Henry understand; but no—
I'll leave, as Spenser says, with many mo,
This secret in the pregnant womb of time,[3]
Too vast a matter for so weak a rhyme.   105

And here like some weird Archimage[4] sit I,
Plotting dark spells, and devilish enginery,
The self-impelling steam-wheels of the mind
Which pump up oaths from clergymen, and grind
The gentle spirit of our meek reviews   110
Into a powdery foam of salt abuse,
Ruffling the ocean of their self-content—
I sit—and smile or sigh as is my bent,
But not for them—Libeccio[5] rushes round
With an inconstant and an idle sound,   115
I heed him more than them—the thunder-smoke
Is gathering on the mountains, like a cloak
Folded athwart their shoulders broad and bare;
The ripe corn under the undulating air
Undulates like an ocean—and the vines   120
Are trembling wide in all their trellised lines—
The murmur of the awakening sea doth fill
The empty pauses of the blast—the hill
Looks hoary through the white electric rain,
And from the glens beyond, in sullen strain,   125
The interrupted thunder howls—above
One chasm of Heaven smiles, like the eye of Love
On the unquiet world—while such things are,
How could one worth your friendship heed the war
Of worms?—the shriek of the world's carrion jays,   130
Their censure, or their wonder, or their praise?

You are not here . . . the quaint witch Memory sees,
In vacant chairs, your absent images,

---

mathematical physics; *Sims* is either
Thomas Simpson (1710–1761), who wrote
treatises on the laws of chance and the
theory of fluctuations, as well as text-
books on algebra, geometry, and trigo-
nometry, or Robert Simson (1687–1768),
who wrote books on geometry and conic
sections.
2. Baron François de Tott's *Mémoires
sur les Turcs et les Tartares* (1785;
English trans., 1786).
3. Shelley coalesces Spenser's phrase

"many mo" (*Faerie Queene*, IV.i.8)
with "many events in the womb of time,"
in Shakespeare's *Othello*, I.iii.377.
4. Archimago is the evil wizard or ma-
gician in *The Faerie Queene*. Shelley
sardonically describes his imagination as
evil because it ruffles the feelings of the
clergymen (like his Eton and Oxford
contemporary, the Rev. Henry Hart Mil-
man) who wrote for the establishment
Quarterly Review.
5. The southwest wind.

And points where once you sat, and now should be
But are not.—I demand if ever we   135
Shall meet as then we met—and she replies,
Veiling in awe her second-sighted eyes;
"I know the past alone—but summon home
My sister Hope,—she speaks of all to come."
But I, an old diviner, who know well   140
Every false verse of that sweet oracle,[6]
Turned to the sad enchantress once again,
And sought a respite from my gentle pain,
In citing every passage o'er and o'er
Of our communion—how on the sea shore   145
We watched the ocean and the sky together,
Under the roof of blue Italian weather;
How I ran home through last year's thunder-storm,
And felt the transverse lightning linger warm
Upon my cheek—and how we often made   150
Feasts for each other, where good will outweighed
The frugal luxury of our country cheer,
As well it might, were it less firm and clear
Than ours must ever be—and how we spun
A shroud of talk to hide us from the Sun   155
Of this familiar life, which seems to be
But is not—or is but quaint mockery
Of all we would believe, and sadly blame
The jarring and inexplicable frame
Of this wrong world:—and then anatomize[7]   160
The purposes and thoughts of men whose eyes
Were closed in distant years—or widely guess
The issue of the earth's great business,
When we shall be as we no longer are—
Like babbling gossips safe, who hear the war   165
Of winds, and sigh, but tremble not—or how
You listened to some interrupted flow
Of visionary rhyme,[8] in joy and pain
Struck from the inmost fountains of my brain,
With little skill perhaps—or how we sought   170
Those deepest wells of passion or of thought
Wrought by wise poets[9] in the waste of years,
Staining their sacred waters with our tears;
Quenching a thirst ever to be renewed!
Or how I, wisest lady! then indued   175
The language of a land which now is free,[1]
And winged with thoughts of truth and majesty

6. That is, Hope; the *sad enchantress* (142) is Memory.
7. Analyze minutely.
8. Shelley had read *Prometheus Unbound* to the Gisbornes the previous autumn.
9. Maria Gisborne had taught Shelley to read Spanish; together they had read several plays by Pedro Calderón de la Barca.
1. In January 1820 there had been an almost bloodless revolution in Spain that had resulted in the abolition of the Inquisition and the establishment of a constitutional monarchy.

Flits round the tyrant's sceptre like a cloud,
And bursts the peopled prisons—cries aloud,
"My name is Legion!"[2]—that majestic tongue   180
Which Calderon over the desart flung
Of ages and of nations, and which found
An echo in our hearts, and with the sound
Startled Oblivion—thou wert then to me
As is a nurse—when inarticulately   185
A child would talk as its grown parents do.
If living winds the rapid clouds pursue,
If hawks chase doves through the ætherial way,
Huntsmen the innocent deer, and beasts their prey,
Why should not we rouse with the spirit's blast   190
Out of the forest of the pathless past
These recollected pleasures?[3]

                                        You are now
In London, that great sea whose ebb and flow
At once is deaf and loud, and on the shore
Vomits its wrecks, and still howls on for more.   195
Yet in its depth what treasures! You will see
That which was Godwin,—greater none than he
Though fallen—and fallen on evil times[4]—to stand
Among the spirits of our age and land
Before the dread Tribunal of *to come*   200
The foremost . . . while Rebuke cowers pale and dumb.
You will see Coleridge—he who sits obscure
In the exceeding lustre and the pure
Intense irradiation of a mind
Which, with its own internal lightning blind,   205
Flags wearily through darkness and despair—
A cloud-encircled meteor of the air,
A hooded eagle among blinking owls.—
You will see Hunt[5]—one of those happy souls
Who are the salt of the Earth, and without whom   210
This world would smell like what it is, a tomb—
Who is, what others seem—his room no doubt
Is still adorned with many a cast from Shout,[6]
With graceful flowers tastefully placed about,

---

2. I.e., "innumerable" (Mark 5:9; Matthew 26:53).
3. Lines 132–192 treat the past and Memory (traditionally the mother of the Muses). The next section (192–253) is a flight of the imagination across space, rather than time, to London in the present.
4. Shelley describes his father-in-law—once his mentor but now his bitter accuser—in a phrase that Milton used of himself (*Paradise Lost*, VII.25) and with a generous appreciation of Godwin's place in intellectual history. Maria Gisborne and her first husband Willey Reveley had in the 1790s been members of London intellectual circles that included Godwin and Samuel Taylor Coleridge (202–208), both, in 1820, at the low ebb of their literary reputations.
5. James Henry Leigh Hunt (1784–1859), Shelley's closest friend, was a poet and journalist who at this period was best known as editor of the *Examiner*, a weekly political and literary newspaper.
6. Robert Shout was a London maker of plaster copies of great statues, like the Venus de Medici and the Apollo Belvedere.

And coronals[7] of bay from ribbons hung,   215
And brighter wreaths in neat disorder flung,
The gifts of the most learn'd among some dozens
Of female friends, sisters-in-law and cousins.
And there is he with his eternal puns,
Which beat the dullest brain for smiles, like duns[8]   220
Thundering for money at a poet's door.
Alas, it is no use to say "I'm poor!"
Or oft in graver mood, when he will look
Things wiser than were ever read in book,
Except in Shakespeare's wisest tenderness.—   225
You will see Hogg[9]—and I cannot express
His virtues, though I know that they are great,
Because he locks, then barricades the gate
Within which they inhabit—of his wit
And wisdom, you'll cry out when you are bit.   230
He is a pearl within an oyster shell,
One of the richest of the deep. And there
Is English Peacock,[1] with his mountain fair,
Turned into a Flamingo, that shy bird
That gleams i' the Indian air—have you not heard   235
When a man marries, dies, or turns Hindoo,
His best friends hear no more of him?—but you
Will see him, and will like him too, I hope,
With the milk-white Snowdonian antelope
Matched with this cameleopard[2]—his fine wit   240
Makes such a wound, the knife is lost in it;
A strain too learned for a shallow age,
Too wise for selfish bigots—let his page
Which charms the chosen spirits of the time
Fold itself up for the serener clime   245
Of years to come, and find its recompense
In that just expectation.—Wit and sense,
Virtue and human knowledge, all that might
Make this dull world a business of delight,
Are all combined in Horace Smith.[3]—And these,   250
With some exceptions, which I need not tease
Your patience by descanting on,—are all
You and I know in London.[4]

              I recall
My thoughts, and bid you look upon the night.
As water does a sponge, so the moonlight   255

---

7. Garlands worn on the head.
8. Collection agents.
9. Thomas Jefferson Hogg (1792–1862), Shelley's closest friend at Oxford, now grown somewhat distant from him.
1. Thomas Love Peacock (1785–1866), Shelley's friend and a comic novelist, had recently taken a post at the East India Company and married Jane Gryffydh from the area of northwest

Wales called Snowdonia (239).
2. A giraffe.
3. Famous as one of the authors (with his brother James) of *Rejected Addresses* (1812), which included parodies of many famous writers of the day, Horace Smith (1779–1849) was a poet, stockbroker, wit, and later a novelist.
4. That is, all their mutual friends who lived in London.

Fills the void, hollow, universal air—
What see you?—unpavilioned heaven is fair
Whether the moon, into her chamber gone,
Leaves midnight to the golden stars, or wan
Climbs with diminished beams the azure steep,   260
Or whether clouds sail o'er the inverse deep
Piloted by the many-wandering blast,
And the rare stars rush through them dim and fast—
All this is beautiful in every land—
But what see you beside?—a shabby stand   265
Of Hackney coaches,[5] a brick house or wall
Fencing some lonely court, white with the scrawl
Of our unhappy politics; or worse—
A wretched woman reeling by, whose curse
Mixed with the watchman's, partner of her trade,[6]   270
You must accept in place of serenade—
Or yellow-haired Pollonia murmuring
To Henry, some unutterable thing.[7]—
I see a chaos of green leaves and fruit
Built round dark caverns, even to the root   275
Of the living stems that feed them—in whose bowers
There sleep in their dark dew the folded flowers;
Beyond, the surface of the unsickled corn
Trembles not in the slumbering air, and borne
In circles quaint, and ever changing dance,   280
Like winged stars the fire-flies flash and glance
Pale in the open moonshine, but each one
Under the dark trees seems a little sun,
A meteor tamed, a fixed star gone astray
From the silver regions of the Milky Way;—   285
Afar the contadino's[8] song is heard,
Rude, but made sweet by distance—and a bird
Which cannot be the Nightingale, and yet
I know none else that sings so sweet as it
At this late hour—and then all is still—   290
Now Italy or London—which you will!

    Next winter you must pass with me; I'll have
My house by that time turned into a grave
Of dead despondence and low-thoughted care
And all the dreams which our tormentors are.   295
Oh, that Hunt, Hogg, Peacock and Smith were there,
With everything belonging to them fair!
We will have books, Spanish, Italian, Greek;
And ask one week to make another week

---

5. Horse-drawn carriages for hire.
6. I.e., the watchman pimps for the prostitute.
7. Apollonia Ricci, daughter of the Gis-bornes' landlord in Leghorn, had a crush on Henry Reveley, as Mary Shelley repeatedly reminded him in teasing letters.
8. Italian peasant or farmhand.

As like his father as I'm unlike mine,[9]   300
Which is not his fault, as you may divine.
Though we eat little flesh and drink no wine,
Yet let's be merry! we'll have tea and toast;
Custards for supper, and an endless host
Of syllabubs[1] and jellies and mince-pies,   305
And other such lady-like luxuries—
Feasting on which we will philosophize!
And we'll have fires out of the Grand Duke's wood,[2]
To thaw the six weeks' winter in our blood.
And then we'll talk—what shall we talk about?   310
Oh, there are themes enough for many a bout
Of thought-entangled descant;—as to nerves,
With cones and parallelograms and curves
I've sworn to strangle them if once they dare
To bother me—when you are with me there,   315
And they shall never more sip laudanum,
From Helicon or Himeros;[3]—well, come,
And in despite of God and of the devil
We'll make our friendly philosophic revel
Outlast the leafless time—till buds and flowers   320
Warn the obscure inevitable hours
Sweet meeting by sad parting to renew—
"To-morrow to fresh woods and pastures new."[4]

Peter Bell the Third

Wordsworth's *Peter Bell*, which appeared at the end of April 1819, tells the story of an itinerant potter named Peter Bell, who leads a completely immoral life until a series of natural events, centering on an ass that is dumbly faithful to his dead master, so work upon the ignorant man's superstitious imagination that he "Forsook his crimes, renounced his folly,/ And, after ten months' melancholy,/ Became a good and honest man." In a scathing review in the *Examiner* for May 2, 1819, Leigh Hunt charged that the moral of the poem (a "didactic little horror") was "founded on the bewitching principles of fear, bigotry, and diseased impulse," and after quoting the stanza Shelley takes as his epigraph, he asks whether "Mr. Wordsworth is earnest . . . in thinking that his fellow-creatures are to be damned?" (*The Romantics Reviewed*, ed. D. H. Reiman [New York, 1972], Part A, II, 538–539.)

In June 1819, Shelley read Hunt's review, together with a review by Keats that had appeared in the April 25 issue of the *Examiner* of John Hamilton Reynolds' parody entitled *Peter Bell; A Lyrical Ballad* (which

---

9. Shelley alludes to his estrangement from his own father, Sir Timothy Shelley.
1. A sweetened drink or dish made from milk (often freshly drawn from the cow) and cider or wine.
2. Ferdinand III was the Grand Duke of Tuscany.
3. Laudanum was a liquid form of opium, used figuratively here. Shelley

says (312–317) that he will *strangle* his *nerves* with mathematical studies rather than use the opiates of writing poetry (the summit of *Helicon* contains the sanctuary of the Muses and the spring of poetic inspiration) or falling in love. *Himeros:* "A synonym of Love" (Shelley's note).
4. The final line of Milton's *Lycidas*.

Reynolds had contrived without seeing Wordsworth's poem and published just before "the real Simon Pure"). Mary Shelley wrote in 1839, "A critique on Wordsworth's Peter Bell reached us at Leghorn, which amused Shelley exceedingly and suggested this poem." She does not say—but scholars have recently argued—that Shelley read Wordsworth's poem itself before writing his reply (see Cameron, *Shelley: The Golden Years*, pp. 626–627). In any case, Shelley takes up Peter's story at a point deriving from the inferences of Hunt's review rather than the end of *Peter Bell* itself.

Shelley creates a Methodist Peter Bell, predestined to damnation, whose career resembles, in a wild way, Wordsworth's own career. By Sunday, October 24, 1819, Shelley had completed his poem and read it to Mary, who transcribed it for the press by October 28. Shelley mailed it to Leigh Hunt on November 2 with instructions to ask Charles Ollier "to print & publish immediately . . . NOT however with my name . . . as I have only expended a few days on this party squib . . . & I am about to publish more serious things this winter" (*Letters*, II, 135). On December 15, Shelley asked Ollier what he had done with the poem, adding, "I think *Peter* not bad in his way; but perhaps no one will believe in anything in the shape of a joke from me" (*Letters*, II, 164).

Though Shelley later tried to stimulate Ollier to publish it, the poem remained unknown to the public until Mary added it to the one-volume second edition of Shelley's *Poetical Works* late in 1839. There Mary, who had earlier omitted the poem because she found its humor at the expense of Wordsworth and Coleridge somewhat embarrassing amid the proper solemnity of Victorian high seriousness, added to her apologetic remarks: "No poem contains more of Shelley's peculiar views, with regard to the errors into which many of the wisest have fallen, and of the pernicious effects of certain opinions on society. Much of it is beautifully written— and though . . . it must be looked on as a plaything, it has so much merit and poetry—so much of *himself* in it, that it cannot fail to interest greatly. . . ."

Our text is based directly on the Bodleian manuscript (MS. Shelley adds. c.5, ff. 50–68), transcribed for the press by Mary Shelley in October 1819, with headings, some notes, and corrections in Shelley's hand. Part of the Preface (suppressed by Mary in 1839 because it attacked the powerful house of John Murray) is here printed for the first time, and numerous readings have been corrected to conform to Shelley's manifest intention.

Peter Bell the Third

By Miching Mallecho, Esq.

Is it a party in a parlour—
Crammed just as they on earth
   were crammed,
Some sipping punch—some sip-
   ping tea;
But, as you by their faces see,
All silent and all——damned!
Peter Bell, by W. WORDSWORTH.[1]

Ophelia: What means this, my lord?
Hamlet: Marry, this is miching mallecho; it means mischief.
                               SHAKESPEARE.[2]

Dedication

To Thomas Brown, Esq., The Younger, H.F.[3]

Dear Tom—Allow me to request you to introduce Mr. Peter Bell to the respectable family of the Fudges; although he may fall short of those very considerable personages in the more active properties which characterize the Rat and the Apostate,[4] I suspect that even you their historian will be forced to confess that he surpasses them in the more peculiarly legitimate qualification of intolerable dulness.

You know Mr. Examiner Hunt. That murderous and smiling villain at the mere sound of whose voice our susceptible friend the *Quarterly* fell into a paroxysm of eleutherophobia and foamed so much acrid gall that it burned the carpet in Mr. Murray's upper room,[5] and eating a hole in the floor fell like rain upon our poor friend's head,[6] who was scampering from room to room like a bear with a swarm of bees on his nose:—it caused an incurable ulcer and our poor friend has worn a wig ever since. Well, this monkey[7] suckled with tyger's milk, this odious thief, liar, scoundrel, coxcomb and monster presented me to two of the Mr. Bells. Seeing me in his presence they of course uttered very few words and those with much caution. I scarcely need observe that they only kept company

---

1. The stanza, later omitted by Wordsworth on the remonstrance of friends, appeared in the first edition on page 39, the fourth stanza from the end of Part I. Shelley's text is punctuated as he found it in the *Examiner*.
2. Shakespeare, *Hamlet*, III.ii.148–149. Ophelia's question follows the opening scene of the dumb show that reenacts Claudius' murder of Hamlet's father. Scholars have glossed "miching malle-cho" as "lying in wait for the evildoer." Shelley, like Hamlet, presumably hoped to "catch the conscience" of his political foes by drawing self-exposing reactions to his poem.
3. I.e., Thomas Moore, who had written popular doggerel satires including *The*

Twopenny Post-Bag (1813) and *The Fudge Family in Paris* (1818) under the name "Thomas Brown, the Younger." "H.F." ("Historian of Fudges") plays off Wordsworth's Dedication to "Robert Southey, Esq., P.L." (Poet Laureate).
4. Pressumably the "Rat" is Reynold's "antenatal Peter" and the "Apostate" is Wordsworth's legitimate one.
5. William Gifford, who edited the Tory *Quarterly Review* in an upper room at John Murray's Albemarle Street publishing house, was Hunt's greatest enemy; *eleutherophobia:* fear of freedom (*eleuthero*, Greek for "free").
6. I.e., John Murray's.
7. I.e., Leigh Hunt.

with him—at least I can certainly answer for one of them—in order to observe whether they could not borrow colours from any particulars of his private life for the denunciation they mean to make of him, as the member of an "infamous and black conspiracy for diminishing the authority of that venerable canon, which forbids any man to mar his grandmother"; the effect of which in this on our moral and religious nation is likely to answer the purpose of the controversy. My intimacy with the younger Mr. Bell naturally sprung from this introduction to his brothers. And in presenting him to you, I have the satisfaction of being able to assure you that he is considerably the dullest of the three.

There is this particular advantage in an acquaintance with any one of the Peter Bells; that if you know one Peter Bell, you know three Peter Bells; they are not one but three, not three but one. An awful mystery after having caused torrents of blood, and having been hymned by groans enough to deafen the music of the spheres is at length illustrated to the satisfaction of all parties in the theological world, by the nature of Mr. Peter Bell.

Peter is a polyhedric Peter, or a Peter with many sides. He changes colours like a chameleon, and his coat like a snake. He is a Proteus[8] of a Peter. He was at first sublime, pathetic, impressive, profound; then dull; then prosy and dull; and now dull—o so dull! it is an ultra-legitimate dulness.

You will perceive that it is not necessary to consider Hell and the Devil as supernatural machinery. The whole scene of my epic is in "this world which is"—so Peter informed us before his conversion to *White Obi*[9]—

> the world of all of us, *and where*
> *We find our happiness, or not at all.*

Let me observe that I have spent six or seven days[1] in composing this sublime piece;—the orb of my moonlike genius has made the fourth part of its revolution round the dull earth which you inhabit, driving you mad whilst it has retained its calmness and its splendour, and I have been fitting this its last phase "to occupy a permanent station in the literature of my country."

---

8. Greek demigod of the sea who could change shape at will.
9. Christianity. Among blacks in the West Indies, "Obi" was the name of a magical power that sorcerers used to afflict their enemies; the "White Obi" would be white magic, or religion. The indented quotation is from Wordsworth's "The French Revolution as It Appeared to Enthusiasts at Its Commencement," which first appeared in Coleridge's *The*

Friend (1809). It was reprinted with the collected poems of 1815, and was finally incorporated into *The Prelude* (XI.142–144).
1. Wordsworth had taken pains with his *Peter Bell* since 1798 "to make the production less unworthy of a favourable reception; or, rather, to fit it for filling *permanently* a station however humble, in the Literature of my Country."

Your works, indeed, dear Tom, Sell better; but mine are far superior. The public is no judge; posterity sets all to rights.

Allow me to observe that so much has been written of Peter Bell, that the present history can be considered only, like the *Iliad*, as a continuation of that series of cyclic poems which have already been candidates for bestowing immortality upon, at the same time that they receive it from, his character and adventures. In this point of view, I have violated no rule of syntax in beginning my composition with a conjunction; the full stop which closes the poem continued by me being, like the full stops at the end of the *Iliad* and *Odyssey*, a full stop of a very qualified import.

Hoping that the immortality which you have given to the Fudges, you will receive from them; and in the firm expectation that when London shall be an habitation of bitterns,[2] when St. Paul's and Westminster Abbey shall stand, shapeless and nameless ruins in the midst of an unpeopled marsh; when the piers of Waterloo bridge shall become the nuclei of islets of reeds and osiers[3] and cast the jagged shadows of their broken arches on the solitary stream,— some transatlantic commentator will be weighing in the scales of some new and now unimagined system of criticism, the respective merits of the Bells and the Fudges, and of their historians; I remain, Dear Tom, Yours sincerely,

Miching Mallecho.

December 1, 1819.

P.S. Pray excuse the date of place; so soon as the profits of this publication come in, I mean to hire lodgings in a more respectable street.[4]

Prologue

Peter Bells, one, two and three,
O'er the wide world wandering be.—
First, the antenatal Peter,
Wrapt in weeds of the same metre,
The so long predestined raiment   5
Clothed in which to walk his way meant
The second Peter; whose ambition
Is to link the proposition
As the mean of two extremes—
(This was learnt from Aldric's themes)[5]   10

2. Marsh-dwelling birds related to the heron.
3. Willow trees.
4. I.e., Miching Mallecho does not include his address, as did Tom Brown in his *Fudge Family in Paris* (the fashionable "245, Piccadilly").
5. *Artis Logicae Compendium*, written in 1691 by Henry Aldrich (1647–1710), remained the standard school logic text until the late nineteenth century.

Shielding from the guilt of schism
The orthodoxal syllogism:
The First Peter—he who was
Like the shadow in the glass
Of the second, yet unripe;   15
His substantial antitype.—
Then came Peter Bell the Second,
Who henceforward must be reckoned
The body of a double soul—
And that portion of the whole   20
Without which the rest would seem
Ends of a disjointed dream.—
And the third is he who has
O'er the grave been forced to pass
To the other side, which is,—   25
Go and try else,—just like this.

Peter Bell the First was Peter
Smugger, milder, softer, neater,
Like the soul before it is
Born from *that* world into *this*.[6]   30
The next Peter Bell was he
Predevote[7] like you and me
To good or evil as may come;
His was the severer doom,—
For he was an evil Cotter[8]   35
And a polygamic[9] Potter.[1]
And the last is Peter Bell,
Damned since our first Parents fell,
Damned eternally to Hell—
Surely he deserves it well!   40

Part First

DEATH

And Peter Bell, when he had been
    With fresh-imported Hell-fire warmed,
Grew serious—from his dress and mien
'Twas very plainly to be seen
    Peter was quite reformed.   5

6. The idea underlying this "antenatal
Peter" is the Platonic (or Pythagorean)
transmigration of souls, which are reborn
in various bodies.
7. Predestined, foredoomed.
8. A Scottish peasant renting a cottage
and small plot of ground; a *potter* (36)
makes and sells ceramic pots.

9. Having many wives.
1. "The oldest scholiasts read—
         A *dodecagamic* Potter.
This is at once descriptive and more
megalophonous.—but the alliteration of
the text had captivated the vulgar ears of
the herd of later commentators" (Shel-
ley's note).

His eyes turned up, his mouth turned down;
　His accent caught a nasal twang;
He oiled his hair;[2] there might be heard
The grace of God in every word
　Which Peter said or sang.　　　　　　　　10

But Peter now grew old, and had
　An ill no doctor could unravel;
His torments almost drove him mad;—
Some said it was a fever bad—
　Some swore it was the gravel.[3]　　　　15

His holy friends then came about
　And with long preaching and persuasion,
Convinced the patient, that without
The smallest shadow of a doubt
　He was predestined to damnation.　　　20

They said—"Thy name is Peter Bell;
　Thy skin is of a brimstone hue;
Alive or dead—ay, sick or well—
The one God made to rhyme with hell;
　The other, I think, rhymes with you."[4]　25

Then Peter set up such a yell!—
　The nurse, who with some water gruel
Was climbing up the stairs, as well
As her old legs could climb them—fell,
　And broke them both—the fall was cruel.　30

The Parson from the casement leapt
　Into the lake of Windermere[5]—
And many an eel—though no adept
In God's right reason for it—kept
　Gnawing his kidneys half a year.　　　35

And all the rest rushed through the door,
　And tumbled over one another,
And broke their skulls.—Upon the floor
Meanwhile sate Peter Bell, and swore,
　And cursed his father and his mother;　40

2. "To those who have not duly appreciated the distinction between *Whale* and *Russia* oil this attribute might rather seem to belong to the Dandy than the Evangelic. The effect, when to the windward, is indeed so similar, that it requires a subtle naturalist to discriminate the animals. They belong, however, to distinct genera" (Shelley's note). "Russia oil" was oil of the birch tree imported from Russia and sold to the upper classes; whale oil, the common man's cheap substitute.
3. A disease involving aggregations of urinary crystals; popularly used to indicate pain or difficulty in passing urine.
4. *one . . . other:* I.e., "Peter *Bell*" and "brimstone hue."
5. A large lake in Westmorland that appears frequently in Wordsworth's poetry.

And raved of God, and sin, and death,
  Blaspheming like an infidel;
And said, that with his clenched teeth
He'd seize the earth from underneath,
  And drag it with him down to Hell.   45

As he was speaking came a spasm,
  And wrenched his gnashing teeth asunder,
Like one who sees a strange phantasm
He lay,—there was a silent chasm
  Between his upper jaw and under.   50

And yellow death lay on his face;
  And a fixed smile that was not human
Told, as I understand the case,
That he was gone to the wrong place:—
  I heard all this from the old woman.   55

Then there came down from Langdale Pike[6]
  A cloud with lightning, wind and hail;
It swept over the mountains like
An Ocean,—and I heard it strike
  The woods and crags of Grasmere vale.[7]   60

And I saw the black storm come
  Nearer, minute after minute,
Its thunder made the cataracts[8] dumb,
With hiss, and clash, and hollow hum
  It neared as if the Devil was in it.   65

The Devil *was* in it:—he had bought
  Peter for half a crown; and when
The storm which bore him vanished, nought
That in the house that storm had caught
  Was ever seen again.   70

The gaping neighbours came next day—
  They found all vanished from the shore:
The Bible, whence he used to pray,
Half scorched under a hen-cooplay;
  Smashed glass—and nothing more!   75

Part Second

THE DEVIL

The Devil, I safely can aver,
  Has neither hoof, nor tail, nor sting;
Nor is he, as some sages swear,
A spirit, neither here nor there,
  In nothing—yet in every thing.   80

6. The Langdale Pikes (or Peaks) are a group of mountains east of Grasmere.
7. Wordsworth lived in the village of Grasmere, near the lake of the same name, from Dec. 1799 until May 1813.
8. Waterfalls of considerable size.

He is—what we are; for sometimes
   The Devil is a gentleman;
At others a bard bartering rhymes
For sack;[9] a statesman spinning crimes,
   A swindler, living as he can;   85

A thief, who cometh in the night,
   With whole boots and net pantaloons,
Like some one whom it were not right
To mention;—or the luckless wight
   From whom he steals nine silver spoons.   90

But in this case he did appear
   Like a slop-merchant[1] from Wapping
And with smug face, and eye severe
On every side did perk and peer
   Till he saw Peter dead or napping.   95

He had on an upper Benjamin
   (For he was of the driving schism)[2]
In the which he wrapt his skin
From the storm he travelled in,
   For fear of rheumatism.   100

He called the ghost out of the corse;[3]—
   It was exceedingly like Peter,—
Only its voice was hollow and hoarse—
It had a queerish look of course—
   Its dress too was a little neater.   105

The Devil knew not, his name and lot;
   Peter knew not that he was Bell:
Each had an upper stream of thought,
Which made all seem as it was not;
   Fitting itself to all things well.   110

Peter thought he had parents dear,
   Brothers, sisters, cousins, cronies,
In the fens o' Lincolnshire;
He perhaps had found them there
   Had he gone and boldly shewn his   115

Solemn phiz[4] in his own village;
   Where he thought, oft when a boy
He'd clombe[5] the orchard walls to pillage
The produce of his neighbour's tillage,
   With marvellous pride and joy.   120

9. The Poet Laureate (at this time Robert Southey) was paid in sack, a class of white and amber wines, including sherries, imported from Spain and the Canary Islands.
1. A dealer in cheap sailor's clothes; *Wapping:* A poor seamen's quarter (and traditional place of executions) in the East End of London, along the Thames.
2. I.e., one of his great pleasures was driving his own carriage, like Sir Telegraph Paxarett in Peacock's *Melincourt; upper Benjamin:* short overcoat.
3. Corpse.
4. Face (short for "physiognomy").
5. Climbed.

And the Devil thought he had,
   'Mid the misery and confusion
Of an unjust war, just made
A fortune by the gainful trade
Of giving soldiers rations bad—   125
   The world is full of strange delusion.

That he had a mansion planned
   In a square like Grosvenor square,[6]
That he was aping fashion, and
That he now came to Westmoreland   130
   To see what was romantic there.

And all this, though quite ideal,—
   Ready at a breath to vanish,—
Was a state not more unreal
Than the peace he could not feel,   135
   Or the care he could not banish.

After a little conversation
   The Devil told Peter, if he chose
He'd bring him to the world of fashion
By giving him a situation   140
   In his own service—and new clothes.

And Peter bowed, quite pleased and proud,
   And after waiting some few days
For a new livery—dirty yellow
Turned up with black—the wretched fellow   145
   Was bowled to Hell in the Devil's chaise.

Part Third

HELL

Hell is a city much like London—
   A populous and a smoky city;
There are all sorts of people undone,
And there is little or no fun done;   150
   Small justice shown, and still less pity.

There is a Castles, and a Canning,
   A Cobbett, and a Castlereagh;[7]

6. Then a relatively new section of London, inhabited by the *nouveaux riches*, including John Westbrook, the wealthy coffeehouse owner who was Shelley's first father-in-law, and William Gifford, editor of the *Quarterly Review*, who had begun as a dependent of Lord Grosvenor.

7. John Castle(s), a government spy and *agent provocateur*, led workmen into conspiracies and then betrayed them; George Canning, brilliant Tory wit of the *Anti-Jacobin*, government official, and later prime minister; William Cobbett, popular journalist and demagogue, whose *Political Register* urged radical reform; John Stewart, Viscount Castlereagh, an Anglo-Irish politician who at this time, as foreign secretary, was the strong man in the reactionary government. Shelley groups them to show they are equally unsavory, no matter what their politics.

All sorts of caitiff corpses planning
All sorts of cozening for trepanning[8]   155
   Corpses less corrupt than they.

There is a * * *,[9] who has lost
   His wits, or sold them, none knows which;
He walks about a double ghost,
And though as thin as Fraud almost—   160
   Ever grows more grim and rich.

There is a Chancery Court,[1] a King,
   A manufacturing mob; a set
Of thieves who by themselves are sent
Similar thieves to represent;[2]   165
   An Army;—and a public debt.

Which last is a scheme of Paper money,
   And means—being interpreted—
"Bees, keep your wax—give us the honey
And we will plant while skies are sunny   170
   Flowers, which in winter serve instead."[3]

There is a great talk of Revolution—
   And a great chance of despotism—
German soldiers[4]—camps—confusion—
Tumults—lotteries—rage—delusion—   175
   Gin—suicide and methodism;

Taxes too, on wine and bread,
   And meat, and beer, and tea, and cheese,[5]
From which those patriots pure are fed
Who gorge before they reel to bed   180
   The tenfold essence of all these.

There are mincing women, mewing,
   (Like cats, who *amant misere*,)[6]
Of their own virtue, and pursuing
Their gentler sisters to that ruin,   185
   Without which—what were chastity?[7]

---

8. *caitiff:* vile, base, mean; *cozening:* deception or defrauding by deceit; *trepanning:* cheating, entrapping.
9. Possibly Eldon, the Lord Chancellor, who appears as "Fraud" in "The Mask of Anarchy," line 14.
1. The court presided over by the Lord Chancellor that decided matters of equity between individuals. Shelley's children by Harriet were taken from him in a Chancery Court trial.
2. The unreformed Parliament.
3. Shelley attacked the evils arising from the standing army, the national debt, and paper money in his *Philosophical View of Reform* (see *Shelley and his Circle*, VI, 945ff.).
4. The liberals repeatedly feared that the Georges, Electors of Hanover as well

as kings of England, would bring in German soldiers to suppress dissent among the English people.
5. New regressive commodity taxes passed in 1817 to pay the interest on the national debt put an added burden on the poor.
6. Love misery. "One of the attributes in Linnaeus's description of the Cat. To a similar cause the caterwauling of more than one species of this genus is to be referred;—except indeed that the poor quadruped is compelled to quarrel with its own pleasures, whilst the biped is supposed only to quarrel with those of others" (Shelley's note).
7. "What would this husk and excuse for a Virtue be without its kernal prostitution, or the kernal prostitution without

Lawyers—judges—old hobnobbers[8]
    Are there—Bailiffs—Chancellors—
Bishops—great and little robbers—
Rhymesters—pamphleteers—stock-jobbers[9]—   190
    Men of glory in the wars,—

Things whose trade is, over ladies
    To lean, and flirt, and stare, and simper,
Till all that is divine in woman
Grows cruel, courteous,[1] smooth, inhuman,   195
    Crucified 'twixt a smile and whimper.

Thrusting, toiling, wailing, moiling,[2]
    Frowning, preaching—such a riot!
Each with never ceasing labour
Whilst he thinks he cheats his neighbour   200
    Cheating his own heart of quiet.

And all these meet at levees;[3]—
    Dinners convivial and political;—
Suppers of epic poets;—teas,
Where small talk dies in agonies;—   205
    Breakfasts professional and critical;

Lunches and snacks so aldermanic
    That one would furnish forth ten dinners,
Where reigns a Cretan-tongued[4] panic
Lest news Russ, Dutch, or Alemannic[5]   210
    Should make some losers, and some winners

At conversazioni[6]—balls—
    Conventicles[7] and drawing-rooms.
Courts of law—committees—calls
Of a morning—clubs—book stalls—   215
    Churches—masquerades and tombs.

And this is Hell—and in this smother
    All are damnable and damned;
Each one damning, damns the other;
They are damned by one another,   220
    By none other are they damned.

---

this husk of a Virtue? I wonder the Women of the Town do not form an association, like the Society for the Suppression of Vice, for the support of what may be considered the 'King, church, and Constitution' of their order. But this subject is almost too horrible for a joke" (Shelley's note).

8. Those who drink together or to each other, or who are on familiar terms.

9. Stockbrokers and speculators.

1. I.e., with manners that befit the court of a prince.

2. Drudging, working in wet and mire.

3. In Great Britain, assemblies held in the early afternoon by the sovereign or his representative, at which men only are received.

4. Lying. The Cretans were proverbial as liars at least as early as the time of the New Testament (see Titus 1:12).

5. German.

6. Social assemblies, often with discussions of literature, art, or science.

7. Nonconformist or dissenting meeting-houses, or the meetings themselves.

'Tis a lie to say, "God damns!"[8]
   Where was Heaven's Attorney General
When they first gave out such flams?[9]
Let there be an end of shams,   225
   They are mines of poisonous mineral.

Statesmen damn themselves to be
   Cursed; and lawyers damn their souls
To the auction of a fee;
Churchmen damn themselves to see   230
   God's sweet love in burning coals.

The rich are damned beyond all cure
   To taunt, and starve, and trample on
The weak and wretched: and the poor
Damn their broken hearts to endure   235
   Stripe on stripe,[1] with groan on groan.

Sometimes the poor are damned indeed
   To take,—not means for being blessed,—
But Cobbett's snuff, revenge;[2] that weed
From which the worms that it doth feed   240
   Squeeze less than they before possessed.

And some few, like we know who,
   Damned—but God alone knows why—
To believe their minds are given
To make this ugly Hell a Heaven;   245
   In which faith they[3] live and die.

Thus, as in a Town, plague-stricken,
   Each man be he sound or no
Must indifferently sicken;
As when day begins to thicken   250
   None knows a pigeon from a crow,—

So good and bad, sane and mad,
   The oppressor and the oppressed;
Those who weep to see what others
Smile to inflict upon their brothers;   255
   Lovers, haters, worst and best;

All are damned—they breathe an air,
   Thick, infected, joy-dispelling:
Each pursues what seems most fair,
Mining like moles, through mind, and there   260
Scoop palace-caverns vast, where Care
   In throned state is ever dwelling.

8. "This libel on our national oath, and this accusation of all our countrymen of being in the daily practise of solemnly asseverating the most enormous falsehood I fear deserves the notice of a more active Attorney General than that here alluded to" (Shelley's note).
9. Deception, humbug.

1. A stroke or lash with a whip or scourge.
2. Alluding to journalistic calls for revenge on the ruling class in Cobbett's *Political Register*.
3. I.e., Hunt, Shelley himself, and other idealistic reformers.

Part Fourth

SIN

Lo, Peter in Hell's Grosvenor square,
　　A footman in the Devil's service!
And the misjudging world would swear　　　265
That every man in service there
　　To virtue would prefer vice.

But Peter, though now damned, was not
　　What Peter was before damnation.
Men oftentimes prepare a lot　　　　　270
Which ere it finds them, is not what
　　Suits with their genuine station.

All things that Peter saw and felt
　　Had a peculiar aspect to him;
And when they came within the belt　　　275
Of his own nature, seemed to melt
　　Like cloud to cloud, into him.

And so the outward world uniting
　　To that within him, he became
Considerably uninviting　　　　　280
To those, who meditation slighting,
　　Were moulded in a different frame.

And he scorned them, and they scorned him;
　　And he scorned all they did; and they
Did all that men of their own trim[4]　　　285
Are wont to do to please their whim,
　　Drinking, lying, swearing, play.

Such were his fellow servants; thus
　　His virtue, like our own, was built
Too much on that indignant fuss　　　290
Hypocrite Pride stirs up in us
　　To bully one another's guilt.

He had a mind which was somehow
　　At once circumference and centre
Of all he might or feel or know;　　　295
Nothing went ever out, although
　　Something did ever enter.

He had as much imagination
　　As a pint-pot:—he never could
Fancy another situation　　　　　300
From which to dart his contemplation,
　　Than that wherein he stood.

4. Nature, character, or manner.

Yet his was individual mind,
    And new created all he saw
In a new manner, and refined   305
Those new creations, and combined
    Them, by a master-spirit's law,

Thus—though unimaginative,
    An apprehension clear, intense,
Of his mind's work, had made alive   310
The things it wrought on; I believe
    Wakening a sort of thought in sense.[5]

But from the first 'twas Peter's drift
    To be a kind of moral eunuch
He touched the hem of Nature's shift,   315
Felt faint—and never dared uplift
    The closest, all-concealing tunic.

She laughed the while, with an arch smile,
    And kissed him with a sister's kiss,
And said—"My best Diogenes,[6]   320
I love you well—but, if you please,
    Tempt not again my deepest bliss.

"'Tis you are cold—for I, not coy,
    Yield love for love, frank, warm and true:
And Burns, a Scottish Peasant boy,—   325
His errors prove it—knew my joy
    More, learned friend, than you.

"*Bocca baciata non perde ventura*
    Anzi rinnuova come fa la luna:[7]—
So thought Boccaccio, whose sweet words might cure a   330
Male prude like you from what you now endure, a
    Low-tide in soul, like a stagnant laguna."

Then Peter rubbed his eyes severe,
    And smoothed his spacious forehead down
With his broad palm;—'twixt love and fear,   335
He looked, as he no doubt felt, queer,
    And in his dream sate down.

The Devil was no uncommon creature;
    A leaden-witted thief—just huddled
Out of the dross and scum of nature;   340
A toadlike lump[8] of limb and feature,
    With mind, and heart, and fancy muddled.

5. Lines 293–312 can probably be taken as Shelley's true (if somewhat sardonically expressed) evaluation of Wordsworth's genius.
6. The Cynic philosopher of Athens; the name itself suggests that Peter is unwilling to seek ultimate truths.
7. "A mouth that's been kissed does not lose its charm;/Rather, it renews itself as does the moon" (Boccaccio, *Decameron*, Second Day, end of the Seventh Novella).
8. In two stanzas Shelley has coalesced reminiscences of two classic passages—*Paradise Lost*, IV.799ff., where guardian angels discover Satan "Squat like a Toad, close at the eare of *Eve*," and Pope's character of Sporus in "Epistle to Dr. Arbuthnot" (lines 305–333), where Pope echoes the same passage in Milton.

He was that heavy, dull, cold thing
    The spirit of evil well may be:
A drone[9] too base to have a sting;   345
Who gluts, and grimes his lazy wing,
    And calls lust, luxury.

Now he was quite, the kind of wight[1]
    Round whom collect, at a fixed æra,[2]
Venison, turtle, hock[3] and claret,—   350
Good cheer—and those who come to share it—
    And best East Indian madeira!

It was his fancy to invite
    Men of science, wit and learning
Who came to lend each other Light:—   355
He proudly thought that his gold's might
    Had set those spirits burning.

And men of learning, science, wit,
    Considered him as you and I
Think of some rotten tree, and sit   360
Lounging and dining under it,
    Exposed to the wide sky.

And all the while, with loose fat smile
    The willing wretch sat winking there,
    Believing 'twas his power that made   365
That jovial scene—and that all paid
    Homage to his unnoticed chair.

Though to be sure this place was Hell;
    He was the Devil—and all they—
What though the claret circled well,   370
And Wit, like ocean, rose and fell?—
    Were damned eternally.

Part Fifth

GRACE

Among the guests who often staid
    Till the Devil's petits soupers,[4]
A man[5] there came, fair as a maid,   375
And Peter noted what he said,
    Standing behind his master's chair.

9. The nonworking male honeybee whose function is to impregnate the queen; hence, a lazy idler or sluggard.
1. A person; here used with contempt.
2. A memorable or important date.
3. White German wine.
4. Little suppers to which only intimates are admitted.

5. Samuel Taylor Coleridge. Shelley, who admired Coleridge's writings, may have heard him lecture but seems never to have met him socially; he had certainly heard much of him from such mutual friends and acquaintances as Southey, Godwin, Hunt, Byron, and Maria Gisborne.

He was a mighty poet—and
   A subtle-souled Psychologist;
All things he seemed to understand   380
Of old or new—of sea or land—
   But his own mind—which was a mist.

This was a man who might have turned
   Hell into Heaven—and so in gladness
A Heaven unto himself have earned;   385
But he in shadows undiscerned
   Trusted,—and damned himself to madness.

He spoke of poetry, and how
   "Divine it was—a light—a love—
A spirit which like wind doth blow   390
As it listeth, to and fro;
   A dew rained down from God above

"A power which comes and goes like dream,
   And which none can ever trace—
Heaven's light on Earth—Truth's brightest beam."   395
And when he ceased there lay the gleam
   Of those words upon his face.

Now Peter, when he heard such talk
   Would, heedless of a broken pate
Stand like a man asleep, or baulk   400
Some wishing guest of knife or fork,[6]
   Or drop and break his master's plate.

At night oft would start and wake
   Like a lover, and began
In a wild measure songs to make   405
On moor, and glen, and rocky lake,
   And on the heart of man.

And on the universal sky—
   And the wide earth's bosom green,—
And the sweet, strange mystery   410
Of what beyond these things may lie
   And yet remain unseen.

For in his thought he visited
   The spots in which, ere dead and damned,
He his wayward life had led;   415
Yet knew not whence the thoughts were fed
   Which thus his fancy crammed.

And these obscure remembrances
   Stirred such harmony in Peter,
That, whensoever he should please,   420
He could speak of rocks and trees
   In poetic metre.

6. I.e., intentionally omit the silverware.

For though it was without a sense
    Of memory, yet he remembered well
Many a ditch and quickset fence;   425
Of lakes he had intelligence
    He knew something of heath and fell.[7]

He had also dim recollections
    Of pedlars tramping on their rounds,
Milk pans and pails, and odd collections   430
Of saws,[8] and proverbs, and reflexions
    Old parsons make in burying-grounds.

But Peter's verse was clear, and came
    Announcing from the frozen hearth
Of a cold age, that none might tame   435
The soul of that diviner flame
    It augured to the Earth:

Like gentle rains, on the dry plains,
    Making that green which late was grey,
Or like the sudden moon, that stains   440
Some gloomy chamber's windowpanes
    With a broad light like day.

For language was in Peter's hand
    Like clay while he was yet a potter;
And he made songs for all the land   445
Sweet both to feel and understand
    As pipkins[9] late to mountain Cotter.

And Mr.——, the Bookseller,[1]
    Gave twenty pounds for some:—then scorning
A footman's yellow coat to wear,   450
Peter, too proud of heart I fear,
    Instantly gave the Devil warning.

Whereat the Devil took offence,
    And swore in his soul a great oath then,
"That for his damned impertinence,   455
He'd bring him to a proper sense
    Of what was due to gentlemen!"

Part Sixth

DAMNATION

"O that mine enemy had written
    A book!"—cried Job:[2]—A fearful curse;
If to the Arab, as the Briton,   460
'Twas galling to be critic-bitten:—
    The Devil to Peter wished no worse.

---

7. *heath:* a flat, uncultivated land covered with low herbage; *fell:* an elevated stretch of waste or pasture land.
8. Traditional maxims.
9. Small earthenware pots or pans.
1. Shelley alludes to Joseph Cottle's pur-

chase (for 30 guineas) of the copyright to *Lyrical Ballads*, though he may not have known all the details.
2. Job 31:35; Job's "adversary" was God.

When Peter's next new book found vent,
  The Devil to all the first Reviews
A copy of it slyly sent   465
With five-pound note as compliment,
  And this short notice—"Pray abuse"[3]

Then *seriatim*,[4] month and quarter,
  Appeared such mad tirades.—One said—
"Peter seduced Mrs. Foy's daughter,   470
Then drowned the Mother in Ullswater,[5]
  The last thing as he went to bed."

Another—"Let him shave his head!
  Where's Dr. Willis?[6]—Or is he joking?
What does the rascal mean or hope,   475
No longer imitating Pope,
  In that barbarian Shakespeare poking?"

One more,—"Is incest not enough,
  And must there be adultery too?
Grace after meat? Miscreant[7] and Liar!   480
Thief! Blackguard! Scoundrel! Fool! Hellfire
  Is twenty times too good for you.

"By that last book of yours WE think
  You've double damned yourself to scorn:
We warned you whilst yet on the brink   485
You stood. From your black name will shrink
  The babe that is unborn."

All these Reviews the Devil made
  Up in a parcel, which he had
Safely to Peter's house conveyed.   490
For carriage ten-pence Peter paid—
  Untied them—read them—went half mad.

"What!"—Cried he, "this is my reward
  For nights of thought, and days of toil?
Do poets, but to be abhorred   495
By men of whom they never heard,
  Consume their spirits' oil?

3. The leading "Reviews" of Shelley's day (as opposed to "magazines" and weekly "newspapers") were the quarterly *Edinburgh Review* (1802ff.), *Quarterly Review* (1809ff.), and *British Review* (1811–1825), and the monthly *Monthly Review* (1749–1845), *Critical Review* (1756–1817), and *British Critic* (1793–1826). Though Francis Jeffrey's attacks on Wordsworth in the *Edinburgh Review* are the most (in)famous, Wordsworth's *Poems: In Two Volumes* (1807) was roughly handled by most reviewers. (For facsimiles of these and other contemporary reviews of the Romantic poets, see *The Romantics Reviewed*, ed. Donald H. Reiman [9 vols., New York, 1972].)

4. One by one in succession.
5. Betty Foy is the mother of Wordsworth's "Idiot Boy" (she has no daughter); *Ullswater:* one of the larger lakes in the Lake Country of Westmorland and Cumberland counties.
6. Francis Willis (1718–1807) and his sons John (1751–1835) and Robert Darling Willis (1760–1821) were all physicians specializing in the treatment of mental illness; all treated King George III. (The better known writer on insanity, Robert Willis (1799–1878), was too young for Shelley to have known of him.)
7. Vile wretch or villain.

"What have I done to them?—and Who
   Is Mrs. Foy? 'Tis very cruel
To speak of me and Betty so!   500
Adultery! God defend me! Oh!
   I've half a mind to fight a duel.

"Or," cried he, a grave look collecting,
   "Is it my genius, like the moon,
Sets those who stand her face inspecting,   505
(That face within their brain reflecting,)
   Like a crazed bell chime, out of tune?"[8]

For Peter did not know the town,
   But thought, as country readers do,
For half a guinea or a crown,   510
He bought oblivion or renown
   From God's own voice[9] in a review.

All Peter did on this occasion
   Was, writing some sad stuff in prose.[1]
It is a dangerous invasion   515
When Poets criticise: their station
   Is to delight, not pose.

The Devil then sent to Leipsic fair,
   For Born's translation of Kant's book;[2]
A world of words, tail foremost, where   520
Right—wrong—false—true—and foul and fair
   As in a lottery wheel are shook.

Five thousand crammed octavo pages
   Of German psychologics,—he
Who his *furor verborum*[3] assuages   525
Thereon, deserves just seven months' wages
   More than will e'er be due to me.

I looked on them nine several days,
   And then I saw that they were bad;
A friend, too, spoke in their dispraise,—   530
He never read them;—with amaze
   I found Sir William Drummond had.[4]

---

8. Cf. Shakespeare, *Hamlet*, III.i.165–166: "Now see that noble and most sovereign reason,/Like sweet bells jangled, out of tune and harsh."

9. "*Vox populi, vox dei.* As Mr. Godwin truly observes of a more famous saying, of *some merit as a popular maxim, but totally destitute of philosophical accuracy*" (Shelley's note). *Vox populi, vox dei:* The voice of the people [is] the voice of god.

1. Wordsworth's preface to *Lyrical Ballads* (1800) and his preface to the collected *Poems* of 1815 (I,vii–xlii) and the "Essay, Supplementary to the Preface"

in the same volume (I,341–375).

2. F. G. Born's Latin translation of Kant's works: *Opera ad philosophiam criticam pertinentia* (4 vols., Leipzig, 1796–1798). Immanuel Kant (1724–1804), who spent his life in Koenigsberg, Prussia, was the leading moral and metaphysical philosopher of the late eighteenth century.

3. The inspired frenzy of poets and prophets.

4. Sir William Drummond (1770–1828) criticized Kant's ideas in *Academical Questions* (London, 1805), a book that greatly influenced Shelley.

When the book came, the Devil sent
    It to P. Verbovale[5] Esquire,
With a brief note of compliment,   535
By that night's Carlisle mail. It went
    And set his soul on fire.

Fire; which *ex luce præbens fumum*,[6]
    Made him beyond the bottom see
Of truth's clear well—when I and you, Ma'am,   540
Go, as we shall do, *subter humum*,[7]
    We may know more than he.

Now Peter ran to seed in soul
    Into a walking paradox;—
For he was neither part nor whole,   545
Nor good, nor bad—nor knave, nor fool,
    —Among the woods and rocks

Furious he rode, where late he ran,
    Lashing and spurring his tame hobby;
Turned to a formal Puritan,   550
A solemn and unsexual man,—
    He half believed W*hite Obi*![8]

This steed in vision he would ride,
    High trotting over nine-inch bridges,
With Flibbertigibbet,[9] imp of pride,   555
Mocking and mowing by his side—
    A mad brained goblin[1] for a guide—
    Over cornfields, gates and hedges.

After these ghastly rides, he came
    Home to his heart, and found from thence   560
Much stolen of its accustomed flame:
His thoughts grew weak, drowsy, and lame
    Of their intelligence.

To Peter's view, all seemed one hue;
    He was no Whig, he was no Tory: 565
No Deist[2] and no Christian he;—
He got so subtle, that to be
    Nothing, was all his glory.

---

5. "Quasi, *Qui valet verba:—i.e.* all the words which have been, are, or may be expended by, for, against, with, or on him. A sufficient proof of the utility of this History. Peter's progenitor who selected this name seems to have possessed *a pure anticipated cognition* of the nature and modesty of this ornament of his posterity" (Shelley's note).
6. "From light he then gives smoke" (an inversion of Horace's *Ars poetica*, 143–144: "His thought is not to give flame first and then smoke, but from smoke to let light appear").
7. Under the ground, i.e., die.
8. See note 9, p. 324.
9. The name of a devil or fiend (see Shakespeare, *King Lear*, III.iv.120).
1. Will-o'-the-wisp, the elusive light-goblin who leads travelers astray.
2. One who believes in a deity that created the universe and rules it through natural law, but who does not believe in divine intervention in human affairs (or in the divinity of Jesus).

One single point in his belief
  From his organization sprung,   570
The heart enrooted faith, the chief
Ear in his doctrine's blighted sheaf,
  That "happiness is wrong,"

So thought Calvin and Dominic;[3]
  So think their fierce successors, who   575
Even now would neither stint nor stick
Our flesh from off our bones to pick,
  If they might "do their do."

His morals thus were undermined:—
  The old Peter—the hard, old Potter—   580
Was born anew within his mind:
He grew dull, harsh, sly, unrefined,
  As when he tramped beside the Otter.[4]

In the death hues of agony
  Lambently[5] flashing from a fish,   585
Now Peter felt amused to see
Shades, like a rainbow's, rise and flee,
  Mixed with a certain hungry wish.[6]

So in his Country's dying face
  He looked—and, lovely as she lay,   590
Seeking in vain his last embrace,
Wailing her own abandoned case,
  With hardened sneer he turned away:

And coolly to his own soul said;—
  "Do you not think that we might make   595
A poem on her when she's dead?—
Or, no—a thought is in my head—
  Her shroud for a new sheet I'll take:

"My wife wants one.—Let who will bury
  This mangled corpse!—And I and you,   600

3. John Calvin (1509–1564), the Geneva Protestant theologian, and St. Dominic (1170–1221), Spanish founder of the Catholic Dominican order.
4. "A famous river in the new Atlantis of the Dynastophylic Pantisocratists" (Shelley's note). *Otter:* The River Otter near Coleridge's boyhood home to which he addressed one sonnet; he also wrote sonnets praising Pantisocracy, the plan he, Southey, their wives (the Fricker sisters), and other friends had concocted in 1794 to establish a utopian community on the banks of the Susquehanna River in Pennsylvania. *Dynastophylic* refers to Southey's and Coleridge's later support of the established dynasties of Europe.
5. Gilding over a surface.
6. "See the description of the beautiful colours produced during the agonising death of a number of trout, in the fourth part of a long poem in blank verse, published within a few years. [*The Excursion*, VIII.568–71.] That poem contains curious evidence of the gradual hardening of a strong but circumscribed sensibility, of the perversion of a penetrating but panic stricken understanding. The Author might have derived a lesson which he had probably forgotten from these sweet and sublime verses:—

This lesson, Shepherd, let us two divide,
Taught both by what she* shews and
  what conceals,
Never to blend our pleasure or our pride
With sorrow of the meanest thing that
  feels." (Shelley's note).
  * Nature.

My dearest Soul, will then make merry,
    As the Prince Regent did with Sherry,[7]—"
      "Ay—and at last desert me too."

And so his Soul would not be gay,
    But moaned within him; like a fawn,   605
Moaning within a cave, it lay
Wounded and wasting, day by day,
    Till all its life of life was gone.

As troubled skies stain waters clear;
    The storm in Peter's heart and mind,   610
Now made his verses dark and queer:
They were the ghosts of what they were;
    Shaking dim grave clothes in the wind.

For he now raved enormous folly,
    Of Baptisms, Sunday-schools and Graves,   615
'Twould make George Colman[8] melancholy
To have heard him, like a male Molly,[9]
    Chaunting those stupid staves.

Yet the Reviews, who heaped abuse
    On Peter, while he wrote for freedom,   620
So soon as in his song they spy
The folly which soothes Tyranny,
    Praise him, for those who feed 'em.

"He was a man, too great to scan;—
    A planet lost in truth's keen rays:—   625
His virtue, awful and prodigious;—
He was the most sublime, religious,
    Pure-minded Poet of these days."

As soon as he read that—cried Peter,
    "Eureka! I have found the way   630
To make a better thing of metre
Than e'er was made by living creature
    Up to this blessed day."

Then Peter wrote odes to the Devil;—
    In one of which he meekly said:—   635
    "May Carnage and Slaughter,
    Thy niece and thy daughter,[1]

---

7. Richard Brinsley Sheridan (1751–1816), dramatist, wit, and liberal Whig member of Parliament, was a friend and drinking companion of George IV in his younger days as Prince of Wales. As Regent, George turned reactionary and abandoned Sheridan; (false) rumor had it that George allowed "Sherry" to be arrested for debt and die in poverty without attempting to assist him.
8. George Colman, the Younger (1762–1836), an important dramatist and writer of farces, was noted for his wit and off-color humor.
9. *male Molly:* an effeminate man or sodomite; *staves:* stanzas.
1. Cf. lines 636–637 with Wordsworth's "Ode, 1815" (celebrating the defeat of Napoleon at Waterloo): ". . . Almighty God!/. . . Thy most dreaded instrument,/ In working out a pure intent,/Is Man—arrayed for mutual slaughter,/—Yea, Carnage is thy daughter." Wordsworth drastically revised the lines for the edition of 1845.

May Rapine and Famine,
Thy gorge ever cramming,[2]
Glut thee with living and dead!   640

"May death and Damnation,
And Consternation,
Flit up from Hell with pure intent!
Slash them at Manchester,[3]
Glasgow, Leeds and Chester;   645
Drench all with blood from Avon to Trent.

"Let thy body-guard yeomen
Hew down babes and women,
And laugh with bold triumph till Heaven be rent!
When Moloch[4] in Jewry   650
Munched children with fury
It was thou, Devil, dining with pure intent."[5]

Part Seventh

DOUBLE DAMNATION

The Devil now knew his proper cue.—
    Soon as he read the ode, he drove
To his friend Lord MacMurderchouse's,[6]   655
A man of interest in both houses,
    And said:—"For money or for love

"Pray find some cure or sinecure,
    To feed from the superfluous taxes
A friend of ours—a Poet—fewer   660
Have fluttered tamer to the lure
    Than he."—His Lordship stands and racks his

Stupid brains, while one might count
    As many beads as he had boroughs,—
At length replies;—from his mean front,   665
Like one who rubs out an account,
    Smoothing away the unmeaning furrows:—

2. Pronounced "crammin."
3. An allusion to the Peterloo Massacre; see "The Mask of Anarchy," pp. 301–310.
4. A Canaanite god to whom children were sacrificed as burnt offerings (Leviticus 18:21); one of Milton's devils in *Paradise Lost* (II.43). Moloch means "king" in Hebrew (as Milton knew).
5. "It is curious to observe how often extremes meet. Cobbett and Peter use the same language for a different purpose: Peter is indeed a sort of metrical Cobbett. Cobbett is however more mischievous than Peter, because he pollutes a holy and now unconquerable cause with the principles of legitimate murder; whilst the other only makes a bad one ridiculous and odious.
    "If either Peter or Cobbett should see this note, each will feel more indignation at being compared to the other than at any censure implied in the moral perversion laid to their charge" (Shelley's note).
6. *Chouse:* to cheat or swindle, or (as a noun) one who is a swindler. The nobleman who actually obtained a government position for Wordsworth was (as Shelley knew) William Lowther, Earl of Lonsdale, the son of ("Mac-") the nobleman who had cheated Wordsworth's family.

"It happens fortunately, dear Sir,
　　I can. I hope I need require
No pledge from you, that he will stir. 670
In our affairs;—like Oliver,[7]
　　That he'll be worthy of his hire."

These words exchanged, the news sent off
　　To Peter:—home the Devil hied;
Took to his bed; he had no cough, 675
No doctor,—meat and drink enough,—
　　Yet that same night he died.

The Devil's corpse was leaded down.—
　　His decent heirs enjoyed his pelf;[8]
Mourning-coaches, many a one, 680
Followed his hearse along the town:—
　　Where was the Devil himself?

When Peter heard of his promotion
　　His eyes grew like two stars for bliss:
There was a bow of sleek devotion 685
Engendering in his back; each motion
　　Seemed a Lord's shoe to kiss.

He hired a house,[9] bought plate, and made
　　A genteel drive up to his door,
With sifted gravel neatly laid,— 690
As if defying all who said
　　Peter was ever poor.

But a disease soon struck into
　　The very life and soul of Peter—
He walked about—slept—had the hue 695
Of health upon his cheeks—and few
　　Dug better—none a heartier eater.

And yet, a strange and horrid curse
　　Clung upon Peter, night and day—
Month after month the thing grew worse, 700
And deadlier than in this my verse
　　I can find strength to say.

Peter was dull—he was at first
　　Dull—O, so dull—so very dull!
Whether he talked, wrote, or rehearsed— 705
Still with this dulness was he cursed—
　　Dull—beyond all conception—dull.—

---

7. W. J. Richards ("Oliver") was a
government spy and agent like Castle
(line 152).
8. A deprecatory term for money or
wealth.
9. In 1813, Wordsworth received a gov-
ernment appointment as Distributor of
[Tax] Stamps for Westmorland and
Cumberland counties and moved into
Rydal Mount, the larger house he was
to occupy till his death.

No one could read his books—no mortal,
  But a few natural friends, would hear him:—
The parson came not near his portal;—   710
His state was like that of the immortal
  Described by Swift[1]—no man could bear him.

His sister, wife, and children yawned,
  With a long, slow and drear ennui,
All human patience far beyond;   715
Their hopes of Heaven each would have pawned,
  Anywhere else to be.

But in his verse, and in his prose,
  The essence of his dullness was
Concentred and compressed so close,   720
'Twould have made Guatimozin doze
  On his red gridiron of brass.[2]

A printer's boy, folding those pages,
  Fell slumbrously upon one side:
Like those famed seven who slept three ages.   725
To wakeful frenzy's vigil rages
  As opiates were the same applied.

Even the Reviewers who were hired
  To do the work of his reviewing,
With adamantine nerves, grew tired;—   730
Gaping and torpid they retired,
  To dream of what they should be doing.

And worse and worse, the drowsy curse
  Yawned in him—till it grew a pest—
A wide contagious atmosphere,   735
Creeping like cold through all things near;
  A power to infect, and to infest.

His servant maids and dogs grew dull;
  His kitten, late a sportive elf;
The woods and lakes, so beautiful,   740
Of dim stupidity were full,
  All grew dull as Peter's self.

The earth under his feet—the springs,
  Which lived within it a quick life—
The Air, the Winds of many wings—   745
That fan it with new murmurings,
  Were dead to their harmonious strife.

1. One of the Struldbruggs, who are doomed to live forever, in *Gulliver's Travels*, Part III, chap. X.
2. The nephew and successor of Montezuma led the Aztec defense of Mexico City against Cortes; after his capture he and a friend were tortured on a hot metal grid. In order to keep up his companion's courage, Guatimozin said, "Am I now reposing on a bed of flowers?"

The birds and beasts within the wood,
   The insects, and each creeping thing,
Were now a silent multitude;   750
Love's work was left unwrought—no brood
   Near Peter's house took wing.

And every neighbouring Cottager
   Stupidly yawned upon the other;
No jackass brayed;—no little cur   755
Cocked up his ears;—no man would stir
   To save a dying mother.

Yet all from that charmed district went
   But some half idiot and half knave,
Who, rather than pay any rent,   760
Would live, with marvellous content,
   Over his father's grave.

No bailiff dared within that space,
   For fear of the dull charm, to enter:
A man would bear upon his face,   765
For fifteen months, in any case,
   The yawn of such a venture.

Seven miles above—below—around—
   This pest of dulness holds its sway:
A ghastly life without a sound;   770
To Peter's soul the spell is bound—
   How should it ever pass away?

The Witch of Atlas

In August 1820, Shelley went on foot from Lucca to a shrine high in the Apennines atop Monte San Pellegrino, completing the entire journey in three days (August 11–13). Inspired during this walk, Shelley spent the next three days (August 14–16) writing "The Witch of Atlas."

The poem is written in the *ottava rima* stanzas of Italian seriocomic poetry. In June and July, Shelley and Mary had been reading aloud *Il Ricciardetto* (1738) by Niccolò Forteguerri, an imitator of Luigi Pulci, whose *Morgante Maggiore* had been the ultimate source of Byron's style in *Beppo, Don Juan*, and *A Vision of Judgment*. But Shelley's *ottava rima* in "The Witch of Atlas" (and in the Homeric "Hymn to Mercury," which he translated during this period) is as distinctively different from Byron's *ottava rima* as it is from Keats's use of the same form in *Isabella*.

The Witch—another embodiment of the Ideal—is treated seriously but with lightness and without a note of sentimentality. Yet she plays pranks with mortal creatures, and they—including the poet and his readers—are aware that the consequences of her actions are not as satisfactory to humankind as they might be. The tone holds the reader's feelings in suspension, as the poet describes the incomparable beauty and perfection of the Witch and, at the same time, her lack of understanding sympathy with the problems of mortal creatures.

Though most of such "plot" as the poem exhibits is self-explanatory, a few comments on particular matters may be helpful. According to some classical geographers, the Atlas Mountains, which were the Witch's home, were the source of one branch of the Nile River, which was imagined to loop from Morocco below the Sahara Desert and flow eastward into the Sudan. So the Witch's final journey down the populated Nile Valley has some connection with her childhood among the remote mountains. The Witch's flight into the skies of the Southern Hemisphere (423–448) has never been explained satisfactorily. Though there had been some current interest in Antarctica since Captain James Cook's second voyage (1772–1775)—reflected in the voyage of Coleridge's Ancient Mariner to the southern land of "mist and snow"—Shelley's portrait of an "Austral lake" that is a calm haven seems to have its origins in myth rather than in exploration. The only hint we can find in previous literature is Ulysses' account of his final questing voyage in Dante's *Inferno* (Canto XXVI), where he and his crew cross the equator and come within sight of the Mount of Purgatory looming to the southwest.

Mary Shelley transcribed "The Witch of Atlas" in December 1820, and Shelley mailed the poem to Ollier on January 20, 1821. On February 22 he instructed Ollier to publish it with his name—but not to include it with *Julian and Maddalo*. Ollier neglected issuing "The Witch," and it was first published by Mary Shelley in Shelley's *Posthumous Poems* (1824), though without the introductory stanzas in which Shelley mocks Mary, the critics, and Wordsworth's *Peter Bell*. Besides the first edition and Mary's subsequent collected editions of 1839, the chief textual authorities are Shelley's intermediate fair copy (Bodleian MS. Shelley d.1, ff.15–32) and a transcript in Mary's hand that Forman collated in his edition of 1876. Shelley's fair copy is missing some lines and phrases, as is Mary's transcript, which obviously derives from it. The fair copy by Mary sent to Ollier in January 1821 presumably served as press copy for *Posthumous Poems* (1824); it is now lost. The transcript by Mary that Forman collated may have been done in Italy after Shelley's death, before Mary had retrieved the completed version sent to Ollier. We have followed 1824 on most verbal differences but have followed the manuscripts on several matters of spelling, capitalization, and punctuation and on a few verbal points where the 1824 reading could have resulted from Mary's error in transcribing Shelley's manuscript or the typesetter's in setting Mary's transcript.

The Witch of Atlas

To Mary

(ON HER OBJECTING TO THE FOLLOWING POEM, UPON THE SCORE
OF ITS CONTAINING NO HUMAN INTEREST)

I

How, my dear Mary, are you critic-bitten
    (For vipers kill, though dead)[1] by some review,
That you condemn these verses I have written
    Because they tell no story, false or true?

---

1. We have been unable to identify the source of this belief in Shelley's reading.

What, though no mice are caught by a young kitten,   5
   May it not leap and play as grown cats do,
Till its claws come? Prithee, for this one time,
Content thee with a visionary rhyme.

II

What hand would crush the silken-winged fly,[2]
   The youngest of inconstant April's minions,[3]   10
Because it cannot climb the purest sky
   Where the swan sings, amid the sun's dominions?[4]
Not thine. Thou knowest tis its doom to die
   When Day shall hide within her twilight pinions[5]
The lucent[6] eyes, and the eternal smile,   15
Serene as thine, which lent it life awhile.

III

To thy fair feet a winged Vision[7] came
   Whose date should have been longer than a day,
And o'er thy head did beat its wings for fame
   And in thy sight its fading plumes display;   20
The watery bow burned in the evening flame,
   But the shower fell,—the swift Sun went his way.
And that is dead:[8] O, let me not believe
That anything of mine is fit to live!

IV

Wordsworth informs us he was nineteen years   25
   Considering and retouching Peter Bell;[9]
Watering his laurels[1] with the killing tears
   Of slow, dull care, so that their roots to hell
Might pierce, and their wide branches blot the spheres
   Of Heaven, with dewy leaves and flowers; this well   30
May be, for Heaven and Earth conspire to foil
The over busy gardener's blundering toil.

V

My Witch indeed is not so sweet a creature
   As Ruth or Lucy,[2] whom his graceful praise
Clothes for our grandsons—but she matches Peter   35
   Though he took nineteen years, and she three days
In dressing. Light the vest of flowing metre
   She wears: he, proud as dandy with his stays,
Has hung upon his wiry limbs a dress
Like King Lear's "looped and windowed raggedness."[3]   40

---

2. Ephemerid, or dayfly, which lives only for a few hours to a few days (see "The Sensitive-Plant," II.49).
3. Favorites or darlings.
4. In classical mythology the swan, believed to sing shortly before its death, was sacred to Apollo (the *sun*); the swan appears in astronomy as the northern constellation Cygnus.
5. Wings.
6. Shining or bright.

7. Shelley alludes to his longest poem, *Laon and Cythna* (*The Revolt of Islam*).
8. Both the sales and the reviews of *The Revolt* disappointed Shelley.
9. For Wordsworth's *Peter Bell*, see the headnote to *Peter Bell the Third*, above.
1. The emblem of distinction in poetry.
2. Idealized girls in Wordsworth's *Lyrical Ballads*.
3. The reference is to Shakespeare, *King Lear*, III.iv.31.

VI

If you strip Peter, you will see a fellow
    Scorched by Hell's hyperequatorial climate
Into a kind of a sulphureous yellow,
    A lean mark hardly fit to fling a rhyme at;
In shape a Scaramouch, in hue Othello.[4]   45
    If you unveil my Witch, no Priest or Primate
Can shrive[5] you of that sin, if sin there be
In love, when it becomes idolatry.

The Witch of Atlas

I

Before those cruel Twins, whom at one birth
    Incestuous Change bore to her father Time,   50
Error and Truth, had hunted from the earth
    All those bright natures which adorned its prime,
And left us nothing to believe in, worth
    The pains of putting into learned rhyme,
A lady-witch there lived on Atlas' mountain[6]   55
Within a cavern, by a secret fountain.

II

Her mother was one of the Atlantides[7]—
    The all-beholding Sun[8] had ne'er beholden
In his wide voyage o'er continents and seas
    So fair a creature, as she lay enfolden   60
In the warm shadow of her loveliness . . .
    He kissed her with his beams, and made all golden
The chamber of grey rock in which she lay—
She, in that dream of joy, dissolved away.[9]

III

'Tis said, she first was changed into a vapour,   65
    And then into a cloud, such clouds as flit,
Like splendour-winged moths about a taper,
    Round the red West when the sun dies in it:
And then into a meteor,[1] such as caper
    On hill-tops when the moon is in a fit:[2]   70
Then, into one of those mysterious stars
Which hide themselves between the Earth and Mars.

4. Probably the puppet representing the stock character in Italian farce, Scaramouche, a coward and boaster constantly being cudgeled by Harlequin; *Othello:* i.e., black.
5. Impose penance on and administer absolution for.
6. The Atlas Mountains run from southwestern Morocco to northeastern Algeria. According to the myth, Atlas, a brother of Prometheus, when shown Medusa's head by Perseus, was changed into the mountain; he was believed to support the heavens on his shoulders.
7. Daughters of Atlas and Hesperus or Pleione, the *Atlantides* (also called Hesperides or Pleiades) were nymphs or goddesses made into a constellation after their deaths.
8. I.e., Apollo; see line 293 and note.
9. *The all-beholding . . . dissolved away:* The circumstances of the Witch's birth are very similar to those of Spenser's Belphoebe and Amoret (*Faerie Queene*, III.vi.7ff.).
1. Aurora or halo.
2. An interval of inaction; hence, the period when the moon is not visible.

IV

Ten times the Mother of the Months[3] had bent
   Her bow beside the folding-star,[4] and bidden
With that bright sign the billows[5] to indent   75
   The sea-deserted sand—like children chidden
At her command they ever came and went—
   Since in that cave a dewy splendour hidden
Took shape and motion: with the living form   80
Of this embodied Power, the cave grew warm.

V

A lovely lady garmented in light
   From her own beauty—deep her eyes, as are
Two openings of unfathomable night
   Seen through a Temple's cloven roof—her hair
Dark—the dim brain whirls dizzy with delight   85
   Picturing her form—her soft smiles shone afar,
And her low voice was heard like love, and drew
All living things towards this wonder new.

VI

And first the spotted cameleopard[6] came,
   And then the wise and fearless elephant;   90
Then the sly serpent, in the golden flame
   Of his own volumes intervolved;[7]—all gaunt
And sanguine[8] beasts her gentle looks made tame—
   They drank before her at her sacred fount—
And every beast of beating heart grew bold,   95
Such gentleness and power even to behold.

VII

The brinded[9] lioness led forth her young
   That she might teach them how they should forego
Their inborn thirst of death—the pard[1] unstrung
   His sinews at her feet, and sought to know   100
With looks whose motions spoke without a tongue
   How he might be as gentle as the doe.
The magic circle of her voice and eyes
All savage natures did imparadise.

VIII

And old Silenus,[2] shaking a green stick   105
   Of lilies, and the wood-gods in a crew
Came, blithe, as in the olive copses thick
   Cicadæ[3] are, drunk with the noonday dew:

3. I.e., the moon; nine full months she bent her bow by filling out from a thin crescent to the full moon.
4. Venus, the evening star, rising at folding time (when sheep are put into their folds for the night).
5. A great wave of air.
6. Giraffe.
7. Wound up within his coils (*volumes*).
8. Bloody; i.e., carnivorous or predatory.

9. Tawny or brownish color, marked with streaks of a different hue.
1. Leopard or panther.
2. A demigod, attendant of Bacchus. See *Prometheus Unbound*, II.ii; *wood-gods:* probably the Sileni—fauns and satyrs in general.
3. Locusts with large, transparent wings, often erroneously identified as grasshoppers; the male makes a shrill chirping sound.

And Dryope and Faunus⁴ followed quick,
    Teasing the God to sing them something new   110
Till in this cave they found the lady lone,
Sitting upon a seat of emerald stone.

IX

And Universal Pan,⁵ 'tis said, was there,
    And though none saw him,—through the adamant
Of the deep mountains, through the trackless air,   115
    And through those living spirits, like a want⁶
He past out of his everlasting lair
    Where the quick heart of the great world doth pant—
And felt that wondrous lady all alone—
And she felt him upon her emerald throne.   120

X

And, every Nymph of stream and spreading tree
    And every shepherdess of Ocean's flocks⁷
Who drives her white waves over the green Sea;
    And Ocean with the brine on his grey locks,
And quaint Priapus⁸ with his company   125
    All came, much wondering how the enwombed rocks
Could have brought forth so beautiful a birth;—
Her love subdued their wonder and their mirth.

XI

The herdsmen and the mountain maidens came
    And the rude kings of Pastoral Garamant⁹—   130
Their spirits shook within them, as a flame
    Stirred by the air under a cavern gaunt:
Pigmies, and Polyphemes,¹ by many a name,
    Centaurs and Satyrs,² and such shapes as haunt
Wet clefts,—and lumps neither alive nor dead,   135
Dog-headed, bosom-eyed³ and bird-footed.

XII

For she was beautiful—her beauty made
    The bright world dim, and every thing beside
Seemed like the fleeting image of a shade:
    No thought of living spirit could abide—   140

---

4. *Dryope:* a nymph; the name designates both the Arcadian mother of Pan by Mercury and an Italian nymph who was the mother of Tarquitus by *Faunus*, the brave and wise legendary ruler of Italy, who was revered as a satyr-deity.
5. As god of shepherds, huntsmen, and inhabitants of Arcadia (an area in Greece in the center of the Peloponnesus), *Pan* (sometimes identified with *Faunus*) was a ruddy, flat-nosed, horned man with the feet and legs of a goat—a satyr.
6. Need.
7. Daughters of Oceanus, the Oceanides, who also protected seamen.
8. The deity of gardens and genitalia, *Priapus* was the deformed son of Aphrodite and Dionysus; he is represented with a human face, goat's ears, a stick to drive away birds, and a pruning hook.
9. The Garamantes were an African (north central Libya) people who lived in common and "scarce clothed themselves" because of the warm climate.
1. One-eyed giants; after Polyphemus, the Cyclops (*Odyssey*, IX).
2. *Centaurs:* a race of imaginary creatures, half man and half horse, of Thessaly; *Satyrs:* see note 5, above. These creatures are both lascivious and generally playful.
3. The syntax of the entire line indicates that the creatures have eyes like bosoms—i.e., bulging eyes, not (as has been suggested) breasts filled with eyes.

Which to her looks had ever been betrayed,
   On any object in the world so wide,
On any hope within the circling skies,
But on her form, and in her inmost eyes.

XIII

Which when the lady knew she took her spindle   145
   And twined three threads of fleecy mist, and three
Long lines of light such as the Dawn may kindle
   The clouds and waves and mountains with, and she
As many star-beams, ere their lamps could dwindle
   In the belated moon, wound skilfully;   150
And with these threads a subtle veil she wove—
A shadow for the splendour of her love.

XIV

The deep recesses of her odorous dwelling
   Were stored with magic treasures—Sounds of air,
Which had the power all spirits of compelling,   155
   Folded in cells[4] of chrystal silence there;
Such as we hear in youth, and think the feeling
   Will never die—yet ere we are aware,
The feeling and the sound are fled and gone,
And the regret they leave remains alone.   160

XV

And there lay Visions swift and sweet and quaint,
   Each in its thin sheath like a chrysalis,[5]
Some eager to burst forth, some weak and faint
   With the soft burthen of intensest bliss;
It was its work to bear to many a saint   165
   Whose heart adores the shrine which holiest is,
Even Love's—and others white, green, grey and black,
And of all shapes—and each was at her beck.

XVI

And odours in a kind of aviary
   Of ever blooming Eden-trees she kept,   170
Clipt[6] in a floating net a love-sick Fairy
   Had woven from dew beams while the moon yet slept—
As bats at the wired window of a dairy
   They beat their vans;[7] and each was an adept,
When loosed and missioned, making wings of winds,   175
To stir sweet thoughts or sad, in destined minds.

XVII

And liquors clear and sweet, whose healthful might
   Could medicine the sick soul to happy sleep
And change eternal death into a night
   Of glorious dreams—or if eyes needs must weep,   180
Could make their tears all wonder and delight,
   She in her chrystal vials did closely keep—

---

4. Small rooms in monasteries.   6. Embraced or held tightly.
5. Cocoon.   7. Wings.

If men could drink of those clear vials, 'tis said
The living were not envied of[8] the dead.

XVIII

Her cave was stored with scrolls of strange device,   185
    The works of some Saturnian Archimage,
Which taught the expiations at whose price
    Men from the Gods might win that happy age
Too lightly lost, redeeming native vice[9]—
    And which might quench the earth-consuming rage   190
Of gold and blood—till men should live and move
Harmonious as the sacred stars above.

XIX

And how all things that seem untameable,
    Not to be checked and not to be confined,
Obey the spells of wisdom's wizard skill;   195
    Time, Earth and Fire—the Ocean and the Wind
And all their shapes—and man's imperial Will—
    And other scrolls whose writings did unbind
The inmost lore of Love—let the prophane[1]
Tremble to ask what secrets they contain.   200

XX

And wondrous works of substances unknown,
    To which the enchantment of her father's power
Had changed those ragged blocks of savage stone,
    Were heaped in the recesses of her bower;
Carved lamps and chalices and phials which shone   205
    In their own golden beams—each like a flower
Out of whose depth a fire fly shakes his light
Under a cypress in the starless night.

XXI

At first she lived alone in this wild home,
    And her own thoughts were each a minister,   210
Clothing themselves or[2] with the Ocean foam,
    Or with the wind, or with the speed of fire,
To work whatever purposes might come
    Into her mind; such power her mighty Sire
Had girt them with, whether to fly or run,   215
Through all the regions which he shines upon.

XXII

The Ocean-Nymphs and Hamadryades,
    Oreads and Naiads with long weedy locks,
Offered to do her bidding through the seas,
    Under the earth, and in the hollow rocks,   220
And far beneath the matted roots of trees
    And in the knarled heart of stubborn oaks,

---

8. By.
9. Unlike Archimago's books, which contain recipes for evil charms (Spenser's *Faerie Queene*, I.i.36), the Witch's *scrolls* show how men can return to *that happy age:* the Golden Age of Saturn or the time before the Fall, when men acquired *native vice* or original sin. (Cf. "Letter to Maria Gisborne," lines 106ff.)
1. The uninitiated.
2. Either.

So they might live forever in the light
Of her sweet presence—each a satellite.[3]

XXIII

"This may not be—" the wizard Maid replied;   225
  "The fountains where the Naiades bedew
Their shining hair at length are drained and dried;
  The solid oaks forget their strength, and strew
Their latest leaf upon the mountains wide;
  The boundless Ocean like a drop of dew   230
Will be consumed—the stubborn centre must
Be scattered like a cloud of summer dust—

XXIV

"And ye with them will perish one by one—
  If I must sigh to think that this shall be—
If I must weep when the surviving Sun   235
  Shall smile on your decay—Oh, ask not me
To love you till your little race is run;
  I cannot die as ye must . . . over me
Your leaves shall glance—the streams in which ye dwell
Shall be my paths henceforth, and so, farewell!"   240

XXV

She spoke and wept—the dark and azure well
  Sparkled beneath the shower of her bright tears,
And every little circlet where they fell
  Flung to the cavern-roof inconstant spheres
And intertangled lines of light—a knell[4]   245
  Of sobbing voices came upon her ears
From those departing Forms, o'er the serene
Of the white streams and of the forest green.

XXVI

All day the wizard lady sate aloof
  Spelling out scrolls of dread antiquity,   250
Under the cavern's fountain-lighted roof;
  Or broidering the pictured poesy
Of some high tale upon her growing woof,[5]
  Which the sweet splendour of her smiles could dye
In hues outshining Heaven—and ever she   255
  Added some grace to the wrought poesy.

XXVII

While on her hearth lay blazing many a piece
  Of sandal wood, rare gums and cinnamon;
Men scarcely know how beautiful fire is—
  Each flame of it is as a precious stone   260
Dissolved in ever moving light, and this
  Belongs to each and all who gaze upon.

---

3. I.e., an attendant to an important person. The nymphs are beautiful young girls and inferior deities, each of whom lasts only as long as her special habitat: forests and trees (*Hamadryades*), mountains (*Oreads*), and fountains and streams (*Naiads*).

4. A doleful cry or dirge, reminiscent of a funeral bell.
5. The weft, or threads that cross at right angles to the warp (the lengthwise threads on the loom). In "Mont Blanc" (44) Shelley calls Poesy a witch.

The Witch beheld it not, for in her hand
She held a woof that dimmed the burning brand.[6]

XXVIII

This lady never slept, but lay in trance   265
    All night within the fountain—as in sleep. .
Its emerald crags glowed in her beauty's glance:
    Through the green splendour of the water deep
She saw the constellations reel and dance
    Like fire-flies—and withal[7] did ever keep   270
The tenour[8] of her contemplations calm,
With open eyes, closed feet and folded palm.

XXIX

And when the whirlwinds and the clouds descended
    From the white pinnacles of that cold hill
She past at dewfall to a space extended   275
    Where in a lawn of flowering asphodel
Amid a wood of pines and cedars blended
    There yawned an inextinguishable well
Of crimson fire, full even to the brim
And overflowing all the margin trim.   280

XXX

Within the which she lay when the fierce war
    Of wintry winds shook that innocuous liquor[9]
In many a mimic[1] moon and bearded star[2]
    O'er woods and lawns—the serpent heard it flicker
In sleep, and dreaming still, he crept afar—   285
    And when the windless snow descended thicker
Than autumn leaves she watched it as it came
Melt on the surface of the level flame.

XXXI

She had a Boat which some say Vulcan wrought
    For Venus, as the chariot of her star;[3]   290
But it was found too feeble to be fraught
    With all the ardours in that Sphere which are,
And so she sold it, and Apollo[4] bought
    And gave it to this daughter: from a car
Changed to the fairest and the lightest boat   295
Which ever upon mortal[5] stream did float.

XXXII

And others say, that when but three hours old
    The first-born Love out of his cradle leapt,[6]
And clove dun Chaos with his wings of gold,

6. Wood burning on the hearth; *woof:*
here, a piece of woven fabric.
7. Nevertheless.
8. The procedure or course of progress.
9. The fire.
1. An artistic or playful imitation of.
2. A comet with its tail (which always
points away from the sun) preceding it.
3. *Venus* is goddess of beauty, laughter,
grace, and pleasure, and mother of Love;

Vulcan, craftsman among the gods, is
her deformed husband.
4. The sun and inventor and god of the
fine arts, including medicine, poetry,
music, and eloquence.
5. I.e., accessible to human beings, as
opposed to the sphere of Venus.
6. Cf. Shelley's translation of Plato's
Symposium: "Hesiod says . . . that after
Chaos these two were produced, the

And like an horticultural adept,   300
Stole a strange seed, and wrapt it up in mould
    And sowed it in his mother's star,[7] and kept
Watering it all the summer with sweet dew,
And with his wings fanning it as it grew.

XXXIII

The plant grew strong and green—the snowy flower   305
    Fell, and the long and gourd-like fruit began
To turn the light and dew by inward power
    To its own substance; woven tracery ran
Of light firm texture, ribbed and branching, o'er
    The solid rind, like a leaf's veined fan—   310
Of which Love scooped this boat—and with soft motion
Piloted it round the circumfluous[8] Ocean.

XXXIV

This boat she moored upon her fount, and lit
    A living spirit within all its frame,
Breathing the soul of swiftness into it—   315
    Couched on the fountain, like a panther tame,
One of the twain at Evan's[9] feet that sit—
    Or as on Vesta's[1] sceptre a swift flame—
Or on blind Homer's heart a winged thought—
    In joyous expectation lay the Boat.   320

XXXV

Then by strange art she kneaded fire and snow
    Together, tempering the repugnant mass
With liquid love—all things together grow
    Through which the harmony of love can pass;
And a fair Shape out of her hands did flow—   325
    A living Image, which did far surpass
In beauty that bright shape of vital stone
Which drew the heart out of Pygmalion.[2]

XXXVI

A sexless thing it was, and in its growth
    It seemed to have developed no defect   330
Of either sex, yet all the grace of both—
    In gentleness and strength its limbs were decked;

Earth and Love"; *clove dun Chaos:* i.e., split (*clove*) the dark or murky (*dun*) void (*Chaos*).
7. The *star*, called Lucifer or the morning star, is actually the planet Venus. Here Shelley combines the myth from Hesiod with that of Cupid, the son of Venus.
8. Flowing around; in ancient geography, Ocean was thought to be a river flowing around the land.
9. *Evan's:* Bacchus' (Dionysus').
1. Roman goddess of the sacred hearth, which was tended by the vestal virgins.
2. *Pygmalion*, a legendary king of Cyprus, after he had vowed never to love a woman or to marry, sculptured and

fell in love with a beautiful statue, which Venus changed into a living (*vital*) woman in response to his prayers. (Ovid, *Metamorphoses*, X.) In the classical legend Hermaphroditus was the son of Hermes (Mercury) and Aphrodite (Venus); a nymph united her body with his, giving Hermaphroditus the perfect beauty of both sexes. Though the Witch's hermaphrodite is made of snow like the wicked witch's False Florimell in *The Faerie Queene*, III.viii.6, Spenser's creation is inhabited by an evil Sprite and contains wax, mercury, and vermilion instead of fire.

The bosom swelled lightly with its full youth—
   The countenance was such as might select
Some artist that his skill should never die,   335
Imaging forth such perfect purity.

XXXVII

From its smooth shoulders hung two rapid wings,
   Fit to have borne it to the seventh sphere,[3]
Tipt with the speed of liquid lightenings—
   Dyed in the ardours of the atmosphere—   340
She led her creature to the boiling springs
   Where the light boat was moored, and said: "Sit here!"
And pointed to the prow, and took her seat
Beside the rudder, with opposing feet.

XXXVIII

And down the streams which clove those mountains vast   345
   Around their inland islets, and amid
The panther-peopled forests, whose shade cast
   Darkness and odours and a pleasure hid
In melancholy gloom, the pinnace[4] past
   By many a star-surrounded pyramid   350
Of icy crag cleaving the purple sky
And caverns yawning round unfathomably.

XXXIX

The silver noon into that winding dell
   With slanted gleam athwart the forest tops
Tempered like golden evening, feebly fell;   355
   A green and glowing light like that which drops
From folded lilies in which glow worms dwell
   When Earth over her face night's mantle wraps;
Between the severed mountains lay on high
Over the stream, a narrow rift[5] of sky.   360

XL

And ever as she went, the Image lay
   With folded wings and unawakened eyes;
And o'er its gentle countenance did play
   The busy dreams, as thick as summer flies,
Chasing the rapid smiles that would not stay,   365
   And drinking the warm tears, and the sweet sighs
Inhaling, which, with busy murmur vain,
They had aroused from that full heart and brain.

XLI

And ever down the prone[6] vale, like a cloud
   Upon a stream of wind, the pinnace went;   370
Now lingering on the pools, in which abode
   The calm and darkness of the deep content

---

3. The transparent hollow globe carrying Saturn; this sphere was next to that of the fixed stars, according to classical and medieval astronomy.

4. A small boat.
5. Shelley reverses the normal usage: a break in the clouds or mist.
6. Having a descending slope.

In which they paused, now o'er the shallow road
  Of white and dancing waters all besprent[7]
With sand and polished pebbles . . mortal Boat   375
In such a shallow rapid could not float.

XLII

And down the earthquaking cataracts[8] which shiver
  Their snowlike waters into golden air,
Or under chasms unfathomable ever
  Sepulchre[9] them, till in their rage they tear   380
A subterranean portal for the river,
  It fled . . the circling sunbows[1] did upbear
Its fall down the hoar[2] precipice of spray,
Lighting it far upon its lampless way.

XLIII

And when the wizard lady would ascend   385
  The labyrinths of some many winding vale
Which to the inmost mountain upward tend—
  She called "Hermaphroditus!"—and the pale
And heavy hue which slumber could extend
  Over its lips and eyes, as on the gale   390
A rapid shadow from a slope of grass,
Into the darkness of the stream did pass.

XLIV

And it unfurled its heaven-coloured pinions[3]
  With stars of fire spotting the stream below;
And from above into the Sun's dominions   395
  Flinging a glory, like the golden glow
In which Spring clothes her emerald-winged minions,[4]
  All interwoven with fine feathery snow
And moonlight splendour of intensest rime[5]
With which Frost paints the pines in winter time.   400

XLV

And then it winnowed the Elysian[6] air
  Which ever hung about that lady bright,
With its ætherial vans—and speeding there
  Like a star up the torrent of the night
Or a swift eagle in the morning glare   405
  Breasting the whirlwind with impetuous flight,
The pinnace, oared by those enchanted wings,
Clove the fierce streams towards their upper springs.

XLVI

The water flashed, like sunlight by the prow
  Of a noon-wandering meteor[7] flung to Heaven;   410

---

7. Sprinkled or scattered.
8. Large waterfalls.
9. Entomb; the subject is *which* (377).
1. An arch of prismatic colors like a rainbow, formed by refraction of light in mist or vapor.
2. Grayish white.

3. *it:* the boat; *pinions:* wings.
4. Favorites or darlings.
5. Frozen mist.
6. Gloriously fragrant, as in Elysium, the Greek abode of the honorable dead; *winnowed:* beat or flapped.
7. A flash or reflection of light.

The still air seemed as if its waves did flow
    In tempest down the mountains—loosely driven
The lady's radiant hair streamed to and fro:
    Beneath, the billows[8] having vainly striven
Indignant and impetuous, roared to feel   415
The swift and steady motion of the keel.

XLVII

Or, when the weary moon was in the wane
    Or in the noon of interlunar[9] night
The lady-witch in visions could not chain
    Her spirit; but sailed forth under the light   420
Of shooting stars, and bade extend amain[1]
    Its storm-outspeeding wings, th' Hermaphrodite;
She to the Austral[2] waters took her way
Beyond the fabulous Thamondocana,[3]—

XLVIII

Where like a meadow which no scythe has shaven,   425
    Which rain could never bend, or whirl-blast shake,
With the Antarctic constellations paven,
    Canopus[4] and his crew, lay th' Austral lake—
There she would build herself a windless haven
    Out of the clouds whose moving turrets make   430
The bastions of the storm, when through the sky
The spirits of the tempest thundered by.

XLIX

A haven beneath whose translucent floor
    The tremulous stars sparkled unfathomably,
And around which, the solid vapours hoar,   435
    Based on the level waters, to the sky
Lifted their dreadful crags; and like a shore
    Of wintry mountains, inaccessibly
Hemmed in with rifts and precipices grey
And hanging crags, many a cove and bay.   440

L

And whilst the outer lake beneath the lash
    Of the wind's scourge,[5] foamed like a wounded thing,
And the incessant hail with stony clash
    Ploughed up the waters, and the flagging wing
Of the roused cormorant[6] in the lightning flash   445
    Looked like the wreck of some wind-wandering
Fragment of inky thundersmoke,—this haven
Was as a gem to copy Heaven engraven.[7]—

---

8. Great waves.
9. The period between the old and the new moon.
1. With full force and speed.
2. Of the Southern Hemisphere.
3. The ancient name for Tombouctou (Timbuktu), located in Mali, south of the Sahara Desert.

4. One of the brightest stars in the southern sky, in the constellation Argo.
5. A flail or whip.
6. Black sea bird about three feet long, noted for its voracious appetite.
7. I.e., was like a gem engraved with a copy of heaven.

LI

On which that lady played her many pranks,
　　Circling the image of a shooting star,　　　　　450
Even as a tyger on Hydaspes'[8] banks
　　Outspeeds the antelopes which speediest are,
In her light boat; and many quips[9] and cranks
　　She played upon the water, till the car
Of the late moon, like a sick matron wan,　　　　455
To journey from the misty east began.

LII

And then she called out of the hollow turrets
　　Of those high clouds, white, golden and vermilion,
The armies of her ministering Spirits—
　　In mighty legions million after million　　　　460
They came, each troop emblazoning its merits
　　On meteor flags,[1] and many a proud pavilion
Of the intertexture of the atmosphere
They pitched upon the plain of the calm mere.[2]

LIII

They framed the imperial tent of their great Queen　　465
　　Of woven exhalations,[3] underlaid
With lambent[4] lightning-fire, as may be seen
　　A dome of thin and open ivory inlaid
With crimson silk . . cressets[5] from the Serene
　　Hung there, and on the water for her tread　　470
A tapestry of fleecelike mist was strewn
Dyed in the beams of the ascending moon.

LIV

And on a throne o'erlaid with starlight, caught
　　Upon those wandering isles of aëry dew
Which highest shoals of mountain shipwreck not　　475
　　She sate, and heard all that had happened new
Between the earth and moon, since they had brought
　　The last intelligence—and now she grew
Pale as that moon lost in the watery night—
And now she wept and now she laughed outright.　　480

LV

These were tame pleasures—She would often climb
　　The steepest ladder of the crudded rack[6]
Up to some beaked cape of cloud sublime,
　　And like Arion on the dolphin's back[7]

8. A river of northeast Pakistan, now called the Jhelum; it marked the eastern limit of Alexander's conquests.
9. Fanciful turns of speech; *cranks:* odd or fantastic actions. The expression is from Milton's *L'Allegro*, 27.
1. I.e., inscribing conspicuously (*emblazoning*) on flashes of lightning (*meteor flags*). Shelley follows Milton's description of an "Empyreal Host of Angels" in *Paradise Lost*, V.583–594.
2. Lake.
3. Cf. Milton's Pandemonium: "a Fabric huge/Rose like an Exhalation" (*Paradise Lost*, I.710–711).
4. Shining with a soft, clear light without fierce heat.
5. Iron lamps (Milton's Pandemonium also contains cressets).
6. A bank of clouds (*rack*) resembling coagulated curds (*crudded*).
7. *Arion*, seventh-century B.C. lyric poet and musician, was threatened with death for his riches while aboard a ship but was saved when dolphins attracted by his music carried him away.

Ride singing through the shoreless air. Ofttime   485
   Following the serpent lightning's winding track
She ran upon the platforms of the wind
And laughed to hear the fireballs[8] roar behind.

LVI

And sometimes to those streams of upper air
   Which whirl the earth in its diurnal round   490
She would ascend, and win the spirits there
   To let her join their chorus. Mortals found
That on those days the sky was calm and fair,
   And mystic snatches of harmonious sound[9]
Wandered upon the earth where'er she past,   495
And happy thoughts of hope too sweet to last.

LVII

But her choice sport was, in the hours of sleep
   To glide adown old Nilus,[1] where he threads
Egypt and Æthiopia, from the steep
   Of utmost Axumè,[2] until he spreads,   500
Like a calm flock of silver-fleeced sheep,
   His waters on the plain: and crested heads
Of cities and proud temples gleam amid
And many a vapour[3]-belted pyramid.

LVIII

By Mœris and the Mareotid lakes,[4]   505
   Strewn with faint blooms like bridal chamber floors,
Where naked boys bridling tame Water snakes
   Or charioteering ghastly alligators
Had left on the sweet waters mighty wakes
   Of those huge forms—within the brazen doors   510
Of the great Labyrinth[5] slept both boy and beast,
Tired with the pomp of their Osirian feast.[6]

LIX

And where within the surface of the River
   The shadows of the massy[7] temples lie
And never are erased—but tremble ever   515
   Like things which every cloud can doom to die

---

8. Lightning in a globular form.
9. Lines 489–494 allude to the music of the spheres. (Cf. *Prometheus Unbound*, IV.186–188, and "With a Guitar. To Jane," 75–78.)
1. The Nile River.
2. Probably the present site of Aksum in mountainous northeast Ethiopia.
3. Mist or fog.
4. Lake Mareotis is located in the Nile Delta; Lake Moeris (now called Birket-Qarun) is southwest of Cairo and about 120 miles southeast of Lake Mareotis.
5. A magnificent tomb and commemorative structure of Egyptian royalty, containing 3,000 chambers.
6. Osiris, one of the chief Egyptian gods,
was variously considered to be a son of Jupiter or Saturn. In legends he is depicted as a wise and good king of Egypt who taught his people agriculture, good morals, and civilized ways and, as a bloodless conqueror (like Dionysus) of other peoples, bringing them civilization. The most important religious myths depict him as a vegetation god, killed and cut to pieces by Set or Typhon and then brought together and revived by his wife Isis and their son Horus. Thus he was identified by comparative mythologists with Adonis and with various aspects of Christ.
7. Massive.

Through lotus-pav'n canals, and wheresoever
   The works of man pierced that serenest sky
With tombs, and towers, and fanes,[8] 'twas her delight
To wander in the shadow of the night.   520

LX

With motion like the spirit of that wind
   Whose soft step deepens slumber, her light feet
Past through the peopled haunts of humankind;
   Scattering sweet visions from her presence sweet
Through fane and palace court and labyrinth mined   525
   With many a dark and subterranean street
Under the Nile, through chambers high and deep
She past, observing mortals in their sleep.—

LXI

A pleasure sweet doubtless it was to see
   Mortals subdued in all the shapes of sleep.   530
Here lay two sister-twins in infancy;
   There, a lone youth who in his dreams did weep;
Within, two lovers linked innocently
   In their loose locks which over both did creep
Like ivy from one stem—and there lay calm   535
Old age with snow bright hair and folded palm.

LXII

But other troubled forms of sleep she saw,
   Not to be mirrored in a holy song—
Distortions foul of supernatural awe,
   And pale imaginings of visioned wrong   540
And all the code of custom's lawless law
   Written upon the brows of old and young:
"This," said the wizard maiden, "is the strife
Which stirs the liquid[9] surface of man's life."

LXIII

And little did the sight disturb her soul—   545
   We, the weak mariners of that wide lake
Where'er its shores extend or billows roll,
   Our course unpiloted and starless make
O'er its wild surface to an unknown goal—
   But she in the calm depths her way could take   550
Where in bright bowers immortal forms abide
Beneath the weltering[1] of the restless tide.

LXIV

And she saw princes couched under the glow
   Of sunlike gems, and round each temple-court
In dormitories ranged, row after row,   555
   She saw the priests asleep—all of one sort
For all were educated to be so—
   The peasants in their huts, and in the port

---

8. Temples.   1. Surging.
9. I.e., changeable in shape.

The sailors she saw cradled on the waves,
And the dead lulled within their dreamless graves.   560

LXV

And all the forms in which those spirits lay
   Were to her sight like the diaphanous
Veils, in which those sweet ladies oft array
   Their delicate limbs, who would conceal from us
Only their scorn of all concealment: they   565
   Move in the light of their own beauty thus.
But these and all now lay with sleep upon them
And little thought a Witch was looking on them.

LXVI

She, all those human figures breathing there
   Beheld as living spirits—to her eyes   570
The naked beauty of the soul lay bare,
   And often through a rude and worn disguise
She saw the inner form most bright and fair—
   And then, she had a charm of strange device,
Which murmured on mute lips with tender tone,   575
Could make that Spirit mingle with her own. ·

LXVII

Alas, Aurora! what wouldst thou have given
   For such a charm when Tithon became grey?[2]
Or how much, Venus, of thy silver Heaven
   Wouldst thou have yielded, ere Proserpina   580
Had half (oh! why not all?) the debt forgiven
   Which dear Adonis had been doomed to pay,[3]
To any witch who would have taught you it?
The Heliad[4] doth not know its value yet.

LXVIII

Tis said in after times her spirit free   585
   Knew what love was, and felt itself alone—
But holy Dian could not chaster be
   Before she stooped to kiss Endymion[5]
Than now this lady—like a sexless bee[6]
   Tasting all blossoms and confined to none—   590
Among those mortal forms the wizard-maiden
Passed with an eye serene and heart unladen.

2. Aurora (Eos in Greek), goddess of the dawn, loved Tithonus and at her request Zeus gave him immortality, but she forgot to ask also for the gift of eternal youth. When old age made him decrepit, she changed him into a cicada (see note to line 108).
3. Adonis, beloved of Venus, was killed while hunting a wild boar; Proserpina (Greek Persephone), queen of the underworld and wife of Pluto (Hades), restored Adonis to life on the condition that he spend six months with Venus and the rest of the year with her.
4. The Witch of Atlas; literally, child of Helius, or the sun.
5. Diana, goddess of the moon, was so enamored by the beauty of Endymion, a shepherd of Caria (modern Turkey), that she descended nightly from heaven to make love to him as he slept his eternal sleep on Mt. Latmos.
6. The undeveloped female (neuter) bee is the worker that produces wax, collects honey, and stores it up for food in the winter.

LXIX

To those she saw most beautiful, she gave
　　Strange panacea[7] in a chrystal bowl . . .
They drank in their deep sleep of that sweet wave—　　595
　　And lived thenceforward as if some control
Mightier than life, were in them; and the grave
　　Of such, when death oppressed the weary soul,
Was as a green and overarching bower
Lit by the gems of many a starry flower.　　600

LXX

For on the night that they were buried, she
　　Restored the embalmer's ruining, and shook
The light out of the funeral lamps, to be
　　A mimic[8] day within that deathly nook;
And she unwound the woven imagery　　605
　　Of second childhood's swaddling bands and took
The coffin, its last cradle, from its niche
And threw it with contempt into a ditch.

LXXI

And there the body lay, age after age,
　　Mute, breathing, beating, warm and undecaying　　610
Like one asleep in a green hermitage
　　With gentle smiles about its eyelids playing
And living in its dreams beyond the rage
　　Of death or life, while they were still arraying
In liveries ever new, the rapid, blind　　615
And fleeting generations of mankind.

LXXII

And she would write strange dreams upon the brain
　　Of those who were less beautiful, and make
All harsh and crooked purposes more vain
　　Than in the desert is the serpent's wake　　620
Which the sand covers—all his evil gain
　　The miser in such dreams would rise and shake
Into a beggar's lap—the lying scribe[9]
Would his own lies betray without a bribe.

LXXIII

The priests would write an explanation full,　　625
　　Translating hieroglyphics into Greek,
How the god Apis, really was a bull[1]
　　And nothing more; and bid the herald stick
The same against the temple doors, and pull
　　The old cant down; they licensed all to speak　　630

---

7. A medicine reputed to heal all diseases.
8. Artistic imitation.
9. A public official in charge of writing and keeping accounts.

1. A bull, supposedly the Egyptian god Apis, with special marking was much venerated, with a festival, consultation for omens, and offerings of money.

Whate'er they thought of hawks and cats and geese[2]
By pastoral letters to each diocese.

LXXIV

The king would dress an ape up in his crown
  And robes, and seat him on his glorious seat,[3]
And on the right hand of the sunlike throne   635
  Would place a gaudy mock-bird to repeat
The chatterings of the monkey.—Every one
  Of the prone courtiers crawled to kiss the feet
Of their great Emperor when the morning came,
And kissed—alas, how many kiss the same!   640

LXXV

The soldiers dreamed that they were blacksmiths, and
  Walked out of quarters in somnambulism,
Round the red anvils you might see them stand
  Like Cyclopses in Vulcan's sooty abysm,[4]
Beating their swords to ploughshares[5]—in a band   645
  The jailors sent those of the liberal schism
Free through the streets of Memphis, much, I wis,[6]
To the annoyance of king Amasis.[7]

LXXVI

And timid lovers who had been so coy
  They hardly knew whether they loved or not,   650
Would rise out of their rest, and take sweet joy
  To the fulfillment of their inmost thought;
And when next day the maiden and the boy
  Met one another, both, like sinners caught,
Blushed at the thing which each believed was done   655
Only in fancy[8]—till the tenth moon shone;

LXXVII

And then the Witch would let them take no ill:
  Of many thousand schemes which lovers find
The Witch found one,—and so they took their fill
  Of happiness in marriage warm and kind;   660
Friends who by practice of some envious skill,
  Were torn apart, a wide wound, mind from mind!
She did unite again with visions clear
Of deep affection and of truth sincere.

---

2. The hawk was sacred to Horus. Diana
Bubastis transformed herself into a cat
when the gods fled into Egypt. Though
the sacred geese of Juno's temple were
famous for warning the besieged Ro-
mans of the Gauls' attack on the Capito-
line Hill, the reference to geese as
Egyptian gods may be intended as the
reductio ad absurdum of animal wor-
ship, because "goose" was a name com-
monly applied in Shelley's time to a
foolish person ("silly goose").
3. Cf. Spenser's *Prosopopoia*, in which
the Ape "upon his head/The Crowne,
and on his backe the skin he did,/And

the false Foxe him helped to array"
(1061–1063).
4. Vulcan, god of fire and patron of
artists who worked metals, forged Jupi-
ter's thunderbolts and arms for heroes
and gods with the aid of the Cyclopes
under Mt. Aetna in Sicily.
5. Micah 4:3.
6. I.e., "I know"; a corruption of "iwis,"
an adverb meaning "certainly."
7. Amasis (570–526 B.C.), according to
Herodotus (II.161ff.), was a man who
rose from a common soldier to king of
Egypt.
8. Fantasy or dream.

LXXVIII

These were the pranks she played among the cities 665
 Of mortal men, and what she did to sprites
And gods, entangling them in her sweet ditties
 To do her will, and shew their subtle slights,
I will declare another time; for it is
 A tale more fit for the weird winter nights 670
Than for these garish summer days, when we
Scarcely believe much more than we can see.

Song of Apollo[1]

The sleepless Hours who watch me as I lie
 Curtained with star-enwoven tapestries
From the broad moonlight of the open sky;
 Fanning the busy dreams from my dim eyes,
Waken me when their mother, the grey Dawn, 5
Tells them that Dreams and that the moon is gone.

Then I arise; and climbing Heaven's blue dome,
 I walk over the mountains and the waves,
Leaving my robe upon the Ocean foam.
 My footsteps pave the clouds with fire; the caves 10
Are filled with my bright presence, and the air
Leaves the green Earth to my embraces bare.

The sunbeams are my shafts with which I kill
 Deceit, that loves the night and fears the day.
All men who do, or even imagine ill 15
 Fly me;[2] and from the glory of my ray
Good minds, and open actions take new might
Until diminished, by the reign of night.

I feed the clouds, the rainbows and the flowers
 With their ætherial colours; the moon's globe 20
And the pure stars in their eternal bowers
 Are cinctured[3] with my power as with a robe;
Whatever lamps on Earth or Heaven may shine
Are portions of one spirit; which is mine.

1. The following two "Songs" were written in 1820 by Shelley for inclusion in Mary Shelley's mythological drama *Midas*. In Mary's blank verse play, as in the well-known account in Ovid's *Metamorphoses* (Book XI, fables 4 and 5), Midas arrives on the scene just as Tmolus, spirit of the mountain of the same name, is about to judge a singing contest between Apollo and Pan. In Ovid's version Pan sings first and Apollo overpowers him; Mary Shelley reverses the order of the contest, having Apollo perform first and leaving the last word to Pan. Shelley's poems, each thirty-six lines long, tend to give static power and dignity (along with considerable self-satisfaction) to Apollo and a historical progression toward a tragedy (and, hence, considerable human sympathy) to Pan.

 Mary could not find a publisher for her verse drama and published Shelley's poems under the titles "Hymn of Apollo" and "Hymn of Pan" in Shelley's *Posthumous Poems* (1824). The present texts are based on Shelley's draft in Bodleian MS. Shelley adds. e.6, pp. 23–29.

2. Flee from me.

3. Encircled, girdled.

I stand at noon upon the peak of Heaven;   25
 Then with unwilling steps, I linger down
Into the clouds of the Atlantic even.
 For grief that I depart they weep and frown—
What look is more delightful, than the smile
With which I soothe them from the Western isle?   30

I am the eye with which the Universe
 Beholds itself, and knows it is divine.
All harmony of instrument and verse,
 All prophecy and medicine are mine;
All light of art[4] or nature—to my song   35
Victory and praise, in its own right, belong.

Song of Pan

From the forests and highlands
 We come, we come,
From the river-girt islands
 Where loud waves were dumb
Listening my sweet pipings.   5
  The wind in the reeds and the rushes,
  The bees on the bells of thyme,
  The birds in the myrtle bushes,
  The cicadæ above in the lime,
   And the lizards below in the grass,   10
Were silent as even old Tmolus was,
  Listening my sweet pipings.

Liquid Peneus was flowing—
 And all dark Tempe lay
In Olympus' shadow,[5] outgrowing   15
 The light of the dying day,
 Speeded with my sweet pipings.
  The sileni and sylvans and fauns[6]
  And the nymphs of the woods and the waves,
  To the edge of the moist river-lawns   20
  And the brink of the dewy caves,
   And all that did then attend and follow
Were as silent for love, as you now, Apollo,
  For envy of my sweet pipings.

---

4. Apollo, god of the fine arts, music, poetry, eloquence, and medicine, received from Jupiter the power of knowing the future and was the only god whose oracles were in general repute throughout the ancient world.
5. *Peneus:* a river in Thessaly that flows northeastward through the beautiful Val-ley of *Tempe,* which lies between Mt. *Olympus* to the northwest and Mt. Ossa to the southeast.
6. *sileni, sylvans,* and *fauns* are various male woodland and rural demigods, like satyrs. The *nymphs* are their (beautiful) female equivalents.

I sang of the dancing stars, 25
  I sang of the dædal[7] Earth,
And of Heaven, and the giant wars,[8]
  And Love and Death and Birth;
    And then I changed my pipings,
    Singing how, down the vales of Mænalus 30
    I pursued a maiden and clasped a reed.[9]
  Gods and men, we are all deluded thus!—
  It breaks in our bosom and then we bleed;
    They wept as, I think, both ye[1] now would,
If envy or age had not frozen your blood, 35
    At the sorrow of my sweet pipings.

The Indian Girl's Song[2]

I arise from dreams of thee
In the first sleep of night—
The winds are breathing low
And the stars are burning bright.
I arise from dreams of thee— 5
And a spirit in my feet
Has borne me—Who knows how?
To thy chamber window, sweet!—

The wandering airs they faint
On the dark silent stream— 10
The champak[3] odours fail
Like sweet thoughts in a dream;
The nightingale's complaint—
It dies upon her heart—
As I must die on thine 15
O beloved as thou art!

7. Intricately, artistically wrought (after Daedalus).
8. The giants, who first aided Zeus (Jupiter) and the Olympians in their overthrow of the Titans, later rose up and attacked the Olympian gods, who—after a severe fright—defeated them with the help of Hercules.
9. The nymph Syrinx, when Pan tried to make love to her, was turned into a reed (from which Pan made his musical pipes). *Mænalus:* a mountain in Arcadia sacred to Pan.
1. Apollo and Tmolus; the first is accused of being silent through *envy*, the second because of *age*.
2. The title of this poem has proved to be the key to its meaning. For some years critics hostile to Shelley's poetry used this minor lyric as an example of Shelley's "sentimental" poetry. Students

of Shelley's major works realized that this was unfair, pointing out the titles under which the poem had been known—"Song, Written for an Indian Air" (as first published in the *Liberal*, no. II, 1823), "Lines to an Indian Air" (*Posthumous Poems*, 1824), and "The Indian Serenade" (transcripts by Mary Shelley in *The Harvard Shelley Notebook* and the Pierpont Morgan Library). The reemergence in 1962 of Shelley's own fair copy entitled "The Indian Girl's Song" (first published by Chernaik, *The Lyrics of Shelley*, 1972) shows that the poem is purely dramatic. On the general problem of dramatic personae in Shelley's poetry see G. M. Matthews' essay "Shelley's Lyrics," pp. 681–694 below.
3. One species of magnolia, a tree of India bearing highly fragrant orange flowers.

O lift me from the grass!
I die, I faint, I fail!
Let thy love in kisses rain
On my lips and eyelids pale.   20
My cheek is cold and white, alas!
My heart beats loud and fast.
Oh press it close to thine again
Where it will break at last.

Song[4]

Rarely, rarely comest thou,
    Spirit of Delight!
Wherefore hast thou left me now
    Many a day and night?
Many a weary night and day   5
'Tis since thou art fled away.

How shall ever one like me
    Win thee back again?
With the joyous and the free
    Thou wilt scoff at pain.   10
Spirit false! thou hast forgot
All but those who need thee not.

As a lizard with the shade
    Of a trembling leaf,
Thou with sorrow art dismayed;   15
    Even the sighs of grief
Reproach thee, that thou art not near,
And reproach thou wilt not hear.

Let me set my mournful ditty
    To a merry measure;   20
Thou wilt never come for pity—
    Thou wilt come for pleasure;
Pity then will cut away
Those cruel wings, and thou wilt stay.—

I love all that thou lovest,   25
    Spirit of Delight!
The fresh Earth in new leaves drest,
    And the starry night,
Autumn evening, and the morn
When the golden mists are born.   30

4. Shelley's holograph fair copy of this poem in *The Harvard Shelley Notebook* is dated "Pisa—May—1820." The lyric gives every indication of being a highly successful conventional exercise; Shelley did not, apparently, think this poem important enough to include among those he had Mary transcribe for inclusion in *Prometheus Unbound* in mid-May 1820. It first appeared in *Posthumous Poems* (1824).

> I love snow, and all the forms
>   Of the radiant frost;
> I love waves and winds and storms—
>   Every thing almost
> Which is Nature's and may be   35
> Untainted by man's misery.

> I love tranquil Solitude,
>   And such society
> As is quiet, wise and good;
>   Between thee and me   40
> What difference? but thou dost possess
> The things I seek—not love them less.

> I love Love—though he has wings,
>   And like light can flee—
> But above all other things,   45
>   Spirit, I love thee—
> Thou art Love and Life! O come,
> Make once more my heart thy home.

Epipsychidion

In late November 1820, Mary Shelley and Claire Clairmont were introduced to Teresa Viviani, the nineteen-year-old daughter of the governor of Pisa, who was confined in the Convent of St. Anna there. Shelley—always aroused by the sight of teen-age girls confined by strict (or tyrannical) fathers—took an interest in Teresa; he, Mary, and Claire all visited and corresponded with her until her arranged marriage (September 8, 1821). Teresa's biographer has argued that the Shelleys referred to her as "Emilia" because her position in a triangle involving two suitors was analogous to that of Emilia, the heroine of Boccaccio's *Teseida* (the story that was the model for Chaucer's *Knight's Tale*).

Shelley composed the lines that were to become *Epipsychidion* amid a welter of other verses that were later sorted out to form two fragmentary narrative poems on Italian themes—"Ginevra" and "Fiordispina." On February 16, 1821, Shelley sent the (now lost) fair copy of *Epipsychidion* to his publisher Charles Ollier, asking him to publish it anonymously: "indeed, in a certain sense, it is a production of a portion of me already dead; and in this sense the advertisement is no fiction" (*Letters*, II, 262–263). After Shelley's death Ollier told Mary Shelley that "it was the wish of Mr. Shelley that the whole of the 'Epipsychidion' should be suppressed"; he turned over to John Hunt (on Mary's instructions) a remainder of 160 copies. (This shows that at least 200 or 250 copies were printed.) One reason for the poem's suppression is cited in a letter published in *Blackwood's Edinburgh Magazine* over the pseudonym "John Johnes," who was apparently Ollier himself: "The poem was published anonymously, but as people began to apply it to a certain individual, and make their own inferences, it was, I believe, suddenly withdrawn from circulation." Shelley later wrote to John Gisborne: "The 'Epipsychidion' I cannot look at; . . .

If you are anxious, however, to hear what I am and have been, it will tell you something thereof. It is an idealized history of my life and feelings" (*Letters*, II, 434).

In addition to Shelley's indications of deep personal involvement in the sentiments of *Epipsychidion* (and Mary Shelley's failure to write a note on this alone among Shelley's major poems), we have the evidence of the text itself that it involves the core of Shelley's personal aspirations. Kenneth Neill Cameron's essay "The Planet-Tempest Passage in *Epipsychidion*," reprinted below (pp. 637–658), judiciously sorts out the probable significance of some of the allegorized autobiography. At the same time, it has been cogently argued that the poem is essentially about the role of poetry as the most appropriate object of human desires. Those who accept this view base their analysis on the comparison of this work with Dante's *Vita Nuova*, to which Shelley calls attention in his Advertisement, and with the biblical Song of Solomon or Song of Songs, to the language and imagery of which there are frequent parallels in *Epipsychidion*.

In the absence of a fair copy manuscript, our sole textual authority of any consequence is the first edition of 1821. We have normalized a few spellings according to Shelley's consistent practice (e.g., *Ay* to *Aye* in line 33) and have adopted a few minor or conventional changes included in other editions (such as italicizing the words "*Vita Nuova*" in the Advertisement), but have otherwise followed the printed text that is based on Shelley's final holograph.

Epipsychidion can be divided into the following major sections: (1) lines 1–189 tell of the poet's relationship to "Emily"—first in an invocation (1–71), then in an allegorical history of his encounter with her (72–129), and finally in an address to her about the nature of love (130–189); (2) lines 190–383 form the main part of the "idealized history of [Shelley's] life and feelings," concluding with an address to Emily, Mary Shelley, and (probably) Claire Clairmont under the symbols Sun, Moon, and Comet, respectively; (3) after a short transitional prayerful address to Emily, Shelley concludes the poem proper with a proposal that Emily elope with him to an island paradise; and (4) the concluding envoy addressed to the poem.

Shelley's title is coined from the Greek preposition *epi-* (upon) and the diminutive noun *psychidion* ("little soul") and means "On the Subject of the Soul" (as in the Emperor Hadrian's poem *De animula*).

Epipsychidion:

VERSES ADDRESSED TO THE NOBLE AND UNFORTUNATE LADY,
EMILIA V———, NOW IMPRISONED IN THE CONVENT OF ———

L'anima amante si slancia fuori del creato, e si crea nel infinito un
Mondo tutto per essa, diverso assai da questo oscuro e pauroso baratro.
HER OWN WORDS.[1]

ADVERTISEMENT

The Writer of the following Lines died at Florence, as he was preparing for a voyage to one of the wildest of the Sporades, which he had bought, and where he had fitted up the ruins of an old building, and where it was his hope to have realised a scheme of life, suited perhaps to that happier and better world of which he is now an inhabitant, but hardly practicable in this. His life was singular; less on account of the romantic vicissitudes which diversified it, than the ideal tinge which it received from his own character and feelings. The present Poem, like the *Vita Nuova* of Dante, is sufficiently intelligible to a certain class of readers without a matter-of-fact history of the circumstances to which it relates; and to a certain other class it must ever remain incomprehensible, from a defect of a common organ of perception for the ideas of which it treats. Not but that, *gran vergogna sarebbe a colui, che rimasse cosa sotto veste di figura, o di colore rettorico: e domandato non sapesse denudare le sue parole da cotal veste, in guisa che avessero verace intendimento.*[2]

The present poem appears to have been intended by the Writer as the dedication to some longer one. The stanza on the opposite page[3] is almost a literal translation from Dante's famous Canzone

> *Voi, ch' intendendo, il terzo ciel movete, etc.*

The presumptuous application of the concluding lines to his own composition will raise a smile at the expense of my unfortunate friend: be it a smile not of contempt, but pity.   S.

> My Song, I fear that thou wilt find but few
> Who fitly shall conceive thy reasoning,
> Of such hard matter dost thou entertain;

1. The quotation from Teresa Viviani may be translated: "The loving soul launches beyond creation, and creates for itself in the infinite a world all its own, far different from this dark and terrifying gulf."
2. "Great would be his shame who should rhyme anything under the garb of metaphor or rhetorical figure; and, being requested, could not strip his words of this dress so that they might have a true meaning."
3. I.e., the nine lines that follow, which are translated from the final lines of the first *canzone* of Dante's *Convito*, Trattato II. The opening line may be translated, "Ye who intelligent, the third sphere move . . ." (see note to line 117).

Whence, if by misadventure, chance should bring
Thee to base company (as chance may do),
Quite unaware of what thou dost contain,
I prithee, comfort thy sweet self again,
My last delight! tell them that they are dull,
And bid them own that thou art beautiful.

EPIPSYCHIDION

Sweet Spirit! Sister of that orphan one,
Whose empire is the name thou weepest on,[4]
In my heart's temple I suspend to thee
These votive[5] wreaths of withered memory.

Poor captive bird! who, from thy narrow cage,   5
Pourest such music, that it might assuage
The rugged hearts of those who prisoned thee,
Were they not deaf to all sweet melody;
This song shall be thy rose: its petals pale
Are dead, indeed, my adored Nightingale!   10
But soft and fragrant is the faded blossom,
And it has no thorn left to wound thy bosom.

High, spirit-winged Heart! who dost for ever
Beat thine unfeeling bars with vain endeavour,
'Till those bright plumes of thought, in which arrayed   15
It over-soared this low and worldly shade,
Lie shattered; and thy panting, wounded breast
Stains with dear blood its unmaternal nest!
I weep vain tears: blood would less bitter be,
Yet poured forth gladlier, could it profit thee.   20

Seraph of Heaven![6] too gentle to be human,
Veiling beneath that radiant form of Woman
All that is insupportable in thee
Of light, and love, and immortality!
Sweet Benediction in the eternal Curse!   25
Veiled Glory of this lampless Universe!
Thou Moon beyond the clouds! Thou living Form
Among the Dead! Thou Star above the Storm!
Thou Wonder, and thou Beauty, and thou Terror!
Thou Harmony of Nature's art! Thou Mirror   30
In whom, as in the splendour of the Sun,

4. From Shelley's own Italian version of
these lines, it appears that the *orphan
one* is Shelley's soul, to which Teresa's
Sweet Spirit is a sister. The word
"Percy" means "lost" (*persi*) in Italian.
A contrary explanation sees *that orphan
one* as Mary Shelley's soul, in which
case the *empire* would be the name of
"wife" or "Mrs. Shelley." In Teresa's
correspondence with Shelley and Mary
she called and referred to them as her
"Brother" and "Sister."
5. Consecrated or dedicated, in fulfill-
ment of a vow.
6. In medieval and Renaissance theology
the Seraphim, excelling in love, were
the highest of the nine orders of angels,
just above the Cherubim (who excelled
in wisdom). Milton first used the singu-
lar form "seraph" in English (*Paradise
Lost*, III.667).

All shapes look glorious which thou gazest on!
Aye, even the dim words which obscure thee now
Flash, lightning-like, with unaccustomed glow;
I pray thee that thou blot from this sad song   35
All of its much mortality and wrong,
With those clear drops, which start like sacred dew
From the twin lights thy sweet soul darkens through,
Weeping, till sorrow becomes ecstasy:
Then smile on it, so that it may not die.   40

    I never thought before my death to see
Youth's vision thus made perfect. Emily,
I love thee; though the world by no thin name
Will hide that love from its unvalued[7] shame.
Would we two had been twins of the same mother![8]   45
Or, that the name my heart lent to another
Could be a sister's bond for her and thee,
Blending two beams of one eternity!
Yet were one lawful and the other true,
These names, though dear, could paint not, as is due,   50
How beyond refuge I am thine. Ah me!
I am not thine: I am a part of *thee*.

    Sweet Lamp! my moth-like Muse has burnt its wings;
Or, like a dying swan who soars and sings,[9]
Young Love should teach Time, in his own grey style,   55
All that thou art. Art thou not void of guile,
A lovely soul formed to be blest and bless?
A well of sealed and secret happiness,
Whose waters like blithe light and music are,
Vanquishing dissonance and gloom? A Star   60
Which moves not in the moving Heavens, alone?[1]
A smile amid dark frowns? a gentle tone
Amid rude voices? a beloved light?
A Solitude, a Refuge, a Delight?
A lute, which those whom love has taught to play   65
Make music on, to soothe the roughest day
And lull fond[2] grief asleep? a buried treasure?
A cradle of young thoughts of wingless pleasure?
A violet-shrouded grave of Woe?[3]—I measure
The world of fancies, seeking one like thee,   70
And find—alas! mine own infirmity.

7. Extremely great.
8. Cf. the Song of Songs: "O that thou wert as my brother, that sucked the breasts of my mother! . . . I would kiss thee; yea, I should not be despised" (8:1).
9. According to classical and medieval fables, the swan, mute in its lifetime, was supposed to fly and sing a beautiful, plaintive song just before its death ("swan song").
1. I.e., the polestar, around which all the other "fixed" stars seem to move as the earth rotates and revolves around the sun.
2. Trivial or unreasonable.
3. The violet, a persistent perennial which blooms early in the spring, recurs as one of Shelley's symbols of rebirth and hope.

She met me, Stranger,[4] upon life's rough way,
And lured me towards sweet Death; as Night by Day,
Winter by Spring, or Sorrow by swift Hope,
Led into light, life, peace. An antelope,   75
In the suspended impulse of its lightness,
Were less ethereally light: the brightness
Of her divinest presence trembles through
Her limbs, as underneath a cloud of dew
Embodied in the windless Heaven of June   80
Amid the splendour-winged stars, the Moon
Burns, inextinguishably beautiful:
And from her lips, as from a hyacinth full
Of honey-dew,[5] a liquid murmur drops,
Killing the sense with passion; sweet as stops   85
Of planetary music[6] heard in trance.
In her mild lights the starry spirits dance,
The sun-beams of those wells which ever leap
Under the lightnings of the soul—too deep
For the brief fathom-line[7] of thought or sense.   90
The glory of her being, issuing thence,
Stains the dead, blank, cold air with a warm shade
Of unentangled intermixture, made
By Love, of light and motion: one intense
Diffusion, one serene Omnipresence,   95
Whose flowing outlines mingle in their flowing,
Around her cheeks and utmost fingers glowing
With the unintermitted blood,[8] which there
Quivers, (as in a fleece of snow-like air
The crimson pulse of living morning quiver,)   100
Continuously prolonged, and ending never,
Till they are lost, and in that Beauty furled
Which penetrates and clasps and fills the world;
Scarce visible from extreme loveliness.
Warm fragrance seems to fall from her light dress,   105
And her loose hair; and where some heavy tress
The air of her own speed has disentwined,
The sweetness seems to satiate the faint wind;
And in the soul a wild odour is felt,
Beyond the sense, like fiery dews that melt   110
Into the bosom of a frozen bud.—
See where she stands! a mortal shape indued
With love and life and light and deity,
And motion which may change but cannot die;
An image of some bright Eternity;   115

4. From Shelley's draft it is clear that "Stranger" is the unknown reader of the poem, addressed directly.
5. A sweet, sticky substance found on plants in very hot weather (Shelley repeats the phrase at 262; it also appears in Coleridge's "Kubla Khan," 53).
6. The harmonious music of the spheres was supposed to have been audible by human beings in the state of innocence, or, since then, in ecstasy.
7. A weighted line thrown over the side of a boat to measure the depth of water.
8. Uninterrupted.

A shadow of some golden dream; a Splendour
Leaving the third sphere pilotless;[9] a tender
Reflection of the eternal Moon of Love
Under whose motions life's dull billows move;
A Metaphor of Spring and Youth and Morning;   120
A Vision like incarnate April, warning,
With smiles and tears, Frost the Anatomy[1]
Into his summer grave.

            Ah, woe is me!
What have I dared? where am I lifted? how
Shall I descend, and perish not? I know   125
That Love makes all things equal: I have heard
By mine own heart this joyous truth averred:
The spirit of the worm beneath the sod
In love and worship, blends itself with God.

Spouse! Sister! Angel! Pilot of the Fate   130
Whose course has been so starless! O too late
Beloved! O too soon adored, by me!
For in the fields of immortality[2]
My spirit should at first have worshipped thine,
A divine presence in a place divine;   135
Or should have moved beside it on this earth,
A shadow of that substance, from its birth;
But not as now:—I love thee; yes, I feel
That on the fountain of my heart a seal[3]
Is set, to keep its waters pure and bright   140
For thee, since in those *tears* thou hast delight.
We—are we not formed, as notes of music are,
For one another, though dissimilar;
Such difference without discord, as can make
Those sweetest sounds, in which all spirits shake   145
As trembling leaves in a continuous air?

Thy wisdom speaks in me, and bids me dare
Beacon the rocks on which high hearts are wreckt.
I never was attached to that great sect,
Whose doctrine is, that each one should select   150
Out of the crowd a mistress or a friend,
And all the rest, though fair and wise, commend
To cold oblivion, though it is in the code
Of modern morals, and the beaten road
Which those poor slaves with weary footsteps tread,   155
Who travel to their home among the dead

9. *Splendour . . . pilotless: Splendor* is
one of Dante's words for angels; the
third sphere in Dante's cosmology was
that of Venus, the realm of lovers (cf.
Advertisement).

1. Skeleton.
2. The Elysian fields, the classical abode
of the blessed after death.
3. Symbol of a covenant.

By the broad highway of the world, and so
With one chained friend, perhaps a jealous foe,
The dreariest and the longest journey go.

True Love in this differs from gold and clay, 160
That to divide is not to take away.
Love is like understanding, that grows bright,
Gazing on many truths; 'tis like thy light,
Imagination! which from earth and sky,
And from the depths of human phantasy, 165
As from a thousand prisms and mirrors, fills
The Universe with glorious beams, and kills
Error, the worm, with many a sun-like arrow
Of its reverberated lightning.[4] Narrow
The heart that loves, the brain that contemplates, 170
The life that wears, the spirit that creates
One object, and one form, and builds thereby
A sepulchre for its eternity.

Mind from its object differs most in this:
Evil from good; misery from happiness; 175
The baser from the nobler; the impure
And frail, from what is clear and must endure.
If you divide suffering and dross,[5] you may
Diminish till it is consumed away;
If you divide pleasure and love and thought, 180
Each part exceeds the whole; and we know not
How much, while any yet remains unshared,
Of pleasure may be gained, of sorrow spared:
This truth is that deep well, whence sages draw
The unenvied light of hope; the eternal law 185
By which those live, to whom this world of life
Is as a garden ravaged,[6] and whose strife
Tills for the promise of a later birth
The wilderness of this Elysian earth.

There was a Being whom my spirit oft 190
Met on its visioned wanderings, far aloft,
In the clear golden prime of my youth's dawn,
Upon the fairy isles of sunny lawn,
Amid the enchanted mountains, and the caves
Of divine sleep, and on the air-like waves 195
Of wonder-level dream, whose tremulous floor
Paved her light steps;—on an imagined shore,
Under the grey beak of some promontory
She met me, robed in such exceeding glory,

4. An allusion to Apollo's slaying of
Python, a monstrous serpent.
5. Worthless, impure matter.

6. See "The Sensitive-Plant," pp. 210–
219.

That I beheld her not. In solitudes   200
Her voice came to me through the whispering woods,
And from the fountains, and the odours deep
Of flowers, which, like lips murmuring in their sleep
Of the sweet kisses which had lulled them there,
Breathed but of *her* to the enamoured air;   205
And from the breezes whether low or loud,
And from the rain of every passing cloud,
And from the singing of the summer-birds,
And from all sounds, all silence. In the words
Of antique verse and high romance,—in form,   210
Sound, colour—in whatever checks that Storm
Which with the shattered present chokes the past;[7]
And in that best philosophy,[8] whose taste
Makes this cold common hell, our life, a doom[9]
As glorious as a fiery martyrdom;   215
Her Spirit was the harmony of truth.—

    Then, from the caverns of my dreamy youth
I sprang, as one sandalled with plumes of fire,
And towards the loadstar[1] of my one desire,
I flitted, like a dizzy moth, whose flight   220
Is as a dead leaf's in the owlet light,[2]
When it would seek in Hesper's setting sphere[3]
A radiant death, a fiery sepulchre,
As if it were a lamp of earthly flame.—
But She, whom prayers or tears then could not tame,   225
Past, like a God throned on a winged planet,
Whose burning plumes to tenfold swiftness fan it,
Into the dreary cone of our life's shade;[4]
And as a man with mighty loss dismayed,
I would have followed, though the grave between   230
Yawned like a gulph whose spectres are unseen:
When a voice said:—"O thou of hearts the weakest,
The phantom is beside thee whom thou seekest."
Then I—"where?"—the world's echo answered "where!"
And in that silence, and in my despair,   235
I questioned every tongueless wind that flew
Over my tower of mourning, if it knew
Whither 'twas fled, this soul out of my soul;[5]
And murmured names and spells which have controul

---

7. *that Storm . . . past:* The apparent meaning is that the random experience of everyday current activity (*shattered present*) ordinarily obscures the great achievements scattered through cultural history.
8. Shelley probably refers not to any particular philosophical school but to a general attitude, described in 213–215, that sees suffering as meaningful.

9. Fate or destiny.
1. More commonly "lodestar"—a "guiding star."
2. The dim light in which owls fly about.
3. The planet Venus as the evening star.
4. The "cone of night" or shadow cast by the earth away from the sun.
5. See Shelley's essay "On Love," pp. 473–474.

Over the sightless tyrants of our fate; 240
But neither prayer nor verse could dissipate
The night which closed on her; nor uncreate
That world within this Chaos, mine and me,
Of which she was the veiled Divinity,
The world I say of thoughts that worshipped her: 245
And therefore I went forth, with hope and fear
And every gentle passion sick to death,
Feeding my course with expectation's breath,
Into the wintry forest of our life;[6]
And struggling through its error with vain strife, 250
And stumbling in my weakness and my haste,
And half bewildered by new forms, I past,
Seeking among those untaught foresters[7]
If I could find one form resembling hers,
In which she might have masked herself from me. 255
There,—One,[8] whose voice was venomed melody
Sate by a well, under blue night-shade bowers;[9]
The breath of her false mouth was like faint flowers,
Her touch was as electric poison,—flame
Out of her looks into my vitals came, 260
And from her living cheeks and bosom flew
A killing air, which pierced like honey-dew
Into the core of my green heart, and lay
Upon its leaves; until, as hair grown grey
O'er a young brow, they hid its unblown[1] prime 265
With ruins of unseasonable time.

In many mortal forms I rashly sought
The shadow of that idol of my thought.[2]
And some were fair—but beauty dies away:
Others were wise—but honeyed words betray: 270
And One was true—oh! why not true to me?
Then, as a hunted deer that could not flee,
I turned upon my thoughts, and stood at bay,
Wounded and weak and panting;[3] the cold day
Trembled, for pity of my strife and pain. 275
When, like a noon-day dawn, there shone again
Deliverance. One stood on my path who seemed
As like the glorious shape which I had dreamed,

---

6. The image of the hero's journey of
life passing through a dark, hostile
forest appears at the opening of Dante's
Divine Comedy, among other works.
7. I.e., other human beings who had not
experienced such a revelation.
8. The relationship with a woman de-
picted symbolically in lines 256ff. has
been variously interpreted as an en-
counter with a prostitute or simply the
first serious arousal of the youth's sexual
desires.

9. A poisonous plant, probably deadly
nightshade (belladonna).
1. Not yet flowered.
2. For a detailed discussion of the bio-
graphical elements in 267–383, see K. N.
Cameron's essay, pp. 511–519, below.
3. For Shelley's other uses of this image
of the Actaeon-like poet pursued by his
own thoughts (hounds), see *Prometheus
Unbound*, I.454–457, and *Adonais*, 274–
279.

As is the Moon, whose changes ever run
Into themselves, to the eternal Sun;   280
The cold chaste Moon, the Queen of Heaven's bright isles,
Who makes all beautiful on which she smiles,
That wandering shrine of soft yet icy flame
Which ever is transformed, yet still the same,
And warms not but illumines. Young and fair   285
As the descended Spirit of that sphere,
She hid me, as the Moon may hide the night
From its own darkness, until all was bright
Between the Heaven and Earth of my calm mind,[4]
And, as a cloud charioted by the wind,   290
She led me to a cave in that wild place,
And sate beside me, with her downward face
Illumining my slumbers, like the Moon
Waxing and waning o'er Endymion.[5]
And I was laid asleep, spirit and limb,   295
And all my being became bright or dim
As the Moon's image in a summer sea,
According as she smiled or frowned on me;
And there I lay, within a chaste cold bed:
Alas, I then was nor alive nor dead:—   300
For at her silver voice came Death and Life,
Unmindful each of their accustomed strife,
Masked like twin babes, a sister and a brother,
The wandering hopes of one abandoned mother,
And through the cavern without wings they flew,   305
And cried "Away, he is not of our crew."
I wept, and though it be a dream, I weep.

What storms then shook the ocean of my sleep,
Blotting that Moon, whose pale and waning lips
Then shrank as in the sickness of eclipse;—   310
And how my soul was as a lampless sea,
And who was then its Tempest; and when She,
The Planet of that hour, was quenched, what frost
Crept o'er those waters, 'till from coast to coast
The moving billows of my being fell   315
Into a death of ice, immoveable;—
And then—what earthquakes made it gape and split,
The white Moon smiling all the while on it,
These words conceal:—If not, each word would be
The key of staunchless tears. Weep not for me!   320

---

4. I.e., the poet's mind is between heaven and earth, like the cloud used in the following simile.
5. In the traditional myth Jupiter granted the shepherd Endymion immortality and eternal youth on the condition that he should sleep forever. Diana, the moon goddess, fell in love with his sleeping form and made love to him every night. (See "The Witch of Atlas," line 588 and note.)

At length, into the obscure Forest[6] came
The Vision I had sought through grief and shame.
Athwart that wintry wilderness of thorns[7]
Flashed from her motion splendour like the Morn's,
And from her presence life was radiated   325
Through the grey earth and branches bare and dead;
So that her way was paved, and roofed above
With flowers as soft as thoughts of budding love;
And music from her respiration spread
Like light,—all other sounds were penetrated   330
By the small, still, sweet spirit of that sound,
So that the savage winds hung mute around;
And odours warm and fresh fell from her hair
Dissolving the dull cold in the froze air:
Soft as an Incarnation of the Sun,   335
When light is changed to love, this glorious One
Floated into the cavern where I lay,
And called my Spirit, and the dreaming clay
Was lifted by the thing that dreamed below
As smoke by fire, and in her beauty's glow   340
I stood, and felt the dawn of my long night
Was penetrating me with living light:
I knew it was the Vision veiled from me
So many years—that it was Emily.

Twin Spheres of light who rule this passive Earth,   345
This world of love, this *me*; and into birth
Awaken all its fruits and flowers, and dart
Magnetic might into its central heart;
And lift its billows and its mists, and guide
By everlasting laws, each wind and tide   350
To its fit cloud, and its appointed cave;
And lull its storms, each in the craggy grave
Which was its cradle, luring to faint bowers
The armies of the rainbow-winged showers;
And, as those married lights, which from the towers   355
Of Heaven look forth and fold the wandering globe
In liquid sleep and splendour, as a robe;
And all their many-mingled influence blend,
If equal, yet unlike, to one sweet end;—
So ye, bright regents, with alternate sway   360
Govern my sphere of being, night and day!
Thou, not disdaining even a borrowed might;
Thou, not eclipsing a remoter light;
And, through the shadow of the seasons three,
From Spring to Autumn's sere maturity,   365

---

6. I.e., dark forest (the *selva oscura* in Dante's *Inferno*, I.2).
7. As in the mechanics' performance of "Pyramus and Thisbe" in Shakespeare's *A Midsummer Night's Dream*, a "bush of thorn" was a traditional property of the moon, as well as of the dark forest of life.

Light it into the Winter of the tomb,
Where it may ripen to a brighter bloom.
Thou too, O Comet beautiful and fierce,
Who drew the heart of this frail Universe
Towards thine own; till, wreckt in that convulsion,   370
Alternating attraction and repulsion,
Thine went astray and that was rent in twain;
Oh, float into our azure heaven again!
Be there love's folding-star[8] at thy return;
The living Sun will feed thee from its urn   375
Of golden fire; the Moon will veil her horn
In thy last smiles; adoring Even and Morn
Will worship thee with incense of calm breath
And lights and shadows; as the star of Death
And Birth[9] is worshipped by those sisters wild   380
Called Hope and Fear—upon the heart are piled
Their offerings,—of this sacrifice divine
A World shall be the altar.

                    Lady mine,
Scorn not these flowers of thought, the fading birth
Which from its heart of hearts that plant puts forth   385
Whose fruit, made perfect by thy sunny eyes,
Will be as of the trees of Paradise.

    The day is come, and thou wilt fly with me.
To whatsoe'er of dull mortality
Is mine, remain a vestal sister still;   390
To the intense, the deep, the imperishable,
Not mine but me, henceforth be thou united
Even as a bride, delighting and delighted.[1]
The hour is come:—the destined Star has risen
Which shall descend upon a vacant prison.   395
The walls are high, the gates are strong, thick set
The sentinels—but true love never yet
Was thus constrained: it overleaps all fence:
Like lightning, with invisible violence
Piercing its continents; like Heaven's free breath,   400
Which he who grasps can hold not; liker Death,
Who rides upon a thought, and makes his way
Through temple, tower, and palace, and the array
Of arms: more strength has Love than he or they;
For it can burst his charnel, and make free   405
The limbs in chains, the heart in agony,
The soul in dust and chaos.

8. Venus as the evening star—"The Star that bids the Shepherd fold [his sheep]" (Milton, *Comus*, 93). See also "The Witch of Atlas," 74, and *Hellas*, 1029.
9. Venus, as both the morning and the evening star. (Cf. "The Triumph of Life," 412–419.)

1. Lines 389–393, with their reference to the vestal virgins (see "The Witch of Atlas," 318), have been cited to prove that the overt sexual imagery in the last part of the poem is not to be taken literally.

Emily,
A ship is floating in the harbour now,
A wind is hovering o'er the mountain's brow;
There is a path on the sea's azure floor,   410
No keel has ever ploughed that path before;
The halcyons[2] brood around the foamless isles;
The treacherous Ocean has forsworn its wiles;
The merry mariners are bold and free:
Say, my heart's sister, wilt thou sail with me?   415
Our bark[3] is as an albatross, whose nest
Is a far Eden of the purple East;
And we between her wings will sit, while Night
And Day, and Storm, and Calm, pursue their flight,
Our ministers, along the boundless Sea,   420
Treading each other's heels, unheededly.
It is an isle under Ionian skies,[4]
Beautiful as a wreck of Paradise,
And, for[5] the harbours are not safe and good,
This land would have remained a solitude   425
But for some pastoral people native there,
Who from the Elysian,[6] clear, and golden air
Draw the last spirit of the age of gold,
Simple and spirited; innocent and bold.
The blue Ægean girds this chosen home,   430
With ever-changing sound and light and foam,
Kissing the sifted sands, and caverns hoar;
And all the winds wandering along the shore
Undulate with the undulating tide:
There are thick woods where sylvan forms abide;   435
And many a fountain, rivulet, and pond,
As clear as elemental diamond,
Or serene morning air; and far beyond,
The mossy tracks made by the goats and deer
(Which the rough shepherd treads but once a year,)   440
Pierce into glades, caverns, and bowers, and halls
Built round with ivy, which the waterfalls
Illumining, with sound that never fails
Accompany the noon-day nightingales;[7]
And all the place is peopled with sweet airs;   445
The light clear element which the isle wears

---

2. According to the myth, when Ceyx and Alcyone were turned into king-fishers (*halcyons*), Alcyone's father, Aeolus, god of the winds, granted his daughter "seven days of calm in winter [in which] Alcyone broods on the sea, wings outstretched over her nest" (Ovid, *Metamorphoses*, XI.10).
3. A small ship.
4. Though the Ionian Sea lies between southern Italy and western Greece, the area called Ionia in classical times was the western coast of Asia Minor, together with the adjacent islands in the Aegean Sea, which had been colonized by Greeks who spoke the Ionian dialect. Among these islands were the Sporades (see Shelley's Advertisement).
5. Because.
6. Having the quality of the Elysian fields, the classical version of paradise (see note to 133).
7. Ordinarily the nightingale sings only at night.

Is heavy with the scent of lemon-flowers,
Which floats like mist laden with unseen showers,
And falls upon the eye-lids like faint sleep;
And from the moss violets and jonquils peep,   450
And dart their arrowy odour through the brain
'Till you might faint with that delicious pain.
And every motion, odour, beam, and tone,
With that deep music is in unison:
Which is a soul within the soul—they seem   455
Like echoes of an antenatal dream.—
It is an isle 'twixt Heaven, Air, Earth, and Sea,
Cradled, and hung in clear tranquillity;
Bright as that wandering Eden Lucifer,[8]
Washed by the soft blue Oceans of young air.   460
It is a favoured place. Famine or Blight,
Pestilence, War and Earthquake, never light
Upon its mountain-peaks; blind vultures, they
Sail onward far upon their fatal way:
The winged storms, chaunting their thunder-psalm   465
To other lands, leave azure chasms of calm
Over this isle, or weep themselves in dew,
From which its fields and woods ever renew
Their green and golden immortality.[9]
And from the sea there rise, and from the sky   470
There fall, clear exhalations, soft and bright,
Veil after veil, each hiding some delight,
Which Sun or Moon or zephyr draw aside,
Till the isle's beauty, like a naked bride
Glowing at once with love and loveliness,   475
Blushes and trembles at its own excess:
Yet, like a buried lamp, a Soul no less
Burns in the heart of this delicious isle,
An atom[1] of th' Eternal, whose own smile
Unfolds itself, and may be felt not seen   480
O'er the grey rocks, blue waves, and forests green,
Filling their bare and void interstices.—
But the chief marvel of the wilderness
Is a lone dwelling, built by whom or how
None of the rustic island-people know: 485
'Tis not a tower of strength, though with its height
It overtops the woods; but, for delight,
Some wise and tender Ocean-King,[2] ere crime
Had been invented, in the world's young prime,
Reared it, a wonder of that simple time,   490

8. Venus as the morning star ("Light-Bearer") is imagined as the home of unfallen Eden.
9. The ever-renewing of the seasonal cycle of green foliage and golden harvests is cited as a kind of immortality.
1. The smallest possible particle.

2. One underlying myth may be that of Nereus, the eldest son of Oceanus; Hesiod in the *Theogony* says that Nereus "is always right and always gentle; he never forgets the laws, and is full of just and gentle wisdom." His wife, Doris, was also a child of Oceanus.

An envy of the isles, a pleasure-house
Made sacred to his sister and his spouse.
It scarce seems now a wreck of human art,
But, as it were Titanic;[3] in the heart
Of Earth having assumed its form, then grown   495
Out of the mountains, from the living stone,
Lifting itself in caverns light and high:
For all the antique and learned imagery
Has been erased, and in the place of it
The ivy and the wild-vine interknit   500
The volumes[4] of their many twining stems;
Parasite flowers illume with dewy gems
The lampless halls, and when they fade, the sky
Peeps through their winter-woof of tracery
With Moon-light patches, or star atoms keen,   505
Or fragments of the day's intense serene;—
Working mosaic on their Parian floors.[5]
And, day and night, aloof, from the high towers
And terraces, the Earth and Ocean seem
To sleep in one another's arms, and dream   510
Of waves, flowers, clouds, woods, rocks, and all that we
Read in their smiles, and call reality.

This isle and house are mine, and I have vowed
Thee to be lady of the solitude.—
And I have fitted up some chambers there   515
Looking towards the golden Eastern air,
And level with the living winds, which flow
Like waves above the living waves below.—
I have sent books and music there, and all
Those instruments with which high spirits call   520
The future from its cradle, and the past
Out of its grave, and make the present last
In thoughts and joys which sleep, but cannot die,
Folded within their own eternity.
Our simple life wants little, and true taste   525
Hires not the pale drudge Luxury, to waste
The scene it would adorn, and therefore still,
Nature, with all her children, haunts the hill.
The ring-dove, in the embowering ivy, yet
Keeps up her love-lament, and the owls flit   530
Round the evening tower, and the young stars glance
Between the quick bats in their twilight dance;
The spotted deer bask in the fresh moon-light
Before our gate, and the slow, silent night

---

3. The origins are set back into the era of the Titans—Kronus (Saturn) and his siblings—before the advent of Zeus (Jupiter) and the Olympian gods, who introduced *crime* as a category of thought.
4. Coils.
5. Of fine white marble from the island of Paros in the Cyclades.

Is measured by the pants of their calm sleep.   535
Be this our home in life, and when years heap
Their withered hours, like leaves, on our decay,
Let us become the over-hanging day,
The living soul of this Elysian isle,
Conscious, inseparable, one. Meanwhile   540
We two will rise, and sit, and walk together,
Under the roof of blue Ionian weather,
And wander in the meadows, or ascend
The mossy mountains, where the blue heavens bend
With lightest winds, to touch their paramour;[6]   545
Or linger, where the pebble-paven shore,
Under the quick, faint kisses of the sea
Trembles and sparkles as with ecstasy,—
Possessing and possest by all that is
Within that calm circumference of bliss,   550
And by each other, till to love and live
Be one:—or, at the noontide hour, arrive
Where some old cavern hoar seems yet to keep
The moonlight of the expired night asleep,
Through which the awakened day can never peep;   555
A veil for our seclusion, close as Night's,
Where secure sleep may kill thine innocent lights;
Sleep, the fresh dew of languid love, the rain
Whose drops quench kisses till they burn again.
And we will talk, until thought's melody   560
Become too sweet for utterance, and it die
In words, to live again in looks, which dart
With thrilling tone into the voiceless heart,
Harmonizing silence without a sound.
Our breath shall intermix, our bosoms bound,   565
And our veins beat together; and our lips
With other eloquence than words, eclipse
The soul that burns between them, and the wells
Which boil under our being's inmost cells,
The fountains of our deepest life, shall be   570
Confused in passion's golden purity,
As mountain-springs under the morning Sun.[7]
We shall become the same, we shall be one
Spirit within two frames, oh! wherefore two?
One passion in twin-hearts, which grows and grew,   575
'Till like two meteors of expanding flame,
Those spheres instinct with[8] it become the same,
Touch, mingle, are transfigured; ever still
Burning, yet ever inconsumable:

6. Lover; i.e., the island.
7. *wells . . . morning sun:* Accompanying the fairly explicit sexual imagery is an allusion to the myth of Alpheus, the river-god, who pursued Arethusa, a virgin nymph who served Diana. Both became streams, and Alpheus followed Arethusa from Greece under the ocean to Sicily, where their waters finally mingled. (Shelley wrote two versions of a poem on Arethusa.)
8. Animated by.

In one another's substance finding food,   580
Like flames too pure and light and unimbued[9]
To nourish their bright lives with baser prey,
Which point to Heaven and cannot pass away:
One hope within two wills, one will beneath
Two overshadowing minds, one life, one death,   585
One Heaven, one Hell, one immortality,
And one annihilation. Woe is me!
The winged words on which my soul would pierce
Into the height of love's rare Universe,
Are chains of lead around its flight of fire.—   590
I pant, I sink, I tremble, I expire!

Weak Verses, go, kneel at your Sovereign's[1] feet,
And say:—"We are the masters of thy slave;[2]
What wouldest thou with us and ours and thine?"
Then call your sisters from Oblivion's cave,   595
All singing loud: "Love's very pain is sweet,
But its reward is in the world divine
Which, if not here, it builds beyond the grave."
So shall ye live when I am there. Then haste
Over the hearts of men, until ye meet   600
Marina, Vanna, Primus,[3] and the rest,
And bid them love each other and be blest:
And leave the troop which errs, and which reproves,
And come and be my guest,—for I am Love's.[4]

Adonais

Shelley learned of John Keats's serious consumptive illness from Leigh Hunt and from John and Maria Gisborne during their visit to England. Late in July 1820, Shelley wrote, inviting Keats to visit him in Italy. Keats conditionally accepted, and he and Joseph Severn sailed for Naples in mid-September 1820, reached there on October 21, proceeded to Rome on November 7 or 8, where they arrived on November 15, and took lodgings on the Piazza di Spagna. There Keats died on February 23, 1821. Shelley did not learn of this event until April 11, 1821, and almost immediately began his elegy on Keats's death. By June 8, 1821, Shelley wrote to Charles Ollier that he had completed his poem "of about forty Spenser stanzas"; he finished the entire fifty-five stanzas, had the poem printed in Pisa, and sent a copy to the Gisbornes on July 13. Though Shelley instructed Ollier to have another edition printed in England, *Adonais* sold so poorly that Ollier did no more than sell the copies he had received (probably less than one hundred).

Shelley called *Adonais* "a highly wrought piece of art" and "the least

---

9. Unstained.
1. I.e., Emily.
2. The poet.
3. *Marina, Vanna, Primus:* Mary Shelley, Jane (Gio*vanna*) Williams, Edward Wil-

liams (Shelley's *first* [i.e., primary] friend).
4. This envoy, addressed to the poem in Dante's manner, restates the central theme of the entire composition.

imperfect of my compositions." Later poets and critics have generally agreed, and its artistry, its place in the long, distinguished tradition of the pastoral elegy, and its subject have made it the most widely known of Shelley's book-length poems. That is not to say that *Adonais* has been easily understood; though earlier commentators—particularly W. M. Rossetti in his Clarendon Press Series edition of the poem (1891)—had pointed out the poem's numerous parallels to Bion's Greek "Lament for Adonis" and the "Elegy for Bion" attributed to Moschus, only recently have critics been able to demonstrate the unity of the poem's imagery and structure. Both Wasserman and Reiman see a symmetrical structure; Wasserman divides the poem into three movements of seventeen, twenty-one, and seventeen stanzas, and Reiman elaborates this by separating out the three central stanzas (27–29) to leave sections of seventeen, nine, three, nine, and seventeen stanzas. Silverman finds the key to the poem's structure in that of *Astrophel*, Spenser's pastoral elegy on the death of Sir Philip Sidney.

As the epigraph from the elegy for Bion suggests, there are two chief biographical focuses in the poem—one being Keats and the other the anonymous *Quarterly* reviewer, whom Shelley believed to be Robert Southey. The relevance to *Adonais* of Shelley's relations with Southey is shown in Kenneth Neill Cameron's "Shelley vs. Southey: New Light on an Old Quarrel" (*PMLA*, 1942), and Reiman gives the fullest treatment of the other question in "Keats and Shelley: Personal and Literary Relations" (*Shelley and his Circle*, V).

There being no surviving fair copy manuscript, the chief authorities for the text are the first edition, which, Shelley wrote to Ollier, "is beautifully printed, & what is of more consequence, correctly . . ." (*Letters*, II, 311), and Mary Shelley's first edition of 1839, which contains (along with several errors) at least three verbal changes that must have Shelley's authority behind them. We have printed book titles in the Preface in italics, altered a few minor points of orthography to conform to the consistent practice in Shelley's manuscripts (e.g., *ancient* to *antient*, *gray* to *grey*), and changed the possessive *it's* to *its*, to conform to the correct usage of Shelley's day as found in his poems printed in England.

Adonais

An Elegy on the Death of John Keats, Author of
Endymion, Hyperion, Etc.

Ἀστὴρ πρὶν μὲν ἔλαμπες ἐνὶ ζωοῖσιν Ἑῷος·
νῦν δὲ θανὼν λάμπεις Ἕσπερος ἐν φθιμένοις.—PLATO[1]

PREFACE

Φάρμακον ἦλθε, Βίων, ποτὶ σὸν στόμα, φάρμακον εἶδες.
πῶς τευ τοῖς χείλεσσι ποτέδραμε, κοὐκ ἐγλυκάνθη;
τίς δὲ βροτὸς τοσσοῦτον ἀνάμερος, ἢ κεράσαι τοι,
ἢ δοῦναι λαλέοντι το φάρμακον; ἔκφυγεν ᾠδάν.
—MOSCHUS, EPITAPH. BION.[2]

IT is my intention to subjoin to the London edition of this poem, a
criticism upon the claims of its lamented object to be classed among
the writers of the highest genius who have adorned our age. My
known repugnance to the narrow principles of taste on which
several of his earlier compositions were modelled, prove, at least
that I am an impartial judge. I consider the fragment of *Hyperion*,
as second to nothing that was ever produced by a writer of the same
years.[3]

John Keats, died at Rome of a consumption, in his twenty-fourth
year, on the —— of —— 1821; and was buried in the romantic and
lonely cemetery of the protestants in that city, under the pyramid
which is the tomb of Cestius, and the massy walls and towers, now
mouldering and desolate, which formed the circuit of antient Rome.
The cemetery is an open space among the ruins covered in winter
with violets and daisies. It might make one in love with death, to
think that one should be buried in so sweet a place.[4]

The genius of the lamented person to whose memory I have
dedicated these unworthy verses, was not less delicate and fragile
than it was beautiful; and where cankerworms abound, what wonder

1. An epigram attributed to Plato, which
Shelley translated:

Thou wert the morning star among the
living,
  Ere thy fair light had fled—
Now, having died, thou are as Hesperus,
giving
  New splendour to the dead.

2. From the "Elegy for Bion" (attrib-
uted to Moschus): "Poison came, Bion,
to thy mouth—poison didst thou eat.
How could it come to such lips as thine
and not be sweetened? What mortal was
so cruel as to mix the drug for thee, or
to give it to thee, who heard thy voice?
He escapes [shall be nameless in] my
song." The poem's next clause, not

given by Shelley, states: "Yet justice
overtakes all."
3. Shelley, thinking that Keats died in
his twenty-fourth year (before his twenty-
fourth birthday), and reading in the
Advertisement to the *Lamia* volume
(dated June 26, 1820) that *Hyperion*
had been left unfinished because of the
unfavorable reception of *Endymion*
(1818), must have thought that the frag-
mentary *Hyperion* had been written by
Keats by late 1818 or early 1819, when
(according to Shelley's information) he
would have been only twenty-one years
old.
4. Shelley's son William had been buried
there in 1819, as he himself was to be in
1822.

if its young flower was blighted in the bud? The savage criticism on his *Endymion,* which appeared in the *Quarterly Review,* produced the most violent effect on his susceptible mind; the agitation thus originated ended in the rupture of a blood-vessel in the lungs;[5] a rapid consumption ensued, and the succeeding acknowledgements from more candid critics,[6] of the true greatness of his powers, were ineffectual to heal the wound thus wantonly inflicted.

It may be well said, that these wretched men know not what they do. They scatter their insults and their slanders without heed as to whether the poisoned shaft lights on a heart made callous by many blows, or one, like Keats's composed of more penetrable stuff. One of their associates, is, to my knowledge, a most base and un-principled calumniator. As to *Endymion,* was it a poem, whatever might be its defects, to be treated contemptuously by those who had celebrated, with various degrees of complacency and panegyric, *Paris,* and *Woman,* and a *Syrian Tale,* and Mrs. Lefanu, and Mr. Barrett, and Mr. Howard Payne, and a long list of the illustrious obscure?[7] Are these the men, who in their venal good nature, pre-sumed to draw a parallel between the Rev. Mr. Milman and Lord Byron? What gnat did they strain at here, after having swallowed all those camels? Against what woman taken in adultery, dares the foremost of these literary prostitutes to cast his opprobrious stone?[8] Miserable man! you, one of the meanest, have wantonly defaced one of the noblest specimens of the workmanship of God. Nor shall it be your excuse, that, murderer as you are, you have spoken dag-gers, but used none.[9]

The circumstances of the closing scene of poor Keats's life were nòt made known to me until the Elegy was ready for the press.[1]

5. Shelley wrote to Byron on May 4, 1821: "Hunt tells me that in the first paroxysms of his disappointment he burst a blood-vessel; and thus laid the founda-tion of a rapid consumption" (*Letters,* II, 289). The review in question appeared in the April 1818 number of the *Quar-terly,* which was published in September 1818. See Reiman, *The Romantics Re-viewed,* Part C, II, 767–770.
6. Shelley may allude to Francis Jef-frey's favorable review of *Endymion* and the *Lamia* volume that appeared in the *Edinburgh Review* for August 1820 (see *The Romantics Reviewed,* Part C, I, 385–390).
7. *Paris in 1815* (1817) by the Rev. George Croly was published anony-mously and favorably reviewed in the *Quarterly* for April 1817. (Croly wrote a vicious review of *Adonais* for the *Literary Gazette.*) A later edition of *Woman* (1810) by Eaton Stannard Bar-rett, a Tory wit, was reviewed by the *Quarterly* in the April 1818 number.

John Howard Payne, an American drama-tist who later courted the widowed Mary Shelley, was reviewed harshly, not favor-ably, in the *Quarterly* for January 1820. Works by the Rev. Henry Hart Milman (Shelley's contemporary at both Eton and Oxford) were favorably reviewed in the *Quarterly* issues dated April 1816, July 1818, and May 1820. (Milman him-self was a reviewer for the *Quarterly,* and Shelley later came to suspect him of having written the scurrilous attack on *Laon and Cythna* in the number for April 1819.)
8. The language of this sentence, like that of the one that precedes it and the first sentence in the paragraph, comes straight from the New Testament; see Luke 23:34, Matthew 23:24, and John 8:3–11.
9. Shakespeare, *Hamlet,* III.ii.414.
1. Shelley alludes to a letter to John Gisborne from the Rev. Robert Finch, who gave a sentimentalized account of Keats's last days.

I am given to understand that the wound which his sensitive spirit had received from the criticism of *Endymion*, was exasperated by the bitter sense of unrequited benefits; the poor fellow seems to have been hooted from the stage of life, no less by those on whom he had wasted the promise of his genius, than those on whom he had lavished his fortune and his care. He was accompanied to Rome, and attended in his last illness by Mr. Severn, a young artist of the highest promise, who, I have been informed "almost risked his own life, and sacrificed every prospect to unwearied attendance upon his dying friend." Had I known these circumstances before the completion of my poem, I should have been tempted to add my feeble tribute of applause to the more solid recompense which the virtuous man finds in the recollection of his own motives. Mr. Severn can dispense with a reward from "such stuff as dreams are made of."[2] His conduct is a golden augury of the success of his future career— may the unextinguished Spirit of his illustrious friend animate the creations of his pencil, and plead against Oblivion for his name!

1

I weep for Adonais—he is dead!
O, weep for Adonais! though our tears
Thaw not the frost which binds so dear a head!
And thou, sad Hour,[3] selected from all years
To mourn our loss, rouse thy obscure compeers,   5
And teach them thine own sorrow, say: with me
Died Adonais; till the Future dares
Forget the Past, his fate and fame shall be
An echo and a light[4] unto eternity!

2

Where wert thou mighty Mother,[5] when he lay,   10
When thy Son lay, pierced by the shaft which flies
In darkness?[6] where was lorn[7] Urania
When Adonais died? With veiled eyes,
'Mid listening Echoes, in her Paradise
She sate, while one,[8] with soft enamoured breath,   15
Rekindled all the fading melodies,
With which, like flowers that mock the corse[9] beneath,
He had adorned and hid the coming bulk of death.

2. Shakespeare, *The Tempest*, IV.i.156–157.
3. As in *Prometheus Unbound*, Shelley follows the classical poetic convention of personifying the Horae (Hours), goddesses of the seasons.
4. The distinction between the senses of sound and sight plays a significant part in the poem's symbolism.
5. Urania (line 12), a name used for the Muse of astronomy, the "Heavenly Muse" invoked by Milton in *Paradise Lost* (Books I, VII), and Uranian Venus, the goddess seen as patroness of ideal love.
6. Cf. "Thou shalt not be afraid for the terror by night; nor for the arrow that flieth by day" (Psalms 91:5). Shelley alludes to the anonymous attack on Keats's *Endymion* in the *Quarterly Review*, XIX (April 1818), 204–208.
7. Forsaken.
8. One of the personified Echoes.
9. Corpse.

3

O, weep for Adonais—he is dead!
Wake, melancholy Mother, wake and weep!   20
Yet wherefore? Quench within their burning bed
Thy fiery tears, and let thy loud heart keep
Like his, a mute and uncomplaining sleep;
For he is gone, where all things wise and fair
Descend;—oh, dream not that the amorous Deep[1]   25
Will yet restore him to the vital air;
Death feeds on his mute voice, and laughs at our despair.

4

Most musical of mourners, weep again!
Lament anew, Urania![2]—He died,
Who was the Sire of an immortal strain,   30
Blind, old, and lonely, when his country's pride,
The priest, the slave, and the liberticide,
Trampled and mocked with many a loathed rite
Of lust and blood;[3] he went, unterrified,
Into the gulph of death; but his clear Sprite   35
Yet reigns o'er earth; the third among the sons of light.[4]

5

Most musical of mourners, weep anew!
Not all to that bright station dared to climb;
And happier they their happiness who knew,
Whose tapers yet burn through that night of time   40
In which suns perished;[5] others more sublime,
Struck by the envious wrath of man or God,
Have sunk, extinct in their refulgent prime;
And some yet live, treading the thorny road,
Which leads, through toil and hate, to Fame's serene abode.[6] 45

6

But now, thy youngest, dearest one, has perished
The nursling of thy widowhood,[7] who grew,
Like a pale flower by some sad maiden cherished,
And fed with true love tears, instead of dew;[8]
Most musical of mourners, weep anew!   50
Thy extreme hope, the loveliest and the last,
The bloom, whose petals nipt before they blew[9]
Died on the promise of the fruit, is waste;
The broken lily lies—the storm is overpast.

1. An unfathomable abyss.
2. I.e., Milton.
3. Lines 31–34 refer to the Restoration of the Stuart monarchy, when the "regicides"—those responsible for executing King Charles I—were killed.
4. In *A Defence of Poetry*, Shelley says that Milton was the third great epic poet, along with Homer and Dante; *Sprite:* spirit.
5. Lines 38–41 characterize minor poets who were content to have minor fame during their lifetime.
6. *some . . . serene abode:* Byron and Shelley, among others.
7. Keats as a poet is depicted as the posthumous child of Milton (Sire of line 30). Shelley admired Keats's *Hyperion*, his most Miltonic poem.
8. Lines 48–49 allude to the story of Keats's poem "Isabella; or, The Pot of Basil."
9. Bloomed or achieved perfection.

7

To that high Capital,[1] where kingly Death   55
Keeps his pale court in beauty and decay,
He came; and bought, with price of purest breath,
A grave among the eternal.—Come away!
Haste, while the vault of blue Italian day
Is yet his fitting charnel-roof! while still   60
He lies, as if in dewy sleep he lay;
Awake him not! surely he takes his fill
Of deep and liquid rest, forgetful of all ill.

8

He will awake no more, oh, never more!—
Within the twilight chamber spreads apace,   65
The shadow of white Death, and at the door
Invisible Corruption waits to trace
His extreme way to her dim dwelling-place;
The eternal Hunger sits, but pity and awe
Soothe her pale rage, nor dares she to deface   70
So fair a prey, till darkness, and the law
Of change, shall o'er his sleep the mortal curtain draw.[2]

9

O, weep for Adonais!—The quick Dreams,[3]
The passion-winged Ministers of thought,
Who were his flocks, whom near the living streams   75
Of his young spirit he fed, and whom he taught
The love which was its music, wander not,—
Wander no more, from kindling brain to brain,
But droop there, whence they sprung; and mourn their lot
Round the cold heart, where, after their sweet pain,[4]   80
They ne'er will gather strength, or find a home again.

10

And one[5] with trembling hands clasps his cold head,
And fans him with her moonlight wings, and cries;
"Our love, our hope, our sorrow, is not dead;
See, on the silken fringe of his faint eyes,   85
Like dew upon a sleeping flower, there lies
A tear some Dream has loosened from his brain."
Lost Angel of a ruined Paradise!
She knew not 'twas her own; as with no stain
She faded, like a cloud which had outwept its rain.   90

11

One from a lucid[6] urn of starry dew
Washed his light limbs as if embalming them;
Another clipt her profuse locks, and threw

1. Rome, the Eternal City, where Keats died.
2. In the first edition this line read: "Of mortal change, shall fill the grave which is her maw."
3. I.e., "living Dreams"; Shelley personifies various aspects of Keats's mental life as his *flocks*, according to the tradition of the pastoral elegy.
4. Such use of oxymoron is common in Keats's poetry, but relatively unusual in Shelley's.
5. One of the Dreams, etc., of stanza 9.
6. Luminous.

The wreath upon him, like an anadem,[7]
Which frozen tears instead of pearls begem;   95
Another in her wilful grief would break
Her bow and winged reeds,[8] as if to stem
A greater loss with one which was more weak;
And dull the barbed fire against his frozen cheek.

12

Another Splendour[9] on his mouth alit,   100
That mouth, whence it was wont to draw the breath
Which gave it strength to pierce the guarded wit,
And pass into the panting heart beneath
With lightning and with music: the damp death
Quenched its caress upon his icy lips;   105
And, as a dying meteor stains a wreath
Of moonlight vapour, which the cold night clips,[1]
It flushed through his pale limbs, and past to its eclipse.

13

And others came . . . Desires and Adorations,
Winged Persuasions and veiled Destinies,   110
Splendours, and Glooms, and glimmering Incarnations
Of hopes and fears, and twilight Phantasies;
And Sorrow, with her family of Sighs,
And Pleasure, blind with tears, led by the gleam
Of her own dying smile instead of eyes,   115
Came in slow pomp;—the moving pomp might seem
Like pageantry of mist on an autumnal stream.[2]

14

All he had loved, and moulded into thought,
From shape, and hue, and odour, and sweet sound,
Lamented Adonais. Morning sought   120
Her eastern watchtower, and her hair unbound,
Wet with the tears which should adorn the ground,
Dimmed the aerial eyes that kindle day;
Afar the melancholy thunder moaned,
Pale Ocean in unquiet slumber lay,   125
And the wild winds flew round, sobbing in their dismay.

15

Lost Echo sits amid the voiceless mountains,
And feeds her grief with his remembered lay,
And will no more reply to winds or fountains,
Or amorous birds perched on the young green spray,   130
Or herdsman's horn, or bell at closing day;
Since she can mimic not his lips, more dear
Than those for whose disdain she pined away

---

7. Garland for the head, usually of flowers.
8. I.e., arrows; Shelley is here paraphrasing Bion's "Lament for Adonis," where the mourning creatures are Loves (Cupids) rather than *Dreams, Ministers*

of thought, etc.
9. Cf. Dante's word *splendori* (*Paradiso*, XXIII.82).
1. Embraces.
2. Lines 116–117 allude to Keats's "To Autumn."

Into a shadow of all sounds:[3]—a drear
Murmur, between their songs, is all the woodmen hear.   135

16

Grief made the young Spring wild, and she threw down
Her kindling buds, as if she Autumn were,
Or they dead leaves; since her delight is flown
For whom should she have waked the sullen year?
To Phœbus was not Hyacinth so dear[4]   140
Nor to himself Narcissus, as to both
Thou Adonais: wan they stand and sere[5]
Amid the faint companions of their youth,
With dew all turned to tears; odour, to sighing ruth.[6]

17

Thy spirit's sister, the lorn nightingale[7]   145
Mourns not her mate with such melodious pain;
Not so the eagle, who like thee could scale
Heaven, and could nourish in the sun's domain
Her mighty youth with morning,[8] doth complain,
Soaring and screaming round her empty nest,   150
As Albion[9] wails for thee: the curse of Cain[1]
Light on his head who pierced thy innocent breast,
And scared the angel soul that was its earthly guest!

18

Ah woe is me! Winter is come and gone,
But grief returns with the revolving year;   155
The airs and streams renew their joyous tone;
The ants, the bees, the swallows reappear;
Fresh leaves and flowers deck the dead Seasons' bier;
The amorous birds now pair in every brake,
And build their mossy homes in field and brere:[2]   160
And the green lizard, and the golden snake,
Like unimprisoned flames, out of their trance awake.

19

Through wood and stream and field and hill and Ocean
A quickening life from the Earth's heart has burst
As it has ever done,[3] with change and motion,   165

3. When the nymph Echo was rebuffed by Narcissus, whom she loved, she faded into an echo of sounds; Narcissus scorned Echo, fell in love with his own reflection, and was transformed into a flower.
4. Hyacinthus was a youth beloved by Phoebus Apollo, who mourned him when jealous Zephyrus caused his death. Apollo turned Hyacinthus into a flower.
5. Dry or withered.
6. Pity.
7. Besides echoing the elegy on Bion, this image alludes to Keats's "Ode to a Nightingale."
8. *eagle . . . morning:* According to tradition, the eagle could renew its youthful vision by first flying toward the sun

(which burned the scales from its eyes) and then diving into a fountain.
9. England.
1. The first murderer was cursed to be "a fugitive and a vagabond . . . in the earth."
2. The original form of "brier"; thorny bushes in general, or wild rosebushes; *brake:* thicket or clump of bushes.
3. The renewal of the animal and vegetable species in the spring, contrasted with the linear termination of the individual human life, leads to a lament (in the manner of the late Latin poem *Pervigilium Veneris*) that destroys the comfort earlier provided by the myth in which Adonais was reborn annually.

From the great morning of the world when first
God dawned on Chaos; in its steam immersed
The lamps of Heaven flash with a softer light;
All baser things pant with life's sacred thirst;
Diffuse themselves; and spend in love's delight,   170
The beauty and the joy of their renewed might.

20

The leprous corpse touched by this spirit tender
Exhales itself in flowers of gentle breath;[4]
Like incarnations of the stars, when splendour
Is changed to fragrance, they illumine death   175
And mock the merry worm that wakes beneath;
Nought we know, dies. Shall that alone which knows[5]
Be as a sword consumed before the sheath
By sightless[6] lightning?—th'intense atom glows
A moment, then is quenched in a most cold repose.   180

21

Alas! that all we loved of him should be,
But for our grief, as if it had not been,
And grief itself be mortal! Woe is me!
Whence are we, and why are we? of what scene
The actors or spectators? Great and mean   185
Meet massed in death, who lends what life must borrow.
As long as skies are blue, and fields are green,
Evening must usher night, night urge the morrow,
Month follow month with woe, and year wake year to sorrow.

22

He will awake no more, oh, never more!   190
"Wake thou," cried Misery, "childless Mother, rise
Out of thy sleep, and slake,[7] in thy heart's core,
A wound more fierce than his with tears and sighs."
And all the Dreams that watched Urania's eyes,
And all the Echoes whom their sister's song[8]   195
Had held in holy silence, cried: "Arise!"
Swift as a Thought by the snake Memory stung,
From her ambrosial rest the fading Splendour sprung.

23

She rose like an autumnal Night, that springs
Out of the East, and follows wild and drear   200
The golden Day, which, on eternal wings,
Even as a ghost abandoning a bier,
Had left the Earth a corpse. Sorrow and fear
So struck, so roused, so rapt Urania;
So saddened round her like an atmosphere   205
Of stormy mist; so swept her on her way
Even to the mournful place where Adonais lay.

---

4. Anemones, or windflowers.
5. The human mind.
6. Both invisible and blind, amoral.

7. Render less acute or painful.
8. The sister is Echo (127), who repeated Adonais' poem.

24

Out of her secret Paradise she sped,
Through camps and cities rough with stone, and steel,
And human hearts, which to her aery tread   210
Yielding not, wounded the invisible
Palms⁹ of her tender feet where'er they fell:
And barbed tongues, and thoughts more sharp than they
Rent the soft Form they never could repel,
Whose sacred blood, like the young tears of May,   215
Paved with eternal flowers that undeserving way.

25

In the death chamber for a moment Death
Shamed by the presence of that living Might
Blushed to annihilation, and the breath
Revisited those lips, and life's pale light   220
Flashed through those limbs, so late her dear delight.
"Leave me not wild and drear and comfortless,
As silent lightning leaves the starless night!
Leave me not!" cried Urania: her distress
Roused Death: Death rose and smiled, and met her vain caress.225

26

"Stay yet awhile! speak to me once again;
Kiss me, so long but as a kiss may live;
And in my heartless breast and burning brain
That word, that kiss shall all thoughts else survive
With food of saddest memory kept alive,   230
Now thou art dead, as if it were a part
Of thee, my Adonais! I would give
All that I am to be as thou now art!
But I am chained to Time, and cannot thence depart!

27

"Oh gentle child, beautiful as thou wert,   235
Why didst thou leave the trodden paths of men
Too soon, and with weak hands though mighty heart
Dare the unpastured dragon¹ in his den?
Defenceless as thou wert, oh where was then
Wisdom the mirrored shield,² or scorn the spear?   240
Or hadst thou waited the full cycle, when
Thy spirit should have filled its crescent³ sphere,
The monsters of life's waste had fled from thee like deer.

28

"The herded wolves, bold only to pursue;
The obscene ravens, clamorous o'er the dead;   245
The vultures to the conqueror's banner true
Who feed where Desolation first has fed,

9. Shelley's use of *palm* for "sole" of the foot here and in *Prometheus Unbound* (IV.123) and "The Triumph of Life" (361) is, so far as we can discover, entirely without precedent.
1. The hostile critic(s) who, Shelley believed, had crushed Keats's spirit.
2. A mirrored shield appears in the legend of Perseus, who succeeds in slaying Medusa by viewing her only indirectly in the shield.
3. Growing.

And whose wings rain contagion;—how they fled,
When like Apollo, from his golden bow,
The Pythian of the age[4] one arrow sped   250
And smiled!—The spoilers tempt no second blow,
They fawn on the proud feet that spurn them lying low.[5]

29

"The sun comes forth, and many reptiles spawn;
He sets, and each ephemeral insect[6] then
Is gathered into death without a dawn,   255
And the immortal stars awake again;
So is it in the world of living men:
A godlike mind soars forth, in its delight
Making earth bare and veiling heaven, and when
It sinks, the swarms that dimmed or shared its light   260
Leave to its kindred lamps[7] the spirit's awful night."

30

Thus ceased she: and the mountain shepherds[8] came
Their garlands sere, their magic mantles rent;
The Pilgrim of Eternity,[9] whose fame
Over his living head like Heaven is bent,   265
An early but enduring monument,
Came, veiling all the lightnings of his song
In sorrow; from her wilds Ierne sent
The sweetest lyrist of her saddest wrong,[1]
And love taught grief to fall like music from his tongue.   270

31

Midst others of less note, came one frail Form,[2]
A phantom among men; companionless
As the last cloud of an expiring storm
Whose thunder is its knell; he, as I guess,
Had gazed on Nature's naked loveliness,   275
Actæon-like, and now he fled astray
With feeble steps o'er the world's wilderness,
And his own thoughts, along that rugged way,
Pursued, like raging hounds, their father and their prey.[3]

---

4. Byron, his *one arrow* being *English Bards and Scotch Reviewers*, which silenced the critics as Apollo killed the Python.

5. The first edition read "as they go" instead of *lying low*; Mary Shelley's emendation of this line and line 72 certainly reflects Shelley's wishes.

6. For Shelley's other uses of the ephemerid, see "The Sensitive-Plant" (II.49) and "The Witch of Atlas" (9).

7. The stars (other creative minds) that the glare of sunlight, diffused through the atmosphere, had "veiled" (258).

8. In pastoral elegies the fellow poets of the poet being mourned are also characterized as shepherds; here they are mountain shepherds because of the traditional associations of mountains with

independence and liberty (see especially Milton's *L'Allegro*, 36, and Wordsworth's poetry *passim*).

9. Byron, alluding particularly to *Childe Harold's Pilgrimage*.

1. Thomas Moore from Ireland (*Ierne*), famous for his *Irish Melodies*, his translations of the love songs of Anacreon, and his anti-government satirical poetry (see notes to the Dedication of *Peter Bell the Third*).

2. I.e., Shelley.

3. For the association of the Actaeon myth (in which the hunter Actaeon was destroyed by his own dogs because he saw Diana naked) with the Shakespearean image of thoughts pursuing their *father*-mind, see note to *Prometheus Unbound*, I.454–457.

32

A pardlike⁴ Spirit beautiful and swift—   280
A Love in desolation masked;—a Power
Girt round with weakness;—it can scarce uplift
The weight of the superincumbent hour;⁵
It is a dying lamp, a falling shower,
A breaking billow;—even whilst we speak   285
Is it not broken? On the withering flower
The killing sun smiles brightly: on a cheek
The life can burn in blood, even while the heart may break.

33

His head was bound with pansies overblown,
And faded violets, white, and pied, and blue;   290
And a light spear topped with a cypress cone,
Round whose rude shaft dark ivy tresses grew⁶
Yet dripping with the forest's noonday dew,
Vibrated, as the ever-beating heart
Shook the weak hand that grasped it; of that crew   295
He came the last, neglected and apart;
A herd-abandoned deer struck by the hunter's dart.

34

All stood aloof, and at his partial⁷ moan
Smiled through their tears; well knew that gentle band
Who in another's fate now wept his own;   300
As in the accents of an unknown land,
He sung new sorrow; sad Urania scanned
The Stranger's mien, and murmured: "who art thou?"
He answered not, but with a sudden hand
Made bare his branded and ensanguined brow,   305
Which was like Cain's or Christ's⁸—Oh! that it should be so!

35

What softer voice is hushed over the dead?
Athwart what brow is that dark mantle thrown?
What form leans sadly o'er the white death-bed,
In mockery of monumental stone,⁹   310
The heavy heart heaving without a moan?
If it be He,¹ who, gentlest of the wise,
Taught, soothed, loved, honoured the departed one;
Let me not vex, with inharmonious sighs
The silence of that heart's accepted sacrifice.   315

4. A *pard* is a panther or leopard, sacred to Dionysus (Bacchus).
5. Lines 281–283: The "overlying" or "overhanging" *hour* is that which marks the death of Adonais (see 4–9); this hour masks Cupid (*Love*) with *desolation*, godlike *Power* with *weakness*.
6. The thyrsus, a staff tipped with an evergreen cone and wrapped with ivy or grape leaves. In the Dionysia, the festival honoring Dionysus, the Greeks carried the thyrsus (which had clear phallic symbolism) and garlanded their heads with ivy, violets, and other flowers.

7. Having a bias.
8. The forehead of Cain was *branded* by God with a mark to distinguish him; the crown of thorns bloodied (*ensanguined*) Christ's brow.
9. The figure leans silent and still, posing like a memorial statue, yet *mocking* such a statue because his *heart* continues to beat.
1. Leigh Hunt, Keats's first literary patron and champion; he took Keats into his house and cared for him at the beginning of his final illness.

36

Our Adonais has drunk poison—oh!
What deaf and viperous murderer could crown
Life's early cup with such a draught of woe?[2]
The nameless worm[3] would now itself disown:
It felt, yet could escape the magic tone   320
Whose prelude held all envy, hate, and wrong,
But what was howling in one breast alone,
Silent with expectation of the song,
Whose master's hand is cold, whose silver lyre unstrung.

37

Live thou, whose infamy is not thy fame!   325
Live! fear no heavier chastisement from me,
Thou noteless blot on a remembered name!
But be thyself, and know thyself to be!
And ever at thy season be thou free
To spill the venom when thy fangs o'erflow: 330
Remorse and Self-contempt shall cling to thee;
Hot Shame shall burn upon thy secret brow,
And like a beaten hound tremble thou shalt—as now.

38

Nor let us weep that our delight is fled
Far from these carrion kites[4] that scream below;   335
He wakes or sleeps with the enduring dead;
Thou canst not soar where he is sitting now.[5]—
Dust to the dust! but the pure spirit shall flow
Back to the burning fountain whence it came,[6]
A portion of the Eternal, which must glow   340
Through time and change, unquenchably the same,
Whilst thy cold embers choke the sordid hearth of shame.

39

Peace, peace! he is not dead, he doth not sleep—
He hath awakened from the dream of life—
'Tis we, who lost in stormy visions, keep   345
With phantoms an unprofitable strife,
And in mad trance, strike with our spirit's knife
Invulnerable nothings.—*We* decay
Like corpses in a charnel; fear and grief
Convulse us and consume us day by day,   350
And cold hopes swarm like worms within our living clay.

2. Throughout this and the following stanza Shelley attacks the anonymous author of the *Quarterly Review*'s attack on Keats. Shelley believed him to be Robert Southey, who (Shelley thought) was also the hostile reviewer of works by Hunt and himself. The actual reviewer of Keats was John Wilson Croker, while the attacks on Hunt and Shelley had been written by John Taylor Coleridge, nephew of S. T. Coleridge.
3. Snake.
4. Birds of the hawk family.

5. Again addressing the *Quarterly* reviewer, Shelley adapts (and inverts the implications of) an image from *Paradise Lost*, IV.828–829, in which fallen Satan rebukes Ithuriel and Zephon for failing to recognize him, who had once been "sitting where ye durst not soare."
6. The concept of spirit as a fiery emanation flowing from the divine fire appears in the writings of the neoplatonic philosopher Plotinus (*Enneads*, IV.iii.9–10) and had been widely disseminated in in the Platonic tradition.

40

He has outsoared the shadow of our night;[7]
Envy and calumny and hate and pain,
And that unrest which men miscall delight,
Can touch him not and torture not again;   355
From the contagion of the world's slow stain
He is secure, and now can never mourn
A heart grown cold, a head grown grey in vain;[8]
Nor, when the spirit's self has ceased to burn,
With sparkless ashes load an unlamented urn.   360

41

He lives, he wakes—'tis Death is dead, not he;
Mourn not for Adonais.—Thou young Dawn
Turn all thy dew to splendour, for from thee
The spirit thou lamentest is not gone;
Ye caverns and ye forests, cease to moan!   365
Cease ye faint flowers and fountains, and thou Air
Which like a mourning veil thy scarf hadst thrown
O'er the abandoned Earth, now leave it bare
Even to the joyous stars which smile on its despair![9]

42

He is made one with Nature: there is heard   370
His voice in all her music, from the moan
Of thunder, to the song of night's sweet bird;[1]
He is a presence to be felt and known
In darkness and in light, from herb and stone,
Spreading itself where'er that Power[2] may move   375
Which has withdrawn his being to its own;
Which wields the world with never wearied love,
Sustains it from beneath, and kindles it above.

43

He is a portion of the loveliness
Which once he made more lovely: he doth bear   380
His part, while the one Spirit's plastic[3] stress
Sweeps through the dull dense world, compelling there,
All new successions to the forms they wear;
Torturing th'unwilling dross that checks its flight
To its own likeness, as each mass may bear;   385
And bursting in its beauty and its might
From trees and beasts and men into the Heaven's light.

---

7. The shadow cast by the earth away from the sun. That shadow can eclipse the moon but none of the planets.
8. Shelley undoubtedly thought of Southey, whose youthful liberalism had hardened into conservatism by the time Shelley met him at Keswick late in 1811.
9. If there were no moisture-laden air to diffuse sunlight into a general glow, the stars would be visible in daytime, as well as at night.
1. The nightingale.
2. Power was the eighteenth-century philosophical term for an impersonal God (note the pronoun *its* in line 376).
3. Capable of shaping or molding formless matter.

44

The splendours of the firmament of time[4]
May be eclipsed, but are extinguished not;
Like stars to their appointed height they climb   390
And death is a low mist which cannot blot
The brightness it may veil. When lofty thought
Lifts a young heart above its mortal lair,
And love and life contend in it, for what
Shall be its earthly doom, the dead live there[5]   395
And move like winds of light on dark and stormy air.

45

The inheritors of unfulfilled renown[6]
Rose from their thrones, built beyond mortal thought,
Far in the Unapparent. Chatterton
Rose pale, his solemn agony had not   400
Yet faded from him; Sidney, as he fought
And as he fell and as he lived and loved
Sublimely mild, a Spirit without spot,
Arose; and Lucan, by his death approved:
Oblivion as they rose shrank like a thing reproved.   405

46

And many more, whose names on Earth are dark
But whose transmitted effluence[7] cannot die
So long as fire outlives the parent spark,
Rose, robed in dazzling immortality.
"Thou art become as one of us," they cry,   410
"It was for thee yon kingless sphere has long
Swung blind in unascended majesty,
Silent alone amid an Heaven of song.[8]
Assume thy winged throne, thou Vesper of our throng!"

---

4. Adonais and other creative spirits are now called *splendours*, which at line 100 was the term used to designate one of Adonais' mental creations.

5. The examples of the illustrious dead influence the lives of young imaginative persons torn between the ideals pursued by their desires (*love*) and the sordid realities of everyday *life*; *doom:* destiny.

6. Those who died young before receiving their just recognition. Thomas *Chatterton*, to whose memory Keats had dedicated *Endymion*, committed suicide in 1770 at the age of seventeen while facing starvation, after writing brilliant poetry (purporting to be the work of a medieval monk named Thomas Rowley). Sir Philip *Sidney* (1554–1586), courtier and poet, while dying from wounds, directed that a cup of water intended for himself be given to a wounded common soldier, saying, "Thy necessity is yet greater than mine." He is the subject of Spenser's pastoral elegy *Astrophel*. *Lucan:* Marcus Annaeus Lucanus (39–65 A.D.) was the author of the *Pharsalia* (*Bellum Civile*), which praised the republican ideals of Pompey and Cato in their war against Caesar; forced to commit suicide when his role in a plot against Nero was discovered, Lucan recited a passage from his own poetry to his friends while bleeding to death.

7. Emanation.

8. Traditionally each *sphere* that encircled the earth was thought to be piloted by a particular god or genius— a spirit that gave vitality to it. Adonais is to be the genius of the third sphere of Venus, also known as Lucifer (morning star) and Hesperus or *Vesper* (evening star).

47

Who mourns for Adonais? oh come forth   415
Fond[9] wretch! and know thyself and him aright.
Clasp with thy panting soul the pendulous Earth;[1]
As from a centre, dart thy spirit's light
Beyond all world's, until its spacious might
Satiate the void circumference:[2] then shrink   420
Even to a point within our day and night;
And keep thy heart light lest it make thee sink
When hope has kindled hope, and lured thee to the brink.[3]

48

Or go to Rome,[4] which is the sepulchre
O, not of him, but of our joy: 'tis nought   425
That ages, empires, and religions there
Lie buried in the ravage they have wrought;
For such as he can lend,—they[5] borrow not
Glory from those who made the world their prey;
And he is gathered to the kings of thought   430
Who waged contention with their time's decay,
And of the past are all that cannot pass away.

49

Go thou to Rome,—at once the Paradise,
The grave, the city, and the wilderness;
And where it wrecks like shattered mountains rise,[6]   435
And flowering weeds, and fragrant copses dress
The bones of Desolation's nakedness
Pass, till the Spirit of the spot shall lead
Thy footsteps to a slope of green access
Where, like an infant's smile,[7] over the dead,   440
A light of laughing flowers along the grass is spread.[8]

50

And grey walls[9] moulder round, on which dull Time
Feeds, like slow fire upon a hoary brand;[1]

9. Unreasonable or foolish.
1. The earth is like a pendulum in that its orbit is irregular and from a cosmic vantage point it would appear to be oscillating at the end of its cone-shaped shadow (umbra).
2. "Poetry is indeed something divine. It is at once the centre and circumference of knowledge . . ." (*Defence of Poetry*, p. 503).
3. The edge of a precipice or a grave.
4. When the imagination *shrinks* to a single *point*, a *centre*, after having reached out to scan the universe in stanza 47, the poet suggests Rome as the proper point within time (*our day and night*) to explore.
5. I.e., those *such as he*, creative spirits as opposed to political and ecclesiastical rulers, who merely *ravage* the world.
6. The remains of Nero's palace and other imperial buildings, the city walls,

and the Baths of Caracalla, where Shelley wrote *Prometheus Unbound*, were overgrown with vegetation and almost seemed to have returned to natural hills.
7. Shelley's and Mary's eldest son, William Shelley, had died in Rome on June 7, 1819; his grave was in the Protestant Cemetery (Cimitero Acattolico) near the spot where Keats was later buried.
8. Before he died, Keats had asked Severn to look at the cemetery, and he had expressed pleasure at the "description of the locality . . ., particularly the innumerable violets" and the daisies among the grass.
9. The twelve-mile walls of Rome begun under Aurelian (emperor, 270–275 A.D.) form one boundary of the cemetery; the Porta San Paolo is the nearby gate in the Aurelian wall.
1. A log that has been covered with white ash while burning on the hearth.

And one keen pyramid with wedge sublime,[2]
Pavilioning the dust of him who planned   445
This refuge for his memory, doth stand
Like flame transformed to marble; and beneath,
A field is spread, on which a newer band
Have pitched in Heaven's smile their camp of death[3]
Welcoming him we lose with scarce extinguished breath.   450

51

Here pause: these graves are all to young as yet
To have outgrown the sorrow which consigned
Its charge to each; and if the seal is set,
Here, on one fountain of a mourning mind,[4]
Break it not thou! too surely shalt thou find   455
Thine own well full, if thou returnest home,
Of tears and gall. From the world's bitter wind[5]
Seek shelter in the shadow of the tomb.
What Adonais is, why fear we to become?

52

The One remains, the many change and pass;   460
Heaven's light forever shines, Earth's shadows fly;
Life, like a dome of many-coloured glass,
Stains the white radiance of Eternity,
Until Death tramples it to fragments.[6]—Die,
If thou wouldst be with that which thou dost seek!   465
Follow where all is fled!—Rome's azure sky,
Flowers, ruins, statues, music, words, are weak
The glory they transfuse with fitting truth to speak.

53

Why linger, why turn back, why shrink, my Heart?
Thy hopes are gone before;[7] from all things here   470
They have departed; thou shouldst now depart!
A light is past from the revolving year,
And man, and woman; and what still is dear
Attracts to crush, repels to make thee wither.
The soft sky smiles,—the low wind whispers near: 475
'Tis Adonais calls! oh, hasten thither,
No more let Life divide what Death can join together.

---

2. The pyramidal tomb of Caius Cestius, praetor and tribune of Rome during the latter half of the first century B.C., had been incorporated into the Aurelian wall.

3. One common name for a cemetery in Italy is *camposanto*, "holy camp." Shelley is punning seriously on the Italian word.

4. Shelley alludes to his sorrow at the death of his son.

5. William Shelley died in an epidemic of *malaria* (Italian for "bad [or evil] air"), possibly another Italian-English serious pun.

6. As the atmosphere refracts the sun's white light into the colors of the rainbow, Life distorts the universal *One* into *many* imperfect particulars, *until* Death permits the individual to reunite with the One.

7. Shelley at this period regretted the deaths of his children William and Clara (as well as the legal loss of his children by Harriet), alienation from Mary Shelley, animosity from the reviewers, neglect by his publisher and the reading public, and exile from his country and his few closest friends. Most of his early hopes, personal and political, had apparently failed.

54

That Light whose smile kindles the Universe,[8]
That Beauty in which all things work and move,
That Benediction which the eclipsing Curse   480
Of birth can quench not, that sustaining Love
Which through the web of being blindly wove
By man and beast and earth and air and sea,
Burns bright or dim, as each are mirrors of
The fire for which all thirst; now beams on me,   485
Consuming the last clouds of cold mortality.

55

The breath whose might I have invoked in song
Descends on me; my spirit's bark is driven,
Far from the shore, far from the trembling throng
Whose sails were never to the tempest given;[9]   490
The massy earth and sphered skies are riven!
I am borne darkly, fearfully, afar;
Whilst burning through the inmost veil of Heaven,
The soul of Adonais, like a star,
Beacons from the abode where the Eternal are.   495

Hellas

In December 1820, Professor Francesco Pacchiani (who was then bringing Teresa Viviani to the Shelleys' attention) introduced them to a group of exiled Greek aristocrats living in Pisa, the leading figure of whom was Prince Alexandros Mavrokordatos (1791–1865). Mavrocordato (as his name was usually Westernized) remained friendly with the Shelleys—especially Mary, to whom he taught Greek in return for English lessons. In April 1821 news reached Pisa that the Greeks, who had been subject to Turkey for several centuries, had revolted and declared their independence. In June, Mavrocordato left Italy to take part in the fight, which continued in various forms until 1832 and in which he was to have a major role; Mavrocordato later served as prime minister of independent Greece on four different occasions between 1833 and 1855.

Shelley wrote most of his poem on the War of Greek Independence during the first three weeks of October 1821. As early as October 11, Shelley wrote to Ollier that his "dramatic poem called 'Hellas' will soon be ready" (Edward Williams' suggestion of the name to Shelley on October 25 was, therefore, after the fact). Williams transcribed *Hellas* for the press, November 6–10, and on November 11, Shelley, after correcting it, mailed it to London with a cover letter instructing Ollier to "send the Ms. instantly to a Printer, & the moment you get a proof, dispatch it to me by the Post," but also giving the publisher "liberty to suppress" anything in the *notes* he considered dangerous under the laws of the time. Ollier canceled some lines in the poem as well as passages in the notes, he did

---

8. This line and several others in stanza 54 echo the opening lines of Dante's *Paradiso*: "The glory of him who moves all things penetrates throughout the universe and rekindles [glows again] in one part more, and in another less. I have been in that sphere which most receives his light."

9. Lines 488–490 echo but recast the idea of the opening lines of Canto II of Dante's *Paradiso:* "O ye who in your little skiff [*barca*], longing to hear, have followed behind my keel that goes singing, turn back to your own shores; do not give yourself to the open sea, lest, losing me, you would remain lost."

not send proofs for Shelley to read, and *Hellas* had not been printed by February 19, 1822, according to Maria Gisborne; but when a copy first reached Pisa early in April, Shelley wrote to Ollier that it was "prettily printed, & with fewer mistakes than any poem I ever published." In another letter written to Ollier the following day Shelley did include several important errata (some errors in the manuscript rather than the printing), but the text of *Hellas* is relatively authoritative because both the press copy manuscript and the errata list have survived (both at the Henry E. Huntington Library, HM 329).

Hellas is based, as Shelley himself states, on *The Persians* of Aeschylus. That play, the only surviving Greek drama to deal with contemporary historical events, relates the Greek defeat of the Persian grand army led by Xerxes. A series of messengers bearing the bad news to the Persian capital, where Atossa, the queen mother, and a chorus of Persian elders—counseled by the ghost of Darius the Great summoned by his widow from the dead— lament the misdirected pride of Xerxes and the destruction of their empire's greatness.

Shelley's drama is purely Greek in its external form, observing perfectly the unities of time (twenty-four hours), place (the Sultan's palace in Constantinople), and action (news of the fortunes of the war between the Greeks and the Turks). Structurally, it consists of seven sections—four of choral lyrics flanking three long sections of blank verse dialogue. For a discussion of the political implications of the drama, see the excerpt from Carl Woodring's *Politics in English Romantic Poetry*, pages 675–681; for the grim realities of the War of Greek Independence, of which Shelley (like other outsiders) was totally ignorant, see William St. Clair, *That Greece Might Still Be Free* (Oxford University Press, 1972).

Hellas

A Lyrical Drama

ΜΑΝΤΙΣ 'ΕΙΜ' 'ΕΣΘΛΩΝ 'ΑΓΩΝΩΝ.—OEDIP. COLON.*

To His Excellency

Prince Alexander Mavrocordato

late Secretary for foreign affairs to the Hospodar of Wallachia

The drama of Hellas is inscribed as an
imperfect token of the admiration,
sympathy, and friendship of
the Author.

Pisa, November 1st, 1821.

PREFACE

THE Poem of *Hellas*, written at the suggestion of the events of the moment, is a mere improvise, and derives its interest (should it be

---

* "I am a prophet of glorious struggles." Sophocles, *Oedipus at Colonus*, 1080.

found to possess any) solely from the intense sympathy which the Author feels with the cause he would celebrate.

The subject in its present state, is insusceptible of being treated otherwise than lyrically, and if I have called this poem a drama from the circumstance of its being composed in dialogue, the licence is not greater than that which has been assumed by other poets who have called their productions epics, only because they have been divided into twelve or twenty-four books.

The Persæ of Æschylus afforded me the first model of my conception, although the decision of the glorious contest now waging in Greece being yet suspended forbids a catastrophe parallel to the return of Xerxes and the desolation of the Persians. I have, therefore, contented myself with exhibiting a series of lyric pictures, and with having wrought upon the curtain of futurity which falls upon the unfinished scene such figures of indistinct and visionary delineation as suggest the final triumph of the Greek cause as a portion of the cause of civilization and social improvement.

The drama (if drama it must be called) is, however, so inartificial that I doubt whether, if recited on the Thespian waggon to an Athenian village at the Dionysiaca, it would have obtained the prize of the goat.[1] I shall bear with equanimity any punishment greater than the loss of such a reward which the Aristarchi[2] of the hour may think fit to inflict.

The only *goat-song* which I have yet attempted has, I confess, in spite of the unfavourable nature of the subject, received a greater and a more valuable portion of applause than I expected or than it deserved.

Common fame is the only authority which I can alledge for the details which form the basis of the poem, and I must trespass upon the forgiveness of my readers for the display of newspaper erudition to which I have been reduced. Undoubtedly, until the conclusion of the war, it will be impossible to obtain an account of it sufficiently authentic for historical materials; but poets have their privilege, and it is unquestionable that actions of the most exalted courage have been performed by the Greeks, that they have gained more than one naval victory, and that their defeat in Wallachia[3] was signalized by circumstances of heroism, more glorious even than victory.

The apathy of the rulers of the civilized world to the astonishing circumstance of the descendants of that nation to which they owe their civilization rising as it were from the ashes of their ruin is something perfectly inexplicable to a mere spectator of the shews of

1. The word "tragedy" is generally supposed to derive from the Greek for "goat-song," and the common explanation is that the winner of a dramatic competition at the festival of Dionysus received a goat as prize.

2. Aristarchus of Samothrace (ca. 220–143 B.C.) was an Alexandrian grammarian and critic noted for his harsh criticisms of the Greek classics.

3. A Turkish province north of the Danube; now part of Rumania.

this mortal scene. We are all Greeks—our laws, our literature, our religion, our arts have their root in Greece. But for Greece, Rome, the instructor, the conqueror, or the metropolis of our ancestors would have spread no illumination with her arms, and we might still have been savages, and idolaters; or, what is worse, might have arrived at such a stagnant and miserable state of social institution as China and Japan possess.

The human form and the human mind attained to a perfection in Greece which has impressed its image on those faultless productions whose very fragments are the despair of modern art, and has propagated impulses which cannot cease, through a thousand channels of manifest or imperceptible operation to ennoble and delight mankind until the extinction of the race.

The modern Greek is the descendant of those glorious beings whom the imagination almost refuses to figure to itself as belonging to our Kind, and he inherits much of their sensibility, their rapidity of conception, their enthusiasm, and their courage. If in many instances he is degraded, by moral and political slavery to the practise of the basest vices it engenders, and that below the level of ordinary degradation; let us reflect that the corruption of the best produces the worst, and that habits which subsist only in relation to a peculiar state of social institution may be expected to cease so soon as that relation is dissolved. In fact, the Greeks, since the admirable novel of *Anastasius*[4] could have been a faithful picture of their manners, have undergone most important changes; the flower of their Youth, returning to their Country from the universities of Italy, Germany and France have communicated to their fellow citizens the latest results of that social perfection of which their ancestors were the original source. The university of Chios contained before the breaking out of the Revolution eight hundred students, and among them several Germans and Ámericans. The munificence and energy of many of the Greek princes and merchants, directed to the renovation of their country with a spirit and a wisdom which has few examples, is above all praise.

The English permit their own oppressors to act according to their natural sympathy with the Turkish tyrant, and to brand upon their name the indelible blot of an alliance with the enemies of domestic happiness, of Christianity and civilization.

Russia desires to possess not to liberate Greece, and is contented to see the Turks, its natural enemies, and the Greeks, its intended slaves, enfeeble each other until one or both fall into its net. The wise and generous policy of England would have consisted in establishing the independence of Greece, and in maintaining it both

---

4. *Anastasius; or, Memoirs of a Greek*, a three-volume novel by Thomas Hope published anonymously in 1819.

against Russia and the Turk;—but when was the oppressor generous or just?

Should the English people ever become free they will reflect upon the part which those who presume to represent their will, have played in the great drama of the revival of liberty, with feelings which it would become them to anticipate. This is the age of the war of the oppressed against the oppressors, and every one of those ringleaders of the privileged gangs of murderers and swindlers, called Sovereigns, look to each other for aid against the common enemy and suspend their mutual jealousies in the presence of a mightier fear. Of this holy alliance all the despots of the earth are virtual members. But a new race has arisen throughout Europe, nursed in the abhorrence of the opinions which are its chains, and she will continue to produce fresh generations to accomplish that destiny which tyrants foresee and dread.[5]

The Spanish peninsula is already free. France is tranquil in the enjoyment of a partial exemption from the abuses which its unnatural and feeble government are vainly attempting to revive. The seed of blood and misery has been sown in Italy and a more vigorous race is arising to go forth to the harvest. The world waits only the news of a revolution of Germany to see the Tyrants who have pinnacled themselves on its supineness precipitated into the ruin from which they shall never arise. Well do these destroyers of mankind know their enemy when they impute the insurrection in Greece to the same spirit before which they tremble throughout the rest of Europe, and that enemy well knows the power and the cunning of its opponents, and watches the moment of their approaching weakness and inevitable division to wrest the bloody sceptres from their grasp.—

Dramatis Personæ

Mahmud.	Daood.
Hassan.	Ahasuerus, a Jew.

Chorus of Greek Captive Women.
Messengers, Slaves, and Attendants.
Scene, Constantinople.   Time, Sunset.

SCENE. A terrace on the Seraglio.[6] Mahmud sleeping, an Indian slave sitting beside his couch.

Chorus of Greek Captive Women.

We strew these opiate flowers
     On thy restless pillow,—

---

5. This paragraph, deleted by Ollier from the first edition, was first published by H. Buxton Forman in his Aldine Edition of Shelley's *Poetical Works* (1892).

6. Turkish palace (or, sometimes, the palace in which the harem was located).

They were stript from Orient bowers,
　　By the Indian billow.
　　　　Be thy sleep　　　　　　　　　5
　　　　Calm and deep,
Like theirs who fell, not ours who weep!

Indian.

Away, unlovely dreams!
　　Away, false shapes of sleep!
Be his, as Heaven seems　　　　　　　10
　　Clear and bright and deep!
Soft as love, and calm as death,
Sweet as a summer night without a breath.

Chorus.

Sleep, sleep! our song is laden
　　With the soul of slumber;　　　　　15
It was sung by a Samian[7] maiden
　　Whose lover was of the number
　　　　Who now keep
　　　　That calm sleep
Whence none may wake, where none shall weep.　20

Indian.

I touch thy temples pale!
　　I breathe my soul on thee!
And could my prayers avail,
　　All my joy should be
Dead, and I would live to weep,　　　　25
So thou might'st win one hour of quiet sleep.

Chorus.

　　Breathe low, low!
The spell of the mighty mistress now
When Conscience lulls her sated snake
And Tyrants sleep, let Freedom wake.　　30
　　Breathe! low—low
The words which like secret fire shall flow
Through the veins of the frozen earth—low, low!

Semichorus I.

Life may change, but it may fly not;
Hope may vanish, but can die not;　　　35
Truth be veiled but still it burneth;
Love repulsed,—but it returneth!

---

7. From the Aegean island of Samos, off the coast of Asia Minor.

Semichorus II.

Yet were Life a charnel where
Hope lay coffined with despair;
Yet were Truth a sacred lie,   40
Love were Lust—

Semichorus I.

If Liberty
Lent not Life its soul of light,
Hope its iris of delight,
Truth its prophet's robe to wear,
Love its power to give and bear.   45

Chorus.

In the great Morning of the world
The spirit of God with might unfurled
The flag of Freedom over chaos,
    And all its banded anarchs[8] fled
Like Vultures frighted from Imaus[9]   50
    Before an Earthquake's tread.—
So from Time's tempestuous dawn
Freedom's splendour burst and shone:—
Thermopylæ and Marathon[1]
Caught, like mountains beacon-lighted,   55
    The springing Fire.—The winged Glory
On Philippi[2] half-alighted,
    Like an eagle on a promontory.
Its unwearied wings could fan
The quenchless ashes of Milan.[3]   60
From age to age, from man to man,
    It lived; and lit from land to land
    Florence, Albion,[4] Switzerland.

Then Night fell—and as from night
Re-assuming fiery flight   65
From the West swift Freedom came
    Against the course of Heaven and doom,
A second sun arrayed in flame
    To burn, to kindle, to illume.

---

8. Tyrants in a group or pack (cf. *Adonais*, 244).
9. A mountain in central Asia; in *Paradise Lost*, Milton describes Satan as "a Vultur on *Imaus bred*" (III.431).
1. In 490 B.C. eleven thousand Athenians and Plataeans destroyed the much larger invading Persian army of Darius I on the plain of Marathon; ten years later (480 B.C.) the Spartans and their allies under Leonidas held the host of Xerxes at bay in the narrow defile of Thermopylae, between the mountains and the sea, for three bloody days until Leonidas and all the Spartans had been killed.
2. A city in Macedonia where, in 42 B.C., Mark Antony and Octavius Caesar put an end to the power of the senatorial (republican) party by defeating the army of Brutus and Cassius.
3. In the twelfth and thirteenth centuries Milan was the leading city of the Lombard League of Italian democratic communes that defied and eventually defeated the Holy Roman Emperor Frederick I (Barbarossa).
4. England.

From far Atlantis[5] its young beams 70
Chased the shadows and the dreams
France, with all her sanguine steams[6]
 Hid but quench'd it not; again
 Through clouds its shafts of glory rain
 From utmost Germany to Spain. 75

As an eagle fed with morning
Scorns the embattled tempest's warning
When she seeks her aiëry hanging
 In the mountain-cedar's hair
And her brood expect the clanging 80
 Of her wings through the wild air
Sick with famine—Freedom so
To what of Greece remaineth now
Returns; her hoary ruins glow
Like orient mountains lost in day. 85
 Beneath the safety of her wings
Her renovated nurslings prey,
 And in the naked lightnings
Of truth they purge their dazzled eyes.
Let Freedom leave, where'er she flies, 90
A Desart or a Paradise:
 Let the beautiful and the brave
 Share her glory, or a grave.

   Semichorus I.

 With the gifts of gladness
  Greece did thy cradle strew— 95

   Semichorus II.

 With the tears of sadness
  Greece did thy shroud bedew!

   Semichorus I.

 With an orphan's affection
  She followed thy bier through Time

   Semichorus II.

 And at thy resurrection 100
  Reappeareth, like thou, sublime!

   Semichorus I.

 If Heaven should resume thee,
  To Heaven shall her spirit ascend;

5. The United States of America.   6. The French Revolution.

Semichorus II.

If Hell should entomb thee,
 To Hell shall her high hearts bend.   105

Semichorus I.

If annihilation——

Semichorus II.

Dust let her glories be!
And a name and a nation
Be forgotten, Freedom, with thee!

Indian

His brow grows darker—breathe not—move not! 110
He starts—he shudders—ye that love not,
 With your panting loud and fast,
 Have awakened him at last.

Mahmud (starting from his sleep). Man the Seraglio-guard!—make
 fast the gate.
What! from a cannonade of three short hours?   115
'Tis false! that breach towards the Bosphorus[7]
Cannot be practicable yet—who stirs?
Stand to the match! that when the foe prevails
One spark may mix in reconciling ruin
The conqueror and the conquered! Heave the tower 120
Into the gap—wrench off the roof!
 (*Enter* HASSAN.)   Ha! what!
The truth of day lightens upon my dream
And I am Mahmud, still,—
 Hassan.   Your sublime highness
Is strangely moved.
 Mahmud.   The times do cast strange shadows
On those who watch and who must rule their course, 125
Lest they being first in peril as in glory
Be whelmed in the fierce ebb:—and these are of them.
Thrice has a gloomy vision hunted me
As thus from sleep into the troubled day;
It shakes me as the tempest shakes the sea,   130
Leaving no figure upon memory's glass.
Would that——no matter—thou didst say thou knewest
A Jew, whose spirit is a chronicle
Of strange and secret and forgotten things.
I bade thee summon him—'tis said his tribe   135
Dream, and are wise interpreters of dreams.
 Hassan. The Jew of whom I spake is old—so old
He seems to have outlived a world's decay;

---

7. Constantinople is on the west side of
the Bosporus, the strait that connects
the Black Sea with the Sea of Marmara
(which, in turn, connects with the Aegean
through the Dardanelles).

The hoary mountains and the wrinkled ocean
Seem younger still than he—his hair and beard 140
Are whiter than the tempest-sifted snow.
His cold pale limbs and pulseless arteries
Are like the fibres of a cloud instinct[8]
With light, and to the soul that quickens them
Are as the atoms of the mountain-drift 145
To the winter wind—but from his eye looks forth
A life of unconsumed thought which pierces
The present, and the past, and the to-come.
Some say that this is he whom the great prophet
Jesus, the Son of Joseph, for his mockery 150
Mocked with the curse of immortality.—
Some feign that he is Enoch[9]—others dream
He was preadamite and has survived
Cycles of generation and of ruin.
The sage, in truth, by dreadful abstinence 155
And conquering penance of the mutinous flesh,
Deep contemplation, and unwearied study
In years outstretched beyond the date of man,
May have attained to sovereignty and science[1]
Over those strong and secret things and thoughts 160
Which others fear and know not.
 Mahmud.   I would talk
With this old Jew.
 Hassan.   Thy will is even now
Made known to him, where he dwells in a sea cavern
Mid the Demonesi,[2] less accessible
Than thou or God! He who would question him 165
Must sail alone at sunset where the stream
Of ocean sleeps around those foamless isles,
When the young moon is westering as now
And evening airs wander upon the wave;
And when the pines of that bee-pasturing isle, 170
Green Erebinthus, quench the fiery shadow
Of his gilt prow within the sapphire water.
Then must the lonely helmsman cry aloud,
Ahasuerus! and the caverns round
Will answer Ahasuerus! If his prayer 175
Be granted, a faint meteor will arise
Lighting him over Marmora,[3] and a wind
Will rush out of the sighing pine forest
And with the wind a storm of harmony
Unutterably sweet, and pilot him 180
Through the soft twilight to the Bosphorus:

8. Imbued or inflamed.
9. "And Enoch walked with God: and he was not; for God took him" (Genesis 5:24); this ambiguous poetic phrasing has led some commentators to say that Enoch (the father of Methuselah) never died but was taken alive by God.
1. Mastery.
2. Islands in the Sea of Marmara.
3. Small "sea" between the Dardanelles and the Bosporus.

Thence at the hour and place and circumstance
Fit for the matter of their conference
The Jew appears. Few dare and few who dare
Win the desired communion—but that shout   185
Bodes——   [*a shout within.*
   Mahmud. Evil doubtless like all human sounds.
Let me converse with spirits.
   Hassan.   That shout again.
   Mahmud. This Jew whom thou hast summoned—
   Hassan.   Will be here—
   Mahmud. When the omnipotent hour to which are yoked
He, I, and all things shall compel—enough.   190
Silence those mutineers—that drunken crew,
That crowd about the pilot in the storm.
Aye! strike the foremost shorter by a head.—
They weary me and I have need of rest.
Kings are like stars—they rise and set, they have   195
The worship of the world but no repose.   [*exeunt severally.*

         Chorus.[4]
   Worlds on worlds are rolling ever
     From creation to decay,
   Like the bubbles on a river
     Sparkling, bursting, borne away.   200
     But *they* are still immortal
     Who through Birth's orient portal
And Death's dark chasm hurrying to and fro,
     Clothe their unceasing flight
     In the brief dust and light   205
Gathered around their chariots as they go;
     New shapes they still may weave,
     New Gods, new Laws receive,
Bright or dim are they as the robes they last
     On Death's bare ribs had cast.   210

   A Power from the unknown God,
     A Promethean Conqueror,[5] came;
   Like a triumphal path he trod
     The thorns of death and shame.

4. "The popular notions of Christianity are represented in this chorus as true in their relation to the worship they superseded, . . . without considering their merits in a relation more universal. The first stanza contrasts the immortality of the living and thinking beings which inhabit the planets, and to use a common and inadequate phrase, *clothe themselves in matter,* with the transcience of the noblest manifestations of the external world.

"The concluding verses indicate a progressive state of more or less exalted existence, according to the degree of perfection which every distinct intelligence may have attained. Let it not be supposed that I mean to dogmatise upon a subject, concerning which all men are equally ignorant, or that I think the Gordian knot of the origin of evil can be disentangled by that or any similar assertions. . . . as it is the province of the poet to attach himself to those ideas which exalt and ennoble humanity, let him be permitted to have conjectured the condition of that futurity towards which we are all impelled by an inextinguishable thirst for immortality" (Shelley's note).
5. Jesus Christ.

A mortal shape to him 215
Was like the vapour dim
Which the orient planet[6] animates with light;
Hell, Sin, and Slavery came
Like bloodhounds mild and tame,
Nor preyed, until their Lord had taken flight; 220
The moon of Mahomet[7]
Arose, and it shall set,
While blazoned as on Heaven's immortal noon
The cross leads generations on.[8]

Swift as the radiant shapes of sleep 225
From one whose dreams are Paradise
Fly, when the fond wretch wakes to weep,
And Day peers forth with her blank eyes;
So fleet, so faint, so fair,
The Powers of earth and air 230
Fled from the folding star[9] of Bethlehem;
Apollo, Pan, and Love,
And even Olympian Jove
Grew weak, for killing Truth had glared on them;[1]
Our hills and seas and streams, 235
Dispeopled of their dreams,
Their waters turned to blood, their dew to tears,
Wailed for the golden years.

Enter MAHMUD, HASSAN, DAOOD, *and others.*

   Mahmud. More gold? our ancestors bought gold with victory,
And shall I sell it for defeat?
   Daood.   The Janizars[2] 240
Clamour for pay—
   Mahmud.   Go! bid them pay themselves
With Christian blood! Are there no Grecian virgins
Whose shrieks and spasms and tears they may enjoy?
No infidel children to impale on spears?
No hoary priests after that Patriarch[3] 245
Who bent the curse against his country's heart,
Which clove his own at last? Go! bid them kill—

---

6. Venus as the morning star.
7. The crescent moon is the chief symbol of Islam.
8. The Roman emperor Constantine I (who named Constantinople) was converted to Christianity, according to his own account, when he saw a cross of light superimposed on the noonday sun.
9. The evening star, which appears about the time shepherds bring their sheep back to the fold.
1. In this stanza Shelley alludes to the story Milton tells in "On the Morning of Christ's Nativity" (165–236) of the downfall of the pagan gods.

2. The janizaries were, from the end of the fourteenth century on, the chief standing army of the Turkish Empire; they were originally recruited from Christian children who were demanded as tribute, converted to Islam, and trained as soldiers by the Turks. In 1826, Mahmud II abolished the corps of janizaries.
3. After the Greeks rebelled and slew Turks among them, the Turks retaliated by massacring the Greeks in Asia Minor, including Gregorios, the Orthodox Patriarch of Constantinople, who was hanged on April 22, 1821.

Blood is the seed of gold.
   Daood.   It has been sown,
And yet the harvest to the sicklemen
Is as a grain to each.
   Mahmud.   Then, take this signet.   250
Unlock the seventh chamber in which lie
The treasures of victorious Solyman,[4]—
An Empire's spoil stored for a day of ruin.
O spirit of my sires, is it not come?
The prey-birds and the wolves are gorged and sleep,   255
But these, who spread their feast on the red earth,
Hunger for gold, which fills not—see them fed;
Then, lead them to the rivers of fresh death.   [*Exit* DAOOD.
O, miserable dawn after a night
More glorious than the day which it usurped!   260
O, faith in God! O power on earth! O word
Of the great prophet, whose o'ershadowing wings
Darkened the thrones and idols of the West:
Now bright!—for thy sake cursed be the hour,
Even as a father by an evil child   265
When th'orient moon of Islam roll'd in triumph
From Caucasus to white Ceraunia![5]
Ruin above, and anarchy below;
Terror without, and treachery within;
The chalice of destruction full, and all   270
Thirsting to drink, and who among us dares
To dash it from his lips? and where is hope?
   Hassan. The lamp of our dominion still rides high,
One God is God—Mahomet is his prophet.
Four hundred thousand Moslems, from the limits   275
Of utmost Asia, irresistibly
Throng, like full clouds at the Sirocco's[6] cry;
But not like them to weep their strength in tears:
They bear destroying lightning and their step
Wakes earthquake to consume and overwhelm   280
And reign in ruin. Phrygian Olympus,
Tmolus and Latmos and Mycale[7] roughen
With horrent arms; and lofty ships even now
Like vapours anchored to a mountain's edge,
Freighted with fire and whirlwind, wait at Scala[8]   285
The convoy of the ever-veering wind.

---

4. Suleiman I, the Magnificent (sultan, 1520–1566), had defeated Persia, conquered Hungary (threatening Austria), Rhodes, and Venetian strongholds in southern Greece, and defeated the combined fleets of Spain and Venice off Preveza (1538). His reign also saw the highest achievements of the Ottoman Empire in law, literature, art, and architecture.
5. The Caucasus Mountains between the Black Sea and the Caspian Sea separated Russia from Turkey; the Ceraunian (or Acroceraunian) Mountains of Epirus in northwestern Greece mark the separation of the Ionian Sea from the Adriatic.
6. The sultry southeast wind.
7. Mountains in northwestern Asia Minor, the Ottoman homeland.
8. The port of Scala Tyriorum in Phoenicia.

Samos is drunk with blood;—the Greek has paid
Brief victory with swift loss and long despair.
The false Moldavian[9] serfs fled fast and far
When the fierce shout of Allah-illa-allah![1]   290
Rose like the war-cry of the northern wind
Which kills the sluggish clouds, and leaves a flock
Of wild swans struggling with the naked storm.
So were the lost Greeks on the Danube's day![2]
If night is mute, yet the returning sun   295
Kindles the voices of the morning birds;
Nor at thy bidding less exultingly
Than birds rejoicing in the golden day,
The Anarchies of Africa[3] unleash
Their tempest-winged cities of the sea   300
To speak in thunder to the rebel world.
Like sulphurous clouds half shattered by the storm
They sweep the pale Ægean, while the Queen
Of Ocean,[4] bound upon her island-throne
Far in the West sits mourning that her sons   305
Who frown on Freedom spare a smile for thee.
Russia still hovers as an Eagle might
Within a cloud, near which a kite and crane
Hang tangled in inextricable fight,
To stoop upon the victor—for she fears   310
The name of Freedom even as she hates thine.
But recreant[5] Austria loves thee as the Grave
Loves Pestilence, and her slow dogs of war
Fleshed with the chase come up from Italy
And howl upon their limits; for they see   315
The panther Freedom fled to her old cover
'Mid seas and mountains and a mightier brood
Crouch round. What anarch wears a crown or mitre,
Or bears the sword, or grasps the key of gold,
Whose friends are not thy friends, whose foes thy foes? 320
Our arsenals and our armouries are full;
Our forts defy assault—ten thousand cannon
Lie ranged upon the beach, and hour by hour
Their earth-convulsing wheels affright the city;
The galloping of fiery steeds makes pale   325
The Christian merchant; and the yellow Jew
Hides his hoard deeper in the faithless earth.
Like clouds and like the shadows of the clouds,

9. Moldavia or Bessarabia, now part of the USSR, lies between Rumania and the Ukraine; it was then a dependency of the Turks and a buffer against Russia.
1. The Islamic war cry: "There is no god but God."
2. Alexandros Ypsilantis began the War of Greek Independence by crossing from Russia into Moldavia in March 1821, but was soon defeated and fled to Austria, where he was imprisoned until 1827.
3. The corsair or pirate states of Algiers, Tunis, and Tripoli.
4. Great Britain.
5. Cowardly.

Over the hills of Anatolia[6]
Swift in wide troops the Tartar chivalry   330
Sweep—the far flashing of their starry lances
Reverberates the dying light of day.
We have one God, one King, one hope, one law;
But many-headed Insurrection stands
Divided in itself, and soon must fall.   335
    Mahmud. Proud words when deeds come short are seasonable.
Look, Hassan, on yon crescent moon emblazoned
Upon that shattered flag of fiery cloud
Which leads the rear of the departing day,
Wan emblem of an empire fading now.   340
See! How it trembles in the blood-red air
And like a mighty lamp whose oil is spent
Shrinks on the horizon's edge while from above
One star[7] with insolent and victorious light
Hovers above its fall, and with keen beams   345
Like arrows through a fainting antelope
Strikes its weak form to death.
    Hassan.   Even as that moon
Renews itself——
    Mahmud.   Shall we be not renewed!
Far other bark[8] than ours were needed now
To stem the torrent of descending time;   350
The spirit that lifts the slave before his lord
Stalks through the capitals of armed kings
And spreads his ensign in the wilderness,
Exults in chains, and when the rebel falls
Cries like the blood of Abel[9] from the dust;   355
And the inheritors of the earth, like beasts
When earthquake is unleashed, with idiot fear
Cower in their kingly dens—as I do now.
What were Defeat when Victory must appal?
Or Danger when Security looks pale?   360
How said the messenger who from the fort
Islanded in the Danube, saw the battle
Of Bucharest?[1]—that—
    Hassan.   Ibrahim's scymitar
Drew with its gleam swift victory from heaven,
To burn before him in the night of battle—   365
A light and a destruction——
    Mahmud.   Aye! the day
Was ours—but how?——
    Hassan.   The light Wallachians,
The Arnaut, Servian, and Albanian allies

6. The central plateau of Asia Minor.
7. Venus as the evening star.
8. Small ship.
9. The second son of Adam, who was killed by his brother, Cain.
1. Though Alexandros Ypsilantis held Bucharest briefly, he had retreated in the face of the advancing Turks, and his decisive defeat, which Shelley describes in the following passage, took place at Drăgasăni, about one hundred miles to the west-northwest.

Fled from the glance of our artillery
Almost before the thunderstone alit.   370
One half the Grecian army made a bridge
Of safe and slow retreat with Moslem dead;
The other—
    Mahmud. Speak—tremble not.—
    Hassan.   Islanded
By victor myriads formed in hollow square .
With rough and steadfast front, and thrice flung back   375
The deluge of our foaming cavalry;
Thrice their keen wedge of battle pierced our lines.
Our baffled army trembled like one man
Before a host, and gave them space, but soon
From the surrounding hills the batteries blazed,   380
Kneading them down with fire and iron rain:
Yet none approached till like a field of corn
Under the hook of the swart sickleman
The band, intrenched in mounds of Turkish dead,
Grew weak and few—then said the Pacha, "Slaves,   385
Render yourselves—they have abandoned you,
What hope of refuge, or retreat or aid?
We grant your lives." "Grant that which is thine own!"
Cried one, and fell upon his sword and died!
Another—"God, and man, and hope abandon me   390
But I to them and to myself remain
Constant"—he bowed his head and his heart burst.
A third exclaimed, "There is a refuge, tyrant,
Where thou darest not pursue and canst not harm
Should'st thou pursue; there we shall meet again."   395
Then held his breath and, after a brief spasm
The indignant spirit cast its mortal garment
Among the slain;—dead earth upon the earth!
So these survivors, each by different ways,
Some strange, all sudden, none dishonorable,   400
Met in triumphant death; and when our army
Closed in, while yet wonder and awe and shame
Held back the base hyenas of the battle
That feed upon the dead and fly the living,
One rose out of the chaos of the slain: 405
And if it were a corpse which some dread spirit
Of the old saviours of the land we rule
Had lifted in its anger, wandering by;—
Or if there burned within the dying man
Unquenchable disdain of death, and faith   410
Creating what it feigned;—I cannot tell—
But he cried, "Phantoms of the free, we come!
Armies of the Eternal, ye who strike
To dust the citadels of sanguine[2] kings,
And shake the souls throned on their stony hearts   415

2. Bloody.

And thaw their frostwork diadems like dew;—
O ye who float around this clime, and weave
The garment of the glory which it wears,
Whose fame though earth betray the dust it clasped,
Lies sepulchred in monumental thought;—   420
Progenitors of all that yet is great,
Ascribe to your bright senate, O accept
In your high ministrations, us, your Sons.
Us first, and the more glorious yet to come!
And ye, weak conquerors! giants who look pale   425
When the crushed worm rebels beneath your tread,
The vultures and the dogs, your pensioners tame,
Are overgorged, but like oppressors, still
They crave the relic of destruction's feast;
The exhalations and the thirsty winds   430
Are sick with blood; the dew is foul with death;
Heaven's light is quenched in slaughter; thus, where'er
Upon your camps, cities, or towers, or fleets
The obscene birds the reeking remnants cast
Of these dead limbs,—upon your streams and mountains,   435
Upon your fields, your gardens, and your housetops,
Where'er the winds shall creep or the clouds fly
Or the dews fall or the angry sun look down
With poisoned light—Famine and Pestilence
And Panic shall wage war upon our side;   440
Nature from all her boundaries is moved
Against ye;—Time has found ye light as foam;
The Earth rebels; and Good and Evil stake
Their empire o'er the unborn world of men
On this one cast;—but ere the die be thrown   445
The renovated Genius[3] of our race,
Proud umpire of the impious game, descends,
A seraph-winged Victory, bestriding
The tempest of the Omnipotence of God
Which sweeps all things to their appointed doom   450
And you to oblivion!"—More he would have said
But—
     Mahmud. Died—as thou should'st ere thy lips had painted
Their ruin in the hues of our success—
A rebel's crime gilt with a rebel's tongue!
Your heart is Greek, Hassan.
     Hassan.   It may be so: 455
A spirit not my own wrenched me within
And I have spoken words I fear and hate;
Yet would I die for—
     Mahmud.   Live! O live! outlive
Me and this sinking Empire. But the fleet—
     Hassan. Alas!——

3. Protective guiding spirit.

Mahmud.   The fleet which like a flock of clouds 460
Chased by the wind flies the insurgent banner.
Our winged castles from their merchant ships!
Our myriads before their weak pirate bands![4]
Our arms before their chains! our years of Empire
Before their centuries of servile fear! 465
Death is awake! Repulse is on the waters!
They own no more the thunder-bearing banner
Of Mahmud; but like hounds of a base breed,
Gorge from a stranger's hand and rend their master.
Hassan. Latmos, and Ampelos and Phanæ[5] saw 470
The wreck——
Mahmud.   The caves of the Icarian isles
Told each to the other in loud mockery,
And with the tongue as of a thousand echoes
First of the sea convulsing fight—and, then,—
Thou darest to speak—senseless are the mountains; 475
Interpret thou their voice!
Hassan.   My presence bore
A part in that day's shame. The Grecian fleet
Bore down at day-break from the North, and hung,
As multitudinous on the ocean line
As cranes upon the cloudless Thracian wind. 480
Our squadron convoying ten thousand men
Was stretching towards Nauplia[6] when the battle
Was kindled.—
First through the hail of our artillery
The agile Hydriote[7] barks with press of sail 485
Dashed—ship to ship, cannon to cannon, man
To man were grappled in the embrace of war,
Inextricable but by death or victory—
The tempest of the raging fight convulsed
To its chrystalline depths that stainless sea 490
And shook Heaven's roof of golden morning clouds
Poised on a hundred azure mountain-isles.
In the brief trances of the artillery
One cry from the destroyed and the destroyer
Rose, and a cloud of desolation wrapt 495
The unforeseen event till the north wind
Sprung from the sea lifting the heavy veil
Of battle-smoke—then Victory—Victory!

4. For many years the Turkish navy had depended upon the seamanship of subject Greek sailors and navigators, who during the war either deserted or could not be trusted. The irregular Greek ships outsailed and frequently defeated the Turks early in the war.
5. Latmos and Ampelos are mountains and Phanae is a mountainous promontory on the mainland of Asia Minor to the east; the Icarian isles are to the north and south of the island of Icaria and the Icarian Sea (near Samos).
6. Nauplia, at the head of the Gulf of Argolis, on the east coast of the Peloponnesus, the Greek peninsula south of the Gulf of Corinth, was the center of Greek rebels led by Dimitrios Ypsilantis (younger brother of Alexandros).
7. From the island of Hydra (Idhra), off the eastern coast of the Peloponnesus.

For as we thought three frigates from Algiers
Bore down from Naxos[8] to our aid, but soon   500
The abhorred cross glimmered behind, before,
Among, around us; and that fatal sign
Dried with its beams the strength in Moslem hearts,
As the sun drinks the dew—what more? We fled!—
Our noonday path over the sanguine foam   505
Was beaconed,—and the glare struck the sun pale
By our consuming transports; the fierce light
Made all the shadows of our sails blood red
And every countenance blank. Some ships lay feeding
The ravening fire even to the water's level;   510
Some were blown up—some settling heavily
Sunk; and the shrieks of our companions died
Upon the wind that bore us fast and far
Even after they were dead—Nine thousand perished!
We met the vultures legioned in the air   515
Stemming the torrent of the tainted wind;
They, screaming from their cloudy mountain peaks,
Stooped through the sulphurous battle-smoke and perched
Each on the weltering carcase that we loved
Like its ill angel or its damned soul,   520
Riding upon the bosom of the sea.
We saw the dog-fish hastening to their feast,
Joy waked the voiceless people of the sea,
And ravening Famine left his ocean cave
To dwell with war, with us and with despair.   525
We met Night three hours to the west of Patmos[9]
And with Night, tempest——
    Mahmud.   Cease!—

                Enter a Messenger.
    Messenger.   Your sublime Highness,
That Christian hound, the Muscovite Ambassador,
Has left the city—if the rebel fleet
Had anchored in the port, had Victory   530
Crowned the Greek legions in the hippodrome,[1]
Panic were tamer—Obedience and Mutiny
Like giants in contention, planet-struck,[2]
Stand gazing on each other—there is peace
In Stamboul—
    Mahmud.   Is the grave not calmer still?   535
Its ruins shall be mine.
    Hassan.   Fear not the Russian:
The tiger leagues not with the stag at bay
Against the hunter—cunning, base, and cruel,

8. A large island of the Cyclades, half-way between Rhodes and Nauplia.
9. An island to the east-northeast of Naxos.

1. A *hippodrome* was the site of chariot races in classical times.
2. Paralyzed with fear.

He crouches watching till the spoil be won
And must be paid for his reserve in blood.   540
After the war is fought yield the sleek Russian
That which thou can'st not keep, his deserved portion
Of blood, which shall not flow through streets and fields,
Rivers and seas, like that which we may win,
But stagnate in the veins of Christian slaves!   545

Enter second Messenger.
    Second Messenger. Nauplia, Tripolizza, Mothon, Athens,
Navarin, Artas, Monembasia,[3]
Corinth and Thebes are carried by assault
And every Islamite who made his dogs
Fat with the flesh of Galilean slaves   550
Passed at the edge of the sword; the lust of blood
Which made our warriors drunk, is quenched in death;
But like a fiery plague breaks out anew
In deeds which make the Christian cause look pale
In its own light. The garrison of Patras[4]   555
Has store but for ten days, nor is there hope
But from the Briton; at once slave and tyrant
His wishes still are weaker than his fears
Or he would sell what faith may yet remain
From the oaths broke in Genoa and in Norway;[5]   560
And if you buy him not, your treasury
Is empty even of promises—his own coin.—
The freedman of a western poet chief[6]
Holds Attica with seven thousand rebels
And has beat back the Pacha of Negropont[7]—   565
The aged Ali sits in Yanina[8]

3. *Tripolizza* (Tripolis) was in the interior of the Peloponnesus, not far from Nauplia (see note to line 482); *Mothon* (Methoni) and *Navarin* (Pilos) were near the southwest corner of the peninsula (off which the decisive Battle of Navarino was to be fought in 1827 in which the Turkish and Egyptian fleets were destroyed by French and British fleets). *Artas* (Arta) was far to the northwest in southern Epirus, and *Monembasia* (Monemvasia) is in the far southeast corner of the Peloponnesus. Things, the messenger says, are going badly for the Turks all over Greece.
4. Patras (Pátrai) is on the northwest coast of the Peloponnesus, just outside the narrows of the Gulf of Corinth. The British held a protectorate over the nearby Ionian Islands.
5. During the Napoleonic Wars, Sir William Bentinck had promised the restoration of the Genovese Republic, leading the people to revolt against the French, only to have their city given to the kingdom of Sardinia. In 1814 Sweden took Norway (formerly a Danish possession), but the Norwegians rebelled and set up a constitutional monarchy; this independence was partially quelled by a Swedish invasion in 1818, to which Britain and the Holy Alliance acquiesced.
6. "A Greek who had been Lord Byron's servant commands the insurgents in Attica. This Greek, Lord Byron informs me, though a poet and an enthusiastic patriot, gave him rather the idea of a timid and unenterprising person. It appears that circumstances make men what they are . . ." (Shelley's note).
7. Euboea, a large island in the Aegean off the coast of Attica.
8. Ali (1741–1822), pacha or governor in Albania, was a famous warrior, intriguer, and murderer who had by 1810 or so established a virtually independent state with Yanina (Ioannina) as his capital. He was finally defeated and killed by the army of Sultan Mahmud II in May 1822.

A crownless metaphor of empire:
His name, that shadow of his withered might,
Holds our besieging army like a spell
In prey to Famine, Pest, and Mutiny;   570
He, bastioned in his citadel, looks forth
Joyless upon the sapphire lake that mirrors
The ruins of the city where he reigned
Childless and sceptreless. The Greek has reaped
The costly harvest his own blood matured,   575
Not the sower, Ali—who has bought a truce
From Ypsilanti[9] with ten camel loads
Of Indian gold—

                    Enter a third Messenger.
   Mahmud.   What more?
   Third Messenger.   The Christian tribes
Of Lebanon and the Syrian wilderness
Are in revolt—Damascus, Hems, Aleppo   580
Tremble—the Arab menaces Medina,
The Ethiop has intrenched himself in Senaar,
And keeps the Egyptian rebel well employed
Who denies homage, claims investiture
As price of tardy aid—Persia demands   585
The cities on the Tigris, and the Georgians
Refuse their living tribute.[1] Crete and Cyprus
Like mountain-twins that from each other's veins
Catch the volcano-fire and earthquake spasm,
Shake in the general fever. Through the city   590
Like birds before a storm the Santons[2] shriek
And prophesyings horrible and new
Are heard among the crowd—that sea of men
Sleeps on the wrecks it made, breathless and still.
A Dervise[3] learned in the Koran preaches   595
That it is written how the sins of Islam
Must raise up a destroyer even now.
The Greeks expect a Saviour from the West[4]
Who shall not come, men say, in clouds and glory:
But in the omnipresence of that spirit   600
In which all live and are. Ominous signs
Are blazoned broadly on the noonday sky.
One saw a red cross stamped upon the sun;
It has rained blood, and monstrous births declare

---

9. Alexandros Ypsilantis (see notes to lines 289 and 294) had begun the invasion of Moldavia to take advantage of the conflict between the Sultan and Ali Pacha. It is quite possible that (as Shelley must have heard) Ali and Ypsilantis had cooperated against their common enemy.
1. Georgia, in the Caucasus Mountains (now a Soviet state), was famous for the beautiful girls who were sent for the Sultan's harem.
2. Mohammedan holy men or dervishes.
3. A Mohammedan holy man who has taken vows of poverty and austere life.
4. "It is reported that this Messiah had arrived at a seaport near Lacedaemon in an American brig. The association of names and ideas is irresistibly ludicrous, but the prevalence of such a rumour strongly marks the state of popular enthusiasm in Greece" (Shelley's note).

The secret wrath of Nature and her Lord.   605
The army encamped upon the Cydaris,[5]
Was roused last night by the alarm of battle
And saw two hosts conflicting in the air,
The shadows doubtless of the unborn time
Cast on the mirror of the night;—while yet   610
The fight hung balanced, there arose a storm
Which swept the phantoms from among the stars.
At the third watch the spirit of the plague
Was heard abroad flapping among the tents;
Those who relieved watch found the sentinels dead.   615
The last news from the camp is that a thousand
Have sickened, and——

Enter a fourth Messenger.

   Mahmud.   And, thou, pale ghost, dim shadow
Of some untimely rumour—speak!
   Fourth Messenger.   One comes
Fainting with toil, covered with foam and blood:
He stood, he says, on Chelonites'   620
Promontory,[6] which o'erlooks the isles that groan
Under the Briton's frown, and all their waters
Then trembling in the splendour of the moon—
When as the wandering clouds unveiled or hid
Her boundless light, he saw two adverse fleets   625
Stalk through the night in the horizon's glimmer,
Mingling fierce thunders and sulphurious gleams,
And smoke which strangled every infant wind
That soothed the silver clouds through the deep air.
At length the battle slept, but the Sirocco   630
Awoke and drove his flock of thunder clouds
Over the sea-horizon, blotting out
All objects—save that in the faint moon-glimpse
He saw, or dreamed he saw, the Turkish admiral
And two the loftiest of our ships of war   635
With the bright image of that Queen of Heaven
Who hid, perhaps, her face for grief, reversed;
And the abhorred cross——

Enter an Attendant.

   Attendant.   Your sublime highness,
The Jew, who——
   Mahmud.   Could not come more seasonably:
Bid him attend—I'll hear no more! too long   640
We gaze on danger through the mist of fear,
And multiply upon our shattered hopes
The images of ruin—come what will!
Tomorrow and tomorrow are as lamps

---

5. Not identified.
6. The westernmost point on the main-   land of the Peloponnesus (in Elis, in the northwest part of the peninsula).

Set in our path to light us to the edge 645
Through rough and smooth, nor can we suffer aught
Which he inflicts not in whose hand we are. [*exeunt.*

Semichorus I.

Would I were the winged cloud
Of a tempest swift and loud,
I would scorn 650
The smile of morn
And the wave where the moon rise is born!
I would leave
The spirits of eve
A shroud for the corpse of the day to weave 655
From other threads than mine!
Bask in the deep blue noon divine.
Who would,—not I.

Semichorus II.

Whither to fly?

Semichorus I.

Where the rocks that gird th' Ægean 660
Echo to the battle pæan[7]
Of the free—
I would flee,
A tempestuous herald of Victory,
My golden rain
For the Grecian slain
Should mingle in tears with the bloody main
And my solemn thunder knell
Should ring to the world the passing bell
Of tyranny! 670

Semichorus II.

Ha king! wilt thou chain
The rack[8] and the rain,
Wilt thou fetter the lightning and hurricane?
The storms are free
But we?

Chorus.

O Slavery! thou frost of the world's prime,
Killing its flowers and leaving its thorns bare!
Thy touch has stamped these limbs with crime,
These brows thy branding garland bear,
But the free heart, the impassive soul 680
Scorn thy controul!

7. In Greek antiquity a war song in advancing to battle, addressed to Ares (Roman Mars).

8. Cloud mass in the upper air driven by the wind.

Semichorus I.

Let there be light! said Liberty,
And like sunrise from the sea,
Athens arose!—around her born,
Shone like mountains in the morn   685
Glorious states,—and are they now
Ashes, wrecks, oblivion?

Semichorus II.

Go,
Where Thermæ and Asopus swallowed
Persia,[9] as the sand does foam.
Deluge upon deluge followed,—   690
Discord, Macedon and Rome:
And lastly Thou!

Semichorus I.

Temples and towers,
Citadels and marts and they
Who live and die there, have been ours
And may be thine, and must decay,   695
But Greece and her foundations are
Built below the tide of war,
Based on the chrystalline sea
Of thought and its eternity;
Her citizens, imperial spirits,   700
Rule the present from the past,
On all this world of men inherits
Their seal is set—

Semichorus II.

Hear ye the blast
Whose Orphic[1] thunder thrilling calls
From ruin her Titanian walls?   705
Whose spirit shakes the sapless bones
Of Slavery? Argos, Corinth, Crete
Hear, and from their mountain thrones
The dæmons and the nymphs[2] repeat
The harmony.

Semichorus I.

I hear! I hear!   710

9. The rivers near which were fought
Thermopylae (480 B.C.) and Plataea (479
B.C.)—the first and last land battles
during Xerxes' unsuccessful invasion of
Greece.
1. Associated with Orpheus, the mythical
Thracian whose music charmed all of
nature.
2. In Greek mythology, supernatural
beings intermediate between gods and
men.

Semichorus II.

The world's eyeless charioteer,
    Destiny, is hurrying by!
What faith is crushed, what empire bleeds
Beneath her earthquake-footed steeds?
What eagle winged victory sits   715
At her right hand? what shadow flits
    Before? what splendour rolls behind?
      Ruin and Renovation cry
"Who but we?"

Semichorus I.

      I hear! I hear.
  The hiss as of a rushing wind,   720
The roar as of an ocean foaming,
The thunder as of earthquake coming.
      I hear! I hear!
The crash as of an empire falling,
The shrieks as of a people calling   725
"Mercy? Mercy!" how they thrill!
Then a shout of "Kill! Kill! Kill!"
And then a small still voice, thus—

Semichorus II.

                  For
Revenge and wrong bring forth their kind,
  The foul cubs like their parents are,   730
Their den is in the guilty mind
    And Conscience feeds them with despair.—

Semichorus I.

In sacred Athens, near the fane
  Of Wisdom, Pity's altar stood.
Serve not the unknown God in vain,   735
But pay that broken shrine again,
    Love for hate and tears for blood!

Enter MAHMUD *and* AHASUERUS.

Mahmud. Thou art a man, thou sayest, even as we.
Ahasuerus. No more!
Mahmud.   But raised above thy fellow men
By thought, as I by power.
Ahasuerus.   Thou sayest so.   740
Mahmud. Thou art an adept in the difficult lore
Of Greek and Frank[3] philosophy; thou numberest

---

3. The Greeks, Turks, and other peoples of the eastern Mediterranean referred to all those from western Europe as "Franks" (the Germanic tribe from which France takes its name).

The flowers, and thou measurest the stars;
Thou severest element from element;
Thy spirit is present in the past, and sees   745
The birth of this old world through all its cycles
Of desolation and of loveliness,
And when man was not, and how man became
The monarch and the slave of this low sphere,
And all its narrow circles—it is much—   750
I honour thee, and would be what thou art
Were I not what I am—but the unborn hour,
Cradled in fear and hope, conflicting storms,
Who shall unveil? Nor thou, nor I, nor any
Mighty or wise. I apprehended not   755
What thou has taught me, but I now perceive
That thou art no interpreter of dreams;
Thou dost not own that art, device, or God,
Can make the future present—let it come!
Moreover thou disdainest us and ours;   760
Thou art as God whom thou contemplatest.
    Ahasuerus. Disdain thee? not the worm beneath thy feet!
The Fathomless has care for meaner things
Than thou canst dream, and has made Pride for those
Who would be what they may not, or would seem   765
That which they are not—Sultan! talk no more
Of thee and me, the future and the past;
But look on that which cannot change—the One,
The unborn and the undying. Earth and ocean,
Space and the isles of life or light that gem   770
The sapphire floods of interstellar air,
This firmament pavilioned upon chaos,
With all its cressets[4] of immortal fire
Whose outwall bastioned impregnably
Against the escape of boldest thoughts, repels them   775
As Calpe[5] the Atlantic clouds—this Whole
Of suns, and worlds, and men, and beasts, and flowers
With all the silent or tempestuous workings
By which they have been, are, or cease to be,
Is but a vision—all that it inherits   780
Are motes[6] of a sick eye, bubbles and dreams;
Thought is its cradle and its grave, nor less
The future and the past are idle shadows
Of thought's eternal flight—they have no being.
Nought is but that which feels itself to be.   785
    Mahmud. What meanest thou? thy words stream like a tempest
Of dazzling mist within my brain—they shake

4. Vessels of burning oil used for illumination, usually atop a pole or suspended from a roof.
5. The old name for the Rock of Gibraltar, a promontory in southern Spain
that marks the end of the Straits of Gibraltar and the beginning of the Mediterranean Sea.
6. The small dust particles visible in a sunbeam.

The earth on which I stand, and hang like night
On Heaven above me. What can they avail?
They cast on all things surest, brightest, best,   790
Doubt, insecurity, astonishment.
 Ahasuerus. Mistake me not! All is contained in each.
Dodona's forest[7] to an acorn's cup
Is that which has been, or will be, to that
Which is—the absent to the present. Thought   795
Alone, and its quick elements, Will, Passion,
Reason, Imagination, cannot die;
They are, what that which they regard, appears,
The stuff whence mutability can weave
All that it hath dominion o'er, worlds, worms,   800
Empires and superstitions—what has thought
To do with time or place or circumstance?
Would'st thou behold the future?—ask and have!
Knock and it shall be opened—look and lo!
The coming age is shadowed on the past   805
As on a glass.
 Mahmud. Wild—wilder thoughts convulse
My spirit—did not Mahomet the Second[8]
Win Stamboul?
 Ahasuerus. Thou would'st ask that giant spirit
The written fortunes of thy house and faith—
Thou would'st cite one out of the grave to tell   810
How what was born in blood must die—
 Mahmud.   Thy words
Have power on me!—I see——
 Ahasuerus.   What hearest, thou?
 Mahmud. A far whisper——
Terrible silence—
 Ahasuerus. What succeeds?
 Mahmud.   The sound
As of the assault of an imperial city[9]——   815
The hiss of inextinguishable fire,—
The roar of giant cannon;—the earthquaking
Fall of vast bastions and precipitous towers,
The shock of crags shot from strange engin'ry,
The clash of wheels, and clang of armed hoofs   820
And crash of brazen mail as of the wreck
Of adamantine mountains—the mad blast

---

7. Dodona, in Epirus (northwest Greece), was in ancient times the site of a famous oak grove surrounding an oracle of Zeus (Jupiter). The rustling of the leaves of these trees was interpreted by the oracle as messages from the god.
8. Sultan Mohammed II (1451–1481), "the Conqueror," captured Constantinople (Istanbul) in 1453.
9. "The manner of the invocation of the spirit of Mahomet the Second will be censured. as over subtle. . . . I have preferred to represent the Jew as disclaiming all pretension, or even belief, in supernatural agency, and as tempting Mahmud to that state of mind in which ideas may be supposed to assume the force of sensations . . ." (from Shelley's note).

Of trumpets, and the neigh of raging steeds,
The shrieks of women whose thrill[1] jars the blood
And one sweet laugh most horrible to hear   825
As of a joyous infant waked and playing
With its dead mother's breast, and now more loud
The mingled battle cry,—ha! hear I not
"Ἐν τούτῳ νίκη—" "Allah-Illa, Allah!"[2]
   Ahasuerus. The sulphurous mist is raised thou see'st—
   Mahmud.   A chasm   830
As of two mountains in the wall of Stamboul
And in that ghastly breach the Islamites
Like giants on the ruins of a world
Stand in the light of sunrise. In the dust
Glimmers a kingless diadem, and one   835
Of regal port has cast himself beneath
The stream of war: another proudly clad
In golden arms spurs a Tartarian barb[3]
Into the gap and with his iron mace
Directs the torrent of that tide of men   840
And seems—he is, Mahomet!
   Ahasuerus.   What thou see'st
Is but the ghost of thy forgotten dream.
A dream itself, yet, less, perhaps, than that
Thou callest reality. Thou mayest behold
How cities, on which empire sleeps enthroned,   845
Bow their tower'd crests to Mutability.
Poised by the flood, e'en on the height thou holdest,
Thou may'st now learn how the full tide of power
Ebbs to its depths.—Inheritor of glory,
Conceived in darkness, born in blood, and nourished   850
With tears and toil, thou see'st the mortal throes
Of that whose birth was but the same. The Past
Now stands before thee like an Incarnation
Of the To-come; yet would'st thou commune with
That portion of thyself which was ere thou   855
Didst start for this brief race whose crown is death,
Dissolve with that strong faith and fervent passion
Which called it from the uncreated deep
Yon cloud of war with its tempestuous phantoms
Of raging death; and draw with mighty will   860
The imperial shade hither—   [*Exit* AHASUERUS. *The
            Phantom of* MAHOMET THE SECOND *appears.*
   Mahmud.   Approach!
   Phantom.   I come
Thence whither thou must go! the grave is fitter
To take the living than give up the dead;

1. Vibration.
2. The war cries of the Byzantine Greeks ("In this [sign], Victory") and the Turks ("There is no god but God!").
3. Horse, noted for speed and endurance, from Tartary.

Yet has thy faith prevailed and I am here.
The heavy fragments of the power which fell   865
When I arose like shapeless crags and clouds
Hang round my throne on the abyss, and voices
Of strange lament soothe my supreme repose,
Wailing for glory never to return——
   A later Empire nods in its decay: 870
The autumn of a greener faith is come,
And wolfish Change, like winter howls to strip
The foliage in which Fame, the eagle, built
Her aiëry, while Dominion whelped below.
The storm is in its branches, and the frost   875
Is on its leaves, and the blank deep expects
Oblivion on oblivion, spoil on spoil,
Ruin on ruin—thou art slow my son;
The Anarchs of the world of darkness keep
A throne for thee round which thine empire lies   880
Boundless and mute, and for thy subjects thou,
Like us, shalt rule the ghosts of murdered life,
The phantoms of the powers who rule thee now—
Mutinous passions, and conflicting fears
And hopes that sate themselves on dust and die,   885
Stript of their mortal strength, as thou of thine.
Islam must fall, but we will reign together
Over its ruins in the world of death—
And if the trunk be dry, yet shall the seed
Unfold itself even in the shape of that   890
Which gathers birth in its decay—Woe! woe!
To the weak people tangled in the grasp
Of its last spasms.
   Mahmud.   Spirit, woe to all!—
Woe to the wronged and the avenger! woe
To the destroyer; woe to the destroyed!   895
Woe to the dupe; and woe to the deceiver!
Woe to the oppressed; and woe to the oppressor!
Woe both to those that suffer and inflict,
Those who are born and those who die! but say,
Imperial shadow of the thing I am,   900
When, how, by whom, Destruction must accomplish
Her consummation?
   Phantom.   Ask the cold pale Hour
Rich in reversion of impending death
When he shall fall upon whose ripe grey hairs
Sit Care and Sorrow and Infirmity,   905
The weight which Crime whose wings are plumed with years
Leaves in his flight from ravaged heart to heart
Over the heads of men, under which burthen
They bow themselves unto the grave: fond wretch!
He leans upon his crutch and talks of years   910

To come, and how in hours of youth renewed
He will renew lost joys, and——
    Voice without.   Victory! Victory!
                          [*The Phantom vanishes.*
  Mahmud. What sound of the importunate earth has broken
My mighty trance?
    Voice without. Victory! Victory!
    Mahmud. Weak lightning before darkness! poor faint smile   915
Of dying Islam! Voice, which art the response
Of hollow weakness! Do I wake and live?
Were there such things or may the unquiet brain,
Vexed by the wise mad talk of the old Jew,
Have shaped itself these shadows of its fear?   920
It matters not!—for nought we see or dream,
Possess or lose or grasp at can be worth
More than it gives or teaches. Come what may,
The Future must become the Past, and I
As they were to whom once this present hour,   925
This gloomy crag of Time to which I cling
Seemed an Elysian isle of peace and joy
Never to be attained.——I must rebuke
This drunkenness of triumph ere it die
And dying, bring despair. Victory? poor slaves!   [*Exit* MAHMUD.
    Voice without. Shout in the jubilee of death! the Greeks   931
Are as a brood of lions in the net
Round which the kingly hunters of the earth
Stand smiling. Anarchs, ye whose daily food
Are curses, groans and gold, the fruit of death   935
From Thule[4] to the Girdle of the World,
Come, feast! the board groans with the flesh of men;
The cup is foaming with a nation's blood,
Famine and Thirst await! eat, drink and die!

Semichorus I.

    Victorious Wrong with vulture scream   940
  Salutes the risen sun, pursues the flying day!
    I saw her, ghastly as a tyrant's dream,
  Perch on the trembling pyramid of night
  Beneath which earth and all her realms pavilioned lay
  In Visions of the dawning undelight.—   945
      Who shall impede her flight?
      Who rob her of her prey?

    Voice without. Victory! Victory! Russia's famished Eagles
Dare not to prey beneath the crescent's light.[5]
Impale the remnant of the Greeks? despoil?   950
Violate! make their flesh cheaper than dust!

4. The type of the extreme limit of travel and discovery.
5. The flag of Russia under the Romanov czars featured a double-headed eagle; the Turkish flag, the crescent moon.

Semichorus II.

Thou Voice which art
The herald of the ill in splendour hid!
  Thou echo of the hollow heart
Of monarchy, bear me to thine abode   955
  When Desolation flashes o'er a world destroyed.
O bear me to those isles of jagged cloud
  Which float like mountains on the earthquake, mid
The momentary oceans of the lightening,
  Or to some toppling promontory proud   960
  Of solid tempest whose black pyramid,
Riven, overhangs the founts intensely brightening
  Of those dawn-tinted deluges of fire
  Before their waves expire
When Heaven and Earth are light, and only light   965
  In the thunder night!

Voice without. Victory! Victory! Austria, Russia, England
And that tame Serpent, that poor shadow, France,
Cry Peace, and that means Death when monarchs speak.[6]
Ho, there! bring torches,—sharpen those red stakes,   970
These chains are light, fitter for slaves and poisoners
Than Greeks. Kill, plunder, burn! let none remain.

Semichorus I.

Alas! for Liberty!
If numbers, wealth or unfulfilling years
  Or fate can quell the free!   975
  Alas! for Virtue when
Torments or contumely or the sneers
  Of erring judging men
  Can break the heart where it abides.
Alas! if Love whose smile makes this obscure world splendid   980
  Can change with its false times and tides,
    Like hope and terror,—
    Alas for Love!
And Truth, who wanderest lone and unbefriended,
If thou can'st veil thy lie consuming mirror   985
  Before the dazzled eyes of Error,[7]
  Alas for thee! Image of the Above.

Semichorus II.

Repulse, with plumes from Conquest torn,
Led the Ten Thousand from the limits of the morn
  Through many an hostile Anarchy!   990

6. In this line and 1008, Shelley echoes the famous sentence Tacitus puts into the mouth of Galgacus, one of the leaders of the Britons fighting for their freedom against the Romans: "They make a desert [or solitude] and call it peace" (*Life of Agricola*, 30).
7. As Arthur's shield dazzles Duessa (Spenser, *Faerie Queene*, I.VIII.XX).

At length they wept aloud and cried, "The sea! the sea!"[8]
    Through exile, persecution and despair,
        Rome was, and young Atlantis[9] shall become
        The wonder, or the terror or the tomb
Of all whose step wakes Power lulled in her savage lair: 995
    But Greece was as a hermit child,
        Whose fairest thoughts and limbs were built
      To woman's growth, by dreams so mild,
        She knew not pain or guilt;
And now—O Victory, blush! and Empire, tremble   1000
        When ye desert the free—
        If Greece must be
A wreck, yet shall its fragments reassemble
And build themselves again impregnably
        In a diviner clime   1005
To Amphionic music[1] on some cape sublime
Which frowns above the idle foam of Time.

Semichorus I.

Let the tyrants rule the desart they have made[2]—
    Let the free possess the paradise they claim,
Be the fortune of our fierce oppressors weighed   1010
    With our ruin, our resistance and our name!

Semichorus II.

Our dead shall be the seed of their decay,
    Our survivors be the shadow of their pride,
Our adversity a dream to pass away—
    Their dishonour a remembrance to abide!   1015

Voice without. Victory! Victory! The bought Briton sends
The Keys of Ocean to the Islamite—
Now shall the blazon of the cross be veiled
And British skill directing Othman might,
Thunderstrike rebel Victory. O keep holy   1020
This jubilee of unrevenged blood—
Kill, crush, despoil! Let not a Greek escape!

Semichorus I.

Darkness has dawned in the East
    On the noon of Time:
The death-birds descend to their feast,   1025
    From the hungry clime.—

8. The reference is to the retreat of the ten thousand Greek mercenaries from Persia as described by Xenophon in his *Anabasis.*
9. The United States of America.

1. Amphion, fabled son of Zeus by Antiope, supposedly built the walls of Thebes simply by playing his lyre.
2. See note to 969.

Let Freedom and Peace flee far
To a sunnier strand,
And follow Love's folding star[3]
To the Evening-land![4]   1030

Semichorus II.

The young moon has fed
Her exhausted horn
With the sunset's fire.
The weak day is dead,
But the night is not born,   1035
And like Loveliness panting with wild desire
While it trembles with fear and delight,
Hesperus flies from awakening night
And pants in its beauty, and speed with light
Fast flashing, soft and bright.   1040
Thou beacon of love, thou lamp of the free!
Guide us far, far away,
To climes where now veiled by the ardour of day
Thou art hidden
From waves on which weary noon   1045
Faints in her summer swoon
Between Kingless continents sinless as Eden,
Around mountains and islands inviolably
Prankt[5] on the sapphire sea.

Semichorus I.

Through the sunset of Hope   1050
Like the shapes of a dream
What Paradise islands of glory gleam!
Beneath Heaven's cope,[6]
Their shadows more clear float by—
The sound of their oceans, the light of their sky,   1055
The music and fragrance their solitudes breathe
Burst, like morning on dream, or like Heaven on death,
Through the walls of our prison;
And Greece which was dead is arisen!

Chorus.[7]

The world's great age begins anew,   1060
The golden years return,[8]

---

3. Venus as Hesperus (1038), the evening star, which appears at the time sheep are returned to the fold.
4. The West generally (German: *Abendland*); more specifically, America.
5. Set, as jewels.
6. Vault or canopy.
7. "The final chorus is indistinct and obscure. . . . Prophecies of wars . . . may safely be made by poet or prophet in any age, but to anticipate however darkly a period of regeneration and happiness is a more hazardous exercise. . . . It will remind the reader . . . of Isaiah and Virgil, whose ardent spirits overleaping the actual reign of evil which we endure and bewail, already saw the possible and perhaps approaching state of society in which the '*lion shall lie down with the lamb*' . . ." (from Shelley's note).
8. The mythical reign of Saturn, which the Greeks believed had been a Golden Age.

The earth doth like a snake renew
   Her winter weeds[9] outworn;
Heaven smiles, and faiths and empires gleam
Like wrecks of a dissolving dream.   1065

A brighter Hellas rears its mountains
   From waves serener far,
A new Peneus[1] rolls his fountains
   Against the morning-star,
Where fairer Tempes bloom, there sleep   1070
Young Cyclads[2] on a sunnier deep.

A loftier Argo[3] cleaves the main,
   Fraught with a later prize;
Another Orpheus sings again,
   And loves, and weeps, and dies;[4]   1075
A new Ulysses leaves once more
Calypso for his native shore.[5]

O, write no more the tale of Troy,
   If earth Death's scroll must be!
Nor mix with Laian rage[6] the joy   1080
   Which dawns upon the free;
Although a subtler Sphinx renew
Riddles of death Thebes never knew.

Another Athens shall arise,
   And to remoter time   1085
Bequeath, like sunset to the skies,
   The splendour of its prime,
And leave, if nought so bright may live,
All earth can take or Heaven can give.

Saturn and Love their long repose   1090
   Shall burst,[7] more bright and good
Than all who fell, than One who rose,
   Than many unsubdued;

---

9. Clothing (i.e., skin).
1. A river in Thessaly (northeastern Greece) that flowed through the valley of *Tempe* (1070), famed for its beauty.
2. The Cyclades, a chain of about fifty islands in the Aegean southeast of Attica.
3. The ship in which Jason and the Argonauts sailed in the quest for the Golden Fleece.
4. Reputed by some to be the son of Apollo by the muse Calliope, Orpheus charmed all natural things with the music of his lyre. He wept for the double loss of his wife Eurydice—first when she died and afterwards when he failed to rescue her from the realm of Hades when he looked back too soon. He was torn apart by maenads—maddened female devotees of Dionysus (Bacchus).
5. In the *Odyssey*, Odysseus leaves the island of Calypso, the nymph who has loved him and detained him for seven years, so that he can return to his island-kingdom of Ithaca and his wife, Penelope.
6. King Laius of Thebes ordered the death of his son, Oedipus, but the infant grew up to slay his father in an argument, solve the riddle of the monstrous *Sphinx* (1082), and become king of Thebes and wife of his mother, Jocasta.
7. "Saturn and Love were among the deities of a real or imaginary state of innocence and happiness. *All* those *who fell*, . . . the Gods of Greece, Asia, and Egypt; the *One who rose*, . . . Jesus Christ . . .; and *the many unsubdued*, . . . the monstrous objects of the idolatry of China, India, the Antarctic islands, and the native tribes of America . . ." (from Shelley's note).

Not gold, not blood their altar dowers
But votive tears and symbol flowers.   1095

O cease! must hate and death return?
    Cease! must men kill and die?
Cease! drain not to its dregs the urn
    Of bitter prophecy.
The world is weary of the past,   1100
O might it die or rest at last!

Written on Hearing the News of the Death of Napoleon[1]

1

What! alive and so bold, oh Earth?
    Art thou not overbold?
    What! leapest thou forth as of old
In the light of thy morning mirth,
The last of the flock of the starry fold?   5
Ha! leapest thou forth as of old?
Are not the limbs still when the ghost is fled,
And canst thou move, Napoleon being dead?

2

How! is not thy quick heart cold?
    What spark is alive on thy hearth?[2]   10
How! is not *his* death-knell knolled?
    And livest *thou* still, Mother Earth?
Thou wert warming thy fingers old
O'er the embers covered and cold
Of that most fiery spirit, when it fled—   15
What, Mother, do you laugh now he is dead?

3

"Who has known me of old," replied Earth,
    "Or who has my story told?
    It is thou who art overbold."
And the lightning of scorn laughed forth   20

1. Napoleon Buonaparte died on May 5, 1821, on the island of St. Helena in the south Atlantic, but it was some weeks before the news of his death reached Europe. Claire Clairmont at Florence first heard the official report on July 16 (*Journals*, p. 242). Shelley sent his poetic reaction to Ollier with the manuscript of *Hellas* on November 11, 1821, with instructions to print it "at the end"; Ollier followed those instructions, and this poem was the last lyric by Shelley to reach print during his lifetime.

Though the title usually given is "*Lines* Written on Hearing . . . [etc.]," we have followed both Mary Shelley's transcript (now in the Huntington Library, HM 330), which Shelley approved as press copy for *Hellas*, and the first edition in the *Hellas* volume (1821). The eight-line stanzas, as R. D. Havens pointed out (*PMLA*, 1950), are intricately woven, using only three basic rhymes and repeating the rhyme words in different patterns in the manner of the sestina. Shelley himself referred to the poem as "the ode to Napoleon."

2. Vesta (identified with Tellus) was one of the names under which the ancients worshiped the earth.

As she sung, "To my bosom I fold
All my sons when their knell is knolled
And so with living motion all are fed
And the quick spring like weeds out of the dead.

4

"Still alive and still bold," shouted Earth,   25
    "I grow bolder and still more bold.
    The dead fill me ten thousand fold
Fuller of speed and splendour and mirth.
I was cloudy, and sullen, and cold,
Like a frozen chaos uprolled   30
Till by the spirit of the mighty dead
My heart grew warm. I feed on whom I fed.

5

"Aye, alive and still bold," muttered Earth,
    "Napoleon's fierce spirit rolled,
    In terror, and blood, and gold,   35
A torrent of ruin to death from his birth.
Leave the millions who follow to mould
The metal before it be cold,
And weave into his shame, which like the dead
Shrouds me, the hopes that from his glory fled."   40

The Flower That Smiles Today[3]

The flower that smiles today
    Tomorrow dies;
All that we wish to stay
    Tempts and then flies;
What is this world's delight?   5
Lightning, that mocks the night,
    Brief even as bright.—

Virtue, how frail it is!—
    Friendship, how rare!—
Love, how it sells poor bliss   10
    For proud despair!
But these though soon they fall,
Survive their joy, and all
    Which ours we call.—

Whilst skies are blue and bright,   15
    Whilst flowers are gay,
Whilst eyes that change ere night
    Make glad the day;

3. First published in *Posthumous Poems* under the title "Mutability," this lyric has recently been reedited by Judith Chernaik from the fair copy by Shelley, Bodleian MS Shelley adds. e.7, p. 154 (*The Lyrics of Shelley*, pp. 252–253). We have gone to the holograph fair copy for our text. On the origin of the poem as a dramatic lyric intended for *Hellas*, see G. M. Matthews, "Shelley's Lyrics," p. 690.

Whilst yet the calm hours creep,
Dream thou—and from thy sleep   20
Then wake to weep.

When Passion's Trance Is Overpast[4]

When passion's trance is overpast,
If tenderness and truth could last
Or live—whilst all wild feelings keep
Some mortal slumber, dark and deep—
I should not weep, I should not weep!   5

It were enough to feel, to see
Thy soft eyes gazing tenderly . . .
And dream the rest—and burn and be
The secret food of fires unseen,
Could[5] thou but be what thou hast been!   10

After the slumber of the year
The woodland violets reappear;
All things revive in field or grove
And sky and sea, but two, which move
And form all others—life and love.—   15

To ———[6]

Music, when soft voices die,
Vibrates in the memory.—
Odours, when sweet violets sicken,
Live within the sense they quicken.—

Rose leaves, when the rose is dead,   5
Are heaped for the beloved's bed—
And so thy thoughts, when thou art gone,
Love itself shall slumber on. . . .

Memory

Rose leaves, when the rose is dead,
Are heaped for the beloved's bed,
And so thy thoughts, when thou art gone,
Love itself shall slumber on. . . .

4. This lyric, first published in 1824 in *Posthumous Poems*, was placed by Mary Shelley among Shelley's poems written in 1821. Our text follows the only known contemporary manuscript, Shelley's draft (Bodleian MS. Shelley adds, e.12, pp. 7 and 6). The poem strongly reflects Shelley's estrangement from Mary during their last years together.
5. The verb is subjunctive.

6. "To———" and "Memory" are different versions of a poem Shelley drafted—or began to draft—in Bodleian MS. Shelley adds. e.8, p. 154 *reverso*. The first version was published by Mary Shelley in *Posthumous Poems* (1824) and the second by Irving Massey in *JEGP*, 59 (1960), 430–438. We consider evidence of the manuscript on the order of the two stanzas to be inconclusive.

Music, when soft voices die, 5
Vibrates in the memory.—
Odours, when sweet violets sicken,
Live within the sense they quicken.—

To Jane. The Invitation[7]

Best and brightest, come away—
Fairer far than this fair day
Which like thee to those in sorrow
Comes to bid a sweet good-morrow
To the rough year just awake 5
In its cradle on the brake.[8]—
The brightest hour of unborn spring
Through the winter wandering
Found, it seems, this halcyon morn
To hoar February born; 10
Bending from Heaven in azure mirth
It kissed the forehead of the earth
And smiled upon the silent sea,
And bade the frozen streams be free
And waked to music all their fountains, 15
And breathed upon the frozen mountains,
And like a prophetess of May
Strewed flowers upon the barren way,
Making the wintry world appear
Like one on whom thou smilest, dear. 20

Away, away from men and towns
To the wild wood and the downs,
To the silent wilderness
Where the soul need not repress
Its music lest it should not find 25
An echo in another's mind,
While the touch of Nature's art
Harmonizes heart to heart.—
I leave this notice on my door
For each accustomed visitor— 30

7. The two poems known as "To Jane. The Invitation" and "To Jane. The Recollection" were originally published by Mary Shelley in Shelley's *Posthumous Poems* (1824) from Shelley's rough draft as a single poem entitled "The Pine Forest of the Cascine, near Pisa." The fair copy manuscripts of the two, which had been given to Jane Williams, came to Mary's attention later, and she included the finished versions in the second (one-volume) edition of her collected *Poetical Works of Percy Bysshe Shelley* (1839). There had been a hitherto unnoted printing of "To Jane. The Invitation" in the short-lived *New Anti-Jacobin*,

No. 2 (May 1833), 196–197.

Jane and Mary's other friends had not brought these poems to Mary's attention earlier because, though the walk that inspired them on January 2, 1822, was taken by Mary, Jane, and Shelley together, Jane alone evoked Shelley's happiness and the bittersweet memories of the departed joys here commemorated.

Shelley's fair copies—that of "The Invitation" in Cambridge University Library and "The Recollection" in the British Museum—are the bases of our texts.

8. Thicket.

"I am gone into the fields
To take what this sweet hour yields.
Reflexion, you may come tomorrow,
Sit by the fireside with Sorrow—
You, with the unpaid bill, Despair,   35
You, tiresome verse-reciter Care,
I will pay you in the grave,
Death will listen to your stave—
Expectation too, be off!
To-day is for itself enough—   40
Hope, in pity mock not woe
With smiles, nor follow where I go;
Long having lived on thy sweet food,
At length I find one moment's good
After long pain—with all your love   45
This you never told me of."

Radiant Sister of the day,
Awake, arise and come away
To the wild woods and the plains
And the pools where winter-rains   50
Image all their roof of leaves,
Where the pine its garland weaves
Of sapless green and ivy dun
Round stems that never kiss the Sun—
Where the lawns and pastures be   55
And the sandhills of the sea—
Where the melting hoar-frost wets
The daisy-star that never sets,
And wind-flowers, and violets
Which yet join not scent to hue   60
Crown the pale year weak and new,
When the night is left behind
In the deep east dun and blind
And the blue noon is over us,
And the multitudinous   65
Billows murmur at our feet
Where the earth and ocean meet,
And all things seem only one
In the universal Sun.—

To Jane. The Recollection

Feb. 2, 1822

Now the last day of many days,
All beautiful and bright as thou,
The loveliest and the last, is dead.
Rise, Memory, and write its praise!
Up to thy wonted work! come, trace   5

The epitaph of glory fled;
For now the Earth has changed its face,
A frown is on the Heaven's brow.

1.

We wandered to the pine forest
   That skirts the ocean foam;   10
The lightest wind was in its nest,
   The Tempest in its home;
The whispering waves were half asleep,
   The clouds were gone to play,
And on the bosom of the deep   15
   The smile of Heaven lay;
It seemed as if the hour were one
   Sent from beyond the skies,
Which scattered from above the sun
   A light of Paradise.   20

2.

We paused amid the pines that stood
   The giants of the waste,
Tortured by storms to shapes as rude
   As serpents interlaced,
And soothed by every azure breath   25
   That under Heaven is blown
To harmonies and hues beneath,
   As tender as its own;
Now all the tree-tops lay asleep
   Like green waves on the sea,   30
As still as in the silent deep
   The Ocean woods may be.

3.

How calm it was! the silence there
   By such a chain was bound
That even the busy woodpecker   35
   Made stiller with her sound
The inviolable quietness;
   The breath of peace we drew
With its soft motion made not less
   The calm that round us grew.—   40
There seemed from the remotest seat
   Of the white mountain-waste,
To the soft flower beneath our feet
   A magic circle traced,
A spirit interfused around   45
   A thrilling silent life,
To momentary peace it bound
   Our mortal nature's strife;—
And still I felt the centre of
   The magic circle there   50
Was one fair form that filled with love
   The lifeless atmosphere.

4.

We paused beside the pools that lie
    Under the forest bough—
Each seemed as 'twere, a little sky   55
    Gulphed in a world below;
A firmament of purple light
    Which in the dark earth lay
More boundless than the depth of night
    And purer than the day,   60
In which the lovely forests grew
    As in the upper air,
More perfect, both in shape and hue,
    Than any spreading there;
There lay the glade, the neighboring lawn,   65
    And through the dark green wood
The white sun twinkling like the dawn
    Out of a speckled cloud.

5.

Sweet views, which in our world above
    Can never well be seen,   70
Were imaged in the water's love
    Of that fair forest green;
And all was interfused beneath
    With an Elysian glow,
An atmosphere without a breath,   75
    A softer day below—
Like one beloved, the scene had lent
    To the dark water's breast,
Its every leaf and lineament
    With more than truth exprest;   80
Until an envious wind crept by,
    Like an unwelcome thought
Which from the mind's too faithful eye
    Blots one dear image out.—
Though thou art ever fair and kind   85
    And forests ever green,
Less oft is peace in S[helley]'s mind
    Than calm in water seen.

One Word Is Too Often Profaned[9]

One word is too often profaned
    For me to profane it,
One feeling too falsely disdained
    For thee to disdain it;

9. Mary Shelley first published this poem in *Posthumous Poems* (1824) from a fair copy she had made in one of her notebooks (Bodleian MS. Shelley adds. d.7). It is almost the only lyric of Shelley's later years for which no manuscript in the poet's own hand is known to exist. Critics have often associated the poem with Jane Williams.

One hope is too like despair 5
    For prudence to smother,
And pity from thee more dear
    Than that from another.

I can give not what men call love,
    But wilt thou accept not 10
The worship the heart lifts above
    And the Heavens reject not,—
The desire of the moth for the star,
    Of the night for the morrow,
The devotion to something afar 15
    From the sphere of our sorrow?

The Serpent Is Shut Out from Paradise[1]

1

The serpent is shut out from Paradise[2]—
    The wounded deer must seek the herb no more
      In which its heart's cure lies—
    The widowed dove must cease to haunt a bower
Like that from which its mate with feigned sighs 5
      Fled in the April hour.—
    I, too, must seldom seek again
Near happy friends a mitigated pain.

2

Of hatred I am proud,—with scorn content;
    Indifference, which once hurt me, now is grown 10
      Itself indifferent.
    But not to speak of love, Pity alone
Can break a spirit already more than bent.
      The miserable one
    Turns the mind's poison into food: 15
Its medicine is tears, its evil, good.

1. Shelley gave these stanzas, enclosed in a note, to Edward Williams on January 26, 1822, with the injunction that he show them to no one else but Jane—and preferably not even her. Williams noted in his journal, "S sent us some beautiful but too melancholy lines," the *us* suggesting that he and Jane both read them. The poem, on its first book publication in John Ascham's two-volume pirated edition of 1834, was entitled simply, "Stanzas to * * * *"; William Michael Rossetti supplied its popular title, "To Edward Williams," in his edition of 1870, but it can be argued—particularly on the basis of lines 17–20—that the poem was written primarily with Jane in mind.

The text has always been reprinted in a corrupt state deriving from the Ascham copy, though Shelley's fair copy manuscript, which has been available for years in the University of Edinburgh Library, shows no less than five significant verbal variants from the Oxford Standard Authors text. (A more or less correct transcription is found in Shelley, *Letters*, II, 385–386.) The present text is based on Shelley's holograph.

2. See Genesis 3:14,24. Shelley was at this time called "the snake" by Byron and others in the Pisan circle—probably a pun on the name "Bysshe Shelley" and the Italian *bischelli*, a small snake.

3

Therefore, if now I see you seldomer,
    Dear friends, dear *friend*,[3] know that I only fly
      Your looks, because they stir
    Griefs that should sleep, and hopes that cannot die.   20
The very comfort which they minister
      I scarce can bear; yet I,
      (So deeply is the arrow gone)
Should quickly perish if it were withdrawn.

4

When I return to my cold home, you ask   25
    Why I am not as I have lately been?
      You spoil me for the task
    Of acting a forced part in life's dull scene.
Of wearing on my brow the idle mask
      Of author, great or mean,   30
      In the world's carnival. I sought
Peace thus, and but in you I found it not.

5

Full half an hour, to-day, I tried my lot
    With various flowers, and every one still said,
      "She loves me, loves me not."   35
    And if this meant a Vision long since fled—
If it meant Fortune, Fame, or Peace of thought,
      If it meant—(but I dread
      To speak what you may know too well)
Still there was truth in the sad oracle.   40

6

The crane o'er seas and forests seeks her home.
    No bird so wild, but has its quiet nest,
      When it no more would roam.
    The sleepless billows on the Ocean's breast
Break like a bursting heart, and die in foam   45
      And thus, at length, find rest.
      Doubtless there is a place of peace
Where *my* weak heart and all its throbs will cease.

7

I asked her[4] yesterday if she believed
    That I had resolution. One who *had*   50
      Would ne'er have thus relieved
    His heart with words, but what his judgment bade
Would do, and leave the scorner unrelieved.—
      These verses were too sad
      To send to you, but[5] that I know,   55
Happy yourself, you feel another's woe.

---

3. The plural certainly refers to Jane and Edward Williams; the reference in the emphatic singular is less clear, but it is difficult to understand why Edward's *looks* would "stir/Griefs that should sleep, and *hopes* that cannot die."

4. I.e., Mary Shelley.

5. Except; *were* (54): subjunctive verb to express a condition contrary to fact.

With a Guitar.
To Jane.[6]

Ariel to Miranda;—Take
This slave of music for the sake
Of him who is the slave of thee;
And teach it all the harmony,
In which thou can'st, and only thou,   5
Make the delighted spirit glow,
'Till joy denies itself again
And too intense is turned to pain;
For by permission and command
Of thine own prince Ferdinand   10
Poor Ariel sends this silent token
Of more than ever can be spoken;
Your guardian spirit Ariel, who
From life to life must still pursue
Your happiness, for thus alone   15
Can Ariel ever find his own;
From Prospero's enchanted cell,
As the mighty verses tell,
To the throne of Naples he
Lit you o'er the trackless sea,   20
Flitting on, your prow before,
Like a living meteor.
When you die, the silent Moon
In her interlunar[7] swoon
Is not sadder in her cell   25
Than deserted Ariel;
When you live again on Earth
Like an unseen Star of birth[8]
Ariel guides you o'er the sea
Of life from your nativity;   30
Many changes have been run
Since Ferdinand and you begun
Your course of love, and Ariel still
Has tracked your steps and served your will;

6. Shelley purchased an Italian guitar for
Jane Williams, accompanying the gift
with an urbane poem depicting her,
Edward Williams, and Shelley himself
in the roles of Miranda, her beloved
Ferdinand, and the spirit Ariel from
Shakespeare's *The Tempest.*
   Edward John Trelawny, who came
upon Shelley drafting the poem in a
secluded retreat in the marshy pine
forest near Pisa, described the initial
draft as a "frightful scrawl" that he
found virtually illegible. The copy Shel-
ley gave to Jane, beautifully written and
punctuated in his best copying hand,
is now in the Bodleian Library (MS.
Shelley adds. e.3). Our text follows that
manuscript; the earliest published texts
(the first in the *Athenæum*, October 20,
1832) derive from copies made by
Thomas Medwin.
7. The period between the old and the
new moon.
8. According to various astrological tra-
ditions, each individual lives under the
influence of a natal star that shapes his
temperament and destiny.

Now, in humbler, happier lot   35
This is all remembered not;
And now, alas! the poor sprite[9] is
Imprisoned for some fault of his
In a body like a grave:—
From you, he only dares to crave   40
For his service and his sorrow
A smile today, a song tomorrow.

The artist who this idol[1] wrought
To echo all harmonious thought
Felled a tree, while on the steep   45
The woods were in their winter sleep
Rocked in that repose divine
On the wind-swept Apennine;
And dreaming, some of autumn past
And some of spring approaching fast,   50
And some of April buds and showers
And some of songs in July bowers
And all of love,—and so this tree—
O that such our death may be—
Died in sleep, and felt no pain,   55
To live in happier form again,
From which, beneath Heaven's fairest star,[2]
The artist wrought this loved guitar,
And taught it justly to reply
To all who question skilfully   60
In language gentle as thine own;
Whispering in enamoured tone
Sweet oracles of woods and dells
And summer winds in sylvan cells
For it had learnt all harmonies   65
Of the plains and of the skies,
Of the forests and the mountains,
And the many-voiced fountains,
The clearest echoes of the hills,
The softest notes of falling rills,   70
The melodies of birds and bees,
The murmuring of summer seas,
And pattering rain and breathing dew
And airs of evening;— and it knew
That seldom heard mysterious sound,   75
Which, driven on its diurnal[3] round
As it floats through boundless day
Our world enkindles on its way—
All this it knows, but will not tell
To those who cannot question well   80

---

9. In *The Tempest*, Ariel is a disem-
bodied spirit of the elements of fire and
air.
1. I.e., the guitar.

2. Venus, the evening/morning star of
love.
3. Daily.

The spirit that inhabits it:
It talks according to the wit
Of its companions, and no more
Is heard than has been felt before
By those who tempt it to betray   85
These secrets of an elder day.—
But, sweetly as its answers will
Flatter hands of perfect skill,
It keeps its highest holiest tone
For our beloved Jane alone.—   90

To Jane[4]

The keen stars were twinkling
And the fair moon was rising among them,
      Dear Jane.
The guitar was tinkling
But the notes were not sweet 'till you sung them   5
      Again.—
As the moon's soft splendour
O'er the faint cold starlight of Heaven
      Is thrown—
So your voice most tender   10
To the strings without soul had then given
      Its own.

The stars will awaken,
Though the moon sleep a full hour later,
      Tonight;   15
No leaf will be shaken
While the dews of your melody scatter
      Delight.
Though the sound overpowers
Sing again, with your dear voice revealing   20
      A tone
Of some world far from ours,
Where music and moonlight and feeling
      Are one.

4. The draft of this poem—written at Lerici during the last month of Shelley's life—is scattered in three separate folios of the Bodleian manuscript of "The Triumph of Life" (Bod. MS. Shelley adds. c.4, 56, 33v, and 38v *reverso*). A holograph fair copy is in the University of Manchester Library. The first printed version, entitled "An Ariette for Music," published by Thomas Medwin in the *Athenæum* (November 17, 1832) and *The Shelley Papers* (1833), was incomplete. Mary Shelley followed this text in her first edition of Shelley's *Poetical Works* (1839); in her second one-volume edition of *Poetical Works* (1840) she finally published a complete text. Our text is taken from the fair copy holograph, which also contains this note from Shelley to Jane: "I sate down to write some words for an ariette which might be profane—but it was in vain to struggle with the ruling spirit, who compelled me to speak of things sacred to yours & Wilhelmeister's [i.e., Edward Williams'] indulgence—I commit them to your secrecy & your mercy & will try & do better another time."

Lines written in the Bay of Lerici[5]

Bright wanderer,[6] fair coquette of Heaven,
To whom alone it has been given
To change and be adored for ever. . . .
Envy not this dim world, for never
But once within its shadow grew   5
One fair as [thou], but far more true.
She left me at the silent time
When the moon had ceased to climb
The azure dome of Heaven's steep,
And like an albatross asleep,   10
Balanced on her wings of light,
Hovered in the purple night,
Ere she sought her Ocean nest
In the chambers of the west.—
She left me, and I staid alone   15
Thinking over every tone,
Which though now silent to the ear
The enchanted heart could hear
Like notes which die when born, but still
Haunt the echoes of the hill: 20
And feeling ever—O too much—
The soft vibrations of her touch
As if her gentle hand even now
Lightly trembled on my brow;
And thus although she absent were   25
Memory gave me all of her
That even fancy dares to claim.—
Her presence had made weak and tame
All passions, and I lived alone,
In the time which is our own;   30
The past and future were forgot
As they had been, and would be, not.—
But soon, the guardian angel gone,
The demon reassumed his throne

5. Shelley probably wrote this unfinished lyric, which has Jane Williams as its main subject, two or three weeks before his death. Drafted on two conjugate leaves of the paper on which Shelley wrote "The Triumph of Life" and still kept with that MS (Bodleian MS. Shelley adds. c.4, ff.35–36), it was probably composed before lines 373ff. of "The Triumph" and presumably dates from between June 16 and June 30, 1822 (see Reiman, *Shelley's "The Triumph of Life": A Critical Study*, pp. 244–250). The poem was first published, and its title devised, by Richard Garnett in a truncated version in *Macmillan's Magazine*, VI (June 1862), 122–123, and— with the opening lines of it given as a separate fragment—in Garnett's *Relics of Shelley* (London, 1862). The first complete text was published by G. M. Matthews in "Shelley and Jane Williams," *RES*, n.s. XII (February 1961), 40–48. Later emendations were proposed by Reiman in the book cited and by Chernaik in *The Lyrics of Shelley*. We believe that since the last couplet in the draft is manifestly incomplete, the poem probably unfinished in its present state, in spite of aphoristic endings devised by imaginative editors.
6. The moon.

In my faint heart . . . I dare not speak   35
My thoughts; but thus disturbed and weak
I sate and watched the vessels glide
Along the ocean bright and wide,
Like spirit-winged chariots sent
O'er some serenest element   40
To ministrations strange and far;
As if to some Elysian star
They sailed for drink to medicine
Such sweet and bitter pain as mine.
And the wind that winged their flight   45
From the land came fresh and light,
And the scent of sleeping flowers
And the coolness of the hours
Of dew, and the sweet warmth of day
Was scattered o'er the twinkling bay;   50
And the fisher with his lamp
And spear, about the low rocks damp
Crept, and struck the fish who came
To worship the delusive flame:
Too happy, they whose pleasure sought   55
Extinguishes all sense and thought
Of the regret that pleasure [   ][7]
Destroying life alone not peace.

The Triumph of Life

The Triumph of Life · Written, probably in May and June 1822, at Casa Magni, San Terenzo, on the Bay of Lerici, "The Triumph of Life" was Shelley's final major effort. Though most of it was left in a very unfinished state in a rough draft manuscript, the poem exhibits such vitality and incisiveness that even Mary Shelley, who disliked the dark tone and "lack of human interest" (i.e., the philosophical nature) of the fragment, gave it a prominent place among Shelley's *Posthumous Poems* (1824). In the twentieth century it has been hailed by T. S. Eliot as Shelley's finest work.

"The Triumph of Life" is written in *terza rima*, the interlocking rhyme scheme that Dante employs in the *Divine Comedy* and that Petrarch uses in his *Trionfi*, or *Triumphs* (a sequence of seven poems celebrating the successive "Triumphs" of Love over Man, Chastity over Love, Death over Chastity, Fame over Death, Time over Fame, and God over Time). Besides Dante and Petrarch, Milton, Wordsworth, Lucretius, and Plato figure prominently as recognizable influences on the thought and language of particular passages. Also important both as an epitomizing character in the poem and as a literary influence on it is Jean Jacques Rousseau, whose novel *Julie; ou, La Nouvelle Héloïse* provides the organizing metaphor for

---

7. Various editors have added a concluding word to line 57 and/or read a slightly different version of line 58 to come up with the following final couplets:

    Of the regret that pleasure leaves

    Destroying life alone not peace.
                  (Garnett)

    Of the regret that pleasure [   ]
    Seeking Life alone *not peace.*
                  (Matthews)

a large section of the poem. In Book IX of his *Confessions*, Rousseau wrote of the year 1756: "I believed that I was approaching the end of my days almost without having tasted to the full any of the pleasures for which my heart thirsted, . . . without having ever tasted that passion which, through lack of an object, was always suppressed. . . . The impossibility of attaining the real persons precipitated me into the land of chimeras; and seeing nothing that existed worthy of my exalted feelings, I fostered them in an ideal world which my creative imagination soon peopled with beings after my own heart." (*The Confessions of Jean-Jacques Rousseau*, trans. J. M. Cohen [Penguin Books, 1954], pp. 396, 398). Out of these reveries grew *Julie*, in which a young tutor named Saint-Preux falls in love with his pupil Julie (as the medieval French theologian Peter Abelard fell in love with his pupil Héloïse). After their love has been consummated once, Julie sends Saint-Preux away and—out of a sense of duty—marries her father's friend Wolmar. Saint-Preux later returns to Vevey, where Julie and Wolmar are living quietly, and he eventually learns to control his passions sufficiently to achieve happiness, if not ecstasy, as a friend and confidant of his beloved. This temporary happiness ends for all the idealized circle (including Julie's friend Claire and Saint-Preux's English friend Lord Bomston) when Julie drowns in Lake Geneva. As Rousseau tells in his *Confessions*, his writing of *Julie* was intertwined with his last great passion—that for the Countess d'Houdetot, a passion that remained chaste because of Mme. d'Houdetot's love for Rousseau's friend Saint-Lambert. As Shelley's lyrics to Jane Williams indicate, there was a parallel between Shelley's situation in 1822, in which his partial estrangement from Mary was accompanied by attachment to both Jane and Edward Williams, while the two couples were living in isolation at Casa Magni.

In "The Triumph of Life," Rousseau, who represents the generation that prepared for the modern age centering on the French Revolution, acts as the interpreter of the pageant seen by Shelley's persona, just as Virgil guides Dante through the Inferno and as Love's Triumph is explained to Petrarch by a Florentine acquaintance in the pageant. Shelley uses Rousseau to comment on recent events and the historical process and also, through Rousseau's symbolic autobiography (which is abstracted from *Julie*), to provide an analogue of Shelley's own quest for ideal love (cf. *Epipsychidion*), together with a warning concerning the pursuit of shadows. In both the political sphere and in love, Rousseau warns, it is a mistake both to run to extremes of optimism and to give way to despair when idealized expectations fail.

Though left incomplete by Shelley's sudden death, "The Triumph of Life" as it exists shows a firm structural development: after an introduction (1–40) focusing on the Poet and his unstated personal crisis, which is set against the harmony of nature, there is the Poet's first encounter with the visionary triumphal pageant (1–175); his desire to know more explicitly the meaning of what he has seen evokes the shade of Rousseau, who identifies many of the great in the train of Life and warns the Poet against giving way to inaction because of despair by distinguishing relative degrees of resistance to Life's evil influence (176–295). In the last completed section of the fragment (296–543) Rousseau tells his own story through a series of allegories. Another question by the Poet—"Then, what is Life?"—has just introduced another major section of the poem when the fragment breaks off in the first few words of Rousseau's reply. Critics disagree about how—or even whether—Shelley would have continued the poem.

Mary Shelley published "The Triumph of Life" in Shelley's *Posthumous Poems* (1824), and this text—slightly modified by Mary herself in 1839 and by other editors over the years—remained standard until the 1960s, when new redactions were published by G. M. Matthews (in *Studia Neophilologica*, 32 [1960], 271–309) and Donald H. Reiman (in *Shelley's "The Triumph of Life"* [Urbana, Ill., 1965]), who independently reexamined the Bodleian manuscript on which Mary's texts were based. The present text is based on Reiman's text, slightly revised in the light of both suggestions by Matthews in his review of Reiman (*JEGP*, 1967) and a discussion by Matthews and Reiman held at the Bodleian Library in August 1971 with the manuscript before them.

The Triumph of Life

Swift as a spirit hastening to his task
   Of glory and of good, the Sun sprang forth
Rejoicing in his splendour, and the mask

Of darkness fell from the awakened Earth.
The smokeless altars of the mountain snows   5
   Flamed above crimson clouds, and at the birth

Of light, the Ocean's orison arose
   To which the birds tempered their matin lay.[1]
All flowers in field or forest which unclose

Their trembling eyelids to the kiss of day,   10
Swinging their censers[2] in the element,
   With orient incense lit by the new ray

Burned slow and inconsumably, and sent
   Their odorous sighs up to the smiling air,
And in succession due, did Continent,   15

Isle, Ocean, and all things that in them wear
The form and character of mortal mould
   Rise as the Sun their father rose, to bear

Their portion of the toil which he of old
   Took as his own and then imposed on them;   20
But I, whom thoughts which must remain untold

Had kept as wakeful as the stars that gem
The cone of night,[3] now they were laid asleep,
   Stretched my faint limbs beneath the hoary stem

1. A morning song; *orison:* a prayer.
2. Vessels in which incense is burned.

3. The cone-shaped shadow (umbra) cast by the earth away from the sun.

Which an old chestnut flung athwart the steep   25
    Of a green Apennine:[4] before me fled
The night; behind me rose the day; the Deep

    Was at my feet, and Heaven above my head
When a strange trance over my fancy grew
    Which was not slumber, for the shade it spread   30

Was so transparent that the scene came through
    As clear as when a veil of light is drawn
O'er evening hills they[5] glimmer; and I knew

That I had felt the freshness of that dawn,
Bathed in the same cold dew my brow and hair   35
    And sate as thus upon that slope of lawn

Under the self same bough, and heard as there
    The birds, the fountains and the Ocean hold
Sweet talk in music through the enamoured air.
    And then a Vision on my brain was rolled. . . .   40

—————————

As in that trance of wondrous thought I lay
    This was the tenour of my waking dream.
Methought I sate beside a public way

    Thick strewn with summer dust, and a great stream
Of people there was hurrying to and fro   45
    Numerous as gnats upon the evening gleam,

All hastening onward, yet none seemed to know
    Whither he went, or whence he came, or why
He made one of the multitude, yet so

    Was borne amid the crowd as through the sky   50
One of the million leaves of summer's bier.[6]—
    Old age and youth, manhood and infancy,

Mixed in one mighty torrent did appear,
    Some flying from the thing they feared and some
Seeking the object of another's fear,   55

    And others as with steps towards the tomb
Pored on the trodden worms that crawled beneath,
    And others mournfully within the gloom

4. A peak of the Apennines, a mountain range constituting most of the Italian peninsula south of the Po Valley.
5. I.e., the hills.
6. The phrase *public way* (43) and the comparison of the souls of men with crowds of *gnats* (46) are found in Petrarch's "Triumph of Death" and Dante's *Inferno*, respectively; the simile comparing the dead with fallen leaves had earlier been used by Homer, Virgil, Dante, and Milton.

Of their own shadow walked, and called it death . . .
  And some fled from it[7] as it were a ghost,   60
Half fainting in the affliction of vain breath.

  But more with motions which each other crost
Pursued or shunned the shadows the clouds threw
  Or birds within the noonday ether lost,

Upon that path where flowers never grew;   65
  And weary with vain toil and faint for thirst
Heard not the fountains whose melodious dew

  Out of their mossy cells forever burst
Nor felt the breeze which from the forest told
  Of grassy paths, and wood lawns interpersed   70

With overarching elms and caverns cold,
  And violet banks where sweet dreams brood, but they
Pursued their serious folly as of old. . . .

  And as I gazed methought that in the way
The throng grew wilder, as the woods of June   75
  When the South wind[8] shakes the extinguished day.—

And a cold glare, intenser than the noon
  But icy cold, obscured with [   ] light[9]
The Sun as he the stars. Like the young Moon

  When on the sunlit limits of the night   80
Her white shell trembles amid crimson air
  And whilst the sleeping tempest gathers might

Doth, as a herald of its coming, bear
  The ghost of her dead Mother, whose dim form
Bends in dark ether from her infant's chair,[1]   85

  So came a chariot on the silent storm
Of its own rushing splendour, and a Shape
  So sate within as one whom years deform

Beneath a dusky hood and double cape
  Crouching within the shadow of a tomb,   90
And o'er what seemed the head a cloud like crape[2]

  Was bent, a dun and faint etherial gloom
Tempering the light; upon the chariot's beam
  A Janus-visaged[3] Shadow did assume

---

7. I.e., shadow.
8. The *libeccio*, the southwest wind in Italy, is the wind of hot storms and of the evening onshore breeze on the western coast.
9. Mary Shelley filled this blank with the adjective "blinding."
1. The image in lines 79–85 is that of the crescent new moon (shaped like a chariot body) with the shadow of the rest of the moon over it; Coleridge, in "Dejection: An Ode," quotes the "Ballad of Sir Patrick Spence" on "the new Moon,/With the old Moon in her arms" as the sign of an approaching storm.
2. *cloud* (91) is the subject of *Was bent*; *crape* (91): black material worn on the clothes of those in mourning.
3. Janus, the Roman god of beginnings and endings, was represented in art as having either two faces (*Janus Bifrons*) or four faces, one on each side of his head (*Janus Quadrifrons*).

The guidance of that wonder-winged team.   95
   The Shapes which drew it in thick lightnings
Were lost: I heard alone on the air's soft stream

   The music of their ever moving wings.
All the four faces of that charioteer
   Had their eyes banded . . . little profit brings   100

Speed in the van and blindness in the rear,
   Nor then avail the beams that quench the Sun[4]
Or that these banded eyes could pierce the sphere

   Of all that is, has been, or will be done.—
So ill was the car guided, but it past   105
   With solemn speed majestically on . . .

The crowd gave way, and I arose aghast,
   Or seemed to rise, so mighty was the trance,
And saw like clouds upon the thunder blast

   The million with fierce song and maniac dance   110
Raging around; such seemed the jubilee
   As when to greet some conqueror's advance

Imperial Rome poured forth her living sea
   From senatehouse and prison and theatre
When Freedom left those who upon the free   115

   Had bound a yoke which soon they stooped to bear.[5]
Nor wanted here the just similitude
   Of a triumphal pageant, for where'er

The chariot rolled a captive multitude
   Was driven; all those who had grown old in power   120
Or misery,—all who have their age[6] subdued,

   By action or by suffering, and whose hour
Was drained to its last sand in weal or woe,
   So that the trunk survived both fruit and flower;

All those whose fame or infamy must grow   125
   Till the great winter lay the form and name
Of their own earth with them forever low—

4. I.e., the *cold glare* of line 77.
5. *jubilee . . . stooped to bear:* Though in the Old Testament the Year of Jubilee was the "year of release" in which slaves were freed (Deuteronomy 15), Shelley ironically uses *jubilee* to describe a Roman triumph, in which a victorious army displayed the people they had conquered, forcing them to march under a yoke to symbolize their subservience. Such public triumphs began about the end of the Republic, when the Romans themselves were enslaved by emperors, and variants of them continued in Western civilization, both in literature, as in triumphal processions of Lucifera (*Faerie Queene*, I.iv.2) and Dulness (Pope, *Dunciad*, IV), where the associations were often evil, and in life, as in the pageantry in London in 1815 celebrating the fall of Napoleon.
6. Era, historical period.

All but the sacred few who could not tame
Their spirits to the Conqueror, but as soon
   As they had touched the world with living flame   130

Fled back like eagles to their native noon,
   Or those who put aside the diadem
Of earthly thrones or gems, till the last one

   Were there; for they of Athens and Jerusalem[7]
Were neither mid the mighty captives seen   135
   Nor mid the ribald crowd that followed them

Or fled before. . . . Swift, fierce and obscene
   The wild dance maddens in the van, and those
Who lead it, fleet as shadows on the green,

   Outspeed the chariot and without repose   140
Mix with each other in tempestuous measure
   To savage music. . . . Wilder as it grows,

They, tortured by the agonizing pleasure,
   Convulsed and on the rapid whirlwinds[8] spun
Of that fierce spirit, whose unholy leisure   145

   Was soothed by mischief since the world begun,
Throw back their heads and loose their streaming hair,
   And in their dance round her who dims the Sun

Maidens and youths fling their wild arms in air
   As their feet twinkle; now recede and now   150
Bending within each other's atmosphere

   Kindle invisibly; and as they glow
Like moths by light attracted and repelled,
   Oft to new bright destruction come and go,

Till like two clouds into one vale impelled   155
   That shake the mountains when their lightnings mingle
And die in rain,—the fiery band which held

   Their natures, snaps . . . ere the shock cease to tingle
One falls and then another in the path
   Senseless, nor is the desolation single,   160

Yet ere I can say *where* the chariot hath
   Past over them; nor other trace I find
But as of foam after the Ocean's wrath

   Is spent upon the desert shore.—Behind,
Old men, a women foully disarrayed   165
   Shake their grey hair in the insulting wind,

7. The *sacred few* (128) include the leading representatives of the Hellenic and Hebraic civilization, among them Socrates and Jesus.

8. The carnal sinners of the Second Circle in Dante's Inferno (Canto V) are blown about by whirling winds.

Limp in the dance and strain with limbs decayed
    To reach the car of light which leaves them still
Farther behind and deeper in the shade.

But not the less with impotence of will   170
They wheel, though ghastly shadows interpose
    Round them and round each other, and fulfill

Their work and to the dust whence they arose
    Sink and corruption veils them as they lie—
And frost in these performs what fire in those.[9]   175

Struck to the heart by this sad pageantry,
Half to myself I said, "And what is this?
    Whose shape is that within the car? & why"—

I would have added—"is all here amiss?"
    But a voice answered . . "Life" . . . I turned and knew   180
(O Heaven have mercy on such wretchedness!)

That what I thought was an old root which grew
To strange distortion out of the hill side
    Was indeed one of that deluded crew,

And that the grass which methought hung so wide   185
    And white, was but his thin discoloured hair,
And that the holes it vainly sought to hide

Were or had been eyes.—"If thou canst forbear
To join the dance, which I had well forborne,"
    Said the grim Feature,[1] of my thought aware,   190

"I will tell all that which to this deep scorn
    Led me and my companions, and relate
The progress of the pageant since the morn;

"If thirst of knowledge doth not thus abate,
Follow it even to the night, but I   195
    Am weary" . . . Then like one who with the weight

Of his own words is staggered, wearily
    He paused, and ere he could resume, I cried,
"First who art thou?" . . . "Before thy memory

"I feared, loved, hated, suffered, did, and died,[2]   200
And if the spark with which Heaven lit my spirit
    Earth had with purer nutriment supplied

9. The coldness (*frost*) of the *old men and women* (165) destroys them just as the uncontrolled passions (*fire*) destroy the *maidens and youths* (149). J. C. Maxwell has pointed out that the line echoes *Paradise Lost*, II.595.
1. The shade of Rousseau (see 204);

Milton describes Death in *Paradise Lost* (X.279) as a "grim Feature," using "feature" in the sense of its Latin root-word, *factura*, as a "shaped," or "created," thing.
2. Jean Jacques Rousseau lived from 1712 to 1778.

"Corruption would not now thus much inherit
    Of what was once Rousseau—nor this disguise
Stained that within which still disdains to wear it.—   205

"If I have been extinguished, yet there rise
A thousand beacons from the spark I bore."—
    "And who are those chained to the car?" "The Wise,

"The great, the unforgotten: they who wore
    Mitres and helms and crowns, or wreathes of light,[3]   210
Signs of thought's empire over thought; their lore

"Taught them not this—to know themselves; their might
Could not repress the mutiny within,
    And for the morn of truth they feigned, deep night

"Caught them ere evening." "Who is he with chin   215
    Upon his breast and hands crost on his chain?"
"The Child of a fierce hour;[4] he sought to win

"The world, and lost all it did contain
Of greatness, in its hope destroyed; and more
    Of fame and peace than Virtue's self can gain   220

"Without the opportunity which bore
    Him on its eagle's pinion to the peak
From which a thousand climbers have before

"Fall'n as Napoleon fell."—I felt my cheek
Alter to see the great form pass away   225
    Whose grasp had left the giant world so weak

That every pigmy kicked it as it lay—
    And much I grieved to think how power and will
In opposition rule our mortal day—

And why God made irreconcilable   230
Good and the means of good;[5] and for despair
    I half disdained mine eye's desire to fill

With the spent vision of the times that were
    And scarce have ceased to be . . . "Dost thou behold,"
Said then my guide, "those spoilers spoiled, Voltaire,   235

"Frederic, and Kant, Catherine, and Leopold,
Chained hoary anarchs, demagogue and sage
    Whose name the fresh world thinks already old[6]—

---

3. The headgear respectively of bishops, warriors, kings, and (as 211 explains) sages.
4. Napoleon.
5. Compare with this sentiment of the Poet (a view contradicted by Rousseau in their continuing dialogue) the torturing of Prometheus by the Furies, who tried to drive him to despair (*Prometheus Unbound*, I.625–631).
6. King Frederick II, "the Great," of Prussia (1712–1786), Czarina Catherine II, "the Great," of Russia (1729–1796), and Leopold II (1747–1792), Grand Duke of Tuscany and later Holy Roman Emperor. These are three of the "enlightened despots"; Shelley called such self-willed absolute rulers *anarchs* following Milton's use of the word for Chaos in *Paradise Lost* (II.988), and Pope's use of it for Chaos in *The Dunciad* (IV. 655). Voltaire (1694–1778), who led these despots intellectually, is the *demagogue*, Immanuel Kant (1724–1804), the *sage*.

"For in the battle Life and they did wage
　　She remained conqueror—I was overcome　　　　240
By my own heart alone, which neither age

"Nor tears nor infamy nor now the tomb
Could temper to its object."—"Let them pass"—
　I cried—"the world and its mysterious doom

"Is not so much more glorious than it was　　　　245
　　That I desire to worship those who drew
New figures on its false and fragile glass

"As the old faded."—"Figures ever new
Rise on the bubble, paint them how you may;
　　We have but thrown, as those before us threw,　　250

"Our shadows on it as it past away.
　　But mark, how chained to the triumphal chair
The mighty phantoms of an elder day—

"All that is mortal of great Plato there
Expiates the joy and woe his master knew not;　　255
　　That star that ruled his doom was far too fair[7]—

"And Life, where long that flower of Heaven grew not,
　　Conquered the heart by love which gold or pain
Or age or sloth or slavery could subdue not—

"And near [　　] walk the [　　] twain.[8]　　　　260
The tutor and his pupil, whom Dominion
　　Followed as tame as vulture in a chain.—

"The world was darkened beneath either pinion
Of him whom from the flock of conquerors
　　Fame singled as her thunderbearing minion;　　265

"The other long outlived both woes and wars,
Throned in new thoughts of men,[9] and still had kept
　　The jealous keys of truth's eternal doors

"If Bacon's spirit[1] [　　] had not leapt
Like lightning out of darkness; he compelled　　270
The Proteus shape[2] of Nature's as it slept

7. Socrates (Plato's *master*) refrained
from passionate love affairs with boys,
but Plato loved a youth named Aster
(which means "star" in Greek and is
the name of a flower—hence, *flower of
heaven*). See the epigram attributed to
Plato that Shelley uses as the epigraph
to *Adonais*.
8. Mary Shelley filled in the first blank
with "him"; a later editor suggested
"Macedonian" as a proper adjective for
twain, inasmuch as the *tutor and his
pupil* are Aristotle and Alexander the
Great.

9. Sir Francis Bacon wrote of Aristotle:
"I will think of him that he learned the
humour of his scholar, with whom it
seemeth he did emulate, the one to
conquer all opinions, as the other to
conquer all nations."
1. Bacon's introduction of the founda-
tions of scientific methodology broke the
hold of scholastic dogmatism.
2. In *The Wisdom of the Ancients*,
Bacon discusses the myth of Proteus as
an allegory of physical matter and its
transformations.

"To wake and to unbar the caves that held
The treasure of the secrets of its reign[3]—
   See the great bards of old[4] who inly quelled

"The passions which they sung, as by their strain   275
   May well be known: their living melody
Tempers[5] its own contagion to the vein

   "Of those who are infected with it—I
Have suffered what I wrote, or viler pain!—

   "And so my words were seeds of misery—   280
Even as the deeds of others."[6]—"Not as theirs,"[7]
   I said—he pointed to a company

In which I recognized amid the heirs
   Of Cæsar's crime from him to Constantine.[8]
The Anarchs old whose force and murderous snares   285

   Had founded many a sceptre bearing line
And spread the plague of blood and gold abroad,
   And Gregory and John[9] and men divine

Who rose like shadows between Man and god
   Till that eclipse, still hanging under Heaven,   290
Was worshipped by the world o'er which they strode

   For the true Sun it quenched.—"Their power was given
But to destroy," replied the leader—"I
   Am one of those who have created, even

"If it be but a world of agony."—   295
   "Whence camest thou and whither goest thou?
How did thy course begin," I said, "and why?

   "Mine eyes are sick of this perpetual flow
Of people, and my heart of one sad thought.—
   Speak." "Whence I came, partly I seem to know,   300

"And how and by what paths I have been brought
   To this dread pass, methinks even thou mayst guess;
Why this should be my mind can compass not;

---

3. These are allusions to the Cave of Mammon in Spenser's *Faerie Queene* (II.vii) and to Bacon's quotation from Democritus that "the truth of nature lieth hid in certain deep mines and caves."

4. A canceled reading in the manuscript: "Homer & his brethren."

5. Restrains or checks.

6. Whereas the classical writers suppressed their passions, as their harmonious poetry shows (see *Defence of Poetry*, pp. 492–493), Rousseau acted out his passions before writing them, so that his writings lack tranquillity, and therefore they enflame others as ill-considered actions do.

7. The Poet answers Rousseau that his writings are not as bad as the political and ecclesiastical rulers of the Roman Empire and medieval Europe.

8. Julius Caesar founded the power of the Roman emperors; Constantine first made Christianity the state religion in the empire, combining the political and ecclesiastical tyranny.

9. Gregory VII (Hildebrand) established the temporal power of the papacy; John was the name most commonly used by popes.

"Whither the conqueror hurries me still less.
But follow thou, and from spectator turn   305
    Actor or victim in this wretchedness,

"And what thou wouldst be taught I then may learn
    From thee.—Now listen . . . In the April prime
When all the forest tops began to burn

"With kindling green, touched by the azure clime   310
Of the young year, I found myself asleep
    Under a mountain, which from unknown time

"Had yawned into a cavern high and deep,
    And from it came a gentle rivulet
Whose water like clear air in its calm sweep   315

"Bent the soft grass and kept for ever wet
The stems of the sweet flowers, and filled the grove
    With sound which all who hear must needs forget

"All pleasure and all pain, all hate and love,
    Which they had known before that hour of rest: 320
A sleeping mother then would dream not of

"The only child who died upon her breast
At eventide, a king would mourn no more
    The crown of which his brow was dispossest

"When the sun lingered o'er the Ocean floor   325
    To gild his rival's new prosperity.—
Thou wouldst forget thus vainly to deplore

"Ills, which if ills, can find no cure from thee,
The thought of which no other sleep will quell
    Nor other music blot from memory—   330

"So sweet and deep is the oblivious[1] spell.—
    Whether my life had been before that sleep
The Heaven which I imagine, or a Hell

"Like this harsh world in which I wake to weep,
I know not. I arose and for a space   335
    The scene of woods and waters seemed to keep,

"Though it was now broad day, a gentle trace
    Of light diviner than the common Sun
Sheds on the common Earth, but all the place

"Was filled with many sounds woven into one   340
Oblivious melody, confusing sense
    Amid the gliding waves and shadows dun;

1. Attended by forgetfulness.

"And as I looked the bright omnipresence
  Of morning through the orient cavern flowed,
And the Sun's image radiantly intense   345

"Burned on the waters[2] of the well that glowed
Like gold, and threaded all the forest maze
  With winding paths of emerald fire—there stood

"Amid the sun, as he amid the blaze
  Of his own glory, on the vibrating   350
Floor of the fountain, paved with flashing rays,

"A shape all light,[3] which with one hand did fling
Dew on the earth, as if she were the Dawn
  Whose invisible rain forever seemed to sing

"A silver music on the mossy lawn,   355
  And still before her on the dusky grass
Iris[4] her many coloured scarf had drawn.—

"In her right hand she bore a chrystal glass
Mantling with bright Nepenthe;[5]—the fierce splendour
  Fell from her as she moved under the mass   360

"Of the deep cavern, and with palms[6] so tender
  Their tread broke not the mirror of its billow,
Glided along the river, and did bend her

"Head under the dark boughs, till like a willow
Her fair hair swept the bosom of the stream   365
  That whispered with delight to be their pillow.[7]—

"As one enamoured is upborne in dream
  O'er lily-paven lakes mid silver mist
To wondrous music, so this shape might seem

"Partly to tread the waves with feet which kist   370
The dancing foam, partly to glide along
  The airs that roughened the moist amethyst,

"Or the slant morning beams that fell among
  The trees, or the soft shadows of the trees;
And her feet ever to the ceaseless song   375

"Of leaves and winds and waves and birds and bees
And falling drops moved in a measure new
  Yet sweet, as on the summer evening breeze

2. The sun, symbol of the deity, is reflected from water, symbol of mortality.
3. Literally the glare of the light from the *Sun* (345) reflected from the *waters of the well* (346)—the Ideal creativity reflected by an earthly medium (the human imagination).
4. The rainbow.
5. In *Comus*, 63–66, 672–677, Milton describes Comus, the evil magician who is the son of Circe, the daughter of the Sun, as seducing virtuous travelers by offering them "orient liquor in a Crystal Glasse" that is greater than "that *Nepenthes*," a drug to erase all pain, anger, and sorrow, which Helen of Troy gives to Telemachus (*Odyssey*, IV).
6. See *Adonais*, 212 and note.
7. The *shape all light* (352) assumes the shape of a rainbow.

"Up from the lake a shape of golden dew
    Between two rocks, athwart the rising moon,   380
Dances i' the wind where eagle never flew.—

"And still her feet, no less than the sweet tune
To which they moved, seemed as they moved, to blot
    The thoughts of him who gazed on them, and soon

"All that was seemed as if it had been not,   385
    As if the gazer's mind was strewn beneath
Her feet like embers, and she, thought by thought,

"Trampled its fires into the dust of death,
As Day upon the threshold of the east
    Treads out the lamps of night, until the breath   390

"Of darkness reillumines even the least
    Of heaven's living eyes—like day she came,
Making the night a dream; and ere she ceased

"To move, as one between desire and shame
Suspended, I said—'If, as it doth seem,   395
    Thou comest from the realm without a name,

" 'Into this valley of perpetual dream,
    Shew whence I came, and where I am, and why—
Pass not away upon the passing stream.'

" 'Arise and quench thy thirst,' was her reply.   400
And as a shut lily, stricken by the wand
    Of dewy morning's vital alchemy,

"I rose; and, bending at her sweet command,
    Touched with faint lips the cup she raised,
And suddenly my brain became as sand   405

"Where the first wave had more than half erased
The track of deer on desert Labrador,
    Whilst the fierce wolf from which they fled amazed

"Leaves his stamp visibly upon the shore
    Until the second bursts—so on my sight   410
Burst a new Vision never seen before.—

"And the fair shape waned in the coming light
As veil by veil the silent splendour drops
    From Lucifer,[8] amid the chrysolite

"Of sunrise ere it strike the mountain tops—   415
    And as the presence of that fairest planet
Although unseen is felt by one who hopes

8. Lucifer, the Light-Bearer, is the morn-
ing star (always the planet Venus in
Shelley's poetry); *Chrysolite* is a gem,
olivine, of pale yellowish-green color.

"That his day's path may end as he began it
In that star's smile,[9] whose light is like the scent
   Of a jonquil when evening breezes fan it,   420

"Or the soft notes in which his dear lament
   The Brescian shepherd breathes,[1] or the caress
That turned his weary slumber to content.—

"So knew I in that light's severe excess
   The presence of that shape which on the stream   425
   Moved, as I moved along the wilderness,

"More dimly than a day appearing dream,
   The ghost of a forgotten form of sleep,
A light from Heaven whose half extinguished beam

"Through the sick day in which we wake to weep   430
Glimmers, forever sought, forever lost.—
   So did that shape its obscure tenour keep

"Beside my path, as silent as a ghost;
   But the new Vision, and its cold bright car,
With savage music, stunning music, crost   435

"The forest, and as if from some dread war
Triumphantly returning, the loud million
   Fiercely extolled the fortune of her star.—

"A moving arch of victory the vermilion
   And green and azure plumes of Iris had   440
Built high over her wind-winged pavilion,[2]

"And underneath ætherial glory clad
The wilderness, and far before her flew
   The tempest of the splendour which forbade

"Shadow to fall from leaf or stone;—the crew   445
   Seemed in that light like atomies[3] that dance
Within a sunbeam.—Some upon the new

"Embroidery of flowers that did enhance
The grassy vesture of the desart, played,
   Forgetful of the chariot's swift advance;   450

"Others stood gazing till within the shade
   Of the great mountain its light left them dim.—
Others outspeeded it, and others made

---

9. Venus, as morning and evening star.
1. "The favorite song, 'Stanco di pas-
colar le peccorelle,' [I am weary of
pasturing my sheep] is a Brescian na-
tional air," (Mary Shelley's note).
Brescia is a city in northern Italy, di-
rectly west of Verona (and thus almost
due west of Venice).
2. The rainbow forms an arch of tri-
umph for the conquering chariot of Life.
3. Tiny particles (motes) of dust.

"Circles around it like the clouds that swim
Round the high moon in a bright sea of air,   455
   And more did follow, with exulting hymn,

"The chariot and the captives fettered there,
   But all like bubbles on an eddying flood
Fell into the same track at last and were

"Borne onward.—I among the multitude   460
Was swept; me sweetest flowers delayed not long,
   Me not the shadow nor the solitude,

"Me not the falling stream's Lethean[4] song,
   Me, not the phantom of that early form
Which moved upon its motion,—but among   465

"The thickest billows of the living storm
I plunged, and bared my bosom to the clime
   Of that cold light, whose airs too soon deform.—

"Before the chariot had begun to climb
   The opposing steep of that mysterious dell,   470
Behold a wonder worthy of the rhyme

"Of him[5] who from the lowest depths of Hell
Through every Paradise and through all glory
   Love led serene, and who returned to tell

"In words of hate and awe the wondrous story   475
   How all things are transfigured, except Love;
For deaf as is a sea which wrath makes hoary

"The world can hear not the sweet notes that move
The sphere whose light is melody to lovers—
   A wonder worthy of his rhyme—the grove   480

"Grew dense with shadows to its inmost covers,
   The earth was grey with phantoms,[6] and the air
Was peopled with dim forms, as when there hovers

"A flock of vampire-bats before the glare
Of the tropic sun, bringing ere evening   485
   Strange night upon some Indian isle,—thus were

"Phantoms diffused around, and some did fling
   Shadows of shadows, yet unlike themselves,
Behind them, some like eaglets on the wing

4. According to Greek mythology, the River Lethe has the power to produce forgetfulness of the past when its water is drunk.

5. Dante; *who* is, properly, the object of *Love led* (474), and some editors alter the word to "whom," but the awkward sound of "him whom" might well have led Shelley to find another solution, even to retaining the ungrammatical *who*.

6. In Book IV of *De rerum natura*, Lucretius describes how ideas, superstitions, and passions are given off by men in the form of *simulacra* or masks that peel off and float around in the air. Contrast the reversal of this procedure in *Prometheus Unbound*, III.iv.

"Were lost in the white blaze, others like elves 490
Danced in a thousand unimagined shapes
  Upon the sunny streams and grassy shelves;

"And others sate chattering like restless apes
  On vulgar paws and voluble like fire.
Some made a cradle of the ermined capes 495

  "Of kingly mantles, some upon the tiar[7]
Of pontiffs sate like vultures, others played
  Within the crown which girt with empire

"A baby's or an idiot's brow, and made
  Their nests in it; the old anatomies[8] 500
Sate hatching their bare brood under the shade

  "Of demon wings, and laughed from their dead eyes
To reassume the delegated power
  Arrayed in which these worms did monarchize

"Who make this earth their charnel.[9]—Others more 505
  Humble, like falcons sate upon the fist
Of common men, and round their heads did soar,

  "Or like small gnats and flies, as thick as mist
On evening marshes, thronged about the brow
  Of lawyer, statesman, priest and theorist, 510

"And others like discoloured flakes of snow
  On fairest bosoms and the sunniest hair
Fell, and were melted by the youthful glow

  "Which they extinguished; for like tears, they were
A veil to those from whose faint lids they rained 515
  In drops of sorrow.—I became aware

"Of whence those forms proceeded which thus stained
  The track in which we moved; after brief space
From every form the beauty slowly waned,

  "From every firmest limb and fairest face 520
The strength and freshness fell like dust, and left
  The action and the shape without the grace

"Of life; the marble brow of youth was cleft
  With care, and in the eyes where once hope shone
Desire like a lioness bereft 525

  "Of its last cub, glared ere it died; each one
Of that great crowd sent forth incessantly
  These shadows, numerous as the dead leaves blown

---

7. Tiara or triple crown, symbolic of the sovereignty and dignity of the papacy.
8. Skeletons.

9. A charnel house, where bones of the dead are kept.

"In Autumn evening from a poplar tree—
   Each, like himself and like each other were,[1]   530
At first, but soon distorted, seemed to be

"Obscure clouds moulded by the casual air;
And of this stuff the car's creative ray
   Wrought all the busy phantoms that were there

"As the sun shapes the clouds—thus, on the way   535
   Mask after mask fell from the countenance
And form of all, and long before the day

"Was old, the joy which waked like Heaven's glance
The sleepers in the oblivious valley, died,
   And some grew weary of the ghastly dance   540

"And fell, as I have fallen by the way side,
   Those soonest from whose forms most shadows past
And least of strength and beauty did abide."—

"Then, what is Life?" I said . . . the cripple cast
His eye upon the car which now had rolled   545
   Onward, as if that look must be the last,

And answered. . . . "Happy those for whom the fold
   Of

---

1. Each shadow was like *himself* who gave them off, and each shadow resembled all the other *simulacra* given off by the same person.

The Prose

On Love[1]

What is Love?—Ask him who lives what is life; ask him who adores what is God.

I know not the internal constitution of other men, or even of thine whom I now address. I see that in some external attributes they resemble me, but when misled by that appearance I have thought to appeal to something in common and unburthen my inmost soul to them, I have found my language misunderstood like one in a distant and savage land. The more opportunities they have afforded me for experience, the wider has appeared the interval between us, and to a greater distance have the points of sympathy been withdrawn. With a spirit ill fitted to sustain such proof, trembling and feeble through its tenderness, I have every where sought, and have found only repulse and disappointment.

Thou demandest what is Love. It is that powerful attraction towards all that we conceive or fear or hope beyond ourselves when we find within our own thoughts the chasm of an insufficient void and seek to awaken in all things that are, a community with what we experience within ourselves. If we reason, we would be understood; if we imagine, we would that the airy children of our brain were born anew within another's; if we feel, we would that another's nerves should vibrate to our own, that the beams of their eyes should kindle at once and mix and melt into our own, that lips of motionless ice should not reply to lips quivering and burning with the heart's best blood. This is Love. This is the bond and the sanction which connects not only man with man, but with every thing which exists. We are born into the world and there is something within us which from the instant that we live and move thirsts after its likeness. It is probably in correspondence with this law that the infant drains milk from the bosom of its mother; this propensity developes itself with the developement of our nature. We dimly see within our intellectual nature a miniature as it were of our entire self, yet deprived of all that we condemn or despise, the ideal prototype of every thing excellent or lovely that we are capable of conceiving as

1. The original draft of "On Love" appears on pp. 1–9 of Bodleian MS. Shelley adds. e.11, having been written (as the contents of the notebook suggest) in the summer of 1818—very likely between July 20 and 25, after Shelley finished his translation of Plato's *Symposium* and before he began "Discourse of the Manners of the Antient Greeks Relative to the Subject of Love." Mary Shelley first published the essay in the annual *Keepsake for 1829* (1828), from which it was immediately reprinted in England and translated in a French periodical. Thomas Medwin published a somewhat different version in *The Shelley Papers* (1833). For a full discussion of the essay's date, text, and ideas, see *Shelley and his Circle, VI* (1973), 633–647. Our text is based on Shelley's Bodleian holograph.

belonging to the nature of man. Not only the portrait of our external being, but an assemblage of the minutest particulars of which our nature is composed:[2] a mirror whose surface reflects only the forms of purity and brightness: a soul within our soul that describes a circle around its proper Paradise which pain and sorrow and evil dare not overleap. To this we eagerly refer all sensations, thirsting that they should resemble or correspond with it. The discovery of its antitype: the meeting with an understanding capable of clearly estimating the deductions of our own, an imagination which should enter into and seize upon the subtle and delicate peculiarities which we have delighted to cherish and unfold in secret, with a frame whose nerves, like the chords of two exquisite lyres strung to the accompaniment of one delightful voice, vibrate with the vibrations of our own; and of a combination of all these in such proportion as the type within demands: this is the invisible and unattainable point to which Love tends; and to attain which, it urges forth the powers of man to arrest the faintest shadow of that, without the possession of which there is no rest or respite to the heart over which it rules. Hence in solitude, or in that deserted state when we are surrounded by human beings and yet they sympathise not with us, we love the flowers, the grass and the waters and the sky. In the motion of the very leaves of spring in the blue air there is then found a secret correspondence with our heart. There is eloquence in the tongueless wind and a melody in the flowing of brooks and the rustling of the reeds beside them which by their inconceivable relation to something within the soul, awaken the spirits to a dance of breathless rapture, and bring tears of mysterious tenderness to the eyes like the enthusiasm of patriotic success or the voice of one beloved singing to you alone. Sterne says that if he were in a desert he would love some cypress. . .[3] So soon as this want or power is dead, man becomes the living sepulchre of himself, and what yet survives is the mere husk of what once he was.—

On Life[1]

Life, and the world, or whatever we call that which we are and feel, is an astonishing thing. The mist of familiarity obscures

2. "These words are inefficient and metaphorical—Most words so—No help—" (Shelley's note).

3. David Lee Clark has found this sentiment expressed not in Sterne but in Dugald Stewart's *Philosophy of the Active and Moral Powers of Man.* This book was not, however, published until 1828, and Shelley's source remains unidentified.

1. Shelley's fragmentary essay "On Life" grew directly from an early passage in his *Philosophical View of Reform* and was written, sometime late in 1819, in the back of the notebook in which he drafted *A Philosophical View.* The leaves containing "On Life" were later removed from the notebook and are now in the Pierpont Morgan Library. Thomas Medwin first published a version of "On

from us the wonder of our being. We are struck with admiration at some of its transient modifications; but it is itself the great miracle. What are changes of empires, the wreck of dynasties with the opinions which supported them; what is the birth and the extinction of religions and of political systems to life? What are the revolutions of the globe which we inhabit, and the operations of the elements of which it is composed, compared with life? What is the universe of stars and suns [of] which this inhabited earth is one and their motions and their destiny compared with life? Life, the great miracle, we admire not, because it is so miraculous. It is well that we are thus shielded by the familiarity of what is at once so certain and so unfathomable from an astonishment which would otherwise absorb and overawe the functions of that which is [its] object.

If any artist (I do not say had executed) but had merely conceived in his mind the system of the sun and stars and planets, they not existing, and had painted to us in words or upon canvas, the spectacle now afforded by the nightly cope of Heaven and illustrated it by the wisdom of astronomy, how great would be our admiration. Or had he imagined the scenery of this earth, the mountains, the seas and the rivers, and the grass and the flowers and the variety of the forms and masses of the leaves of the woods and the colours which attend the setting and the rising sun, and the hues of the atmosphere, turbid or serene, these things not before existing, truly we should have been astonished and it would have been more than a vain boast to have said of such a man, "Non merita nome di creatore, sennon Iddio ed il Poeta."[2] But now these things are looked on with little wonder and to be conscious of them with intense delight is esteemed to be the distinguishing mark of a refined and extraordinary person. The multitude of those men care not for them. It is thus with Life—that which includes all.

What is life? Thoughts and feelings arise, with or without our will, and we employ words to express them. We are born, and our birth is unremembered and our infancy remembered but in fragments. We live on, and in living we lose the apprehension of life. How vain is it to think that words can penetrate the mystery of our being. Rightly used they may make evident our

Life" in the *Athenæum* for September 29, 1832, and again the next year in *The Shelley Papers*. Mary Shelley provided a more correct version in her edition of Shelley's *Essays, Letters from Abroad*, etc. (1840). Our text is based on Shelley's manuscript in the Pierpont Morgan Library and contains several important changes from previous texts.

For a discussion of the ideas and implications of "On Life," see the critical selections from C. E. Pulos's *The Deep Truth* and Donald H. Reiman's *Shelley's "The Triumph of Life,"* pp. 110–116.

2. "None deserves the name of Creator except God and the Poet." Shelley quotes from a saying attributed to the Italian epic poet Tasso in Pierantonio Serassi's *Life of Torquato Tasso.*

ignorance to ourselves, and this is much. For what are we? Whence do we come, and whither do we go? Is birth the commencement, is death the conclusion of our being? What is birth and death?

The most refined abstractions of logic conduct to a view of life which, though startling to the apprehension, is in fact that which the habitual sense of its repeated combinations has extinguished in us. It strips, as it were, the painted curtain from this scene of things. I confess that I am one of those who am unable to refuse my assent to the conclusions of those philosophers, who assert that nothing exists but as it is perceived.

It is a decision against which all our persuasions struggle, and we must be long convicted, before we can be convinced that the solid universe of external things is "such stuff as dreams are made of."[3]—The shocking absurdities of the popular philosophy of mind and matter, and its fatal consequences in morals, their violent dogmatism concerning the source of all things, had early conducted me to materialism. This materialism is a seducing system to young and superficial minds. It allows its disciples to talk and dispenses them from thinking. But I was discontented with such a view of things as it afforded; man is a being of high aspirations "looking both before and after,"[4] whose "thoughts that wander through eternity,"[5] disclaim alliance with transience and decay, incapable of imagining to himself annihilation, existing but in the future and the past, being, not what he is, but what he has been, and shall be. Whatever may be his true and final destination, there is a spirit within him at enmity with nothingness and dissolution (change and extinction). This is the character of all life and being.—Each is at once the centre and the circumference; the point to which all things are referred, and the line in which all things are contained.—Such contemplations as these materialism and the popular philosophy of mind and matter, alike forbid; they are consistent only with the intellectual system.

It is absurd to enter into a long recapitulation of arguments sufficiently familiar to those enquiring minds whom alone a writer on abstruse subjects can be conceived to address. Perhaps the most clear and vigorous statement of the intellectual system is to be found in Sir W. Drummond's Academical Questions.[6] After such an exposition it would be idle to translate into other words what could only lose its energy and fitness by the change. Examined point by point and word by word, the most discrimi-

3. Shakespeare, *The Tempest*, IV.i.156–57.
4. Shakespeare, *Hamlet*, IV.iv.37. See also, "To a Sky-Lark," 86–87.
5. Milton, *Paradise Lost*, II.148.

6. For the influence on Shelley of Sir William Drumond's *Academical Questions* (1805), see Pulos, pages 519–524, below.

nating intellects have been able to discover no train of thoughts in the process of its reasoning, which does not conduct inevitably to the conclusion which has been stated.

What follows from the admission? It establishes no new truth, it gives us no additional insight into our hidden nature, neither its action, nor itself. Philosophy, impatient as it may be to build, has much work yet remaining as pioneer[7] for the overgrowth of ages. It makes one step towards this object; it destroys error, and the roots of error. It leaves, what is too often the duty of the reformer in political and ethical questions to leave, a vacancy. It reduces the mind to that freedom in which it would have acted, but for the misuse of words and signs, the instruments of its own creation.—By signs, I would be understood in a wide sense, including what is properly meant by that term, and what I peculiarly mean. In this latter sense almost all familiar objects are signs, standing not for themselves but for others, in their capacity of suggesting one thought, which shall lead to a train of thoughts.— Our whole life is thus an education of error.

Let us recollect our sensations as children. What a distinct and intense apprehension had we of the world and of ourselves. Many of the circumstances of social life were then important to us, which are now no longer so. But that is not the point of comparison on which I mean to insist. We less habitually distinguished all that we saw and felt from ourselves. They seemed as it were to constitute one mass. There are some persons who in this respect are always children. Those who are subject to the state called reverie feel as if their nature were dissolved into the surrounding universe, or as if the surrounding universe were absorbed into their being. They are conscious of no distinction. And these are states which precede or accompany or follow an unusually intense and vivid apprehension of life. As men grow up, this power commonly decays, and they become mechanical and habitual agents. Their feelings and their reasonings are the combined result of a multitude of entangled thoughts, of a series of what are called impressions, planted by reiteration.

The view of life presented by the most refined deductions of the intellectual philosophy, is that of unity. Nothing exists but as it is perceived. The difference is merely nominal between those two classes of thought which are vulgarly distinguished by the names of ideas and of external objects. Pursuing the same thread of reasoning, the existence of distinct individual minds similar to that which is employed in now questioning its own nature, is likewise found to be a delusion. The words, I, *you, they,* are not

---

7. A foot soldier who went ahead to clear a path for the main body of troops.

signs of any actual difference subsisting between the assemblage of thoughts thus indicated, but are merely marks employed to denote the different modifications of the one mind.

Let it not be supposed that this doctrine conducts to the monstrous presumption, that I, the person who now write and think, am that one mind. I am but a portion of it. The words *I*, and *you* and *they* are grammatical devices invented simply for arrangement and totally devoid of the intense and exclusive sense usually attached to them. It is difficult to find terms adequately to express so subtle a conception as that to which the intellectual philosophy has conducted us. We are on that verge where words abandon us, and what wonder if we grow dizzy to look down the dark abyss of—how little we know.

The relations of things remain unchanged by whatever system. By the word *things* is to be understood any object of thought, that is, any thought upon which any other thought is employed, with an apprehension of distinction. The relations of these remain unchanged; and such is the material of our knowledge.

What is the cause of life?—that is, how was it produced, or what agencies distinct from life, have acted or act upon life? All recorded generations of mankind have wearily busied themselves in inventing answers to this question. And the result has been . . Religion. Yet, that the basis of all things cannot be, as the popular philosophy alledges, mind is sufficiently evident. Mind, as far as we have any experience of its properties, and beyond that experience how vain is argument, cannot create, it can only perceive. It is said also to be the Cause? But cause is only a word expressing a certain state of the human mind with regard to the manner in which two thoughts are apprehended to be related to each other.— If any one desires to know how unsatisfactorily the popular philosophy employs itself upon this great question, they need only impartially reflect upon the manner in which thoughts develope themselves in their minds.—It is infinitely improbable that the cause of mind, that is, of existence, is similar to mind. It is said that mind produces motion and it might as well have been said that motion produces mind.

A Defence of Poetry   In the first (and only) issue of *Ollier's Literary Miscellany* (1820), a periodical published by Charles Ollier, Shelley's friend Thomas Love Peacock published a half-serious essay entitled "The Four Ages of Poetry." Peacock argued that poetry passed through repeated four-stage cycles: first, an iron age, in which literature was crude and simple (the period of court bards, folk ballads, and romances, both primitive and medieval); an age of gold, in which genius develops the great epic and tragic forms (from Homer to Euripides and from Dante to Milton); a silver age of polished and civilized, but derivative, poetry governed by fixed rules (the Augustan age in Rome and the English Augustan age from Dryden to Pope); and, finally, the age of brass, in which the narrow vein of polished social poetry and satire having been exhausted, poets seek novelty in pseudo-simplicity. This is the age Peacock saw in the England of his own time: "Mr. Scott digs up the poachers and cattle-stealers of the ancient border. Lord Byron cruizes for thieves and pirates on the shores of the Morea and among the Greek islands. . . . Mr. Wordsworth picks up village legends from old women and sextons; and Mr. Coleridge, to the valuable information acquired from similar sources, superadds the dreams of crazy theologians and the mysticisms of German metaphysics . . ."

Peacock, who had failed as a poet and had recently begun work at the East India Company, urged intelligent men to stop wasting their time writing poetry and apply themselves to the new sciences, including economics and political theory, which would improve the world.

Shelley wrote his answer in February and March 1821, hoping to have it appear in a subsequent issue of the *Literary Miscellany*. Later he wished to have it issued as a pamphlet, but he died before he could complete the arrangements. Late in 1822, Mary Shelley tried to include the paper in the *Liberal*, but that periodical, too, failed before the *Defence* could appear. Finally, Mary included it in *Essays, Letters from Abroad, Translations and Fragments* (1840), without the references to Peacock's by then long forgotten essay.

The *Defence of Poetry* exists in four major manuscripts—a rough draft (Bodleian MS. Shelley d.1) and a partial fair copy (Bod. MS. Shelley adds. e.20) in Shelley's hand and two transcripts by Mary, one containing Shelley's corrections and sent as press copy to Ollier in 1821 (Bod. MS. Shelley e.6) and the other from Mary's transcript book of 1822–1824, which was removed to serve as press copy for the 1840 first edition (Bod. MS. Shelley adds. d.8). Most early texts derived from the first edition; some recent texts—notably John E. Jordan's carefully edited text in the Bobbs-Merrill Library of the Liberal Arts—use Shelley's fair copy as their copy text. It seems clear, however, that the transcript by Mary with Shelley's corrections that was sent to Ollier in 1821 is later than Shelley's fair copy and is in some ways more authoritative than any other surviving manuscript, since it is the only version Shelley himself approved for publication. We have, therefore, followed Bodleian MS. Shelley e.6, correcting some spelling and punctuation from Shelley's holographs and restoring a few words in Shelley's fair copy that may have been accidentally omitted by Mary while transcribing. Since completing our edition, we have consulted Fanny Delisle's *Study of Shelley's "A Defence of Poetry": A Textual and Critical Evaluation* (2 vols. Salzburg, 1974) and have altered a few points on the basis of her suggestions.

A Defence of Poetry
or Remarks Suggested by an Essay
Entitled "The Four Ages of Poetry"

According to one mode of regarding those two classes of mental action, which are called reason and imagination, the former may be considered as mind contemplating the relations borne by one thought to another, however produced; and the latter, as mind acting upon those thoughts so as to colour them with its own light, and composing from them, as from elements, other thoughts, each containing within itself the principle of its own integrity. The one is the τὸ ποιεῖν, or the principle of synthesis, and has for its objects those forms which are common to universal nature and existence itself; the other is the τὸ λογίζειν,[1] or principle of analysis, and its action regards the relations of things, simply as relations; considering thoughts, not in their integral unity, but as the algebraical representations which conduct to certain general results. Reason is the enumeration of quantities already known; imagination is the perception of the value of those quantities, both separately and as a whole. Reason respects the differences, and imagination the similitudes of things. Reason is to Imagination as the instrument to the agent, as the body to the spirit, as the shadow to the substance.

Poetry, in a general sense, may be defined to be "the expression of the Imagination": and poetry is connate with the origin of man. Man is an instrument over which a series of external and internal impressions are driven, like the alternations of an ever-changing wind over an Æolian lyre, which move it by their motion to ever-changing melody. But there is a principle within the human being, and perhaps within all sentient beings, which acts otherwise than in the lyre, and produces not melody, alone, but harmony, by an internal adjustment of the sounds or motions thus excited to the impressions which excite them. It is as if the lyre could accommodate its chords to the motions of that which strikes them, in a determined proportion of sound; even as the musician can accommodate his voice to the sound of the lyre. A child at play by itself will express its delight by its voice and motions; and every inflexion of tone and every gesture will bear exact relation to a corresponding antitype in the pleasurable impressions which awakened it; it will be the reflected image of that impression; and as the lyre trembles and sounds after the wind has

1. The two Greek terms can be transliterated (and translated) *poiein* (making) and *logizein* (reasoning).

died away, so the child seeks, by prolonging in its voice and motions the duration of the effect, to prolong also a consciousness of the cause. In relation to the objects which delight a child, these expressions are, what poetry is to higher objects. The savage (for the savage is to ages what the child is to years) expresses the emotions produced in him by surrounding objects in a similar manner; and language and gesture, together with plastic or pictorial imitation, become the image of the combined effect of those objects, and of his apprehension of them. Man in society, with all his passions and his pleasures, next becomes the object of the passions and pleasures of man; an additional class of emotions produces an augmented treasure of expressions; and language, gesture, and the imitative arts, become at once the representation and the medium, the pencil and the picture, the chisel and the statue, the chord and the harmony. The social sympathies, or those laws from which as from its elements society results, begin to develope themselves from the moment that two human beings coexist; the future is contained within the present as the plant within the seed; and equality, diversity, unity, contrast, mutual dependence, become the principles alone capable of affording the motives according to which the will of a social being is determined to action, inasmuch as he is social; and constitute pleasure in sensation, virtue in sentiment, beauty in art, truth in reasoning, and love in the intercourse of kind. Hence men, even in the infancy of society, observe a certain order in their words and actions, distinct from that of the objects and the impressions represented by them, all expression being subject to the laws of that from which it proceeds. But let us dismiss those more general considerations which might involve an enquiry into the principles of society itself, and restrict our view to the manner in which the imagination is expressed upon its forms.

In the youth of the world, men dance and sing and imitate natural objects, observing in these actions, as in all others, a certain rhythm or order. And, although all men observe a similar, they observe not the same order, in the motions of the dance, in the melody of the song, in the combinations of language, in the series of their imitations of natural objects. For there is a certain order or rhythm belonging to each of these classes of mimetic representation, from which the hearer and the spectator receive an intenser and purer pleasure than from any other: the sense of an approximation to this order has been called taste, by modern writers. Every man in the infancy of art, observes an order which approximates more or less closely to that from which this highest delight results: but the diversity is not sufficiently marked, as that its gradations should be sensible, except in those

instances where the predominance of this faculty of approximation
to the beautiful (for so we may be permitted to name the rela-
tion between this highest pleasure and its cause) is very great.
Those in whom it exists in excess are poets, in the most universal
sense of the word; and the pleasure resulting from the manner in
which they express the influence of society or nature upon their
own minds, communicates itself to others, and gathers a sort of
reduplication from that community. Their language is vitally
metaphorical; that is, it marks the before unapprehended relations
of things, and perpetuates their apprehension, until the words
which represent them, become through time signs for portions
or classes of thoughts[2] instead of pictures of integral thoughts;
and then if no new poets should arise to create afresh the associa-
tions which have been thus disorganized, language will be dead
to all the nobler purposes of human intercourse. These similitudes
or relations are finely said by Lord Bacon to be "the same foot-
steps of nature impressed upon the various subjects of the world"[3]—
and he considers the faculty which perceives them as the store-
house of axioms common to all knowledge. In the infancy of
society every author is necessarily a poet, because language itself
is poetry; and to be a poet is to apprehend the true and the beau-
tiful, in a word the good which exists in the relation, subsisting,
first between existence and perception, and secondly between
perception and expression. Every original language near to its
source is in itself the chaos of a cyclic poem: the copiousness of
lexicography and the distinctions of grammar are the works of a
later age, and are merely the catalogue and the form of the crea-
tions of Poetry.

But Poets, or those who imagine and express this indestructible
order, are not only the authors of language and of music, of the
dance and architecture and statuary and painting: they are the
institutors of laws, and the founders of civil society and the
inventors of the arts of life and the teachers, who draw into
a certain propinquity with the beautiful and the true that partial
apprehension of the agencies of the invisible world which is called
religion. Hence all original religions are allegorical, or susceptible
of allegory, and like Janus[4] have a double face of false and true.
Poets, according to the circumstances of the age and nation in
which they appeared, were called in the earlier epochs of the world
legislators or prophets:[5] a poet essentially comprises and unites
both these characters. For he not only beholds intensely the

2. I.e., abstract concepts.
3. Bacon, *The Advancement of Learning*, Book III, chap. 1.
4. Roman god of beginnings (January) and endings, represented with two (or sometimes four) faces on a single head.
5. As Sir Philip Sidney pointed out in his *Apologie for Poetrie* (1505), *vates*, the Romans' term for poet, means "a diviner, fore-seer, or Prophet."

present as it is, and discovers those laws according to which present things ought to be ordered, but he beholds the future in the present, and his thoughts are the germs of the flower and the fruit of latest time. Not that I assert poets to be prophets in the gross sense of the word, or that they can foretell the form as surely as they foreknow the spirit of events: such is the pretence of superstition which would make poetry an attribute of prophecy, rather than prophecy an attribute of poetry. A Poet participates in the eternal, the infinite, and the one; as far as relates to his conceptions, time and place and number are not. The grammatical forms which express the moods of time, and the difference of persons and the distinction of place are convertible with respect to the highest poetry without injuring it as poetry, and the choruses of Æschylus, and the book of Job, and Dante's Paradise would afford, more than any other writings, examples of this fact, if the limits of this essay did not forbid citation. The creations of sculpture, painting, and music, are illustrations still more decisive.

Language, colour, form, and religious and civil habits of action are all the instruments and materials of poetry; they may be called poetry by that figure of speech which considers the effect as a synonime of the cause. But poetry in a more restricted sense expresses those arrangements of language, and especially metrical language, which are created by that imperial faculty, whose throne is curtained within the invisible nature of man. And this springs from the nature itself of language, which is a more direct representation of the actions and passions of our internal being, and is susceptible of more various and delicate combinations, than colour, form, or motion, and is more plastic and obedient to the controul of that faculty of which it is the creation. For language is arbitrarily produced by the Imagination and has relation to thoughts alone; but all other materials, instruments and conditions of art, have relations among each other, which limit and interpose between conception and expression. The former is as a mirror which reflects, the latter as a cloud which enfeebles, the light of which both are mediums of communication. Hence the fame of sculptors, painters and musicians, although the intrinsic powers of the great masters of these arts, may yield in no degree to that of those who have employed language as the hieroglyphic of their thoughts, has never equalled that of poets in the restricted sense of the term; as two performers of equal skill will produce unequal effects from a guitar and a harp. The fame of legislators and founders of religions, so long as their institutions last, alone seems to exceed that of poets in the restricted sense; but it can scarcely be a question whether, if we deduct the celebrity which their flattery of the gross opinions of the vulgar usually conciliates, together with that which belonged to them in their higher character of poets, any excess will remain.

We have thus circumscribed the meaning of the word Poetry within the limits of that art which is the most familiar and the most perfect expression of the faculty itself. It is necessary however to make the circle still narrower, and to determine the distinction between measured and unmeasured language; for the popular division into prose and verse is inadmissible in accurate philosophy.

Sounds as well as thoughts have relation both between each other and towards that which they represent, and a perception of the order of those relations has always been found connected with a perception of the order of the relations of thoughts. Hence the language of poets has ever affected a certain uniform and harmonious recurrence of sound, without which it were not poetry, and which is scarcely less indispensable to the communication of its influence, than the words themselves, without reference to that peculiar order. Hence the vanity of translation; it were as wise to cast a violet into a crucible that you might discover the formal principle of its colour and odour, as seek to transfuse from one language into another the creations of a poet. The plant must spring again from its seed or it will bear no flower—and this is the burthen of the curse of Babel.

An observation of the regular mode of the recurrence of this harmony in the language of poetical minds, together with its relation to music, produced metre, or a certain system of traditional forms of harmony of language. Yet it is by no means essential that a poet should accommodate his language to this traditional form, so that the harmony which is its spirit, be observed. The practise is indeed convenient and popular, and to be preferred, especially in such composition as includes much form and action: but every great poet must inevitably innovate upon the example of his predecessors in the exact structure of his peculiar versification. The distinction between poets and prose writers is a vulgar error. The distinction between philosophers and poets has been anticipated. Plato was essentially a poet—the truth and splendour of his imagery and the melody of his language is the most intense that it is possible to conceive. He rejected the measure of the epic, dramatic, and lyrical forms, because he sought to kindle a harmony in thoughts divested of shape and action, and he forbore to invent any regular plan of rhythm which would include, under determinate forms, the varied pauses of his style. Cicero[6] sought to imitate the cadence of his periods but with little success. Lord

6. Marcus Tullius Cicero (106–43 B.C.), Roman statesman and man of letters, most famous for his speeches in law courts and before the Senate.

Bacon was a poet.[7] His language has a sweet and majestic rhythm, which satisfies the sense, no less than the almost superhuman wisdom of his philosophy satisfies the intellect; it is a strain which distends, and then bursts the circumference of the hearer's mind, and pours itself forth together with it into the universal element with which it has perpetual sympathy. All the authors of revolutions in opinion are not only necessarily poets as they are inventors, nor even as their words unveil the permanent analogy of things by images which participate in the life of truth; but as their periods are harmonious and rhythmical and contain in themselves the elements of verse; being the echo of the eternal music. Nor are those supreme poets, who have employed traditional forms of rhythm on account of the form and action of their subjects, less capable of perceiving and teaching the truth of things, than those who have omitted that form. Shakespeare, Dante and Milton (to confine ourselves to modern writers) are philosophers of the very loftiest power.

A poem is the very image of life expressed in its eternal truth. There is this difference between a story and a poem, that a story is a catalogue of detached facts, which have no other bond of connexion than time, place, circumstance, cause and effect; the other is the creation of actions according to the unchangeable forms of human nature, as existing in the mind of the creator, which is itself the image of all other minds. The one is partial, and applies only to a definite period of time, and a certain combination of events which can never again recur; the other is universal, and contains within itself the germ of a relation to whatever motives or actions have place in the possible varieties of human nature. Time, which destroys the beauty and the use of the story of particular facts, stript of the poetry which should invest them, augments that of Poetry, and for ever develops new and wonderful applications of the eternal truth which it contains. Hence epitomes have been called the moths of just history;[8] they eat out the poetry of it. The story of particular facts is as a mirror which obscures and distorts that which should be beautiful: Poetry is a mirror which makes beautiful that which is distorted.

The parts of a composition may be poetical, without the composition as a whole being a poem. A single sentence may be considered as a whole though it be found in a series of unassimilated

7. "See the *Filium Labyrinthi* and the *Essay on Death* particularly" (Shelley's note). Francis Bacon, Baron Verulam and Viscount St. Albans (1561–1626), Lord Chancellor of England, was a leading philosopher and man of letters who developed the essay in English.

8. Bacon, *Advancement of Learning*, II. ii.4: "As for the corruptions and moths of history, which are epitomes, the use of them deserveth to be banished."

portions; a single word even may be a spark of inextinguishable thought. And thus all the great historians, Herodotus, Plutarch, Livy, were poets;[9] and although the plan of these writers, especially that of Livy, restrained them from developing this faculty in its highest degree, they make copious and ample amends for their subjection, by filling all the interstices of their subjects with living images.

Having determined what is poetry, and who are poets, let us proceed to estimate its effects upon society.

Poetry is ever accompanied with pleasure: all spirits on which it falls, open themselves to receive the wisdom which is mingled with its delight. In the infancy of the world, neither poets themselves nor their auditors are fully aware of the excellence of poetry: for it acts in a divine and unapprehended manner, beyond and above consciousness; and it is reserved for future generations to contemplate and measure the mighty cause and effect in all the strength and splendour of their union. Even in modern times, no living poet ever arrived at the fulness of his fame; the jury which sits in judgement upon a poet, belonging as he does to all time, must be composed of his peers: it must be impanelled by Time from the selectest of the wise of many generations. A Poet is a nightingale, who sits in darkness and sings to cheer its own solitude with sweet sounds; his auditors are as men entranced by the melody of an unseen musician, who feel that they are moved and softened, yet know not whence or why.[1] The poems of Homer and his contemporaries were the delight of infant Greece; they were the elements of that social system which is the column upon which all succeeding civilization has reposed. Homer embodied the ideal perfection of his age in human character; nor can we doubt that those who read his verses were awakened to an ambition of becoming like to Achilles, Hector and Ulysses: the truth and beauty of friendship, patriotism and persevering devotion to an object, were unveiled to the depths in these immortal creations: the sentiments of the auditors must have been refined and enlarged by a sympathy with such great and lovely impersonations, until from admiring they imitated, and from imitation they identified themselves with the objects of their admiration. Nor let it be objected, that these characters are remote from moral perfection, and that they can by no means be considered as edifying patterns for general imitation. Every epoch under names more or less specious

9. Herodotus (fifth century B.C.) wrote the first Greek history in nine books outlining the events in all the kingdoms of the eastern Mediterranean leading up to the wars between the Greek states and the Persian Empire; Plutarch (ca. 46–

120 A.D.) wrote the *Parallel Lives* of eminent Greeks and Romans in Greek; Titus Livius (ca. 59 B.C.–A.D. 17) wrote a history of Rome in 142 books, 35 of which survive.
1. Cf. "To a Sky-Lark," lines 36–40.

has deified its peculiar errors; Revenge is the naked Idol of the worship of a semi-barbarous age; and Self-deceit is the veiled Image of unknown evil before which luxury and satiety lie prostrate. But a poet considers the vices of his contemporaries as the temporary dress in which his creations must be arrayed, and which cover without concealing the eternal proportions of their beauty. An epic or dramatic personage is understood to wear them around his soul, as he may the antient armour or the modern uniform around his body; whilst it is easy to conceive a dress more graceful than either. The beauty of the internal nature cannot be so far concealed by its accidental vesture, but that the spirit of its form shall communicate itself to the very disguise, and indicate the shape it hides from the manner in which it is worn. A majestic form and graceful motions will express themselves through the most barbarous and tasteless costume. Few poets of the highest class have chosen to exhibit the beauty of their conceptions in its naked truth and splendour; and it is doubtful whether the alloy of costume, habit, etc., be not necessary to temper this planetary music[2] for mortal ears.

The whole objection however of the immorality of poetry rests upon a misconception of the manner in which poetry acts to produce the moral improvement of man. Ethical science arranges the elements which poetry has created, and propounds schemes and proposes examples of civil and domestic life: nor is it for want of admirable doctrines that men hate, and despise, and censure, and deceive, and subjugate one another. But Poetry acts in another and diviner manner. It awakens and enlarges the mind itself by rendering the receptable of a thousand unapprehended combinations of thought. Poetry lifts the veil from the hidden beauty of the world, and makes familiar objects be as if they were not familiar; it reproduces all that it represents, and the impersonations clothed in its Elysian light stand thenceforward in the minds of those who have once contemplated them, as memorials of that gentle and exalted content which extends itself over all thoughts and actions with which it coexists. The great secret of morals is Love; or a going out of our own nature, and an identification of ourselves with the beautiful which exists in thought, action, or person, not our own.[3] A man, to be greatly good, must imagine

2. The "music of the spheres," supposedly accompanying the movements of the planets, could not (according to tradition) be heard by men in their fallen condition since Adam's sin.
3. In Plato's *Symposium*, Socrates explains to Agathon that love arises not from richness and fulfillment, but from lack and need. One of Socrates' key sentences in Shelley's translation of the dialogue reads: "Love, therefore, and every thing else that desires anything, desires that which is absent and beyond his reach, that which it has not, that which is not itself, that which it wants . . ." (James Notopoulos, *The Platonism of Shelley* [Durham, N.C., 1949], p. 440).

intensely and comprehensively; he must put himself in the place of another and of many others; the pains and pleasures of his species must become his own. The great instrument of moral good is the imagination; and poetry administers to the effect by acting upon the cause. Poetry enlarges the circumference of the imagination by replenishing it with thoughts of ever new delight, which have the power of attracting and assimilating to their own nature all other thoughts, and which form new intervals and interstices whose void for ever craves fresh food. Poetry strengthens that faculty which is the organ of the moral nature of man, in the same manner as exercise strengthens a limb. A Poet therefore would do ill to embody his own conceptions of right and wrong, which are usually those of his place and time, in his poetical creations, which participate in neither. By this assumption of the inferior office of interpreting the effect, in which perhaps after all he might acquit himself but imperfectly, he would resign the glory in a participation in the cause. There was little danger that Homer, or any of the eternal poets, should have so far misunderstood themselves as to have abdicated this throne of their widest dominion. Those in whom the poetical faculty, though great, is less intense, as Euripides, Lucan,[4] Tasso, Spenser, have frequently affected a moral aim, and the effect of their poetry is diminished in exact proportion to the degree in which they compel us to advert to this purpose.

Homer and the cyclic poets were followed at a certain interval by the dramatic and lyrical Poets of Athens, who flourished contemporaneously with all that is most perfect in the kindred expressions of the poetical faculty; architecture, painting, music, the dance, sculpture, philosophy, and we may add the forms of civil life. For although the scheme of Athenian society was deformed by many imperfections which the poetry existing in Chivalry and Christianity have erased from the habits and institutions of modern Europe;[5] yet never at any other period has so much energy, beauty, and virtue, been developed; never was blind strength and stubborn form so disciplined and rendered subject to the will of man, or that will less repugnant to the dictates of the beautiful and the true, as during the century which preceded the death of Socrates. Of no other epoch in the history of our species have we records and fragments stamped so visibly with the image of the divinity in man. But it is Poetry alone, in form, in action, or in language, which has rendered this epoch memorable above all others, and the storehouse of examples to everlasting time. For written poetry existed at that epoch simultaneously with the other

4. For Lucan, see *Adonais*, 404, and note.
5. Shelley elsewhere identifies the two chief blots on Athenian society as slavery and the subjugation of women.

arts, and it is an idle enquiry to demand which gave and which received the light, which all as from a common focus have scattered over the darkest periods of succeeding time. We know no more of cause and effect than a constant conjunction of events: Poetry is ever found to coexist with whatever other arts contribute to the happiness and perfection of man. I appeal to what has already been established to distinguish between the cause and the effect.

It was at the period here adverted to, that the Drama had its birth; and however a succeeding writer may have equalled or surpassed those few great specimens of the Athenian drama which have been preserved to us, it is indisputable that the art itself never was understood or practised according to the true philosophy of it, as at Athens. For the Athenians employed language, action, music, painting, the dance, and religious institutions, to produce a common effect in the representation of the highest idealisms of passion and of power; each division in the art was made perfect in its kind by artists of the most consummate skill, and was disciplined into a beautiful proportion and unity one towards another. On the modern stage a few only of the elements capable of expressing the image of the poet's conception are employed at once. We have tragedy without music and dancing; and music and dancing without the highest impersonations of which they are the fit accompaniment, and both without religion and solemnity. Religious institution has indeed been usually banished from the stage. Our system of divesting the actor's face of a mask, on which the many expressions appropriated to his dramatic character might be moulded into one permanent and unchanging expression, is favourable only to a partial and inharmonious effect; it is fit for nothing but a monologue, where all the attention may be directed to some great master of ideal mimicry. The modern practice of blending comedy with tragedy, though liable to great abuse in point of practise, is undoubtedly an extension of the dramatic circle; but the comedy should be as in King Lear, universal, ideal, and sublime. It is perhaps the intervention of this principle which determines the balance in favour of King Lear against the Œdipus Tyrannus or the Agamemnon, or, if you will the trilogies with which they are connected; unless the intense power of the choral poetry, especially that of the latter, should be considered as restoring the equilibrium.[6] King Lear, if it can sustain this comparison, may be judged to be the most perfect specimen of the dramatic art existing in the world; in spite of the

6. Shakespeare's *King Lear* is compared with plays by Sophocles and Aeschylus, each the first play of a trilogy—Sophocles' Theban cycle of *Oedipus the King*, *Antigone*, and *Oedipus at Colonus* and Aeschylus' trilogy of Argos, known as the *Oresteia—Agamemnon*, *The Libation-Bearers*, and *The Eumenides*.

narrow conditions to which the poet was subjected by the ignorance of the philosophy of the Drama which has prevailed in modern Europe. Calderon in his religious Autos has attempted to fulfil some of the high conditions of dramatic representation neglected by Shakespeare; such as the establishing a relation between the drama and religion, and the accommodating them to music and dancing; but he omits the observation of conditions still more important, and more is lost than gained by a substitution of the rigidly-defined and ever-repeated idealisms of a distorted superstition for the living impersonations of the truth of human passion.[7]

But we digress.—The Author of the Four Ages of Poetry has prudently omitted to dispute on the effect of the Drama upon life and manners. For, if I know the knight by the device of his shield, I have only to inscribe Philoctetes[8] or Agamemnon or Othello upon mine to put to flight the giant sophisms which have enchanted him, as the mirror of intolerable light, though on the arm of one of the weakest of the Paladins, could blind and scatter whole armies of necromancers and pagans. The connexion of scenic exhibitions with the improvement or corruption of the manners of men, has been universally recognized: in other words, the presence or absence of poetry in its most perfect and universal form has been found to be connected with good and evil in conduct and habit. The corruption which has been imputed to the drama as an effect, begins, when the poetry employed in its constitution, ends: I appeal to the history of manners whether the periods of the growth of the one and the decline of the other have not corresponded with an exactness equal to any other example of moral cause and effect.

The drama at Athens, or wheresoever else it may have approached to its perfection, coexisted with the moral and intellectual greatness of the age. The tragedies of the Athenian poets are as mirrors in which the spectator beholds himself, under a thin disguise of circumstance, stript of all but that ideal perfection and energy which every one feels to be the internal type of all that he loves, admires, and would become. The imagination is enlarged by a sympathy with pains and passions so mighty, that they distend in their conception the capacity of that by which they are conceived; the good affections are strengthened by pity, indignation, terror and sorrow; and an exalted calm is prolonged from the satiety of this high exercise of them into the tumult of familiar life; even crime is disarmed of half its horror and all its contagion by being represented as the fatal consequence of

---

7. Shelley learned Spanish primarily to read the plays and *autos sacramentales* (allegorical or religious dramas) of Pedro Calderón de la Barca (1600–1681).

8. A tragedy by Sophocles.

the unfathomable agencies of nature; error is thus divested of its wilfulness; men can no longer cherish it as the creation of their choice. In a drama of the highest order there is little food for censure or hatred; it teaches rather self-knowledge and self-respect. Neither the eye nor the mind can see itself, unless reflected upon that which it resembles. The drama, so long as it continues to express poetry, is as a prismatic and many-sided mirror, which collects the brightest rays of human nature and divides and reproduces them from the simplicity of these elementary forms, and touches them with majesty and beauty, and multiplies all that it reflects, and endows it with the power of propagating its like wherever it may fall.

But in periods of the decay of social life, the drama sympathizes with that decay. Tragedy becomes a cold imitation of the form of the great masterpieces of antiquity, divested of all harmonious accompaniment of the kindred arts; and often the very form misunderstood: or a weak attempt to teach certain doctrines, which the writer considers as moral truths; and which are usually no more than specious flatteries of some gross vice or weakness with which the author in common with his auditors are infected. Hence what has been called the classical and domestic drama. Addison's "Cato" is a specimen of the one; and would it were not superfluous to cite examples of the other! To such purposes Poetry cannot be made subservient. Poetry is a sword of lightning, ever unsheathed, which consumes the scabbard that would contain it. And thus we observe that all dramatic writings of this nature are unimaginative in a singular degree; they affect sentiment and passion: which, divested of imagination, are other names for caprice and appetite. The period in our own history of the grossest degradation of the drama is the reign of Charles II when all forms in which poetry had been accustomed to be expressed became hymns to the triumph of kingly power over liberty and virtue. Milton stood alone illuminating an age unworthy of him. At such periods the calculating principle pervades all the forms of dramatic exhibition, and poetry ceases to be expressed upon them. Comedy loses its ideal universality: wit succeeds to humour; we laugh from self-complacency and triumph instead of pleasure; malignity, sarcasm and contempt, succeed to sympathetic merriment; we hardly laugh, but we smile. Obscenity, which is ever blasphemy against the divine beauty in life, becomes, from the very veil which it assumes, more active if less disgusting: it is a monster for which the corruption of society for ever brings forth new food, which it devours in secret.

The drama being that form under which a greater number of modes of expression of poetry are susceptible of being combined than any other, the connexion of poetry and social good is more observable in the drama than in whatever other form: and it is indisputable that the highest perfection of human society has ever corresponded with the highest dramatic excellence; and that the corruption or the extinction of the drama in a nation where it has once flourished, is a mark of a corruption of manners, and an extinction of the energies which sustain the soul of social life. But, as Machiavelli says of political institutions, that life may be preserved and renewed, if men should arise capable of bringing back the drama to its principles. And this is true with respect to poetry in its most extended sense: all language, institution and form, require not only to be produced but to be sustained: the office and character of a poet participates in the divine nature as regards providence, no less than as regards creation.

Civil war, the spoils of Asia, and the fatal predominance first of the Macedonian, and then of the Roman arms were so many symbols of the extinction or suspension of the creative faculty in Greece. The bucolic writers, who found patronage under the lettered tyrants of Sicily and Egypt, were the latest representatives of its most glorious reign.[9] Their poetry is intensely melodious; like the odour of the tuberose, it overcomes and sickens the spirit with excess of sweetness; whilst the poetry of the preceding age was as a meadow-gale of June which mingles the fragrance of all the flowers of the field, and adds a quickening and harmonizing spirit of its own which endows the sense with a power of sustaining its extreme delight. The bucolic and erotic delicacy in written poetry is correlative with that softness in statuary, music, and the kindred arts, and even in manners and institutions which distinguished the epoch to which we now refer. Nor is it the poetical faculty itself, or any misapplication of it, to which this want of harmony is to be imputed. An equal sensibility to the influence of the senses and the affections is to be found in the writings of Homer and Sophocles: the former especially has clothed sensual and pathetic images with irresistible attractions. Their superiority over these succeeding writers consists in the presence of those thoughts which belong to the inner faculties of our nature, not in the absence of those which are connected with the external; their incomparable perfection consists in an harmony of the union of all. It is not what the erotic writers have, but what they have not, in which their imperfection consists. It is not inasmuch as they were Poets, but inasmuch as they were not Poets, that they can be considered with any plausibility as con-

9. Theocritus (ca. 310–250 B.C.), Callimachus (fl. 260 B.C.), Moschus (fl. 150 B.C.), and Bion (fl. 100 B.C.) were poets writing in Greek who lived in Alexandria, Egypt, under the Ptolemy kings or at Syracuse in Sicily. They developed the slighter forms of Greek poetry, including the pastoral idyll.

nected with the corruption of their age. Had that corruption availed so as to extinguish in them the sensibility to pleasure, passion and natural scenery, which is imputed to them as an imperfection, the last triumph of evil would have been atchieved. For the end of social corruption is to destroy all sensibility to pleasure; and therefore it is corruption. It begins at the imagination and the intellect as at the core, and distributes itself thence as a paralyzing venom, through the affections into the very appetites, until all become a torpid mass in which sense hardly survives. At the approach of such a period, Poetry ever addresses itself to those faculties which are the last to be destroyed, and its voice is heard, like the footsteps of Astræa, departing from the world.[1] Poetry ever communicates all the pleasure which men are capable of receiving: it is ever still the light of life; the source of whatever of beautiful, or generous, or true can have place in an evil time. It will readily be confessed that those among the luxurious citizens of Syracuse and Alexandria who were delighted with the poems of Theocritus, were less cold, cruel and sensual than the remnant of their tribe. But corruption must have utterly destroyed the fabric of human society before Poetry can ever cease. The sacred links of that chain have never been entirely disjoined, which descending through the minds of many men is attached to those great minds, whence as from a magnet the invisible effluence is sent forth, which at once connects, animates and sustains the life of all. It is the faculty which contains within itself the seeds at once of its own and of social renovation. And let us not circumscribe the effects of the bucolic and erotic poetry within the limits of the sensibility of those to whom it was addressed. They may have perceived the beauty of those immortal compositions, simply as fragments and isolated portions: those who are more finely organized, or born in a happier age, may recognize them as episodes to that great poem, which all poets, like the co-operating thoughts of one great mind, have built up since the beginning of the world.

The same revolutions within a narrower sphere had place in antient Rome; but the actions and forms of its social life never seem to have been perfectly saturated with the poetical element. The Romans appear to have considered the Greeks as the selectest treasuries of the selectest forms of manners and of nature, and to have abstained from creating in measured language, sculpture,

---

1. Astraea, variously said to be the daughter of Astraeus, the Titan king of Arcadia, of Titan (Saturn's brother) by Aurora, or of Zeus (Jupiter) and Themis ("law"), she was the goddess of justice, and was sometimes identified with Rhea, wife of Saturn. During the Golden Age she lived on earth, but the evil of men drove her into heaven as the zodiacal constellation Virgo. She is represented as a stern virgin holding balance scales in one hand and a sword in the other.

music or architecture, anything which might bear a particular relation to their own condition, whilst it should bear a general one to the universal constitution of the world. But we judge from partial evidence; and we judge perhaps partially. Ennius, Varro, Pacuvius, and Accius, all great poets, have been lost.[2] Lucretius is in the highest, and Virgil in a very high sense, a creator. The chosen delicacy of the expressions of the latter is as a mist of light which conceals from us the intense and exceeding truth of his conceptions of nature. Livy is instinct with poetry. Yet Horace, Catullus, Ovid, and generally the other great writers of the Virgilian age, saw man and nature in the mirror of Greece. The institutions also and the religion of Rome were less poetical than those of Greece, as the shadow is less vivid than the substance. Hence poetry in Rome, seemed to follow rather than accompany the perfection of political and domestic society. The true Poetry of Rome lived in its institutions; for whatever of beautiful, true and majestic they contained could have sprung only from the faculty which creates the order in which they consist. The life of Camillus, the death of Regulus; the expectation of the Senators, in their godlike state, of the victorious Gauls; the refusal of the Republic to make peace with Hannibal after the battle of Cannae, were not the consequences of a refined calculation of the probable personal advantage to result from such a rhythm and order in the shews of life, to those who were at once the poets and the actors of these immortal dramas.[3] The imagination beholding the beauty of this order, created it out of itself according to its own idea: the consequence was empire, and the reward ever-living fame. These things are not the less poetry, *quia carent vate sacro*.[4] They are the episodes of the cyclic poem written by Time upon the memories of men. The Past, like

2. Quintus Ennius (239–169 B.C.), the fathering genius of Latin literature, wrote his epic entitled *Annales* in Latin hexameter verse adapted from the Greek; about 600 lines survive. Of his nineteen tragedies, 420 lines remain. Marcus Pacuvius (220–ca. 130 B.C.), his nephew, was the first important Latin tragic dramatist; of his thirteen known plays, only 400 lines survive. Marcus Terentius Varro (116–27 B.C.), the leading scholar of his day, wrote seventy-four works, of which only his *Res rusticae*, a dialogue about managing a farm, survives intact. Lucius Accius or Attius (170–ca. 85 B.C.) was the greatest Roman tragic poet. Of his forty or more plays, only 700 lines survive.
3. Marcus Furius Camillus (fl. 396 B.C., d. 365 B.C.), though rejected by the Roman common people, continued to return to aid the young republic when-

ever it was threatened; his humanity to conquered enemy cities gained Rome many allies. Marcus Atilius Regulus, captured in 255 B.C., was paroled by the Carthaginians in order to have him persuade his Roman countrymen to make peace; instead, he urged them to continue the war. Then, to honor the terms of his parole, he returned to Carthage, where he was tortured to death. When the Gauls entered Rome in 390 B.C., the Senators sat so still in such a dignified manner that the Gauls at first mistook them for statues. After Hannibal had destroyed two Roman armies (217 and 216 B.C.), many of Rome's Italian allies went over to the Carthaginians, but the Romans persisted until the defeat of Carthage.
4. "Because they lack a sacred poet" (Horace, *Odes*, IX.28).

an inspired rhapsodist, fills the theatre of everlasting generations with their harmony.

At length the antient system of religion and manners had fulfilled the circle of its revolution. And the world would have fallen into utter anarchy and darkness, but that there were found poets among the authors of the Christian and Chivalric systems of manners and religion, who created forms of opinion and action never before conceived; which, copied into the imaginations of men, became as generals to the bewildered armies of their thoughts. It is foreign to the present purpose to touch upon the evil produced by these systems: except that we protest, on the ground of the principles already established, that no portion of it can be imputed to the poetry they contain.

It is probable that the astonishing poetry of Moses, Job, David, Solomon and Isaiah had produced a great effect upon the mind of Jesus and his disciples. The scattered fragments preserved to us by the biographers of this extraordinary person, are all instinct with the most vivid poetry. But his doctrines seem to have been quickly distorted. At a certain period after the prevalence of a system of opinions founded upon those promulgated by him, the three forms into which Plato had distributed the faculties of mind underwent a sort of apotheosis, and became the object of the worship of the civilized world. Here it is to be confessed that "Light seems to thicken," and

> The crow makes wing to the rooky wood,
> Good things of day begin to droop and drowze,
> And night's black agents to their preys do rouze.[5]

But mark how beautiful an order has sprung from the dust and blood of this fierce chaos! how the World, as from a resurrection, balancing itself on the golden wings of knowledge and of hope, has reassumed its yet unwearied flight into the Heaven of time. Listen to the music, unheard by outward ears, which is as a ceaseless and invisible wind, nourishing its everlasting course with strength and swiftness.

The poetry in the doctrines of Jesus Christ, and the mythology and institutions of the Celtic[6] conquerors of the Roman empire, outlived the darkness and the convulsions connected with their growth and victory, and blended themselves into a new fabric of manners and opinion. It is an error to impute the ignorance of the dark ages to the Christian doctrines or the predominance of the Celtic nations. Whatever of evil their agencies may have

---

5. Shakespeare, *Macbeth*, III.ii.50–53.
6. Shelley always uses "Celt" and "Celtic" in the original Greek meaning: barbarian tribes to the north of the Mediterranean civilizations.

contained sprung from the extinction of the poetical principle, connected with the progress of despotism and superstition. Men, from causes too intricate to be here discussed, had become insensible and selfish: their own will had become feeble, and yet they were its slaves, and thence the slaves of the will of others: lust, fear, avarice, cruelty and fraud, characterised a race amongst whom no one was to be found capable of *creating* in form, language, or institution. The moral anomalies of such a state of society are not justly to be charged upon any class of events immediately connected with them, and those events are most entitled to our approbation which could dissolve it most expeditiously. It is unfortunate for those who cannot distinguish words from thoughts, that many of these anomalies have been incorporated into our popular religion.

It was not until the eleventh century that the effects of the poetry of the Christian and Chivalric systems began to manifest themselves. The principle of equality had been discovered and applied by Plato in his Republic, as the theoretical rule of the mode in which the materials of pleasure and of power produced by the common skill and labour of human beings ought to be distributed among them. The limitations of this rule were asserted by him to be determined only by the sensibility of each, or the utility to result to all. Plato, following the doctrines of Timæus and Pythagoras, taught also a moral and intellectual system of doctrine comprehending at once the past, the present, and the future condition of man.[7] Jesus Christ divulged the sacred and eternal truths contained in these views to mankind, and Christianity, in its abstract purity, became the exoteric expression of the esoteric doctrines of the poetry and wisdom of antiquity. The incorporation of the Celtic nations with the exhausted population of the South, impressed upon it the figure of the poetry existing in their mythology and institutions. The result was a sum of the action and reaction of all the causes included in it; for it may be assumed as a maxim that no nation or religion can supersede any other without incorporating into itself a portion of that which it supersedes. The abolition of personal and domestic slavery, and the emancipation of women from a great part of the degrading restraints of antiquity were among the consequences of these events.

The abolition of personal slavery is the basis of the highest political hope that it can enter into the mind of man to conceive. The freedom of women produced the poetry of sexual love. Love

7. Pythagoras (fl. ca. 530 B.C.), a Greek from Samos, founded a religio-philosophical sect at Crotona in southern Italy, which was influential in ancient thought in mathematics, music, and science and in morals and religion. The Timaeus mentioned here was probably Pythagoras' pupil, who wrote a (still extant) treatise on the nature and soul of the world.

became a religion, the idols of whose worship were ever present. It was as if the statues of Apollo and the Muses had been endowed with life and motion and had walked forth among their worshippers; so that earth became peopled by the inhabitants of a diviner world. The familiar appearance and proceedings of life became wonderful and heavenly; and a paradise was created as out of the wrecks of Eden. And as this creation itself is poetry, so its creators were poets; and language was the instrument of their art: "Galeotto fù il libro, e chi lo scrisse."[8] The Provençal Trouveurs, or inventors, preceded Petrarch, whose verses are as spells, which unseal the inmost enchanted fountains of the delight which is in the grief of Love. It is impossible to feel them without becoming a portion of that beauty which we contemplate: it were superfluous to explain how the gentleness and the elevation of mind connected with these sacred emotions can render men more amiable, more generous, and wise, and lift them out of the dull vapours of the little world of self. Dante understood the secret things of love even more than Petrarch. His *Vita Nuova* is an inexhaustible fountain of purity of sentiment and language: it is the idealized history of that period, and those intervals of his life which were dedicated to love. His apotheosis of Beatrice in Paradise and the gradations of his own love and her loveliness, by which as by steps he feigns himself to have ascended to the throne of the Supreme Cause, is the most glorious imagination of modern poetry. The acutest critics have justly reversed the judgement of the vulgar, and the order of the great acts of the "Divine Drama," in the measure of the admiration which they accord to the Hell, Purgatory and Paradise. The latter is a perpetual hymn of everlasting love. Love, which found a worthy poet in Plato alone of all the antients, has been celebrated by a chorus of the greatest writers of the renovated world; and the music has penetrated the caverns of society, and its echoes still drown the dissonance of arms and superstition. At successive intervals, Ariosto, Tasso, Shakespeare, Spenser, Calderon, Rousseau, and the great writers of our own age, have celebrated the dominion of love, planting as it were trophies in the human mind of that sublimest victory over sensuality and force. The true relation borne to each other by the sexes into which human kind is distributed has become less misunderstood; and if the error which confounded diversity with inequality of the powers of the two sexes has become partially recognized in the opinions and institutions of modern Europe,

8. "Gallehaut [Galahad] was the book and he who wrote it" (Dante, *Inferno*, V.137). Since in medieval romances Galahad introduced Lancelot and Guinevere, Dante and other Italians used the name (as English-speaking readers use Pandarus) to signify a go-between in arranging illicit romance.

we owe this great benefit to the worship of which Chivalry was the law, and poets the prophets.

The poetry of Dante may be considered as the bridge thrown over the stream of time, which unites the modern and antient world. The distorted notions of invisible things which Dante and his rival Milton have idealized, are merely the mask and the mantle in which these great poets walk through eternity enveloped and disguised. It is a difficult question to determine how far they were conscious of the distinction which must have subsisted in their minds between their own creeds and that of the people. Dante at least appears to wish to mark the full extent of it by placing Riphæus, whom Virgil calls *justissimus unus*, in Paradise,[9] and observing a most heretical caprice in his distribution of rewards and punishments. And Milton's poem contains within itself a philosophical refutation of that system of which, by a strange and natural antithesis, it has been a chief popular support. Nothing can exceed the energy and magnificence of the character of Satan as expressed in Paradise Lost. It is a mistake to suppose that he could ever have been intended for the popular personification of evil. Implacable hate, patient cunning, and a sleepless refinement of device to inflict the extremest anguish on an enemy, these things are evil; and although venial in a slave are not to be forgiven in a tyrant; although redeemed by much that ennobles his defeat in one subdued, are marked by all that dishonours his conquest in the victor. Milton's Devil as a moral being is as far superior to his God as one who perseveres in some purpose which he has conceived to be excellent in spite of adversity and torture, is to one who in the cold security of undoubted triumph inflicts the most horrible revenge upon his enemy, not from any mistaken notion of inducing him to repent of a perseverance in enmity, but with the alleged design of exasperating him to deserve new torments. Milton has so far violated the popular creed (if this shall be judged to be a violation) as to have alleged no superiority of moral virtue to his God over his Devil. And this bold neglect of a direct moral purpose is the most decisive proof of the supremacy of Milton's genius. He mingled as it were the elements of human nature, as colours upon a single pallet, and arranged them into the composition of his great picture according to the laws of epic truth; that is, according to the laws of that principle by which a series of actions of the external universe and of intelligent and ethical beings is calculated to excite the sympathy of succeed-

9. Riphaeus, whom Virgil's Aeneas in his tale to Dido called the "one man who was most just" among the Trojans and whose senseless death led the Trojan hero to reflect that "the gods' ways are not as ours" (*Aeneid*, II.424–427), appears in Dante's *Paradiso* in the Circle of the Just: "Who would believe, in the erring world below, that Ripheus the Trojan would be in this circle the fifth of the holy lights?" (XX.67–69).

ing generations of mankind. The Divina Commedia and Paradise Lost have conferred upon modern mythology a systematic form; and when change and time shall have added one more superstition to the mass of those which have arisen and decayed upon the earth, commentators will be learnedly employed in elucidating the religion of ancestral Europe, only not utterly forgotten because it will have been stamped with the eternity of genius.

Homer was the first, and Dante the second epic poet: that is, the second poet the series of whose creations bore a defined and intelligible relation to the knowledge, and sentiment, and religion, and political conditions of the age in which he lived, and of the ages which followed it, developing itself in correspondence with their developement. For Lucretius had limed the wings of his swift spirit in the dregs of the sensible world; and Virgil, with a modesty which ill became his genius, had affected the fame of an imitator even whilst he created anew all that he copied; and none among the flock of mock-birds, though their notes were sweet, Apollonius Rhodius, Quintus Calaber Smyrnaeus, Nonnus, Lucan, Statius, or Claudian,[1] have sought even to fulfil a single condition of epic truth. Milton was the third Epic Poet. For if the title of epic in its highest sense be refused to the Æneid, still less can it be conceded to the Orlando Furioso, the Gerusalemme Liberata, the Lusiad, or the Fairy Queen.[2]

Dante and Milton were both deeply penetrated with the antient religion of the civilized world; and its spirit exists in their poetry probably in the same proportion as its forms survived in the unreformed worship of modern Europe. The one preceded and the other followed the Reformation at almost equal intervals. Dante was the first religious reformer, and Luther surpassed him rather in the rudeness and acrimony, than in the boldness of his censures of papal usurpation. Dante was the first awakener of entranced Europe; he created a language in itself music and persuasion out of a chaos of inharmonious barbarisms. He was the congregator of those great spirits who presided over the resurrection of learning; the Lucifer[3] of that starry flock which in the thirteenth century shone forth from republican Italy, as from a heaven,

1. Apollonius of Rhodes (born ca. 295 B.C.) wrote his Greek romance-epic, the *Argonautica*, in Alexandria. Quintus Smyrnaeus (fl. ca. A.D. 375) was called "Calaber" because the manuscript of his *Posthomerica*, a fourteen-book Greek sequel to Homer's *Iliad*, was discovered in Calabria. Nonnus (fl. ca. A.D. 425–450) wrote *Dionysiaca*, a Greek epic in forty-eight books about Dionysus' conquest of India. (He was a favorite poet of Peacock, who in "The Four Ages of Poetry" labeled the classical "bronze age" of poetry the "Nonnic" age.) For Lucan, author of the *Pharsalia*, see the note to *Adonais*, 404. Publius Papinius Statius (ca. A.D. 45–96), a Roman court poet, wrote two Latin epics, the finished twelve-book one entitled *Thebais*, on the struggle between Polynices and Eteocles for Thebes. Claudius Claudianus (ca. A.D. 370–404) wrote a mythological Latin epic on the rape of Proserpine.

2. Romance epics by Ariosto and Tasso in Italian, Luis de Camoens in Portuguese, and Spenser.

3. "Light-Bearer," or morning star.

into the darkness of the benighted world. His very words are instinct with spirit; each is as a spark, a burning atom of inextinguishable thought; and many yet lie covered in the ashes of their birth, and pregnant with a lightning which has yet found no conductor. All high poetry is infinite; it is as the first acorn, which contained all oaks potentially. Veil after veil may be undrawn, and the inmost naked beauty of the meaning never exposed. A great Poem is a fountain for ever overflowing with the waters of wisdom and delight; and after one person and one age has exhausted all its divine effluence which their peculiar relations enable them to share, another and yet another succeeds, and new relations are ever developed, the source of an unforeseen and an unconceived delight.

The age immediately succeeding to that of Dante, Petrarch, and Boccaccio, was characterized by a revival of painting, sculpture, music, and architecture. Chaucer caught the sacred inspiration, and the superstructure of English literature is based upon the materials of Italian invention.

But let us not be betrayed from a defence into a critical history of Poetry and its influence on Society. Be it enough to have pointed out the effects of poets, in the large and true sense of the word, upon their own and all succeeding times and to revert to the partial instances cited as illustrations of an opinion the reverse of that attempted to be established in the Four Ages of Poetry.

But poets have been challenged to resign the civic crown to reasoners and mechanists on another plea. It is admitted that the exercise of the imagination is most delightful, but it is alleged that that of reason is more useful. Let us examine as the grounds of this distinction, what is here meant by Utility. Pleasure or good in a general sense, is that which the consciousness of a sensitive and intelligent being seeks, and in which when found it acquiesces.[4] There are two kinds of pleasure, one durable, universal, and permanent; the other transitory and particular. Utility may either express the means of producing the former or the latter. In the former sense, whatever strengthens and purifies the affections, enlarges the imagination, and adds spirit to sense, is useful. But the meaning in which the Author of the Four Ages of Poetry seems to have employed the word utility is the narrower one of banishing the importunity of the wants of our animal nature, the surrounding men with security of life, the

---

4. Shelley's real challenge is to the growing school of radical reformers (not yet called "utilitarians") who followed Jeremy Bentham (1748–1832) and argued that the goal of life was to provide the greatest quantity of "good"—always defined simply as "pleasure"—to the greatest number of people. Shelley here anticipates John Stuart Mill's interest in *qualitative* as well as *quantitative* elements in the calculation of pleasure.

dispersing the grosser delusions of superstition, and the conciliating such a degree of mutual forbearance among men as may consist with the motives of personal advantage.

Undoubtedly the promoters of utility in this limited sense, have their appointed office in society. They follow the footsteps of poets, and copy the sketches of their creations into the book of common life. They make space, and give time. Their exertions are of the highest value so long as they confine their administration of the concerns of the inferior powers of our nature within the limits due to the superior ones. But whilst the sceptic destroys gross superstitions, let him spare to deface, as some of the French writers have defaced, the eternal truths charactered upon the imaginations of men. Whilst the mechanist abridges, and the political œconomist combines, labour, let them beware that their speculations, for want of correspondence with those first principles which belong to the imagination, do not tend, as they have in modern England, to exasperate at once the extremes of luxury and want. They have exemplified the saying, "To him that hath, more shall be given; and from him that hath not, the little that he hath shall be taken away."[5] The rich have become richer, and the poor have become poorer; and the vessel of the state is driven between the Scylla and Charybdis[6] of anarchy and despotism. Such are the effects which must ever flow from an unmitigated exercise of the calculating faculty.

It is difficult to define pleasure in its highest sense; the definition involving a number of apparent paradoxes. For, from an inexplicable defect of harmony in the constitution of human nature, the pain of the inferior is frequently connected with the pleasures of the superior portions of our being. Sorrow, terror, anguish, despair itself are often the chosen expressions of an approximation to the highest good. Our sympathy in tragic fiction depends on this principle; tragedy delights by affording a shadow of the pleasure which exists in pain. This is the source also of the melancholy which is inseparable from the sweetest melody. The pleasure that is in sorrow is sweeter than the pleasure of pleasure itself. And hence the saying, "It is better to go to the house of mourning, than to the house of mirth."[7] Not that this highest species of pleasure is necessarily linked with pain. The delight of love and friendship, the extacy of the admiration of nature, the joy of the perception and still more of the creation of poetry is often wholly unalloyed.

The production and assurance of pleasure in this highest sense

---

5. One of the sayings of Jesus (Matthew 25:29; Mark 4:25; Luke 8:18, 19:26).
6. A legendary group of rocks and a whirlpool that flanked the Straits of Messina, between Sicily and the toe of Italy, and endangered ships (Homer's *Odyssey*, XII); the names came to represent dangers from any two opposite extremes.
7. Cf. Ecclesiastes 7:2.

is true utility. Those who produce and preserve this pleasure are Poets or poetical philosophers.

The exertions of Locke, Hume, Gibbon, Voltaire, Rousseau,[8] and their disciples, in favour of oppressed and deluded humanity, are entitled to the gratitude of mankind. Yet it is easy to calculate the degree of moral and intellectual improvement which the world would have exhibited, had they never lived. A little more nonsense would have been talked for a century or two; and perhaps a few more men, women, and children, burnt as heretics. We might not at this moment have been congratulating each other on the abolition of the Inquisition in Spain.[9] But it exceeds all imagination to conceive what would have been the moral condition of the world if neither Dante, Petrarch, Boccaccio, Chaucer, Shakespeare, Calderon, Lord Bacon, nor Milton, had ever existed; if Raphael and Michael Angelo had never been born; if the Hebrew poetry had never been translated; if a revival of the study of Greek literature had never taken place; if no monuments of antient sculpture had been handed down to us; and if the poetry of the religion of the antient world had been extinguished together with its belief. The human mind could never, except by the intervention of these excitements, have been awakened to the invention of the grosser sciences, and that application of analytical reasoning to the aberrations of society, which it is now attempted to exalt over the direct expression of the inventive and creative faculty itself.

We have more moral, political and historical wisdom, than we know how to reduce into practise; we have more scientific and œconomical knowledge than can be accommodated to the just distribution of the produce which it multiplies. The poetry in these systems of thought, is concealed by the accumulation of facts and calculating processes. There is no want of knowledge respecting what is wisest and best in morals, government, and political œconomy, or at least, what is wiser and better than what men now practise and endure. But we let "*I dare not* wait upon *I would*, like the poor cat i' the adage."[1] We want the creative faculty to imagine that which we know; we want the generous impulse to act that which we imagine; we want the poetry of life: our calculations have outrun conception; we have eaten more than we can digest. The cultivation of those sciences which have enlarged the limits of the empire of man over the external world, has, for want of the poetical faculty, proportionally cir-

8. "I follow the classification adopted by the author of the Four Ages of Poetry. But Rousseau was essentially a poet. The others, even Voltaire, were mere reasoners" (Shelley's note).

9. The Spanish Inquisition had been suppressed after the Spanish Revolution of 1820; it was restored in 1823 and finally abolished in 1834.

1. Shakespeare, *Macbeth*, I.vii.44–45.

cumscribed those of the internal world; and man, having enslaved the elements, remains himself a slave. To what but a cultivation of the mechanical arts in a degree disproportioned to the presence of the creative faculty, which is the basis of all knowledge, is to be attributed the abuse of all invention for abridging and combining labour, to the exasperation of the inequality of mankind? From what other cause has it arisen that the discoveries which should have lightened, have added a weight to the curse imposed on Adam?[2] Poetry, and the principle of Self, of which money is the visible incarnation, are the God and the Mammon of the world.[3]

The functions of the poetical faculty are two-fold; by one it creates new materials of knowledge, and power and pleasure; by the other it engenders in the mind a desire to reproduce and arrange them according to a certain rhythm and order which may be called the beautiful and the good. The cultivation of poetry is never more to be desired than at periods when, from an excess of the selfish and calculating principle, the accumulation of the materials of external life exceed the quantity of the power of assimilating them to the internal laws of human nature. The body has then become too unwieldy for that which animates it.

Poetry is indeed something divine. It is at once the centre and circumference of knowledge; it is that which comprehends all science, and that to which all science must be referred. It is at the same time the root and blossom of all other systems of thought: it is that from which all spring, and that which adorns all; and that which, if blighted, denies the fruit and the seed, and withholds from the barren world the nourishment and the succession of the scions of the tree of life. It is the perfect and consummate surface and bloom of things; it is as the odour and the colour of the rose to the texture of the elements which compose it, as the form and the splendour of unfaded beauty to the secrets of anatomy and corruption. What were Virtue, Love, Patriotism, Friendship &c.—what were the scenery of this beautiful Universe which we inhabit—what were our consolations on this side of the grave—and what were our aspirations beyond it—if Poetry did not ascend to bring light and fire from those eternal regions where the owl-winged faculty of calculation dare not ever soar? Poetry is not like reasoning, a power to be exerted according to the determination of the will. A man cannot say, "I will compose poetry." The greatest poet even cannot say it: for the mind

---

2. "In the sweat of thy face shalt thou eat bread, till thou return unto the ground; for out of it wast thou taken: for dust thou art, and unto dust shalt thou return" (Genesis 3:19).
3. "No man can serve two masters: for either he will hate the one, and love the other; or else he will hold to the one, and despise the other. Ye cannot serve God and mammon" (Matthew 6:24; see also Luke 16:13).

in creation is as a fading coal which some invisible influence, like an inconstant wind, awakens to transitory brightness: this power arises from within, like the colour of a flower which fades and changes as it is developed, and the conscious portions of our natures are unprophetic either of its approach or its departure. Could this influence be durable in its original purity and force, it is impossible to predict the greatness of the results: but when composition begins, inspiration is already on the decline, and the most glorious poetry that has ever been communicated to the world is probably a feeble shadow of the original conception of the poet. I appeal to the greatest Poets of the present day, whether it be not an error to assert that the finest passages of poetry are produced by labour and study. The toil and the delay recommended by critics can be justly interpreted to mean no more than a careful observation of the inspired moments, and an artificial connexion of the spaces between their suggestions by the intertexture of conventional expressions; a necessity only imposed by a limitedness of the poetical faculty itself. For Milton conceived the Paradise Lost as a whole before he executed it in portions. We have his own authority also for the Muse having "dictated" to him the "unpremeditated song,"[4] and let this be an answer to those who would allege the fifty-six various readings of the first line of the Orlando Furioso. Compositions so produced are to poetry what mosaic is to painting. This instinct and intuition of the poetical faculty is still more observable in the plastic and pictorial arts: a great statue or picture grows under the power of the artist as a child in the mother's womb, and the very mind which directs the hands in formation is incapable of accounting to itself for the origin, the gradations, or the media of the process.

Poetry is the record of the best and happiest moments of the happiest and best minds. We are aware of evanescent visitations of thought and feeling sometimes associated with place or person, sometimes regarding our own mind alone, and always arising unforeseen and departing unbidden, but elevating and delightful beyond all expression: so that even in the desire and the regret they leave, there cannot but be pleasure, participating as it does in the nature of its object. It is as it were the interpenetration of a diviner nature through our own; but its footsteps are like those of a wind over a sea, which the coming calm erases, and whose traces remain only as on the wrinkled sand which paves it. These and corresponding conditions of being are experienced

4. ". . . my Celestial Patroness, who deignes/Her nightly visitation unimplor'd, /And dictates to me slumb'ring, or inspires/Easie my unpremeditated Verse" (Milton, *Paradise Lost*, IX.21–24).

principally by those of the most delicate sensibility and the most enlarged imagination; and the state of mind produced by them is at war with every base desire. The enthusiasm of virtue, love, patriotism, and friendship is essentially linked with these emotions; and whilst they last, self appears as what it is, an atom to a Universe. Poets are not only subject to these experiences as spirits of the most refined organization, but they can colour all that they combine with the evanescent hues of this etherial world; a word, a trait in the representation of a scene or a passion, will touch the enchanted chord, and reanimate, in those who have ever experienced these emotions, the sleeping, the cold, the buried image of the past. Poetry thus makes immortal all that is best and most beautiful in the world; it arrests the vanishing apparitions which haunt the interlunations of life, and veiling them or in language or in form sends them forth among mankind, bearing sweet news of kindred joy to those with whom their sisters abide— abide, because there is no portal of expression from the caverns of the spirit which they inhabit into the universe of things.[5] Poetry redeems from decay the visitations of the divinity in man.

Poetry turns all things to loveliness; it exalts the beauty of that which is most beautiful, and it adds beauty to that which is most deformed: it marries exultation and horror, grief and pleasure, eternity and change; it subdues to union under its light yoke all irreconcilable things. It transmutes all that it touches, and every form moving within the radiance of its presence is changed by wondrous sympathy to an incarnation of the spirit which it breathes; its secret alchemy turns to potable gold the poisonous waters which flow from death through life; it strips the veil of familiarity from the world, and lays bare the naked and sleeping beauty which is the spirit of its forms.

All things exist as they are perceived: at least in relation to the percipient. "The mind is its own place, and of itself can make a heaven of hell, a hell of heaven."[6] But poetry defeats the curse which binds us to be subjected to the accident of surrounding impressions. And whether it spreads its own figured curtain or withdraws life's dark veil from before the scene of things, it equally creates for us a being within our being. It makes us the inhabitants of a world to which the familiar world is a chaos. It reproduces the common universe of which we are portions and percipients, and it purges from our inward sight the film of familiarity which obscures from us the wonder of our being. It compels us to feel that which we perceive, and to imagine that which we know. It creates anew the universe after it has been

5. I.e., all have kindred visions, but most people remain unable to express or com-

municate them.
6. Milton, *Paradise Lost*, I.254–255.

annihilated in our minds by the recurrence of impressions blunted by reiteration. It justifies that bold and true word of Tasso—*Non merita nome di creatore, se non Iddio ed il Poeta.*[7]

A Poet, as he is the author to others of the highest wisdom, pleasure, virtue and glory, so he ought personally to be the happiest, the best, the wisest, and the most illustrious of men. As to his glory, let Time be challenged to declare whether the fame of any other institutor of human life be comparable to that of a poet. That he is the wisest, the happiest, and the best, inasmuch as he is a poet, is equally incontrovertible: the greatest poets have been men of the most spotless virtue, of the most consummate prudence, and, if we could look into the interior of their lives, the most fortunate of men: and the exceptions, as they regard those who possessed the poetic faculty in a high yet inferior degree, will be found on consideration to confirm rather than destroy the rule. Let us for a moment stoop to the arbitration of popular breath, and usurping and uniting in our own persons the incompatible characters of accuser, witness, judge and executioner, let us decide without trial, testimony, or form, that certain motives of those who are "there sitting where we dare not soar"[8] are reprehensible. Let us assume that Homer was a drunkard, that Virgil was a flatterer, that Horace was a coward, that Tasso was a madman, that Lord Bacon was a peculator, that Raphael was a libertine, that Spenser was a poet laureate.[9] It is inconsistent with this division of our subject to cite living poets, but Posterity has done ample justice to the great names now referred to. Their errors have been weighed and found to have been dust in the balance; if their sins "were as scarlet, they are now white as snow"; they have been washed in the blood of the mediator and the redeemer Time. Observe in what a ludicrous chaos the imputations of real or fictitious crime have been confused in the contemporary calumnies against poetry and poets; consider how little is, as it appears—or appears, as it is; look to your own motives, and judge not, lest ye be judged.

Poetry, as has been said, in this respect differs from logic, that it is not subject to the controul of the active powers of the mind, and that its birth and recurrence has no necessary connexion with consciousness or will. It is presumptuous to determine that these are the necessary conditions of all mental causation, when mental effects are experienced insusceptible of being referred to them. The frequent recurrence of the poetical power,

7. "None deserves the name of Creator except God and the Poet." Quoted in Pierantonio Serassi's Italian *Life of Torquato Tasso* (1785).
8. Milton, *Paradise Lost*, IV.829. See also *Adonais*, 337.
9. Shelley believed that Robert Southey, then Poet Laureate, had slandered him in articles and reviews.

it is obvious to suppose, may produce in the mind an habit of order and harmony correlative with its own nature and with its effects upon other minds. But in the intervals of inspiration, and they may be frequent without being durable, a poet becomes a man, and is abandoned to the sudden reflux of the influences under which others habitually live. But as he is more delicately organized than other men, and sensible to pain and pleasure, both his own and that of others, in a degree unknown to them, he will avoid the one and pursue the other with an ardour proportioned to this difference. And he renders himself obnoxious to calumny, when he neglects to observe the circumstances under which these objects of universal pursuit and flight have disguised themselves in one another's garments.

But there is nothing necessarily evil in this error, and thus cruelty, envy, revenge, avarice, and the passions purely evil, have never formed any portion of the popular imputations on the lives of poets.

I have thought it most favourable to the cause of truth to set down these remarks according to the order in which they were suggested to my mind by a consideration of the subject itself, instead of following that of the treatise that excited me to make them public. Thus although devoid of the formality of a polemical reply; if the view they contain be just, they will be found to involve a refutation of the Four Ages of Poetry, so far at least as regards the first division of the subject. I can readily conjecture what should have moved the gall of the learned and intelligent author of that paper; I confess myself like him unwilling to be stunned by the Theseids of the hoarse Codri of the day. Bavius and Mævius undoubtedly are, as they ever were, insufferable persons.[1] But it belongs to a philosophical critic to distinguish rather than confound.

The first part of these remarks has related to Poetry in its elements and principles; and it has been shewn, as well as the narrow limits assigned them would permit, that what is called poetry, in a restricted sense, has a common source with all other forms of order and of beauty according to which the materials of human life are susceptible of being arranged, and which is poetry in an universal sense.

The second part will have for its object an application of these principles to the present state of the cultivation of Poetry, and a defence of the attempt to idealize the modern forms of manners and opinion, and compel them into a subordination to the imaginative and creative faculty. For the literature of England, an ener-

1. Codrus, author of the *Theseid*, Bavius, and Maevius were inferior Latin poets castigated by Juvenal, Virgil, and Horace.

getic developement of which has ever preceded or accompanied a great and free developement of the national will, has arisen as it were from a new birth. In spite of the low-thoughted envy which would undervalue contemporary merit, our own will be a memorable age in intellectual achievements, and we live among such philosophers and poets as surpass beyond comparison any who have appeared since the last national struggle for civil and religious liberty. The most unfailing herald, companion, and follower of the awakening of a great people to work a beneficial change in opinion or institution, is Poetry. At such periods there is an accumulation of the power of communicating and receiving intense and impassioned conceptions respecting man and nature. The persons in whom this power resides, may often, as far as regards many portions of their nature, have little apparent correspondence with that spirit of good of which they are the ministers. But even whilst they deny and abjure, they are yet compelled to serve, the Power which is seated upon the throne of their own soul. It is impossible to read the compositions of the most celebrated writers of the present day without being startled with the electric life which burns within their words. They measure the circumference and sound the depths of human nature with a comprehensive and all-penetrating spirit, and they are themselves perhaps the most sincerely astonished at its manifestations, for it is less their spirit than the spirit of the age. Poets are the hierophants of an unapprehended inspiration, the mirrors of the gigantic shadows which futurity casts upon the present, the words which express what they understand not; the trumpets which sing to battle, and feel not what they inspire: the influence which is moved not, but moves. Poets are the unacknowledged legislators of the World.

Criticism

General Studies

KENNETH NEILL CAMERON

The Social Philosophy of Shelley†

It is a lamentable, but indubitable, fact, that, in spite of the efforts of a number of socially-minded scholars from H. Buxton Forman to Newman Ivey White, the prevalent view of Shelley is still that of a mystic visionary,—the "ineffectual angel" of Matthew Arnold, the winsome "child" of Francis Thompson, the impulsive Ariel of Andre Maurois. If any doubt that this is so, let him but consult those stolid barometers of average academic opinion, the textbooks and anthologies. The anthologies he will find interminably reprinting the same minor lyrics—"To A Skylark," "To Night," "When the lamp is shattered" etc., etc.,— lyrics which are entirely unrepresentative of the major channels of Shelly's philosophy. The textbooks he will find re-echoing (with unimportant and pedestrian variations) the catch-phrases of Arnold, Thompson, Hogg, Clutton Brock and their ilk.

Upon what postulates, we may inquire, is this view based? Only one of its proponents, so far as I can find, has been sufficiently rash to advance any, namely George Santayana, who, in *Winds of Doctrine*, has the following to offer:

Shelley was one of those spokesmen of the *a priori*, one of those nurslings of the womb, like a bee or a butterfly; a dogmatic, inspired, perfect and incorrigible creature. . . . Being a finished child of nature, not a joint product, like most of us, of nature, history and society, he abounded miraculously in his own clear sense but was obtuse to the droll, miscellaneous lessons of fortune. The cannonade of hard, inexplicable facts that knocks into most of us what little wisdom we have, left Shelley dazed and sore, perhaps, but uninstructed. When the storm was over he began chirping again his own natural note. If the world continued to confine and oppress him, he hated the world, and gasped for freedom. Being incapable of understanding reality, he revelled in creating world after world in idea.

† First published in *The Sewanee Review*, L, 4 (Autumn, 1942). Reprinted with the permission of the University of the South.

The view of the angelic school, then, rests upon two postulates: Shelly was not, like other human beings, a product of a social environment but a mystic outgrowth of nature, "like a bee or a butterfly"; Shelley's philosophy is, likewise, not the product of a social environment—or, apparently, of an intellectual one either —but is of the pure substance of his own mind, a dream fantasy, "creating world after world in idea".

It is in the hope of driving one more nail into the coffin of this apparently unburiable view that I undertake the present brief outline of Shelley's social philosophy, a philosophy which both Shelley and Mary looked upon as expressing the essence of his message to mankind.

Shelley, fortunately, has left us a picture of this philosophy not in his poetry alone, but also—as has been insufficiently noted —in his prose, where it is presented with an expository directness which is inevitably lacking in the more symbolic medium of poetry. The key to the understanding of the poetry, in fact, is to be found in the prose.

The main inspirational force in Shelley's work, as many critics have recognized, though they have not always expressed it in quite these terms, is his theory of historical evolution. The essence of this theory, as given in the first chapter of A *Philosophical View of Reform* and other works, is that history is essentially a struggle between two sets of forces, the forces of liberty and the forces of despotism. Sometimes the despotic forces were in the ascendent—as in ancient Rome or the England of Charles I; sometimes the forces of liberty—as in Athens or the medieval Italian states or the England of Cromwell. In recent times two events had raised the power of the forces of liberty to tidal wave proportions,—the American Revolutionary War and the French Revolution.

> The system of government in the United States of America— wrote Shelley (in 1819)—is the first practical illustration of the new philosophy. Sufficiently remote, it will be confessed, from the accuracy of ideal excellence, is that representative system which will soon cover the extent of that vast Continent. But it is scarcely less remote from the insolent and contaminating tyrannies under which, with some limitations of these terms as regards England, Europe groaned at the period of the successful rebellion of America. America holds forth the victorious example of an immensely populous, and as far as the external arts of life are concerned, a highly civilized community administered according to republican forms. . . . The just and successful Revolt of America corresponded with a state of public opinion in Europe of which it was the first result. The French Revolution was the second.

These two advances of the forces of liberty, Shelley believed, were of such a magnitude as to make any future repression of them but temporary. Specifically applied to the contemporary European scene, this meant that the extensive counter-revolutionary network of Metternich, Castlereagh and the Quadruple Alliance would eventually be torn asunder. Shelley—running against the tide of pessimism then so common among liberal thinkers—believed that he could perceive signs of such an awakening in Europe, especially in the revolutionary events in Spain, Naples and Greece (1820 and 1821). As he wrote in 1821, the year before his death—at a time when, according to some critics, he had ceased to be a revolutionary and had become a mystic—

> This is the age of the war of the oppressed against the oppressors, and every one of those ringleaders of the privileged gangs of murderers and swindlers, called Sovereigns, look to each other for aid against the common enemy and suspend their mutual jealousies in the presence of a mightier fear. Of this holy alliance all the despots of the earth are virtual members. But a new race has arisen throughout Europe, nursed in the abhorrence of the opinions which are its chains, and she will continue to produce fresh generations to accomplish that destiny which tyrants foresee and dread.
>
> The Spanish Peninsula is already free. France is tranquil in the enjoyment of a partial exemption from the abuses which its unnatural and feeble government are vainly attempting to revive. The seed of blood and misery has been sown in Italy, and a more vigorous race is arising to go forth to the harvest. The world waits only the news of a revolution in Germany to see the tyrants who have pinnacled themselves on its supineness precipitated into the ruin from which they shall never arise. Well do these destroyers of mankind know their enemy, when they impute the insurrection in Greece to the same spirit before which they tremble throughout the rest of Europe, and that enemy well knows the power and cunning of its opponents, and watches for the moment of their approaching weakness and inevitable division to wrest the bloody sceptres from their grasp.

It is in this theory of historical development—from ancient Greece to his own times and beyond—that we have the basis for what is usually called Shelley's "optimism", that chirping after the storm of which Professor Santayana speaks. That it was not at all, however, a purely emotional, subjective optimism but was based on a study of historical movements is shown by the fact that a little more than a quarter of a century after Shelley uttered these words, the aristocratic-militaristic Europe of Metternich had been torn to shreds under the impetus of those two celebrated years of revolutions, 1830 and 1848, and the more democratic states, which Shelley anticipated, were either established, or had, at least, had their foundations laid.

Shelley did not believe that the historical forces unloosed by the American and French revolutions would stop with the establishment of democratic republics, but they would continue beyond this form of state into an equalitarian society, a society, that is to say, in which every person would possess an equal amount of private property. This he looked upon as a matter for the rather remote future, and urged his contemporaries to concentrate their attention upon the problems of the present.

> Equality in possessions must be the last result of the utmost refinements of civilization; it is one of the conditions of that system of society, toward which with whatever hope of ultimate success, it is our duty to tend. We may and ought to advert to it as to the elementary principle, as to the goal unattainable, perhaps by us, but which, as it were, we revive in our posterity to pursue. We derive tranquillity and courage and grandeur of soul from contemplating an object which is, because we will it, and must be if succeeding generations of the enlightened sincerely and earnestly seek it. . . . But our present business is with the difficult and unbending realities of actual life, and when we have drawn inspiration from the great object of our hopes it becomes us with patience and resolution to apply ourselves to accommodating our theories to immediate practice.

Nor did Shelley himself fail to "accommodate his theories to immediate practice." In regard to the continent of Europe he felt that the existing despotic governments could be overthrown only by revolution, and his letters and work show a constant attention to the development of such movements—in Spain, in Naples, in Paris, in Greece, as well as in Mexico, South America and Ireland (which he had visited as a youth in advocacy of the repeal of the union with England and the establishment of Catholic Emancipation). In regard to England he hoped that a democratic state could be achieved by peaceful means and wrote three political tracts in support of the movement for the reform of parliament. For a time he supported that group known as the moderate reformers, who demanded the vote only for those who paid property taxes, in preference to the radical reformers, who demanded the vote for all adult males. His reason for doing so was not that he accepted limited suffrage as a final objective, but that he believed complete suffrage could best be obtained in two stages; and this, we might note, was how it finally did happen: limited suffrage was established in 1832 and extended in 1867 and 1885, until complete male suffrage was achieved.

Such, then, in brief, is the essence of Shelley's social philosophy as expressed in his prose works. It seems hardly the kind of philosophy that one would suck from nature "like a bee or a butterfly." The belief that the progressive people would overthrow the aristocratic, dictatorial states by revolution on the continent and by reform in England was no "creating world after world in idea". These views were the result of an analysis of the contemporary international situation, the product of a mind shaped by the forces of the French Revolution and the English reform movement. They were views, moreover, shared in large part by such advanced political thinkers as Holbach, Condorcet, Volney, Paine, Godwin, Mary Wollstonecraft, Leigh Hunt, William Cobbett, Sir Francis Burdett and Jeremy Bentham. Were all these thinkers, too, we might legitimately inquire, obsessed by subjective dream fantasies, "ineffectual angels"?

Nor can it be claimed that Shelley had one social philosophy for his prose and another for his poetry. I have discussed the prose first simply as a matter of convenience, but everything brought out in relation to the one applies also to the other. Shelley's analysis of the contemporary situation in England and its reform movement will be found in "The Mask of Anarchy" and "Swellfoot The Tyrant"; his views on the revolutionary movement on the continent, in the "Ode Written in October, 1819", the "Ode to Liberty"—on the Spanish revolution of 1820—the "Ode to Naples"—on the war of the Kingdom of Naples against Austrian domination—and "Hellas"—on the Greek struggle for liberation from the Turkish empire; his interpretation of the rise and fall of the French Revolution and the emergence of the tyranny of the Quadruple Alliance, in "The Revolt of Islam"; his general theory of historical evolution, in "Queen Mab" and "Prometheus Unbound".

To glance briefly at one of Shelley's poems on affairs in England: the central thought of "The Mask of Anarchy" is that if the ruling aristocratic class continued its policy of repression (as at "Peterloo") social anarchy would result, and such a disaster could be prevented only if the people of England would rally around the central issues of the reform movement for a peaceful transference of power. This, too, is the main thought of chapters two and three of A *Philosophical View of Reform*; and like A *Philosophical View of Reform* the poem ends on a sterner note:

> Rise like lions after slumber
> In unvanquishable number—
> Shake your chains to earth like dew
> Which in sleep had fallen on you—
> Ye are many—they are few.

The most encouraging and significant event on the continent, Shelley felt, was the beginning, in 1821, of the revolutionary war of the Greek people, significant because it represented the first major cracking of the Metternich system, and hence a culminating point in the historical evolution of the forces of liberty. It is in this perspective that he treats the Greek revolution in "Hellas" putting into flaming lyrical verse the same concept of historical development we have already noted in his prose.

> In the great morning of the world,
> The Spirit of God with might unfurled
> The flag of Freedom over Chaos,
>   And all its banded anarchs fled,
> Like vultures frighted from Imaus,
>   Before an earthquake's tread,—
> So from Time's tempestuous dawn
> Freedom's splendour burst and shone:—
> Thermopylae and Marathon
> Caught like mountains beacon-lighted,
>   The springing Fire.—The winged glory
> On Philippi half-alighted
>   Like an eagle on a promontory.
> Its unwearied wings could fan
> The quenchless ashes of Milan.
> From age to age, from man to man,
> It lived, and lit from land to land
> Florence, Albion, Switzerland.
>
> Then night fell; and, as from night,
> Reassuming fiery flight,
> From the West swift Freedom came,
> Against the course of Heaven and doom,
> A second sun arrayed in flame,
>   To burn, to kindle, to illume.
> From far Atlantis, its young beams
> Chased the shadows and the dreams.
> France, with all her sanguine streams,
>   Hid, but quenched it not; again
>   Through clouds its shafts of glory rain
> From utmost Germany to Spain.
> As an eagle fed with morning
> Scorns the embattled tempest's warning,
> When she seeks her aerie hanging
>   In the mountain-cedar's hair,
> And her brood expect the clanging
>   Of her wings through the wild air,
> Sick with famine;—Freedom so
> To what of Greece remaineth now
> Returns; her hoary ruins glow

Like Orient mountains lost in day;
  Beneath the safety of her wings
Her renovated nurslings prey
  And in the naked lightenings
Of truth they purge their dazzled eyes.
Let Freedom leave—where'er she flies,
A Desert or a Paradise:
Let the beautiful and the brave
Share her glory or a grave.

It is clear that Shelley is not, as his critics usually assume, treating the Greek revolution as an isolated event, but in terms of an integrated philosophy of historical evolution.

In "The Revolt of Islam" Shelley depicts what he calls a *beau ideal* of the French Revolution and its aftermath, basing his picture upon Volney, Mary Wollstonecraft and other historians of the revolution. He gives a striking picture of the people under tyrannical oppression, grave and hoary demagogues sent among them to prove that "among mankind/The many to the few belong,/By heaven and nature and necessity." He traces the victorious rise of the (French) people and their inspired establishment of a new order based upon wisdom, love and equality, as a result of which the other nations of Europe will likewise attain freedom, for "Thoughts have gone forth whose powers can sleep no more!" Then comes the treacherous attack of the king and his fellow rulers, followed by bloody warfare—the Napoleonic wars—and ended by a peace more horrible than the war itself:

Peace in the desert fields and villages,
Between the glutted beasts and mangled dead!
Peace in the silent streets.

In the midst of these horrors the rulers call a meeting (parallel to the Congress of Vienna):

Ye Princes of the Earth, ye sit aghast
Amid the ruin which yourselves have made,
Yes, Desolation heard your trumpet's blast
And sprang from sleep!—dark Terror has obeyed
Your bidding. . . .

It is a terrible and powerful picture, but no more terrible than the reality of a Europe bloody from a quarter century of wars and revolutions, which inspired it.

In "Prometheus Unbound" Shelley takes a still broader canvas, depicting the vast movement of historical evolution from a period immediately before the outbreak of the French Revolution into the immediate future of the overthrow of the despotic state, and the remoter future, of the equalitarian society. The struggle of Prometheus is the struggle of the leader of humanity—specifically the peoples of post-war Europe—against the despotic state (Jupiter) —specifically the rule of the Quadruple Alliance. In this struggle humanity is assisted by the forces of historical evolution (Demogorgon) and by the strength of human love and comradeship (Asia). Aided by these forces mankind overthrows the despotic state and advances into the new order.

Because of the very vastness of the subject, Shelley does not use the detailed method he employs in "The Revolt of Islam" but treats it in more general terms, a technique which has proved misleading to a number of critics, for they have viewed what are really generalizations of actual historical movements as pure abstractions. A detailed study of the poem and its symbolism reveals the same theories and interpretations that we have already noted in the other poems and the prose. To give an example: the Furies represent, in their historical-political significance, the same thing that the armies of the despots do in "The Revolt of Islam", namely the allied armies of the Napoleonic Wars. The Furies, we remember, come "From the ends of the earth, from the ends of the earth,/Where the night has its grave and the morning its birth"; the armies in "The Revolt of Islam:"

> From every nations of the earth they came,
> The multitude of heartless moving things,
> Whom slaves call men; obediently they came.

These armies, in "The Revolt of Islam," are joined by the forces of other tyrants—a reference, mainly, to the English declaration of war on France—"Myriads had come—millions were on their way"; of the Furies, too, one group comes first and calls to its fellows:

> We are steaming up from Hell's wide gate
> And we burthen the blast of the atmosphere,
> But vainly we toil till ye come here.

To give a second example: When, in *A Philosophical View of Reform,* Shelley writes that in spite of the defeat of the revolution, France will rise again—"But the military project of the great tyrant [Napoleon] having failed, and there being no attempt— and, if there were any attempt, there being not the remotest possibility of reestablishing the enormous system of tyranny abolished by the Revolution, France, is as it were, regenerated"— we have the same basic conception as in the song of the spirits to Prometheus at the conclusion of the first act when they indicate to him that the forces of liberty will again triumph in Europe following the crushing of the French Revolution, a message which Shelley expresses also in the "Ode To The West Wind":

O thou,
Who chariotest to their dark wintry bed

The winged seeds, where they lie cold and low,
Each like a corpse within its grave, until
Thine azure sister of the Spring shall blow

Her clarion o'er the dreaming earth, and fill
(Driving sweet buds like flocks to feed in air)
With living hues and odour plain and hill:

Wild Spirit, which are moving everywhere;
Destroyer and Preserver; hear, oh, hear!

The "winged seeds" are the dormant forces of democratic progress; the "wild spirit", the "destroyer and preserver", the "West Wind" is the mighty tide of historical evolution gathering to sweep away the old order of aristocratic despotism.

C. E. PULOS

[The Role of Scepticism in Shelley's Thought]†

During the years 1811–1816 much of Shelley's reading in philosophy was devoted to sceptics. Hume and Drummond familiarized him with the most recent developments in sceptical thought—developments interpreted by Hume's chief British adversaries, the Common Sense school of thinkers, as the logical and inevitable result of a doctrine pervading nearly all modern speculation. Cicero and Diogenes Laertius introduced Shelley to the scepticism of antiquity; Sir Thomas Browne and Montaigne, to the scepticism of the Renaissance. The impact on the poet's mind of the sceptical tradition, as variously represented by these authors, is largely responsible for those modifications in his thought which critics have long recognized as distinguishing the mature from the young Shelley.

To appreciate, however, the possibility of this conclusion, it is necessary to bear in mind that the sceptical tradition, from its origin down to Shelley's own time, possesses a positive side as well as a negative, and that the former rests on disparate principles. On its negative side scepticism attempts to demonstrate the limitations of reason and knowledge. Sceptics differ on this point only in degree, that is, in the thoroughness and depth of their argu-

† Reprinted from *The Deep Truth: A Study of Shelley's Scepticism* (chap. VII, "Conclusion," pp. 105–112), by C. E. Pulos, by permission of the University of Nebraska Press, © 1954 by the University of Nebraska.

ments. But on its positive side scepticism branches off into dissimilar principles; sceptics disagree in their sceptical solutions to doubt. Some rely mainly on custom, others on faith, still others on the doctrine of probability. The main difference lies between the first and the last of these solutions, while the second is compatible with either of the other two. The reliance on custom naturally leads to the adoption of conservative ideas. Probabilism, on the other hand, may and often does conduct to unorthodox views.

The fundamental doctrine on the negative side of Shelley's scepticism is a theory of causation—a theory that the poet first encountered in Godwin; its full implications, however, did not dawn on him until after he read and reread Hume and Drummond. All knowledge, according to this theory, depends on the relationship which we call cause and effect. But a scrupulous examination of this relationship reveals that the concept is founded on habit, that it arises from our experience of the constant conjunction of objects. Such an analysis of cause and effect banishes at once all possibility of certitude on any matter whatsoever. A provisional science, based on the observation of the constant conjunction of objects, is altogether possible. But where the opportunity of observing the constant conjunction of objects is denied us—which is the case in cosmological, ontological, and theological speculations—reasoning from cause to effect collapses into an exercise of the fancy. Thus reason conducts us to an astonishing awareness of our ignorance; in Shelley's words, we reach "the verge where words abandon us, and what wonder if we grow dizzy to look down the dark abyss of how little we know" (p. 478).

But like every sceptic before him, Shelley cultivated a sceptical solution to doubt, even to the extent of expressing various degrees of assent to propositions regarding ultimate reality. He nowhere relies on custom to escape the sceptic's dilemma, as conformity to the *status quo* was quite incompatible with his social philosophy, his passion for reforming the world. But either faith or the doctrine of probability is implicit in all of his affirmations regarding the transcendent. By overlooking their tentative character or conditional nature, we may confound these with otherwise similar affirmations in Coleridge or Wordsworth or Emerson; Shelley's affirmations, however, are not dogmatic intuitions but aspects of his sceptical solution to doubt. And it is their character as such that gives them their distinctive quality and effect.

The charges of inconsistency not infrequently made against Shelley's thought . . . are the direct result of the overlooking of this distinction. These charges appear baseless when the poet's thought is interpreted, as it should be interpreted, partly in the light of the sceptical tradition. It is true, of course, that Holbach's necessarianism and Berkeley's idealism can hardly be integrated into a coherent metaphysics. That Shelley's thought sometimes reflects such irreconcilable elements rests on two assumptions: that the poet rejected common-sense materialism through Berkeley's influence and that his concept of Necessity agrees with that of the French materialists. Both of these assumptions, however, are erroneous.

There is not the slightest evidence that Berkeley had any significant influence on Shelley's rejection of common-sense materialism. In fact, the poet plainly tells us that Berkeley's arguments did not impress him. What led Shelley to reject common-sense materialism was Hume's theory of causation as applied by both Hume and Drummond to the question of the independent existence of external objects: we cannot assume the existence of a material world as the cause of our sensations, for all we know of cause is the constant conjunction of ideas in our own mind; the cause of our sensations is unknown.

It is true, of course, that Shelley makes affirmations regarding this unknown reality; but these have the sceptical character of resting on faith or probability. Furthermore, his clearest positive remark about ultimate reality is that it must differ from mind; for it is supremely creative, while mind is largely passive. Nothing could be further from Berkeley than this doctrine. On the other hand, Shelley's theory of the "one mind," of which all individual minds are a portion, resembles Berkeley; but the resemblance is quite superficial: Shelley's concept refers to something less than "the basis of all things" or reality; hence, it is quite unlike Berkeley's idea of an infinite mind acting as the cause of phenomena.

Just as Shelley's scepticism renders his idealism significantly unlike Berkeley's, so it makes his doctrine of Necessity significantly unlike that of the French materialists. Shelley's doctrine is not dogmatic, nor does it subsume a materialist world-view. Its source was Hume's theory of causation and the restatement of that theory in Godwin and Drummond. As an historical concept, Shelley's Necessity refers to the constant conjunction of events observable in the evolution of society.[1] As a metaphysical concept, which is the main concern here, it is the unknown cause of our sensations, the mysterious principle that governs the universe. The poet's interpretation of this unknown power as favoring the triumph of good over evil is partly the expression of faith, partly a form of probabilism based on the study of historical evolution.

1. Cf. Kenneth Neill Cameron, "The Social Philosophy of Shelley," *Sewanee Review*, L (1942), 457–466. [See preceding essay.]

Due attention to Shelley's scepticism disposes not only of the alleged inconsistency between his idealism and necessarianism, but also of his alleged pseudo-Platonism. By liberating him from the prejudices against the Greek philosopher which he had inherited from the *philosophes*, scepticism was to an important degree responsible for the renascence of Platonism which occurred in Shelley in 1817. But it was responsible also for the poet's considerable deviation from Plato. Shelley's concept of Beauty, unlike Plato's, is not dialectically arrived at; nor does it involve a theory of ultimate reality—except the sceptic's denial of the possibility of man's knowing ultimate reality. It is essentially an "unknown and awful" power, which man apprehends only as an ecstasy "within his heart" (*Hymn to Intellectual Beauty*). Sometimes Shelley expresses the faith that death will reveal to us this "unknown and awful power" in all its splendor (*Adonais*), but this tendency of thought is counterbalanced by the opposite one of seeking Beauty in a concrete and mortal form (*Epipsychidion*). In brief, Shelley is not a pseudo-Platonist but a consistent Platonist in the sceptical tradition.

But while scepticism presented Plato to Shelley in a new light, it had little effect on his hostility toward organized Christianity. As a sceptic, the poet agreed with the fideists that the main bulwark of any religion is faith, not reason. But this admission did not imply the result one might expect: the sceptic Shelley is almost as hostile toward organized Christianity as the materialist Shelley had been. From his early reading of anti-Christian authors and from his own experience of the reactionary and intolerant character of early nineteenth-century Christianity, Shelley had come to entertain certain moral objections to the Christian religion. These would have remained obstacles to his reconciliation with his ancestral creed regardless of what metaphysical views he later embraced. He was willing, as a sceptic, to accept as much of the Christian religion as was free from his moral objections to it. But the qualification included too much of the Christian religion to allow any real departure from his original unfavorable attitude. The references to "God" in his later poems—which suggest to some critics that the poet was becoming more orthodox in his religious opinions—probably refer to the deity whom he thought Christ worshipped: a mysterious and inconceivable being, differing from man and the mind of man. Shelley's acceptance of God in this sense in no way contradicts his continued strictures against the Christian religion.

Read, then, in the light of the sceptical tradition, Shelley's philosophy reveals itself as remarkably consistent and coherent. The assertion that the poet "never lost a piece of intellectual baggage which he had at any time collected" has no foundation in fact: Shelley did not "collect" ideas in the mechanical manner implied; furthermore, he did discard ideas—like those essential to materialism—in the course of his intellectual development. Nor was Shelley "an enthusiast" who adopted any attractive idea "without first ascertaining whether it was consistent with others previously avowed." On the contrary, he resisted a new idea, as the history of his attitude toward immaterialism suggests, until the relation of that idea to others previously avowed became perfectly clear to him; or he modified ideas before adopting them, as the sceptical quality of his Platonism indicates, if in their original form they were inconsistent with his established convictions.

What bearing, one may now enquire, has this monograph upon the evaluation of Shelley as a poet?

A theoretical world-view is not essential to great poetry: the *Iliad* and *The Book of Job* both antedate the emergence of philosophy. On the other hand, any respectable theoretical system of thought is compatible with the highest poetic achievement: materialism served Lucretius as well as scholasticism served Dante.[2] Yet nothing incorporated in a poem is logically irrelevant to the evaluation of that poem. If form and content are inseparable in a given work of art, any irreconcilable philosophical elements in it, unless they serve a special purpose, must be viewed as a defect. "Between artistic coherence . . . and philosophical coherence there is some kind of correlation."[3]

If this principle of literary theory is in general sound, Shelley's scepticism is important because it provides us with a possible clue to the unity of his thought in all its variety. To begin with, scepticism is quite compatible with the four main traditions that shaped his mind—political radicalism, empiricism, Platonism, and Christianity. While scepticism is in conflict with the metaphysical views of most radicals, it is not conflict with political radicalism as such. Scepticsm and empiricism are also harmonious; in fact, all the more elaborate forms of scepticism are inseparable from empirical premises. Not unrelated, too, are scepticism and Platonism; for an idealist may make profound concessions to scepticism, while a sceptic may develop the positive side of his thought into a qualified idealism. So closely related, finally, are the sceptical and Christian traditions that the real problem here is to explain why sometimes, as in the case of Shelley, their reconciliation is incomplete.

But scepticism not only is quite compatible with the main

2. Cf. Stephen C. Pepper, *The Basis of Criticism in the Arts* (Cambridge, 1946).
3. René Wellek and Austin Warren, *The* *Theory of Literature* (New York, 1949), p. 27.

traditions known to have profoundly influenced Shelley, but also is capable of reconciling two of those traditions that normally stand in disagreement. The central conflict in Shelley's philosophy is that between his empiricism and his Platonism. The poet's resolution of this conflict could have been suggested only by a philosopher who had dealt with the same problem; this consideration eliminates a host of philosophers known to have influenced Shelley in other respects, including Plato and Hume. The most plausible theory to date is that in this question Shelley was a disciple of Berkeley. But Shelley's relation to Hume invalidates this theory—a theory that can only lead to the conclusion that the poet was a confused follower of Berkeley. There remains, however, the possibility of reconciling empiricism and Platonism through the positive issues of scepticism—probability and faith. This mode of reconciling the empirical and Platonic traditions was implied in Drummond's *Academical Questions*. That Shelley employed the same mode is supported by his admiration for Drummond, by his relation to Hume and the sceptical tradition, and by a certain note in his idealism—a note ranging from the tentative to the mystical. In other words, scepticism had consequences in Shelley which it did not have in Hume; and it is in these consequences, not in the mere agreement with Hume, that the real significance of the poet's scepticism is to be found.

EARL R. WASSERMAN

[Shelley's Use of Myth][†]

Man's works of art, according to Prometheus, are

> the mediators
> Of that best worship, love, by him and us
> Given and returned. (III. iii. 58–60)

Art mediates, that is, between the mutable diversity and division of the human mind on the one hand and the immutable unity of the One Mind, or absolute Existence, on the other; and the radical principle of the *Defence of Poetry*—order, arrangement, combination, relation, harmony, or rhythm—is the human means of shaping diversity into an approximation of perfect unity, which is truth, beauty, and goodness. The poetic imagination is—as Shelley considered himself to be—a revolutionist and reformer, first shaking

† From *Shelley: A Critical Reading*, by Earl R. Wasserman, (Baltimore: The Johns Hopkins University Press, 1971), pp. 269–275. Copyright © 1971 by The Johns Hopkins University Press. Reprinted by permission of the publisher.

"Thought's stagnant chaos" (IV. 380), shattering false and imperfect arrangements of thought, and then striving to rearrange the liberated elements into the formal perfection they ought to have according to a poetics which is also an ethics. In *Prometheus Unbound* this doctrine of the workings and purpose of the plastic imagination is responsible for the transformation and syncretism of the myths that constitute the body of the drama.

Peacock reports that Shelley once commented on Spenser's giant who holds the scales and wishes to "rectify the physical and moral evils which result from inequality of condition."[1] Artegall, Shelley explained, "argues with the Giant; the Giant has the best of the argument; Artegall's iron man knocks him over into the sea and drowns him. This is the usual way in which power deals with opinion." When Peacock objected that this is not the lesson Spenser intended, Shelley replied, "Perhaps not; it is the lesson which he conveys to me. I am of the Giant's faction."[2] In the giant's intention to reduce all things "unto equality," Spenser saw the impending dissolution of hierarchy and the return to chaos; from Shelley's point of view Spenser's conception of order was wrong and therefore the ordering of his myth was wrong, for what to Spenser was necessary superiority and subordination was to republican Shelley the frustration of all possibility of perfect unity. The occasion for Peacock's note was a letter in which Shelley alluded to Artegall's giant in order, it is significant, to define the purpose of the recently completed Act I of *Prometheus Unbound*: the act, Shelley writes, is an attempt to "cast what weight I can into the right scale of that balance which the Giant (of Arthegall) holds."[3] For egalitarian Shelley was engaged in reforming and reinterpreting the myth of god-fearing Aeschylus at least as radically as he did that of Spenser, the defender of hierarchism, and to the same end of perfect order. Recasting that myth into the shape and proportions that, according to his imaginative vision, it ought to have as the highest unity of which its components are capable meant to Shelley not only the achievement of the highest formal beauty but also— since it amounts to the same thing—the purging of error and the attainment of truth.

To Shelley myth is not fanciful fable. Whatever its genesis, it is not mistaken for external fact, and therefore it is more truly real than the sensory world that man falsely believes to reside outside his mind. Since "things" actually exist for man only as thoughts, the elements organized by the poet are thoughts recog-

1. *Letters*, II, 71n.
2. Peacock adds that Shelley also "held that the Enchanter in the first canto [of Thomson's *Castle of Indolence*] was a true philanthropist, and the Knight of Arts and Industry in the second an oligarchical impostor overthrowing truth by power" (*ibid.*).
3. To Peacock [23–24 January 1819] (*Letters*, II, 71).

nized as wholly mental and not mistaken for any independent externality. The thoughts composed by the imagination are those upon which the mind has already acted "so as to colour them with its own light,"[4] which is a reflection of the light of the perfect One. Or, as Shelley expresses the same idea in *Prometheus Unbound*, the poet does not heed objects as external "things," but first watches the "lake-reflected sun illume" them and then organizes ("creates") these transfigured thoughts into "Forms more real than living man, / Nurslings of immortality!" (I. 744–49). The elements of myth, being unmistakably mental apprehensions of "things," are pre-eminently thoughts and therefore pre-eminently the valid materials to which the poet is obliged to give the "purest and most perfect shape."

But if the constituent details of myths are especially real for Shelley, it follows that the component elements of one myth are as valid as those of any other, since they are all thoughts. Syncretic mythology had been revitalized in the eighteenth century, especially by those deists who, arguing for the common basis of all faiths, had attempted to demonstrate the interconvertibility of all myths.[5] This tradition of syncretism was part of Shelley's intellectual heritage, and his mentalistic ontology provided it with a special philosophic justification. If, then, all mythic data, from Jupiter to King Bladud, are real and valid, the various received myths are not to be thought of as discrete narratives or distinct national faiths, but only as variant efforts of the mind to apprehend the same truth. Hence, the stuff of all myths is, collectively and indiscriminately, available to the mythopoeist for his task of compelling thoughts to their most nearly perfect structure. Indeed, directly after announcing to Peacock the completion of the first act of his mythopoeic drama and directly before his idiosyncratic interpretation of Artegall's giant, Shelley wrote that he could conceive of a "great work," not of poetry but of moral and political science, "embodying the discoveries of all ages, & harmonizing the contending creeds by which mankind have been ruled." For it is Shelley's assumption that if all creeds, or their mythic embodiments, were shaped into the highest form they admit, they would be precisely translatable into each other. Despite his modest disclaimer—"Far from me is such an attempt"—the syncretism of this "great work" is at the heart of *Prometheus Unbound*.

Moreover, given Shelley's interpretation of "thought," it follows that empirical science, folk science, legends, and all literature that has been assimilated as an operative part of human culture are

---

4. *Defence of Poetry* (Julian, VII, 109).
5. See Albert J. Kuhn, "English Deism and the Development of Romantic Mytho-logical Syncretism," *PMLA*, 71 (1956), 1094–1116.

also mental configurations of thoughts that recognize the mental nature of "things"; they, at least as much as conventional myths, are also permanently real in the sense that supposedly objective things are not. Consequently, all these thoughts, too, are among the materials for the poet's imagination to syncretize and interlock into the most nearly perfect form. *Adonais*, for example, is not merely another variant of the Venus and Adonis myth; it recasts that myth into a new and presumably true system of interrelationships, but it also organically integrates the reformed myth with the ancient belief that souls derive from stars, with astronomy scientific and fabular, with the science of optics, and with various traditional metaphors and symbols, all of them having the same kind and degree of eternal reality because they are the mind's conceptions, rather than perceptions, of things. Myth so inclusively defined is not an assemblage of accepted fictional terms supporting an accretion of rich connotations, as it was for Dryden and Pope; nor merely a fiction that reveals truth better than facts; nor an upsurging from the unconscious. Its components are indestructible and eternal mental possessions. Consequently, however diverse and unrelated their traditional contexts, they ask, like all other thoughts, to be interwoven into a beautiful whole "containing within itself the principle of its own integrity." If the structures of given myths are already beautiful and true, Shelley held, they are integral thoughts having "the power of attracting and assimilating to their own nature all other thoughts,"[6] and thus any conventional myth so organized is inexhaustibly capable of rendering truths for a poet by giving its shape to them. On the other hand, since error, ugliness, and evil are but various modes of disorder, the task of the imagination is also to reform erroneous, misshapen myths according to the model of the mind's extraordinary apprehensions of perfect unity.

Such a conception of myth and of the function of the imagination entails an especially ambiguous relation between the traditional form of a legend or myth and the poet's use of it, and demands of the reader an equally ambiguous frame of mind. When, in his *Rape of the Lock*, Pope calls Thalestris to Belinda's aid, the mere appearance of this queen of the Amazons tacitly attaches to Belinda an unnatural displacement in the sexual hierarchy, a belligerent rejection of men, and the Amazonian ideal of a self-sufficient female society, just as Pope's casting Clarissa's advice in the form of Sarpedon's speech seriocomically elevates that advice to heroic stature and demands of Belinda quasi-heroic deeds. Through knowledge already in the reader's mind, traditional qualities and

6. *Defence of Poetry* (Julian, VII, 118).

meanings outside the poem attach themselves to elements in the poem. Or, for ironic purposes, the likening of Belinda's apotheosized lock to Berenice's evokes the reader's knowledge that Catullus' Berenice sacrificed her hair that her husband might be returned to her, and the clash between that intimated fact outside the poem and Belinda's rejection of the Baron within the poem is central to what the poem is saying. In either kind of instance, the established structures of the myths upon which Pope draws operate allusively in the poem, and the reader, when called upon, must bring them to bear so that they may perform upon the text their acts of supplying, amplifying, and complicating significances. But according to the implications of Shelley's theory, the myths that appear in his poetry, however traditional, are to be understood as really having no inherited contexts at all. As either actually or potentially true-beautiful organizations of thought, they are universal and eternal forms that become limited only insofar as they are thought of as specific myths; and any particular previous appearance of the myth is not a locus for literary allusion but merely another instance of the actual or potential archetypal form.

For example, the myth of Aurora, goddess of the dawn, and her union with the beautiful mortal, Tithonus, is recognizable behind Shelley's account of the creation of works of art:

> And lovely apparitions, dim at first,
> Then radiant, as the mind, arising bright
> From the embrace of beauty, whence the forms
> Of which these are the phantoms, casts on them
> The gathered rays which are reality.   (III. iii. 49–53)

Yet in the more important sense the myth is not present at all behind the symbols of dawn and light, which are themselves adequate to incorporate the meaning; and although the myth does provide an additional propriety to the word "embrace," Shelley certainly does nothing to evoke the myth as an efficient reverberating echo. The Aurora myth is not to be understood as a particular narrative generally current in Western culture; it is the mind's composition of thoughts into an integral and self-sustaining thought that, because of its beauty and truth as a composition, has here assimilated to its own form another body of thoughts—or, rather, has given its form to a body of thoughts and thus lost its own special identity. Awareness of the myth will allow the reader to recognize the patterning source; and yet the end product of this recognition is, paradoxically, that he think as though no myth were present, but only the perfect archetypal arrangement, of which the story of Aurora and Tithonus is a limited instance. Of the same order is Shelley's adaptation of the legend of King Bladud, the mythical founder of Bath, who stumbled upon the curative hot springs when, a banished leper, he followed one of his afflicted swine, and whose dramatic return after his cure enraptured his mother.[7] Hate, fear, and pain, Shelley writes, are to

> Leave Man, even as a leprous child is left,
> Who follows a sick beast to some warm cleft
> Of rocks, through which the might of healing springs is poured;
> Then when it wanders home with rosy smile,
> Unconscious, and its mother fears awhile
> It is a spirit, then, weeps on her child restored.   (IV. 388–93)

Although this is Bladud's legendary history in every detail, the poet's refusal to call it into conscious attention makes present only a beautiful pattern, not a special allusion. Nor in the following speech does Shelley borrow from *King Lear* the term "thought-executing" in order to call up some functional reaction between the plot of *Lear* and the relation of Jupiter to Prometheus, whose words these are:

>   Evil minds
> Change good to their own nature. I gave all
> He [Jupiter] has; and in return he chains me here
> Years, ages, night and day . . .
> Whilst my beloved race is trampled down
> By his thought-executing ministers.
> Such is the tyrant's recompense: 'tis just:
> He who is evil can receive no good;
> And for a world bestowed, or a friend lost,
> He can feel hate, fear, shame; not gratitude:
> He but requites me for his own misdeed.
> Kindness to such is keen reproach, which breaks
> With bitter stings the light sleep of Revenge.
> Submission, thou dost know I cannot try.[8]   (I. 380–95)

An interpretation of Lear's relation to his daughter is, I think, formally present and yet otherwise inoperative; it is present for the poet—and the critic—not for the "pure" reader that the play hypothesizes, who is to experience the work as though it is autonomous, not allusive. The assumption behind the creative act is that Shakespeare formed a beautiful and true arrangement of thoughts, and Shelley is fulfilling his doctrine that such mythic orderings are always capable of attracting other truths to their shape; but he is not engaging Shakespeare's play in his text to illuminate it or to complicate its meaning. These are, admittedly,

7. The allusion has been pointed out by G. M. Matthews, "Shelley's Grasp upon the Actual," *Essays in Criticism*, 4 (1954), 329. The legend is recorded in full in Richard Warner's *History of Bath* (Bath, 1801).

8. The basis of this speech, but not of its form or thematic elaboration, is *Prometheus Bound* 223–27.

extreme examples of Shelley's assimilation of myths as archetypal orderings, but they are symptomatic of his mythopoeic methods and indicate the paradoxical informed ignorance they demand for the most complete reading.

We have seen, however, that Shelley conceives of the poet as not merely an assimilator of beautiful mythic forms: inasmuch as he is creative, he is a mythopoeist, not by inventing myths, but by reconstituting the imperfect ones that already exist. His creations are "beautiful and new, not because the portions of which they are composed had no previous existence in the mind of man or in nature," but because of "the whole produced by their combination." Virgil was not an imitator of Homer, Shelley wrote in an unused passage of the Preface to *Prometheus Unbound*; "the <ideal> conceptions had been new modelled within his mind, they had been born again."[9] Indeed, just as Shelley held that all human minds are portions of the One Mind, so he believed that, because of the interconnection and interdependence of all poems, each is a fragment of, or partial movement toward, "that great poem, which all poets, like the co-operating thoughts of one great mind, have built up since the beginning of the world."[1] Evidence of his respect for this position is to be found not only in his resort to traditional materials but even in his refraining from forging new links to regroup and interrelate diverse myths; for his implicit assumption is that the true and beautiful relationships of wholeness already exist potentially in the qualities of the given materials, waiting to be properly drawn out. Consequently, he rather strictly confines himself to the inherent syntactical potentials, however minor or neglected they may be in the conventional myths, and his mythopoeic art lies especially in eliciting and exploiting these potentials to form new combinations.

DONALD H. REIMAN

The Purpose and Method of Shelley's Poetry[†]

Fundamental and central to all of Shelley's writings—poetry and prose—was the moral law that Shelley found within himself. It is, perhaps, profitless to speculate about what aspects of his childhood training and experience formed the young Shelley's conscience or

9. Zillman, p. 636, where "new" inaccurately reads "now."
1. *Defence of Poetry* (Julian, VII, 124).
† From *Shelley's "The Triumph of Life": A Critical Study* (Urbana, Ill., 1965),
pp. 3–18. Copyright © 1965 by Donald H. Reiman. Reprinted by permission of the author and the University of Illinois Press.

how his later readings in the eighteenth-century humanitarian authors like Godwin molded his concepts of virtue and justice. Shelley recorded in the Dedication to *The Revolt of Islam* (iii-v) a boyhood experience in which he imagined that the sound of voices "from the near schoolroom . . ./ Were but one echo from a world of woes," but he whose ear could thus catch the still sad music of humanity had listened attentively long before that "fresh May-dawn" dispersed "the clouds which wrap this world from youth." Shelley's early formative influences, like those of most men, are shrouded in obscurity; only the results of those lost experiences remained in the cast of his adult mind.

The moral law that governed Shelley's mature thought and action insisted upon both the right and the duty of each individual to rule his own destiny: Each human being was entitled to the liberty to seek his own happiness, but, at the same time, he was obligated to do all in his power to secure this freedom for the less fortunate. From these axioms Shelley dedicated his efforts to the destruction of tyranny in all its forms—the tyranny of marital, parental, pedagogical, political, and religious authoritarianism, the tyranny of poverty and ignorance. He believed that the individual human spirit was the measure of all values within the limitations of mortal experience and that institutions were good only insofar as they promoted the welfare of the individual. Societies and institutions were abstractions, whereas men were real, and a family, a church, or a nation derived its only value from the benefit it conferred on the men and women who constituted it.[1] Like the ethical philosophy of Kant, Shelley's ideas depend ultimately upon the single, categorical imperative that human beings must be treated always as ends, never as means.

Besides the doctrines of benevolence and sympathy, derived from philosophers of the eighteenth century, which gave shape to Shelley's humanitarian ideals,[2] Shelley (again like Kant) inherited the epistemological dilemma of the British empirical philosophers. After reading Locke, Berkeley, Hume, and Sir William Drummond, he concluded that there are no innate ideas, that sense impressions initiate the learning process, and that, since one cannot be certain that the impressions of the senses correspond to an external reality, one must remain ultimately sceptical on all

1. "Government can have no rights: it is a delegation for the purpose of securing them to others. . . . The strength of government is the happiness of the governed. All government existing for the happiness of others is just only so far as it exists by their consent, and useful only so far as it operates to their well-being." *Proposals for an Associa-*tion of Philanthropists . . . ., *Shelley's Prose,* ed. David Lee Clark (Albuquerque, 1954), p. 64. See also *A Declaration of Rights, Prose,* p. 70.

2. See Roy R. Male, Jr., "Shelley and the Doctrine of Sympathy," *University of Texas Studies in English,* XXIX (1950), 183–203.

ontological questions.[3] Such a sceptical epistemology thwarted Shelley's desire to discover a firm metaphysical foundation for the moral values that he found so strong within himself. At the same time, however, the limitations of human knowledge made it impossible for experience or reason to destroy his hope that the ultimate character of the universe was good rather than evil, for even if all empirical evidence and all rational arguments indicated that human moral values were an anomaly in an amoral universe, that evidence and those reasonings, the products of fallible cognitive powers, might yet be mistaken. Shelley's severe intellectual honesty forced him to write an "Essay on a Future State," in which he concluded that there was absolutely no evidence of immortality and that something akin to the physical law of inertia, a "desire to be for ever as we are, the reluctance to a violent and unexperienced change which is common to all the animated and inanimate combinations of the universe," was the sole origin of the hope for "a future state" (*Prose*, p. 178); but with his sceptical distrust of human reasoning, he could continue to hope that beyond the ken of mortal understanding the "Everlasting No" of ordinary human experience would give place to the "Everlasting Yea" of a realm in which the Good, the True, and the Beautiful would triumph.

Shelley sought support for his ethical ideals in the inner caverns of the human mind. An acute observer of the events of nature and society (as his letters from abroad, for example, prove), he could portray in concrete terms the interactions of people and things about him, and sometimes, when it furthers his purpose, he does so; but as a student of the natural sciences who saw behind the appearances of these events to their underlying psychological or physical causes, he often describes the operations of these hidden forces, and as a follower of the "intellectual philosophy"[4] that denied the authority of the senses and even postulated the ultimate unreality of the physical universe, he often turned to an examina-

---

3. The antecedents and nature of Shelley's scepticism have been admirably outlined by Pulos in *The Deep Truth: A Study of Shelley's Scepticism*. Professor Pulos' claims for the influence on Shelley of Sir William Drummond's *Academical Questions* (London, 1805) are conservative; the sceptical ideas and attitudes expressed by Drummond seem to permeate every area of Shelley's philosophy, though Shelley found it impossible to accept fideistic theism, Drummond's implicit solution to the sceptical dilemma.

4. Shelley speaks repeatedly of the "intellectual system" and "Intellectual Philosophy" in his "Essay on Life," where he says, "Perhaps the most clear and vigorous statement of the intellectual system is to be found in Sir William Drummond's *Academical Questions*" (*Prose*, p. 173). C. E. Pulos has demonstrated that the term "intellectual philosophy" was used to designate the thought of Berkeley and Hume as contrasted to the "common sense" philosophy that reacted against them. Drummond and Shelley, as classicists, connected Hume's scepticism with the Greek sceptics of the New Academy, with Cicero, and with Bacon and Montaigne and the Renaissance revival of scepticism. See Pulos, *The Deep Truth*, chaps. 2, 3.

tion of the processes of the mind, from which, he believed, one could learn more about the relationship between the impressions apprehended by the mind and the nature of reality. Through examination of the instrument that responds to sensory impressions and molds them into organic relationships, Shelley attempted to gather knowledge that external impressions themselves could not give. His best poems fuse three levels of experience into images that at the "phenomenal" level describe in detail an event or scene (often one that Shelley has actually witnessed), at the "scientific" level suggest the underlying physical or psychological causes of the phenomenon, and at the "philosophical" level infer its hidden moral implications.[5]

One cannot understand Shelley's philosophical position—ethical, epistemological, or ontological—without a thorough knowledge of his prose. Once the main outlines of his thought are clear, the corpus of Shelley's poetry, together with the prefaces and notes he himself supplied, is usually sufficient to clarify the theme of any single poem, but when one wishes to plumb its subtleties, not only Shelley's essays, letters, and recorded conversations, but even the books he read illuminate modulations of meaning.[6] No English poet is more allusive than Shelley, and certainly few read more widely or brought to their poetry a more varied range of symbolic reference: He knew the literature, history, and science of Western civilization from Homer and the Pentateuch to Goethe and Colèridge. He read ceaselessly and omnivorously, devouring books on agricultural chemistry, the histories of Gibbon and Sismondi, the myths of Plato and the scepticism of Hume, the dramas of Athens and England, Calderón and Alfieri, the theological and philosophical works of Aristotle and Augustine, Lucretius and Spinoza—all in their original languages, which he mastered so that he might not lose the harmonious sounds and subtleties of diction.[7] Shelley,

5. Elsewhere I have attempted to show how these three levels are integrated in one of Shelley's earlier poems: "Structure, Symbol, and Theme in 'Lines Written among the Euganean Hills,' " *PMLA*, LXXVII (September 1962), 404–413.
6. Though it may be, in our day, superfluous to justify poetic obscurity, the writings of most poets contain many references that are meaningless to the casual reader. Obscurities resulting from recondite biographical, historical, or literary allusions or from the author's individual symbolic vocabulary can usually be explained after intensive study of the author's life, works, and reading. The sole difference, between legitimate obscurity and the other kind is that the former results from complexity rather than from indistinctness or confusion of poetic attitude and conception. Shelley's

allusions, almost without exception, enrich and modify the surface statements of his poetry, usually in such a manner that one cannot imagine the same subtlety and complexity being achieved by more direct means.
7. ". . . the language of poets has ever affected a certain uniform and harmonious recurrence of sound, without which it were not poetry, and which is scarcely less indispensable to the communication of its influence than the words themselves, without reference to that peculiar order. Hence the vanity of translation" (*A Defence of Poetry, Prose*, p. 280). See also Shelley's letter "To a Lady," Spring, 1821 (Julian, X, 267–268), where he inveighs at length against studying a literary work in any but its original language.

far from becoming merely eclectic, however, integrated with his personal philosophical perspective the knowledge and wisdom he garnered from his studies.

Throughout his maturity Shelley never changed his basic attitudes and ideals; he persisted in his desire to extend liberty of thought under the guidance of benevolent love to every human being, and he continued also to hold the sceptical epistemology that prevented him from declaring categorically that the ideal to which he aspired was in fact congruent with an objective reality. He attempted, therefore, to portray through his poetry the ideals that he found both within himself and in the records of the greatest human spirits. The conceptions of man, nature, history, and immortality in Shelley's poems are not declared to be objectively true, but are, like the myths of Plato, poetic "guesses at truth"; of the problem of evil and the immortality of the soul Shelley wrote: "Let it not be supposed that I mean to dogmatise upon a subject, concerning which all men are equally ignorant. . . . [but] as it is the province of the poet to attach himself to those ideas which exalt and ennoble humanity, let him be permitted to have conjectured the condition of that futurity towards which we are all impelled by an inextinguishable thirst for immortality."[8] To "exalt and ennoble humanity," to embody the highest human ideas in such attractive forms that men will desire the good, and to image evil in such repulsive forms that they will abhor it, in short, to familiarize men "with beautiful idealisms of moral excellence"[9]—this was the purpose of Shelley's poetry. He could honestly declare that didactic poetry was his abhorrence because he never pretended to "teach" in an intellectual sense; despite the vast range of knowledge he brought to his poetry, his purpose was never to discuss the nature of things, scientifically or philosophically. He attempted, rather, to purify and stretch the imaginations of his readers through self-acknowledged myths that tell not what exists, or even what within the limitations of the mortal world *can* exist, but what according to the profoundest moral insights of Western civilization *should* exist; Shelley, unlike most poets, never confused the realm of "is" with that of "ought." Those critics who have concluded that Shelley's picture of human history in a poem like *Prometheus Unbound* is "unrealistic" had only to turn to Shelley's Preface to

8. Note to *Hellas*, Shelley, *Poetical Works*, Oxford Standard Authors edition ("*P.W.*"), p. 478.
9. Preface to *Prometheus Unbound*, *P.W.*, p. 207. Cf. Sir William Drummond: "If you wish to make men virtuous, endeavour to inspire into them the love of virtue. Show them the beauty of order, and the fitness of things. . . .

Represent vice, as indignant virtue will always represent it, as hideous, loathsome, and deformed. . . . will cannot be changed, while sentiment remains unaltered. There is no power, by which men can create, or destroy their feelings. Sensation alone overcomes sensation." *Academical Questions*, pp. 20–21.

find him admitting as much.[1] In *The Cenci* Shelley exhibits the "sad reality" of the world that "is," a world starkly contrasting with the moral world of "ought" that appears in *Prometheus*. This sharp division between "is" and "ought," between the hard limitations of the human situation and man's apprehension of ideal perfection, remained for Shelley the basic ethical dilemma, and the poet's problem was to find a language through which the two worlds, irreconcilably disparate in "phenomenal" human experience, might be harmonized—or at least related—in the artistic universe of the poem.

Since 1900 when William Butler Yeats wrote his significant essays on "The Philosophy of Shelley's Poetry,"[2] critics have recognized with more or less perception that Shelley transmits his meaning partly through a system of symbols that remain relatively consistent from poem to poem. . . .

For him, as for other poets, subtleties of diction were the heart and soul of poetry.[3] Anyone who has worked with the manuscripts of Shelley's poetry—or who has read the criticism of those who have —ought to be aware that Shelley corrected and revised in a never ending search for the exact words to convey his meaning, though in his struggle to communicate his apprehensions exactly as they came to him, he became cognizant of the limitations of language and the difficulty of communication: "These words are ineffectual and metaphorical. Most words are so—No help!"[4] Although in *A Defence of Poetry* Shelley first designates as "poetry" any product of human imagination, he soon narrows his definition, first to "those arrangements of language and especially metrical language which are created by that imperial faculty. . . ."[5] As a sceptic who denied that there was a necessary correspondence between

---

1. ". . . it is a mistake to suppose that I dedicate my poetical compositions solely to the direct enforcement of reform, or that I consider them in any degree as containing a reasoned system on the theory of human life. Didactic poetry is my abhorrence; nothing can be equally well expressed in prose that is not tedious and supererogatory in verse. My purpose has hitherto been simply to familiarise the highly refined imagination of the more select classes of poetical readers with beautiful idealisms of moral excellence; aware that until the mind can love, and admire, and trust, and hope, and endure, reasoned principles of moral conduct are seeds cast upon the highway of life which the unconscious passenger tramples into dust, although they would bear the harvest of his happiness" (Preface to *Prometheus Unbound*, *P.W.*, p. 207).
2. First published in *The Dome* (July 1900); reprinted in *Ideas of Good and*

Evil and, more recently, in *Essays and Introductions* (New York, 1961).
3. A contrary opinion has recently been expressed—though in no respect documented—by David Perkins in *The Quest for Permanence* (Cambridge, Mass., 1959), p. 109. Shelley's own statements on the value of language are unequivocal: see *A Defence of Poetry*, *Prose*, pp. 279–280; Letter "To a Lady," Julian, X, 267–268.
4. Note to "Essay on Love," *Prose*, p. 170. But although Shelley recognized the metaphorical—we would say "symbolic" —nature of language, he did not impugn its value within his sceptical epistemology; though it is "vain . . . to think that words can penetrate the mystery of our being . . . rightly used they may make evident our ignorance to ourselves, and this is much ("Essay on Life," *Prose*, p. 172).
5. *Prose*, p. 279.

the mind's impressions and any external causes, Shelley believed that the "nature itself of language" could provide "a more direct representation of the actions and passions of our internal being and is susceptible of more various and delicate combinations than color, form, or motion . . ." because language, the medium of thought itself, "is more plastic and obedient to the control of that faculty of which it is the creation. For language is arbitrarily produced by the imagination and has relation to thoughts alone; but all other materials, instruments, and conditions of art" have physical relations and properties "which limit and interpose between conception and expression."[6] Moreover, the sounds of language, he believed, constitute a sensory medium apart from the intellectual content of words and have relations both with one another and with the ideas they represent; the poetic mind must, therefore, perceive "the order of those relations" at the same time that it perceives "the order of those relations of thoughts."[7] Since, therefore, the imagination will harmonize not only the ideas of words but their sounds as well into meaningful relationships, "the authors of revolutions in opinion are not only necessarily poets as they are inventors, nor even as their words unveil the permanent analogy of things by images which participate in the life of truth but as their periods are harmonious and rhythmical . . ." (*Prose*, p. 281).

The poetic imagination for Shelley thus perfectly integrated three aspects of language: first, the relations of words to "ideas," their complex denotative and connotative significance; second, the relations through analogies or metaphors of these verbal concepts to the "impressions" that a nonsceptic would term "objective reality"; and third, the relations of both the "ideas" and the "impressions" of words to their sounds. For Shelley, then, the best poetry first exhibits unity of conception as an organic creation according to the laws of an integrated imagination; it expresses this truth in images that have coherent analogical relations to the "things of nature" or the world of sensory apprehension; and, finally, it orders the sounds of the words in a way that not only commends its meaning through the delight of pleasant harmonies but supports that meaning wherever possible by onomatopoeic effects.

The relation of two of these three aspects requires some elaboration and explanation. That Shelley sought coherent analogical relations between the terms in his poems and the natural objects or beings commonly designated by those words does not mean that

6. *Prose*, pp. 279–280.
7. *Prose*, p. 280. See note 7 above. In Shelley's discussions of the nature of poetry, he discusses only the aural characteristics of language, never the visual appearance or arrangement of words on the printed page.

he used words "naturalistically" or "realistically." On the contrary, Shelley did not believe in the truth of relations between words and the so-called "physical" entities they designated (their referents) but only between words and the concepts of the mind that the words expressed; that is, because the reality of external nature must remain ever doubtful to the limited human mind, words take their significance not from an external world but from the ordered laws of the mind itself. Man's understanding of the phenomenal world is continually in flux, as science describes and postulates more and more about the behavior of animals, the causes of meteorological phenomena, and the like, but the individual human mind retains conceptions and attitudes that give to each word connotations quite distinct from the "objective" nature of its referent. In most instances, however, the connotative "idea" designated by the word bears some relation to the qualities of the "external object" also designated by the word. The lion, for example, may not in fact be the King of Beasts: it may actually fear the rhinoceros or the elephant. But its regal appearance and its carnivorous habits lend to it associations that justify the "idea" of the lion as King of Beasts. Shelley, therefore, never restricted his use of referential words to the empirical nature or behavior of their referents, though he did utilize such scientific "facts" as would contribute to the "idea" of the word. He drew his poetic symbol of the eagle, for example, more from Pliny's *Natural History* and from Biblical and bestiary tradition than from nineteenth-century knowledge of the eagle's nature and habits, because the ancient traditions gave moral and symbolic dimensions to the bird that Shelley—like the American republic[8]—found useful in symbolizing his ideas. Inasmuch as he did not assign symbolic values to his words and images on empirical grounds, his mind could chart a consistent significance for each word.[9] From his reading and his own experience Shelley came to associate various words with particular phases of man's moral life. Heat and cold, light and darkness, owls and eagles, violets and roses, sun and moon, all came to symbolize certain moral and epistemological concepts. To communicate his ideas

8. Benjamin Franklin, an eighteenth-century rationalist, attempted to overthrow this traditional symbolism and to prevent the United States from adopting the bald eagle as its national bird, preferring the turkey, whose characteristic habits he found more in accord with the ideals of the American republic.

9. Since Shelley was not especially concerned with the referents of words, but with language itself, which "is arbitrarily produced by the imagination and has relation to thoughts alone" (*Prose*, p. 279), he often gives synonyms quite different symbolic connotations in his poetry. For example, as I shall try to show in my explication of "The Triumph of Life," the word "Sun" has good associations, whereas the word "day" has bad connotations. Or, to turn to the eagle again, in *Prometheus Unbound*, where Jupiter is evil, Jupiter's sacred bird cannot be called an "eagle" (which, in spite of continued misreading, always carries good connotations in Shelley's poetry); instead, the bird is referred to as "Heaven's winged hound" (I.34). Hounds, like wolves, are always symbols of evil in Shelley's poetry.

to the reader, he drew these symbolic significances from earlier poetic tradition, modifying the usages of earlier poets only as he had to in order to express his individualized conceptions of man and the universe.

Shelley's symbolic universe will be fully elucidated only after scholars have examined dozens of key words in various contexts in his poetry (and prose) and have then studied the associations of these same words in the philosophical, religious, and literary writings that are known to have impressed Shelley. Because such study of his symbolism is still in its infancy, readers of his poetry have often been unable to grasp the significance of a recurring word or phrase that seems to symbolize something beyond itself. Some critics have assumed that many of Shelley's symbols were original and arbitrary, having little relation to those of other writers, while others have attempted to trace all of his symbols to a single tradition, usually Platonism. Recent studies of Shelley's use of Lucretius and of Bacon,[1] however, joined with previous recognition of his debts to the Bible, Plato, Æschylus, Spenser, Milton, Dante, Calderón, Goethe, and others, demonstrate the variety of Shelley's sources, and Earl R. Wasserman's brilliant reading of *Adonais* shows the complexity with which Shelley syncretized symbolic overtones from many sources into his highly original poetry.[2]

In the "Essay on Life" (perhaps the most important single document of Shelley's intellectual development), Shelley divides natural phenomena into two major categories: First he speaks of "the system of the sun, and the stars, and planets . . . the spectacle now afforded by the nightly cope of heaven," and then of "the scenery of this earth. . . ."[3] This distinction between celestial and terrestrial phenomena—between the "cope of heaven" and the "scenery of this earth"—plays an important role in Shelley's symbolism. Shelley adopted for poetic purposes a pre-Copernican cosmology that considered all created things beneath the moon subject to mutability, whereas the sun, planets, and stars beyond the moon existed in a realm of permanence. The moon, "to whom alone it has been given/ To change and be adored forever,"[4] was mutable

1. William O. Scott, "Shelley's Admiration for Bacon," *PMLA*, LXXII (June 1958), 228–236; Paul Turner, "Shelley and Lucretius," *RES*, n.s., X (August 1959), 269–282.

2. "*Adonais*: Progressive Revelation as a Poetic Mode," *ELH*, XXI (December 1954), 274–326. Slightly revised and reprinted in *The Subtler Language*.

3. *Prose*, p. 172. Clark, in a headnote to the "Essay on Life," dates it 1812–14, an error that his first footnote refutes. (He shows that in 1818 Shelley probably first saw the quotation from Tasso that

he uses in the essay.) The holograph of "Essay on Life" (now in the Pierpont Morgan Library) was originally part of the same notebook (now in the Carl H. Pforzheimer Library) that contained the holograph of *A Philosophical View of Reform* (1819–20) (see Kenneth Neill Cameron, *Shelley and His Circle: 1773–1822*, II, 897).

4. "Lines Written in the Bay of Lerici," 2–3 (see G. M. Matthews, "Shelley and Jane Williams," *RES*, n.s., XII (Feb. 1961), p. 41).

but eternal and regular in its mutations; it governed the sublunar world and was the abiding symbol of its limitations. Whereas the celestial bodies consisted of but the single element of fire, terrestrial creation contained the four elements—fire, air, water, and earth. Earth—often referred to as dust—represented inert matter; water symbolized purely mortal or terrestrial generation; fire, the element of the sun and stars, symbolized spiritual energy; and the air, which existed between the earth and waters of the mutable and the fires of the eternal, was the realm of those ideas and abstractions that raise men above the merely mortal perspective but which are limited and distorted by the imperfections of human condition.

Besides distinguishing between the pure fires of Heaven and the sublunar creation, Shelley recognized two subdivisions within terrestrial nature. The quotation from the "Essay on Life" continues: "the scenery of this earth, the mountains, the seas, and the rivers; the grass, and the flowers, and the variety of the forms and masses of the leaves of the woods, and the colors which attend the setting and the rising sun, and the hues of the atmosphere, turbid or serene . . ." (*Prose*, p. 172). As the punctuation of this passage indicates,[5] Shelley distinguished those elemental natural forms such as mountain, sea, and river (that consist of a single one of the three terrestial elements of earth, water, and air) from those slighter phenomena such as cloud, wave, leaf, dew, mist, rainbow, moth, and flower.

A terrestrial feature like an ocean, a continent, or even a river or a mountain, exhibits the qualities of its element (water or earth) in a general or abstract way. The sea or ocean in Shelley's poetry, for example, often symbolizes the realm of temporal existence upon which man pursues his voyage of life.[6] Sometimes a small stream symbolizes the course of life of some particular individual, whereas a river may signify the history of some particular community.[7] The smaller, ephemeral terrestrial creatures frequently image a particular aspect of man, or man in a specific condition or situation. The cloud, for example, is a recurring symbol of the human mind or soul, a product of the moisture of mortal generation but existing above the merely mortal and vivified by the light of the celestial bodies. Or, a mimosa, the "sensitive plant," becomes the symbol of man, with his unfulfilled longings for the Good, the True, and the

---

5. I have examined a photostat of the Pierpont Morgan MS of "On Life," which does not have the same punctuation as Clark's edition, but in this instance there is clearly a division between the two types of terrestrial phenomena such as that indicated by Clark's punctuation. Shelley scholars require a new critical edition of the prose based where possible on Shelley's MSS, but this undertaking will not be feasible on a full scale until the Pforzheimer papers have been published.

6. "Lines Written among the Euganean Hills," 1–26 (*P.W.*, p. 554), and "Time" (*P.W.*, p. 637).

7. "Euganean Hills," 184 (*P.W.*, p. 556), and "Evening: Ponte al Mare, Pisa," 13–16 (*P.W.*, p. 654).

Beautiful, as contrasted with the other transitory creatures, whose natures seem fulfilled and satisfied within the realm of temporal experience.[8]

Occupying a unique position in Shelley's symbolic universe was the wind, which in its wilder manifestations as "storm," "tempest," or "whirlwind" was Shelley's symbol of Necessity. As a follower of Hume and Drummond, Shelley rejected the Aristotelian-Thomistic theory of causation and believed that the mere conjunction of two sensory impressions (even when they conjoined repeatedly) demonstrated no necessary causation of the second by the first. Because Shelley held that the causes for both sensory "impressions" and psychic "ideas" were unknown and unknowable, he used the wind, which "blows where it wills" though nobody knows "whence it comes or whither it goes," to symbolize the concept that philosophers had postulated to explain the relations between series of physical, historical, or psychological events. Because air is the element symbolizing human concepts and ideas, the wind, a connected movement of this element, proves an effective sceptical symbol of the concept of Necessity that had played so large a part in eighteenth-century thought. Among the celestial symbols the moon, which "as Mother of the Months"[9] is associated with time and mutability, is also "the planet of frost, so cold and bright" that makes things "wan with her borrowed light"[1] and is usually identifiable with reason, the analytic faculty, which in A Defence of Poetry Shelley distinguishes from imagination, the vital, synthetic faculty. In a proposed letter to Ollier answering Peacock's Four Ages of Poetry, Shelley wrote: "He would extinguish Imagination which is the Sun of life, and grope his way by the cold and uncertain and borrowed light of that moon which he calls Reason, stumbling over the interlunar chasm of time where she deserts us, and an owl, rather than an eagle, stare with dazzled eyes on the watery orb which is the Queen of his pale Heaven."[2] In Epipsychidion he speaks of

> The cold chaste Moon, the Queen of Heaven's bright isles,
> Who makes all beautiful on which she smiles,
> That wandering shrine of soft yet icy flame
> Which ever is transformed, yet still the same,
> And warms not but illumines.

> 281–285; P.W., pp. 417–418

In a fragment "To the Moon" Shelley asked,

> Art thou pale for weariness
> Of climbing heaven and gazing on the earth,
> Wandering companionless

8. Wasserman, The Subtler Language, p. 257.
9. "The Witch of Atlas," 73 (P.W., p. 373).
1. "To Constantia," 5–6 (P.W., p. 541).
2. ?March 1821. Julian, X, 246.

> Among the stars that have a different birth,—
> And ever changing, like a joyless eye
> That finds no object worth its constancy?
>
> P.W., p. 621

The moon in Shelley's poetry is beautiful but cold, pale, and inconstant, of a different order from the stars, giving one only the borrowed, secondary light of rational analysis, which is eternal but not immutable and shines only upon certain aspects of our experience.

The Sun, on the other hand, is associated with the vivifying creative imagination, a burning fountain of warmth and light out of which flow the spiritual natures of created things. At the universal level the Sun signifies the Deity; in the world of human experience it represents Imagination, the divine in man. Shelley always distinguishes, however, between the light of the celestial Sun and the same light as filtered through the earth's atmosphere. In the first note to *Queen Mab* he wrote: "Beyond our atmosphere the sun would appear a rayless orb of fire in the midst of a black concave. The equal diffusion of its light on earth is owing to the refraction of the rays by the atmosphere, and their reflection from other bodies."[3] Thus, the earth is surrounded by a "veil of light," and the white radiance of pure sunlight is broken into the colors of the visible spectrum. The rainbow, product solely of the distortion of the white light of the One Reality into the multiple colors of this earth, symbolizes the unreal appearances of earthly life, a "painted veil" that hides from human vision the nature of things-in-themselves, and, with the epistemological dilemma clearly in his thoughts, Shelley speaks of the human mind as diffusing truth and casting "rainbow hues" over the external world.[4] The cosmic Sun thus plays what seems to be an ambiguous role in Shelley's symbolism. In itself it vivifies and illuminates in the highest sense, but because of the double distortion by the earth's atmosphere (the conditions of limited, terrestrial existence) and by the cloudy human mind, the light of the sun cannot be trusted; in "Letter to Maria Gisborne" Shelley recalls

> . . . how we spun
> A shroud of talk to hide us from the sun
> Of this familiar life, which seems to be
> But is not:—or is but quaint mockery
> Of all we would believe, and sadly blame
> The jarring and inexplicable frame
> Of this wrong world. . . .
>
> 154–160; P.W., pp. 366–367

3. *P.W.*, p. 800.
4. See "Fragment: To the Mind of Man" (*P.W.*, pp. 634–635). Because water droplets act as light-refracting prisms, such phenomena as dew, mist, and cloud assume symbolic overtones that relate them both to the human mind (*Hellas*, 215–217; "The Sunset," 1–4, *P.W.*, p. 528) and to the mind's distortion of reality.

The sun as seen by men is deceptive, and in such later poems as "The Sensitive Plant" and "To Night," Shelley praises the night and its dreams as fountains of higher knowledge.

The "fixed stars" symbolize the immutable realm of Being that enjoys all the conditions for which men long but which are impossible in this life under the rule of "Fate, Time, Occasion, Chance, and Change." In the terrestrial realm of cyclical necessity, not only do individuals prosper and suffer, live and die, without regard for moral differences, but there is no discernible permanent progress in history: If "the world's great age begins anew," it too shall pass away to be succeeded by a return of "hate and death."[5] The stars, shining with an unchanging light that does not obscure them in their own bright veil (as does the Sun, deity itself), offer the hope to mortals that they, too, can rise above the mutability of this existence into an unchanging fulfillment of the highest human aspirations. In *Adonais* the stars symbolize the souls of great and good men of the past, "the splendours of the firmament of time" who "may be eclipsed, but are extinguished not."[6] Since the true Sun is obscured by its veil of light, man depends upon the inner sun of his own imagination (which partakes of the nature of the Divine but is subject to the limitations of the terrestrial world) and upon the example of those noble dead who, like stars, beacon "from the abode where the Eternal are" (*Adonais*, 495).

Finally, the planet Venus receives considerable attention throughout Shelley's poetry. Shelley believed strongly in two of the "theological virtues," Hope and Love, though "Faith" was always a term of opprobrium in his vocabulary because of what he regarded as the black moral record of all fideisms, Pagan, Christian, or Moslem.[7] For him full use of human reason was a moral responsibility, even though reason's ultimate success lay in defining the narrow limits of its own competence. In the "Essay on Life" he says of the "intellectual philosophy" (Humean scepticism): "It establishes no new truth, it gives us no additional insight into our hidden nature, neither in its actions nor itself. Philosophy, impatient as it may be to build, has much work yet remaining as pioneer for the overgrowth of ages. It makes one step towards this object: it destroys error and the roots of error. It leaves, what is too often the duty of the reformer in political and ethical questions to leave, a vacancy" (*Prose*, p. 173). But whereas "Faith" was, in Shelley's eyes, a moral liability, "Love" and "Hope" were the cornerstones of his ethical philosophy, Love its motivating

---

5. Final Chorus of *Hellas* (*P.W.*, pp. 477–478).
6. *Adonais*, 388–389 (*P.W.*, p. 441). Allan H. Gilbert has pointed out to me that Shelley probably derived his use of

"splendours" from Dante's *Paradiso*, e.g., Canto XXI, 32.
7. See Shelley's note (8) to *Hellas*, 1090–91 (*P.W.*, p. 480).

force, and Hope for the ultimate triumph of Good over Evil the sustainer of its energy. Venus, as the morning star Lucifer (the light-bearer), was the sign of man's regeneration within his earthly life—his awakening to spiritual Love; as Hesperus or Vesper, the evening star, it promised fulfillment of man's aspirations beyond the grave and thus symbolized Hope; as Dante's "third sphere"[8] it also symbolized Love in its highest manifestations.

The celestial symbols remain relatively consistent in their associations throughout Shelley's poetry, as do many of the terrestrial symbols. Each individual poem, however, develops its particular symbolic universe, drawing nuances and associations from specific traditions (the pastoral elegiac tradition in *Adonais*), from literary models (the *Persae* of Æschylus in *Hellas*), or from relevant historical events (the Peterloo Massacre in *The Mask of Anarchy*), and (since the symbolic force is primarily "philosophical") also from the "scientific" and the "phenomenal" levels of meaning. In explicating Shelley's individual poems, then, one cannot impose his "symbolic universe" in a Procrustean fashion; one must read each work on its own terms, keeping in mind the approximate values of these symbols and observing how they interrelate within the poem. The symbolism is consistent, but it evolves in forms as individual as Shelley's poetry is different from the literary sources he used.

* * *

The temptation for the critic of Shelley, friendly or hostile, is immediately to give him or his individual poems a rank or niche in the English poetic tradition. Unfortunately, the present state of Shelley studies does not permit this, for until one knows what the poet actually wrote and what it means, one can hardly determine whether his poetry is better or worse than that of other poets (whose work may or may not be better understood). Until all of Shelley's works are scrutinized anew, beginning with a reconsideration of the authority of their texts and concluding with a line-by-line, word-by-word explication of literal, "scientific," and symbolic-philosophical implications, every effort to determine Shelley's place in the Romantic movement or to evaluate his poetic achievement must remain perilously tentative and approximate. . . . Some criticisms of Shelley's poetic theory and practice and of his philosophical ideas have been based upon misunderstanding of his works, but to point out that a group of critics may have been mistaken about this or that aspect of his work does not, obviously, prove that Shelley was a great poet or a profound thinker; it means only that those who value the qualities that

8. *Paradiso*, VIII–IX; cf. also Shelley's translation of the First Canzone of the *Convito*: "Ye who intelligent the Third Heaven move . . ." (*P.W.*, p. 726).

actually characterize Shelley's poetry be able to appreciate it more when they recognize these qualities in it. If, as I believe, Shelley belongs to the great tradition of Western writers that includes Dante, Shakespeare, and Milton, the proper explication of his works ought to go far toward reestablishing his literary reputation; if not, then his writings deserve, perhaps, to remain less read than abused.

Studies of Individual Works

EVAN K. GIBSON

Alastor: A Reinterpretation[†]

Few of Shelley's poems have received a wider variety of explanations and interpretations than *Alastor*. Most critics would probably admit that the poem is difficult, and some would even go so far as to say that a clear understanding of it is impossible, agreeing with Havens that "the reader of *Alastor* is confused because its author was confused."[1] Hoffman attempts to explain it as largely auto-biographical,[2] while Mueschke and Griggs come to the conclusion that the prototype of the poet is Wordsworth.[3] The poet's vision has also been interpreted in a number of ingenious ways. Woodberry calls it "Alastor or evil genius," which "drives him on in search of its own phantasm till he dies."[4] Du Bois describes it as "a materialization of an ideal man, free, true, beautiful, loving poetry,"[5] and Forman believes that it is the ideal of female perfection.[6] The Preface has also given difficulty. Havens complains that the statements of the Preface are at variance with the action of the poem,[7] Du Bois believes that there is no inconsistency,[8] and Stevens, Beck, and Snow that the difference is only one of emphasis.[9] It is hoped that the present discussion will add clarity rather than confusion to the understanding of this early example of Shelley's deep-set convictions and powers of imagery.

This paper will attempt, first, a reinterpretation of the poet's vision, contending that past critics have erred chiefly in over-personification of the word *spirit*; there is no certain indication that Shelley intended any supernatural beings but the "Mother of this

† Reprinted by permission of the Modern Language Association of America from *PMLA*, LXII (1947), pp. 1022–1042.

1. Raymond D. Havens, "Shelley's 'Alastor,'" *PMLA*, XLV (1930), 1108.
2. Harold L. Hoffman, *An Odyssey of the Soul: Shelley's Alastor* (New York: Columbia University Press, 1933).
3. Paul Mueschke and Earl L. Griggs, "Wordsworth as Prototype of the Poet in Shelley's 'Alastor,'" *PMLA*, XLIX (1934), 229–245.
4. G. E. Woodberry, *Shelley's Complete Poetical Works* (Boston: Houghton, 1901), p. 615.
5. Arthur E. Du Bois, "Alastor: The Spirit of Solitude," *JEGP*, XXXV (1936), 538–539.
6. H. Buxton Forman, *Complete Works of Shelley* (London: Reeves, 1880), I, 26n.
7. *Op. cit.*, pp. 1108–1109.
8. *Op. cit.*, p. 537.
9. J. Stevens, E. L. Beck, and R. H. Snow, *English Romantic Poets* (New York: American Book Company, 1933), p. 886.

unfathomable world" (l. 18) as characters in the story. Second, it will point out what appears to be a natural allegory of the approach of death and the span of human life which takes up more than half the poem and which, heretofore, appears to have been overlooked by the critics. Although the poem may lack in structural organization, it does, we believe, contain unity of thought throughout and does not include, as Havens contends, "pictures of nature for their own sake."[1]

The Preface

In 1812 Shelley wrote to Godwin: "Though I begin a subject in writing with no definite view, it presently assumes a definite form, in consequence of the method that grows out of the induced train of thought."[2] If this declaration is an accurate self-criticism, it would be logical to assume that in most cases the last statements in connection with one of Shelley's artistic productions would be the clearest and most perfectly formed. As the Preface was, presumably, written after the poem was completed (December 14, 1815), it should contain the most complete expression of the idea which took form as Shelley developed the story. Although, as will be shown later, the Preface does not discuss in detail the entire poem, we must assume that Shelley intended it as an explanation of the instructional elements in this picture "not barren of instruction to actual men." Perhaps recognizing the difficulty of the poem for the average reader, Shelley wrote the Preface as a clarification and expected the poem to be read in the light of the Preface rather than, as too many have done, the Preface to be read in the light of the poem. Therefore, a careful examination of this prose piece should be fruitful.

The Preface is divided into two paragraphs, the first of which deals with the story of the poem and the second with explanation and general comment on the theme. The chief character of the story is represented as a youth greatly to be admired—"of uncorrupted feelings and adventurous genius." He possesses "an imagination inflamed and purified through familiarity with all that is excellent and majestic," and by it is led to a contemplation of the ultimate, the essence of the universe. He acquires a vast accumulation of knowledge and develops great intellectual qualities—and his appetite grows by what it feeds on. He becomes, also, extremely sensitive to the world of nature, the magnificence and beauty of

1. *Op. cit.*, p. 1109.
2. Roger Ingpen and Walter E. Peck, *The Complete Works of Percy Bysshe* *Shelley* (New York: Scribner's, 1926), VII, 280.

which enlarge and modify the conceptions of his mind to an infinite extent. Thus, his goal, his aim in life, instead of being a definite object, is an ever widening infinity in the realm of knowledge and of natural beauty. And in this condition he is happy.

But a change comes over him. These objects of the natural world and of the mind cease to minister to the need for companionship in his nature. Shelley's fragment, *On Love*, . . . sheds considerable light on the Preface at this point.

> We are born into the world, and there is something within us which, from the instant that we live, more and more thirsts after its likeness. It is probably in correspondence with this law that the infant drains milk from the bosom of its mother; this propensity develops itself with the development of our nature. We dimly see within our intellectual nature a miniature as it were of our entire self, yet deprived of all that we condemn or despise, the ideal prototype of everything excellent or lovely that we are capable of conceiving as belonging to the nature of man.[3]

And so in the poet that "something within" "thirsts after its own likeness" or, as the Preface states it, "His mind is at length suddenly awakened and thirsts for intercourse with an intelligence similar to itself." As a consequence of this thirst "*he images to himself* the Being whom he loves." It is important to note that this is a creation of his own mind and not, as some writers have stated, a vision sent to him by an outside agency. Because of his vast mental development and familiarity with speculations approaching the ideal, "the vision in which he embodies his own imaginations" is a combination of the ideal of the poet, the philosopher, and the lover—a unity of the wonderful, the wise, and the beautiful.

In other human beings, says Shelley, either the intellectual faculties or the imagination or the functions of sense call forth sympathetic powers in the being loved. In the poet all these faculties are supremely united, and therefore all are attached to the vision. For such a vision, to refer again to the fragment, *On Love*, is

> a miniature as it were of our entire self, . . . a mirror whose surface reflects only the forms of purity and brightness; a soul within our soul that describes a circle around its proper paradise, which pain, and sorrow, and evil dare not overleap.[4]

The vision, then, according to the Preface, is an "epipsychidion" —a soul out of his soul—and not something outside the poet's own nature. As such an image of love is not to be found in this life, for it is "the invisible and unattainable point to which Love tends" (*On Love*), the youth's search for a prototype of the vision is

3. *Ibid.*, VI, 201–202.   4. *Ibid.*

doomed to failure. Therefore, he dies "blasted by his disappointment."

Such, apparently, is Shelley's brief outline of the story as he thought he had written it in the poem; not the story of a youth pursued by a supernatural spirit of solitude, Alastor, who, as an avenger, "drives him on in search of its own phantasm till he dies";[5] not "the plan that the invisible spirit of solitude should tempt the poet to destroy himself;[6] not that Alastor or the gods, jealous of his knowledge of the thrilling secrets of the birth of time "sent him a baneful dream";[7] but, rather, the story of a youth who, after living a life of solitude, falls in love with a vision of his "soul mate," a creation of his own mind, and perishes of disappointment, apart from any other influence either human or divine. If other interpretations of the poem are true, they must be established elsewhere than in Shelley's own digest of the story.

The second half of the Preface deals with the cause of the poet's death but widens the discussion to explain the necessity of human sympathy in general and the evils of the solitary life. The statement of Du Bois that "It is significant that 'solitude' is a necessity, as Shelley's Preface has shown,"[8] which is just the opposite of Shelley's statement, is another illustration of the need of a careful analysis of this apparently confusing piece of prose. We are told that all the lasting misery and loneliness of the world are to be found among those who attempt to exist without human sympathy. It is important to realize that, in this paragraph, Shelley is not discussing all humanity, but only the loveless ones. Of these, there are two classes. One, a vast multitude, are the selfish, blind, and torpid, who love nothing on this earth and cherish no hope beyond, who rejoice neither in human joy nor mourn with human grief. These are morally dead and, living unfruitful lives, "prepare for their old age a miserable grave."

The second group who attempt to live without human sympathy, of whom the youth of the poem is one, are the pure and tender-hearted who "perish through the intensity and passion of their search" for the communities of human sympathy when, too late, "the vacancy of their spirit suddenly makes itself felt." These, as contrasted with the selfish, blind, and torpid, are deluded by a generous error, instigated by a sacred thirst for doubtful knowledge, or duped by an illustrious superstition.

Shelley appears fearful that the reader will misunderstand his thought. He, therefore, attempts in this paragraph to make it clear that there are others than "the luminaries of the world" who

5. Woodberry, loc. cit.
6. Havens, op. cit., p. 1102.
7. M. C. Wier, "Shelley's Alastor Again," PMLA, XLVI (1931), 950.
8. Op. cit., p. 535n.

suffer from living without love, that the law he is illustrating is universal. The poet, although deluded by a "generous error," is not the worst example of the loveless life. The delinquency of those "meaner spirits" is "more contemptible and pernicious." They, with no excuse for keeping "aloof from sympathies with their kind," are "morally dead." The universal power of love is irresistible. All those who "dare to abjure its dominion" constitute "the lasting misery and loneliness of the world," and either (if pure and tenderhearted) "perish through the intensity and passion of their search after its communities," or (if of the unforeseeing multitude) are doomed "to a slow and poisonous decay . . . because none feel with them their common nature."

It is not the search for knowledge or the love of nature which Shelley deplores but the fact that the youth tried to live without human sympathy. As one of the pure and tenderhearted, he is driven to speedy ruin by "the furies of an irresistible passion" created by his own nature. He brings about his own destruction by a conflict with one of the immutable laws of life; for, when, of necessity, "that Power" of human sympathy suddenly awakens him to "too exquisite a perception" of the influences of love, he is consumed by despair in the attempt to fill the vacancy of his spirit, not with flesh and blood companionship but with an impossibility —that "too exquisite perception."

Thus, we find that, contrary to Haven's assumption,[9] Shelley does not say that the poet seeks for a copy of the vision in the actual world. "He seeks in vain for a *prototype* of his conception." That is, he seeks for the pattern or original of the vision itself, the antitype. Although the Preface does not say where or how the poet seeks, we certainly would not expect a philosopher of his surpassing powers to make the blunder of expecting to find the prototype, the original of his vision, in the realm of the physical. Nor do the furies of an irresistible passion come from searching in the actual world. (Indeed, such a search might have saved him.) But they come from attempting to find the "communities of love" without a personal bond or kinship with mankind. This was the vacancy of spirit in which he perished.

This, it would appear, is what Shelley felt he had presented in the poem when he wrote the Preface—a tragedy of misdirected genius brought to inevitable defeat by the innocent neglect of one of the most necessary elements in the human soul. It would be indeed strange if Shelley, in writing this explanation, should so completely miss the point of his own poem or forget the significant details of its development, as much past criticism has inferred. One

9. *Op. cit.*, pp. 1102–1103.

must reject the possibility of a contradiction in the two until all attempts at reconciliation are exhausted.

The Solitary

After an invocation in which Shelley calls upon the "Mother of this unfathomable world" (l. 18) to inspire him, the main body of the poem begins with a lament. The story is to be a tragedy—the tragedy of a lovely youth, gentle, brave, and generous, who lived, died, and sang in solitude. And yet his songs had stirred deeply in the hearts of those unknown to him—strangers had wept and virgins pined, but he passed on unaware of them. Now his mute music is locked in the rugged cell of Silence, who has also become enamoured of his voice.

Then follows a careful description of his character and training. From earliest youth every sight of earth and air had sent its "choicest impulses," and of "divine philosophy" all the worth which the sacred past presented "he felt and knew." That is, he intuitively received the emanations of nature and the wisdom of the ancients. But the values of human companionship were unknown to him, even in his own home:

> When early youth had passed, he left
> His cold fireside and alienated home   (ll. 75–76)

This love of the beauty and majesty of the physical world led him to search in unknown and inaccessible regions to obtain the deepest secrets of nature—the deep caves of priceless treasure; the fields of snow and pinnacles of ice; the majestic dome of heaven; the green earth, where in lonesome vales animal life accepted him into its fellowship. Of this observation of the marvelous in nature he never tired. It never "lost in his heart its claims to love and wonder" (ll. 97–98). His thirst for divine philosophy caused him to travel, also, to the sites of ancient learning, Athens, Babylon, Egypt, to study the wisdom of men—men in the youth of the world who understood "the thrilling secrets of the birth of time." After visiting these places of mystery and knowledge and opening his soul to their influences, meaning "like strong inspiration" flashed upon "his vacant mind" (a mind receptive to emanations of truth) until he, too, saw those thrilling secrets (ll. 125–128).

Shelley has thus far described a youth certainly to be admired for his personal attractiveness, his high intellectual pursuits, and his love and sensitiveness to the beauty and wonder of nature. But during this time he had lived a solitary life—a life untouched by human love. Finding in nature and "divine philosophy" an overwhelming interest, he did not realize his need of anything else.

Shelley gives no indication that he deliberately refused to accept human love and sympathy. Rather, he was merely unaware of its significance or personal value to him. So engrossed was he in his pursuit of truth and beauty that he was not conscious of the virgins who "pined and wasted for fond love of his wild eyes" (ll. 62–63) nor of the love of the Arab maid who watched his nightly sleep and did not dare "for deep awe to speak her love" (ll. 133–134). The references to the strangers who wept, the virgins who pined, and the Arab maid, are used to show not a deliberate, willful rejection of human companionship but an innocent neglect of a vital part of the human soul. This "generous error" (Preface) arose from a desire which must be highly admired—the desire to find truth, to find the meaning of life and of the universe. And what heightens the tragedy of the poet's death is the fact that it was caused by an exclusive emphasis upon this very quality which was so commendable in his life.

The eleven lines (ll. 129–139) referring to the Arab maid have been given undue significance by some writers. Du Bois, for instance, objects to the lack of conflict between the Arab maid and the vision.[1] But Shelley did not intend nor desire such a conflict. He appears to have included these lines merely to reiterate and re-emphasize, just before the appearance of the vision, the fact that the youth was unaware of his opportunities and of the importance of human companionship. He seems hardly conscious of her presence, entirely taken up as he was with discovering "the thrilling secrets of the birth of time," (l. 128) and, while she returned to her father's tent "wildered and wan, and panting," this noble, brave, and generous youth continued on in his explorations through Arabie and Persia with no indication that he realized the pain and unhappiness he had caused.

But finally his human nature asserts itself in a desire for companionship with one like himself. If we are to believe the Preface, "he images to himself the Being whom he loves," a being who unites in a single image the sympathetic demands in the poet of "the intellectual faculties, the imagination, the functions of sense." And such a three-fold division is just what is found in the description of the vision (ll. 149–191). Havens, complaining of contradictions between the Preface and the poem itself, says that "an attentive reader may find some hints" in the poem of the Being of the Preface.[2] But thirty lines of carefully organized detail is certainly more than a hint to an inattentive reader. First she spoke in "low solemn tones" to "his inmost sense" like the voice of his own soul and talked of those things which had been most dear to him, intellectual pursuits: knowledge, truth, and virtue, divine

1. *Op. cit.*, p. 545.　　　　　2. *Op. cit.*, p. 1107.

liberty, and poetry—being herself a poet. Then her mood changed. The contemplation of these thoughts most dear to him kindled the imagination, and she raised "wild numbers," creating strangely moving music from the harp in her hands. The voice stifled in tremulous sobs, the beating heart heard in the pauses of the song, the tumultuous breath, all contribute to show the influence of the imagination upon the affectionate phase of the soul. But the imagination does not deal entirely with concepts. It stimulates the creation of sense perceptions. She ceased singing, and the poet turned and beheld her for the first time. Before, she had been veiled —"her fair hands were bare alone" (ll. 165–166), and he had been aware of her only as she communed with his intellectual and imaginative nature. But now "the functions of the sense" (Preface) imaged the perceptive forms which made the vision complete. Through "the sinuous veil of woven wind" he saw the bare arms, the floating locks, the beamy, bending eyes, the trembling lips— a perfection of sense details.

The sensuousness of the vision has been objected to. Mrs. Campbell says that she is "much too earthly and realistic; she who should have been but a symbol of the soul's desire steps out of the land of imagery like some scantily dressed beauty of a society ball."[3] But such an objection disregards the statement of the Preface. "The Poet" says Shelley "is represented as uniting these requisitions, and attaching them to a single image." Thus, we see that the vision is a three-fold creation of "the intellectual faculties, the imagination, the functions of sense." The omission of the sense details would have left the image incomplete.

As explained by the passage previously quoted from *On Love*, that "something within" which thirsts after its own likeness, and which the poet had never been conscious of before, made itself felt for the first time by awakening his mind to "thirst for intercourse with an intelligence similar to itself" (Preface). This "dream of hopes that never yet had flushed his cheek" (ll. 150–151) was the imaging forth of the "epipsychidion" of the poet, that "miniature as it were of our entire self" (*On Love*). One must understand, however, that the vision is not the poet's own soul. He does not fall in love with himself as Hoffman believes, who makes the vision the poet's own inner self. "Shelley's poet is unable to separate his ideas of a beloved woman from his consciousness of himself except in the matter of physical form."[4] But there is no basis for such a conclusion. The Preface states that all love is sympathy with like qualities in others. The vision is a creation *by* his soul of an ideal "soul-mate," one who will respond to every characteristic of his soul on all three planes.

3. O. W. Campbell, *Shelley and the Un-romantics* (London: Methuen, 1924), p. 190.

4. *Op. cit.*, p. 34.

However, the objection which many would have to this interpretation is that, while is may be in entire agreement with the Preface and the rest of the poem, it is contradicted by lines 203–205, which follow the description of the vision:

> The spirit of sweet human love has sent
> A vision to the sleep of him who spurned
> Her choicest gifts.

Perhaps because of a misunderstanding of Peacock's explanation of the title, many critics have regarded these lines as pivotal in motivating the action of the story, interpreting "the spirit of sweet human love" as some supernatural being who punishes the youth by sending an evil dream. But is not this interpretation an overpersonification of what Shelley meant to be only slightly figurative? Although *spirit* does mean "an intelligent but immaterial being," it may also mean "the essential principle of some emotion as governing action." Used in the latter sense it is in entire agreement with the Preface and the rest of the poem. That is, the dormant spirit of sweet human love in the poet's own nature, sent the vision—that spirit of human sympathy which, according to the Preface, makes itself felt at some time in all those who are not morally dead. Shelley does slightly personify the word by the use of the feminine pronoun and the verb *sent*, but such momentary personification is not uncommon, particularly as he regarded the spirit of love as a universal feeling of human sympathy and, therefore, not improper for personification. Certainly there is little basis, in the light of the rest of the poem, for regarding these lines as the entrance of a supernatural character into the plot.

The title of the poem, as we know from Peacock's note, was selected after the poem was completed. It contains, quite certainly, a reference to a supernatural being. But Alastor is not one of the characters of the poem. He is a personification of the theme of the poem as the sub-title indicates. A spirit of solitude, the ruling temper of the poet's life, causes his destruction. This is the theme of the poem. Nor is there anything in Peacock's explanation to indicate that he understood the title to mean any more than this:

> He [Shelley] was at a loss for a title, and I proposed that which he adopted: *Alastor; or the spirit of Solitude*. The Greek word, ’Αλάστωρ, is an evil genius. . . . The poem treated the spirit of solitude as a spirit of evil. I mention the true meaning of the word because many have supposed *Alastor* to be the name of the hero.[5]

There is little reason for agreeing with Wier that, because the poet had roamed too long in the ruins of antiquity and "saw the

5. Thomas Love Peacock, *Memoirs of Shelley* (London: Frowde, 1909), pp. 55–66.

thrilling secrets of the birth of time," therefore the gods or Alastor, jealous of his knowledge, sent him a baneful dream.[6] Such conclusions come from reading the poem with one eye on *Prometheus Unbound*. The vision in no sense of the word is evil nor exerts an evil influence on him. Shelley believes that all (or at least the pure and tenderhearted) carry such an ideal in the soul (*On Love*). The imaging forth of this ideal was inevitable—one of the laws of the universe. The evil which followed the vision was the result of "the Poet's self-centered seclusion" (Preface).

The effect of the vision upon the poet, though tragic, is what should be expected. Awakening from his dream he suddenly becomes aware of his loneliness in the midst of nature—of his lack of companionship with a being like himself. The nature which had so delighted him now only emphasizes the solitariness of his own existence:

> Whither have fled
> . . . The sounds that soothed his sleep,
> The mystery and majesty of Earth
> The Joy, the exultation? His wan eyes
> Gaze on the empty scene as vacantly
> As ocean's moon looks on the moon in heaven.
>
> (ll. 196–202)

It is not that the poet comes to hate nature but that it has an emptiness about it which he had not realized before the appearance of the vision. Later, as he sees the swan wing its way to its nest (ll. 275–280), he comments upon the companionship of like with like and recognizes the gulf between himself and nature.

> And what am I that I should linger here,
> With voice far sweeter than thy dying notes,
> Spirit more vast than thine, frame more attuned
> To beauty, wasting these surpassing powers
> In the deaf air, to the blind earth, and heaven
> That echoes not my thoughts? (ll. 285–290)

The desire for "a community with what we experience within ourselves" (*On Love*) causes the poet to realize that there can be no actual communion between the divine spirit of man and the deaf, blind, and thoughtless physical world. There may be an appreciation of nature's beauties and even a mystic sense or emotional reaction to the majesty and mystery of nature, but these will not substitute for companionship with thinking, imagining, sentient beings. This was the fatal lesson the poet learned from the vision. To Shelley this was such an important truth that he carries it through to the end of the poem.

6. *Op. cit.*, pp. 949–950.

In lines 412–419, as the poet's boat drifts into the peaceful cove after escaping the abyss, the influences of nature touch him, and he longs to deck his withered hair with the bright flowers on the bank:

> But on his heart its solitude returned
> And he forbore.

The longing for the vision created by "the strong impulse" of sweet human love had not yet performed its ministry. The influence of "those flushed checks, bent eyes, and shadowy frame" hung upon the poet's spirit till death, when the floods of night closed over it.

Even later, in the most perfect natural surroundings, when the very Spirit of Nature seemed to stand beside him and to speak through the medium of

> undulating woods, and silent well,
> And leaping rivulet, and evening gloom
> Now deepening the dark shades,

even here the "two starry eyes" of the vision, from the intense pensiveness of his own "gloom of thought," beckoned him away from this vale of nature to follow the light that shone within his soul (ll. 479–494). For the speech of nature in woods and rivulet and evening gloom, however emotionally real and intuitively sensed, is still that of the deaf air, the blind earth, and the thoughtless sky (ll. 289–290). It cannot substitute for the "two starry eyes" of human companionship, even though an emotional kinship or "mystic sympathy" (l. 652) with nature's movements may be present till the very end of life.

And so, although the poet had felt companionship with nature before the appearance of the vision, after he awakens he is a solitary indeed, finding sympathy nowhere. His first thought is a desire to be reunited with this maiden of the vision. Overleaping the bounds between sleeping and waking, he pursues her into the actual world, only to find that she is lost forever in the pathless desert of dim sleep (l. 210). The thought of sleep immediately suggests a related concept, and the poet wonders if the vision may be found in death. "Does the dark gate of death conduct to thy mysterious paradise, O sleep?" (ll. 211–213) But who knows to what realms death conducts? Perhaps our hopes for the fulfillment of desires in a future state are but wishful thinking. Perhaps, as Shelley says later when the poet gazes into the reflection in the well,

> the human heart,
> Gazing in dreams over the gloomy grave,
> Sees its own treacherous likeness there.   (ll. 472–474)

And here the same image is used. The calm lake, reflecting the arch of clouds and pendant mountains, leads only to blackness and watery nothingness. May not our belief in life after death be but a reflection of our hopes? And yet the loathsome vapors and foul grave may hide something more beautiful than they—perhaps, the delightful realms of sleep. If death is the opposite of life, may not the images represent opposite results? The ebb and flow of these thoughts, motivated by the poet's intense desire, stung his heart with alternate hope and despair (ll. 221–222).

Both Havens and Hoffman labor over this passage and come to opposite conclusions as to whether the image means there is or is not a life after death.[7] But Shelley's intention was to leave the question unanswered. "This *doubt*" flowed on his heart and hope stung like despair. In fact, the latter half of the poem was written mainly to show that the question is unanswerable. We know not the future; we must find what we can of our ideals here.

But the poet is driven on by "hope and despair, the torturers" (l. 639) not in an attempt to find in a human maiden the likeness of his vision but in a blind attempt to escape the torture of intense desire controlled by alternate hope and despair. This is made clear by the image of the eagle and the serpent:

> As an eagle grasped
> In folds of the green serpent, feels her breast
> Burn with the poison, and precipitates
> Through night and day, tempest and calm, and cloud,
> Frantic with dizzying anguish, her blind flight
> O'er the wide aëry wilderness: thus driven
> By the bright shadow of that lovely dream,
> . . . .
> He fled. (ll. 227–237)

Here, certainly, is no search for an earthly maiden. The question of the poet's search in this world for a copy of the vision, which has concerned several writers in recent years, must, of necessity, be answered in the negative. If the poet at this point turned to the world of mankind for love and companionship, the story would be without a theme, and the Preface would, indeed, be inconsistent with it. As we have already pointed out, the Preface states that "He seeks in vain for a prototype of his conception." Hoping intensely that there is a prototype, an archetype, in the ideal world for this "bright shadow" which his mind has conceived, he turns immediately to the two avenues by which man has hoped to reach the ideal world—sleep and death. The former is transitory. Through it the vision came to him but is now lost. "For sleep, he knew,

---

7. Havens, *op. cit.*, p. 1099; Hoffman, *op. cit.*, pp. 36–37.

kept most relentlessly its precious charge" (ll. 292–293). Death is most uncertain, "faithless perhaps as sleep," (l. 294) and yet the only other possibility. It is in these two areas only that the youth seeks for a prototype. The search is first an intellectual one and is presented mainly in lines 205–222, dealing with the image of the calm lake reflecting the world of the senses but leading to nothing but watery blackness. Again the two possible domains of the ideal are referred to in lines 290–295, partially quoted above.

> A gloomy smile
> Of desperate hope wrinkled his quivering lips.
> For sleep, he knew, kept most relentlessly
> Its precious charge, and silent death exposed,
> Faithless perhaps as sleep, a shadowy lure,
> With doubtful smile mocking its own strange charms.

Finally, after the consuming flames of desire have brought him to the edge of the grave, he decides to venture into this unknown and doubtful area of the ideal, and so embarks in the little shallop to "meet lone Death on the drear ocean's waste" (l. 305). As we hope to show later, Shelley carries the poet, from this section on to the end of the poem, through a natural allegory of death and the span of life as he continues his search for the vision beyond this life. The youth's hopes are high while on the stormy sea, and, as he sees the yawning cavern, he cries:

> Vision and Love! . . . I have beheld
> The path of thy departure. Sleep and death
> Shall not divide us long!   (ll. 366–369)

But such hopes of finding our ideals beyond this life are without basis. As the Preface says, the search is a vain one. The passion eventually burns itself out, until at the poet's death "hope and despair, the torturers, slept" (ll. 639–640). The "two starry eyes" cease to beckon him, and his last moments are given "to images of the majestic past" (l. 629).

Such is the search—a search for avenues to the ideal world. At no point in the poem does Shelley indicate that the poet considers any other realms but those of sleep and death as areas in which to seek for the prototype of his vision. And, as Havens has rightly said, it is the vision and the vision alone which the poet seeks, not an earthly, partial copy.[8] This however, as we have shown, is not inconsistent with the Preface, as Havens thinks; for it does not state that the poet seeks for a physical maiden in the physical world but for a prototype of an ideal vision, which must certainly, be found only in the ideal world.

8. *Op. cit.*, p. 1102.

Hoffman has argued at some length that the search is presented in the youth's wanderings among the cottagers in lines 254–271.[9] But to prove his point he very wisely omits any mention of the preceding thirty-four lines (ll. 221–254), which give the image of the eagle and serpent and represent the poet as wandering wildly "where the desolated tombs of Parthian kings scatter to every wind their wasting dust,"—hardly a place to find a soul-mate.

The youthful maidens which Hoffman thinks the poet scrutinized as candidates to take the place of the vision are presented, as was the earlier Arab maid, to show that the youth still did *not* search in the actual world. He was just as solitary after the vision as before. They called him by false names of "brother" and "friend" (ll. 268–269)—false because the name they wished to call him was "lover," showing his further opportunities for love. And, taught by nature, they only interpreted half his woe because they realized that the woe was caused by the pangs of love but not that it was the love of an ideal and not of an actual maiden. Just as the youth, earlier, was hardly conscious of the Arab maid who watched his nightly sleep, so enrapt was he in contemplating the intellectual wonders of the universe, now he is scarcely aware of these cottage maidens, tortured as he is by the intense desire for an impossible, ideal concept of love.

The desire to fill a suddenly felt need for companionship (what the Preface calls the vacancy of his spirit) with a perfect creation of the mind, which the poet knows he will never find in this life, causes the "blasting" which brings about his death. The emotional stress which drives him on past desolated tombs and from cottage to cottage, unaware of the joys of actual human companionship, finally consumes his physical life and completely destroys him. By the time he reaches the Chorasmian shore (l. 272) his body is a very frail and leaky receptacle for the essence of life. The effects of "the brooding care" are described in lines 248–254:

> And now his limbs were lean; his scattered hair
> Sered by the autumn of strange suffering
> Sung dirges in the wind; his listless hand
> Hung like dead bone within its withered skin;
> Life, and the lustre that consumed it, shone
> As in a furnace burning secretly
> From his dark eyes alone.

There is little hope of the continuance of mortality in such a body as this. And so, when the poet contemplates meeting death by embarking in the leaky shallop, he is not contemplating suicide, as Havens says,[1] but, realizing that his life is at an end, is merely

9. *Op. cit.*, pp. 38–39.   1. *Op. cit.*, p. 1100.

seeking his final resting place. The doubtful lure, perhaps faithless, of meeting his ideal in death causes him to consider "the drear ocean's waste" as the most favorable approach to that undiscovered country:

> For well he knew that mighty Shadow loves
> The slimy caverns of the populous deep.   (ll. 306–307)

Havens believes that "morally he was a suicide" and that Shelley held, "vaguely and intermittently," the plan that Alastor "should tempt the poet to destroy himself in order to enjoy the companionship of the ideal being whom he had imaged as his love."[2] Du Bois, attacking the same problem, comes to the opposite conclusion. He says, "The theme of *Alastor* is the triumph of an individual genius over the fear of death."[3] We fail to see that Shelley was concerned with the problem of suicide or the fear of death. As we have shown, death is upon the poet. In a few hours he actually expires in the quiet nook, nor is his death due to his venture on the sea or any other subsequent action. His movements are those of a dying man. The fear of death is not mentioned in the early portion of the poem, nor is there an indication that the poet conquers that fear. He proceeds calmly to death merely because it is a necessity and because he has no desire to live any longer, as the vision has turned this world to ashes. His attitude toward death is not a problem except as an avenue to the ideal world.

The Allegories of Death and Life

When Shelley brings his poet to the shore of this vast sea and to the contemplation of death, he, apparently, changes his method of presentation. Before, he has introduced the youth and illustrated his character and attitudes in the world of the actual or at least the possible. While the events and descriptions as a whole may be representative or in a sense didactic (this is inferred in the Preface), the reader receives the impression that, thus far, the happenings were a part of the actual life of the poet and not merely figures of speech in an allegorical system. However, from here on, the poem presents many physical impossibilities. It is hard to believe, for instance, that Shelley expected the reader to accept the poet's crossing of the sea in the boat as a literal experience. This little shallop whose sides

> Gaped wide with many a rift, and its frail joints
> Swayed with the undulations of the tide   (ll. 302–303)

2. *Ibid.*, p. 1102.   3. *Op. cit.*, p. 537.

carries him across a wide sea, through a raging storm of waves and boiling torrents, down a yawning cavern of winding depth, and finally through a tremendous maelstrom into a quiet cove. And at no time does the boat appear inadequate for the journey.

Such objects and events must have more significance than that of an adventurous section of a surface narrative which, up to this point, has been at least romantically plausible. Before venturing a speculation as to their meaning one ought to consider Shelley's general habits of imagery and allegorical presentation. An attentive reading of Shelley's poetry will demonstrate the fact that repetition of imagery was a common characteristic of his writing. The repetition occurs not merely from one poem to another but within the same poem, the image often appearing later with a word of explanation which shows the metaphor intended. This imaginative tenacity is not, of course, an indication of paucity of thought but of vividness and conviction as to the correct poetic figure.

Another question which should be examined here is the reason for Shelley's change of method. If he has not used an allegorical system thus far, why should he introduce one now? A consideration of the problem of the search for the vision should provide the answer. If death is the only possible area of union with the vision, and if, as we hope to show, Shelley intends to conduct the poet into the realms of death, how else but by allegory may the material be presented? From this point on, the problems treated are not in the sentient world, but in that of death and immortality. A system of figures is the only possible way to continue the story.

At this point, then, the poet, prematurely aged and ready for the grave, stands on the shore, a wide waste of putrid marshes from which a sluggish stream empties into the sea. May not this setting represent the end of mortal existence when the stream of life enters the ocean of eternity? Such an interpretation is given support by the repetition of the image later in the poem with a definite explanation of its meaning. The stream which rises in the well (ll. 477–479) and empties in the immeasurable void (ll. 567–569) is, we are told, an image of life (l. 505). If this portion of the setting represents the passage from this life, other details may also contribute to the representation. The swan which rises as he approaches the shore (l. 276) may represent the departure of the senses and affections at death, the loss of consciousness of the world of physical nature. Certainly the little boat with its gaping sides and frail joints is suggestive of the bodily condition of the poet. Obeying the restless impulse of his soul, he leaps into the boat, which is swept out across the tranquil sea by the wind which sweeps strongly from the shore. The suggestive imagery of unconsciousness and approaching death is strengthened by the next lines:

> As one that in a silver vision floats
> Obedient to the sweep of odorous winds
> Upon resplendent clouds, so rapidly
> Along the dark and ruffled waters fled
> The straining boat.   (ll. 316–320)

The "restless impulse," (l. 304) which urges him to embark and meet lone Death, evidently comes from "his eager soul," (l. 311) which he follows by leaping into the boat and which earlier held "a strong impulse" (l. 274) that urged him toward the seashore. These lines seem to represent the willingness and even eagerness with which the poet's soul is ready to leave this life when death approaches. They also suggest the fatal necessity of the forces of life and death—the "restless impulse" which drives the soul to its appointed end. In the natural allegory this idea of necessity is continued by the wind, which soon becomes a hurricane. At this point there appears no chance of turning back into life, for, although "the day was fair and sunny" (l. 308) and life still had its beauty and charm, yet "the wind swept strongly from the shore, blackening the waves" (ll. 309–310). The poet, following his eager soul, and like one "obedient to the sweep of odorous winds," is driven by these winds of necessity across the blackened waves, which earlier were described as leading only to a black and watery depth (ll. 215–216) and compared to death's blue vault. That the winds represent the necessity of death—the irresistible laws of disintegration in the universe—is strengthened by the use of the same image near the end of the poem, where the poet actually dies:

> O, storm of death!
> Whose sightless speed divides this sullen night:
> And thou, colossal Skeleton, that still
> Guiding its irresistible career
> In thy devastating omnipotence,
> Art king of this frail world.   (ll. 609–614)

The winds which drive the boat first over a tranquil sea like a cloud before a hurricane soon may be truly described as a "storm of death." The experience of losing consciousness as in a silver vision swept by odorous winds is changed to a fierce conflict of tossing waves and scourging tempest—the final struggle as life is subdued by death. But through it all the soul, typified by the poet himself, rides confident, safely carried in its fragile physical receptacle until the fatal moment when the laws of life and death give it release.

The storm continues for some time, but finally the struggle ends as the boat is carried into a yawning cavern—the jaws of death—and on a calmer surface approaches the end of its journey.

That the cavern represents the jaws of death is made quite probable by other uses of the same image. Shelley speaks of "the dark gate of death" (l. 211) and of the "stony jaws" at the end of the stream of life (l. 551). That the poet recognizes the cavern as the dark gate of death is shown by his own words as it looms before him:

> Vision and Love! . . . I have beheld
> The path of thy departure. Sleep and death
> Shall not divide us long! (ll. 366–369)

The conflict is over. The storm of death has subsided. What lies beyond? But Shelley is not prepared to give the answer. The theme of his poem deals with the here and now, not the hereafter. Nor does he believe that man knows the answer. There may be a happy existence beyond this life, and there may be nothing but oblivion awaiting the soul after death. Who knows? And so he presents both possibilities in the allegory, choosing the more optimistic for purposes of the story.

At the end of the windings of the cavern is a vast whirlpool, and

> I' the midst was left,
> Reflecting, yet distorting every cloud,
> A pool of treacherous and tremendous calm.
> (ll. 384–386)

The whirlpool suggests the possibility of complete oblivion, utter annihilation of personality after death. The reflecting pool of calm at the end of the maelstrom, tremendous and yet treacherous, is a repetition of the same image used earlier and again later. As was pointed out above, the reflections of this life seen on the surface of water suggest the wishful thinking which may be the only basis for our belief in an individual existence after death. The surface of the lake, reflecting the arch of rainbow clouds, but leading only to watery blackness is compared to death's blue vault (ll. 213–218). And, later, the reflections in the well are compared to the possibility that

> the human heart
> Gazing in dreams over the gloomy grave,
> Sees its own treacherous likeness there. (ll. 472–474)

And so, here, the maelstrom leading to oblivion has at its center a *treacherous* calm, reflecting and yet distorting the life of this physical, sentient world. But it is only a reflection. Beyond black nothingness. Such, Shelley seems to say, is one possibility.

But it is not the only one. The belief in the retention of personality may be more than wishful thinking. There may be a

quiet cove in eternity where the wise and the good will continue
their existence. As the boat is about to be drawn down into the
vortex, "a wandering stream of wind breathed from the west"
(ll. 397–398), perhaps again the winds of necessity, gently forces
the boat into a smooth spot and blows it down a placid opening
into a quiet cove whose meeting banks, drooping flowers, and
murmuring breeze are in startling contrast to the roar of the falling
stream and the dizzy speed of the whirlpool just escaped.

The meaning of these images is again reinforced by repetition.
At the end of the poem the same two possibilities are presented.
The stream of life scatters its waters to the passing winds as it
loses its identity in the "immeasurable void" of oblivion (ll. 569–
570), and yet on the edge of the precipice, overlooking the earth,
is a tranquil nook where the poet finally comes to rest—a spot that
seems to smile even in the lap of horror (ll. 571–578). This quiet
cove or tranquil nook as a haven for the soul appears to represent
Shelley's hope for the retention of personality after death, for in
his essay *On Life,* . . . he says of man:

> Whatever may be his true and final destination, there is a spirit
> within him at enmity with nothingness and dissolution.[4]

But the uncertainty of that hope, as shown in the two images of
oblivion, is expressed in his Journal on July 28, 1814. Meditating
on death he writes, "I hope—but my hopes are not unmixed with
fear for what will befall this inestimable spirit when we die."[5]
That he recognized the possibility of loss of individual being is
also established by a prose fragment, *On the Punishment of Death,*
probably written in 1814 or 1815:

> The opinion that the vital principle within us, in whatever mode
> it may continue to exist, must lose that consciousness of definite
> and individual being which now characterizes it, and become a
> unit in the vast sum of action and of thought which disposes and
> animates the universe, and is called God, seems to belong to that
> class of opinion which has been designated as indifferent.[6]

So the allegory of death comes to an end, and we might expect
the poet actually to expire on the banks of the cove.

The reason the poem does not end at this point is, perhaps, not
at first apparent. The poet has reached his quiet cove in eternity.
What more is there to say? But the last words of the poet ("Vision
and Love . . . " ll. 366–369) had suggested the likelihood of his
reuniting with the vision after death. That had been his hope, and
if he died in the cove with the vision still strong on his mind, we

4. Ingpen and Peck, *op. cit.*, VI, 194.   6. *Ibid.*, VI, 186.
5. *Ibid.*, VI, 361.

would be left with the feeling that he probably was united with her after death. However, that was not Shelley's intention as was shown in the Preface. The danger of neglecting love and sympathy with one's fellow-man in *this* life was to be the theme of the poem. And so the story continues until the passion subsides from the impulse in the cove (ll. 415–419) to the fainter impulse by the well in the two starry eyes (ll. 488–492) and finally dies away when hope and despair sleep (ll. 639–640) and the poet gives his thoughts up to images of the majestic past, his last moments being in complete harmony with his surroundings.

Shelley also wishes to drive home the thought that such a hope of expecting to find one's ideals beyond this life is without any certain foundation. It is as if nature stretched out a vast allegory for the poet to observe to show the futility of his quest. Behold our life! What do we know of it, rising we know not whence and ending we know not whither? And so he presents these images of all that we know of our existence, beginning and ending with hollow caves giving forth a thousand confused voices. We must capture what we can of our ideals in this world. The future is unknown.

In dealing with the second allegory we can begin our analysis with more confidence. There can be little doubt that this section represents the span of human life, for the poet himself recognizes that the various aspects of the setting are types of his mortal existence and appears to draw from it resignation as to the loss of the vision. His words might be regarded as the answer to his "Vision and Love" speech:

> O stream!
> Whose source is inaccessibly profound,
> Whither do thy mysterious waters tend?
> Thou imagest my life. Thy darksome stillness,
> Thy dazzling waves, thy loud and hollow gulfs,
> Thy searchless fountain, and invisible course
> Have each their type in me; and the wide sky,
> And measureless ocean may declare as soon
> What oozy cavern or what wandering cloud
> Contains thy waters, as the universe
> Tell where these living thoughts reside, when stretched
> Upon thy flowers my bloodless limbs shall waste
> I' the passing wind! (ll. 502–514)

With such a positive statement as this it is strange that no one, heretofore, has worked out the detailed system of metaphors by which Shelley pictures our mortal span. Certainly we cannot agree with Havens that "in *Alastor* we have pictures of nature for their own sake."[7] Rather, we are inclined to believe Shelley's own state-

7. *Op. cit.*, p. 1109.

ment in a letter to Elizabeth Hitchener dated June 5, 1811: "My opinion is that all poetical beauty ought to be subordinate to the inculcated moral."[8]

Leaving the boat in the cove the poet walks through a narrow shaded vale (l. 420) where huge caves "respond and roar for ever." These caves at the beginning of the setting find a counterpart at the end of the stream where "black gulfs and yawning caves . . . gave ten thousand various tongues" (ll. 548–549). As these "loud and hollow gulfs" are mentioned by the poet in the passage quoted above, we can be sure that they have typical significance. Coming as they do at the beginning and end of the allegory, they apparently represent the thousands of questions and answers of philosophy and religion as to man's origin before birth and his destination after death. That Shelley had considered many of these questions himself is common knowledge, but it is significant to note his attitude toward them in the fragment, *On Life* . . . :

> How vain it is to think that words can penetrate the mystery of our being! Rightly used they may make evident our ignorance to ourselves, and this is much. For what are we? Is birth the commencement, is death the conclusion of our being? What is birth and death?[9]

And so the poet wanders through this dark yet beautiful forest vale, "as led by love, or dream, or god, or mightier Death" (ll. 427–428). These lines are further indications of uncertainty. What is the controlling force of our mortality? Are we motivated by something within—love or dream (aspirations)? Or is it by something beyond ourselves—the fatal pattern of some god or of mighty, impersonal Death, the necessary workings of the laws of dissolution in the universe?

Leaving, then, these uncertainties, Shelley deals with what we do know of the beginnings of life in the union of male and female and the development of the family. Using the symbolism of trees and vines and flowers, he pictures the scene in which "the oak, expanding its immense and knotty arms, embraces the light beech" (ll. 431–433). The tall cedars overarch and protect the tremulous and pale ash and acacia (ll. 433–438). Around their trunks the parasitic vines flow, and

> as gamesome infants' eyes,
> With gentle meanings, and most innocent wiles,
> Fold their beams round the hearts of those that love,
> These twine their tendrils with the wedded boughs
> Uniting their close union.   (ll. 441–445)

8. Ingpen and Peck, *op. cit.*, VIII, 100.   9. *Ibid.*, VI, 194.

It is by such phrases as "the wedded boughs uniting their close union" and "as gamesome infants' eyes" that Shelley makes certain the intended symbolism throughout the allegory.

Among these symbols of wedded union and gamesome infants, in one dark, lovely, and mysterious glen, a well of most translucent wave

> Images all the woven boughs above,
> And each depending leaf, and every speck
> Of azure sky, darting between their chasms.
>
> (ll. 459–461)

This well, which represents the mysterious source of life and from which flows the stream (ll. 477–479), reflects on its surface the woven boughs of hereditary influence and the impressions that this sentient life receives from the world of nature. As we have pointed out, it is from these impressions that man builds his hope for sentient existence after death (ll. 469–474). After pausing for a moment in this lovely glen beside the well, the poet continues on, for the influence of the vision, those "two starry eyes, hung in the gloom of thought," (l. 490) still causes a separation from nature. The thought of her reminds him that companionship must be in like with like. The rivulet which he follows from the well and which represents the span of mortal life begins wanton and wild "like childhood laughing as it went" (l. 499). But soon the scene changes. Grey rocks, thin spires of dry grass, and "gnarled roots of ancient pines" indicate the influences of age upon life. And yet in old age, man, "branchless and blasted," still clenches this life "with grasping roots" (ll. 527–532):

> A gradual change was here,
> Yet ghastly. For, as fast years flow away,
> The smooth brow gathers, and the hair grows thin
> And white, and where irradiate dewy eyes
> Had shone, gleam stony orbs:—so from his steps
> Bright flowers departed, and the beautiful shade
> Of the green groves, with all their odorous winds
> And musical motions.
>
> (ll. 532–539)

As the stream approaches the end of its existence, it is surrounded by the caves mentioned above, which "gave ten thousand various tongues" (l. 549) concerning the life beyond. Finally it reaches the end of its course as "the pass expands its stony jaws" and an "immeasurable void" is revealed into which the stream scatters "its waters to the passing winds" (ll. 550–570). Beyond the stony jaws of death and across the immeasurable void where lies oblivion, are

Islanded seas, blue mountains, mighty streams,
Dim tracts and vast, robed in the lustrous gloom
Of leaden-coloured even, and fiery hills
Mingling their flames with twilight, on the verge
Of the remote horizon.   (ll. 555–559)

Beyond this mortality seem to stretch unknown lands, but of their significance no man can tell.

However, again Shelley points out the alternative. These grim aspects "were not all;—one silent nook was there" (ll. 571–573). As was illustrated in the figure of the cove beside the maelstrom (ll. 397–408), there may be more than wishful thinking in the hope of individual existence after death. There may be a tranquil nook where at least such surpassing spirits as this youth will rest eternally.

It is in this spot that the poet draws his last breath, expiring just at the instant that the crescent moon, which had filled the foggy air with yellow mist, disappears below the horizon. The moon and its yellow mist apparently represent in the natural allegory that which the vision has represented in the poet's life—mankind's ideal aspirations. This interpretation gains its main support from the fact that, as the moon sinks out of sight, its two horns are the last to be seen, diminishing until "two lessening points of light alone gleamed through the darkness" (ll. 654–655). These two points of light are so similar to the "two starry eyes" (l. 490) that both Kessel[1] and Moore[2] have assumed that they actually refer to the eyes of the vision, but a careful reading will show that they are the two points of "the divided frame of the vast meteor." (ll. 650–651). However, the similarity does make it appear that the moon has such a place in the allegorical system and that when man dies his ideals die with him. At least, there is no assurance that they will be found in death.

The conclusion to the poem is a lament that such a surpassing spirit is lost forever to the world. Mueschke and Griggs find in this section a reference to Wordworth and believe that he is the prototype of the poet throughout the poem. But they suppose that the "one living man" the "vessel of deathless wrath" (ll. 677–678) refers to Shelley's older contemporary.[3] A careful reading of this passage with its allusions to "Medea's wondrous alchemy" which restored old Æson to youth (ll. 672–675) and to "the dream of dark magician" searching for the elixir of eternal life (ll. 681–686), will show that Shelley is speaking here of someone having the gift of everlasting life, that gift being a curse. Quite

1. Marcel Kessel, "The Poet in Shelley's *Alastor*, a Criticism," *PMLA*, LI (1936), 308n.
2. T. V. Moore, *Percy Bysshe Shelley,* an Introduction to the Study of Character (Princeton: Psychological Review Company, 1922), p. 17.
3. *Op. cit.*, p. 230.

obviously this is a reference to the wandering Jew, a figure he used more than once in his poetry. Nor does the theme of the poem apply to Shelley's criticism of Wordsworth, which was concerned with his desertion of the liberal cause.

A more popular interpretation is that the entire poem is autobiographical—that "the over-idealistic poet as described in both the Preface and the poem is undoubtedly Shelley."[4] Now, it cannot be denied that the youth of the poem has a number of characteristics in common with his creator. Attempting to exhibit a character greatly to be admired, possessing but one tragic flaw, Shelley draws largely upon the ideals by which he attempted to pattern his own life and in so doing shows great sympathy and perhaps, at times, even identification with his creation. In this sense we might say that there are autobiographical elements in the poem. But to say that the portrait of this solitary, whose one weakness was a neglect of human sympathy, is a self-criticism of the man who, from the early *Queen Mab* to the mature *Philosophical View of Reform*, waged war against social injustice, and who confessed to have "a passion for reforming the world,"[5] such an attitude is to lose sight of either the character of the author or the theme of the poem. Certainly, if *Epipsychidion* is autobiographical, it cannot be said that Shelley searched for love only in the ideal worlds of sleep and death! We must conclude that the poem deals largely with a problem rather than an actual person—the temptation of the idealist to live a solitary life rather than find partial ideals of love and human companionship in this present world.

The fact that the poem ends on a despairing note rather than with some hint of the theme, which in a cooler moment Shelley discusses in the Preface, would suggest that in the white heat of poetic creation his sympathies with the youth forced him to stress the tragic loss of such a surpassing spirit rather than the central thought of the poem. He may have recognized this weakness when he wrote the Preface.

In conclusion, we cannot agree with Havens that "The poem is not a unity, it does not produce a single impression, it was not the offspring of a single, dominating purpose."[6] Although the poem does not have the balance which some might wish, it is a unity and does have structure, the loose structure of a progressive development of a central theme. And from this theme he does not deviate throughout the poem.

4. N. I. White, *Shelley*, I, 419. Professor White has recently informed me, however, that he did not intend this statement to be understood as a complete interpretation of the poem. It should, therefore, be regarded only as a concise statement of the opinion to be found in a number of recent critical works, e.g., Hoffman, *op. cit.*, or Carl H. Grabo, *The Magic Plant; the Growth of Shelley's Thought* (Chapel Hill: University of North Carolina Press, 1936).

5. Preface to *Prometheus Unbound*.

6. *Op. cit.*, p. 1109.

Apparently, however certain Shelley was in 1821 of his words on idealism:

> . . . Die,
> If thou wouldst be with that which thou dost seek!
> Follow where all is fled—   (*Adonais*, ll. 464–466)

in 1815 when he wrote *Alastor* . . . , he was not at all sure that man's ideals had any returnable value beyond the very important ones of love and sympathy in this present life. It is better to "arrest the faintest shadow" of that love here[7] than to try to find it in a future life which may not exist.

CHARLES H. VIVIAN

The One "Mont Blanc"[†]

The fullest published analysis of Shelley's "Mont Blanc" is a study by I. J. Kapstein which appeared in 1947. Professor Kapstein finds in the poem equivocations and ambiguities—not of the functional, Empsonian variety, but rather inadvertent ambiguities, reflecting a conflict or uncertainty in Shelley's own mind. This uncertainty Professor Kapstein identifies with Shelley's wavering between Liberty and Necessity, or between a conception of the human mind as a free, creative thing and the doctrine of radical empiricism that the mind is nothing but the sum of its sensations.[1] I believe that a different reading is possible: that the element of conflict or struggle in the poem may be interpreted in different terms, and that the poem itself can be shown to be self-consistent.

According to my reading, the conflict between the two conceptions of the mind is not a real problem in the poem. On this issue, at the time when he wrote "Mont Blanc," Shelley had taken a position. It was different from his earlier position, the thoroughgoing empiricism of *Queen Mab*; and it was different from his later position, the thoroughgoing idealism of *Prometheus Unbound*; but within the limits of this one poem, "Mont Blanc," it was fixed and definite. It was, in fact, a perfect mid-point between the other two positions. I shall come back to this matter in a moment, when I turn to the text of the poem and try to prove my contentions. Meanwhile, what kind of conflict or struggle *is* a real problem in the poem?

I believe that what Shelley did in "Mont Blanc"—whether his

7. *On Love, loc. cit.*
† From the *Keats-Shelley Journal*, IV (1955), pp. 55–65. Reprinted by permission of the publisher, The Keats-Shelley Association of America, Inc.
1. "The Meaning of Shelley's 'Mont Blanc,'" *PMLA*, LXII (1947), 1046–1060.

intention to do it was fully or only partly conscious—was give an account of a twofold struggle in his own experience. One element in this struggle was an almost agonizing effort to understand the real nature of the mind. The question of empiricism versus idealism, I have posited, was answered to his temporary satisfaction. But this one answer was like one of Newton's pebbles on the shore; the whole sea of truth still stretched out virtually unexplored. In this poem Shelley records an attempt to do some charting of those waters for himself; he tells how deep they are, and how difficult to sound.

The other element in this twofold struggle was an effort to understand something else. Here again I diverge sharply from Professor Kapstein's interpretation. In his view the chief symbol in the poem, the mountain peak itself, represents Necessity. Now, of course the doctrine of Necessity had been central in Shelley's thought in previous years; and it would be reasonable on *a priori* grounds to presume that this doctrine is the referent—in the poem four times called "power"—of the Mont Blanc symbol. In the poem itself, however, there is nothing which clearly establishes this relationship. I believe that the mountain represents something else—that something else which Shelley was struggling to understand.

Precisely what this something else was, is difficult to say in unfigurative prosaic language; but perhaps a tentative explanation may be given as follows. Shelley's theory of knowledge at this time was a compromise between empiricism and idealism; he was, so to speak, half an empiricist and half an idealist. He was enough of an empiricist so that in trying to get his questions answered he looked ordinarily to sense experience. But he was enough of an idealist so that a problem posed in a non-empirical way might be for him a real problem. A particular problem *was* posed in such a way: he had an intuitive awareness of something permanent, something apart from the flux of sense experience. Now, this kind of awareness is difficult to refine. Intuition, though it may carry strong conviction, is an elusive thing. One may wish fervently to get more of the kind of light which it has given; one may try by his own will to turn it on—but, for the most part anyway, it simply shineth where it listeth. And the other, the ordinary source of knowledge is of little help here: it is difficult or virtually impossible to learn from common experience about that which is apart from common experience. With this particular intuition—this awareness that Shelley had of something permanent—the effect of transitory experience was rather more to obscure it than to cast further light upon it. Here, then, was the problem: to come to any real understanding of the permanent and the single, with nothing to go on but elusive intuition on the one hand and fleeting, multifarious experience on the other. It is this problem that the mountain represents in the poem; or, to speak more precisely, Mont Blanc symbolizes this principle of permanence of which Shelley has awareness and which he is trying to understand. I believe that this phrase, Principle of Permanence, is the best definition that we can give for the referent of the symbol. A short phrase like this will be convenient, in any case—and perhaps its meaning will become clearer—in the following examination of the poem.

Shelley divides the poem into five sections. Sections I and II are devoted chiefly to the first element in his twofold struggle: here he describes his attempt to understand his own mind. At the very outset he gives expression to his compromise theory of knowledge. First comes a brief suggestion of how experience functions in the doctrine of empiricism—"The everlasting universe of things/ Flows through the mind" (lines 1,2)—and then a statement that the mind makes its own independent contribution to consciousness:

> from secret springs
> The source of human thought its tribute brings
> Of waters,—*with a sound but half its own.* (4–6)

I italicize the last phrase because it succinctly characterizes Shelley's epistemological position. The mind neither gives nor takes exclusively; it does both in equal degree—and the product of these operations, consciousness, is quite literally "half its own." Whatever the validity of this position, it is the one which Shelley not only takes at the beginning but maintains throughout the poem. The other passages in which he touches on the same issue, as we shall see later, are consistent with this first one.

It should be noted here that the word "secret" in line 4 introduces a suggestion that the mind, the "source of human thought," is mysterious and difficult of access. The theme of the difficulty of introspection is to be expressed more fully a little farther along in the poem. Meanwhile, the remainder of Section I simply expands by a simile the statement of the epistemological compromise—the mind's having "a sound but half its own."[2]

2. It has been suggested to me that the image presented in this simile implies a compromise somewhat less than fair and equal: "The source of human thought," or the mind, is represented only by a feeble brook; the environment, by a whole combination of waterfalls, woods, winds, and a vast river. I believe, however, that this implication need not be taken. The role of the mind is represented by the sound of the brook. Ordinarily we should consider the sound of a brook as being entirely "its own"; in this context, the imposing combination of other sounds is not greater than what is really necessary to support the idea that the brook itself contributes as little as "only half" to its own sound. The simile is apt: either the brook in the wilderness or the mind in its environment is in one sense almost infinitesimal; and yet, in terms of the auditory image here presented, the compromise between the brook and its surroundings remains fair and equal. The same is true, then, of the mind and its environment.

A simile is sufficient for this, which is no real problem anyway. To express what *is* a real problem—the struggle to understand something further, something about the ultimate nature of the mind—Shelley uses a more elaborate figure: a full-scale symbol. Section I has served another purpose in addition to what we have noted already: it has set the stage for the establishment of this symbol in Section II. The universe of things flows through the mind, and the river Arve flows through its Ravine. In Section I there were "secret springs" of thought, mysterious and obscure; in Section II there is a "dark, deep Ravine" (line 12). This Ravine is a

> many-colored, many-voiced vale,
> Over whose pines, and crags, and caverns sail
> Fast cloud-shadows and sunbeams.   (13–15)

The Ravine is the mind, its "caverns echoing to the Arve's commotion" (line 30)—and so of course the principal symbol of sensation or experience is the river; the shifting lights and shadows in line 15 are minor and supplementary symbols for the ever-changing play of sensations. The "pines, and crags, and caverns" are another group of supplementary symbols; these represent the mind itself or the thoughts in the mind. And once again there is mutual give-and-take between the mind and its environment. Not only do the caverns echo to the sound of the river; not only is the Ravine "pervaded with that ceaseless motion" and "the path of that unresting sound" (lines 32, 33); but also the pines are

> Children of elder time, in whose devotion
> The chainless winds still come and ever came
> To drink their odors, and their mighty swinging
> To hear—an old and solemn harmony.   (21–24)

That is to say, under the figure of scent and sound, that the mind gives something to its environment in return.

Just as in Section I the stage was set for the establishment of the Ravine symbol in Section II, so in this latter section comes the first mention of Power, and the preparation for the later development of the Mont Blanc symbol. The Ravine is an

>   awful scene,
> Where Power in likeness of the Arve comes down
> From the ice-gulfs that gird his secret throne.   (15–17)

Now, it might seem that here is a confusion in the symbolism. The river Arve stands for sense experience; why then should we have "*Power* in likeness of the Arve"? The reason is as follows. True, this Power is to appear later in a symbolic likeness, the mountain peak; but, strictly speaking—and without this symbolism, which has not yet been established—it cannot appear in its own likeness. The Principle of Permanence is not manifested to mortal man, in the midst of his ever-changing sensations, except by intuition. All he can actually contemplate is experience; if he is able to intuit anything about the Principle, the latter can appear to him only as "Power in likeness of the Arve." The next two lines carry on the same idea: the river comes

> Bursting through these dark mountains like the flame
> Of lightning through the tempest. (18,19)

The only real illumination that experience brings into the mind, the only help toward this elusive intuition, is like lightning in a storm. Flashes of insight there are, but thy are fitful, and of only an instant's duration; by their light we can see only in momentary glimpses. A similar suggestion is made once more, a few lines farther on. The Ravine has its

> earthly rainbows stretched across the sweep
> Of the ethereal waterfall, whose veil
> Robes some unsculptured image. (25-27)

The waterfall—made up, of course, of the waters of experience—robes something behind it as with a veil. Under these circumstances, for anyone actually to perceive what lies behind would perhaps not be impossible, but it would be extremely difficult. Here is the problem: to understand the Permanent behind the transitory. The second major problem in the poem has been briefly registered in Section II; its full expression will come later.

Meanwhile, in the remainder of the section, Shelley returns to his first problem and completes its development. Here once more I differ with Professor Kapstein. In this latter part of Section II, if I do not misunderstand him, he regards the Ravine as just a ravine: ". . . the poet's mind," he says, ". . . wandering over the landscape of the Ravine finally settles down to re-creation of the scene in poetry."[3] But the Ravine must be more than just a ravine, on two counts. First, the Ravine has already been clearly established as a symbol of the mind; and, second, at this very juncture the connection is established again:

> Dizzy Ravine! . . . when I gaze on thee,
> I seem as in a trance sublime and strange
> To muse on my own separate fantasy,
> My own, my human mind. (34-37)

When Shelley looks at the Ravine, he thinks of his own mind: here is association of ideas by similarity, which keys in once more

3. P. 1051.

the symbolic identity. Now, this reinforced identification is not important in the next few lines, for Shelley simply goes on to talk about the mind, without employing the symbol. Incidentally, he expresses once again the idea of mutual give-and-take between the external world and the mind:

> my human mind, which passively[4]
> Now renders and receives fast influencings,
> Holding an unremitting interchange
> With the clear universe of things around.　　(37–40)

But the symbolic relationship becomes essential in what follows. By a kind of distributive metonymy the mind now appears as

> One legion of wild thoughts, whose wandering wings
> Now float above thy darkness [i.e., the Ravine's], and now rest
> Where that or thou art no unbidden guest,
> In the still cave of the witch Poesy.　　(41–44)

The mind, the "legion of wild thoughts," may sometimes dwell upon things which are not so mysterious and obscure ("now float above thy darkness"); but sometimes it plunges into a realm of deeper speculation ("the still cave of the witch Poesy")—of speculation which may ultimately be recorded in poetry, even in just such a poem as this one, "Mont Blanc." What kind of speculation is this? It is a realm "Where that or thou art no unbidden guest." And what are "that" and "thou"? They are "thy darkness"[5] and "thou [Ravine]" respectively: in terms of the clearly established symbolism, the mind and its mystery. In other words, sometimes the mind contemplates the mind itself.

And this kind of contemplation is peculiarly difficult, because its object is so elusive. In this pursuit the mind must be struggling and groping,

> Seeking among the shadows that pass by—
> Ghosts of all things that are—some shade of thee
> 　　[thou Ravine, thou human mind],
> Some phantom, some faint image.　　(45–47)[6]

4. For Professor Kapstein (p. 1050) the word "passively" makes an epistemological ambiguity: unless its force is taken to be sharply limited by the word "Now," it implies that the whole "unremitting interchange" in line 39 is always entirely involuntary on the part of the mind—that the entire content of the mind is derivative. In my reading of the passage, a passive rendering is still a rendering, still an independent contribution to consciousness. The pines were passive as the wind swept over them, but the odor which they gave was their own.

5. Here again I differ with Professor Kapstein (p. 1051), who believes the antecedent of "that" to be Shelley's mind, the "legion of wild thoughts."
6. Here, it seems to me, is indisputable proof that in this passage the Ravine must still be regarded as standing for the mind (as object of the mind's contemplation). Otherwise, how can these lines make sense? Why should it be necessary for the contemplating mind to struggle and grope for a shade, a phantom, a faint image, if its object is only a landscape or a scene?

There need be nothing cryptic or ambiguous in the words which follow immediately, "till the breast/From which they fled recalls them, thou art there!" (lines 47–48). The antecedent of "they" is the shadows and ghosts of lines 45 and 46. These are the elusive traces of the mind's mysterious operations: shadows of subliminal mental activity, and ghosts—i.e., reflections or Lockean "ideas"— of "all things that are" in the objective external world. "Till the breast from which they fled recalls them"—that is, as long as the introspecting mind keeps them before itself as objects of active contemplation, and until it allows them to slip back into its own mysterious depths—"thou [Ravine] art there": the mind is there, accessible to examination, or as accessible as it ever can be. But shadowy and ghostly the evidence is; and it is the only evidence available to the mind, the only thing it has to go on, in this examination of itself. The elusive and tenuous nature of the material is what makes introspection so difficult.

On this note Section II ends. Shelley has not arrived at any conclusion about the ultimate nature of the mind. But "Mont Blanc" is not a poem in which the problems are solved. Rather, it is a poem about the very experience of coming to grapple with the problems, and about the nature of the evidence available for dealing with them. If the analogy is not too grotesque, one might compare the poem to a preliminary bibliographical study—not a substantive study—of certain problems in introspective psychology and metaphysics. Perhaps the chief conclusion at which Shelley arrives is that the attempt to solve these problems is necessarily a struggle.

On this same note Section III begins. Now Shelley is about to describe his experience in a different—although a related—realm of speculation; and at the beginning of this account he tells how unsure the footing will seem to be. He looks up at Mont Blanc. Is the intuition represented by this symbol a valid insight into the nature of things, or is his whole experience nothing but a dream? Engrossed in such speculation, the mind feels as helpless and confused as in a dream:

> I look on high;
> Has some unknown Omnipotence unfurled
> The veil of life and death? or do I lie
> In dream, and does the mightier world of sleep
> Spread far around and inaccessibly
> Its circles? for the very spirit fails,
> Driven like a homeless cloud from steep to steep
> That vanishes among the viewless gales!   (52–59)

The mountain is there, the Principle of Permanence—

> Far, far above, piercing the infinite sky,
> Mont Blanc appears,—still, snowy and serene.   (60,61)

But what lies between the mountain and the observer looking up at it? That is, what lies between the Principle and the mind groping toward some understanding of it? All the chaotic welter of experience. Such is the symbolic meaning of the description in lines 62–75, ending with the fanciful questions to which "None can reply."

Now follows the passage in which are made explicit the implications of this relationship between the Permanent and the transitory. "The wilderness has a mysterious tongue"—and the wilderness is the total scene which has just been presented, the single peak above and the chaos all around below it—

> The wilderness has a mysterious tongue
> Which teaches awful doubt, or faith so mild,
> So solemn, so serene, that man may be
> But for such faith with Nature reconciled.   (76–79)

How will it be determined which of the two lessons, doubt or faith, the wilderness will teach to a particular observer? Where he focuses his attention and what he sees is what will make the difference. If he looks at the chaos and not at the peak—if he cannot see past the distracting welter of experience and intuit the Principle beyond—then he will fall into skepticism about the meaning of life itself. If, on the other hand, while of course perceiving the flow of experience, he can discern the Principle and recognize its significance, then he will see all things *sub specie aeternitatis*.[7] The wilderness can teach either faith or doubt, but the mountain can teach only faith:

> Thou hast a voice, great Mountain, to repeal
> Large codes of fraud and woe.   (80,81)

These codes are evil institutions, tyrannies and injustices based upon a short-run view, upon skepticism about those eternal values which "the wise, and great, and good" (line 82) can understand.

Section IV develops further Shelley's account of his groping toward an understanding of this Principle, this One among the Many, this Permanent amidst the Mutable. There are in fact two further stages in the development, one lying within Section IV

---

7. I am reading the phrase "But for such faith" in line 79 to mean not "except for such faith" but "by means of such faith alone." This interpretation is supported by the variant "In such a faith" of the Boscombe MS. It is more reasonable to presume that Shelley made the revision to sharpen the emphasis than to think that he wished to change the meaning diametrically.

and the other running over for its climax into Section V. The first of these two begins with a general description of the cycle of nature—a description not confined to this particular scene in the Vale of Chamouni, but extended to include "all the living things that dwell/Within the daedal earth" (lines 85, 86). This passage concludes with the summary lines

> All things that move and breathe with toil and sound
> Are born and die, revolve, subside and swell.　　　(94,95)

All these things indeed are flux; but

> Power dwells apart in its tranquillity,
> Remote, serene, and inaccessible.　　　(96,97)

The significance of this juxtaposition is clear. In what has immediately preceded, the emphasis was upon cyclical change. In these last two lines, then, that aspect of the Principle which is tacitly emphasized by contrast is its unchangeableness, its permanence.[8] Another important note is struck in the epithet "inaccessible"; this, we shall see, will be picked up in the final section of the poem.

Now comes the second further stage in the development. By contrast once again, Shelley implies,

> *this*, the naked countenance of earth
> On which I gaze, even these primeval mountains,
> Teach the adverting mind.　　　(98–100)

The force of Shelley's italics in the pronoun is to indicate that now he is focusing once more on the foreground, the welter of chaos. He is looking not at *that* single peak beyond but at *this* naked countenance of earth and *these* primeval mountains, or foothills (called "subject mountains" in line 62 above). And what do these things "teach the adverting mind"? The lesson of Mutability. The most vivid description in the poem, and symbolically the most effective, is the passage which continues all through the remainder of Section IV (lines 100–126). Here, change is not something cyclical and evolutionary; rather, it is a titanic force aptly symbolized by the slow but utterly irresistible movement of a glacier. Before this "flood of ruin" (line 107) vast pines and rocks are swept, and even

> 　　　　　The race
> Of man flies far in dread; his work and dwelling
> Vanish, like smoke before the tempest's stream,
> And their place is not known.　　　(117–120)

---

8. Professor Kapstein believes, consistently with his whole analysis of the poem, that the fundamental aspect here is Necessity (pp. 1056, 1057). But, once again, the context seems to me to suggest a different interpretation. That which is *not* born and does *not* die, and which neither revolves, subsides, nor swells, is thereby virtually defined as the permanent.

Following immediately after this descriptive passage—in a juxta-position which is even more dramatic than the one we noted a moment ago, and which therefore emphasizes the implicit contrast even more strongly—the mountain appears again:

> Mont Blanc yet gleams on high: the power is there,
> The still and solemn power of many sights
> And many sounds, and much of life and death.   (127–129)

Yes, Shelley assures himself, the Principle does have being. Despite the chaos of experience, despite the constant change in the cycle of nature, despite the flood of ruin that is mutability, "the power is there"—the power of or the Principle behind the sights and sounds and all the sensations of transitory human life. The intuition represented by the Mont Blanc symbol *is* a valid insight.

But this Principle is like the human mind, in one way: real understanding of it is virtually impossible to gain. In Section IV it was called "inaccessible"; now in Section V the same idea is registered more fully. The Principle does have being, but the mode of that being is mysterious to man. The snows fall on the mountain, but "none beholds them there" (line 132); the winds blow, but in effect they are silent, for no one perceives them either. The springs that fed the source of human thought, the mind, were secret; the Principle too is secret, "the secret strength of things" (line 139).[9] Here again is the central theme of difficulty in these speculations.

But the difficulty must be faced. Here is the force of the last three lines of the poem:[1]

> And what were thou, and earth, and stars, and sea,
> If to the human mind's imaginings
> Silence and solitude were vacancy?   (142–144)

If the human mind did not, in silence and solitude, plunge into these realms of speculation, and pursue its way until finally it came upon these insights and intuitions—then, in effect, the Principle itself ("thou") would have no significance. Neither would

---

9. Here I may perhaps anticipate the strongest criticism of my interpretation. The phraseology here and in the next two lines—

> The secret strength of things,
> Which governs thought, and to the infinite dome
> Of heaven is as a law, inhabits thee!
> (139–141)

may seem to suggest that Necessity is a better referent for the Mont Blanc symbol than my Principle of Permanence. But I believe that the suggestion is not irresistible. The Principle is above experience; it is apart from all the things of which we have ordinary knowledge, including even the heavens themselves. But it alone imparts to these things the only real significance they can have; only when they are conceived under its aspect do they have ultimate meaning. The Principle may, then, not inappropriately be called "the secret strength of things"; as an ordering and synthesizing principle it is like eternal law. And conversely, since an intuitive recognition of it is a necessary basis for all correct interpretation of experience, since only "the wise, and great, and good" who apprehend it can properly understand all other things, it governs the only true thought in the world.

1. It will be sufficiently apparent that I disagree with Professor Kapstein's belief that these lines are anticlimatic (pp. 1057, 1058).

any of our ordinary experience, with the common objects of knowledge ("earth, and stars, and sea"). If no human imaginings ever went this far, there would be no apprehension of the Principle; and without this apprehension no ultimate meaning would be perceived in anything. Faith would never be learned, and the codes of fraud and woe would never be repealed. Like the quest for understanding of the human mind, the quest for understanding of the Principle is necessarily a struggle. The goal is virtually inaccessible; and the means that we ordinarily depend on to help us toward knowledge— our sense experience—can help us little here. Still, Shelley says, he has had a glimpse of the goal—and he gives an account of some of his gropings toward it.

Shelley himself called "Mont Blanc" "an undisciplined overflowing of the soul." Perhaps he was somewhat unkind to his own poem. It is not so tightly knit in form as a satire by Donne, but neither is it by any means completely amorphous. Shelley discusses two problems—or rather, strictly speaking, he discusses his own experience in grappling with them. The problems are related by their both lying in the realms of abstruse speculation—by the common theme of difficulty or struggle. The poem as an organic structure is further integrated by its imagery and its organization. The two central symbols, the mountain peak above and the Ravine below, are carefully established and systematically employed. The five sections of the poem have various unifying cross-relationships. Sections I and II, which develop the first problem, are interlocked by the preparation for and establishment of the Ravine symbol. Section II includes an anticipatory registration of the second problem. Sections III, IV, and V, which are concerned chiefly with this problem, are tied together by the successive stages in its development. I have tried to show that the different statements which deal with the same issue—the relationship between the mind and its environment—are mutually consistent. "Mont Blanc" is one more illustration that the Romantic poets were sometimes more scrupulous artists than we have believed them to be.

DONALD H. REIMAN

Structure, Symbol, and Theme in "Lines written among the Euganean Hills"†

Over forty years ago Oliver Elton wrote of "Lines written among the Euganean Hills": "This poem is perfectly put together, and it is an intellectual pleasure to see its firm development, even apart

† Reprinted by permission of the Modern Language Association of America from *PMLA*, 77 (Sept. 1962), pp. 404–413.

from the rapid, impassioned, shimmering brilliancy of the imagery, which resolves itself into the emotions of the poet." One need not assent to the unqualified absolute of this declaration to recognize the poem as one worthy of serious study, yet during the last half century of intensive Shelley scholarship and criticism there has appeared little to advance our understanding of "Lines written among the Euganean Hills" beyond Professor Elton's own perceptive, but necessarily brief appreciation.[1] An examination of Shelleyana will suggest a number of reasons for this neglect by scholars of a poem that is often anthologized and frequently taught. First, Shelley criticism is a literature filled with polemicism, and "Lines written among the Euganean Hills" has never been controversial: critics and admirers of Shelley alike have conceded or declared, when they mentioned it at all, that it is a good poem. Second, its tetrameter couplets appear "uncharacteristic" of Shelley under the generalizations which govern most discussions of his poetry, thus making the poem "peripheral" to both attackers and defenders of Shelley's poetic achievement. Closely related to the problem of metrics are those of the poem's length and its date of composition: it is too long to be discussed with the lyrics, too short to qualify as a major effort, and written too early for intensive study with Shelley's late poetry. Finally, biographers have been less successful than usual in casting light on those passages—especially lines 45–65—that seem to require additional illumination before a critic can integrate the whole composition.[2]

In this paper I shall attempt to give substance to Oliver Elton's

1. *A Survey of English Literature: 1780–1830* (Second Edition, London, 1920), II, 194–195. Although there exists no complete explication of "Lines written among the Euganean Hills," useful information and incidental criticism can be found in notes to the complete editions of Shelley's poetry (especially that by C. D. Locock); in selections edited by Newman Ivey White (*The Best of Shelley*, New York, 1932), Ellsworth Barnard (*Shelley: Selected Poems, Essays, and Letters*, New York, 1944), Frederick L. Jones (*Percy Bysshe Shelley: Selected Poems*, New York, 1956); in biographies by Carl Grabo (*The Magic Plant*, Chapel Hill, N.C., 1936), Newman Ivey White (*Shelley*, London, 1947), Edmund Blunden (*Shelley: A Life Story*, London, 1946); and in critical studies by Carlos Baker (*Shelley's Major Poetry*, Princeton, 1948), Peter Butter (*Shelley's Idols of the Cave*, Edinburgh, 1954), Milton Wilson (*Shelley's Later Poetry*, New York, 1959), and Desmond King-Hele (*Shelley: His Thought and Work*, London, 1960).

2. Although we have very scant information about the composition of "Lines written among the Euganean Hills," we know that it was begun at Este early in October 1818 and completed at Naples sometime before 20 December 1818, during most of which period Shelley was occupied either in society (with Byron and the Hoppners in Venice, 11–31 October), in travel (from Este to Rome, 5–20 November and from Rome to Naples, 27–29 November), or in sight-seeing. Mary Shelley tells us that " 'Rosalind and Helen,' and 'Lines written among the Euganean Hills,' I found among his papers by chance; and with some difficulty urged him to complete them" (*Poetical Works*, ed. Mrs. Shelley, London, 1839, I, xi). Shelley himself alludes to the poem only in the "Advertisement" to the *Rosalind and Helen* volume and in two letters: to Peacock, April 1819, and to Ollier, postmarked in England 3 August 1819 (*The Complete Works of Percy Bysshe Shelley*, Julian Edition, ed. Roger Ingpen and Walter E. Peck, London and New York, 1926–30, X, 48, 63).

claim for "Lines written among the Euganean Hills." I shall first outline the symmetry of the poem's structure and then overlay this x-ray with the flesh and blood of the poem, its allusions, images, and figures, relating these and showing how theme or meaning grows naturally out of texture, architecture, and even prosody.

"Lines written among the Euganean Hills" falls into three well-defined movements, with the middle one of these again divisible into three. The opening three verse-paragraphs or strophes (ll. 1–89) depict first the predicament of human life and then the poet's temporary release from its painful contemplation one morning in the Euganean Hills. In the seven paragraphs of the second movement the prophet-bard, who in his own imaginative release from the limitations of common humanity is able to view clearly and perceptively the destinies of other men, gazes on Venice, both home and symbol of men sunk into moral depravity (ll. 90–166), and on Padua, symbol of the inevitable destruction that follows moral decay to prepare the way for healthy rebirth (ll. 206–284). The fourth verse-paragraph of this movement—the central paragraph of the poem (ll. 167–205)—idealizes Byron as the Poet, the man of imagination, who alone is able to save Venice (and thus mankind) from its fate. The final three strophes (ll. 285–373) record, with the return of night, the end of the poet's brief respite from the darkness of human suffering and announce his hope for the renewal in himself and extension to all men of the calm and order that his soul has known this day. When we divide the second movement into its three subdivisions, the five parts of the poem exhibit almost pyramidal symmetry: part one, 89 lines; part two, 77 lines; part three, 39 lines; part four, 79 lines; part five, 89 lines.

I

The poem opens with the metaphor—a favorite one with Shelley —of life as a voyage over a dangerous sea of time-mortality.[3] But the traditional metaphor is here extended and explored to reveal more about the human condition than its uncertainty: the human mariner has control over neither his past—which closes immediately and irrevocably behind him (ll. 7–8)—nor his future. Above him heavy clouds keep out the sun, symbol of divine energy and illumination, while behind him winds of Necessity drive him violently,

3. Cf. Earl R. Wasserman, *The Subtler Language* (Baltimore, 1959), pp. 314–315. See also Shelley's lyric "Time," which begins, "Unfathomable Sea! whose waves are years" (*Complete Poetical Works of Percy Bysshe Shelley*, ed. Thomas Hutchinson, London, 1934, p. 637. All quotations and references to Shelley's poetry are to this edition [*Poetical Works*].) I shall confine my discussion to the particular manifestations of the boat-sea-voyage-island complex of symbols in "Lines written among the Euganean Hills" and their appropriateness as vehicles of the poem's theme. For the persistence of this symbolic complex throughout Shelley's poetry, see Carl Grabo, *The Magic Plant*, and Neville Rogers, *Shelley at Work* (Oxford, 1956).

almost immersing him in the purely mortal world until his ship "sinks down, down, like that sleep/When the dreamer seems to be/Weltering through eternity" (ll. 16–18). The simile compares this symbolic drowning in the merely temporal to that ordinary, though unpleasant, psychological phenomenon in which a sleeper dreams of falling endlessly through space. The unpleasant connotations of "weltering" suggest that even a life beyond some of the more obvious limitations of temporal existence may not bring the peace for which man's heart yearns. The simile thus prepares us for the "divided will" which leaves man uncertain whether he is to seek or shun the grave.

Shelley, his academic scepticism clearly operative, does not speculate whether or not there is personal immortality but asks whether, given the unsatisfactory conditions of human life, it makes any *difference* if in the grave "no heart will meet/His with love's impatient beat" (ll. 28–29). If man cannot hope to find in this life escape from his misery "in friendship's smile, in love's caress," then " 'twill wreak him little woe" whether or not these comforts await him after death; at least his suffering will be at an end (ll. 30–44). Thus, when it has been compared with the dark alternative of temporal life, death has assumed a relatively positive aspect. From the phrase "haven of the grave" (l. 26) onward the implication is clear that, were it not for "many a green isle," death and oblivion would be preferable to mortal existence.[4]

All the evidence advanced in the first verse-paragraph is a necessary elaboration and defense of its first four lines:

> Many a green isle needs must be
> In the deep wide sea of Misery,
> Or the mariner, worn and wan,
> Never thus could voyage on—

The human voyager, worn by his struggles to keep above the waves that seek to engulf him and "wan" because separated from the vivifying sunlight, must find moments of respite from his struggle, green isles where he can see the sun and chart his course unhindered by earlier mistakes and regrets, whose cold winds otherwise make death and oblivion the better choice.

The second paragraph describes a death that *was* better than life, the death of Shelley's immediate past. For one trying to interpret lines 45–65, three elements of the opening description require special attention: the "northern sea"; the "seven dry bones"; the absence of any lament for "him . . . Who once clothed with life and thought" the heap of bones. If the dry bones were those of Fanny Godwin, Harriet, or Shelley's infant daughter Clara, it

---

4. Cf. "Julian and Maddalo," ll. 315–319, 494–499.

would hardly be accurate to describe this person's fate as un-lamented, inasmuch as Shelley would, in the very act of describing the tragic death of such a loved one, be lamenting that fate. The spirit of the dead person is, moreover, clearly masculine (ll. 62–65),[5] although study of the biographical evidence has yielded no man whose literal death Shelley might at this time have mourned. As White points out, "the only death that Shelley commonly spoke of as unlamented was his own."[6] Again, it seems unlikely that Shelley would describe the Adriatic even in its northernmost ex-tremity as a "northern sea." If an actual locale was intended, he probably referred to a beach at least as far north as the British Isles; but a "northern sea," distant from the direct rays of the sun, could symbolize a state of human existence like that described in the first paragraph of the poem—dark and unrelated to the cosmic inspiration that alone can make human life meaningful.

The passage becomes clear and integral to the poem only, I think, when we view it as primarily symbolic. Shelley is not alluding to a literal heap of unburied dry bones, as the otherwise inexpli-cable number seven should warn us. He is instead figuratively describing the end of the life he left behind him in England. The seven bones symbolize the seven years between his expulsion from Oxford (March 1811) and his final departure from England (March 1818). Every biographer of Shelley will agree that, how-ever valuable these years and their experiences were in educating him and laying the foundation of his future greatness, they were in themselves extremely painful, both to Shelley and to those he loved. One has only to catalogue the successive mistakes, frustra-tions, and disappointments of this period to realize how regrettable they must have appeared to the poet in retrospect, whether he regarded himself as an innocent victim or as a guilty agent. Such a catalogue will at the same time rescue from the charge of senti-mentality the pessimistic view of human life found in the poem's first forty-four lines.[7] The symbolic death of Shelley's past was necessary before the poet could hope to reach one of those green isles.

Thus, Shelley describes his old self as lying dead on a tempest-torn beach. This dead life is "unburied" (l. 60) because its effects

5. Newman Ivey White apparently be-lieves (*Shelley*, II, 41) that ll. 62–65 apply to Shelley but that ll. 47–49 do not. This leaves as a problem the ante-cedent of "what" in l. 65. "What now moves nor murmurs not" must be the "unburied bones" of l. 60 and thus those of ll. 47–49. For White's earlier view, which more nearly corresponds to mine, see *The Best of Shelley*, p. 478. Other suggestions for interpreting the passage can be found in *The Explicator*: by the

Editors (I, October 1942, 5), who follow White's *Best of Shelley*, and by Louise Schutz Boas (III, November 1944, 14), who thinks that the "wretch" who is the subject of the lines is Frankenstein's creation, dead and abandoned in the Arctic wastes.
6. *Shelley*, II, 41.
7. Cf. "Julian and Maddalo," ll. 320–337, where a less restrained recounting of griefs is prepared for by the dramatic character of the speaker.

still haunt the poet; the whirlwind that howls around it like the voices from a "slaughtered town" points backward to the tempests that drive the human mariner across the temporal sea and points forward to the poem's second movement, where moral Necessity as it is operative in human society will become the primary theme. At this point the wind symbolizes the chains of cause and effect that emanate from the past life of the poet, producing "many a mournful sound" about those yet unforgotten years. The spirit that "once clothed with life and thought" this dead existence is, however, unmourned because in the developmental pattern of the poem that spirit is neither dead nor living. The poet, after passing through the "everlasting no" of the first paragraph, has reached a "center of indifference" through the death of his regrettable past. His spirit is drifting with the tide of consciousness in the pre-dawn darkness.

The third and final strophe of the first movement confirms what was posited at the beginning of the poem as a necessary condition for continuation of human life: "Ay, many flowering islands lie/In the waters of wide Agony" (ll. 66–67). The sunrise pictured in the ensuing description, like all the finest passages in Shelley, is made to exist simultaneously in an external scene and, analogically, in the symbolic world of the poem. At the literal surface a flock of rooks sing a paean to the rising sun even as they take flight and disappear, following the sun-dispersed morning mist into the distance where their cawing is inaudible. The symbolic significance of the birds themselves is clear from Shelley's only other poetic use of the word "rooks":

> Like a flock of rooks at a farmer's gun
> Night's dreams and terrors, every one,
> Fled from the brains which are their prey
> From the lamp's death to the morning ray.
> ("The Boat on the Serchio," ll. 26–29)

Thus on this morning the sun, symbol of divine energy on the cosmic level and the imagination on the human level,[8] disperses both the light-distorting mists that darken men's minds and the "dreams and terrors" that afflict men during their periods of separation from divine illumination; yet these very birds of ill-omen hail the rising of the divinity that is their ultimate source. Aloft

8. Cf. Shelley's "Proposed Letter to the Editor of the Literary Miscellany" in answer to Peacock's "The Four Ages of Poetry" (March 1821): "He would extinguish Imagination which is the Sun of life, and grope his way by the cold and uncertain and borrowed light of that moon which he calls Reason, stumbling over the interlunar chasm of time where she deserts us, and an owl, rather than an eagle, stare with dazzled eyes on the watery orb which is the Queen of his pale Heaven" (Julian Edition, X, 246).

with their black wings appearing "all hoar" in the mist (black seems white in the distorted realm of merely human knowledge), they fly "like gray shades" until the sun bursts over the eastern horizon. Then, as evening clouds borrow colors ("fire and azure") from the sun's last rays, the purple plumage of the birds gleams "with drops of golden rain" as they pass out of hearing, till "all is bright, and clear, and still,/Round the solitary hill" (ll. 88–89). The poet, released in part from the meaningless clamor and false colors of his own limited and divided mind, is ready to experience, in the silence and clarity of a moment of imaginative insight, a universe in which his private and social moral endeavors find their unified significance.

To recapitulate the progression of the poem's first movement: the initial paragraph articulated the problem of human life: what is it that sustains men through the trials and sorrows of this temporal existence when death promises at least an end to their sufferings? The second and third strophes answered that, when one can banish bitter memories of the past, there can come upon the spirit with a fine suddenness moments of brightness, clarity, and calm silence. The remainder of the poem will demonstrate how, within these best and happiest moments, the poet's more-than-human powers of imagination make him the prophet and legislator of the world.

II

The Euganean Hills become, in the second movement of the poem, a metaphorical island amid the green sea of the Lombard plain (ll. 90–93).[9] The first sight that claims the poet's attention as he gazes toward the east is Venice, described successively as "ocean's nursling," "a peopled labyrinth," and "Amphitrite's destined halls." The first and third of these phrases allude to the relationship of Venice to the sea in the past ("Ocean's child, and then his queen," l. 116) and in the future ("And thou soon must be his prey," l. 118); Venice, which has been the child of the sea and, metaphorically, his bride (as was once annually celebrated in the ceremony of the *Sposalizio del Mare*), is destined to perish beneath the waves, to become a home for the creatures that obey Amphitrite and her lord. The phrase "peopled labyrinth" depicts the present state of Venice and her relationship to the sea. Because Minos failed to sacrifice the bull that Poseidon had given him, the sea-god caused Pasiphaë, wife of Minos, to fall in love with the bull, from which union was born the Minotaur, half-man and half-bull. It was to house this creature that Minos directed Daedalus to construct the Cretan Labyrinth. Venice, like Minos, misused

9. Cf. "Julian and Maddalo," ll. 76–79.

the gifts of the sea, and, as a result, her people, too, have degenerated to the level of animals.[1]

The associations of Venice with the sea are sharply contrasted to those of Venice with the burning sun that, rising behind it, silhouettes the city. Its buildings seem to "shine like obelisks of fire" within "a furnace bright." Moving beyond the obvious implications of the purification of gold by fire, the poet describes the spires of the city flickering "from the altar of dark ocean" toward the sky, as flames of sacrifice rose from the marble shrines of the Delphic oracle: "as [if] to pierce the dome of gold/Where Apollo spoke of old" (ll. 113–114). Apollo, the god of poetry as well as lord of the sun and all light, is about to speak through his present-day oracle, the poet, who watches Venice tested by the fires of truth and sees the dross purged away.

There is, in fact, little except dross left within the city, as both the "peopled labyrinth" and the symbolic combustibility of every "column, tower, and dome, and spire" (ll. 104–110) would indicate. Paradoxically, the "sun-girt City" has now come to a darker day; Venice, which rose from the water, to the water must return, "if the power that raised thee here/Hallow so thy watery bier." For Venice, in the second paragraph of this movement, as for the old Shelley himself in the same position of the first movement, death has come, and all that remains is burial. If the cosmic power (the Sun) is merciful, he will allow the city to hide its shame forever beneath the waves of its native element. That would be better than the sad irony of the Spouse of the Sea stooping from its island throne to the slave (Austria) of slaves (the reactionary tyrants of the Holy Alliance, slaves to their own self-will).[2]

At this point occurs a word that Shelley used only twice, the other time earlier in this same poem. Venice will be "a less drear ruin" when "the sea-mew/Flies, as once before it flew,/O'er thine isles depopulate" (ll. 121, 125–127). Shelley borrows the "sea-mew" from Milton's *Paradise Lost*, where Michael, after showing the fallen Adam the destruction of corrupt civilization in the flood, explains the extent of the deluge's ravages:

> then shall this Mount
> Of Paradise by might of Waves be mov'd
> Out of his place, push'd by the horned flood,

1. Cf. Shelley's letter to Peacock, 8 October 1818: "I had no conception of the excess to which avarice, cowardice, superstition, ignorance, passionless lust, and all the inexpressible brutalities which degrade human nature, could be carried, until I had lived a few days among the Venetians" (Julian Edition, IX, 335). Cf. also Shelley to Peacock, 6 November 1818, on the country between Este and Ferrara: "Every here and there one sees people employed in agricultural labours, and the plough, the harrow or the cart drawn by long teams of milk white or dove-coloured oxen of immense size and exquisite beauty. This indeed might be the country of Pasiphaes" (Julian Edition, IX, 338).

2. Cf. *Prometheus Unbound* II.iv.110: "All spirits are enslaved which serve things evil."

With all his verdure spoil'd, and Trees adrift
Down the great River to the op'ning Gulf,
And there take root an Island salt and bare,
The haunt of Seals and Orcs, and Sea-mews' clang.
To teach thee that God áttributes to place
No sanctity, if none be thither brought
By Men who there frequent, or therein dwell.[3]

Although the implications of this allusion for Venice are obvious, the significance of the earlier reference (l. 54) is, perhaps, less so. The crying of gulls and howling of the whirlwind provided the mournful sound on the beach of that northern sea; England, once Eden, had for Shelley become "an Island salt and bare/The haunt of Seals and Orcs, and Sea-mews' clang," and this, too, because men (himself included?) had brought to it no sanctity. As Milton implied in his lines that England stood under judgment at the hour he wrote, Shelley implicates both England and Venice in the tale of the lost paradise become the haunt of gulls. Although Venice's ruin will be *less* drear when she has returned to the sea whence she sprung and when her palace gates, overgrown with sea-flowers, are like other rocks of the Ocean, the site of the ruined city will still arouse dread in the simple fisherman, who "will spread his sail and seize his oar/Till he pass the gloomy shore" (ll. 136–137), for the moral actions of men live after them, hallowing or corrupting the scenes of their victories or their falls.

The third strophe in this movement recapitulates the moral degradation of Venice but suggests that her fate and that of her sister-cities might be changed "if Freedom should awake" and cast off "the Celtic Anarch's hold," a phrase incorporating the concepts of the barbarian and of the tyrant in rebellion against the moral laws of reason and love.[4] If the regeneration occurs,

---

3. *Paradise Lost* XI.829–838. Although Byron used "sea-mew" in "Childe Harold's Good Night" (*Childe Harold's Pilgrimage*, Canto I), there seems to be no connection between his and Shelley's use of the term beyond what is probably a common debt to Milton.

4. By "anarch" Shelley designated, as Ellsworth Barnard says, those rulers who "desecrated and trampled under foot the laws of that spiritual world to which man's higher self aspires" (*Shelley's Religion*, Minneapolis, 1937, p. 243). By "Celtic" Shelley did not mean what Matthew Arnold meant or what we mean by the word. The OED records a sharp distinction between the classical and modern meanings of "Celt": in earlier Greek writers the term was "applied to the ancient peoples of Western Europe." Whether or not "Celt" had by his time achieved wide currency in its modern, ethno-linguistic sense, Shelley clearly uses it to designate non-Graeco-Roman peoples to the north of the Mediterranean basin. That is, Celts were barbarians beyond the pale of the classical culture that was Shelley's ideal.

Cf. Shelley's other three poetic uses of "Celt" or "Celtic": "Ode to Naples," l. 173, where the "Celtic [Austrian] wolves" will flee from the "Ausonian [Italian] shepherds"; *Prometheus Unbound* II.iv.94, where the Celt and the Indian represent the farthest poles of humanity, both geographically and culturally; and "Euganean Hills," l. 223, where "Celt" refers to "the Austrian soldiery" (See *A Lexical Concordance to . . . Shelley*, compiled by F. S. Ellis, pp. 94–95). Cf. also Shelley to Peacock, 8 October 1818: "A horde of German soldiers, as vicious and more disgusting than the Venetians themselves, insult these miserable people" (Julian Edition, IX, 335).

then these cities "might adorn this sunny land," combining remembered glories of the past "with new virtues more sublime;/If not, perish thou and they!" (ll. 156–160). The cities of Italy, of which Venice is but the example, are, in their present state of degradation, "clouds which stain truth's rising day," to be consumed by the sun as were the morning mists around Shelley's mountain-island (ll. 84–89). Thus the dawn, which at the personal level scattered the vapors and the rooks that symbolized Shelley's miseries, from a social perspective represents the dawn of a new age of truth that will dissipate the clouds of ignorance and drive away the birds of vice. Out of the dust of a dead Italy will spring like flowers new nations to usher in "the world's great age."

III

We are told that the strophe on Byron (ll. 167–205) was "interpolated after the completion of the poem."[5] In the not-so-distant past, when it was believed that Shelley's poetry flowed from him without thought or plan, echoing every throb of his sensitive soul, the insertion of these lines might have been explained this way: Shelley, overbrimming with admiration and affection for Byron, wrote an enthusiastic tribute to his friend and then inserted it at this point in the poem because he had last seen Byron at Venice. Fortunately, we now understand enough of the artistic technique of Shelley to realize that these lines have really less to do with his feelings toward Byron than with his attitude toward poetry and the poet. On 22 December 1818 he wrote to Peacock of his mixed feelings on Lord Byron: "I entirely agree with what you say about Childe Harold. The spirit in which it is written is, if insane, the most wicked and mischievous insanity that ever was given forth. It is a kind of obstinate and self-willed folly, in which he hardens himself. . . . But that he is a great poet, I think the address to ocean proves."[6]

The significance of Shelley's tribute in "Lines written among the Euganean Hills" must be sought not in biographical considerations but in the artistic demands of the poem. These lines, occupying the central position in the poem's construction, integrate the various themes of the middle movement and the symbolism of the entire composition. In Shelley's symbolic universe water is emblematic of the mortal world, fire of divine, spiritual energy, dust of inert matter, and air, occupying a middle region between the

5. See the headnote to the poem, *Poetical Works*, p. 554. The manuscript of these lines (which were, of course, already an integral part of the completed version that Shelley sent to Ollier for publication) is now in the Yale University Library, as part of the collection of Professor C. B. Tinker (see *The Tinker Library*, New Haven, 1959, p. 382).

6. Julian Edition, X, 12. Cf. Shelley's other remarks to and on Byron during the months before and during the composition of "Euganean Hills": Julian Edition IX, 299, 301–305, 325–328, 334; X, 8, 10–11, 12–13; "Julian and Maddalo," Preface and ll. 48–52.

fires of heaven and the merely mortal realms, is a symbol of the intellectual and spiritual abstractions attached to the temporal world that both reveal and distort the divinity beyond. Thus, when Shelley refers to perished Venice as a "hearthless sea" (l. 168), he says that although the city may exist as a physical site, the spiritual fires that raise men above the level of beasts have all been extinguished. Let there remain, says Shelley, over this wreck, a memory (a thought, immaterial as the sky) greater in its power to hide the evil recollection of Venice than is the passing of time itself: that Byron (metaphorically represented as a swift, aspiring, beautiful bird of mournful song) "driven from his ancestral streams/By the might of evil dreams,/Found a nest in thee" (ll. 176–178). The next lines, which at the literal level refer to Byron's apostrophe to the ocean in *Childe Harold*, at the symbolic level indicate that the joy Byron experienced at Venice was of a mortal rather than a divine character: Ocean's "joy grew his" (ll. 178–183). The stream of English poetry, unending but ever mutable, lashes "many a sacred Poet's grave" (ll. 184–187), for the ongoing tradition is not always gentle to the remains of its earlier sons. (Pope at this period felt the "lashing" of many a "melodious wave.") Once again the limitations inherent in every manifestation of water are implicit, though they are not, of course, paramount here. We can paraphrase the rhetorical questions thus: what though the stream of English poetry, which is not always kind to dead poets, still mourns the exile of Byron? what though Venice, even with its great past, can now add nothing to Byron's fame as he adds to hers? what though, rather, Venice's "sins and slaveries foul/Overcloud a sunlike soul?" Venice, in its current state of degradation, has not only failed to add to the stature of Byron, but it has actually obscured and corrupted his creative genius. Even with all these reservations, Venice will still be remembered for giving refuge to the English poet. "The ghost of Homer clings/Round Scamander's wasting springs"; Homer's art has long outlived his biography, and the merely mutable waters that he immortalized shall waste away before their fame dies; "Divinest Shakespeare," like the omniscient power (symbolized in the sun) that he mirrored, "fills Avon and the world with light" (ll. 196–199); the love of Petrarch, on the other hand, is a "quenchless lamp by which the heart/Sees things unearthly" (ll. 200–203). Shelley's use of the "mirror" and the "lamp" accords exactly with the theory of Professor Abrams' book. Shelley, to fulfill the rhetorical purpose of his poem, here praises Petrarch above Shakespeare (as the order is climactic rather than chronological); whereas Shakespeare filled the world with the reflection of cosmic light, Petrarch himself burned with the fire of love that both warms *and* illumines. Reflected light is reason, but the illuminating fire of love represents the highest employment of human imagination. Like Homer Byron will remain immortal through his poetry; like Shakespeare he will illuminate the world; like Petrarch he will vivify the world with love; and like all three he will bring fame to the places with which his memory is associated.

This verse-paragraph portrays not the actual Byron but rather the ideal Byron, emancipated from all bondage to sin; Shelley may have hoped, perhaps, through the idealized portrait to bring Byron to his senses, causing the noble poet to reject his sordid companions and pastimes.[7] But it is as a symbol of poetic genius in all its manifestations that Byron shows how even the city whose destruction has been foretold by a prophet of Apollo can in part redeem its memory through hospitality to another of the divine oracles.

IV

The key image of the sections on Venice and Byron was that of fire, befitting the red blaze of sunrise. Now, when "the sun floats up the sky/Like thought-wingèd Liberty" (ll. 206–207), the imagery shifts from "fire" to "light." As the portrayal of Venice centered on wilful perversion and misuse of the Creator's gifts, so that of Padua will focus on the darkness of tyranny that is the wages of such sin.

In a transitional passage (ll. 206–213) the morning advances "till the universal light/Seems to level plain and height"; this essential equality of all things beneath the sun, the sense of brotherhood engendered by the light of "thought-wingèd Liberty," is the standard against which will be measured the social conditions of the Po Valley. Venice, meanwhile, has been swallowed up by a mist from the sea until even her reflected glory from the sun has been lost in "that gray cloud." Near the edge of the mist stands Padua, "a peopled solitude," as Venice was "a peopled labyrinth" (ll. 216, 96). In the tableau before him Shelley had used Venice to represent the city of sin; now he uses Padua to represent the city upon which retribution has already fallen, the bestial labyrinth become a desert.

Before turning to the city itself, however, Shelley describes the "harvest-shining plain" that surrounds it. Amid the great wealth of the land, what most concerns the poet is the social injustice: that "the peasant heaps his grain/In the garner of his foe" (ll. 218–

---

7. Preface to "Julian and Maddalo": "He [Maddalo-Byron] is a person of the most consummate genius, and capable, if he would direct his energies to such an end, of becoming the redeemer of his degraded country [Venice]. But it is his weakness to be proud." Mary Shelley later wrote of Shelley: "He had never read 'Wilhelm Meister,' but I have heard him say that he regulated his conduct towards his friends by a maxim which I found afterwards in the pages of Goethe —'When we take people merely as they are, we make them worse; when we treat them as if they were what they should be, we improve them as far as they can be improved'" (*Essays, Letters from Abroad, Translations and Fragments*, ed. Mrs. Shelley, London, 1840, xxiv).

219). The harvest imagery is brilliantly sustained throughout the remainder of the verse-paragraph. The creaking wagon symbolizes the unstable social structure, weighted down by the oppressions of "purple pride" (cf. ll. 221, 284). Even the "milk-white" color of the oxen that draw the wain (l. 220) may be both fact[8] and symbol, suggesting the pure white truth that plods inexorably toward the rectification of injustice. The sickle that cuts the grain will soon, the prophet of Apollo predicts, be changed into another sharp instrument for the reaping of "many a lord/. . . Sheaves of whom are ripe to come/To destruction's harvest-home" (ll. 226–230). For, says the poet,

> Men must reap the things they sow,
> Force from force must ever flow,
> Or worse; but 'tis a bitter woe
> That love or reason cannot change
> The despot's rage, the slave's revenge. (ll. 231–235)

There is no exultation here, only sadness at the knowledge brought by imaginative insight: what the poet, with the ordered soul represented by his mountain-island vantage point, can clearly envision is unseen by both the tyrant and the slave, blinded by self-will and ignorance and thus captives of Necessity.

The second paragraph on Padua (ll. 236–255) gives us a historical perspective upon her present plight. During the thirteenth-century wars between the Popes and the Emperors, Ezzelino da Romano, vicar of the Emperor Frederick II, became the master of Verona, Vicenza, and Padua (in 1237). For nearly twenty years Ezzelino's tyranny maintained the ascendancy of the Ghibellines, although at the same time his atrocities made Frederick's cause odious throughout Italy. After the emperor's death Ezzelino reaped the harvest of his actions; he was hunted down and killed in 1259. Thus Death finally won Ezzelin from Sin (ll. 236–240).[9] Padua, which during the rule of Ezzelino and the brief period of prosperity following his death had played the tyrant and enslaved its neighbors, also felt the hand of retribution. First the Scalas of Verona conquered the city (1311) and then, after almost a century of independence under the Carrara family, Padua passed permanently under the rule of Venice in 1405. Thus, for more than four hundred years the city had been subject to foreign powers, with Sin acting as Death's "Vice-Emperor" (note the pun) under the Austrian tyranny:

8. See n. 1 above. Cf. also Shelley to Mary, 20 August 1818: "You everywhere meet those teams of beautiful white oxen, which are now labouring the little vine-divided fields with their Virgilian ploughs and carts" (Julian Edition, IX, 323).

9. As has often been pointed out, Shelley borrows Sin and Death from *Paradise Lost* and the game at dice for a man's soul from "The Rime of the Ancient Mariner."

And since that time, ay, long before,
Both have ruled from shore to shore,—
That incestuous pair, who follow
Tyrants as the sun the swallow,
As Repentance follows Crime,
And as changes follow Time.   (ll. 250–255)

The swallow is the fourth and final symbolic bird introduced in the poem. Rooks, emblematic of the poet's "passion, pain, and guilt," had been followed by the sea-mew, symbol of divine retribution; now the swallow serves, as did the reaping and sowing imagery of the previous strophe, to symbolize the necessary consequences of tyranny. Only the man of imagination, a "tempest-cleaving Swan" (l. 174), can successfully struggle against the winds of Necessity; only love and reason could, if they were widespread, stay "the despot's rage, the slave's revenge." As it is, changes must follow time, and those overlords who have sown the wind must surely reap the whirlwind.

The seventh and last strophe of the poem's middle movement, which parallels the third verse-paragraph of the first movement (ll. 66–89), focuses on the hope for a social redemption equal to the personal release felt by the poet at dawn. Padua's university, once the pride of Italy, is no longer a light to the nations, but like an illusory "meteor" (optical phenomenon) "it gleams betrayed and to betray" (l. 260). Newer lamps of knowledge, kindled from Padua's sacred flame, are illuminating the world, "but their spark lies dead in thee,/Trampled out by Tyranny" (ll. 267–268).[1] It is clear now that "light" and "fire" cannot be regarded as separate or distinct. As the flame of the "lamp of learning" both warms and illumines "this cold and gloomy earth," so can there be no separation of the fire of love from the light of reason.[2] Shelley never regards moral action as a necessary consequence of knowledge, but neither will he recognize ignorant goodwill as a virtuous quality. His recurrent use of the sun and the lamp to symbolize cosmic and human creative energy (imagination) precludes a split between reason, will, and emotions.

The final simile, which compares Tyranny engulfed by the light and flames originally sprung from Padua's lamp to a Norwegian

---

1. Although textual emendation without manuscript authority is a dangerous practice, I am inclined to accept C. D. Locock's conjectural emendation of "might" to "night" at the end of l. 266. Shelley was plagued throughout his stay in Italy by inaccuracies in his published poetry that resulted from his being unable to read the proof sheets. That the *Rosalind and Helen* volume was no exception we can gather from his letter to the Olliers, 6 September 1819: "In the 'Rosalind and Helen,' I see there are some few errors, which are so much the worse because they are errors in the sense. If there should be any danger of a second Edition, I will correct them" (Julian Edition, X, 79).

2. Cf. Preface to "Julian and Maddalo": "His passions and his powers are incomparably greater than those of other men; and, instead of the latter having been employed in curbing the former, they have mutually lent each other strength."

woodsman surrounded by the raging forest fire, the source of which he had extinguished, ties together the imagery of the second movement. The power of Necessity is clearly recognized in the spreading flames, and the fire reiterates the sun-hearth-lamp imagery central to the movement; moreover, the scene of the simile is as appropriate to landlocked Padua as was the image of the fisherman (ll. 134–141) that concluded the passage on Venice's watery death.

The first movement portrayed the release of one individual, the poet, from the power of Necessity; it showed how an infusion of divine energy, symbolized in the sunrise, had broken the power of the poet's unhappy past and had freed him from his feelings of guilt and regret. The second movement demonstrated that the same kind of regeneration is possible at the social level. If "Freedom" (l. 150), the "thought-wingèd Liberty" (l. 207) that can spring from a renaissance among the individuals of a society, "should awake," then the resulting love and reason could free men from "the despot's rage, the slave's revenge" (l. 235). Byron, the example of poetic genius, represents the kind of man who, once freed from his own sins and slaveries, will be a "tempest-cleaving Swan," rebuffing the big wind of circumstance and leading others to the light of the new morn of truth. Byron (as symbol rather than as individual) thus forms the link both between personal and social regeneration and between the destructive swing of the cycle of Necessity imagined in the fate of Venice and the rebirth predicted with the downfall of Padua's tyrants.

V

The third movement of "Lines written among the Euganean Hills" begins with the advent of noon. Because at this hour the sun's rays are least diffused and refracted by the earth's atmosphere, noontime was Shelley's symbol of the nearest conjunction between the divine and the mortal, the eternal and the temporal. At noon a new mist of autumn envelops the scene, but one no longer the symbol of evanescent mortality; rather, it has become a "purple mist," a general diffusion of the "purple pride" that had earlier (l. 284) marked the sinful self-will of the tyrants but that now casts a general effluence of value over all things. It seems like a rare gem vaporized or "an air-dissolvèd star" that "fills the overflowing sky" (ll. 287–293). Here the planet Venus, emblem of love, melts into the earth's region of air, that realm of mortal thought, and enriches all things with mingled "light and fragrance" (l. 290).[3] Under the dual influence of the noontide sun of cosmic creativity and the morning-evening star of human love and aspiration, all creation—

3. Cf. *The Triumph of Life*, ll. 416–423. Shelley wrote to Peacock, 16 August 1818: "The weather has been brilliantly fine; and now, among these mountains, the autumnal air is becoming less hot, especially in the mornings and evenings. . . . We see here Jupiter in the east; and Venus, I believe, as the evening star, directly after sunset" (Julian Edition, IX, 321).

plains, leaves, vines, flower, Apennine, Alps, "and of living things each one;/And my spirit"—merge in a mystical unity, "interpenetrated" by "the glory of the sky" (ll. 294–314).[4] What caused this memorable feeling of oneness between the once-isolated human soul and the natural creation around him? Shelley, true to his sceptical epistemology, does not answer categorically but rather names the alternative possibilities (ll. 315–319): the experience may have been generated by a purely physical stimulus (light or odor), by an external metaphysical reality (love, harmony, or the "soul of all"), or by the poet's own active creative spirit, which peoples an empty universe.

At evening the sun disappears to be replaced by the moon and the evening star, symbols of the reason and love that had both been present in the symbolic sun. Both the unity within the poet's soul and the union between him and the surrounding universe have been disrupted. Although the moon of reason (see note 8 above) borrows also "from the sunset's radiant springs," the evening star seems to minister to the moon half of that "crimson light." In other words, even the cold, borrowed, uncertain light that the moon of reason affords us seems to be partly dependent upon the guiding star of love. With the setting of the sun, the "soft dreams of the morn" pass to others, and Pain, the "ancient pilot" of the poet's bark, returns to the helm.[5] "The day is gone, and all its sweets are gone!"

Gone, but not forgotten, for the poet, recalling the joy that surprised him that day among the Euganean Hills, can declare that "other flowering isles must be/In the sea of Life and Agony" (ll. 335–336) and that there must be other spirits, daemon intermediaries between the divine and the human; perhaps even now, dove-like, "with folded wings they waiting sit/For my bark, to pilot it" (ll. 340–341). It may be that they will guide the poet to a cove where, for him and those he loves, will be built a "windless bower," free from the bondage to Necessity, "far from passion, pain, and guilt" (ll. 342–351).

The island-paradise described in these lines is, like the island-havens in other Shelley poems, a figurative and symbolic one. The island of calm lies within the minds of those who live there. Like

---

4. Cf. Shelley to Hunt, April 1818: "no sooner had we arrived at Italy than the loveliness of the earth and the serenity of the sky made the greatest difference in my sensations—I depend on these things for life; for in the smoke of cities and the tumult of human kind and the chilling fogs and rain of our own country I can hardly be said to live" (Julian Edition, IX, 293–294), and Shelley to Hogg, 21 December 1818: "It will be difficult however to live contentedly in England again after the daily contemplation of the sublimest objects of antient art, and the sensations inspired by the enchanting atmosphere which envelopes these tranquil seas and majestic mountains in its radiance" (Julian Edition, X, 8).

5. In 1822 Shelley recorded the death of another brief moment of peace and calm. See "Lines written in the Bay of Lerici" (*Poetical Works*, pp. 673–674), especially ll. 22–29.

hell or heaven, it is not a place but rather a condition of the soul. Let me live, Shelley asks, freed from the stormy passions and feelings of guilt that prevent me from treating others with complete love and understanding. If such a state of soul can be achieved by Shelley and his immediate circle (and the establishment of a harmonious intellectual coterie was one of his most persistent dreams), the Spirits of the Air, those atmospheric limitations of mortality that interpose themselves between the human and the divine, will undoubtedly bring about encounters between this ideal human society and the outside world where the penalties of Necessity continue to be exacted. Perhaps, suggests the poet, the calm and kindness with which we encounter the multitude will affect them more than their passion will us; perhaps we can, through the exercise of love and reason, bring about a regeneration of other individuals; perhaps, under the mild influence of

> the love which heals all strife
> Circling, like the breath of life,
> All things in that sweet abode
> With its own mild brotherhood:
> They, not it, would change; and soon
> Every sprite beneath the moon
> Would repent its envy vain,
> And the earth grow young again.   (ll. 366–373)

Thus the final movement of the poem, even as it records the sad message of the evanescence of those bright moments when the human world seems interpenetrated by the divine, also expresses hope for the return of such experiences and, through their nurture and cultivation by a dedicated community, to the amelioration of all humanity. Venus, which as the evening star bears the promise of the day's return, becomes the key symbol of the third movement; it is both the symbol of creation's unity amid the diffused glare that is caused by the terrestrial atmosphere's refraction of the white radiance of eternity and the symbol of man's hope amid the dark hours of the soul's complete separation from that divine warmth and illumination.

Shelley has created a symbolic universe that skillfully embodies and reverberates his theme: although it is ordinarily man's fate to be the slave and victim of forces beyond his conscious control (a situation so intolerable that death and oblivion are preferable to it), there come to the man of imagination moments in which his soul becomes one with the universe, in which he is able to see, not through a glass darkly but clearly and vitally, the values and end of human existence; such moments, in which a divine infusion of love and reason breaks through the clouds of mortality, have their own kind of inevitability but one that gives their recipient true moral freedom; such moments, if cultivated and trusted, might break the harsh chain of provocation and retribution.

Shelley supports the thematic development of "Lines written among the Euganean Hills" through its prosody. Enid Hamer, who finds in the poem a "heavily stressed line" that "has a monotonous tramp through the major part of the poem," believes that "when Shelley breaks free of the drowsing beat of the endstopped sevens, he can produce effects of extraordinary richness and expressiveness." Of lines 275–284 she declares: "Never have more magnificent harmonies been achieved in the four-foot measure."[6] The truth is that Shelley carefully modulates his versification according to the meaning of the lines. Throughout most of the poem he utilizes the sharply recurrent rhythms and rhymes of the tetrameter couplet to underline his central concern with the power of Necessity; he even increases and punctuates repetitive sounds through the employment of fifteen triplet rhymes and the skillful use of assonance. In the opening lines, for instance, the vowel sounds of the second line echo those of the first almost exactly: "deep" is assonant with "green," "wide" with "isle," and "sea" with "needs," while there are close parallels between "In the" and "Many a," "of" and "must," and "misery" and "be." Whereas the first three lines contain eight, nine, and eight syllables respectively, once the poet begins in the fourth line to describe man's relentless voyage toward the grave, the meter settles into strongly accented, four-beat, seven-syllable lines. Thereafter the seven-syllable norm is varied with untruncated initial iambs or trisyllabic feet in passages where the poet describes or invokes a break in the inexorable march of Necessity (e.g., ll. 66–79, 134–137, 151, 233–235, 275–282, 295–307, 335–340). But the concluding lines, which describe the island-paradise and the regeneration of mankind, return to the seven-syllable pattern in order to lend to the healing powers of love and reason a strength and inevitability equal to that bondage portrayed earlier in the poem.

M. H. ABRAMS

[Shelley's *Prometheus Unbound*][†]

* * * None of Shelley's longer poems is irrelevant to his theme of the human need for love to fulfill what is incomplete and to reintegrate what has been divided, both in the individual psyche

6. *The Metres of English Poetry* (London, 1930), pp. 39–40.
† From *Natural Supernaturalism: Tradition and Revolution in Romantic Literature*, by M. H. Abrams (New York:
W. W. Norton & Company, Inc., 1971), pp. 299–307. Published by W. W. Norton & Company, Inc. and Oxford University Press, London. Reprinted by permission of the publishers.

and in the social order; but I shall discuss only his most detailed and successful rendering of this theme, *Prometheus Unbound*. Like Keats in his exactly contemporary *Hyperion*, Shelley in this poem explored the problem of evil and suffering in terms of the classical myth of the loss of the Golden Age when Saturn was displaced by Jupiter (see II, iv, 32 ff.). And like many other contemporaries Shelley fused the pagan myth of a lost Golden Age with the Biblical design of a fall, redemption, and millennial return to a lost felicity, and gave special prominence to the associated Biblical figure of the exile, return, and marriage of the bride. In his Preface Shelley also tells us that he chose the Titan Prometheus for his protagonist over Satan, "the hero of *Paradise Lost*," because Prometheus has Satan's heroic virtues of courage and firm "opposition to omnipotent force," but without the moral defects which, in Milton's "magnificent fiction," engender "in the mind a pernicious casuistry which leads us to weigh his faults with his wrongs, and to excuse the former because the latter exceed all measure."[1] *Prometheus Unbound*, then, like Wordsworth's *Prelude* and *Home at Grasmere*, Blake's *Milton*, and Keats's *Hyperion*, can be looked upon as a deliberate attempt by a Romantic Miltonist—in his Preface Shelley called his predecessor "the sacred Milton"—to revise Milton's great but no longer adequate imaginative conception of the nature, justification, and mitigation of the evils and agonies of human experience.

Many critics of Shelley's poem assert that Prometheus is an allegorical figure, but they disagree as to what he allegorizes. Earl Wasserman, for example, in a recent and often enlightening monograph, has argued that "Prometheus is the personification of Shelley's concept of the One Mind," as this concept is represented in Shelley's system of metaphysics, and that "the drama is the history of the One Mind's evolution into perfection."[2] In his Preface, however, Shelley himself asserts that Prometheus "is, as it were, the type of the highest perfection of moral and intellectual nature." Shelley's hero, then, is close kin to the agent called "Man" or "Mankind" who is the protagonist in the popular eighteenth-century genre of universal history—a genre which, in its French and English versions, ranked high in Shelley's favorite reading matter. In universal history "Man" is the collective representative (in Shelley's word, "the type") of the intellectual and moral vanguard among human beings, who develops through history toward his perfected human condition. In *Prometheus Unbound* Shelley renders the universal history of man in the dramatic form of visualizable agents and their actions, and he represents man's accession to an earthly paradise not (in the usual eighteenth-century pattern) as the terminus of a long and gradual progress but (by a reversion to

1. *Shelley's Prose*, p. 327. 2. *Shelley's "Prometheus Unbound,"* pp. 195, 30–1.

the Biblical design of history) as a sudden, right-angled break-through from misery to felicity.

Within the frame of Shelley's dramatic fiction Prometheus, like Blake's Albion, is also a descendant of a familiar mythical figure: the one man who was once whole, has fallen into division, and proceeds to redeem his lost integrity. Throughout the work, how-ever, Shelley sustains the bodily separateness of Prometheus and Asia, his divided feminine complement, so that their reunion is not represented as a reintegration of the primal man, but as a culminat-ing marriage. In his drama, furthermore, Shelley clearly distinguishes between his *dramatis personae* proper—Prometheus and the other "Giant Forms" (as Blake would call them) who act out the mythi-cal plot—and the world that these mythical personages and actions figure forth: the real world of ordinary men and women, who are never directly presented in the action of the dramatic poem but whose experiences are reported to us by the Spirit of the Earth and the Spirit of the Hour in the third act, and whose spiritual alteration and accession to an earthly paradise are correlative with the conversion of Prometheus and his reunion with Asia.

When the play begins, Prometheus has already fallen into dis-unity and conflict as a consequence of his moral error in having succumbed, in response to tyranny and injustice, to the divisive passion of hate; the result is that Asia has been exiled from him. Asia is the soul's counterpart which, in his "Essay on Love," Shelley calls the "anti-type."[3] In the play she is characterized as an Aphro-dite figure who embodies the universally integrative and life-restoring power which Shelley called "love." "Most vain all hope but love; and thou art far, Asia!"—in "that far Indian vale," as Panthea explains,

> The scene of her sad exile; rugged once
> And desolate and frozen, like this ravine;
> But now invested with fair flowers and herbs
>   . . . from the aether
> Of her transforming presence, which would fade
> If it were mingled not with thine.   (I, 808–9, 826–33)

Her separation has left Prometheus as the male remnant who mani-fests the power of the will in the highest masculine virtues of resistance and endurance, but remains "eyeless in hate," an isolated and immobilized Samson, in a natural setting which has become alien and lifeless to him:

> Nailed to this wall of eagle-baffling mountain,
> Black, wintry, dead, unmeasured; without herb,
> Insect, or beast, or shape or sound of life.   (I, 9–22)

3. *Shelley's Prose*, p. 170.

Prometheus is represented as having been chained and tortured by Jupiter. We soon learn, however, that all of Jupiter's power has been vested in him by his victim. The implication is that Jupiter is mankind's own worst potentiality—the corruption of affiliative love into self-love, with its concomitant lust for dominion and tyranny— which has been projected by the mind of man in the fantasy of a cruel tyrant-god who dwells aloof in his distant heaven. But if Jupiter is a pseudo-person, he is not the less psychologically real and effective: "I gave all/He has; and in return he chains me here" (I, 381–2). Various clues in the text, moreover, invite us to regard all the *dramatis personae*, except one, as externalized correlatives of the powers, aspects, and activities of Prometheus' own divided and conflicting self, and to regard even the altering natural setting as projections of Prometheus' mental states.[4] The one clear exception is Demogorgon, the "mighty darkness" and shapeless form (II, iv. 2–7) who is the principle, or power, behind all process. This ultimate reason for things not only lies outside of man's mind and its activities but also, Shelley skeptically insists, lies irretrievably outside the limits of man's knowledge, by virtue of the fact that it exceeds the bounds of possible human experience. Accordingly, Demogorgon is simply postulated—like the cognitively inaccessible "Power in likeness of the Arve" in Shelley's great lyric, *Mont Blanc* —as the course of events which is in itself purposeless and amoral, but carries out the ineluctable consequences of man's decisions or acts; whether for good or ill depends on the condition of the human will which makes neutral process the instrument of its own moral purposes. Read in this way *Prometheus Unbound*, like Blake's prophetic poems, is a psycho-drama of the reintegration of the split personality by that annihilation of selfhood which converts divisive hate into affiliative love, in which the action is equally relevant to the mind of each and all of us. And by any valid reading of Shelley's myth, it is plain that man is ultimately the agent of his own fall, the tyrant over himself, his own avenger, and his own potential redeemer; as H. N. Fairchild has described Shelley's intention, justly though disapprovingly, "the mind of man is liberated from its dark delusions solely by the mind of man."[5]

The plot of *Prometheus Unbound* has no precedent in the drastic asymmetry of its construction. It begins not *in medias res* but at the end, for the reversal occurs in the opening soliloquy when Prometheus, his arrogance suddenly dissipating after his long discipline of suffering, substitutes a unifying sentiment for the separative

4. See Harold Bloom's insightful discussion of the divided Prometheus in *The Visionary Company*, pp. 298ff. Wasserman in *Shelley's "Prometheus Unbound"* also suggests that various characters and events of the dramas are "the symbolic externalizing of mental acts and powers"; see, e.g., pp. 2–3.
5. *Religious Trends in English Poetry* (4 vols.; New York, 1939–57), III, 350.

sentiment: pity for hate. (As Blake had put it, "They have divided themselves by Wrath, they must be united by/ Pity . . . in terrors of self annihilation."[6]) Prometheus at once proceeds to "recall"— in the double sense of bringing into the full light of consciousness, and by that very fact revoking—the implications of the curse he had called down upon Jupiter, which serves in the play as the central emblem of his moral flaw. These feet, he cries to Jupiter, might trample thee,

> If they disdained not such a prostrate slave.
> Disdain! Ah no! I pity thee. . . .
>   I speak in grief,
> Not exultation, for I hate no more,
> As then ere misery made me wise. The curse
> Once breathed on thee I would recall. . . .
> Though I am changed so that aught evil wish
> Is dead within; although no memory be
> Of what is hate. . . .   (I, 51–72)

This is all Prometheus, by the reversal of his unaided masculine will, can do, except to remain indomitable against Jupiter's continuing demands for submission. But by substituting compassion for hate Prometheus, although unknowingly, has released his feminine complement, the full power of love, from her long exile.

From the end of the first act on, the plot consists almost entirely of Asia's journey to her reunion with Prometheus. She and Panthea (her sister and lesser self, through whom she has retained some relation to Prometheus in exile) obey the reiterative "Follow! Follow!" which expresses the sweet and irresistible compulsion that has been put in process by Prometheus' change of heart; this is Shelley's version of the yearning toward the apocalyptic bridal union in Revelation: "And the Spirit and the bride say, Come. And let him that heareth say, Come." Asia's movement toward reunion is a spiritual journey which, in consonance with the great Romantic trope, is specifically a *Bildungsreise*, in the course of which she acquires essential knowledge that leaves her radically altered. Prometheus' change from hate to pity had been unpremeditated and instinctive, and, before his reformation can be complete and stable, the principle implicit in this moral act must be brought out as conscious knowledge. But since, by the conditions of Shelley's inherited story, Prometheus must remain fixed to his precipice, the function of the self-educative journey is given over to his alter ego, Asia. In obedience to her inner compulsion Asia descends to Demogorgon's underworld at the dark bases of existence and puts to him the ultimate questions about the "why" of the way things are—the rationale of all human history and experience. In the Induction to Keats's *The Fall of Hyperion*, as the poet ascends the stairs his evolving awareness is educed from him by the progressive alteration of Moneta's charges and comments. Asia's developing insight is similarly projected and dramatized in the form of a colloquy; for Demogorgon, who simply acts as he must without knowing why, responds to her queries with riddling utterances that merely stimulate her to answer her own questions, by specifying as knowledge what she had already possessed as obscure presentiment.

Accordingly it is not Demogorgon but Asia who tells us the prehistory of the drama in which, during the Golden Age under Saturn men had lived in felicity, but a felicity of ignorance, then had suffered under the tyranny of Jupiter, but had been relieved by Prometheus, who brought men science, culture, and the arts. Yet for this act of benevolence Prometheus hangs bound and tortured, and civilized man is become "The wreck of his own will, the scorn of earth/The outcast, the abandoned, the alone." At this point Asia raises the question central to the Romantic, as to the earlier Christian spiritual journey: *unde malum?* "But who rains down/ Evil, the immedicable plague?" To Shelley's skeptical empiricism, this question oversteps the limits of possible human experience. Demogorgon does not know the answer, nor does Asia, nor can any man, for as Demogorgon says, "the deep truth is imageless." He can give her only as much knowledge as she already possesses, below the level of distinct awareness; but this knowledge turns out to be all we need to know—that to "Fate, Time, Occasion, Chance, and Change . . ./All things are subject but eternal Love." To which Asia replies

> So much I asked before, and my heart gave
> The response thou hast given; and of such truths
> Each to itself must be the oracle.   (II, iv. 32–123)

Asia's educational journey, then, like Wordsworth's in *The Prelude*, terminates in the lesson that love is first and chief, as the only available solution to the problem of the good and evil of our mortal state. At the instant of this discovery by Asia, Demogorgon becomes capable of answering the sole question to which he can give a decisive and unambiguous reply, and that merely by a gesture: "When shall the destined hour arrive?" "Behold!" For the destined hour has at that instant arrived.

Taking up her journey back to Prometheus in the car driven by the Spirit of the Hour, Asia in a great lyric describes the correlative inner journey in which her soul, like an enchanted boat, moves up and back through age, manhood, youth, infancy, and "Through Death and Birth, to a diviner day;/A paradise of vaulted bowers"

(II, v. 72–110). This spiritual dying to be reborn is equated, on the mythical level, with her visible outer change back to the pristine form she had manifested when she had risen as Aphrodite from the sea, while "love . . . filling the living world,/Burst from thee"; her transfiguration matches that of Prometheus back to his primal form at the moment when, suspended on the cliff, he had repealed his hate (II, i. 56ff.). Jupiter is hurled by Demogorgon into "the dark void" (III, ii. 10); that is, the projection of man's self-isolating and domineering hate reverts to its original state of potentiality in the human psyche, whence it will reconsolidate and reemerge if man ceases to sustain his integrity by the cohesive force of love. The condition of a reintegrated humanity is signified by the reunion of Prometheus and Asia, which is exactly simultaneous with the annihilation of Jupiter. Mary Shelley's interpretation of the event is too exclusive to be adequate, but it makes salient the parallel between the conclusion of Shelley's myth and the figure of the culminating marriage in Wordsworth and other Romantic writers. Asia, says Mrs. Shelley, in some mythological interpretations was

> the same as Venus and Nature. When the benefactor of mankind is liberated, Nature resumes the beauty of her prime, and is united to her husband, the emblem of the human race, in perfect and happy union.[7]

This marital reunion coincides with the sounding of the conch shell by the Spirit of the Hour (Shelley's version of the last trump in the Book of Revelation), at which "All things . . . put their evil nature off" and man, having become what he might always have been, "made earth like heaven" and, "equal, unclassed, tribeless, and nationless," takes up residence in his achieved paradise. Unlike Grasmere Vale—Wordsworth's "earthly counterpart" of heaven, whose inhabitants differ "but little from the Man elsewhere" in their guilt and suffering—Shelley's envisioned state is one in which man will be "free from guilt or pain . . . for his will made or suffered them." Like Wordsworth's, however, Shelley's is a paradise of this earth, in which man remains inescapably conditioned by passion and by "chance, and death, and mutability"; otherwise he would not be earthly man but a disembodied idea in a Platonic heaven: these mortal conditions are

> The clogs of that which else might oversoar
> The loftiest star of unascended heaven,
> Pinnacled dim in the intense inane.   (III, iv. 54–204)

Shelley added to *Prometheus Unbound* a fourth act in the traditional form of a nuptial masque. The act constitutes an immense

7. *Complete Poetical Works of P. B. Shelley*, ed. Thomas Hutchinson (London, 1939), p. 272.

epithalamion in which the elements of the human mind and of the outer cosmos celebrate the triumph of love and participate, in song, dance, and ritual mimicry, in the union of Prometheus and Asia taking place behind the scenes. The thematic word is "Unite!" and this concept is enacted in the fantastic, yet beautiful, episode of the wooing and love union between the masculine earth and the feminine moon—possibly, Shelley's adaptation of the alchemical marriage between the male and female contraries (symbolically represented as sun and moon, as well as king and queen) which consummates the Hermetic quest for the principle that will transmute all elements to gold and all mankind to the age of gold. Held in its circular course by the embrace of the earth, the cold and sterile moon bursts into restored life and fertility, as the earth's enhanced energy manifests itself in a heightening of its electromagnetic forces and its radiated heat and light—those attributes which in Shelley's spiritual physics are material correlates of the attractive and life-giving powers of universal love. Such dramatic episodes are merely emblematic, however, of the primary union, in which all men are assimilated by love into a unitary mankind. This fulfillment Shelley describes in a statement which is his metaphorical equivalent to the myth of the reintegration of the Universal Man:

> Man, oh, not men! A chain of linkèd thought,
> Of love and might to be divided not. . . .
> Man, one harmonious soul of many a soul,
> Whose nature is its own divine control,
> Where all things flow to all, as rivers to the sea.
>
> (IV, 394–402)

D. J. HUGHES

Potentiality in *Prometheus Unbound*†

Harold Bloom writes of the passages describing the chariot of the moon and the sphere of the earth in the fourth act, "These visions are the mythic culminations of *Prometheus Unbound*."[1] Not all commentators would agree, but most have found these passages worthy of comment, Locock remarking that "the blank verse marks the highest level attained by Shelley."[2] The Biblical and Miltonic sources and analogues of these passages have been studied by

† From *Studies in Romanticism*, II (1963), pp. 107–126. Reprinted by permission of the Trustees of Boston University.

1. *Shelley's Mythmaking* (New Haven, 1959), p. 140.
2. *The Poems of Percy Bysshe Shelley*, ed. C. D. Locock, 2 vols. (London 1911), I, 624.

Wiltrude L. Smith[3] and Ants Oras,[4] the nature of the imagery by R. H. Fogle,[5] while perhaps the best pages yet written on the thematic significance of these two visions remain those of G. Wilson Knight in *The Starlit Dome*,[6] who reads these extraordinary lines (180–318) against the background of the unfolding vision of the total poem. Without such sense of *Prometheus* as a whole, these passages, however brilliant and portentous in themselves, tend to appear more exotic than they are. And, while the examination of Ezekiel and Milton throws some light on how these passages came to be written, the fact remains that the tone of these visions differs widely from Biblical prophecy and the vengeful deity of Milton's chariot. Nothing in Shelley is more characteristic than these visions, and nothing in Shelley brings to better focus the particular and unusual strategies by which he created poems. These two visions in the celebrations of the fourth act of the drama are best read in relation to the poem as a whole and in relation to Shelley's characteristic poetic method.

This method, as it reveals in the most significant poems, is best understood on the analogy of the famous "fading coal" which Shelley uses as a metaphor for the mind in creation.[7] The parts of Shelley's longer poems can be understood as a series of such fading coals, sometimes beginning in full hypostasis, sometimes gathering strength and coherence as the self-discovering image perfects itself, sometimes starting in collapse and ending there, but, whatever the process, the imagistic progression is wholly organic and under some kind of overarching control, even when the particular passage seems to complete itself in a thematic or emotional (*not* formal) collapse. I think this process is everywhere at work in *Prometheus Unbound*, although the vast interwoven complexity of the poem makes it difficult to plot. Such a process is dramatic in a different sense than we normally think of the term, but much of the continuing argument about *Prometheus* as drama might be resolved if we thought of the drama enacted in the poem, not in the Aristotelian sense of character in action, but in the terms Shelley himself set for his poem (often quoted, but seldom understood), "imagery . . . drawn from the operations of the human mind."[8] The poem contains two such large dramatic operations, 1. the events leading to the unchaining of Prometheus, and 2. the building of another process by

3. "An Overlooked Source for *Prometheus Unbound*," *Studies in Philology*, XLVIII (1951), 783–792.

4. "The Multitudinous Orb: Some Miltonic Elements in Shelley," *Modern Language Quarterly*, XVI (1955), 247–257.

5. *The Imagery of Keats and Shelley* (Chapel Hill, 1949), pp. 49–54.

6. *The Starlit Dome* (Oxford, 1941, 1959), pp. 219–224.

7. See my "Coherence and Collapse in Shelley, with particular reference to *Epipsychidion*," *ELH*, XXVIII (Sept. 1961), 260–283, for a reading of that poem from the point of view of the Shelleyan fading coal.

8. *The Complete Poetical Works of Percy Bysshe Shelley*, ed. Thomas Hutchinson (Oxford, 1933), p. 205.

which Prometheus, in his symbolic role, can find a fresh hypostasis, not in the actuality which Shelley is anxious to spiritualize in the poem, but in the Potentiality where the poem finally leaves us. Paul Valéry speaks of the poet as cleansing the verbal situation.[9] Shelley, in his most ambitious poem, can be seen as cleansing the ontological situation, restoring our sense of the potential, turning, through a series of verbal strategies, the actual back upon itself. The world at the end of the poem is a virtual one, with the seeds of decline checked, themselves remaining in potency.

If this general statement about *Prometheus Unbound* has any validity, each part of the poem must bear, microcosmically, some of the pattern of the fading coal, a structure of coherence and collapse. The widest ranging structure in the poem, indeed in Shelley's poetry as a whole, is this section of Act IV describing the visions of the Oceanides. Through these visions we experience the birth and death of a cosmos, beginning with the "thinnest boat" of the potential and ending in the cataclysmic collapse of as much of the actual as the human mind can conceive or bear, indeed, even more than deity wishes to sustain: "some God/Whose throne was in a comet, passed and cried/'Be not!'" (IV.316–318). These 138 lines present in small the process of the poem as a whole, a process which, here, save for the symbolic infants themselves, dispenses with the important dramatis personae of the drama. The subsequent cosmic dance of the masculine earth and feminine moon has been prepared for by the fullest imaginative reach of the Shelleyan strategy. In Bloom's witty view, "In effect, the infants give away the mythic planets in marriage.'[1] The potential, then, arises out of the actual to new forms and dominates it. It is important to keep in mind that these visions occur in the fourth act, *after* the freeing of Prometheus. The "intoxication . . . the complicated and uncontrollable splendour" which C. S. Lewis finds in Act IV[2] express not so much the liberation of suffering mankind from political and psychological repression as from the ontological tyranny of the phenomenal, a task given to the very medium with which the poet works:

> Language is a perpetual Orphic song,
> Which rules with Daedal harmony a throng
> Of thoughts and forms, which else senseless and shapeless were.
> (IV. 415–417)

I

These visions begin in a characteristic Shelleyan absence, the memory of music fled:

9. "Poetry and Abstract Thought," *The Art of Poetry*, Bollingen Series XLIV (New York, 1958), p. 54.

1. Bloom, p. 142.
2. *Rehabilitations* (London, 1939), p. 33.

> *Panthea.* Ha! they are gone!
> *Ione.*   Yet feel you no delight
> From the past sweetness?
> *Panthea.*   As the bare green hill
> When some soft cloud vanishes into rain,
> Laughs with a thousand drops of sunny water
> To the unpavilioned sky!   (IV. 180–184)

This "unpavilioning" is important here because the first three acts of the poem have succeeded in destroying the actuality with which the drama opens: Prometheus chained to his rock. Now, the structuring of further forms in the poem can take place in the ambience of liberated man, who, himself, must be placed against the cosmic, suprahuman content of these visions for the poem to have its widest range. It should be noted, also, that the two visions have dramatic propriety: it is proper that the lesser of the Oceanides, Ione, should, as Bloom points out,[3] have the less terrific vision, a vision of a Potentiality which stays perfectly poised in itself, and that Panthea, the stronger, should be able to bear the larger experience, in which the potential of her vision, the earth-infant, should lead to the fullest actualization and collapse in Shelley—a collapse, of course, perfectly contained within the formal structure of the poem.

The new music encountered by the Oceanides is heard "Kindling within the strings of the waved air/Aeolian modulations" (IV.187–188). Kindle is a highly significant word in Shelley, often signifying the beginning of the Shelleyan process, the awakening of the fading coal. The stasis expressed at the very beginning of these visions recalls and contrasts with the opening stasis of the poem. Compare:

> The crawling glaciers pierce me with the spears
> Of their moon-freezing crystals, the bright chains
> Eat with their burning cold into my bones.   (I. 31–33)

> Clear, silver, icy, keen, awakening tones,
> Which pierce the sense, and live within the soul,
> As the sharp stars pierce winter's crystal air
> And gaze upon themselves within the sea.   (IV. 190–193)

But this happy narcissism, usually signifying points of desired rest in Shelley's work, now gives way to movement as "Two visions of strange radiance" float into view above the runnels of a rivulet which, "like sisters/Who part with sighs that they may meet in smiles," can be identified with Panthea and Ione themselves as they await their major revelations. In Ione's subsequent vision, the moon-chariot is likened to "that thinnest boat,/In which the Mother of Months is borne/By ebbing light into her western cave"

3. Bloom, p. 140.

(IV.206–208). Many commentators have pointed to this image as a picture of the old moon in the new moon's arms,[4] certainly a clear representation of the emergence of the potential from the actual, and the boat imagery, of course, is very familiar in Shelley,[5] best illuminated here, perhaps, by a passage in a letter to Peacock: "rivers are not like roads, the work of the hands of man; *they imitate mind*, which wanders at will over pathless deserts, and flow through nature's loveliest recesses, which are inaccessible to anything besides."[6] The mind that rivers imitate is general or collective mind; the boat is the vehicle or container of the individual mind or consciousness which enables us to participate in, without being overwhelmed by, the Universal. Moreover, the boat-image often arises in Shelley's work from the structural need to keep his poem moving. In this passage, the boat as imitative of thought in the manner suggested, and the boat as a technical device to stir the poem to movement, combine to inaugurate the great visions of Act IV. We should also keep in mind that the boat image has a female significance in these lines. The moon, which will finally be fully hypostatized as female and impregnated by the earth, is seen at this point in the poem in its fragile beginnings—the *thinnest* boat. The movement of Ione's vision must be distinguished, however, from the wild Shelleyan journeys of *Alastor, Epipsychidion,* and *The Witch of Atlas*—and even from Asia's ride at the end of Act II of *Prometheus.* Here Shelley manages to suggest movement within stasis, a "progress" that, paradoxically, creates an image of stillness. The mingling of the solid and the vaporous, which Fogle and others have noticed as characteristic of Shelley's technique, not only enables him to grasp the very difficult material he is dealing with, but helps him to express here, as nowhere else in his work, his sense of the potential of thought as it seeks its form. The infant asleep in the moon-chariot symbolizes the perfection of the potential, a potential which, in its stasis, need not seek completed form. The six repetitions of white in as many lines (IV.219–224) emphasize this magnificently unresolved possibility—the condition of being before the "staining" process of existence takes over, as the famous lines in *Adonais* describe the condition of human life.

4. Both Mr. Bloom and Mr. Richard Harter Fogle seem to me to misread this passage slightly. Bloom speaks of "the new moon in the old moon's arms" when the image is meant to be the opposite, I think, as in Coleridge and elsewhere. The sequence is important for the development of Shelley's imagery of this passage. And Mr. Fogle, using the less acceptable reading of night for light in "By ebbing night into her western cave," distorts the time sequence of the passage.

5. Perhaps the best discussion of Shelley's boat imagery can be found in Neville Rogers, *Shelley at Work* (Oxford, 1956), pp. 91–105.

6. From a letter to Peacock, July 17, 1816. *The Complete Works of Percy Bysshe Shelley*, Julian edition (New York, 1926), IX, 180. The italics are mine.

The infant, however, stands for more than this. Harold Bloom's identification of this figure with the Divine Man of Ezekiel does not seem very useful, but Wilson Knight comes closer, I think, to the full significance of the infant figures in this act. He writes (of the second infant, but I think his remarks are applicable to both): "Here the active and central agent is again the Child, the Earth-Spirit, yet son of man. Shelley is to this extent a humanist: the child is the final fact."[7] This "final fact," of course, cuts deep through English Romanticism, whether we think of the child in terms of Blakean Innocence or of the Wordsworthian prophet-blest. But there are important distinctions to be made between the two infants of Shelley's vision. The first, the infant in the moon-chariot, is akin to Blake's Thel and the chariot is to be associated with the state of Beulah. The second, the infant of the earth-sphere, is more the Child of Apocalypse and the vision of the higher innocence. The infant of the moon-chariot *stays* prematurely in the potential, and the Shelleyan process cannot complete itself. The solid clouds of the chariot's wheels "as they roll/Over the grass, and flowers, and waves, wake sounds,/Sweet as a singing rain of silver dew" (IV.233–235). This is not the "deep music of the rolling world" heard by Panthea in line 186, but is more like the "under-notes" caught by Ione in line 189. We still need the full, self-destroying cosmic music.

Panthea's remarkable vision of the sphere of the earth sets the poetic process going to its inevitable completion. This sphere which, among a dozen other possibilities, can be taken as a description of Shelley's poetry at its best, "Solid as crystal, yet through all its mass/Flow, as through empty space, music and light" (IV.239–240), offers us the full world the moon-chariot was not capable of kindling. Color is awakened: "Purple and azure, white, and green, and golden,/" and sufficient plenitude expressed in one of Shelley's most daring conceits, "and every space between/Peopled with unimaginable shapes,/Such as ghosts dream dwell in the lampless deep,/Yet each inter-transpicuous." The combination here is so remote as to be hardly graspable, yet the syntax is firm and the language exact (*inter-transpicuous* strikes me as incredibly cunning). Moreover, the movement of this vision is one of a "self-destroying swiftness" (the true Shelleyan mode) which will ultimately end in the illumination of a cosmic cataclysm, capable of grinding and kneading the actual back into the potential: "With mighty whirl the multitudinous orb/Grinds the bright brook into an azure mist/Of elemental subtlety, like light." William Empson's criticism of these lines, that Shelley "not being able to think of a comparison fast enough . . . compares the thing to a vaguer or more abstract notion of itself, or points out that it is its own nature, or that it sustains itself by supporting itself,"[8] is an accurate description of Shelley's technique, but his implication that this is somehow inadequate misapprehends the function of Shelley's mode. These materials are notoriously elusive, whether they are emerging into full realization or again passing from realization into a new potential, but this is precisely the area Shelley wishes to grasp: his whole poem centers there. The same technique can be seen at work in the description of the sleeping infant in the sphere who is likened to "a child o'erwearied with sweet toil." The child is a demiurge who has done work and must do more; he is the child of the higher innocence who must illuminate and then transcend the natural processes of experience.

The progress of this orb, leading as it must to the inevitable Shelleyan collapse, disturbs Ione, who, in her ironic comment at line 269, attempts to slow the terrific movement, as she interprets the smiles of the sleeping child, " 'Tis only mocking the orb's harmony." Bloom[9] and Knight[1] have commented well on this line, emphasizing its humanistic irony, the necessity for the human to intrude itself at this point lest the orb turn into something like the crushing chariot of *The Triumph of Life*. I would like to see the function of this line in relation to Shelley's evolving form. Ione's vision of the moon-chariot was read as a premature suspension, a stasis that failed to complete Shelley's form. The deeper music of Panthea's vision of the earth-sphere, with its powerful grinding and kneading, the grinding of the bright brook of the actual into the mist which is the new potential, will, in R. P. Blackmur's Yeatsian verse, "Keep the great gong going" until history and even prehistory are overcome, laid open to the transformative movement of the poem as a whole. Knight is correct when he points out that "these hammers of flame and fierce gyrations . . . are used to show Keats's 'supreme of power' now piercing, revealing, redeeming, and *annihilating* all past agonies of Man and Earth."[2] In order for this to happen, the sphere must complete its revelations, and Ione's vision of the child in Beulah must be transcended by the fierce insight of the apocalyptic child asleep in the earth-sphere. The technique here is essentially ironic, but not in the usual sense. Earl Wasserman, writing on *Adonais*, frames an excellent definition of the ironic mode in that poem which, I think, can be extended to Shelley's work in general: "The evolution of the poem gains its inevitability from ambivalences and inversions

8. *Seven Types of Ambiguity* (New York, rev. ed. 1947), pp. 160–161.
9. Bloom, p. 145.

1. Knight, p. 222.
2. Knight, p. 223.

of such a nature that, while the materials nearly tolerate a coherent interpretation from false perspectives, they are weighted to compel their true ordering and interpretation."[3] Ione's comment is an excellent example of such a false perspective; however beautiful and satisfying in a humanistic sense Ione's slight irony is, it is not enough—it takes us back to the condition of the earlier passage, "Sweet as a singing rain of silver dew." In order for the actual to be overcome by the potential, the process must continue.

Without denying that the scientific allegorizers of the next passage, such as Professor Grabo, may have validity in their readings, I am not so much interested in what these lines (270–318) refer to as in how they advance the action of the poem. The function of this passage is to bring to full reality as much as the mind of an already liberated mankind can conceive. The beams of the flashing star on the forehead of the infant can be identified with the very process of thought, the birth of thought in the brain, which is in Shelley also the beginning of poetry, "swifter than thought." The "sun-like lightenings," the creative mind aflame, fill the abyss of uncreated things, and by revealing them, create them. Notice how this passage moves characteristically from the static to the kinetic, beginning with "Infinite mines of adamant and gold" (IV.280) and moving to "earth's mountaintops" clothed "With kingly, ermine snow" (IV.287). This contains its own collapse because this snow recalls the "sun-awakened avalanche" of Act II, scene iii, whose mass

> Thrice sifted by the storm, had gathered there
> Flake after flake, in heaven-defying minds
> As thought by thought is piled, till some great truth
> Is loosened, and the nations echo round,
> Shaken to their roots, as do the mountains now.
>
> (II. iii. 38–42)

The great truth freed in the second and third acts had social, political, humanistic implications. Here, in Act IV, it is the very structure of things Shelley would dissolve through the action of mind upon matter. This reminiscence sets the process going again and brings to light "the melancholy ruins/Of cancelled cycles." The subsequent vision (ll. 289–318), extraordinary in its harsh diction and recalling the *Ozymandias* mood but now transcending any mere moral pointing, presents "ruin within ruin" to be overcome by the mind; then it moves to the wrecks of cities whose population "was mortal, but not human," and back beyond them to "prodigious shapes/Huddled in gray annihilation," and thence to creatures of the deep, and finally to the behemoths themselves who "Increased

---

3. *The Subtler Language* (Baltimore, 1959), p. 361.

and multiplied like summer worms/On an abandoned corpse." At this point, we witness the most extraordinary completion in Shelley's poetry. The "earth-convulsing behemoth" is the most terrific phenomenon that the Shelleyan method can annihilate, and the apocalyptic deluge that overcomes this suddenly monstrous vision, in which the poetic mind itself seems overborne, is the terrible but necessary "quenching" Shelley has been seeking since this particular process was kindled at line 180. Yet Shelley offers an alternative, and more hopeful, cancellation. The image of the deluge gives way to this: "or some God/Whose throne was in a comet, passed, and cried./'Be not!' And like my words they were no more" (IV. 316–318).

This startling image brings together the strategic devices of the entire section we have been examining. This God can be identified with the enthroned infants of the moon-chariot and the earth-sphere, now grown to full demiurgic stature; moreover, the image serves as a literal *deus ex machina*, outside, paradoxically, the world Shelley's process has been destroying, and, therefore, while *that* world is destroyed, the creative power of continuity is maintained. Above all, we see here the completion of one thrust of the Shelleyan logos. The command "Be not!", which can be taken as the poetic motivation of the entire scene (ll. 180–318), cancels not only the phenomenal world, but also the Word that Shelley has been building throughout. We return to Panthea, "And like my words they were no more." With the ending of Panthea's words, the phenomenal, and the logos behind it, collapse; but a creative, saving power *above* this world has been revealed. This device compares interestingly with two uses of such an image in *Epipsychidion*. In the second part of the poem Shelley describes the fading of the Emily-figure he has been seeking:

> But She, whom prayers or tears then could not tame,
> Passed, like a God throned on a winged planet,
> Whose burning plumes to tenfold swiftness fan it,
> Into the dreary cone of our life's shade. (224–228)

But the God of *Prometheus Unbound* has destroyed this very cone, and the poem need not return to the world. The deity of Panthea's vision is more akin to the Comet of *Epipsychidion*, who, brought into the poem at line 368, "Thou too, O Comet beautiful and fierce," serves to stabilize the Shelleyan process and make possible the invitation to the voyage of the last third of the poem.

With the destruction complete, the exaltation of the marriage rites of the earth and moon has been prepared for, "The joy, the triumph, the delight, the madness!" have been made possible by an ontological reversal unparalleled in English poetry. We have taken the greatest of Shelley's boat rides, in the frailest of all his vehicles, the "thinnest boat," and we have ended in cataclysm, but have emerged safely. The Potential has overcome the Actual.

II

To speak of *Prometheus Unbound* in terms of ontological transformation, we should be able to see such a mode operating at every significant juncture of the poem. I will limit my further examination in this paper to three passages that come immediately to mind when the poem is viewed in this light: Act II, scenes ii and iii, the approach to Demogorgon's cave by Asia and Panthea, and scene v, the end of the second act, the voyage taken by Asia in the enchanted boat.

The first of these passages (II.ii), the approach to Demogorgon's cave by the unseen Oceanides, is a brilliant rendering of Mallarméan absence, the gradual emptying-out of the phenomenal and the suggested and gradual presence of the noumenal. The first Semichorus of Spirits introduces us to what I think is the main purpose of the scene: to draw us toward the potential and away from sense perception, both of sight and hearing. The path taken by Asia and Panthea is "curtained out from Heaven's wide blue," but the Shelleyan beatitudes of transformation are operative: the cloud of dew that "hangs each a pearl in the pale flowers/Of the green laurel, blown anew," and the star that cleaves through those interwoven bowers to let its beams fall, serve as guides to mark the way, while the mind itself becomes like the "frail and fair anemone" that "bends, and then fades silently" (II.ii.12). The close of this first semichorus completes the pattern of withdrawal, both in its sound effects and in its change from visual to tactile sensation: "And the gloom divine is all around,/And underneath is the mossy ground" (II.ii.22–23). Semichorus II, praised by some and damned by others, keeps the scene moving by describing the continuity of the sound that itself must fade into the larger harmonies of "Demogorgon's mighty law." The sexual sense of this lyric about the nightingales is important and has been noted before, but I think Leone Vivante has best described the function of this scene, "in which thought is distinctly represented in its ever-originating character. The new moment takes wing, as it were, out of the *infinite* in which the preceding one dissolves—and in tune with it."[4] The song of the nightingales then moves to a transcending intensity until "Sounds overflow the listener's brain/So sweet, that joy is almost pain" (II.ii.39–40). Each of these first two semichoruses ends in a mild Shelleyan collapse, preparing the way for the largest

4. *English Poetry and Its Contribution to the Knowledge of a Creative Principle* (London, 1950), p. 148.

development in this scene, the third lyric in which, in small com-
pass, the familiar soul-history of Shelley's poetry (cf. *Hymn to
Intellectual Beauty, Epipsychidion*, etc.) is presented as a mani-
festation of the withdrawal from the existent. I take "Demogor-
gon's mighty law," much allegorized and guessed at, to be the very
process of transformation Shelley is describing, the restoration of
the potential to itself. The boat imagery is familiar, as is the call to
prophetic vocation. Of more interest, perhaps, is the nice balance
between the willed and the necessary (like the poetic process itself)
described in lines 53–57, and the completion of the first half of
this scene with the appearance of the fatal mountain of Demogor-
gon. The movement of mind has ranged widely in these passages
from the "frail and fair anemone" of the beginning to the fatal
mountain that this particular fading coal has sought as its termina-
tion.

The conversation between the two fauns that follows is best un-
derstood, I think, in its dramatic function. Shelley is nowhere near
ready to bring Asia's transformation to completion. The fauns serve
as commentators and as quiet points of release, much as do Apollo
and Ocean after the fall of Jupiter. Curiously, considering the fan-
tastic nature of the whole, the fauns bring some realism and solidity
back into the scene, while at the same time they point to the possi-
bility of other transformations like the one just described. Shelley's
common technique of combining the evanescent and the solid, so
magnificently developed in Act IV, finds expression here in the de-
scription of the dwelling place of the spirits who have spoken. They
dwell in the bubbles (here limned as "pavilions") which are taken
back to the sea, and the cycle through which they pass is described
in familiar terms. When noontide has *kindled* the atmosphere,

> these burst, and the thin fiery air
> The which they breathed within those lucent domes,
> Ascends to flow like meteors through the night,
> They ride on them, and rein their headlong speed,
> And bow their burning crests, and glide in fire
> Under the waters of the earth again.   (II. ii. 77–82)

This image-cluster, descriptive of Shelley's poetic method and point-
ing to the comet-riding deity of Act IV, suggests a cyclic process
that must finally give way to completed stasis, but that develop-
ment is a long way off at this point in the poem. The last speech
of this scene points to the future, the freeing of Prometheus that
Silenus, a Shelleyan poet-prophet, will sing of, a song the fauns
wish to hear. In a sense, the fauns are lower beings, outside the
transforming developments of the second act, though they are
aware of the true prophetic note. At the end of this scene, we are

promised a greater music still: "delightful strains which cheer/Our solitary twilights, and which charm/To silence the unenvying night-ingales" (II.ii.95–97). This is the silence towards which the whole scene has been tending, where even the continuous sound of the nightingales must yield to the prophetic voice of liberation.

Act II, scene iii, continues the unwinding process of the whole act, but the reintroduction of Asia and Panthea returns us to those still untransfigured beings who must be overcome. The best description of this scene, I think, is by G. M. Matthews: "the objective setting seems unchallengeable: the nymphs have been attracted (impelled) to the terminal cone of a colossal volcano."[5] The "oracular vapour" which the poet-prophets inhale can be related to the dew of the potential in scene ii, here become active. The "voice which is contagion to the world" (II.iii.10) may be the voice of political revolution, but revolution better understood as metaphysical change, ontological transformation. Asia's Shelleyan gesture, her willingness to fall down in worship before the spirit of whom the scene is but a shadow, "weak, but beautiful," foreshadows the incredible transmutations of the fourth act, where the earth-spirit is encased in the complex machinery already discussed, beautiful, yes, but overcoming all weakness. The much-lauded metaphor that concludes the description here, almost the finest example of Shelley's presentation of matter in terms of mind, sets the process of descent going again, and, as I have already pointed out, recalls the frozen world of the opening of the poem. The imperfectly realized beings that now beckon Asia downward symbolize the proliferation of the possible that waits, and the descent to the cave is the climactic surrender of the actual in the first stages of the poem, although the ultimate transfiguration of Asia will not, of course, take place until the end of this act.

The brilliant lyric of descent that brings Asia and Panthea to Demogorgon's cave takes us further from the actual; such falling will be balanced later by the "horizontal" movement of the en-chanted boat lyric, but, appropriately, the approach to Demogorgon is seen as a terrifying fall. The Shelleyan boat ride, usually symboliz-ing the process of mind seeking its fullest object (often seen as an Elysian isle), would not be appropriate here, since Demogorgon is not a point of hoped-for resolution but rather the beginning of mystery. Asia and Panthea, bound by the spirits who take them to the cave, pass through *both* death and life, thus breaking the natural cycle, freed from the tragic vision of Blake's mental traveller. Shel-ley's travellers let go both appearance and reality to come upon a state that contains them both.

The images of this lyric are images of thought reaching for hypostatization, figures suggested and then denied. "As the fawn draws the hound" suggests the sadomasochistic pursuit by which Shelley often expresses the nature of thought, the best example of which is the Actaeon passage of *Adonais*: "And his own thoughts, along that rugged way,/Pursued, like raging hounds, their father and their prey."[6] The reversal of the grammatical order in the second stanza is part of Shelley's whole strategy of reversal in this act, while the negatives of the third stanza continue this development until the heavens and the cavern-crags are abolished, along with the darkness of earth: "Nor the gloom to Earth given" (II.iii.79). The images of the fourth stanza of this lyric are images of Potentiality, power withheld, seeking a fresh actualization. Such images indicate that this lyric is, in part, "about" the creative process itself, the Shelleyan fading coal. The "veiled lightning asleep" and the "spark nursed in embers" point to the possibility of poetry; the "last look love remembers," as often in Shelley, signifies the creative absence that starts the poem, while the last image, "Like a diamond, which shines/On the dark wealth of mines" (86–87), points to the secret internality of the potential state, as well as to the hardness of its possible form.

The concluding stanza of this lyric shifts the emphasis from the dizzying, downward flight itself to the moral injunction of the spirit. The "weakness" that Asia is urged not to resist is the final giving up of the actual, the release of the merely phenomenal which the entire second act is devoted to spiritualizing. She has already shown herself in this scene willing to fall down and worship the spirit, and her continued surrender is proof of her capacity to be the vehicle of the transforming power of love in the poem. The "meekness" in which she will find strength is the putting off of Blakean-Shelleyan Selfhood, the abandonment of the narrowly-ordering ego that finds forms completed, static, mechanical. If these are surrendered, Demogorgon will "unloose through life's portal" the Doom of Jupiter, "snake-like" because the snake stands for the cyclical development from father to child, that is, from Saturn to Jupiter to Demogorgon, a cycle that comes to an end with the release of Prometheus.[7] The concluding lines, with their hollow O's, and the curious dimeter line that concludes the whole lyric set us down firmly, deep within the world of Demogorgon, an echoing promise of what is to come.

But the transformation of Asia into a potential state is not com-

---

6. For other images of the same kind in Shelley see the antelopes of *Alastor* 103 and *Epipsychidion* 75, and the deer of *The Triumph of Life* 407.

7. I think it might be helpful to see Demogorgon's snake as the cyclical snake, the ouroboros, with its tail in its mouth. This must be distinguished from the amphisbaena of *Prometheus*, III.iv. 119, an image of the cycle overcome, an image of open form, with a head at either end.

plete; she is merely brought into its realm. The two concluding lyrics of Act II, "Life of Life" and "My soul is an enchanted boat," complete this process. These are, of course, very famous moments in the poem and famous in themselves. Yet, for all the discussion these poems have occasioned, critics have been insufficiently aware of their rightness here at the end of the second act and the inevitable relationship they have to each other. After the attempt at hypostasis in the first lyric, with its calculated collapse ("Dizzy, lost, yet unbewailing!"), the impulse towards movement is necessary, and that this should take the form of the boat ride should surprise no one—we see the same development: stabilization, calculated collapse, and then the voyage out in *Epipsychidion* and elsewhere. The "Life of Life" lyric is Shelley's most delicately sustained hypostasis, with the last line of each stanza threatening to break down the very image the stanza has sought to maintain. Then Asia's answer in the enchanted boat lyric is the fully appropriate response, and the inevitable one, as her soul seeks its final point of rest.

The last stanza is our main concern. Whatever its Platonic and Wordsworthian sources or analogues, this return to a pre-existent state represents one of the climaxes of the return to Potentiality in the poem, a journey we have been taking since the first scene of this act. The higher innocence of Blake, the yearning for the primordial waters in Wordsworth, the search for the unitive ground in Coleridge, even the Keatsian ritualistic quest for the finer tone—all bear upon this lyric, one of the key moments, it seems to me, in English Romanticism. Asia, now transfigured by love, about to rejoin the transformed Prometheus, like the Romantic poet must seek out her origins in order that the present time be redeemed. "Age's icy caves" reminds us again of the frozen world of the poem's beginning, and while "Manhood's dark and tossing waves" may be too much of a "public image," as Harold Bloom suggests,[8] the momentum is recaptured in "Youth's smooth ocean, smiling to betray," the confident beginning of the Shelleyan quest that so often gives way to despair. But here the "betrayal" is overcome by the *backward* movement of Asia's boat. She passes beyond "shadow-peopled Infancy,/Through Death and Birth, to a diviner day" (III. v.104–105), and by so doing comes upon the Shelleyan lower Paradise, the Great Good Place which Bloom, I think convincingly, compares with the Blakean Beulah-land.[9] It is also worth noting that this "paradise of vaulted bowers" is seen as a perfect internality, "Lit by downward-gazing flowers" suggesting a higher narcissism, an achieved recovery of a total and undivided state, "Peopled by shapes too bright to see," which walk upon the water, singing— the potential in Shelley often signified by this fortunate combina-

8. Bloom, p. 130.   9. *Ibid.*

tion of light and music. It is also worth remarking that the confused syntax here (I think the sense finds Asia and her pilot "resting," i.e., coming to a stop, and the "thee" to whom she speaks is her pilot, the voice in the air) brings the lyric to, as Locock says, "a wretchedly weak conclusion."[1] This, I think, is not the calculated collapse that closes the "Life of Life" lyric, but a simple failure to bring the voyage to an artistically satisfying conclusion. Shelley has not devised a strategy to keep this coal from fading satisfactorily and, in fact, does not want to suggest finality here. The next two acts of the drama must do this for him; so Asia's trip ends lamely enough. Only in *Adonais*, perhaps, does this kind of Shelleyan voyage reach triumphant port—and even there it is at the cost of personal annihilation.

III

The sections of the poem we have studied, Act IV, lines 180–318, and II, scenes ii, iii, and v, define the characteristic movement of mind in the poem; the cleansing of the actual that a new potential may emerge. The whole poem, I think, could be profitably analyzed from this perspective. Shelley *is* concerned with reform in the poem, but the reform is more metaphysical than political and more ontological than social. The poem, in its movement from the tragic stasis of the opening to the lyrical stasis of the close, proceeds through a series of strategic maneuvers that spiritualize the physical and make possible what has already hardened into fact. All this, of course, is purely mental and manifests perhaps the most inspired wish in English literature. Comparing *The Triumph of Life* with *Prometheus*, Harold Bloom writes precisely:

> The hope here in *Prometheus* is dialectical, but is still hope; Shelley believes in his myth. In *The Triumph of Life* faith in the myth is abandoned. This does not mean that Shelley rejects the myth, thinks it false. The myth itself is aware of its necessary defeat, but affirms human possibility. In *Prometheus* Shelley dwells in possibility, with all its windows and doors. In *The Triumph* . . . the fairer house is deserted for the vision of human probability.[2]

This dwelling in possibility, or, as I have termed it, the return to Potentiality, takes two forms in the passages we have discussed. The second of these, Asia's descent to Demogorgon and her voyage out in the enchanted boat, describes the process of this return in terms of the individual soul; the other passage, the visions of the moonchariot and the sphere of the earth, has more to do with the return to the potential of the very structure of created things. By this

1. Locock, p. 616.   2. Bloom, p. 117.

time in the drama, the recognizably anthropomorphic figures have been put aside. While Prometheus and Asia inhabit their cave, a larger process takes over and completes Shelley's form.

The sources of Asia's enchanted boat ride have long been traced to several Platonic and Neoplatonic texts. Perhaps the most relevant for our purposes is the following from the *Phaedrus*. Speaking of pre-existence, Socrates says:

> And then we beheld the beatific vision and were initiated into a mystery which may be truly called most blessed, celebrated by us in our state of innocence, before we had any experience of evils to come, when we were admitted to the sight of apparitions innocent and simple and calm and happy, which we beheld shining in pure light, pure ourselves and not yet enshrined in that living tomb which we carry about, now that we are imprisoned in the body, like an oyster in his shell. Let me linger over the memory of scenes which have passed away.[3]

This is clearly the situation to which Asia has returned at the end of Act II, and the significance of her return rests in a state of recovered innocence, the higher innocence which so dominates the most characteristic Romantic poetry. The Platonic anamnesis, of which Asia's voyage is a splendid example, is essentially a *psychological* phenomenon, and the cleansing of the human psyche in *Prometheus Unbound* particularly as this is expressed in Act II, points the way to an essentially humanistic concern. But the other passage we have examined, IV, lines 180–318, has less to do with human possibility as with the structure of Being itself as the mind, and particularly the mind of the poet, is able to conceive it.

The extraordinary development from the thinnest boat of the moon-chariot to the comet-enthroned deity who cancels creation is a single movement of thought, precise in its detail and inevitable in its progress. The passage seems to me, as does all of *Prometheus Unbound*, an attempt to mirror the creative mind at full stretch, and ultimately to be self-reflexive, about itself. All the admitted failures and yet continuing attempts to allegorize the poem fail, I think, because of the failure to recognize its organic development in terms of the creative process and the way Shelley apparently wrote and conceived his poems. His remark in the *Defence* that "the most glorious poetry that has ever been communicated to the world is probably a feeble shadow of the original conceptions of the poet" may be a dubious point in the construction of a poetics, but it illuminates the Shelleyan problem exactly. Shelley's poetry seeks the form that will best recover what that form, by actualizing itself, must necessarily lose. This concept of form is best explained by Signor Leone Vivante, whose philosophy of indeterminism as

3. *The Dialogues of Plato*, trans. Benjamin Jowett, 5 vols. (London, 1892), I, 456–457.

expressed in A *Philosophy of Potentiality* and whose chapter on Shelley in his *English Poetry and Its Contribution to the Knowledge of a Creative Principle* have been of great value to the present writer. Vivante views form in this way:

> *Form*—in other words, actualization, consciousness taking shape, *presence*—however essential to value, does not entirely explain it. What is the element which we call image, expression, form, actualization, in comparison with the immensity of sorrow, of love, of sacrifice? What is the pang—the *form*—of a desperate sorrow, as compared with the infinite virtuality which, in that very moment, seems to exceed our consciousness? Form, though it be a primal force and an original motive-value, in which power itself is inflamed, enriched and confirmed, exalted and appeased, cannot be compared with such an infinite intimate urge—which yet does not exist without an element of form and which craves for form. Potentiality, however much it may have its *raison d'être* in actualization, nevertheless exceeds actualization and every existentiality of its own.[4]

Such a conception of the relation between form and that out of which form emerges helps to explain some of the failures in Shelley's poetry and some of those necessary collapses in which the form of his thought itself runs its course to completion, but the poem itself does not fail as an aesthetic structure. We might say that in the great passages of Act IV Potentiality indeed exceeds every existentiality, the destructive progress of the beams from the earth-infant returning us to the fullest Potentiality, an apocalyptic stasis in which time and the cyclical process come to an end.

The Shelleyan form exists to mirror consciousness, not consciousness of any particular object, but the fact of consciousness itself. Again, Signor Vivante offers the best definition for our purposes:

> Consciousness is first of all an immediate value of actualization, beyond any distinction between subject and object. And this not only in germinal or vague, indefinite moments, but in the highest forms of thought. The positing of the object belongs—in tendency—to the processes of external construction and extrinsic causality, where all deep and rich implication of value—all originality, all fecund spontaneity of intelligence is lost. So much so that creative positivity finds an obstacle not only in the object, but in its very form, inasmuch as this tends to objectify itself. The garment of the flame of the spirit falls to ashes as soon as looked at.[5]

We recognize the Shelleyan image here, whether intentional or not, for this account of consciousness is similar to Shelley's theory of the fading coal. Moreover, viewing the Shelleyan process in this light,

4. *A Philosophy of Potentiality* (London, 1955), p. 46.   5. *Ibid.*, pp. 15–16.

we can see that the tendency in Shelley's work to transcend the object is not, as has long been charged, a manifestation of a weak grasp of the actual, but, put positively, should be seen as a demonstration of the poet's profound awareness of the processes of thought and poetry. At its best, Shelley's poetry is of the profoundest value in revealing to us the sources of consciousness and the unity of its concerns.

Prometheus Unbound is the crucial example of this development in Shelley's poetry because it is the most ambitious attempt in his work to *restore* our sense of the beginning of things. The poem seeks to establish a pure present, beyond time, by moving backward to the pre-existent, for, while the whole appears to press towards futurity, it does so not that a new existent may emerge, but that a new Potentiality may sustain itself; it mirrors the mind freed from the causal, purified, transformed. The passages I have examined, Asia's descent to Demogorgon and her final transformation, and the great visions of the fourth act, are vital instances of the true structure of the poem. At first, their motives seem very different: Asia, as Eros, moves *backward* to a prior state of being, recovering the potential through a reflexive act; the visions of the moon-chariot and the earth-sphere move *forward* from the beginning of things, through the destructive process of time, to annihilation. But the end is the same; we arrive at Pure Being. Such a voyage must be distinguished from the transcendence of *Adonais*, which invokes death as the solution to poetic and intellectual form. There is no symbolic dying of this kind in *Prometheus*. The dualism that finally overwhelms Shelley in *The Triumph of Life*, and of which *Adonais* is merely the opposite coin, is absent in *Prometheus*. There, Potentiality reigns.

IRENE H. CHAYES

["Ode to the West Wind"][†]

"Ode to the West Wind" (1819) is as distinctive among Shelley's odes as "Dejection" is among Coleridge's, and the two poems, separated by some seventeen years, are remarkably similar to each other. With the same traditional and Romantic associations as Coleridge's storm-wind, Shelley's West Wind too is a dynamic, destructive, universal force that is ultimately beneficial, both "destroyer" and "preserver." As in "Dejection," the might of the wind

† Reprinted by permission of the Modern Language Association of America from "Rhetoric as Drama: An Approach to the Romantic Ode," *PMLA*, 79 (March 1964), pp. 71–74.

is in contrast to human weakness—the weakness of the speaker himself, who is a poet contemplating the ideal poetic powers from a subjective situation the very opposite of ideal.[1] The extreme negative state that must be transcended here is not only spiritual death, despair, but actual physical death as well. The West Wind is the wind of autumn and death, and the ground metaphor of the ode, introduced in stanza 1, is one that is constant in Shelley's poetry, so fundamental to his way of thinking that "metaphor" is an inadequate name for it: the working out of the seasonal cycle in nature as a continuing process of universal death and regeneration. The problem here is a more urgent version of that posed in *Alastor* and *Adonais*, as well as in "Stanzas Written in Dejection": what is the place of humanity in the grand cosmic order? If, as the familiar Shelleyan imagery implies, there is an analogy between the processes of nature and the life of man, how can the analogy be completed to save man too from extinction at physical death? The answer in "Ode to the West Wind," like Coleridge's approach to a resolution of the situation in "Dejection," takes the form of a dramatic recovery and reversal by way of a pattern of rhetoric.

The whole poem is a single, sustained apostrophe, which begins abruptly, without preamble or descriptive frame, is spoken directly by the poet, and throughout its interwoven tercets keeps the object of address always in the foreground. The first three stanzas are devoted to a formal invocation, in which the wind is characterized, and praised, in its role of destroyer and preserver in nature by its effects on the land vegetation, the sky, and the sea.[2] In stanza IV, the speaker begins what he himself calls a prayer (l. 52), and in the course of this he uses a series of parallel imperatives that make up a progression as significant and dramatically functional as the epithets in stanza VII of "Dejection." Although each is a rhetorical command, or appeal, to the wind, amplifying its power in relation to the man addressing it, the speaker is also expressing his feelings about himself as a human being facing extinction of identity and as a Romantic poet-prophet facing frustration and defeat in his heroically conceived vocation. At first, in the "sore need" out of which he begins to speak, his wish is only to surrender to the wind's superior force, like the nonhuman objects named in the invocation:

1. Shelley's own note describing the setting in which the ode was "conceived and chiefly written" (*Prometheus Unbound, . . . With Other Poems*, London, 1820, p. 188) includes wind and a sunset storm like those in "Dejection." On the beginning state of mind, cf. "Stanzas Written in Dejection, Near Naples" (1818), esp. ll. 19–27.
2. Contrasting the Neoclassical and Romantic odes with respect to their rhetoric, Maclean observes (*Critics and Criticism*,

p. 434) that the famous odes by Wordsworth, Shelley, and Keats "are not artistic constructions designed to the end of amplifying the wonders, respectively, of immortality, wind, and nightingales." Yet to say that "Ode to the West Wind," like stanza VII of "Dejection," is first of all an encomium of wind in the fulness of its natural and symbolic meanings is to make possible all else that may be said about it. On the nightingale, see sec. IV below.

"Oh, lift me as a wave, a leaf, a cloud!" Confessing exhaustion, pain, oppression, despair (ll. 54–56), he in effect accepts death in this stanza, like the Poet at the edge of the precipice in *Alastor* (ll. 625ff.). The elegiac last line assimilates the man to the wind, "One too like thee: tameless, and swift, and proud," but by way of qualities which humanize the wind as well.

The second imperative, "Make me thy lyre, even as the forest is," opens stanza v with a reminder of another archetypal image Shelley shares with Coleridge, which for Shelley usually represents the mind in its passive, receptive functions, or the transience of human life itself.[3] The West Wind, like its counterpart in "Dejection," is conceived now as a performer, transforming man and nature alike into its own kind of art. Like the forest with its falling leaves, the speaker dying is prepared to become part of the wind's "mighty harmonies," adding "a deep, autumnal tone,/Sweet though in sadness" to its "tumult" (ll. 58–61). On the basis of these lines, especially, some critics have too readily assumed that the remainder of the ode merely intensifies an identification between the poet and nature. For instance: "This identification represents, so to speak, the unity which the poem is to win from variety. The individual is to be merged with the general; Shelley [sic] is to become the instrument through which speaks the universal voice."[4] But such an interpretation overlooks the abrupt change in tone and attitude in the third imperative, which follows immediately (ll. 61–62) and for the first time is an outright command: "Be thou, Spirit fierce,/My spirit! Be thou me, impetuous one!" This is by no means an identification by the speaker with the wind in which he loses his individual identity; he does not say "Let me be thee," as he would necessarily be saying if the "individual" here were indeed being "merged with the general."

Like Coleridge in stanza vii of "Dejection," Shelley in the remainder of stanza v draws together and fuses the two sides of the analogy that has been developing in the invocation and the first two imperatives to the wind. The image of the fallen leaves, reintroduced in the reference to the forest (l. 58), has in Shelley a continuing association with death, not only because the leaves mark the end of a seasonal cycle but also because they can be picked up and scattered to dissolution by the destroyer wind.[5] In stanza i of the ode the leaves are "pestilence-stricken multitudes," driven before the wind "like ghosts from an enchanter fleeing," and in the fourth imperative of the later sequence (ll. 63–64) "withered

3. Cf. "A Defence of Poetry," in *Shelley's Prose*, or, *The Trumpet of a Prophecy*, ed. D. L. Clark (Albuquerque, N.M., 1954), p. 277AB; "Essay on a Future State," ibid., p. 176B; *Alastor*, ll. 42–44, 667–668.

4. R. H. Fogle, "The Imaginal Design of Shelley's 'Ode to the West Wind'," *ELH*, XV (1948), 221.

5. Cf. *Alastor*, ll. 583–586.

leaves" becomes an explicit simile for the speaker's "dead thoughts," which he commands the wind to "drive" over the universe. But the whole line includes an additional idea: the "dead thoughts" are to "quicken a new birth," and this brings them also into correspondence with the "wingèd seeds" which in stanza I are carried by the wind to "their dark wintry bed" (l. 6) to await the coming of spring. The speaker's "words," which the wind next is commanded to "scatter" (ll. 65–67), are compared in turn to "ashes and sparks" —a new image that is directly analogous to the dead leaves and wingèd seeds, juxtaposing end and beginning, death and rebirth, in a relation about to be affirmed for the speaker and mankind in general as well as for physical nature.

In the closing lines of stanza v, the rhetorical and dramatic patterns produce a new shift. The verbs in lines 63–67, "drive" and "scatter," are still transitive, like the earlier "lift me," "make me," of the speaker's stages of weakness. Both his "thoughts" and his "words," like the lyre of the first tercet, are to be *acted upon* by the wind, although with a different result. At the same time, the wind is subtly reduced in power by the command that it "scatter" the poet's words, for the medium is to be the poet's own art: "by the incantation of this verse" (l. 65). In the sixth and last command of the sequence the intrusive construction of "Be thou me," which appeared between the "lyre" and "thoughts" passages, returns to mark at once the rhetorical climax of the poem and the dramatic Reversal. In stanza I, a "clarion" was to be blown by the wind of rebirth in springtime to rouse the buried seeds (ll. 9–12). At the conclusion of the last stanza, we find that the autumn wind itself (*not* the poet) is to be the instrument of awakening, and the speaker, the man who a few lines earlier sought to be a passive lyre, is the one who will sound its call: "Be through my lips to unawakened earth/The trumpet of a prophecy!" He does not "become the instrument through which speaks the universal voice," for his is the voice that speaks.[6]

The rhetorical-dramatic progression in Shelley's ode, then, ends in a total inversion of the original relation between the speaker and the West Wind. As in "Dejection" but less equivocally, a downward reversal of condition, or "fortune," in the past is followed by an upward reversal in direction and intention, which negates the first. The man rises from his state of prostrate surrender to join himself to the force of the wind, master it—fulfilling his boyhood ambition

---

6. Here I am in disagreement also with the special interpretation of Bloom, *Shelley's Mythmaking*, pp. 87, 89–90. The progression from leaves to seeds and thoughts to words, concluding in a vocal utterance, has a justification in the tradition of prophecy; cf. *Aeneid* VI.74–76, in which Aeneas prays the Cumaean Sibyl to chant her verses instead of committing them to leaves which may be disordered by the winds.

to "outstrip" it (ll. 50–51)—and turn it into an instrument of his own. Passive becomes active and active, passive; agent and medium, performer and performed upon, change places. The "destroyer" becomes the "preserver" by serving as the means to prophecy, and the liberating prophecy itself is both made possible by and contained in "the incantation of this verse," which is to say *this* verse, or "Ode to the West Wind."[7] Here process and product are identical, as they are not quite in "Dejection," and the composition of the ode is necessary to the resolution of the speaker's situation, which is completed with the formulation of the prophecy. The actual prophecy, when it is finally given in the last line, sums up the Discovery, which the poet has been demonstrating dramatically in the course of the poem. Still addressed to the wind, which has now become a human power as well, it confirms the analogy that has been explored in the imagery of leaves and seeds, thoughts and words, by turning from both man and nature to the seasonal cycle that includes both: "O Wind,/If Winter comes, can Spring be far behind?" If the force of the triumphant enthymeme is somewhat weakened by its being cast in the form of a question, the only one in the ode,[8] this too has a dramatic function, I think. By his uncertainty at the moment he is affirming his victory over his own weakness and despair, the speaker is indicating that he is about to cross the metaphysical boundary line, represented in *Alastor* by the precipice on which the Poet dies, between the individual and universal phases of existence as Shelley conceived it.

In "Dejection," the burden of act is placed on the ambiguous power embodied in the storm-wind; in "Ode to the West Wind," it is assumed by the speaker himself, although he starts from an even lower point than Coleridge's poet. If in "Dejection" the wind descends, or is brought down, to the level of the human, in Shelley's ode the man raises himself to a level above both the human and the mundane natural. The redeeming energy that comes in vision to Coleridge's poet is perhaps closest to the power of divine wrath, momentarily transformed and transferred to the visionary and paving the way for the operation of the human imagination. For Shelley, on the other hand, what is needed in the final extremity is the force of the moral and creative will,[9] the human becoming divine, to enable the products of the imagination to survive and do their work, through which the poet himself will be reborn. In their central addresses to the symbolic winds, both odes are prayers; but

7. As an "incantation," the poem itself replaces the "enchanter" wind saluted in the opening (l. 3).

8. In an early draft the line was declarative: "When Winter comes Spring lags not far behind." (See *Verse and Prose from the Manuscripts of Percy Bysshe Shelley*, ed. Sir J. C. E. Shelley-Rolls and Roger Ingpen, priv. print., London, 1934, p. 58.) Cf. *The Revolt of Islam* IX.xxv.3685–3689.

9. Cf., in slightly different terms, M. T. Wilson, *Shelley's Later Poetry: A Study of His Prophetic Imagination* (New York, 1959), p. 299.

rather than "secularized versions of an older devotional poetry, employed in the examination of the soul's condition as it approaches and retreats from God,"[1] I find them passionate supplications for deliverance, uttered out of the depths of spiritual crises that are not the less profound because they are concerned directly with the activity and functions of the artist. Like the petitioner in Donne's Holy Sonnet, "Batter my heart, three person'd God," Coleridge's poet requires salvation by assault; Shelley's in his own word "strives" with his unequal antagonist, like Jacob of the Old Testament or like the Victorian Jacob in Gerard Manley Hopkins' "Carrion Comfort." In both instances, the prayer becomes the occasion of an experience very close to mystical, but only in "Ode to the West Wind" does it have an outcome in its own terms—nothing less than a resurrection of and through the poetic word.

CARLOS BAKER

[The Cenci][†]

To group Shelley's historical tragedy, *The Cenci*, with such conversation-poems as *Rosalind and Helen* and *Julian and Maddalo* may seem at first glance to involve a violation of the somewhat inelastic laws which govern literary *genres*, for *The Cenci* is obviously a stage-drama, composed to be acted. In other respects, however, *The Cenci* resembles the two pieces which preceded it sufficiently to justify its inclusion here. Like them it is made to serve as a vehicle for Shelley's moral ideas. As in the conversation-poems, Shelley projects his ideas through dramatic dialogue, his method being to place two characters vis-à-vis and to develop opposed points of view by means of impassioned conversational interchange. There are accordingly reasonable grounds for considering *The Cenci* in conjunction with the conversation pieces.

Of the three poems to which the present chapter is devoted, *The Cenci* was by all odds Shelley's strongest bid for popular favor. . . . He toned down the uglier aspects of the original story in order, as he thought, to make it acceptable to a bourgeois theater-going public. He chose a subject which for two centuries had continued to excite wide interest among the Romans. He adopted a plainer style, abjuring high-flown images, and seeking to come as close as his subject allowed to the everyday language of men.

1. Abrams, *English Romantic Poets*, p. 48.
† From Chapter 5, "The Human Heart: The Conversation-Poems of 1818" in Carlos Baker, *Shelley's Major Poetry:*

The Fabric of Vision (copyright 1948 by Princeton University Press), pp. 138–153. Reprinted by permission of Princeton University Press.

Even more than the first two points, the last two seem to have been part of a definite plan in Shelley's mind, both in the year of the conversation-poems and as late as the year of his death. He now sought story-structures which already existed in popular tradition, and which might therefore be expected to exert a stronger grip on the imaginations of the people. This search for "natural" subjects appears to have had something to do with his choice of the Promethean myth. Like the Greek tragedians, he did not feel "bound to adhere to the common interpretation, or to imitate in story as in title" the great treatments which in the past had been accorded this and other myths. In other words, he found precedent among his peers for allowing himself to invent freely within the general framework of a traditional story. At the same time, he could count on his audience's acquaintance with the general shape of a given myth or legend or historical event, and hence assume from the start a certain sympathy between his auditors and his subject. The Job legend, for example, fitted his plans admirably. In selecting the story of the Cenci, he observed that "*King Lear* and the two plays in which the tale of Oedipus is told were stories which already existed in tradition" before Shakespeare and Sophocles gave them permanent literary form. In Rome, at least, he found that everyone knew as much about the Cenci scandal as if it had occurred two years instead of two centuries before. "This national and universal interest" in the affair first suggested to him, he said, its fitness for dramatic purposes.

He was also coming round, for the time being, to an almost Wordsworthian view of poetic language. "I entirely agree with those modern critics," said he, "who assert that in order to move men to true sympathy we must use the familiar language of men. . . . But it must be the real language of men in general, and not that of any particular class to whose society the writer happens to belong."[1] He was plainly in search of what Coleridge, in the recently published *Biographia Literaria*, had called the *lingua communis*. Equally plain is the reason for his choice: he adopts this language "in order to move men to true sympathy." About the introductory and closing sections of *Julian and Maddalo*, he thought in similar though somewhat more limited terms. Sending this poem to Hunt a week after he had finished *The Cenci*, he observed that Hunt ought to like the manner in which it was written. "I have employed," he said, "a certain familiar style of language to express the actual way in which people talk with each other whom education and a certain refinement of sentiment have placed above the use of vulgar idioms."[2]

1. Preface to *The Cenci*.   2. Julian Edition, X, 68. Aug. 15, 1819.

In the three years of life which remained, Shelley never wholly abandoned the belief that one way to enlist popular sympathy was to employ a selection of the language really used by men—provided, of course, that the subject sanctioned it. He continued to write certain poems designed only for the eyes of the esoteric few. He felt that the familiar style was hardly feasible "in the treatment of a subject wholly ideal, or in that part of any subject which relates to common life, where the passion, exceeding a certain limit, touches the boundaries of that which is ideal."[3] Otherwise he believed in, and in such poems as *The Masque of Anarchy* carefully experimented with, the *lingua communis* and the familiar style.[4]

Besides a more or less systematic attempt to enlarge his circle of listeners, Shelley obviously gave some thought in the year of the conversation-poems to the nature of tragedy. *Prometheus Unbound*, though roughly modeled after the Aeschylean original, had not turned out to be a tragedy in the Greek tradition, and certainly not a tragedy in the English sense of that word. Shelley had shown Prometheus rejecting hatred, admitting love and pity, and triumphing at last over the sufferings which beset the human mind when it is not its own sovereign. Of such agony as Prometheus endured he had presumably some personal knowledge, as he had had, for example, personal knowledge of the mental state of the *Alastor* poet. But in writing *The Cenci*, as he later remarked to Trelawny, his object was to see how well he could succeed in describing passions he had never personally felt.

He was also, and again for the time being, focusing his attention more on Elizabethan than on classical models. Wishing to show a true picture of human beings in action instead of treating the kind of subject he called "ideal," he turned from mythology to history, and from his "beautiful idealisms of moral excellence" to the dark realities of mortal turpitude and error. Up to this time, as he told Hunt, his writing had consisted of "little else than visions" which "impersonated" (that is, projected by means of intentionally symbolic personages) his own "apprehensions of the beautiful and the just: . . . dreams of what ought to be or may be." The published pieces (*Queen Mab*, *Alastor*, and *The Revolt of Islam*) showed those "literary defects incidental to youth and impatience." Now he laid aside "the presumptuous attitude of an instructor" and

3. *Ibid.*, pp. 68–69.
4. Had *The Cenci* been phenomenally successful, or had *Julian and Maddalo* been published and popular in his lifetime, Shelley might have done more conversation-poems, or at least poems designed for the people. Work done in the familiar style, besides the *Masque of Anarchy*, would include *Peter Bell the Third*, *Oedipus Tyrannus*, some of the lesser political lyrics, the poem to Mary introducing *The Witch of Atlas*, *The Sensitive Plant*, the *Letter to Maria Gisborne*, and some parts of the fragmentary *Charles I*. The other poems of the period 1819–1822 move in the realm of the "ideal," as in *The Witch of Atlas*, *Adonais*, *Epipsychidion*, *Hellas*, the fragmentary *Magic Plant*, and the fragmentary *Triumph of Life*.

turned to "sad reality." The *Prometheus Unbound* had depicted the results in the human mind of moral reform; *The Cenci* showed the results in human society of moral deformity.

For Shelley, tragedy consisted in moral deformity. At the same time, he believed that no tragedy written for the stage should be "subservient to what is vulgarly termed a moral purpose." He had purposely laid aside the presumptuous attitude of an instructor, which meant that he had abrogated direct moral preachment. "It is nothing," he told Peacock of *The Cenci*, "which by any courtesy of language can be termed either moral or immoral." He felt that had anything like the Promethean kind of moral or poetic justice been employed in telling the story of Beatrice, the effectiveness of the play as tragedy would have been diminished. "Undoubtedly," said he, perhaps with his recent experience of the *Prometheus* in his mind's eye, "the fit return to make to the most enormous injuries is kindness and forbearance and a resolution to convert the injurer from his dark passions by peace and love." Undoubtedly, also, revenge or retaliation or even atonement are "pernicious mistakes." Yet if Beatrice had acted with kindness and forbearance, and if she had used the instruments of peace and love instead of appealing to the hatred which the assassins Marzio and Olimpio bore towards her father, she would not, in Shelley's opinion, have been a tragic character.

In selecting the old Italian story as the subject of a tragedy, the nineteenth-century meliorist became involved with a moral problem for which there was no easy solution. Shelley's dilemma in composing *The Cenci* was that of a writer whose moral disapproval of any act involving bloodshed was close to absolute, yet who was compelled, by the very circumstances of his source-story, to make his heroine resort to bloodshed as the means of extirpating a ruthless and triumphant social and domestic evil which was itself close to absolute. If Shelley were really to write a tragedy, it was unthinkable to invent a denouement in which Beatrice succeeded in converting the injurer "from his dark passions" by the exercise of peace and love. His admiration for Beatrice is evident, and it was necessary to engage the sympathies of the audience by painting Beatrice as a fundamentally admirable character. One might be led to conclude on the basis of Shelley's evident admiration that in his view any act which stamps out evil on earth is not only excusable but also desirable. Such a conclusion would, however, be quite in error. Shelley never sanctioned bloodshed, even when the blood was as black as Count Cenci's. To him Beatrice was admirable in spite of, not because of, her taking arms against a sea of troubles, as Hamlet was admirable in spite of, not because of, his act of vengeance. The words which he applies to Beatrice—"a most gentle and amiable being . . . violently thwarted from her nature by the necessity of circumstance and opinion"—could no doubt with equal justice be applied to Shelley's reading of Hamlet's character.[5]

The contrast between *Prometheus* and *The Cenci* is the contrast between what might be and what is. As in the *Prometheus*, Shelley subjected his central figure to all the diabolical rapier-thrusts and bludgeonings that mind and flesh could bear. But this time the reaction was more complicated, as the individual human being is always more complicated than any symbol which can be devised for him. This time no ethical conversion renovated the world. Instead, under indignities of the most horrible kind, a gentle and innocent girl was turned into an efficient machine of vengeance, coolly planning, imperiously executing, denying her part in, and at last calmly dying for the murder of her father. After it was over, history, that "record of crimes and miseries" in human society, moved on as before.

In the summer of 1819, while he was at work on *The Cenci*, Shelley spoke feelingly of "that ever-present Malthus, Necessity," and the implication is, since Malthus was a thoroughgoing economic determinist, that however much Shelley may have trusted in the regenerative powers of the mind, he still regarded some form of Necessity as a strong and perhaps ineluctable force in human social organization.[6] Under the compulsion of such forces, even nominally virtuous human beings might be driven from the paths of righteousness. He had already anticipated this position during the preceding year in his review of his wife's novel, *Frankenstein*, where he observed that the crimes and malevolence of the monster flowed "irresistibly from certain causes fully adequate to their production." All these crimes, he urged, were the offspring "of Necessity and Human Nature," and they served to emphasize, dramatically, the direct preachment of Mrs. Shelley's novel: "Treat a person ill, and he will become wicked."[7] Although Beatrice becomes "wicked" only long enough to murder her father and to perjure herself at the trial, the moral of *The Cenci* (despite Shelley's disavowal of a moral purpose) is essentially that which Shelley found in *Frankenstein*.

The point has often been made that *The Cenci*, like the *Prometheus*, is designed more for reading than for acting, mainly because Shelley's interest in characterization is greater than his determination that the action shall move forward. As the play stands, the point is well taken. Not only did Shelley think himself better

5. *The Cenci*, preface.
6. Julian Edition, X, 57.
7. *Ibid.*, VI, 264. This is not to be con-
fused with Shelley's preface to the novel, which he wrote at Mary's behest.

qualified for the delineation of minute and subtle distinctions of feeling than for what might be called the kinetographic elements of the drama, but he was also quite ready to admit that in *The Cenci* he had laid considerable emphasis on character-analysis. At one point, Orsino begins a long, self-analytic soliloquy with the following remark:

> 'Tis a trick of this same family
> To analyze their own and other minds.
> Such self-anatomy shall teach the will
> Dangerous secrets; for it tempts our powers,
> Knowing what must be thought, and may be done,
> Into the depth of darkest purposes.

Such pauses for "self-anatomy" as Shelley allows to the count, Beatrice, Giacomo, and Orsino serve to reveal their characters with varying degrees of fullness, but there is no doubt that these pauses act to the detriment of the play as a piece of action.

While it appears to have been generally agreed that if Shelley succeeded as a playwright at all, he succeeded chiefly in the area of character analysis, there have been few attempts to take Shelley at Orsino's word, and to discover precisely what his conception of the leading characters was, or what constitutes the psychological basis of the central struggle. Shelley's desire to anatomize and lay bare the secrets of other minds led him quite literally "into the depth of darkest purposes." To cast what light one can into these depths is basic to a critical study of the play.[8]

The count is a complex character. The widespread belief that his is a motiveless malignity ignores Shelley's careful exposition throughout the play; the father of the Cenci family has three major reasons for his conduct. One basis of his motivation is explicitly a perverted sexual drive. During his first-act conversation with Cardinal Camillo, allusion is made to the count's fiery youth, remorseless manhood, and unrepentant old age. Camillo wonders that such a man is not miserable. But Cenci is miserable only in that the onset of old age has left him less ready than formerly to translate his every thought into immediate action. He is confessedly a "hardened" man. His youth was notorious for sexual promiscuity. When the diet of what he calls "honey" palled, he required stronger stimulants, which he found in the sight and sound of physical suffering in others. But his sadistic appetites took in the end a deeper turn. Now he is satisfied only when he is able to afflict some new victim with extreme mental agony—and be there to watch its outward manifestations. In this last refinement upon his earlier methods of self-gratification, the count has simply habitu-

8. The excellent study of the play by Ernest Sutherland Bates (New York, 1908) seems least satisfactory in the chapter devoted to the characters.

ated himself to what Hawthorne was to exploit fictionally as the unpardonable sin, that is, the desire to finger the soul of another human being, and it appears that the hardening process in the count is now virtually complete. In starting from a groundwork of sexual perversion, Shelley was closely following, though cleaning up considerably, his manuscript source, "The Relation of the Death of the Family of The Cenci," where it is stated that the historical count was a thrice-convicted sodomist.[9]

The second of the count's motives is avarice, a condition of mind the less fortunate for his family in that it frequently comes into conflict with his insatiable appetites. Both in the source and in Shelley's play the count buys immunity for his deeds through the payment of large fines to Pope Clement. The voracity of his desires and the sly vigilance of the Pope's agents are such that his fortune—which he values as a guarantee of future immunity from prosecution—is rapidly diminishing. His wish to conserve it partly explains his maltreatment of his sons, who are a drain upon his resources and have lately received a judgment from the Pope which requires the count to support them. Hence the father's delight when the two boys suffer accidental deaths in Spain, and his reason for stealing, by a legal trick, the dowry-money in the possession of his eldest son, Giacomo.

But Shelley is both refining and enlarging upon his source-manuscript, as his development of a third complicating motive shows. The source explains the count's inhuman treatment of Beatrice as a combination of avarice and sexual perversion. He imprisoned his daughter to prevent her following the example of her sister, who had fled the palace, married, and through the Pope's intercession had extracted from the count a good-sized dowry. According to the source, the count's attempts to debauch Beatrice were far more frequent and ugly than Shelley's play indicates: he sought her naked in bed, compelled her presence during his encounters with sundry courtesans, and tried to persuade her "that children born of the commerce of a father and his daughter were all saints." Shelley either omits or merely hints at such horrors because he wishes to make dramatic capital of a single sexual attack. Moreover his portrait of the count subordinates avarice to a third motive, vengeance.

This is not, as Shelley builds it, a simple block-like vengeance, but a whole nervous complex of deeper drives, where the deepest has no place, except by inference, in the source-account. It appears that the count's desire for vengeance arose from his relations with his first wife, who died, according to the source, "after she had given birth to seven unfortunate children." The count had always

9. The source-manuscript in Shelley's own translation may be consulted in Woodberry's edition of the play, Belles Lettres Series, Boston, 1909.

been a domestic tyrant *in extremis*, and nothing enraged him so much as defiance of his authority, whether as parent or (observe his treatment of his second wife, Lucretia) as husband. Shelley is following his source in saying that from their earliest days he abused his children.[1] When they were too weak to help themselves, Lucretia served them as protector; in recent years the maturing Beatrice has assumed this office. As a result the daughter has been brought into sporadic conflict with a domestic tyrant content only with absolute power over the minds and bodies of his family.

Although the sourcebook is so vague about the vengeance motive that it must be regarded as Shelley's own refinement, the play leaves the impression that the count's hatred of his children and his desire to dominate them stems ultimately from his hatred of their mother. The first wife was "an exceedingly rich lady" who married a complete profligate. If the count in those days was running true to form, he lost no time in establishing his dominance over both her fortune and her person. The fact that she bore him seven children would not in itself suggest a ruthless sexual campaign were it not that the count even now displays his faith that sexual domination is a trustworthy means to the subduing of women. At the close of the banquet scene, the count dismisses his nubile daughter with the boast that he knows a charm to make her meek and mild. The charm he contemplates is sexual intercourse. Why should he imagine that it would render her meek instead of desperately resistant unless his importunate sexuality had produced that very reaction in her mother? It is entirely in character for the count to suppose that through the persecution of his dead wife's offspring he can continue to wreak vengeance upon her memory.

In any event, he is not long in putting his "charm" to work. During his visit to Beatrice's chamber some hours after the banquet he manages, though without overt declaration, to make it clear to Beatrice that he intends to rape her. At that point she is still able to face him down with "a stern and an inquiring brow." But on the following morning, his sudden appearance in a room where she is talking with Lucretia and her younger brother catches her unprepared and opens the first seam in her defiant reserve. Seeing her fear, the count gleefully capitalizes upon it.

> Never again, I think, with fearless eye,
> And brow superior, and unaltered cheek,
> And that lip made for tenderness or scorn,
> Shalt thou strike dumb the meanest of mankind;
> Me least of all. Now get thee to thy chamber!

1. The source states that the abuse began while the children "were yet too young to have given him any real cause of displeasure."

That his joy comes from the satisfaction of a long-postponed desire to break her spirit is clear enough. That he is even then thinking of her mother becomes evident when he immediately turns to her brother Bernardo with the words of dismissal:

> Thou, too, loathed image of thy cursèd mother,
> Thy milky, meek face makes me sick with hate!

It is finally worth noting that as soon as Beatrice and Bernardo have gone he immediately consolidates his feeling of complete domestic mastery by cruelly brow-beating his second wife, Lucretia.

A strong desire for vengeance emanating from the conditions of his first marriage would seem therefore to be a third element in the motivation of Count Cenci. The isolation of these motives, which collaborate in many ways to explain the count's actions, indicates that his malignity is by no means motiveless, while if one simply writes him off as a "devilish incarnation of the principle of evil," one ignores Shelley's careful, though not always perfectly explicit, presentation of the true bases of his character.

The usual reading of the character of Beatrice has also been unsatisfactory. A frequent objection to Shelley's conduct of the fifth act is that Beatrice there appears as an ignoble liar. She steadily denies any part in the murder of the count, even though her associates are being tortured for information, and she displays no compunction when she imperiously compels the hired assassin Marzio to withdraw the confession which has implicated her in the crime. Since this behavior appears to contradict the notion that Beatrice embodies the spirit of good, the fifth act is held to be inconsistent with the remainder of the play, and in reading criticisms of the trial scene one sometimes gains the impression that it is not so much Beatrice as the author himself who is up for judgment.

The critical discomfiture over Beatrice's conduct in the fifth act, like the sneaking suspicion that Count Cenci is far too black to be credible, rests upon a failure to appreciate the intricacies of Shelley's intention. In brief that intention is to display the perhaps inevitable corruption of human saintliness by the conspiracy of social circumstances and the continued operation of a vindictive tyranny. At first glance this intention may seem to refute the ethical conclusions of *Prometheus Unbound*. Actually it only brings those conclusions down to earth and works them out in a specific human situation. Where Prometheus, during several millenniums, falls short of ideal standards of conduct, his conversion is at last accomplished through his act of self-reform, and he emerges as "the type of the highest perfection of moral and intellectual nature." In *The Cenci* this order is reversed.[2] Beatrice begins in a state of almost saintly

2. Compare Shelley's review of *Frankenstein; or, The Modern Prometheus.*

innocence. For long years she lives the Christian life: she is devout, chaste, dutiful, forgiving, and altruistic, and she gains strength and the power to endure through her conviction that she is clothed in the armor of righteousness. Shelley is at some pains to show how, under blows repeated day after day and week after week for years, this armor cracks, until Beatrice is ready to cast it off in favor of the cloak of a murderess. As Prometheus in Act I rejects hatred and vengeance, so Beatrice in Act III embraces both with a determination born, like that of Prometheus, out of prolonged agony. Shelley still believed in the course followed by Prometheus, and specifically blamed Beatrice for not having done likewise. But he was not now seeking to prove an ethical point—he was writing a tragedy. The tragic flaw in Beatrice, in Shelley's mind, was the crack in the armor of her righteousness.

Something analogous to the hardening of soul which Count Cenci describes as his most conspicuous trait now begins in Beatrice. As in the *Prometheus*, the "conversion" when it comes is both sudden and complete, but Shelley's exposition has carefully prepared the way for it. In the past Beatrice has tried every device of moral persuasion upon her father. At first she endured his malice through an innocent belief in the rightness of paternal judgment; then she sought to bend him with love and tears; next she tried prayer; then she petitioned the Pope; finally, at the banquet, she came desperately into the open with a plea for aid from the assembled guests. All these efforts came to nothing because Beatrice had the misfortune to exist in a social milieu from which scruple was absent.

But this is not the only restraint upon Shelley's heroine: she is also held back by her own conscience. When she asks herself the crucial question—"Where shall I turn?"—one wonders why she has not turned to flight. She is, of course, a prisoner in the Cenci Palace just as certainly as Tasso was a prisoner in Santa Anna; yet even if this were not so, she would have chosen to remain: her stepmother and her younger brother must have her assistance. This sense of duty, as well as her religious fear of the consequences, have prevented flight by suicide. Yet she is not defeatist, partly because she believes her armor is strong. As late as the banquet scene she retains her self-possession, and even offers to pray with her father for the salvation of his soul.

Her evident fear of the count on the morning after the banquet is the first sign that her will to endure is beginning to give way before her father's relentless pressure. Her appearance that morning is so deeply altered that Lucretia at once observes it: an unseen visitor's lifting of the doorlatch induces a hysterical response. When the visitor turns out to be, not the count, but a messenger bearing

the false report that the Pope has rejected her petition, she settles
into an utter depression of spirits, a dead center of indifference
best summarized in her statement, " 'Twere better not to struggle
any more." With the count's arrival, his new found mastery be-
comes evident. The formerly imperious girl cringes at sight of him,
and he is not long in following up his advantage. Sometime in the
course of that very night he completes his dominance with an overt
sexual attack.

It is the supreme irony of the drama that the means chosen by
the count to establish final mastery are the best means he could
have fixed on to harden Beatrice's soul to the point where she is
ready to do murder. Out of the darkest experience of her life, the
temporary derangement caused by her father's attack, Beatrice rises
with a resolution:

> Ay, something must be done;
> What, yet I know not.

Suicide is out of the question, and legal action is quickly rejected.
Murder, the bold redress of the insufferably wronged, remains.

In making herself the prime agent of her father's destruction,
Beatrice explicitly rejects the moral position to which she has
hitherto been devoted. There must be no forbearance, no remorse.
For the time being she enters that state of implacable hardness
which is necessary to the fulfillment of her purpose. She becomes,
in her own phrase, "the angel of [God's] wrath," and her only rule
of conduct, until just before her execution, is to play a ruthless
game to the top of her bent—intriguing, bribing, conniving, and
lying, without regret, without remorse, without pity. Only once,
as she hears her death-sentence (to which she responds almost in
the words of Shakespeare's Claudio in the comparable section of
Measure for Measure) does her hard demeanor show signs of
breaking down under the force of fear. Twice her buried life rises
to the surface. Once, with Lucretia's head on her shoulder, she
sings the equivalent of Desdemona's "Willow Song"; again, ready-
ing their necks for the executioner's axe, she and Lucretia bind up
each other's hair, quietly, tenderly, and finally. For the rest, neither
the trial judge, nor Marzio, nor any of the other culprits is able
to penetrate her self-possession. Lady Macbeth, summoning to her
breast the murdering ministers, is not more willfully callous to all
accepted moral codes than she. Nor is the comparison a mere
literary ornament. Every reader of *The Cenci* and *Macbeth* knows
how closely Shelley modeled the count's murder, and its aftermath,
upon the murder of Duncan. It is very probable that through most

of Acts III, IV, and V, Shelley wrote of Beatrice with one eye on Lady Macbeth.[3]

If Shelley's conception of character is in some respects Shakespearean, his management of the action reveals influence from classical tragedy. Bates believes that the conduct of the scenes, which usually consist "in a dialogue between two persons, or of a succession of such dialogues with changed speakers," is more Greek than Elizabethan.[4] Although the idea deserves mention, it should be pointed out that Shelley had handled in this way every major scene in every major poem from *Queen Mab* to *Prometheus Unbound*, so that habit rather than classical influence probably fixed his course in *The Cenci*.

A much clearer instance of classical influence appears in Shelley's handling of the count's fourth-act *hybris*, which so closely resembles that of Jupiter in the third act of *Prometheus Unbound* as to suggest that Shelley was recalling his most recent verse-drama as he led Count Cenci nearer and nearer the brink of disaster. Classical *hybris*, as in the *Hippolytus* of Euripides, is always charged with dramatic irony. Jupiter's fall from the ramparts of Olympus occurs just after he has smugly supposed that Demogorgon's arrival will confirm and perpetuate his nearly absolute dominion over the minds of men. But the audience, which has already overheard Asia's interview with Demogorgon, knows all along that *Ate* is about to descend upon the master of Olympus. When Count Cenci takes his family to Castle Petrella, high on a rock among the loneliest Apennines, he believes himself as secure as Jupiter upon Olympus. There he plans the final stroke in his attack on Beatrice—the establishment of his supremacy not merely over her body (which he accomplished with the assault in Rome) but also over her mind. His single aim at Petrella is to force Beatrice's agreement to his incestuous suit, and thus "to poison and corrupt her soul," to break her stubborn will

> Which, by its own consent, shall stoop as low
> As that which drags it down.

3. That Beatrice resembles Lady Macbeth in her complete resolution and Desdemona in her few moments of tenderness are points which seem to have escaped Bates, whose treatment of Elizabethan and particularly of Shakespearean parallels is otherwise excellent. In his study of *The Cenci*, Bates lists some 13 other passages where Shelley is following *Hamlet*, *Othello*, *Lear*, *Macbeth*, *Measure for Measure*, *King John*, *Richard III*, *Twelfth Night*, and *The Merchant of Venice. Op. cit.*, pp. 54–55. He observes also that Orsino's machinations resemble those of De Flores in Middleton's *The Changeling*, although

Iago seems as good a parallel. He suggests that the trial scene may owe something to the trial of Vittoria in Webster's *The White Devil*. He compares the prison scenes in Act V to those in Milman's *Fazio*, which Shelley saw performed, with Miss O'Neill as Bianca, in 1818. A more recent consideration of Shakespeare's influence on *The Cenci* is in D. L. Clark, "Shelley and Shakespeare," *PMLA* 54 (1939). *The Cenci* is discussed on pp. 278–286. See also S. R. Watson, "*Othello* and *The Cenci*," *PMLA* 55 (1940), 611–614.

4. Bates, *op. cit.*, p. 57.

In this intention he is in effect seeking to attain a Jupiter-like power, for it is Jupiter's dominion over the mind of man which has kept Prometheus bound to the rock. The count's anticipation of success is as firm as that of Jupiter. The real peak of his *hybris* is reached in the midst of his curse upon Beatrice. When the awed Lucretia reminds him that God punishes such prayers, the count tempts Necessity with a supreme histrionic boast: "He does his will, I mine!" Two scenes later he is dead.

* * *

In spite of its lengthening stage history, *The Cenci* has always been treated more like an heirloom extracted from a glass case for temporary exhibit than like a piece of serious stagecraft.[5]

* * *

By and large, *The Cenci*, like the other dialogue-poems, presented Shelley's view of the human predicament as it could be found in history. In *Rosalind and Helen* and the two stories drawn from the Italian past he chose to work in the area of domestic tragedy, projecting on a lesser scale, and in essentially nonpolitical terms, the same sort of unendurable, unrelenting oppression of the weak by the strong, and of the principled by the unscrupulous, which he had writ large in *The Revolt of Islam* and *Prometheus Unbound*. The impression to be gained from these poems is not that of an untroubled world. Malicious intrigue, abuse of power, cruelty, betrayal, false witness, corruption, madness, lust, avarice, and murder: these were the red letters upon the calendar of history as Shelley viewed it, and he was to discover further corroboration for his views in the state of England during the years 1819–1820, even to the extent of implying an ominous parallel between nineteenth-century England and sixteenth-century Italy.

KENNETH NEILL CAMERON

The Planet-Tempest Passage in *Epipsychidion*†

The action of the central autobiographical passage (lines 267–383) of *Epipsychidion* runs roughly as follows. The poet, in his search for love, first encountered several "mortal forms," some of them "fair," others "wise," one of them "not true"; then, for some

---

5. For an excellent . . . account of the stage history of *The Cenci*, see the article of that title by K. N. Cameron and Horst Frenz in *PMLA* 60 (1945), 1080–1105.

† Reprinted by permission of the author and the Modern Language Association of America from *PMLA*, 63 (1948), pp. 950–972. The author also supplied several corrections.

unexplained reason he entered a period of emotional crisis—"stood at bay, wounded and weak and panting" (272–275)—from which he was rescued by one whom he compares to his ideal of love as the Moon to the Sun. At first, we gather, he was enchanted with this moonlike love (276–280) but later began to realize that she was "cold" (281–307):

> And there I lay, within a chaste cold bed;
> Alas, I then was nor alive nor dead.

Shortly after his discovery of the coldness of the Moon he was precipitated into a new crisis, much worse than the one he had experienced just before his encounter with the Moon, a crisis that tore his being apart as an earthquake tears the earth. The ruling deities of this crisis were a Planet and a Tempest (308–320). Some time later—"at length"—he finally met his ideal in human form, "Soft as an incarnation of the Sun" (321–344). And now he wishes that both the Moon and the Sun remain with him and inspire him—"Twin Spheres of light who rule this passive earth"; but, further, he wishes that one more "mortal form" return and share in this influence with the Sun and the Moon—a "Comet beautiful and fierce." This Comet had formerly both attracted and repulsed him, had been "wrecked" and had gone "astray"; but now he fears no such disaster and seems sure that the Comet, Moon, and Sun will exist in a harmonious relationship (345–383).

Although at first sight this passage may sound quite obscure, much of it can readily be interpreted.[1] For instance we have a sure focal point in lines 276–280 describing the encounter with the Moon; for the Moon we know is Mary Shelley. We know this not only from the internal evidence of the poem but also because Mary herself accepted the identification (in a letter to Byron and two

---

1. The first full attempt at an interpretation of *Epipsychidion* appeared in John Todhunter, *A Study of Shelley* (London, 1880), pp. 229–253. Todhunter received suggestions in some of his identifications from William Michael Rossetti (pp. 245, 248); and his work exercised considerable influence on all subsequent studies. . . . In the conclusion of "Shelley's 'Julian and Maddalo'," *Gentleman's Magazine* (Oct. 1887), pp. 329–342, Arabella Shore made some valuable suggestions, some of which were followed up in a brief article in *Poet Lore* in 1890, "The Story of Shelley's Life in 'Epipsychidion'" (pp. 252–233), by F. G. Fleay. In the same year Richard Ackermann in *Quellen, Vorbilder, Stoffe zu Shelley's Poetischen Werken* (Erlanger, Leipzig), pp. 27–28, began his study of the characters of the poem, and further suggestions were made in Helene Richter's *Shelley* (Weimar, 1898).

Ackermann returned to his studies with his edition of *Adonais* and *Epipsychidion* (1900) and his *Shelley, der Mann, der Dichter und seine Werke* (Dortmund, 1906). The most complete of the German interpretations is a lengthy article by Armin Kroder, "Studien zu Shelley's 'Epipsychidion'," *Englische Studien*, XXVII (1900), 365–396. In 1911, C. D. Locock in his edition of Shelley, II, 453–459, summarized part of this previous scholarship and made a few suggestions. More recent interpretations are in Walter Edwin Peck, *Shelley: His Life and Work* (New York, 1927), II, 189–196; Floyd H. Stovall, *Desire and Restraint in Shelley* (Durham, N.C., 1931), pp. 273–276; Carl Grabo, *The Magic Plant* (Chapel Hill, N.C., 1936), pp. 336–345; John Harrington Smith, "Shelley and Claire Clairmont," *PMLA*, LIV (1939), 788–797; Newman I. White, *Shelley* (New York, 1940), II, 255–269.

private journal entries).[2] These lines (276–280), therefore, must refer to the early summer of 1814, when Shelley met Mary. Hence, the previous lines must deal with events that took place prior to the meeting with Mary and the succeeding lines with events following that meeting. The "mortal forms," then—the "wise," the "fair," and the one untrue—must include women with whom Shelley was acquainted before meeting Mary, and such women we know to have been Harriet Grove, Elizabeth Hitchener, Harriet Shelley, Mrs. Boinville, and Cornelia Turner. The most likely identifications are: the "fair"—Harriet Grove and Cornelia Turner; the "wise"—Mrs. Boinville and perhaps Elizabeth Hitchener;[3] and the one untrue—Harriet Grove.[4]

The events reflected in lines 271–285 must be those of Shelley's rejection by Harriet Grove, his unsatisfactory marriage to Harriet Westbrook, and its breakup in the spring of 1814. When the next event occurred, namely, the discovery by the poet of the coldness of the Moon (Mary), we cannot exactly tell. Nor is there any

2. Letter to Byron [? Oct. 21, 1822], *Letters of Mary W. Shelley*, ed. Frederick L. Jones (Univ. of Oklahoma Press, 1946), I, 198: "There might have been something sunny about me then [i.e., when Shelley was alive], now I am truly *cold moonshine*." Journal entry, Oct. 5, 1822, *Shelley Memorials*, ed. Lady Shelley (London, 1875), pp. 332–333: "Well, I shall commence my task, commemorate the virtues of the only creature worth loving or living for, and then, maybe I may join him. Moonshine may be united to her planet, and wander no more, a sad reflection of all she loved on earth." . . . The third journal entry is that of Nov. 11, 1822, quoted in Mrs. Julian Marshall, *Life and Letters of Mary Wollstonecraft Shelley* (London, 1889), II, 53: "A cold heart! Have I a cold heart? God knows! But none need envy the icy region this heart encircles; and at least the tears are hot which the emotions of this cold heart forces me to shed. A cold heart! yes, it would be cold enough if all were as I wished it—cold, or burning in the flame for whose sake I forgive this, and would forgive every other imputation—that flame in which your heart, beloved, lay unconsumed." . . .
3. Rossetti suggested to Todhunter that the "fair" and "wise" were probably references to the Boinville family, but he tangled up the relationships rather badly. Thus, while he correctly believed Cornelia to be included among the "fair," he mistakenly identified her as the wife of Shelley's vegetarian friend John Frank Newton. (Mrs. Boinville, Cornelia's mother, was sister to Newton's wife.) The one who was "not true to me" he identifies as "Mrs. Taylor, a second daughter of Mrs. Boinville, with whom Shelley was hopelessly in love." No

second daughter of Mrs. Boinville is known to Shelley's biographers; so "Mrs. Taylor" is presumably Cornelia Boinville (Mrs. Turner) once again. That Shelley was attracted to Cornelia is true but his comments on her do not indicate that he was ever "hopelessly in love" with her or felt himself betrayed by her. . . . These views of Rossetti were widely accepted by subsequent scholars, even the non-existent Mrs. Taylor enjoying considerable popularity and appearing in Kroder, p. 385; Ackermann, *Quellen Vorbilder Stoffe*, p. 27, and *Shelley*, pp. 297–298; Locock, II, 456; Peck, II, 192. Richter, p. 496, and Kroder, p. 385, add Elizabeth Hitchener to the "wise"; and Richter suggests Mrs. Boinville as the one "not true to me" on the grounds that she became cool to Shelley after his union with Mary. Fleay, p. 228, followed Rossetti's suggestion of Cornelia as the one not true. Peck, II, 192, follows the "Mrs. Boinville, Cornelia Turner, and Mrs. Taylor" pattern for the "fair" and "wise," but suggested Harriet Shelley for the one not true. Stovall, p. 273, sees Harriet Grove among the "fair" and Elizabeth Hitchener among the "wise," and thinks the one not true may be Cornelia Turner. White, II, 262, sees Harriet Westbrook and Cornelia Turner in the "fair," Elizabeth Hitchener and Mrs. Boinville in the "wise," and Harriet Grove as the one not true.
4. Fleay (p. 226) pointed out that Shelley had used a line ("She whom I found was dear but false to me") similar to the "not true to me" line in *Epipsychidion* with apparent reference to Harriet Grove in a canceled passage in the Dedication to *Laon and Cythna* (*The Revolt of Islam*).

sure indication of a date for the Planet-Tempest passage (308–320). The next point of reference comes in lines 321–322:

> At length into the obscure forest came
> The Vision I had sought through grief and shame.

This, as Shelley himself tells us (line 344), refers to the meeting with Emilia Viviani, and this meeting occurred in December, 1820.[5] In the final section of the passage (345–383) we also have a certain date, namely, the date of the composition of the poem (December, 1820, to February, 1821),[6] for the poet is there speaking of the present. The Comet asked to return, therefore, must be someone who was not at that time in the vicinity but who could return; and the reference, as John Harrington Smith and Newman I. White (following a conjecture by Shore in 1887) have demonstrated beyond any reasonable doubt, must be to Claire Clairmont (who was then at Florence), the "alternating attraction and repulsion" referring to a previous entanglement of Shelley and Claire, and the "going astray" and wrecking of the Comet referring to Claire's later affair with Byron.[7]

Three of the five main symbols in this central autobiographical passage, then—the Moon, the Sun, and the Comet—are identifiable, and the events concerning them—the meeting with Mary following the marital crisis in 1814, the meeting with Emilia in the winter of 1820–21, the appeal to Claire to return in the same period, the previous entanglement with Claire (probably in 1815)—are identifiable also. This leaves the Planet-Tempest passage, in challenging isolation. Who are the Planet and the Tempest, and what are the events surrounding them?

The most recent theories are those of John Harrington Smith

---

5. The exact date we do not know; Claire first visited Emilia on Nov. 29; Mary and Claire together on Dec. 1; on Dec. 10 Emilia wrote Shelley a letter which indicates at least one visit from Shelley; so the initial visit recorded by Medwin must fall within those dates. Dowden, *Shelley*, II, 370–373.

6. Shelley sent the poem to Ollier on Feb. 16, 1821 (*Works*, X, 236); hence it was written between the first visit in early December and Feb. 16.

7. Todhunter, pp. 244, 248, guessed the Comet to be Harriet Shelley, and was followed by Kroder, p. 390, White in his notes in *The Best of Shelley* (New York, 1932), pp. 503–504, and Grabo, p. 342. Harriet, however, could not be asked to "float into our azure heaven again" for the simple reason that Harriet was dead; and the context indicates an actual and not an ectoplasmic return. Furthermore, Harriet, while certainly "beautiful," could under no circumstances, either as

person or spirit, be conceived of as "fierce." In 1887 Arabella Shore (pp. 336–337) first conjectured the comet to be Claire, and was followed by Fleay, 228–230; Richter, p. 498; Ackermann, *Epipsychidion*, p. xix, and *Shelley*, p. 298; Stovall, pp. 275–276; J. H. Smith, pp. 788–797; White, *Shelley*, II, 266–267. Peck, II, 193–194, proposes Sophia Stacy as the Comet but gives no evidence to support his view and what we know of Shelley's relations with Sophia makes the assumption ridiculous. Whether Richter came to her conclusion independently or knew of Shore's or Fleay's articles is not indicated. She simply states: "The comet is Claire." No hint of this identification had appeared in previous German scholarship (Druskowitz, Ackermann). But as Shore's article had appeared eleven years previously and Fleay's eight, I presume that she was indebted to one or the other.

(1939) and Newman I. White (1940). Smith, following up a suggestion made by Fleay in 1890, contended that Claire Clairmont was both the Planet and the Tempest; hence the passage reflected the love affair already mentioned between Shelley and Claire (the "quenching" of the Planet referring to Claire's ejection from the household in the spring of 1815, and the "earthquakes" Shelley's distraction at her "desertion" of him for Byron the following year).[8] This explanation, however, is unsatisfactory on two grounds. First, while it is true that Shelley and Claire were emotionally involved in the winter and spring of 1814–15, what evidence we have does not indicate that either that involvement or its possible dissolution resulted in a major catastrophe in Shelley's life such as here depicted. Second, as Shelley refers to his entanglement with Claire later in the poem, in the Comet passage, it is unlikly that he would deal with it twice, each time under a different symbol.[9]

White, rejecting the Fleay-Smith theory, proposed his own.[1] After quoting the passage (307–320) he commented as follows:

This is professedly autobiography, and professedly cryptic. The period it describes must be subsequent to the summer of 1817, when Shelley wrote his introductory poem to *Laon and Cythna*, his earlier spiritual autobiography. In that poem Mary was still his perfect "deliverance" and he was still "asleep," without then knowing it, to her inability to furnish the complete sympathy he sought. When Shelley awoke to this deficiency we have already seen in our discussion of "Julian and Maddalo." That poem, if any poem ever did, records a spiritual storm, and a storm in which Mary was "blotted." Also, like the present passage, it is autobiography that Shelley thought concealed. Shelley's life between 1817 and 1821 is too well known for the storms he described to have been anything except those following Clara Shelley's death and repeated possibly after the death of William Shelley. Under these blows, it is a known fact that Mary's spirits "shrank as in the sickness of eclipse," and Shelley's soul was often "as a lampless sea."

The identity of the Tempest and the Planet is not so certain because the lines in which they are mentioned do not absolutely

8. Fleay, Ackermann, Stovall (pp. 99–101, 275), and Smith consider that Claire is intended by both the Comet and the Planet-Tempest.

9. White (*Shelley*, II, 608) points out also that as Shelley's "astronomical imagery throughout the poem is scientifically correct" he "could hardly have made the ignorant blunder of calling Claire both a Planet and a Comet."

1. In addition to the Fleay-Smith and White theories, several others have been proposed. Todhunter, p. 248, thought the Planet might be the mysterious unknown lady who, Shelley informed Medwin, followed him to Naples, a suggestion followed by Kroder, p. 389, and Peck, II, 192. White, however, has satisfactorily demonstrated the non-existence of this lady (I, 436–437). Richter (pp. 330, 498) suggested that the "Neapolitan child" might be the child of Shelley and the mysterious lady, and that this passage reflected those events; but she attempted no specific identifications. Ackermann, *Quellen, Vorbilder Stoffe*, pp. 27–28, suggested Fanny Godwin as the Planet but in his later works retracted this suggestion in favor of Claire.

exclude any one of three possible meanings. The sentence is phrased so vaguely that the Tempest and the Planet might be the same, or the Planet might be Mary (for in Shelley's astronomy the moon was a planet) or a person otherwise unknown. If we try to resolve this difficulty from the known facts of Shelley's life in 1819 and 1820, Sophia Stacy must be considered a possibility, though there is no indication that she was ever "quenched" or in fact that Shelley ever idealized her to anything like the extent implied in the passage. In an earlier chapter we have seen that not even all of the few poems with which her name is associated were inspired by her. Mary was never "quenched," for Shelley says the "white Moon" continued smiling. Nor could Mary, for the same reason, be a planet only "of that hour."

But Elena Adelaide Shelley, whose life was concealed just as Shelley says the truth behind these allusions is concealed, might well have been a Tempest in the life of Shelley and Mary. She alone was definitely "quenched," and her influence could most properly be limited to "that hour." The "frost" which at her death afflicted Shelley's spirits may be inferred from Shelley's words at the time: "It seems as if the destruction that is consuming me were as an atmosphere which wrapt and *infected* everything connected with me—An ounce of civit good apothecary to sweeten this dunghill of a world." Elena Adelaide fits into this pattern of the passage and of Shelley's life far better than any other known person, but she conforms rather badly to the pattern set by Shelley's other Incarnate Sympathies. Against this may be set the known fact that she entered his life at the precise moment when the need of sympathy was most desperately felt.

The earthquakes that split the ice-pack of the poet's frozen spirit are hard to explain because it is not clear whether they are to be regarded as further catastrophes or a deliverance. If the former, one thinks of the troubles in 1820 over Godwin and Paolo Foggi; if the latter, one thinks of the appearance of Emilia. On the whole it would seem that they were an agency of deliverance. At any rate Emilia immediately appears, "Soft as an Incarnation of the Sun," and Shelley hails her by name as

> . . . the Vision veiled from me
> So many years.[2]

The main weakness in this interpretation is that it provides no really satisfactory identification for the symbols around which the events of the passage revolve, the Planet and the Tempest. White's speculations on Mary or Sophia Stacey[3] are, as he recognizes, tentative; and it is most unlikely that Elena Adelaide Shelley could be intended by the Planet or the Tempest. Shelley would hardly introduce, suddenly and incongruously, a baby in his listing of the

2. White, II, 264–266.
3. See also Peck, II, 161–163, 193–194; almost all we know of the relations of Shelley and Sophia will be found in

Helen Rossetti Angeli, *Shelley and His Friends in Italy* (London, 1911), pp. 95–105.

women who had influenced his life. He was upset by Elena Ade-laide's death, it is true, but less so than by that of Clara or William. A second weakness in this interpretation is that it posits a series of unconnected events quite widely scattered in time: the "storms" represent the grief of Shelley and Mary at the death of Clara (September, 1818) and perhaps also of William (June, 1819); the Planet and Tempest both represent the child Shelley and Mary apparently adopted in Naples in December, 1818, and the "quenching" its death in June, 1820; the earthquakes represent either difficulties with Godwin and Foggi (summer of 1820) or a disturbance over Emilia (December, 1820–February, 1821). There is no real connection or sequencing of events here; yet the passage in the poem gives the impression of a connected sequence of events happening within a relatively short period of time. The events depicted are isolated in one paragraph from the events preceding and following them, and the punctuation and phrasing of the paragraph imply unity.

There is, it seems to me, a fallacy in White's position from which these weaknesses in his theory flow, namely his initial argument that the Planet-Tempest passage must be dated "subsequent to the summer of 1817," or, as he elsewhere (p. 608) more definitely states it, "in 1819 or 1820." Once the passage is dated so late as that, it is impossible to be other than speculative, for we know of no events in Shelley's life following that period which fit the Planet-Tempest passage. Hence it is of importance, if we are to arrive at a more reasonable explanation for the passage, to examine the argument for late dating.

The argument rests essentially upon one point. In the summer of 1817, in the Dedication to *Laon and Cythna* (*The Revolt of Islam*), Shelley speaks of Mary as his "perfect 'deliverance.'" In the "chaste cold bed" passage in *Epipsychidion* he speaks of her as cold. Hence the events and moods reflected in the "chaste cold bed" passage must be later than the summer of 1817. And if the events of the "chaste cold bed" passage are of a later date than the summer of 1817, then the events of the Planet-Tempest passage must be still later, for the Planet-Tempest passage follows the "chaste cold bed" passage.[4] In order to perceive the weight of White's argument here

4. White uses also two subsidiary arguments, the first based on an interpretation of internal evidence: "Shelley is plainly following a chronological series of events in which the episode of the Planet is the last Incarnate Sympathy before Emilia. This could only place the Planet in 1819 or 1820" (II, 608). But Shelley does not state that he met Emilia immediately after the Planet; he states that after the Planet was "quenched" he went through a series of soul-shaking experiences—"a death of ice," "earthquakes"—and that after this "at length" came upon Emilia.

This could clearly, in a creative, symbolic treatment such as is *Epipsychidion*, cover a considerable time sequence.

The Dedication argument White supports by the contention that *Julian and Maddalo*, written in the fall of 1818, reveals Shelley first becoming aware of Mary's coldness. But even if one accepts White's argument (which, it seems to me, he has proved beyond any reasonable doubt) that the "death's dedicated bride" of that poem is Mary, it does not follow that Shelley's words to her (in the guise of the Madman) indicate a first awaken-

let us compare the two passages. I quote first the key stanzas from the Dedication and then the Moon passage from *Epipsychidion*:

> Thou friend, whose presence on my wintry heart
>   Fell, like bright Spring upon some herbless plain;
> How beautiful and calm and free thou wert
>   In thy young wisdom, when the mortal chain
>   Of Custom thou didst burst and rend in twain,
> And walked as free as light the clouds among,
>   Which many an envious slave then breathed in vain
> From his dim dungeon, and my spirit sprung
> To meet thee from the woes which had begirt it long!
>
> No more alone through the world's wilderness,
>   Although I trod the paths of high intent,
> I journeyed now: no more companionless,
>   Where solitude is like despair, I went.—
>   There is the wisdom of a stern content
> When Poverty can blight the just and good,
>   When Infamy dared mock the innocent,
> And cherished friends turn with the multitude
> To trample: this was ours, and we unshaken stood. . . .
>
> And what art thou? I know, but dare not speak:
>   Time may interpret to his silent years.
> Yet in the paleness of thy thoughtful cheek,
>   And in the light thine ample forehead wears,
>   And in thy sweetest smiles, and in thy tears,
> And in thy gentle speech, a prophecy
>   Is whispered, to subdue my fondest fears:
> And through thine eyes, even in my soul I see
> A lamp of vestal fire burning internally.[5]

The Moon passage from *Epipsychidion*:

> One stood on my path who seemed
> As like the glorious shape which I had dreamed
> As is the Moon, whose changes ever run
> Into themselves, to the eternal Sun;

---

ing to her coldness. The Madman episode records a violent quarrel between the two which seems rather to indicate long-standing marital strains than any newly discovered incompatibilities. The castration fantasies of the woman (420–436), in fact, imply a frigidity extending back for several years of union. White is perhaps also somewhat influenced in his dating by his interpretation of the word "conceal" (319): "Also, like the present passage, it is autobiography that Shelley thought concealed." Shelley, however, does not mean that the events he is reflecting in the poem were themselves of a secret or "concealed" nature but simply that the words are concealing the events. The events may have been well

known but he is treating them in symbolic fashion.

5. Stanzas vii–viii, xi. For further sentiments of affection for Mary, see also stanza i: "thou child of love and light"; stanza ii: "But beside thee, where still my heart has ever been"; stanza ix:

> And from thy side two gentle babes
>   are born
> To fill our home with smiles, and thus
>   are we
>   Most fortunate beneath life's beam-
>   ing morn;
> And these delights, and thou, have been
>   to me
> The parents of the Song I consecrate to
>   thee.

The cold chaste Moon, the Queen of Heaven's bright isles,
Who makes all beautiful on which she smiles,
That wandering shrine of soft yet icy flame
Which ever is transformed, yet still the same,
And warms not but illumines. Young and fair
As the descended Spirit of that sphere,
She hid me, as the Moon may hide the night
From its own darkness, until all was bright
Between the Heaven and Earth of my calm mind,
And, as a cloud charioted by the wind,
She led me to a cave in that wild place,
And sate beside me, with her downward face
Illumining my slumbers, like the Moon
Waxing and waning o'er Endymion.
And I was laid asleep, spirit and limb,
And all my being became bright or dim
As the Moon's image in the summer sea,
According as she smiled or frowned on me;
And there I lay, within a chaste cold bed:
Alas, I then was nor alive nor dead:—
For at her silver voice came Death and Life,
Unmindful each of their accustomed strife,
Masked like twin babes, a sister and a brother,
The wandering hopes of one abandoned mother,
And through the cavern without wings they flew,
And cried 'Away, he is not of our crew.'
I wept, and though it be a dream, I weep.

A comparison of these two passages reveals that White is correct
in positing a difference between them. Shelley speaks in both of his
early enthusiasm for Mary: "deliverance" "like a noonday dawn" in
Epipsychidion; "bright spring" in the Dedication; but in *Epipsychidion*, though he pays tribute to her beauty and tenderness, he refers
to her coldness and chasteness, whereas in the Dedication he praises
her enthusiastically. It is not possible, however, to go further and
accept the assumption that because Shelley does not mention Mary's
coldness in the Dedication, he was, therefore, unaware of it at the
time. The fact that a man does not mention his wife's coldness in
a poem cannot, in any case, be taken as proof that he is unaware
of it. And in regard to Shelley and Mary we have the evidence of
another poem written in the same year as the Dedication (1817) to
show that Shelley was then aware of Mary's coldness. This is the
short lyric, *To Constantia*, in which Shelley complains to Claire
Clairmont that Mary is cold, and compares her, in precisely the
image he later used in *Epipsychidion*, to the moon, the "cold,"
"bright" moon, the "planet of frost" which "gazing" down on his
heart "makes it wan." On this poem, White has commented elsewhere in his book: "As early as 1817, in his unfinished poem *To Constantia*, Shelley employed the same symbolism of the moon to

express a feeling of the incompleteness of Mary's love."[6] And the evidence of this poem is supported by the indication of marital strains as early as the winter and spring of 1814–15. Whatever the Hogg-Mary-Shelley-Claire *folie à quatre* of that time—ending in May with the ejection of Claire from the household amid "a turmoil of passion and hatred"[7]—signified, it certainly did not signify a stable marital adjustment between Shelley and Mary. Nor is such an adjustment reflected in the loneliness and despair of *Alastor* in the fall of 1815.

The probability, then, is that Shelley *was* aware of Mary's coldness in 1817 when he penned the Dedication. Nor is there really anything in the Dedication itself to negate such a conclusion. True, Shelley does not there specifically mention coldness; but, on the other hand, there is nothing in his depiction of Mary to exclude such a characteristic. Mary is not hailed as a young and passionate

6. II, 607. White believes that Shelley is speaking throughout in his comments on Mary of the purely spiritual aspects of love, e.g.: "Whatever the meaning of this passage [the "chaste cold bed" passage] in terms of Shelley's life with Mary, it is of all things least likely to be physical, both because it was not true physically and because Shelley has given evidence again and again, both in the poem and out of it, that *Epipsychidion* is the history of spiritual not physical love. . . . The chasteness and coldness was spiritual and was not at first perceived because of the intense brightness of the intellectual light which Mary shed upon him" (*ibid.*, p. 263). But this interpretation is clearly open to question. There is no evidence, nor could there well be any evidence, to show that Shelley and Mary were sexually compatible. On the contrary, their union was sufficiently filled with strains to make some degree of sexual incompatibility probable. Nor does Shelley say that *Epipsychidion* is the "history of spiritual" love only; he wrote to his friend Gisborne simply that it was "an idealized history of my life and feelings," i.e., a picture of actual events and emotions treated in a symbolic creative medium (letter, June 18, 1822, *Works*, X, 401). Furthermore, in this particular passage the language itself has unmistakable sexual overtones. Such phrases as "cold chaste moon," "soft yet icy flame," "chaste cold bed" (within which the poet "lies" "nor alive nor dead"), when applied by a man to his wife give the impression of sexual rather than spiritual coldness. Whether Shelley intended this meaning to be clear to his reader or even whether he was himself conscious of it we cannot certainly tell; but the mere choice of language reveals the existence of sexual thinking at some level of consciousness, and indicates a sexual frustration behind the thinking. And this, it is important to note, is true of the poem as a whole. *Epipsychidion*, even in its most Platonic passages, is essentially a poem springing from deep love starvation.

7. Letter from Claire Clairmont to Fanny Godwin, May 28, 1815, quoted in Mrs. Marshall, *op. cit.*, I, 118. The argument for an affair between Shelley and Claire was first developed by John Harrington Smith, *op. cit.* White (I,694 *et passim*) disagrees that an actual affair took place but admits (II, 267) that at least "on Claire's part it was attended by distinct emotional disturbance." F. L. Jones in "Mary Shelley and Claire Clairmont," *South Atlantic Quart.*, XLII (1943), 409–412, also argued against Smith's conclusions by attempting (unsuccessfully in my opinion) to show from the letters of Mary that she was not jealous of Claire. While Smith's view that Claire was one of the great loves of Shelley's life, affecting, in a major way, such poems as *Alastor, Julian and Maddalo*, and *Epipsychidion*, is difficult to sustain, and leads him, in my judgment, to some misinterpretations of these poems, it is hard to believe that Shelley and Claire did not have an affair sometime in the winter and spring of 1814–15, an affair, one would gather, attended by a good deal of rather immature super-emotionalizing. The Hogg-Mary affair of the same time was first revealed by White (I, 391–393), although he was not allowed to quote the letters which were his source of information. These letters were first printed in *Harriet and Mary*, ed. Walter Sidney Scott, pp. 42–56, and reprinted in Robert Metcalf Smith, *The Shelley Legend* (New York, 1945), pp. 146–163. Smith misdates the final letter in the series (p. 162) "January, 1818" for "April 26, 1815" (see Scott, p. 45).

bride; she is praised for her moral courage and intelligence, her "young wisdom," her companionableness, the "paleness" of her "thoughtful cheek," her "ample forehead," her "gentle speech," the "*vestal* fire" in her "soul." One gets the impression of a rather quietly intellectual young woman who could well be "transformed yet still the same," interested in ideas but never really shaken by them or by her emotions in such a way as to change her whole being. All we can say on the basis of the two passages is that the "cold chaste bed" lines specifically mention a coldness which the Dedication does not mention but does not necessarily exclude, and perhaps, by its very selection of qualities for praise, implies.

Let us assume—as is most probable—that Shelley made the discovery of coldness in the initial months of his union with Mary, and that from early 1815 until the summer of 1817 he had felt this deficiency in an otherwise not unhappy relationship. It does not follow that he would write of that 1815–17 period in the same terms in 1821, when he wrote *Epipsychidion*, as in 1817. In 1821 he and Mary had lived together for six years, in 1817 but three. In 1821 the bonds of marriage were being strained by Shelley's excessive interest in Emilia Viviani; in 1817 those bonds had been drawn closer by mutual suffering and by Mary's loyalty to Shelley through a period of crisis. Between 1817 and 1821 had intervened the violent quarrel recorded in *Julian and Maddalo* which had resulted in the hurling of recriminations that once uttered would not easily die. Furthermore, we must not forget that the 1817 picture occurred in a public Dedication, where its meaning would be clear to all, whereas the 1821 picture occurred in an obscure, symbolic narrative published anonymously. A poet might obviously permit himself greater frankness, under any circumstances, in the latter type of poem than in the former.

To summarize: we have evidence of marital disruption in 1815, and of dissatisfaction with Mary as cold in 1817 (*To Constantia*); the differences between the Dedication and *Epipsychidion* are not contradictions, and are explainable in terms of variance in treatment in different periods and in different kinds of poems. While, therefore, it might at first appear that the variation between the two passages provides a basis for dating the "chaste cold bed" episode subsequent to 1817, further examination reveals that it provides no really sound basis for such dating. And it is upon this point alone of variation between the two poems that the argument for the late dating rests. There is no other serious evidence, either internal or external, to support it.

The internal evidence, on the contrary, follows the external evidence in supporting the view of an early discovery of coldness: the poet meets the moonlady and is enthralled by her (summer of

1814); she leads him off to comfort him in his troubles and he discovers that she is cold. The passage gives no evidence of any considerable lapse of time but rather of a close sequencing of events. And this would fit with the external evidence of marital difficulties in 1815.

Just how soon after this discovery of coldness the Planet-Tempest episode occurred we cannot exactly tell, but the "then" of "What storms then shook the ocean of my sleep," which opens the passage, implies some but not a considerable lapse of time; and hence would indicate a date approximately in the 1816–17 period. And this general indication is supported by the "at length" of line 321, which notes the meeting with Emilia in December, 1820. The Planet-Tempest passage certainly comes within the general range 1815–20 and in all probability towards the earlier and not the latter part of that period. And this is all that we can say from the internal evidence.

If we now turn to these years and look for an event or series of events constituting a major crisis in Shelley's life of the kind evidently reflected in the Planet-Tempest passage, we do not have to look far, for within that period occurred what was undoubtedly the greatest crisis in his life, namely the suicide of Harriet Shelley (December 1816) followed by the painful litigation for the custody of his children and ending with the actual loss of those children (January-March 1817). Even without any real analysis of the passage, the indication that it refers to these events is very strong. Shelley, in *Epipsychidion*, as he told Gisborne, is dealing with the history of his "life and feelings." He could not, in such a history, leave out the central tragedy of his life. And when we find that no other passage in *Epipsychidion* fits these events and that this passage occurs in approximately the chronological position in his recounting of that life where these events occurred, the conclusion is almost inescapable that the passage must reflect them. This conclusion could only be seriously weakened if the symbolic language of the passage could not possibly fit the events. But this is not so; for while all aspects of the passage may not be capable of elucidation, the central symbols and actions do very clearly correspond to the events.

Let us look at the Planet-Tempest passage as a whole in the light of this view:

> What storms then shook the ocean of my sleep,
> Blotting that Moon, whose pale and waning lips
> Then shrank as in the sickness of eclipse;—
> And how my soul was as a lampless sea,
> And who was then its Tempest; and when She,
> The Planet of that hour, was quenched, what frost
> Crept o'er those waters, till from coast to coast

The moving billows of my being fell
Into a death of ice, immovable;—
And then—what earthquakes made it gape and split,
The white Moon smiling all the while on it.
These words conceal:—If not, each word would be
The key of staunchless tears. Weep not for me!

The first, rather obvious point of correspondence between the events and the passage is the suicide of Harriet and Shelley's extremely disturbed state consequent upon it. The "quenching" of the Planet corresponds to the suicide of Harriet even to the very method used, drowning. That Shelley was shaken by that suicide almost to the point of madness, until he may well have felt that the frost of death itself was upon him, we have ample testimony: his disturbed, almost distracted letter of December 16, 1816, with its frantic rationalizations; the statements of Leigh Hunt and Peacock, who were with him much of the time: "It was a heavy blow to him and he never forgot it. For a time it tore his being to pieces";[8] "Harriet's untimely fate occasioned him deep agony of mind, which he felt the more because for a long time he kept the feeling to himself";[9] Thornton Hunt's comment: "I am well aware that he *had* suffered severely, and that he continued to be haunted by certain recollections, partly real and partly imaginative, which pursued him like an Orestes";[1] Trelawny's statement to Rossetti that even in 1822 "the impression of extreme pain which the end of Harriet had caused the poet was still vividly present and operative."[2] The evidence is unmistakable that Shelley went through a period of extreme crisis following the suicide of Harriet which could correspond to the "death of ice" state described here as following the "quenching" of the Planet.[3]

---

8. *Autobiography of Leigh Hunt* (London, 1885), p. 237.
9. Peacock, *Life of Shelley*, ed. Wolfe (London, 1933), p. 347.
1. "Shelley," by One Who Knew Him, *Atlantic Monthly*, XI, (Feb., 1863), 188.
2. Rossetti, *Memoir of Shelley*, p. 69.
3. So far as I have been able to ascertain, it has not been previously suggested that Harriet was the Planet. Why so obvious an identification has not been made it is rather difficult to say. One reason has certainly been the reluctance of critics to believe that Shelley could have been aware of a coldness in Mary at a date so early as 1816 or 1817, a reluctance which existed even before White developed his theory (see, e.g., Kroder, *op. cit.*, p. 389 f.). Another reason has been the interpretation of the influence of the Planet in a personal, romantic sense; "the Planet of that hour" has been generally taken to indicate a woman who by her personal attractions was reigning in the poet's heart, the "last Incarnate Sympathy before Emilia,"

as White, for example, puts it (II, 608). But Shelley means that the Planet was "of that hour" in the sense that her actions, not his feeling for her, were controlling the events of his life. In the concepts of astrology, which Shelley is here using, one need have no particular feeling for the planet which by its influence is directing one's destinies. As a result of this subjective interpretation the critics have perforce hunted for some woman in Shelley's life with whom he might at that time have been in love: Fanny Godwin, Claire Clairmont, the mysterious and (non-existent) lady of rank at Naples—and thought of the eclipsing of the Moon as indicating Mary's being thrust from the poet's heart by the new love and of the quenching as representing the end of the affair. (Since completing this article I have found one suggestion of Harriet as the Planet—in Stopford Brooke's selection of Shelley's poems (1880)—a suggestion apparently overlooked by subsequent critics.)

While the poet was still in this state a second blow, or rather series of blows, struck him: "And then—what earthquakes made it gape and split." If I am correct in my interpretation of the preceding lines, this line can hardly refer to anything but the agony of mind consequent upon the litigation to deprive Shelley of his children, for this litigation is the only major crisis we know of in Shelley's life in the period immediately following the suicide of Harriet. And the evidence indicates that Shelley's disturbance during this period was sufficiently strong to warrant so extreme a concept as a spiritual earthquake. Again we have the evidence of Shelley's letters, that to Mary on January 11, 1817, and that to Byron on January 17, the latter being especially revealing of Shelley's state of mind during the whole period:

> I write to you, my dear Lord Byron, after a series of the most unexpected and overwhelming sorrows, and from the midst of a situation of peril and persecution. . . . My late wife is dead. The circumstances which attended this event are of a nature of such awful and appalling horror, that I dare hardly avert to them in thought. The sister of whom you have heard me speak may be truly said (though not in law, yet in fact) to have murdered her for the sake of her father's money. Thus did an event which I believed quite indifferent to me, following the train of a far severer anguish, communicate a shock to me which I know not how I have survived.[4]

Again we have the testimony of Leigh Hunt:

> . . . His children, a girl and a boy, were taken from him. They were transferred to the care of a clergyman of the Church of England. The circumstance deeply affected Shelley: so much so, that he never afterwards dared to trust himself with mentioning their names in my hearing, though I had stood at his side throughout the business; probably for that reason.[5]

And the revealing anecdote from Thornton Hunt's childhood recollections:

> Sometimes but much more rarely he teased me with exasperating banter; and, inheriting from some of my progenitors a vindictive temper, I once retaliated severely. We were in the sitting room with my father and some others, while I was tortured. The chancery suit was just then approaching its most critical point, and, to inflict the cruellest stroke I could think of, I looked him in the face, and expressed a hope that he would be beaten in the trial and have his children taken from him. I was sitting on his knee, and as I spoke, he let himself fall listlessly back in his chair, without attempting to conceal the shock I had given him.[6]

4. *Works*, IX, 218–219.
5. Hunt, pp. 238–239.
6. Page 187. See also p. 185, where Hunt speaks of Shelley's extreme "depressions" at the time and his need for "support and consolation."

We have the evidence, too, of *Rosalind and Helen* in the "agony" of Rosalind when she is similarly deprived of her children,[7] and in the bitter denunciation and deep disturbance of *To The Lord Chancellor* and *To William Shelley*:

> They have taken thy brother and sister dear,
>   They have made them unfit for thee;
> They have withered the smile and dried the tear
>   Which should have been sacred to me.

The "earthquakes," then, could well correspond to Shelley's state during this period of litigation and the final decree of the Lord Chancellor taking the children from him.

That Shelley was being tormented by thoughts of Harriet and his children may be indicated also in the lines immediately preceding this Planet-Tempest passage:

> And there I lay, within a chaste cold bed:
> Alas, I then was nor alive nor dead:—
> For at her silver voice came Death and Life,
> Unmindful each of their accustomed strife,
> Masked like twin babes, a sister and a brother,
> The wandering hopes of one abandoned mother,
> And through the cavern without wings they flew,
> And cried 'Away, he is not of our crew.'
> I wept, and though it be a dream, I weep.
>
> What storms then shook the ocean of my sleep. . . .

The parallel here between the "abandoned mother" and Harriet, and between the "wandering" children, "a sister and a brother," and Ianthe and Charles can hardly be coincidental. Mary's soothing rationalizations, Shelley seems to be telling us, serve only to bring up the conscience-stabbing images of his abandoned wife and children which drive him even further into his state of semi-being between life and death; and while in this condition he is hurled into the "storms" of suicide and litigation. And that Shelley had indeed been in a state of considerable uneasiness in the weeks preceding Harriet's suicide is shown by his letter to Hookham in November 1816 asking him to discover Harriet's whereabouts.[8]

A third problem of identification is that of the Tempest:

> And how my soul was as a lampless sea,
> And who was then its Tempest; and when She,
> The Planet of that hour, was quenched, what frost
> Crept o'er those waters. . . .

---

7. Lines 484–535; see also the "trial" of Lionel for "blasphemy," ll. 857–901.

8. Dowden, II, 67.

The syntax of the passage allows us to take the Planet and the Tempest either as identical or separate entities. If they are identical, then the Tempest is also Harriet and she is a tempest in the sense that not she herself but her death caused the "storms" that so shook the poet. This explanation, however, is not too satisfying. In the first place the interpretation strains the sense of the concept *tempest*, which gives the impression of an active, not a passive force. In the second place a reference to one character under two such different symbols in such close proximity creates a jarring confusion of metaphor which is not paralleled in the treatment of symbols in the rest of the poem.

If we take the alternative course and presume the two symbols to represent different characters in the drama of Shelley's life, we do not have to look far in the period under discussion for a person whom Shelley regarded as a Tempest responsible for the "storms" which turned his soul into a "lampless sea." Eliza Westbrook is clearly such a person. Shelley not only hated Eliza with an almost pathological hatred but held her responsible for all the "storms" which then shook his life, for the suicide of Harriet equally with the litigation over the children. That he held her responsible for the suicide of Harriet is clear from his letter to Byron quoted above —"The sister . . . may be truly said . . . to have murdered her"— and that to Mary on December 16, 1816: "There can be no question that the beastly viper her sister, unable to gain profit from her connexion with me—has secured to herself the fortune of the old man—who is now dying—by the murder of this poor creature."[9] That he also believed her—and this time probably correctly—to be the guiding genius of the litigation over the children is clear from his letter to Byron:

> The sister has now instituted a Chancery process against me, the intended effect of which is to deprive me of my unfortunate children, now more than ever dear to me; of my inheritance, and to throw me into prison, and expose me in the pillory, on the ground of my being a REVOLUTIONIST, and an *Atheist*. It seems whilst she lived in my house she possessed herself of such papers as go to establish these allegations. The opinion of Counsel is, that she will certainly succeed to a considerable extent, but that I may probably escape entire ruin, in the worldly sense of it.[1]

9. *Works*, IX, 212.
1. *Ibid.*, p. 219. Shelley's letter to Eliza on Dec. 18, 1816 (*Shelley's Lost Letters to Harriet*, ed. Leslie Hotson [London, 1930], pp. 54–56), in which he assures her that he bears her "no malice," does not contravene the evidence of the two letters quoted above. In a letter to Eliza, he would naturally not speak in the same terms as in a letter about her to others; and in this particular letter he had a special motive for restraint. His object in writing was to attempt to get his children back without a lawsuit. That he was guilty of some hypocrisy is undeniable but under such circumstances his conduct is neither inexcusable nor uncommon. We might note, too, that when he wrote to Eliza, her rôle as persecutor-in-chief had not become clear; but when

Eliza, then, clearly fits the rôle of the Tempest; and such an identification is preferable to regarding the Tempest as identical with the Planet (Harriet). Eliza is a real tempest in the active sense and a regarding of the two symbols as separate both avoids straining the syntax or violating the usual distinction of symbols which Shelley elsewhere preserves (the Moon as Mary, the Sun as Emilia, and the Comet as Claire).

The final problem of the passage is that of the "storms" of the initial lines and the rôle of the Moon during these storms:

> What storms then shook the ocean of my sleep,
> Blotting that Moon, whose pale and waning lips
> Then shrank as in the sickness of eclipse;—
>
> . . . .
>
> And then—what earthquakes made it gape and split,
> The white Moon smiling all the while on it.

The "storms," it seems to me, are not intended to be separate experiences to the "sea of ice" or the "earthquakes," but represent a general introductory metaphor for the poet's disturbances throughout the period. It is, however, probable, as Rossetti suggested, that among the storms Shelley had in mind also a previous event which had greatly shaken him, the suicide of Fanny Godwin (October 1816).[2]

Even before considering any possible parallels to the lines on the Moon it is clear that they could well fit what one would imagine to have been Mary's rôle during this whole period (October 1816– March 1817)[3] and Shelley's reaction to her: Shelley's mind was in such turmoil that she was, as it were, "blotted" from his consciousness, and she in her anxiety for him "shrank" in body and

---

he wrote to Byron, a month later (Jan. 17), it had. (The Bill of Complaint against Shelley was filed Jan. 8). Eliza, we may note, appears once more as the Avenging Demon in a letter from Mary to Amelia Curran, Sept. 18, 1819, in which, speaking of the importance of keeping the authorship of *The Cenci* anonymous, she commented: "With S[helley]'s public and private enemies it would certainly fall if known to be his —his sister in law alone would hire enough people to damn it" (*Letters of Mary W. Shelley*, ed. Jones, I, 79). Mary was doubtless also echoing Shelley's sentiments in her postscript to her Dec. 17, 1816 letter: "How it would please me if old Westbrook were to repent in his last moments and leave all his fortune away from that miserable and odious Eliza" (*ibid.*, p. 17); and see, too, her letter of Nov. 22, 1822 to Maria Gisborne (p. 206).

2. Todhunter, *op. cit.*, p. 248. Ackermann once thought Fanny was the Planet but

later dropped this identification in favor of Claire. The conjecture receives some support from Shelley's statement in his Jan. 17, 1817, letter to Byron that the death of Fanny was "a far severer anguish" than that of Harriet. It is possible that Shelley believed this, but more likely that he wished to hide the depth of his feeling about Harriet in a letter to Byron. In any event, time was to show that while Fanny's suicide was a severe shock, it did not become a major tragedy in his life, one to haunt him to the end of his days, as did that of Harriet. It is unlikely, therefore, that Fanny occupies the main rôle in this key passage, but very probable that Shelley was thinking of her death as among the "storms."

3. I do not mean that Shelley's disturbance over the trial for and the loss of the children ceased on the day of the verdict. Here, as elsewhere, I use dates as approximations.

spirit; but she persisted in her loving care and as his mind became normal again he found that she had been "smiling" lovingly on him "all the while." That Mary was eager to help him, even generously urging him to bring his children by Harriet back to her, and yet was extremely worried and disturbed herself we can tell from her letter of December 17, 1816, written in the early stages of the crisis: "You tell me to write a long letter and I would but that my ideas wander and my hand trembles come back to reassure me my Shelley & bring with you your darling Ianthe & Charles."[4]

If we now turn to *Rosalind and Helen* we find a rather striking parallel between a section of it and both the Planet-Tempest and the Moon passages. This section of the poem was almost certainly among those written at Marlow in 1817 or the early winter of 1818,[5] is autobiographical, written as a token of their marriage to Mary (who refers to it with a kind of pleased possessiveness as "my pretty eclogue"),[6] and clearly reflects the events and emotions of the period under discussion. The central character of the poem is Lionel, who has long been recognized as one of Shelley's self portraits. Lionel is a young revolutionary and sceptic who battles against political oppression and religious tyranny. He is, however, driven from his native land by some unfortunate love experience:

> 'Twas said that he had refuge sought
> In love from his unquiet thought
> In distant lands, and been deceived
> By some strange show.   (756–759)

As a result of these experiences "he was striken deep with some disease of mind," and became despondent:

> 'How am I changed! my hopes were once like fire:
> I loved, and I believed that life was love.
> How am I lost! . . .
>   I wake to weep
> And sit the long day gnawing the core
> Of my bitter heart. . . .'   (764–777)

Then he meets Helen (Mary); Helen nurses him back to mental health but his physical health begins to decline and she herself grows ill with worry:

> Our talk was sad and sweet,
> Till slowly from his mien there passed
> The desolation which it spoke. . . .

4. Jones, *op. cit.*, I, 17.
5. Shelley's letters to Peacock in April 1818 (*Works*, IX, 295) and on Aug. 16, 1818 (*ibid.*, pp. 319–320) show that he had begun to send the poem to the printers before he left England (March, 1818). Hence, it was probably completed in the main by that time. R. D. Havens argues plausibly that only the first 218 and last 79 lines were added in Italy in August, 1818—"Rosalind and Helen," *JEGP*, XXX (1931), 218–222.
6. Letter to Shelley, Sept. 26, 1817 (Jones, I, 31).

> And so, his mind
> Was healed, while mine grew sick with fear:
> For ever now his health declined. . . .
>
> The blood in his translucent veins
> Beat, not like animal life, but love
> Seemed now its sullen springs to move,
> When life had failed, and all its pains:
> And sudden sleep would seize him oft
> Like death, so calm, but that a tear,
> His pointed eyelashes between,
> Would gather in the light serene
> Of smiles, whose lustre bright and soft
> Beneath lay undulating there.
> His breath was like inconstant flame,
> So eagerly it went and came;
> And I hung o'er him in his sleep,
> Till, like an image in the lake
> Which rains disturb, my tears would break
> The shadow of that slumber deep:
> And say with flattery false, yet sweet,
> That death and he could never meet,
> If I would never part with him.
> And so we loved, and did unite
> All that in us was yet divided.   (784–845)

Hardly has he begun to recover, however, than he is arrested and put on trial—"a trial, I think, men call it"—for "keen blasphemy." Following the trial he is released and he and Helen are drawn more strongly together. Lionel, however, is again ill and Helen fears for him:

> You might see his colour come and go,
> And the softest strain of music made
> Sweet smiles, yet sad, arise and fade
> Amid the dew of his tender eyes; . . .
>
> And then I fell on a life which was sick with fear
> Of all the woe that now I bear.   (1020–1048)

This time her loving care is to no avail, and Lionel dies.

The parallels between this passage, on the one hand, and the events in Shelley's life and *Epipsychidion*, on the other, are unmistakable. Not that the parallels are exact or that there are no differences; but the general correspondence is clear. One gets the impression from *Rosalind and Helen* of three crises: the mental derangement, the physical illness, and the decline following the trial. The first unfortunate love experience of Lionel, which unbalanced his mind, would clearly correspond to Shelley's last months with Harriet Westbrook and the breakup of their marriage; in

Epipsychidion it parallels the "hunted deer" passage (271–275); in the Dedication to *The Revolt of Islam*, stanza six:

> Alas, that love should be a blight and snare
> To those who seek all sympathies in one!—
> Such once I sought in vain; then black despair,
> The shadow of a starless night, was thrown
> Over the world in which I moved alone.

His recovery, under Helen's gentle care, corresponds to his reaction to Mary's love in the early months of their union; to the "noonday dawn" in *Epipsychidion*, to the "spring" in the Dedication. Following this, we have two periods of crisis, that of the physical decline and that following the trial, during both of which Helen stood loyally by Lionel and watched over him. That the second of these represents Shelley's state following the trial for the custody of the children is reasonably sure for the parallel between the trial in the poem and that in his life cannot be mistaken. Lionel is tried for blasphemy; Shelley told Byron that he was being tried because he was an avowed "atheist" and "revolutionist";[7] the speech which Lionel makes following his trial—"Fear not the tyrants shall rule for ever"—Shelley included in *To William Shelley*, which, as we have seen, centers around the loss of his children: "They have taken thy brother and sister dear." We have here a fairly certain focal point. If, then, I am correct in my interpretation of *Epipsychidion*, this incident must correspond to that of the Moon in the Planet-Tempest episode.[8] And the spirit of the two is similar: in *Rosalind and Helen* the woman works with love and kindness to revive the man's spirits even though she is herself greatly upset:

> And I fell on a life which was sick with fear
> Of all the woe that now I bear.

In *Epipsychidion*, the woman shrinks as in "the sickness of eclipse," but when the man recovers he finds that she has been "smiling all the while" over him.

We can, then, be reasonably certain of these two episodes and their parallels in *Rosalind and Helen* and *Epipsychidion*: the revival of Shelley by Mary following the misfortunes with Harriet (summer of 1814); the tender nursing of him after the trial (spring of 1817). The identification of the intermediary crisis—the physical illness of the man and the nursing by the woman—is less certain, but the most likely explanation is that it refers to the physical illness of Shelley in the summer of 1815: "He had been advised by a phy-

7. Letter, Jan. 17, 1817 (*Works*, IX, 219).
8. Kroder, *op. cit.*, pp. 388–389, first indicated a parallel between *Rosalind and Helen* and *Epipsychidion*.

sician to live as much as possible in the open air . . . He had just recovered from a severe pulmonary attack."[9] I am inclined to think also, that, in spite of differences between the two passages, it refers to the same period as the "cold chaste bed" crisis in *Epipsychidion*. The *Rosalind and Helen* passage does not depict the coldness of the woman, but it does hint at some degree of previous estrangement in the statement that Lionel's troubles brought the two together in such a way as to "unite All that in us was yet divided." There are two rather striking parallels between the two passages: (a) the half-alive condition of the man: "nor alive nor dead" in *Epipsychidion*; the slow beat of the blood, the sudden sleeps "like death," the faint breath in *Rosalind and Helen*; (b) the woman hovering anxiously over the sick man: "sate beside me, with her downward face Illumining my slumbers" in *Epipsychidion*; "And I hung o'er him in his sleep," in *Rosalind and Helen*. Neither *Epipsychidion* nor *Rosalind and Helen* gives the impression of any great lapse of time between these two crises; in *Rosalind and Helen* the physical crisis immediately succeeds the mental crisis; in *Epipsychidion* the "deliverance" seems almost to blend into the "chaste cold bed" crisis.[1]

The indication is that Shelley, following the marital upsets of the spring of 1815, entered a period of physical and psychological crisis, the psychological aspect of the situation being due in part to his growing awareness of the incompleteness of the marriage. In *Rosalind and Helen*—a poem written for Mary and with Mary (Helen) as narrator—he stresses the physical illness; in *Epipsychidion* he stresses the psychological aspect; in *Alastor*, written in the fall of 1815, we find both: physical illness and love starvation.

These passages in *Rosalind and Helen*, then, occurring as they do, in a poem almost as directly autobiographical as *Epipsychidion* itself, provide confirmation of the view that the events reflected in the Moon and Planet-Tempest passages are those from the meeting with Mary in the summer of 1814 to the litigation over the children. In particular they throw light upon the rôles of both Shelley and Mary during those crises. We get a more complete picture of the loving tenderness of Mary to supplement the impression from *Epipsychidion* and we learn that part of the coldness complained of in the "chaste cold bed" passage was due to the emotional

9. Mary Shelley, "Note on the Early Poems," *Works*, III, 120.
1. In one respect the feeling of the woman in this intermediate crisis is closer to the Planet-Tempest passage than to the Moon passage. In *Rosalind and Helen* the woman says that her mind "grew sick with fear," which is similar to the Moon shrinking "as in the sickness of eclipse" in the Planet-Tempest passage. This does not, however, warrant the conclusion that one should parallel these episodes but probably indicates only that both crises had elements in common in the nursing of the man and the anxiety of the woman.

paralysis of the man resulting from physical illness and psychological crises. That this latter phenomenon was an important aspect of the picture as it occurred in life there can be little doubt.

The foregoing interpretation of the Planet-Tempest passage, regardless of whether one accepts it in all its details or not, is, it seems to me, preferable to those so far advanced. The passage not only fits the events but fits them in detail and in sequence: the quenching of the Planet—Harriet's suicide; the frost of despair—the poet's state following that death; the harassing of the sea of his life by the Tempest—his persecution by Eliza Westbrook; the earthquakes—the litigation over the children; the continued smiling of the Moon—Mary's tender care of him. Further, we can produce supplementary evidence from letters and *Rosalind and Helen* and the observations of others to show that Shelley's and Mary's emotional states and reactions during this crisis were similar to those portrayed in the poem. This conclusion could be seriously weakened only by a demonstration that the passage could not represent events of the period of this crisis, but White's arguments to this effect are, as I have attempted to demonstrate, inconclusive. On the contrary, the weight of the evidence, both from external sources and from the poem itself, indicates that the events of the passage do fall within the same period as that of the crisis. This will, perhaps, become clearer if we parallel our initial description of the symbolism of the autobiographical passage as a whole (265–383) with an attempted reconstruction of the events and characters there reflected: in the years 1812–14, Shelley tells us, he knew and admired a number of women who influenced his life, some of them "wise," some of them "fair," the wise probably including Elizabeth Hitchener and Mrs. Boinville, the fair, Harriet Grove and Cornelia Turner (267–270); his marriage with Harriet Westbrook (the one who was "not true") disintegrated and he consequently endured a severe emotional crisis (March–May, 1814; lines 271–275); he was "delivered" from this crisis by Mary (the Moon—summer of 1814), but later (1815–16) discovered that although she was intelligent and affectionate she was "cold" (276–307); he was shortly thereafter precipitated into an even greater crisis in the suicide of Harriet (the Planet) and the vindictive pursuit of him by her sister Eliza (the Tempest), culminating in the loss of his children (December 1816 to March 1817; lines 307–320); "at length" he met Emilia (the Sun—December 1820; 321–344); now (January–February, 1821) he hopes to live happily under the joint influence of Emilia and Mary with Claire Clairmont (the Comet), with whom he hints a previous but now concluded affair, back at home with them (245–383).

ROSS WOODMAN

Adonais†

As an Orphic poet, Shelley could never come to rest in the epic vision of art with its conception of the poet as the unacknowledged legislator of the world. The Orphic apocalypse is intended to free man from the relentless revolutions of the wheel of life by releasing the buried divinity within him. The anagogical vision in the concluding stanzas of *Adonais* presents this final transcendence and, as such, brings to completion Shelley's apocalyptic career.

* * *

The anagogical dimension of *Adonais* provides the focus of the entire poem. It is the energizing principle which compels the poet to press on towards the object of knowledge as distinct from the mythical account which defines the limits of his art. Shelley's goal is the "deep truth" which is "imageless." The dialectic of sacred passion drives the poet, as it drives Dante in the *Paradiso*, beyond imagery to its primal source.

If Plato's *Symposium* provides the model for Shelley's ascent in *Adonais*, then Dante's *Convivio* provides the commentary of ascent in terms of which Shelley was able to structure his vision into what he himself described as a "highly wrought *piece of art*."[1] Specifically, in his description of his elegy, Shelley had in mind Dante's discussion of the four levels of meaning in the second tractate of the *Convivio*, which he studied in 1821, translating the last *canzone* of the fourth tractate and including it in his Advertisement to *Epipsychidion*. It is with reference to Dante's discussion of the four levels that *Adonais* will be examined.

Dante in the *Convivio* distinguishes between the literal, allegorical, moral, and anagogical levels of his own vision. His discussion is neatly summarized in his letter to Can Grande Della Scala, and for this reason it is worth quoting. "For the clarity of what is to be said," he writes,

> one must realize that the meaning of this work [*The Divine Comedy*] is not simple, but rather is to be called polysemous, that is, having many meanings. The first meaning is the one obtained through the letter; the second is the one obtained through the thing signified by the letter. The first is called literal, the second allegorical or moral or anagogical. In order that this man-

† Reprinted from *The Apocalyptic Vision in the Poetry of Shelley* by Ross Woodman by permission of University of Toronto Press, pp. 159–178. © University of Toronto Press, 1964.
1. Julian Edition, X, 270 (letter to John and Maria Gisborne, June 5, 1821).

ner of treatment may appear more clearly, it may be applied to the following verses: "When Israel went out of Egypt, the house of Jacob from a people of strange language, Judah was his sanctuary and Israel his dominion." For if we look to the letter alone, the departure of the children of Israel from Egypt in the time of Moses is indicated to us; if to the allegory, our redemption accomplished by Christ is indicated to us; if to the moral sense, the conversion of the soul from the woe and misery of sin to a state of grace is indicated to us; if to the anagogical sense, the departure of the consecrated soul from the slavery of this corruption to the liberty of eternal glory is indicated. And though these mystic senses may be called by various names, they can generally be spoken of as allegorical, since they are diverse from the literal or the historical.[2]

On the literal or historical level, *Adonais* concerns the death of John Keats as a result of the vicious attack made upon his *Endymion* in the *Quarterly Review*; on the allegorical level, the poem concerns the plight of the visionary in a society controlled by tyrannical forces; on the moral level, it concerns the release of the soul from the corruptions of earthly existence; on the anagogical level, it concerns, to use Dante's words, "the departure of the consecrated soul from the slavery of this corruption to the liberty of eternal glory." The first two levels, the literal and allegorical, are presented within the framework of the myth of the dying and rising vegetation god, Adonis; the last two levels, the moral and anagogical, move beyond the myth of Adonis and find their archetype in Adonai, the Hebrew Lord revealed in, though transcending, His creation. Professor Wasserman has pointed out the significance of the amalgamation of the two words in the title of the poem, and Professor Foakes has noted the dropping of the Adonis myth in the last section of the elegy (stanzas 38–55).[3]

Unlike Dante, Shelley in *Adonais* radically opposes the literal and allegorical to the moral and anagogical dimensions of his poem. Following the characteristic late mediaeval Aristotelian approach to Christianity, Dante places great emphasis upon the literal meaning of his own art. He argues that the literal level is "that sense in the expression of which the others are all included, and without which it would be impossible and irrational to give attention to the other meanings, and most of all to the allegorical."[4] Drawing an analogy from Aristotle's *Physics*, he argues that the literal level may be considered as the matter, while the other levels may be

2. As quoted in Allan H. Gilbert, *Literary Criticism: Plato to Dryden* (New York: American Book Co., 1940), pp. 202–3.
3. Earl R. Wasserman, "Adonais" in *The Subtler Language* (Baltimore: The Johns Hopkins University Press, 1959),

pp. 311–13; R. A. Foakes, *The Romantic Assertion: A Study of the Language of Nineteenth Century Poetry* (London: Methuen & Co., 1958), p. 102.
4. Dante Alighieri, *Convivio*, trans. W. W. Jackson (Oxford: Clarendon Press, 1909), p. 74.

considered as the form. Unless the matter is properly set forth, it will be impossible either to impose a form upon it or to interpret its meaning. Dante, in other words, does not oppose matter and form; rather he sees form arising out of matter, rendering explicit the potential inherent in it. At the end of the *Paradiso*, therefore, he is not left suspended in an "intense inane"; on the contrary, he is able to return to this world, his sense purified and sanctified, and see in earthly love the emblem of God's Grace.

As an Orphic poet, Shelley in *Adonais* opposes flesh to spirit by asserting that the annihilation of flesh is necessary to the release of spirit. Viewed within the framework of spirit, man on earth confronts "invulnerable nothings" (348). The literal level of *Adonais*, therefore, is a vision of the death of Keats seen as the cessation of matter in a state of motion. The literal level finds its source in D'Holbach's materialism, which Shelley with his anagogical focus in mind rejects as sensory delusion.

On the literal level, therefore, Shelley presents a picture similar in many respects to the daemonic vision of *Alastor*. In that poem he relates his own fear of sudden extinction to what he considers the slow and withering decay of Wordsworth's powers. Confronted with the dismal spectacle of Wordsworth's ruin as he sees it revealed in *The Excursion*, Shelley is partially consoled: sudden death is preferable to the fate of those who, as he says in his Preface (p. 15) "prepare for their old age a miserable grave." This same consolation is offered to Keats in *Adonais* (356–60), and in images that echo the earlier *Alastor*:

> From the contagion of the world's slow stain
> He is secure, and now can never mourn
> A heart grown cold, a head grown gray in vain;
> Nor, when the spirit's self has ceased to burn,
> With sparkless ashes load an unlamented urn.

In *Alastor*, the entire daemonic vision comes to a climax in the poet's passive submission to that "colossal Skeleton" that rules "this frail world" with "devastating omnipotence" (611–14). And this same imagistic focus defines the literal level of *Adonais*. Keats has been led to "that high Capital, where kingly Death/Keeps his pale court in beauty and decay" (55–6). He is the victim of that "invisible Corruption" (67) drawn over the curtain of flesh. Shelley describes him as he describes the dead poet in *Alastor*: the "silent, cold, and motionless" (661) form of one "yet safe from the worm's outrage" (702).

Within the materialistic framework of the first seventeen stanzas of *Adonais*, Shelley accepts the fact that there is nothing to mourn in the death of Keats. He is the victim of "the law/Of change"

(71–2); "Death feeds on his mute voice, and laughs at our despair" (27). And here again, his fate is similar to that of the poet in *Alastor* over whose death "no lorn bard/Breathed . . . one melodious sigh" (58–9). Yet Keats, unlike the poet in *Alastor,* has "moulded into thought" (118) his own desires and aspirations. They have, therefore, a legitimate cause for grief; cut off from their source in the physical activity of the brain, they must perish like sheep deserted by the shepherd. And Nature also can mourn the passing of that beauty with which Keats has invested her. Unlike Keats's "Desires and Adorations" (108), however, Nature can survive his passing. Thus Shelley, in the opening stanzas of the second section of his elegy (stanzas 18–37) ironically sets the rebirth of Nature over against the death of Keats. Nature's lament becomes a mock despair. Shelley suggests this by comparing Keats's "fading melodies" to "flowers that mock the corse beneath" (16–17).

When Shelley turns from his contemplation of Keats's annihilation to his attack upon the critics whom he considered responsible, he is forced by the logic of his first hypothesis to recognize that they acted according to the law of Necessity. To condemn them for their murderous action in the *Quarterly Review* is futile. Shelley can no more condemn the critics who murdered Keats than mourn his death. Although their "wings rain contagion" (248), the poison is not something alien to life; rather it is the "contagion of the world's slow stain" (356) to which all men, including critics, must succumb. In the final section of the poem, the critics become an emblem of life itself, a symbol of the human condition to which all men are bound as by a curse.

On the literal level Shelley recreates in *Adonais* his own earlier materialism derived primarily from D'Holbach. From this literal level, he moves on to the allegorical in which he makes use of the myth of a dying and rising god. While the allegorical dimension allows him to view Keats less as a mortal and more as a poet, Shelley is still bound by the very character of his myth to the eternal cycle of Nature. The second movement of the elegy focuses on rebirth, just as the first movement focuses upon death. Both death and rebirth, however, belong within the fallen order of Nature, within the framework of Necessity. For this reason, the second movement is set within the pattern of the first and provides no real advance; there is as yet no principle of transcendence in operation. The first two movements of *Adonais,* which partially recreate the vision of *Alastor,* simply serve to purge "from our inward sight the film of familiarity which obscures from us the wonder of our being."[5] The third movement reveals that wonder, which is the "divinity in Man" released from the law of Necessity.

5. *A Defence of Poetry*, Julian, VII, 137.

On the allegorical level Keats is identified with Adonis, the dying and rising vegetation god of Greek mythology. In the Greek myth, Adonis is a comely youth beloved by Aphrodite. In his infancy, Aphrodite hides him from Ares, his jealous rival, in a chest which she entrusts to Proserpine, Queen of Hades. When Proserpine opens the chest and gazes upon the infant, she is so enamoured of his beauty that she refuses to return him to Aphrodite. The dispute between the two goddesses over who should possess the child is finally decided by Zeus, who decrees that he will dwell with Proserpine for one part of the year and with Aphrodite for the other part.

The joint possession of Adonis by Proserpine and Aphrodite is dramatized in the myth by presenting Adonis as a youthful and eager hunter. Aphrodite, fearing that he will be killed, attempts to persuade him to give up hunting. One day, however, when Aphrodite is absent, presiding over ceremonies in her honour, Adonis returns to the hunt and is mortally wounded by his jealous rival, Ares, who has disguised himself as a wild boar. When Aphrodite is informed of what has happened, she hastens to his side in a futile effort to revive him. Her tears mix with his blood and from that mixture the rich profusion of vegetable life emerges. Thus, the return of Adonis to Proserpine contains in the rebirth of Nature the promise of his resurrection and reunion with Aphrodite.

In Bion's *Lament for Adonis*,[6] which was Shelley's immediate source, all the elements of the myth are present. At the death of Adonis, Aphrodite laments that he must return to Proserpine (or Persephone): "Take thou my husband, Persephone, for thou art mightier far than I, and all that is fair comes down to thee; while I am hapless utterly, a prey to sorrow unassuaged, and weep for my Adonis who is dead, and I fear thee" (52–6). From her tears mixed with Adonis' blood flowers come forth: "As fast from the Paphian flow tears as from Adonis blood, and both on the ground are turned to flowers; of the blood are roses born, and of the tears anemones" (63–5). Finally, the cyclic recurrence of death and resurrection is implied in the last lines: "Cease thy laments to-day, Cytherea; stay thy dirges. Again must thou lament, again must thou weep another year" (97–8).

On the allegorical level, Shelley makes use of Bion's poem. After calling upon Urania (Bion's Aphrodite) to leave her Paradise and weep for Adonais who is dead, he then tells her to quench her "fiery tears" (22). Adonais has returned to Proserpine ("the amorous Deep") "where all things wise and fair/Descend" (24–5). Nevertheless, Urania leaves her "secret Paradise" and laments over the corpse of Adonais (235–43). . . .

6. The quotations that follow are taken from *The Greek Bucolic Poets*, trans., with notes, by A. S. P. Gow (Cambridge: Cambridge University Press, 1933).

At this point, however, the allegory breaks off. Shelley does not go on to describe the resurrection of Adonais in terms of his re-union with Urania. And the reason is evident in Urania's lament (232–4):

> "I would give
> All that I am to be as thou now art!
> But I am chained to Time, and cannot thence depart!"

Bion's Adonis has become Shelley's Adonais, the "divinity in Man" released from the cyclic pattern of Nature.

Within the allegorical framework of the Adonis myth, Shelley describes the fate of the visionary in a hostile society. In the lament of Urania, he argues that had Keats been strong enough to survive the review in the *Quarterly Review*, he might have completed his cycle and filled his "crescent sphere" (242). The cyclic imagery, however, contains within it the suggestion of futility. Shelley argues that Keats's survival depended upon his ability to arm himself with the shield of wisdom and the spear of scorn and join forces with the enemies of tyranny. He would have to "dare the unpastured dragon in his den." Implicit in this battle is the fear that the poet who fights back, as Prometheus fought back, may himself become the victim of his own wrath. This was Prometheus' fate in the first act of *Prometheus Unbound*, and Shelley was unable adequately to resolve it in the third. The central incongruity in the drama lies in Shelley's vision of love, on the one hand, and the awful judgment upon Jupiter, on the other. Jupiter in *Prometheus Unbound* is not redeemed, and, to that extent at least, Promethus' recreative power is limited. The most obvious evidence of that limitation is the fact that Prometheus' imaginative achievement belongs within the cycle of Nature. Necessity must reassert itself. Eternity, "Mother of many acts and hours," has an "infirm hand" (IV, 565–6); Jupiter must inevitably rise again.

In Urania's dubious hope that Adonais, had he lived, might have armed himself to deal with society, Shelley had Byron in mind. Byron is the "Pythian of the age" (250) from whom the critics fled when he loosed in *English Bards and Scotch Reviewers* one spear of scorn upon them. Shelley wrote to Byron after receiving the news of Keats's death telling him of the devastating effect of the criticism of *Endymion* upon Keats's mind. On April 26, 1821, Byron replied:

> I am very sorry to hear what you say of Keats—is it *actually* true? I did not think criticism had been so killing. Though I differ from you essentially in your estimate of his performances, I so much abhor all unnecessary pain, that I would rather he had been seated on the highest peak of Parnassus than have perished

in such a manner. . . . I read the review of "Endymion" in the *Quarterly*. It was severe,—but surely not so severe as many reviews in that and other journals upon others.

I recollect the effect upon me of the *Edinburgh* on my first poem; it was rage, and resistance, and redress—but not despondency nor despair. I grant that those are not amiable feelings; but, in this world of bustle and broil, and especially in the career of writing, a man should calculate his powers of *resistance* before he goes into the arena.[7]

Shelley could not whole-heartedly accept this attitude. While it allowed Byron the strength to deal with a corrupt society, he had paid severely for it in the sacrifice of his own idealism.

* * *

Shelley's optimism . . . finds its counterpart in his hopes for Keats's future. In November, 1820 (Julian Edition, X, 218), several months after the event, he described Keats's reception of the criticism of *Endymion* in a letter to the Editor of the *Quarterly Review*: "The first effects are described to me to have resembled insanity, and it was by assiduous watching that he was restrained from effecting purposes of suicide. The agony of his sufferings at length produced the rupture of a blood-vessel in the lungs, and the usual process of consumption appears to have begun." At the time this news reached Shelley, he believed that if he could see Keats he would be able to help him. He had himself been driven close to insanity in 1814 and during the crisis over Mary Godwin had been driven to attempt suicide. More than that, in 1815 he had been told by his physician that he had not long to live. Out of that despair had emerged *Alastor*, in which the wretched wanderings of the poet parallel in a very real sense the wanderings of Keats's poet in *Endymion*. Moved by the memory of these experiences, Shelley wrote to Keats on July 27, 1820, asking him to come and stay near him in Pisa. After issuing his invitation, he continued:

> I have lately read your "Endymion" again and ever with a new sense of the treasures of poetry it contains, though treasures poured forth with indistinct profusion. This, people in general will not endure, and that is the cause of the comparatively few copies which have been sold. I feel persuaded that you are capable of the greatest things, so you but will. I always tell Ollier to send you copies of my books.—"Prometheus Unbound" I imagine you will receive nearly at the same time with this letter.
> [Julian, X, 194]

But the death of Keats defeated Shelley's hopes, and in that defeat the words which he had attributed to Byron in *Julian and Maddalo* (120–30) must have come home to him with peculiar impact.

7. As quoted in Julian, X, 254n.

Maddalo is moralizing upon the vesper bells ringing from the tower of an asylum:

> "And such,"—he cried, "is our mortality,
> And this must be the emblem and the sign
> Of what should be eternal and divine!—
> And like that black and dreary bell, the soul,
> Hung in a heaven-illumined tower, must toll
> Our thoughts and our desires to meet below
> Round the rent heart and pray—as madmen do
> For what? they know not,—till the night of death
> As sunset that strange vision, severeth
> Our memory from itself, and us from all
> We sought, and yet were baffled."

The impact of Keats's death upon Shelley is explained by his close identification with Keats as a poet. He believed that only Keats and himself among all the Romantics had remained faithful to the pursuit of the ideal. In sending Keats copies of his own poems and in inviting him to Pisa, he hoped that they might support each other in their arduous task. Shelley had attempted to follow in the path of Byron, but he found it temperamentally impossible to develop within himself a defensive satirical scorn for society. He remained, in some sense, as vulnerable as he believed Keats to be. Thus, in his self-portrait in *Adonais*, there is no evidence of the Promethean poet. Instead, there is a vision of the poet "who in another's fate now wept his own" (300). Shelley describes Keats as "a pale flower" (48), its "petals nipped before they blew" (52), and he uses the same image to describe himself: "the withering flower" on which "the killing sun smiles brightly" (286–7). His "power, like Keats's, is "girt round with weakness" (281–2). Instead of the spear of scorn, he carries, again like Keats, "a light spear topped with a cypress cone" (291). As an Orphic poet, he carries the Dionysian thyrsus, thus finding his archetype in the peace-loving Orpheus whose music had the power to tame the wildest beasts. Nevertheless, Shelley remains, as Keats had remained, the victim of "the herded wolves" and "the obscene ravens" (244–5). He believes that his Promethean power has failed him. And for this reason, Shelley returns (274–9) to that early daemonic image of himself which he presented in *Alastor*:

> he, as I guess,
> Had gazed on Nature's naked loveliness,
> Actaeon-like, and now he fled astray
> With feeble steps o'er the world's wilderness,
> And his own thoughts, along that rugged way,
> Pursued, like raging hounds, their father and their prey.

* * *

At first glance it appears impossible that the Urania of *Adonais* who is "chained to Time" (234) is Shelley's "mistress Urania" in whose honour he told Peacock he wrote *A Defence of Poetry*.[8] Professor Wasserman in his analysis of the elegy argues that she is not. Carefully distinguishing between the "quickening life" which springs out of matter (stanza 19) and the "plastic stress" of the one Spirit which descends into matter (stanza 43), Wasserman goes on to separate Urania and the poet by identifying Urania with the former and the poet with the latter.[9] This distinction is reinforced when Shelley in the third section of his elegy describes Keats as having returned to that power "which wields the world with never-wearied love,/Sustains it from beneath, and kindles it above" (377–8). Keats has returned to the power which kindles life "above"; Urania remains sustaining it "from beneath." Urania, in other words, is the poet's shaping spirit of imagination which, like the "quickening life," must spring out of the world of the senses and shape it into an image of the "divinity in Man." Urania creates the vision of apocalypse, but not the apocalypse itself. She is the myth-making power in the poet which constructs the "probable account" of the poet's object. Shelley, therefore, accurately identifies her with Bion's Aphrodite who must share her beloved Adonis with Proserpine, the goddess of Hades. To pursue Urania is to be half in love with death, as Keats recognizes in his *Ode to a Nightingale*.

Because Shelley is preoccupied with the Promethean vision of art in his *Defence of Poetry*, he does not bring into focus the anagogical dimension of his vision. He describes the poet in terms of Urania, which is to say, in terms of his earthly mission as a recreator of the universe. At the same time, however, he clearly anticipates the anagogic when he draws a careful distinction between the poet's "original conceptions" and his actual productions. "But when composition begins," he writes, "inspiration is already on the decline, and the most glorious poetry that has ever been communicated to the world is probably a feeble shadow of the original conception of the Poet" (Julian Edition, VII, 135). Urania is not the poet's conception; she is the poet's fading creativity which, out of that conception, constructs a "feeble shadow." She is, in other words, the "awful shadow of some unseen power" which waxes and wanes in accordance with Nature's mutability. She exists only within the myth of Adonis, and when Shelley abandons the myth, Urania disappears.

One possible reason, therefore, for Shelley's failure to compose the second part of his *Defence* is that he had watched in his own lifetime the waning of creative power among his favourite living

8. In a letter dated Feb. 15, 1821, Julian, X, 234. 9. *The Subtler Language*, p. 331.

poets. He could not, as a result, put to the test his faith in the apocalyptic power of his contemporaries. The best he could do, when confronted by the actual texts, was to recreate the vision of *Alastor* to include not only Wordsworth, but Coleridge and Southey as well. And this, of course, is precisely what Shelley does do in the first two sections of *Adonais*. Urania is deserted; in Keats, her "youngest, dearest one, has perished" (46), and there is no one left to invoke her. All that is left to her is to curse those who robbed her of her prize.

It may therefore be concluded that the Urania of *A Defence of Poetry* is the same Urania who laments the death of Keats in *Adonais*. The change is not in Urania; it is in Shelley, who, in *Adonais*, views her within an anagogical perspective. Shelley, it may be said, abandoned Urania for Proserpine believing that in and through her the object of his quest was to be found. To move from the vision of apocalypse to the apocalypse itself, it is necessary to descend first to the daemonic. The path which Shelley follows in *Adonais* is the path of Dante in *The Divine Comedy*; he descends into the Hell of material annihilation that he may truly rise into the "white radiance of Eternity" (463). Those who remain with Urania, playing with lovely images, ultimately delude themselves.

The moral dimension of Shelley's elegy, therefore, concerns itself with the release of the soul from the "contagion of the world's slow stain" (356). Shelley has anticipated this moral level from the outset. His allusions to Urania have all been ironic. In calling upon her to weep for Adonais, he points out the futility of her tears. In calling upon her to weep again as she had earlier wept for Milton, he points out that Milton "went, unterrified,/Into the gulf of death" (34–5). As for those who yet live, they tread "the thorny road" of "toil and hate" (44–5), even as Urania treads it. At the same time, however, those poets who, like Milton, are willing to follow this path find their reward in "Fame's serene abode" (45). Urania, on the other hand, within her "secret Paradise" (208) sits with "veilèd eyes" rekindling "fading melodies" surrounded by "listening Echoes" (12–15). Like a mistress grown old with time, her only consolation is the memory of her former glory (226–30). . . .

The real crisis, which defines the transition from the allegorical to the moral dimension of the elegy, comes when Shelley in his self-portrait exposes his branded brow which, he says, is "like Cain's or Christ's" (306). The radical ambiguity evident in placing Christ and Cain side by side as prototypes of himself as poet reveals Shelley's increasing misgivings about the nature of his own poetic power. These misgivings may have been further clarified by his reading of Byron's *Cain, A Mystery*, conceived partly under Shelley's influence,[1] and executed during the summer shortly after Shelley completed *Adonais*. Shelley considered the poem "a revelation not before communicated to man";[2] it is therefore worth examining for the possible light which it casts upon Shelley's somewhat Byronic identification with Cain in *Adonais*.

In Byron's vision, Cain, like Shelley's Prometheus, rebels against the Jehovah-Jupiter conception of God. Guided by Lucifer (Shelley's archetypal hero) he journeys into a pre-Adamite underworld and into an empyrean beyond the sun and moon. As the journey unfolds, Lucifer suggests to Cain that death may hold the key to the deepest mysteries which perplex man in his earthly state. Instead, however, of leading Cain to smash the "dome of many-coloured glass" to find the "white radiance of Eternity," Lucifer's suggestion leads him to return to the world and murder his brother, Abel. The murder of Abel vividly (and ironically) dramatizes the rejection of the familiar world in favour of an ideal world beyond the limits of man's mortality.

While Shelley in his letter to Gisborne did not define the precise nature of the "revelation" which the poem offered (beyond describing it as "apocalyptic"), he probably recognized, as indeed Byron likely intended that he should, some mark of identity with Cain and gained from it a richer insight into the daemonic aspect of his own apocalyptic vision which was destined to bear fruit in *The Triumph of Life*. The release of Prometheus required the destruction of Jupiter, even as Cain's vision in Byron's poem required the murder of Abel. The underside of Shelley's apocalyptic vision was the complete destruction of human society in its present form as exemplified in the passive submission of Byron's Abel to the vengeful Jehovah. Byron, unwilling, for example, to expose his natural

1. In a letter to Horace Smith (April 11, 1822) Shelley writes (Julian, X, 377–8): "Amongst other things, however, Moore, after giving Lord B. much good advice about public opinion, etc., seems to deprecate MY influence on his mind, on the subject of religion, and to attribute the tone assumed in 'Cain' to my suggestions. Moore cautions him against my influence on this particular, with the most friendly zeal; and it is plain that his motive springs from a desire of benefiting Lord B., without degrading me. I think you know Moore. Pray assure him that I have not the smallest influence over Lord Byron, in this particular, and if I had, I certainly should employ it to eradicate from his great mind the delusions of Christianity, which, in spite of his reason, seem perpetually to recur, and to lay in ambush for the hours of sickness and distress. 'Cain' was *conceived* many years ago, and begun before I saw him last year at Ra-

venna. How happy should I not be to attribute to myself, however indirectly, any participation in that immortal work!"

In spite of Shelley's assertion that he had no influence upon Byron, it is evident that it is Shelley's view of Christianity that governs many of the speeches of Byron's Cain. Shelley admits to a knowledge of the conception of the poem "many years ago" and, in admitting that he would be happy *not* to be in any sense identified with it, he may be referring to the daemonic light which Byron's poem casts upon his own Promethean vision. Such an interpretation of the last sentence in the above passage would certainly help to explain the significance of the extraordinary juxtaposition of Christ and Cain as prototypes of himself as a Dionysian poet in *Adonais*.

2. In a letter to John Gisborne, Jan. 26, 1822, Julian, X, 354.

child to the influence of the Shelley household, was keenly aware of the danger of Shelley's "atheism," especially when it was lost to sight in the clouds of his soaring idealism. In *Adonais* Shelley questions whether he bears the wounds of the suffering Christ or the mark of the accursed Cain. By rounding his first two movements with the curse of Cain which leads him directly to the question, Shelley, consciously or unconsciously, arrives at the impasse which he faced with Prometheus in the third act of his drama. In *Prometheus Unbound* he was unable to resolve it; he allowed Prometheus both to repent his curse and see it fulfilled.

In *Adonais*, however, Shelley is concerned neither to repent the curse society as embodied in Urania and the critics nor to enjoy the imaginative benefits of seeing it fulfilled. So far as any earthly redemption is concerned he seems to have succumbed to Prometheus' tempter and affirmed that good and the means to good are incompatible. He turns what in Byron's vision amounts to a metaphysical explanation of murder into a metaphysical defence of self-murder. The moral dimension of the elegy resides in a metaphysical defence of suicide (415–23):

> Oh, come forth,
> Fond wretch! and know thyself and him aright.
> Clasp with thy panting soul the pendulous Earth;
> As from a centre, dart thy spirit's light
> Beyond all worlds, until its spacious might
> Satiate the void circumference: then shrink
> Even to a point within our day and night;
> And keep thy heart light lest it make thee sink
> When hope has kindled hope, and lured thee to the brink.

In *Adonais*, Shelley has been lured "to the brink" first by his rejection of materialism, which conducts to annihilation, and then by his rejection of mutability, which traps the poet within the limits of Nature. Beyond both is the "void circumference," which is the realm of pure mind revolving in its own divinity. It is the poet's "ideal prototype" partially discovered in the creation of its "antitype." The "antitype," however, is nothing more than an image shaped by the imagination out of the sensory data offered to the mind. It is the distorting mirror in which the "divinity in Man" first recognizes itself; it cannot, however, truly know itself by gazing upon its own mirror image. Thus, in the stanza quoted above, the divinity within Shelley calls upon the poet to "come forth" from the mirror world of images and know himself "aright." He must dart his spirit beyond the range of his own shaping power, which is the range of Urania, until "its spacious might/Satiate the void circumference." Confronted by this vast abyss, which to the physical eye is nothingness, the heart, so long dependent upon the senses to guide its promptings, must remain detached, lest it sink back into that "pendulous earth" which it is now called upon to abandon. Shelley is describing the suicidal moment seen, not as defeat, but as victory. Death is the awakening to life, to that ultimate self-knowledge which is the goal of Eros and the purpose of the Orphic purification rites. In his own moral defence, Shelley could argue that in his apocalyptic vision he reveals his own "metaphysical anatomy."[3] Within the womb of Urania, which is the womb of time, it takes shape. He is now ready to leave the womb of his "melancholy Mother" (20), sever the umbilical cord that attaches him to the mythological vision of Necessity, and find his proper abode in the kingdom of pure mind. Viewed from within the womb of Urania, the reality of death, which is the awakening to life, cannot be perceived. So long as Shelley functions within that illusory world, his theme in *Adonais* is despair. Once, however, he rids himself of that illusion, he is able completely to reverse his perspective and see not only himself but the universe aright (343–8).

> Peace, peace! he is not dead, he doth not sleep—
> He hath awakened from the dream of life—
> 'Tis we, who lost in stormy visions, keep
> With phantoms an unprofitable strife,
> And in mad trance, strike with our spirit's knife
> Invulnerable nothings.

It is the absence of this apocalyptic awakening from "the dream of life" that largely limits the earlier vision of *Alastor* to the first two movements of *Adonais*. *Alastor* presents, however ambiguously, the triumph of Necessity; *Adonais* presents, however ambiguously, the triumph over Necessity. Viewed within the anagogical perspective of *Adonais*, the poet's vision of the ideal in *Alastor* is indeed a "mad trance" in which the poet struggles with what D'Holbach himself declared to be mere "phantoms," mere "invulnerable nothings." Shelley, striving in *Alastor* to break free of the rational grip of the mechanistic philosophy by exploring the realm of his imagination, presents an image of the poet whose vision, like Rousseau's vision of Iris in *The Triumph of Life*, has turned into a nightmare. Thus, the passion quickened by the poet's vision of the "veilèd maid" (151) is "like the fierce fiend of a distempered dream" (225). The passion burns in his breast like the poison of a "green serpent" (228). It is to this image of the poet that Shelley returns at the end of his career. Indeed, Shelley's portrayal of himself in *Adonais* as one crushed and repelled by that which attracts him is precisely the image which he constructs of the poet in *Alastor*. With this difference, however: Shelley in

---

3. Mrs. Shelley's Preface to 1839 edition of Shelley's poems (*Poetical Works*, p. x).

Adonais views the poet in *Alastor* with the ironic detachment of one who has worked out an affirmative answer to the question that obsesses the poet who found an "untimely tomb" (50):

> Does the dark gate of death
> Conduct to thy mysterious paradise,
> Oh sleep? Does the bright arch of rainbow clouds,
> And pendent mountains seen in the calm lake,
> Lead only to a black and watery depth,
> While death's blue vault, with loathiest vapours hung,
> Where every shade which the foul grave exhales
> Hides its dead eye from the detested day,
> Conducts, O Sleep, to thy delightful realms?[4]

Attached to the power which "kindles from above" (378), Shelley is able in the last section of *Adonais* to view with new understanding its modification in that which "sustains it from beneath." So long as "the many" which "change and pass" can be viewed in the anagogical focus of "the One" which "remains" (460), Shelley can rejoice in the evidence of his own and Keats's spirit in the infinite variety of Nature's music. Both poets have for a time coalesced with Nature's "plastic stress" (381), though neither poet when thus immersed can properly grasp the divine reality, the "ideal prototype," behind what was being shaped.

In his *Defence of Poetry* (*Julian*, VII, 136), Shelley writes: "This instinct and intuition of the poetical faculty is still more observable in the plastic and pictorial arts; a great statue or picture grows under the power of the artist as a child in the mother's womb; and the very mind which directs the hands in formation is incapable of accounting to itself for the origin, the graduations, or the media of the process." What is being shaped by the artist is the image of his own divinity, of which, until he confronts that image, he remains unaware. But once he is aware, the image as such no longer attracts him, for he has awakened to the reality within him that it both conceals and reveals. For this reason, Shelley suggests, the poet leaves his image behind where it may dwell with and in Nature. The divinity in the poet, like God in the great creation myths, creates out of matter His own image and then withdraws into Himself, leaving behind His own visionary form which is the reality both of Nature and of art. In this sense, Keats "is made one with Nature," and his voice is heard "in all her music" (370–1). Beyond that, however, like the God without creation alone in the omnipotence of His own mind, the divinity within Keats resides. This ultimate dimension of Shelley's vision is the anagogic.

From the outset of his early training in the occult, Shelley in-

---

4. *Alastor* (211–19). Shelley in this elegiac poem reveals a dissatisfaction with a mechanistic philosophy for which he had not as yet found a substitute. The poem is perhaps best understood when read in the light of *Adonais*, the first two movements of which recreate its vision.

stinctively sought for some hidden meaning in whatever he read. On the surface, often expressing the poet's conscious intention, he saw "a thin disguise of circumstance" behind which the poet's real intention lay buried. Those who could penetrate below that surface and discover what lay hidden were the elect, whom Shelley defines as "the more select classes of poetical readers."[5] Like so many aristocrats who reject the social hierarchy on the grounds that it is unjust, Shelley found an outlet for his inherited sense of class in the occult, where he was able to recreate on the inner levels of consciousness what he had rejected on the outer. Shelley was perfectly at home in the psychic hierarchy of the occult in which all men were judged not according to the accidents of family or school or economic position, but according to the more fundamental criterion of psychic penetration. While, in theory, Shelley was committed to universal love and brotherhood, in fact he lived and wrote by a rigid code in terms of which men were accepted or rejected according to their degree of spiritual sensibility. Thus Shelley was actively repelled by the gross insensitivity of the familiar world; so acute, in fact, was his repulsion that he spent most of his life as a poet attempting to destroy that world. Of course, like most prophets functioning outside the established order, Shelley hoped that, if he annihilated the world of custom and habit, all men would find their way into his own kingdom of the elect. He was subject to the Romantic illusion that all men were potentially poets, prophets and visionaries. It is not surprising, therefore, that in Shelley's Heaven only the poets are to be found. Shelley's Heaven is an exclusive club to which belong only the aristocrats of the imagination.

Boris Pasternak has vividly described this peculiar character of the Romantic genius, which is at the same time the Romantic failure. "In the poet who imagines himself the measure of life and pays for this with his life," he writes,

> the Romantic conception manifests itself brilliantly and irrefutably in his symbolism, that is in everything which touches upon Orphism and Christianity imaginatively. . . . But outside the legend, the Romantic scheme is false. The poet who is its foundation is inconceivable without the nonpoets who must bring him into relief. . . . Romanticism always needs philistinism and with the disappearance of the petty bourgeosie loses half its poetical content.[6]

So long as Shelley stands in need of the familiar world as something both to oppose and recreate, he has a background in terms of

5. *A Defence of Poetry*, Julian, VII, 121; Preface to *Prometheus Unbound*, p. 207. 6. Boris Pasternak, "The Safe Conduct" in *The Collected Prose Works* (London: Lindsay Drummond, 1945), pp. 115–16. Boris Pasternak is discussing Mayakovsky's art in the passage quoted.

which his dialectic of vision can be seen. He has his materials. When, however, as in the closing stanzas of *Adonais*, his background dissolves and he is left with the "intense inane" (*P.U.*, III, iv, 204), he moves, as he himself realizes, beyond the reach of art. And it is precisely in this anagogical sphere that the contrast between Dante and Shelley comes into sharp relief. While Dante can be blinded by the radiance of his empyrean, he lived in the midst of a tradition which seeks at every turn to reveal the invisible world to the outward sense. For this reason, he can argue that the literal level contains the anagogical. His art is supported by his belief in a God who incarnated Himself in flesh without at the same time losing His divinity. For all his overwhelming sense of mystery and wonder as he scales with Beatrice the circles of Heaven, Dante also knows that he is moving over familiar theological ground at every point open to the intellect. His ascent to the tenth Heaven is a training in revealed theology under the direction of Beatrice issuing ultimately in the intellectual love of God. Shelley, in contrast, is forced to abandon all his sensible and rational supports, and find his sole support in that divine madness which Plato ironically describes in the *Ion*. Writing within an esoteric tradition both alien and isolated from the European traditions of thought which surrounded him, he is forced ultimately to look into himself and find his divinity there. He has somehow to make his poetic faith, which in the end he recognizes as a "willing suspension of disbelief," a matter of religious faith, which is to say, a matter of absolute truth. While, on one level of anagogy, Shelley can declare that Keats has been absorbed into the "white radiance of Eternity," on another level he can see himself, in setting out to join Keats, "borne darkly, fearfully, afar" (492). There is some slight, lingering suggestion of the daemonic in this closing stanza of *Adonais*. Again, as in *Alastor*, he makes use of the image of the little boat hurled upon the tempest to describe his own spirit setting out on its final journey (488–91):

> my spirit's bark is driven,
> Far from the shore, far from the trembling throng
> Whose sails were never to the tempest given;
> The massy earth and spherèd skies are riven!

What emerges in Shelley's vision of death in the closing section of *Adonais* is a revelation of the poet's effort to drive his will towards an anagogical focus. By 1821, the realm of mythopoeic literature had become Shelley's familiar world; in his *Defence of Poetry* he had demonstrated to himself his mastery of it. But now he is forced to admit, as Plato admits in his seventh Epistle, that he has not composed, nor ever can compose, a work which deals with the actual object of his quest. "Acquaintance with it," Plato writes, "must come rather after a long period of attendance or instruction in the subject itself and of close acquaintance when suddenly like a blaze kindled by a leaping spark, it is generated in the soul and at once becomes self-sustaining" (341D). In the concluding stanzas of *Adonais*, Shelley must rely entirely upon that self-sustaining fire within his own soul which had gradually been generated through his period of instruction in the occult. "The fire for which all thirst," he writes, "now beams on me,/Consuming the last clouds of cold mortality" (485–6).

It is, however, those "last clouds" that in some sense hold him back. Thus, he struggles to persuade himself (469–77):

> Why linger, why turn back, why shrink, my Heart?
> Thy hopes are gone before: from all things here
> They have departed; thou shouldst now depart!
> A light is passed from the revolving year,
> And man, and woman; and what still is dear
> Attracts to crush, repels to make thee wither.
> The soft sky smiles,—the low wind whispers near:
> 'Tis Adonais calls! oh, hasten thither,
> No more let Life divide what Death can join together.

And yet he does linger. His spirit moves restlessly, like some caged animal, from Nature where he catches the echoes of Adonais beckoning him, to a vision of Keats assuming his position on the vacant throne among the immortals, to the ruins of Rome and Keats's grave where he seeks "shelter in the shadow of the tomb" (458). Finally, however, he moves beyond all these images of death; the breath of Adonais, suggested in the "low wind," descends upon him. The "soul of Adonais" burns "through the inmost veil of Heaven" (493–4) and, as in the closing lines of *Epipsychidion*, Shelley feels himself consumed in that fire. Setting forth, he sees "Earth's shadows fly" (461) as the "massy earth and spherèd skies are riven" (491). He has smashed the "dome of many-coloured glass." Before him is spread "the white radiance of Eternity" which, in a combination of dread and ecstasy, he images (one final support) as the beacon star of Adonais.

CARL WOODRING

[*Hellas*][†]

For his last dramatic poem Shelley returned to a vision of the beautiful and the just, but a vision grounded in the actual and the contemporaneous. At the age of twenty-nine, he had an opportunity to construct a myth around an actual revolution in progress.

† Reprinted by permission of the publishers from Carl Woodring, *Politics in English Romantic Poetry*, Cambridge, Mass.: Harvard University Press, Copyright 1970, by the President and Fellows of Harvard College, pp. 313–319.

Hellas: A Lyrical Drama, planned and executed almost as rapidly as Coleridge and Southey had composed and published *The Fall of Robespierre,* had a degree of daring beyond the hot topicality that it shared with their ephemeral play.[1] Robespierre, however recently dead, was safely so. The French Revolution continued, but the cycle of events reported in the play by Coleridge and Southey had come to an end with the execution of Robespierre. The uprising by Shelley's Greeks, still in its early stages, was chaotic and seemingly ineffectual. As fervently as he hoped for a Greek victory, he could not prophesy it as a military event of the near future. Nevertheless, he had practical aims in the rapidity of composition. His play was a kind of spiritual benefit for the combatant Greeks. As I hope to show from its references to Britain, it also possessed the material aim of an actor's benefit: to raise funds in a worthy cause.

For his declared model Shelley looked back to *The Persians.* Aeschylus had celebrated the defeat of Xerxes' fleet at Salamis, in the historic present of drama, eight years after the event. As part of the feigned contemporaneity, the Ghost of Darius foretells further defeat at Plataea, which in history follows a few months after Salamis. Without feigning, *Hellas* gives heightened details of current skirmishes between Greek and Turk while the future of the revolution is in strong doubt.

For performance before Greeks as victors, Aeschylus' setting of *The Persians* in a remote hamlet of the suffering enemy is decorously humble. Action reported in *Hellas* scatters geographically from Bucharest to the Sea of Crete, but the performed action occurs in Constantinople, at the seat of the Sultan's power. The immediate need for hope and aspiration, as the converse of a victor's need for humility, explains Shelley's shift from Aeschylus' peripheral place of suffering to the focal place of decisions. Setting supports theme: fear sits on the tyrant's throne.

Shelley followed *The Persians* in awarding the chief roles to the enemy. Although *Hellas* does not stir the audience to pity for the whining but dangerous enslavers of Greece, Shelley refrains from making a monster of Mahmud II. Generously, Aeschylus' chorus also is Persian; Shelley, in contrast, provides his Turks with a chorus of enslaved Greek women. Without Greeks in the cast, no lyrics of affirmation would have been possible.

Amid other parallels, there are further departures from Aeschylus, equally pointed. Aeschylus' Atossa, widow of Darius and mother of Xerxes, recounts her dream of Xerxes' defeat. When Shelley's Mahmud enters with Ahasuerus (Shelley's old friend the Wandering Jew), Mahmud has already told his dream offstage and learned that Ahasuerus has no more power of divination than sages who

1. See Woodring, *Politics in the Poetry of Coleridge,* pp. 194–198.

lack his longevity. (So much for religion; as Manfred puts it to the old abbot, "I say to thee—Retire!") The effective echo of Atossa had occurred earlier in *Hellas,* when Mahmud, in his dark despair, called Hassan's attention to the clouded crescent moon beneath a single insolent star, "Wan emblem of an empire fading now!" So memorably does the Ghost of Darius condemn Xerxes' *hybris* that Shelley can afford to make Mahmud the essence of despair; a mere allusion to Aeschylus' memorable lines suggests the evil of tyrannic pride. And the availability of *The Persians*—in fact the very existence of Aeschylus' historical subject—invites such allusion throughout *Hellas.* A semichorus sings in Mahmud's ear of how Persia was followed by "Discord, Macedon, and Rome" and "lastly thou," where *thou* can be construed interchangeably as Mahmud II or "Slavery! thou frost of the world's prime." *Hellas* traces the law by which the Turks must be driven out as the Persians were driven out.

Four messengers, in addition to Hassan, bring word of reversals that Shelley knew about from Italian newspapers, from Prince Alexander Mavrocordatos, and from insurgents allowed passage through Pisa. Mavrocordatos taught Mary Shelley Greek in return for English until 26 June 1821, when he sailed to join the battle (and later to become the first President of Greece). After he left, one of his cousins kept the Shelleys abreast of news and rumors. With such informants between us and the record, it is pointless to raise questions of historical accuracy in the messengers' reports to Mahmud. More to the point than historical accuracy, the drama bore the clear intent to celebrate the rising of the Greeks in such a way as to arouse English interest, English funds, and patriotic shame at the roles of such diplomats as the English ambassador at Constantinople—tools, to Shelley, of Metternich—in keeping the rest of Europe neutral:

> And now, O Victory, blush! and Empire, tremble
> When ye desert the free—   (1000–1001)

Naturally *Hellas* does not describe the barbaric slaughter then practiced at every opportunity by the Greeks. In this work Shelley tries to persuade.

When he began to write in October 1821, Byron had awakened much of the Continent, as Harold Nicolson noted in *Byron, the Last Journey,* but had not awakened London. The policy of Castlereagh, carried out through Lord Strangford, the ambassador at Constantinople, was to inhabit the Greeks in order to discourage a Russian war against Turkey. When *Hellas* appeared in February 1822, the London supporters of the Greeks were still a small band. A general change of sentiment was yet to come.

One would expect in *Hellas* allusions to other struggles for independence as a way of heightening the theme, and one finds them; but the knowing Second Messenger condemns British "oaths broke in Genoa and in Norway" for a strictly practical purpose. Castlereagh's opponents had protested for six years the ceding of Genoa to Piedmont and of Norway to Bernadotte of Sweden, both by treaties initially secret. *Hellas* argues that abandonment of Greece to the Turks will constitute a betrayal similar to these. In such defenses of independence one notices, incidentally, the shading of cosmopolitanism into nationalism. Freedom for every man becomes freedom for weak countries.

Leigh Hunt, in the "Political Examiner" of 7 October 1821, calls upon English students to raise money for the Greeks. In parallel with the argument of *Hellas*, he bases his plea chiefly on the revival of high respect for Greek literature and sculpture; he quotes *The Revolt of Islam*; he conveys news of the Greeks received through the Shelleys; and he refers scornfully to the rape of Norway. That rape was one of only two previous occasions, says Hunt, when a desire to join the battle overcame his objection to "wars and fightings" as means of solving public differences. *Hellas*, which shares several other specific details with this editorial and obviously has some of the same purposes, was written by a would-be pacifist who has now chosen to praise "wars and fightings." Pacifism turns out to have been a limiting rule of reason.

Assigned the problem of defending a rebellion, *Hellas* starts right off by recognizing the "Spirit of God" in Thermopylae, Marathon, and Philippi as well as in the continued progress of freedom through Milan, Florence, Albion, Switzerland, "far Atlantis," France, Germany, Spain, and now again in Greece. At Philippi, Freedom was like "an eagle on a promontory"; at the right hand of Destiny sits "eagle-wingèd victory." Elsewhere in the drama, too, Russia, although condemned as an eagle hovering over an entangled kite and crane, and furthermore equated with a tiger gloating over the stag at bay, is forced to share the eagle of glory with more attractive states. Given the theory that volcanic eruptions relieve the pressure and thus prevent greater ruin by earthquakes, and given its metaphoric meaning that revolution stops anarchy, then the report of the Third Messenger that Crete and Cyprus catch "from each other's veins" (a pun) both "volcano-fire and earthquake-spasm" serves as an admission, or at least as a recognition, of anarchic devastation by the Greeks.[2]

2. Lines 588–589. Part of this acceptance of violence is simply the theory that "Revenge and Wrong bring forth their kind . . ." (729). In his edition of the poems (London, 1911, II, 471) C. D. Locock found it strange that a "Voice without," obviously hostile to the Greeks, should be invoked in later stages of the play to assure the future shelter of a Greek semichorus. But the Voice speaks for the self-destructive pride of empire. Health for the Greeks must wait on the other side of the self-inflicted ruin. Not only *Hellas*, but also *Prometheus Unbound*, is much concerned with the principle of imperial self-destruction.

Shelley's letters show that, like the Examiner, he did not wish a Greek victory beholden to Russian strength, but *Hellas* condemns Russia not only for the exercise of power but also for her failure to use it against the infidel, when the Patriarch of Constantinople was hanged in retribution for the slaughter of Turks in the Morea. England should take no lessons from Russia, and should exchange no declarations of common concern (lines 307–311, 536–545).

Hellas also shares with Hunt's editorial an unexpectedly favorable treatment of "the philosophical part of Christianity, as distinguished from the dogmas that have hitherto been confounded with and perverted it." As often as Shelley had condemned the union of armed force and religion, the inclination of his presumed readers to support a Christian thrall against a Moslem master was too tempting to ignore. Russia's failure to avenge the archpriest in Constantinople, which Shelley would normally approve, becomes an evil in *Hellas*. Internally, too, the drama generated a more elevated role for Christianity than the author in repose could endorse. Christian truth killed Greek myth, sings the Chorus, although the author interrupts with a note to say that the truth is relative. The Chorus puts it with less offense: "Worlds on worlds are rolling ever/From creation to decay." Again, in the final prophetic lyric, although the Chorus predicts a reawakening of Saturn and Love "more bright and good . . . than One who rose," the author takes the precaution of elucidating: the "sublime human character of Jesus Christ" was deformed among men by identification with Jehovah, whose followers have in fact tortured and murdered the true followers of Christ. Partly Shelley was clarifying the position he had always held; partly he had greatly increased his esteem for Jesus; and partly he had learned to live with His disciples. This change goes hand in glove with his acceptance of violence as the means of securing independence.

The most persuasive excuse for violence in *Hellas* is its concept of Hellenism. The play frees itself from the cage of opportune rhetoric in its celebration of the Hellenic Spirit. The Chorus offers a cyclic view of history. Time, as sometimes depicted in the hand of Saturn, is the *ouroboros*, the snake with its tail in its mouth. In a Humean version of Descartes, Ahasuerus disposes of the future along with the past: "Nought is but that which feels itself to be." Thought is eternal. Empire is the collective error of perceiving man as a part of time, place, circumstance, blood, and matter. Cities, "on which Empire sleeps enthroned," all bow "their towered crests to mutability." Empire and all else that mutability rules must pass. Hellenism, which is freedom of the human spirit, breaks out of this cycle of time, space, and material nothingness. Freedom belongs to Thought, with its "quick elements" Will, Passion, Reason, and Imagination. Thought cannot die; freedom therefore is immortal.

As thought cannot die, eternal Necessity works through it rather than through matter.[3]

Hellenism lives on, as in "young Atlantis" (the United States), which also shows promise of reviving the material strength of ancient Rome (SP, 475:992–995). Yet the final chorus, "The world's great age begins anew," is no more limited to the United States than Hellenism is limited to Troy, Ulysses, and the Argonauts. Hellenism is the freedom to improve on Hellenic history and legend. The fourth stanza of the final chorus ("Oh, write no more the tale of Troy,/If earth Death's scroll must be!") and the last stanza ("Oh, cease! must hate and death return?") do not represent a cancellation of hope that the "world's great age begins anew." If the Greeks win independence or if the spirit of Hellenism prevails anywhere, then the new Athens, wherever it may be geographically, will be free of the blood that marked the fall of Troy and the history of Athens to date. The final chorus puts some of this in the future, some in the conditional, and some in the present tense, because the renovation of Greece is part of a shining idea universally valid, but Shelley expresses wryly, in a note, the limits of this idea when expressed as hope: "Prophecies of wars, and rumours of wars, etc., may safely be made by poet or prophet in any age, but to anticipate however darkly a period of regeneration and happiness is a more hazardous exercise of the faculty which bards possess or feign." The bard sees in the uprising of the Greeks, where it was unlooked for but is uniquely appropriate, a symptom of what may be the ultimate realization of man's continuing hope for peace. In words that conclude "The Sensitive Plant," it is a "modest creed," yet pleasant "if one considers it." Given favorable signs, the bard need not drain the urn of "bitter prophecy" to its dregs.

The two major choral hymns embody speculative hope. The work as a whole, a "mere improvise" according to Shelley's Preface, embodies a lyrical expression of his "intense sympathy" with the Greek cause, which he offers as a replacement for the prevailing policy,

3. Lines 763–806. For a time I was inclined to take Mahmud's expressions of fatalism, as at 642–647, and a Semichorus' assignment of ruin and renovation to Destiny, the world's "eyeless charioteer" (711), as signs of a break in Shelley's doctrine of Necessity. Necessity is taken as equivalent in this poem to "oriental fatalism" by Douglas Bush, *Mythology and the Romantic Tradition in English Poetry* (Harvard University Press, 1937), p. 163. On such matters Bush is seldom wrong, and he goes on to read the conclusion of the poem as the fading of a "radiant mirage" (p. 165). But I now conclude, first, that Mahmud's repeated expressions concerning "the omnipotent hour to which are yoked" all men and things (189) belong to his own character, and second, that the choruses, who protest too much in their search to excuse the expediency of resistance, offer aspects, however inconsistent, of the Shelleyan insistence that apparent retribution is actually inevitable self-destruction: "Revenge and Wrong bring forth their kind . . ." (729).

whereby the English "permit their own oppressors to act according to their natural sympathy with the Turkish tyrant" (SP, 446, 447).

With *Hellas* Shelley published "Lines Written on Hearing the News of the Death of Napoleon," expressing mock surprise that the earth still moves. Mother Earth declares that this life and death, like others, warms her: "I feed on whom I fed." The new revolutions will be better.

> 'Still alive and still bold,' shouted Earth,
> 'I grow bolder and still more bold.'
>
> (SP, 641:25–26)

Earth requires for hope only the endless renewal of the seasons. It is true that she once invested hope in Bonaparte, but she has nothing to lament in the fading of glory that was "terror and blood and gold." The energy of his spirit will pass into glories yet to come.

G. M. MATTHEWS

Shelley's Lyrics†

It is easy to slip into the assumption that 'self-expression' was among the objectives of the early English Romantics. T. S. Eliot may unwittingly have made it easier, by combining a distaste for Romanticism with his principle that 'Poetry is not a turning loose of emotion, but an escape from emotion; it is not the expression of personality, but an escape from personality'; if so, this would be ironical, for it is from the Romantics that his principle derives. When Eliot says: 'the more perfect the artist, the more completely separate in him will be the man who suffers and the mind which creates', he is developing Shelley's view that 'The poet and the man are two different natures';[1] when he affirms, of the poet, that 'emotions which he has never experienced will serve his turn as well as those familiar to him', he is generalizing from Shelley's endeavour in *The Cenci* 'to produce a delineation of passions which I had never participated in'.[2] The word 'self-expression' dates from the nineties, and the idea that an artist wants to express his own 'individuality' in art is alien to the early Romantic poets, all of whom would have repudiated, or did explicitly rule out, any such notion. Shelley would have had difficulty in even making sense of it. Every great poet, he agreed, left the imprint of an individual mind

† Matthews' essay is here reprinted in its entirety from *The Morality of Art: Essays Presented to G. Wilson Knight*, ed. D. W. Jefferson (London: Routledge & Kegan Paul, 1969), pp. 195–209, by permission of the publisher.
1. *The Letters of Percy Bysshe Shelley*, ed. F. L. Jones, Oxford (1964), II. 310.
2. *Letters*, II. 189.

on all his works, but that imprint was the brand of his limitation as much as of his greatness; it was a by-product of his real aims. For an artist to seek, or a critic to praise, 'self-expression' would have seemed absolutely meaningless to him.

This has never deterred critics from assuming not only that the lyrical heart-cry is Shelley's typical utterance, but that he is liable to utter this cry at virtually any moment. Charles Kingsley and F. R. Leavis have recognized even the Catholic murderess Beatrice Cenci as Percy B. Shelley. Turn but a petticoat and start a luminous wing. David Masson decided in 1875 that Shelley's poetry was 'nothing else than an effluence from his personality',[3] and in 1965 the medical psychologist Dr. Eustace Chesser declared that Shelley 'does not even *notice* the existence of the hard, external world which pays no attention to his wishes. His gaze is directed all the time on his own emotional states'.[4] The present essay tries to remove a major obstacle in the way of a more intelligent discussion; and it is first necessary to see in plain figures what Shelley's contribution as a lyrical poet really was.

From *Original Poetry* (1810) to *Hellas* (1822) Shelley published twelve volumes of verse. Seven of these contain no separate lyrics. *Original Poetry* had four 'personal' lyrics,[5] all bearing on Shelley's attachment to Harriet Grove. *Posthumous Fragments of Margaret Nicholson* was artfully-packaged propaganda, and its concluding poem is the only personal one it contains. *Alastor* has ten shorter poems: three addressed to Coleridge, Wordsworth, and Napoleon respectively; two translations; and again one 'personal' lyric, the 'Stanzas.—April 1814', which concern the Boinville-Turner entanglement. *Rosalind and Helen* (1819) has three shorter poems, 'Lines written in the Euganean Hills', 'Hymn to Intellectual Beauty', and 'Ozymandias', the second of which contains a striking autobiographical passage. The 'Euganean Hills' I believe to have even less reference to Shelley himself than Donald Reiman has already ably argued.[6] *Prometheus Unbound* contains nine shorter poems, including the allegorical 'Sensitive Plant';[7] once again, the only lyric with unequivocal personal application is the 'Ode to the West Wind'. A total of seven or eight 'personal' lyrics in twelve volumes of verse, only half of these in the last eleven volumes—a

3. *Wordsworth, Shelley, Keats and other Essays*, p. 129.
4. *Shelley and Zastrozzi: self-revelation of a neurotic*, p. 29.
5. By 'personal' lyrics, I intend (a) short poems that name names ('What would cure, that would kill me, Jane'), and (b) poems that seem recognizably biographical ('Her voice did quiver as we parted'). (b) is, however, a very unsafe category.
6. 'Structure, Symbol, and Theme in "Lines written among the Euganean Hills",' *PMLA*, 77, September 1962, 404–13.
7. 'There is no justification for the frequent definition of the Sensitive Plant as Shelley saw himself or as a special category of man, such as the Poet . . . The Garden . . . is the total animate universe as it is experienced by man, the Sensitive Plant.' (E. R. Wasserman, *The Subtler Language*, Baltimore (1959), pp. 257–8).

modest ration, one might think, for a monotonously self-regarding narcissist whose genius was essentially lyrical. This is not quite the full story, of course. Two volumes had 'personal' dedications; Shelley himself called *Epipsychidion* 'an idealized history of my life and feelings'[8] (though nobody can explain the history it records, and it is not a lyric). Two other proposed volumes would have affected the statistics: the early 'Esdaile' collection (at least 57 poems, of which about 23 have direct personal significance), and *Julian and Maddalo*, intended to contain, Shelley said, 'all my saddest verses raked up into one heap'.[9] But these were not published, and after a few unanswered inquiries Shelley seems to have lost interest. *Epipsychidion*, in an anonymous edition of 100 copies, was suppressed by its author within twelve months.[1] Shelley also cancelled a passage intended for the *Adonais* preface 'relating to my private wrongs'.[2] Medwin's story that the poet's self-portrait in *Adonais* was also 'afterwards expunged from it'[3] may be a muddle, but it is a fact that Shelley had enjoined his publisher to make an '*omission*' in the second edition,[4] while the draft proves that the 'frail Form' who comes to mourn Adonais in stanza 31 was almost certainly not, in conception, Shelley himself but some idealized figure born not later than Buonaparte and contrasted with him—perhaps Rousseau.[5]

From *Alastor* onwards, then, Shelley actually published in book form (excluding dedications) four personal or semi-personal poems: 'Stanzas.—April 1814', 'The Euganean Hills', 'Intellectual Beauty', and the 'West Wind'. His ten poems in periodicals were all offered anonymously; of these only 'On a Faded Violet' and possibly 'The Question' might be called 'personal' ('Sunset' and 'Grief' appeared with all the personal parts omitted). *Epipsychidion* was repudiated and suppressed. Four of *Adonais's* 55 stanzas are personal, but allegorized. Some of *Rosalind and Helen* was suggested by a family friendship. This is all. It now seems necessary to ask: how is it that so reticent a poet has gained a reputation for emotional exhibitionism? Shelley's evolution into a lyricist was accidental. Like most poets, he bestowed, over the years, a few[6] complimentary or occasional verses on his intimates, less in the manner of a celebrity dispensing autographs than of an uncle covertly fishing out tips. They were private gifts, and Shelley often kept no copy. 'For Jane &

8. *Letters*, II. 434.
9. *Letters*, II. 246.
1. *Blackwoods Edinburgh Magazine* II, February 1822, p. 238; Ollier to Mary Shelley, 17 November 1823, *Shelley and Mary* IV. 990–1.
2. *Letters*, II. 306.
3. *Conversations of Lord Byron* (1824), p. 314n.
4. *Letters*, II. 396.
5. Some of the relevant stanzas are nos. I–III, XII–XIV, printed on pp. 37–8, 42–3 of *Verse and Prose from the MSS*, ed. Shelley-Rolls and Ingpen, 1934.
6. Cold statistics are again helpful. From 1816, Shelley is known to have given one poem to Claire Clairmont, and (probably) to Emilia Viviani; two to the Hunts; three to the Gisbornes; four to his wife; six to Sophia Stacey; and ten to the Williamses—twenty-seven altogether, in six years. Two of these were not lyrics, and five others were commissioned contributions to plays.

Williams alone to see', he directed on the manuscript of 'The Magnetic Lady', and 'Do not say it is mine to any one', on that of 'Remembrance'; 'The enclosed must on no account be published' ('Letter to Maria Gisborne'); '—if you will tell no one *whose* they are' ('Lines on a Dead Violet'). Later, his widow tried to retrieve everything possible from his worksheets and acquaintances, and was able to publish about 110 short poems and fragments by 1840, when her second edition of the *Poetical Works* appeared. Many of Shelley's best-known lyrics now first emerged: the 'Stanzas in Dejection', 'O world! O life! O time!', 'I fear thy kisses', 'When the lamp is shattered', 'Music when soft voices die', 'With a Guitar, to Jane'. Mary Shelley was right to print all she could find, but it meant salvaging the equivalents of doodles on the telephone-pad, such as 'O Mary dear, that you were here', as well as drafts whose illegibility made them half-incomprehensible, such as 'Rough wind, that moanest loud'. This has not worried the critics much, who have rarely questioned a poem's origins or purpose, being content merely to find it exquisite or shoddy; some, indeed, outdoing Coleridge, profess to be given most pleasure by Shelley when he is not perfectly understandable. Swinburne hailed one half-completed line as 'a thing to thrill the veins and draw tears to the eyes of all men whose ears were not closed against all harmony',[7] and Donald Davie has found another nonsensical fragment manly and wholesome.[8] So Mary Shelley's conscience is partly responsible for the dogma that besides being trivial and self-obsessed, Shelley was negligent of grammar, syntax, and logical structure, with an incapacity to punctuate verging on feeblemindedness.[9]

Yet although Shelley's negligence is axiomatic, it would not be easy to illustrate by anyone prepared to look into the transmission of his examples. As for self-obsession, Shelley withheld his lyrics from publication for the same reason that Samuel Johnson wrote his private poems in Latin: to keep them private. To treat these intimate verses ('you may read them to Jane, but to no one else,— and yet on second thoughts I had rather you would not') as if they were manifestoes is rather like breaking into a man's bathroom in order to censure his habit of indecent exposure. Still, the reminder that certain poems were printed without Shelley's consent is no defence of their quality. It did not help poor Midas that the secret

7. *Essays and Studies*, 1876, pp. 229–30.
8. 'Shelley's Urbanity' (1953), rptd. in *English Romantic Poets*, ed. M. H. Abrams, New York (1960), p. 318.
9. One experienced modern editor still maintains (*Keats-Shelley Memorial Bulletin* 17, (1966), pp. 20–30) that in a fully representative passage (essentially *Prometheus Unbound* III. iii. 49–62) Shelley's punctuation corrupts the sense. The reader is given no chance to judge the MS. punctuation for himself (Bod. MS. Shelley e.3, f.2Iv), which in my view is careful, intelligible, and better than Hutchinson's. Bridges's punctilious tinkerings make good sense too, but not quite Shelley's.

of his ears was only whispered into a hole in the ground. What that reminder should do is inhibit any pronouncement on a given poem's qualities until the *nature* and *function* of the poem have been inquired into. A straightforward example, not a 'personal' one, is the 'Bridal Song' or 'Epithalamium' of 1821.[1]

Here the reader must first decide which of three 'versions' constitutes the poem. Close consideration will show that neither of the first two versions makes sense; however, as the poet is Shelley, it is perhaps begging the question to suggest that this throws doubt on their integrity. The 'third version' (Hutchinson tells us) derives from Shelley's holograph, and its use as a gloss makes the conjecture a pretty safe one that Versions One and Two represent the foul papers and a Bad Quarto respectively of the authentic Version Three. Nevertheless, one critic has thought it

admirable in its first version. In this first:

> O joy! O fear! what will be done
> In the absence of the sun!

—is as manly and wholesome as Suckling's 'Ballad of a Wedding'. In the last version:

> O joy! O fear! there is not one
> Of us can guess what may be done
> In the absence of the sun . . .

—is just not true. And the familiar tone of 'Come along!' which securely anchors the first version, is merely silly in the others.[2]

The First Version begins by calling down sleep on the lovers in the middle of begetting a child, and goes on to advocate, among other things, what Lionel Trilling once memorably criticized in the Sexual Behaviour of the American Male ('Haste, swift Hour, and thy flight Oft renew'). Professor Davie's stricture on the Third Version bears hardly on Catullus, whose Epithalamium (62) was Shelley's model. Here is the text of the Third Version:

Boys Sing.

> Night! with all thine eyes look down!
>   Darkness! weep thy holiest dew!
> Never smiled the inconstant moon
>   On a pair so true.
> Haste, coy hour! and quench all light,
> Lest eyes see their own delight!
> Haste, swift hour! and thy loved flight
>   Oft renew!

1. *The Complete Poetical Works*, ed. Hutchinson, Oxford (1945), pp. 646–7.
2. 'Shelley's Urbanity', *loc. cit.* Professor Davie has repudiated this essay (*New Statesman* 27 November 1964, p. 840). But the dyslogistic passages, I take it, are still part of his faith.

Girls Sing.

Fairies, sprites, and angels, keep her!
   Holy stars! permit no wrong!
And return, to wake the sleeper,
   Dawn, ere it be long!
O joy! O fear! there is not one
Of us can guess what may be done
In the absence of the sun:—
    Come along!

Boys.

Oh! linger long, thou envious eastern lamp
   In the damp
    Caves of the deep!

Girls.

Nay, return, Vesper! urge thy lazy car!
   Swift unbar
    The gates of Sleep!

Chorus.

The golden gates of Sleep unbar,
   When Strength and Beauty, met together,
Kindle their image, like a star
   In a sea of glassy weather.
May the purple mist of love
Round them rise, and with them move,
Nourishing each tender gem
Which, like flowers, will burst from them.
As the fruit is to the tree
May their children ever be![3]

In a conventional Epithalamium, the desire and misgiving which both partners feel are polarized on to a reluctant bride, with her mock-modest virgin attendants, and an avid groom, incited by his troop of wanton boys. Catullus's girls ask, 'Hespere, qui caelo fertur crudelior ignis?', to which the boys retort, 'Hespere, qui caelo lucet jucundior ignis?'[4] and later (still addressing Hesperus) comment:

> at libet innuptis ficto te carpere questu.
> quid tum si carpunt tacita quem mente requirunt? (36–7)

which Peter Whigham has rendered:

> for maidens' acts belie their mock complaints,
> affecting aversion
> for what they most desire[5]

3. Text from Hutchinson, p. 723, with the singular *gate* corrected in line 23.
4. The girls: "Hesperus, what flame glows more cruelly in heaven?" The boys: "Hesperus, what flame shines more resplendently in heaven?" [Editors' note.]
5. *The Poems of Catullus*, Penguin Classics 1966, p. 133.

Mock-trepidation, 'tender-whimpring-maids',[6] were essential to the ceremony. But the girls' feigned ignorance of what the lovers will do in bed is stressed here for an important reason. This was commissioned work, written for the climactic scene of a play, a wedding-banquet in a 'magnificent apartment' where wealth literally rivals nobility. To compare it with Suckling's mock-turnip 'Ballad of a Wedding' is like comparing a State funeral with Finnegan's wake. The plot is that of Novel IX from the tenth day of the *Decameron*, and concerns a Pavian wife's promise to wait a year, a month, and a day after her husband's departure to the Crusade before remarrying. The time having expired, she unwillingly consents to marry a former suitor; but after the ceremony her consort reappears, the new bridegroom renounces his claim, and the play ends in amity. The girls' declaration, therefore, that not one of them can guess what may be done in the absence of the sun just *is* true: contrary to every expectation, *nothing* will be done—not, at any rate, by those newly licensed to do it. How the 'tone' of a poem can be so confidently criticized without the slightest interest in that poem's provenance or purpose is a mystery darker than Hymen's.

The first line presents in one immediate image the antiphonal unity which structures the poem: the sociable stars are invited to watch the lovers with the *voyeur* relish of the males who are singing, but also with the bashful, downcast gaze of the bride. The lovers are to be seen and unseen at once, hidden in darkness under the eyes of stars, moon, and one another; for this is a supremely social and an intensely private occasion. The weeping of 'holiest dew' suggests both the modest sanctity of the encounter and its fruitful sensuality;[7] and although the darkness weeps, the moon smiles. These opposites re-echo in the two invocations to the hour of union, a *coy* hour from one viewpoint, moonless 'lest eyes see their own delight' (i.e. lest each is abashed to see his own pleasure mirrored on the other's eyes: a variant of Blake), a *swift* hour from the other viewpoint, transient yet renewable like the moon—and an hour which, after all, both sides want to hasten on. The girls' opening appeal, made jointly to fairies and angels, indicates (like Shelley's word *phryghte* written playfully above the text) just how serious it all really is.

As in Catullus, the verbal dance now brings boys and girls into direct opposition. The planet Venus, whose setting as Hesperus and rising as Phosphorus symbolizes the bedding and rising of a married couple, is besought by the boys to stay hidden so as to lengthen the

---

6. Herrick, 'A Nuptiall Song on Sir Clipseby Crew and his Lady', line 91.
7. Compare Herrick:
   These precious-pearly-purling tears
   But spring from ceremonious fears . . .

O! give them [the lovers] active heat
And moisture, both compleat:
   ('An Epithalamie to Sir Thomas
   Southwell and his Ladie').

night, by the girls to return quickly and allow the bride to sleep. Unbarring the gates of sleep—admitting the lovers to their ultimate peace—deftly completes the ceremony whose public end was the shutting of the bedroom door. Finally, both sides drop their feigned postures to join in the traditional invocation for fruitfulness in the marriage: the lovers are to sleep only after duplicating their qualities in a child, as the 'wished starre' of love itself is mirrored in a calm sea. The sea image enters in because it is from across the Mediterranean that 'glassy weather' is even now returning in the person of Adalette's true husband; while the meeting of 'Strength and Beauty' reminds us ironically of the unauthorized union of Mars and Venus, caught in the act by Venus's true husband and exposed to the laughter of the assembled gods. *Golden* gates of sleep and *purple* mist of love sound like poeticisms, but even the make-up matches: these were the colours of the god Hymen, *croceo velatus amictu*, and 'purple' was used atmospherically, in both classical and English epithalamia, of the bliss environing a bridal.[8] The poem is concise, shapely, precisely pointed; mindful of its lineage yet perfectly attuned to its own dramatic purpose. No one would call it an important poem, least of all its author, yet it is almost faultless of its kind, a first-rate piece of craftsmanship.

The kind is not easy to define. It might be called a dramatic imitation into the spirit of which the poet enters with such deceptive wholeness that the pretence—the gap between the playfulness of the role and the absorbed gravity of the manner—constitutes an uncommon sort of poetic wit. A splendid example of this wit is the maligned 'Indian Serenade'. Shelley did not publish this poem either, but the titles of all the existing versions stress that it is *Indian* and for *singing*. It was in fact composed to be sung by Sophia Stacey,[9] and it is a dramatic imitation of an Oriental love-song, not just in atmosphere, the potency of which has always been recognized, but in its entirety. A proper imitation of the mode represented by the following lines required emotional abandonment:

My cries pierce the heavens!
My eyes are without sleep!
Turn to me, Sultana—let me gaze on thy beauty.

Adieu! I go down to the grave.
If you call me I return.
My heart is hot as sulphur;—sigh, and it will flame.

Crown of my life! fair light of my eyes!
　My Sultana! my princess!

8. E.g. at the official wedding of Cupid and Psyche in Apuleius, *Met.* VI. xxiv, 'Horae rosis et ceteris floribus purpurabant omnia'.

9. C. S. Catty, 'Shelley's "I arise from dreams of thee" and Miss Sophia Stacey', *Athenaeum*, 18 April 1908, p. 478.

I rub my face against the earth;—I am drown'd in scalding tears—
   I rave!
Have you no compassion? Will you not turn to look upon me?[1]

It is a very physical as well as a very evocative poem (five parts of
the body are named); its subject is a passionate assignation in
which a dream is about to be made flesh and the languishing
bodily senses are to be revived by physical love as rain revives the
grass. By a hyperbole familiar also in Elizabethan poetry, wind,
magnolia-blossom, and birdsong, faint, fail, and die respectively in
contiguity with the beloved; then the singer herself capitulates with
them ('As I must die on thine'). Her own person embodies the
senses by which she perceives these lesser delights: touch (the wind
on the stream), smell (the champaca), hearing (the nightingale);
but her senses are ungratified, she is a songless nightingale, a per-
fume without scent, a wind without motion ('*I* die! *I* faint! *I* fail!').
Her recent love-dream is melting like the champaca's odour, with
nothing substantial to take its place. Only the beloved's response
will save her, as the effect of *rain* on *grass* lifts the cloying languor
of the night; and three lines from the end the loud, anticipatory
heartbeats of the lover echo and replace the low breathing of the
sleeping winds three lines from the beginning.

The lover in the Turkish poem quoted was a male; Shelley's song
could fit either sex, but the draft of line 11, 'the odours of my
chaplet fail', shows that his singer is a girl.[2] The title on a manu-
script auctioned in 1960, 'The Indian girl's song', confirms what
should have been obvious.

This, too, is perfect of its kind. Its imaginative structure is taut
and sound, its atmospheric versatility astonishing. Its loving exag-
geration, its total absorption in a dramatic pretence, give it some of
the qualities of brilliant parody, yet it is no parody. *Craftsmanship*
is again the only single word to fit it. As an expression of its author's
personality and feelings it is of about the same order as 'Gerontion',
or 'Gretchen am Spinnrade'.

A companion piece is 'From the Arabic: An Imitation' (again
unpublished) which according to Medwin was 'almost a translation
from a translation',[3] in Terrick Hamilton's Arab romance *Antar*
(1819–20). But *Antar* is male-orientated, with a hero as stupend-
ously virile as Kilhwch in the *Mabinogion*, whereas Shelley's poem
takes the Arab woman's point of view, and amounts to a critique

1. Turkish lines translated literally in
Lady Mary Wortley Montagu's letter of
1 April 1717.
2. Bod. MS. Shelley adds. e.7, f.153.
'The strong aromatic scent of the gold-
coloured *Champac* is thought offensive
to the bees . . . but their elegant appear-
ance on the black hair of the *Indian*
women is mentioned by RUMPHIUS;
and both facts have supplied the *Sanscrit*
poets with elegant allusions.' (Sir Wil-
liam Jones, *Works*, 1807, V. 129).
3. *Life of Shelley*, ed. H. B. Forman,
Oxford (1913), p. 351.

of that novel's values. Such a capacity for adopting the female view-point, uncommon in male lyric poets, suggests that others among Shelley's lyrics might repay re-examination. The final stanza of 'Remembrance' ('Swifter far than summer's flight') begins

> Lilies for a bridal bed—
> Roses for a matron's head—
> Violets for a maiden dead—
> Pansies let *my* flowers be:
>
> (Hutchinson p. 718)

Mary Shelley's remorseful letter after Shelley's death has helped to put readers on the wrong track. 'In a little poem of his are these words—*pansies let my flowers* be . . . so I would make myself a locket to wear in eternal memory with the representation of his flower . . .'[4] But in the poem the three flowers, seasons, and birds correspond to three conditions of female life, bride, wife, and spin-ster; the series, therefore, *cannot* culminate in a male poet. *Pansies*, plainly, are the symbol-flowers of a deserted mistress. One possible way round is to assert that in that case the deserted mistress must be Shelley, in the manner of the character in *Alice* who argued that little girls must be a kind of serpent; alternatively, that although his *personae* are distinct from their creator, their attitudes and verbal habits are not. Both arguments are unpromising. For instance, the lyric posthumously entitled 'Mutability' ('The flower that smiles today Tomorrow dies') has seemed a typical expression of Shelley's disillusioned idealism:

> Whilst skies are blue and bright,
>   Whilst flowers are gay,
> Whilst eyes that change ere night
>   Make glad the day;
> Whilst yet the calm hours creep,
> Dream thou—and from thy sleep
> Then wake to weep.   (Hutchinson pp. 640–1)

'Earthly pleasures are delusive—like me, Shelley, you will have a bitter awakening.' But the poem was evidently written for the opening of *Hellas*,[5] to be sung by a favourite slave, who loves him, to the literally sleeping Mahmud before he awakens to find his imperial pleasures slipping from his grasp. This puts the naivety of the sentiment in an unexpected light. Far from voicing a self-pitying bitterness, the poem is really an ironical endorsement, with qualifi-cations, of Mahmud's reversal of fortune. The qualifications arise

---

4. *The Letters of Mary W. Shelley*, ed. F. L. Jones, Norman (1944), I. 176–7.
5. Bod.MS. Shelley adds.e.7, cover ff.1–2, 154. Compare the song actually adopted in the play:

'. . . could my prayers avail,
All my joy should be
Dead, and I would live to weep,
So thou mightst win one hour of quiet sleep.'   (22–6)

from the personal loyalty of the slave to her tyrant master, which complicates the irony of the lament and tempers our gladness at his downfall. Something similar was attempted in *Laon and Cythna*, where the only being who showed any love for the deposed Othman was his child by the slave he had violated (V. xxi–xxx).

The dramatic impulse was at least as strong in Shelley as the lyrical, and the two were often inseparable. An especially interesting puzzle is set by yet another posthumous lyric, 'When the lamp is shattered'. Besides a draft, there are two known manuscripts, including one given to Jane Williams (now in the University Library, Glasgow). This is the only one of the nine poems given to her which is without title or dedication at any known stage of its existence, and her copy has one other curious feature. Between the first pair of stanzas and what would have been (if the final stanza were not missing)[6] the second pair, the words *second part* appear, in Shelley's hand. What can this mean?

The draft throws some light. 'When the lamp is shattered' was undoubtedly written for the 'Unfinished Drama' of early 1822, and is closely related to the lyric printed at the opening of that play, in modern editions. In these editions[7] the drama opens 'before the Cavern of the Indian Enchantress', who sings:

> He came like a dream in the dawn of life,
>   He fled like a shadow before its noon;
> He is gone, and my peace is turned to strife,
>   And I wander and wane like the weary moon.
>   O sweet Echo, wake,
>   And for my sake
> Make answer the while my heart shall break!
>
> But my heart has a music which Echo's lips,
>   Though tender and true, yet can answer not,
> And the shadow that moves in the soul's eclipse
>   Can return not the kiss by his now forgot;
>   Sweet lips! he who hath
>   On my desolate path
> Cast the darkness of absence, worse than death!
>
> (Hutchinson, pp. 482–3)

All that is known about the 'Unfinished Drama' comes from Mrs. Shelley's headnotes. Undertaken, she says, 'for the amusement of the individuals who composed our intimate society', its plot concerned an Enchantress on an Indian island who lures a Pirate, 'a man of savage but noble nature', away from his mortal lover. 'A

6. The final stanza must have existed once, as this text was the source of Medwin's memorial piracy in his *Ahasuerus, the Wanderer* (1823).
7. Beginning with *The Poetical Works*

(1839), IV. 168. The *Posthumous Poems* text has no stage-direction or notes (neither has the draft from which all texts of the play are derived).

good Spirit, who watches over the Pirate's fate, leads, in a mysterious manner, the lady of his love to the Enchanted Isle. She is accompanied by a Youth, who loves the lady, but whose passion she returns only with a sisterly affection.' The text, some of which is unpublished, does imply a kind of lovers' chain, similar to that in Moschus's Idyl VI, or in *Andromaque*. Diagrammatically it seems to go: Indian girl A, deserted by Pirate lover (or husband) B, leaves admirer E and on a magic island meets (not accompanies) boy C, who himself has been deserted by girl D (the Enchantress?). Presumably B and D began this merry-go-round for the sake of each other, and presumably all would have returned in the end to the original truce-lines.[8] Despite the bittersweet atmosphere of *Faust* and *The Tempest* that haunts the context of 'When the lamp is shattered', and may originate in the poet's own situation, it is ludicrous to treat a song written for private theatricals as if it were the cry of Shelley to his own soul. Not the major love-poets but the minor dramatists, Lyly, Fletcher, and the masque-writers, are in its line of descent.

The notation *second part* could have been intended in a semi-musical sense, of a dialogue in which a second voice takes up and answers the first. The imagery changes abruptly in the 'second part', though both pairs of stanzas share a basic idea: in part one, lamp, cloud, lute, and lips with their 'contents', the hollow heart, the empty cell, the lifeless corpse; in part two, the nest with its winged occupant, the heart as cradle, home, and bier, the raftered eyrie, the naked refuge. Because of the idea common to all these, Professor Pottle's attractive defence of *The light in the dust lies dead*, as meaning that the light reflected from the physical environment (the 'light-in-the-dust') stops shining when the source goes out,[9] seems narrowly to miss the mark. Rather, the light is inseparable from the 'dust' of which the physical lamp is composed, and perishes with it; the glory of the rainbow *is* the cloud, and is 'shed' with the cloud's waterdrops; music and the lute are annihilated together.[1] The heart cannot sing—respond emotionally—when the signal to which it resonates, the spirit of love, is 'mute'; it can only echo, passively, and hollowly the noises of wind and water. All these light-and-dust

8. The rehearsals of *Lover's Vows* should warn us that the proposed casting is unlikely to have reflected real alignments, wished or existing. Working backwards from the most tactful final combination we might get: A=Jane Williams, B=Trelawny, C=Edward Williams, D=Mary Shelley, E=Shelley. Shelley, unattached, could thus take the part of the Spirit, fitting in with the role he gave himself in 'With a Guitar. To Jane'.
9. 'The Case of Shelley' (1952), rptd. in *English Romantic Poets*, *op. cit.*, pp. 302–3.
1. 'The common observer . . . contends in vain against the persuasion of the grave, that the dead indeed cease to be . . . The organs of sense are destroyed, and the intellectual operations dependent on them have perished with their sources . . . When you can discover where the fresh colours of the fading flower abide, or the music of the broken lyre, seek life among the dead.' ('Essay on a Future State', *Essays, Letters from Abroad*, etc. ed. Mrs. Shelley, 1840, I. 234–5).

images are analogues of the 'good Spirit's' lodgement at the earth's centre. He is contained in the reality he energizes, as radiance in the lamp, as music in the lute, as words between the lips:

> Within the silent centre of the earth
> My mansion is; where I have lived insphered
> From the beginning, and around my sleep
> Have woven all the wondrous imagery
> Of this dim spot, which mortals call the world;   (15–19)

A cancelled stage-direction hesitates whether to call this Spirit 'Love', but he was evidently to be the Prospero of the island, moving its affairs to their kindliest end.

The whole poem is about the loss of love, and if part one laments that when the physical embodiment is lacking, the essence disappears, part two seems to retort that if the essence is lacking, the physical embodiment disintegrates. It is tempting to guess that the two halves of the poem were intended for the Enchantress and the Lady respectively. This would account for the domestic imagery of the second part, while the ruined cell and the knell for the dead seaman are proper 'currency values' for an Indian Lampedusa on whose shores a pirate-lover has probably been wrecked.

The first word of part two is not *When* but *Where*, so these two lines are a simple inversion: Love leaves the nest where hearts once mingled. It has been asked, In what form are we to imagine Love doing this? To answer, In the form of Love, seems irreverent, but the episode of Cupid and Psyche in Apuleius's *Metamorphoses*, which Shelley much admired, had clearly some influence on this poem.[2] By *first* leaving the nest, the winged form of Love suggests also a fledgling (genuine love is a result as well as a cause of 'mingling'). This stresses the contrasting images of raven and eagle, because the raven was supposed to evict its young from the nest and abandon them, whereas the eagle is famous for the care it takes of its own young. Golden eagles, as Shelley would know, mate for life, and their nest is permanent, literally cradle, home, and bier.

'The weak one is singled' of course has nothing to do with the sad lot of woman; 'the weak one' is the weak heart, and applies to either sex. The paradoxes (*one* is *singled*, the *weak* one must *endure*), and the pun (*singled*, 'picked on', 'divorced'), lead to the ambiguities of 'To endure what it once possessed', which could

2. Cupid and Psyche are happily married, mingling nightly in a love-nest built by Cupid himself, with ivory rafters; Psyche entertains her treacherous sisters with lute and song; a spilt lamp is the cause of Cupid's flight (in Mrs. Tighe's well-known version the lamp shattered: '. . . from her trembling hand extinguished falls the fatal lamp'); he leaves Psyche's bed as a feathered god every morning, and at last deserts it for good; Psyche is then exposed, half-naked, to Venus's mocking laughter and is tormented by the passions of Anxiety and Sorrow; but in the end the lovers are reunited— as no doubt they were in Shelley's play.

have secondary meanings of 'to make indifferent that which it once fascinated', and 'to imprison what it once owned by right', and to the major paradox that 'Love' is now confronted with: why does one who laments 'frailty', transience, choose to nest in 'the frailest of all things', the human heart?

The change of pronoun in the final stanza implies that the speaker has turned to address a human, or superhuman, rival. 'Its passions' (the passions of the heart) will rock *thee*, she says, and reason will only give you clarity without comfort, like the sun in winter. And the epithet *naked* returns to the hint of the fledgling, the product of love's union, not now in voluntary flight but evicted, defenceless, and—perhaps deservedly—laughable.

The parent play is so sketchy that any detailed account of 'When the lamp is shattered' can only be very conjectural. What is essential is to begin with the right questions: what *is* this poem, what was it for? Once the dramatic function is recognized, tone, imagery, emotional mode take on appropriate significances; even if the poem is moving it is not self-expression but artifice, creative play. Shelley's lyrics deserve a fresh—and a more responsible—critical look.

Selected Bibliography

Included below are the studies we consider most valuable for advanced undergraduate and graduate students of Shelley, as well as a few widely disseminated books that require a cautionary word. Bibliographies and footnotes in the recent critical studies will, together with section I below, provide guidance for further study. Publication dates are given for first printings only; many of the books listed have been reprinted in recent years. (Check *Books in Print* and *Paperback Books in Print.*)

I. BIBLIOGRAPHIES AND REFERENCE BOOKS

Ellis, F. S. *A Lexical Concordance to the Poetical Works of Percy Bysshe Shelley.* London: Quaritch, 1892. The first concordance to the works of a Romantic poet, this labor of love by an amateur has been outdated by recent additions to the Shelley canon (notably *The Esdaile Notebook*).

Forman, Harry Buxton. *The Shelley Library, An Essay in Bibliography.* London: Reeves and Turner, 1886.

Wise, Thomas James. *A Shelley Library.* London: Privately printed, 1924. This work supplements Forman's *Shelley Library* for information on first editions and other early printings of Shelley's works.

Keats-Shelley Journal, "Current Bibliography" (1951 to date). The first twelve annual bibliographies were collected and edited by David Bonnell Green and Edwin Graves Wilson, *Keats, Shelley, Byron, Hunt, and Their Circles, A Bibliography: July 1, 1950–June 30, 1962.* Lincoln: University of Nebraska, 1964.

[Matthews, G. M.] "Percy Bysshe Shelley" in *New Cambridge Bibliography of English Literature,* III (Cambridge University Press, 1969), 309–343.

Weaver, Bennett, and Donald H. Reiman. "Shelley" in Frank Jordan, Jr., ed., *The English Romantic Poets: A Review of Research and Criticism,* 3rd. ed. New York: Modern Language Association, 1972.

II. FIRST PUBLICATIONS IN BOOKS OF SHELLEY'S MAJOR POETRY AND PROSE

Queen Mab; A Philosophical Poem: with Notes. London [no publisher], 1813. [anonymous].

Alastor; or, The Spirit of Solitude: and Other Poems. London: Baldwin, Cradock, and Joy; and Carpenter and Son, 1816.

History of a Six Weeks' Tour through a Part of France, Switzerland, Germany, and Holland . . . . London: T. Hookham, Jr., and C. and J. Ollier, 1817. [anonymous, by Shelley and Mary; contains the first printing of "Mont Blanc"].

Laon and Cythna; or, The Revolution of the Golden City; A Vision of the Nineteenth Century. London: Sherwood, Neely, & Jones; and C. and J. Ollier, 1818. [suppressed, emended, and reissued as:] *The Revolt of Islam; A Poem, in Twelve Cantos.* London: C. and J. Ollier, 1818.

Rosalind and Helen, A Modern Eclogue; with Other Poems. London: C. & J. Ollier, 1819.

The Cenci: A Tragedy, in Five Acts. Italy: for C. and J. Ollier, London, 1819.

Prometheus Unbound: A Lyrical Drama in Four Acts, with Other Poems. London: C. and J. Ollier, 1820.

Œdipus Tyrannus: or, Swellfoot the Tyrant. A Tragedy in Two Acts. London: The Author, 1820. [anonymous].

Epipsychidion: Verses Addressed to the Noble and Unfortunate Lady Emilia V—— Now Imprisoned in the Convent of ——. London: C. and J. Ollier, 1821. [anonymous].

Adonais: An Elegy on the Death of John Keats, Author of Endymion, Hyperion etc. Pisa, 1821.

Hellas: A Lyrical Drama. London: Charles and James Ollier, 1822.
Posthumous Poems of Percy Bysshe Shelley [ed. Mary Shelley]. London: John and Henry L. Hunt, 1824.
The Masque of Anarchy. A Poem. Ed. Leigh Hunt. London: Edward Moxon, 1832.
The Shelley Papers. Ed. Thomas Medwin. London: Whittaker, Treacher, & Co., 1833.
The Poetical Works of Percy Bysshe Shelley. Ed. Mrs. Shelley. 4 vols. London: Edward Moxon, 1839.
Essays, Letters from Abroad, Translations and Fragments. Ed. Mrs. Shelley. 2 vols. London: Edward Moxon, 1840.
A Philosophical View of Reform, Now Printed for the First Time. Ed. T. W. Rolleston. London: Oxford University Press, 1920.
The Esdaile Notebook: A Volume of Early Poems. Ed. Kenneth Neill Cameron. New York: Alfred A. Knopf, 1964.

III. CRITICAL EDITIONS AND TEXTUAL STUDIES

Rossetti, William Michael, ed. *The Poetical Works of Percy Bysshe Shelley.* 2 vols. London: Moxon, 1870 (revised in 3 vols., 1878). Rossetti's strength is poetic sensitivity; his weakness is lack of both specific textual information and sound bibliographical and editorial principles.
Forman, Harry Buxton, ed. *The Poetical Works of Percy Bysshe Shelley.* 4 vols. London: Reeves and Turner, 1876 (*Prose Works*, 4 vols., 1880; corrected texts, without notes, 2 vols., 1882, and 5 vols., 1892). An excellent edition by the leading English bibliographer of the later nineteenth century.
Hutchinson, Thomas, ed. *The Complete Poetical Works of Shelley.* Oxford: Clarendon Press, 1904 (reset as Oxford Standard Authors edition, 1905 and 1934; corrected by G. M. Matthews, 1970). Once the best one-volume edition of Shelley's poetry, it is now seriously outdated by newly available evidence.
Locock, C. D., ed. *The Poems of Percy Bysshe Shelley, with an Introduction by A. Clutton-Brock.* 2 vols. London: Methuen, 1911. Useful for its notes but unreliable in textual details.
Ingpen, Roger, and Walter E. Peck, eds. *The Complete Works of Percy Bysshe Shelley.* 10 vols. London: Ernest Benn, 1926–1930 (Julian Edition). The closest thing available to a complete edition of Shelley's works; the four volumes of poetry (I–IV) and three volumes of letters (VIII–X) have been superseded, but the prose volumes (V–VII) are still valuable.
Notopoulos, James A. *The Platonism of Shelley: A Study of Platonism and the Poetic Mind.* Durham: Duke University, 1949. Includes the best texts of Shelley's translations from Plato (supplemented by Notopoulos in "New Texts of Shelley's Plato," *K-SJ*, 15:99–115 [1966]).
Clark, David Lee, ed. *Shelley's Prose; or, The Trumpet of a Prophecy.* Albuquerque: University of New Mexico, 1954. The most easily obtainable edition of Shelley's prose, but very unreliable in both text and annotation. Clark's dating of Shelley's posthumously published prose is, for the most part, fanciful.
Zillman, Lawrence John, ed. *Shelley's "Prometheus Unbound": A Variorum Edition.* Seattle: University of Washington, 1959 (text reedited by Zillman in *Shelley's "Prometheus Unbound": The Text and the Drafts.* New Haven: Yale University, 1969). Both Zillman's editions are valuable for their notes and comments but the texts are based on unsound editorial theories.
Cameron, Kenneth Neill, and Donald H. Reiman, eds. *Shelley and his Circle: 1773–1822.* Cambridge, Mass.: Harvard University; vols. I–II, 1961, vols. III–IV, 1970, vols. V–VI, 1973. A catalogue-edition, with extensive commentaries, of the manuscripts of the Shelleys, Byron, Godwin, Mary Wollstonecraft, Leigh Hunt, Peacock, *et al.* in The Carl H. Pforzheimer Library.
Reiman, Donald H. *Shelley's "The Triumph of Life": A Critical Study, Based on a Text Newly Edited from the Bodleian Manuscript.* Urbana: University of Illinois, 1965.
Jordan, John E., ed. *A Defence of Poetry* [Shelley], *The Four Ages of Poetry* [Peacock]. Indianapolis: Bobbs-Merrill, 1965. Excellent texts and notes.
Chernaik, Judith. *The Lyrics of Shelley.* Cleveland: Case Western Reserve University, 1972. Contains valuable texts of Shelley's major lyrics newly edited from the primary sources, in addition to sensitive interpretations.
Rogers, Neville, ed. *The Complete Poetical Works of Percy Bysshe Shelley.* vol. I. Oxford: Clarendon Press, 1972. This, the first of four projected volumes in an Oxford English Text edition of Shelley, is an editorial disaster, being deficient and unreliable in canon, text, collations, and critical notes.

IV. BIOGRAPHICAL WORKS

A. Primary Materials

Clairmont, Mary Jane Clara. *The Journals of Claire Clairmont*, ed. Marion Kingston Stocking. Cambridge: Harvard University, 1968.

Gisborne, Maria, and Edward E. Williams. *Maria Gisborne & Edward E. Williams, Shelley's Friends: Their Journals and Letters*, ed. Frederick L. Jones. Norman: University of Oklahoma, 1951.

Hunt, [James Henry] Leigh. *Lord Byron and Some of His Contemporaries . . . .* London: Henry Colburn, 1828. The material on Shelley appears, in revised form, in Hunt's *Autobiography* (1850).

Medwin, Thomas. *Life of Percy Bysshe Shelley*. 2 vols. London: Thomas Cautley Newby, 1847 (revised text, ed. Harry Buxton Forman, 1913). Strong on Shelley's literary interests during his school days and his last years.

Shelley, Mary Wollstonecraft. *The Letters of Mary W. Shelley*, ed. Frederick L. Jones. 2 vols. Norman: University of Oklahoma, 1944. Additional relevant letters appear in Jones, "Mary Shelley to Maria Gisborne: New Letters, 1818–1822," *Studies in Philology*, 52:39–74 (1955), and in Cameron and Reiman, *Shelley and his Circle* (see section III above).

———. *Mary Shelley's Journal*, ed. Frederick L. Jones. Norman: University of Oklahoma, 1947. The text of the journal in *Shelley and Mary*, from which Jones worked here, is incomplete and occasionally garbled.

Shelley, Percy Bysshe. *The Letters of Percy Bysshe Shelley*, ed. Frederick L. Jones. 2 vols. Oxford: Clarendon Press, 1964. Additional letters and corrected texts of some letters appear in *Shelley and his Circle* (section III above).

Shelley and Mary. 3 vols. (occasionally 4 vols.). Privately printed [ca. 1880]. Transcriptions (sometimes censored) of letters, journals, and documents then owned by Shelley's son, Sir Percy Florence Shelley.

Wolfe, Humbert, ed. *The Life of Percy Bysshe Shelley, as Comprised in* The Life of Shelley *by Thomas Jefferson Hogg,* The Recollections of Shelley & Byron *by Edward John Trelawny,* Memoirs of Shelley *by Thomas Love Peacock*. 2 vols. London: Dent, 1933. Conveniently collects three of the five valuable firsthand biographies (the others being those by Hunt and Medwin cited above).

B. Critical Biographies

Blunden, Edmund. *Shelley: A Life Story*. London: Collins, 1946.

Cameron, Kenneth Neill. *The Young Shelley: Genesis of a Radical*. New York: Macmillan, 1950. The standard book on Shelley's youth and early intellectual development (through *Queen Mab*).

Dowden, Edward. *The Life of Percy Bysshe Shelley*. 2 vols. London: Kegan Paul, Trench & Co., 1886 (revised in one volume, 1896). This "official" biography, sponsored by Shelley's family, suffers from Victorian reticence, but it is carefully written by one of the greatest scholars ever to interest himself in Shelley.

Ingpen, Roger. *Shelley in England*. London: Kegan Paul, Trench, Trübner & Co., 1917 (sometimes bound as 2 vols.). Important on Shelley's relations with his father and other members of his family.

Peck, Walter E. *Shelley: His Life and Work*. 2 vols. Boston: Houghton Mifflin, 1927. Though inaccurate in many details and somewhat distorted by Peck's own personal enthusiasms, this life is a storehouse of valuable information and documents.

White, Newman Ivey. *Shelley*. 2 vols. New York: Alfred A. Knopf, 1940 (one-volume *Portrait of Shelley*, 1945). The standard biography. Some individual points are corrected in later works, notably in *Shelley and his Circle* (section III above).

V. MAJOR BOOKS ON SHELLEY'S THOUGHT AND ART

In addition to the books listed below, consult those listed in section III by Notopoulos, Reiman, and Chernaik and in section IV.B by Cameron and White.

Baker, Carlos. *Shelley's Major Poetry: The Fabric of a Vision*. Princeton: Princeton University, 1948. A milestone in its treatment of Shelley as primarily an artist in the English poetic tradition, rather than as chiefly a thinker or personality.

Barrell, Joseph. *Shelley and the Thought of His Time: A Study in the History of Ideas*. New Haven: Yale University, 1947. Though superseded in much of its factual content and literary explication, Barrell's analysis of the Godwinian and the Platonic elements in Shelley's thought is a useful corrective to later studies that have overemphasized one or the other.

Bloom, Harold. *Shelley's Mythmaking*. New Haven: Yale University, 1959. Very uneven and based on a false analogy between Shelley and Martin Buber, this book rises to individual insights through Bloom's poetic sensitivity and in spite of the irrelevant systems he feels compelled to impose on his poetic analyses.

Butter, Peter H. *Shelley's Idols of the Cave*. Edinburgh: Edinburgh University, 1954. Drawing upon Yeats's view of Shelley, Butter explores recurring symbols and ideas in Shelley's writings.

Cameron, Kenneth Neill. *Shelley: The Golden Years*. Cambridge: Harvard University, 1974. This sequel to *The Young Shelley* (Section IV.B above) is a detailed study of Shelley's mature ideas and poetry.

Curran, Stuart. *Shelley's "Cenci": Scorpions Ringed with Fire*. Princeton: Princeton University, 1970. A major study, only slightly flawed by over-emphasis on Shelley's moral pessimism.

Grabo, Carl. *The Magic Plant: The Growth of Shelley's Thought*. Chapel Hill: University of North Carolina, 1936. A sensitive, appreciative study, slightly overemphasizing neo-Platonic elements in Shelley's thought.

Pulos, C. E. *The Deep Truth: A Study of Shelley's Scepticism*. Lincoln: University of Nebraska, 1954. This approach to the center of Shelley's thought has been widely influential in recent criticism, especially in the work of Reiman and Wasserman.

Reiman, Donald H. *Percy Bysshe Shelley*. New York: Twayne, 1969. A concise survey of Shelley's entire thought and work, based on primary materials as well as the writings of other scholars.

Wasserman, Earl R. *Shelley: A Critical Reading*. Baltimore: Johns Hopkins University, 1971. A book of such weight (in erudition and prose) and importance that no summary is useful; this book incorporates earlier studies of Shelley from *The Subtler Language* (1959) and *Shelley's "Prometheus Unbound"* (1965). Wasserman's interpretations of many poems are, even when fully understood, controversial.

Wilson, Milton. *Shelley's Later Poetry: A Study of His Prophetic Imagination*. New York: Columbia University, 1959. A sound study of the poems and poetic techniques Shelley created during his years in Italy.

Woodman, Ross Greig. *The Apocalyptic Vision in the Poetry of Shelley*. Toronto: University of Toronto, 1964. More valuable for sensitive individual readings than for its thesis.

Woodring, Carl. *Politics in English Romantic Poetry*. Cambridge: Harvard University, 1970. The chapter on Shelley (pp. 230–330) is, together with Cameron's quite different work, the best exploration of the contemporary political impulse (as distinct from philosophical and purely artistic concerns) in Shelley's work.

Index of Titles and First Lines